MW00834517

MEDIA, FEMINISM, CULTURAL STUDIES

The Sacred Cinema of Andrei Tarkovsky
by Jeremy Mark Robinson

Liv Tyler
by Thomas A. Christie

The Cinema of Hayao Miyazaki
Jeremy Mark Robinson

Stepping Forward: Essays, Lectures and Interviews
by Wolfgang Iser

Wild Zones: Pornography, Art and Feminism
by Kelly Ives

'Cosmo Woman': The World of Women's Magazines
by Oliver Whitehorne

The Cinema of Richard Linklater
by Thomas A. Christie

Walerian Borowczyk
by Jeremy Mark Robinson

Andrea Dworkin
by Jeremy Mark Robinson

Cixous, Irigaray, Kristeva: The Jouissance of French Feminism
by Kelly Ives

The Erotic Object: Sexuality in Sculpture
From Prehistory to the Present Day
by Susan Quinnell

Women in Pop Music
by Helen Challis

Detonation Britain: Nuclear War in the UK
by Jeremy Mark Robinson

Julia Kristeva: Art, Love, Melancholy, Philosophy, Semiotics
by Kelly Ives

Luce Irigaray: Lips, Kissing, and the Politics of Sexual Difference
by Kelly Ives

*Helene Cixous I Love You: The*Jouissance *of Writing*
by Kelly Ives

FORTHCOMING BOOKS

Ghost In the Shell
The Art of Masamune Shirow (3 vols)
Legend of the Overfiend
Fullmetal Alchemist
Death Note
Naruto
Berserk
Bleach
Hellsing
Vampire Knight
Mushishi
One Piece
Nausicaä of the Valley of the Wind
Tsui Hark
The Twilight Saga
Jackie Collins and the Blockbuster Novel
Harry Potter

THE ART OF

KATSUHIRO OTOMO

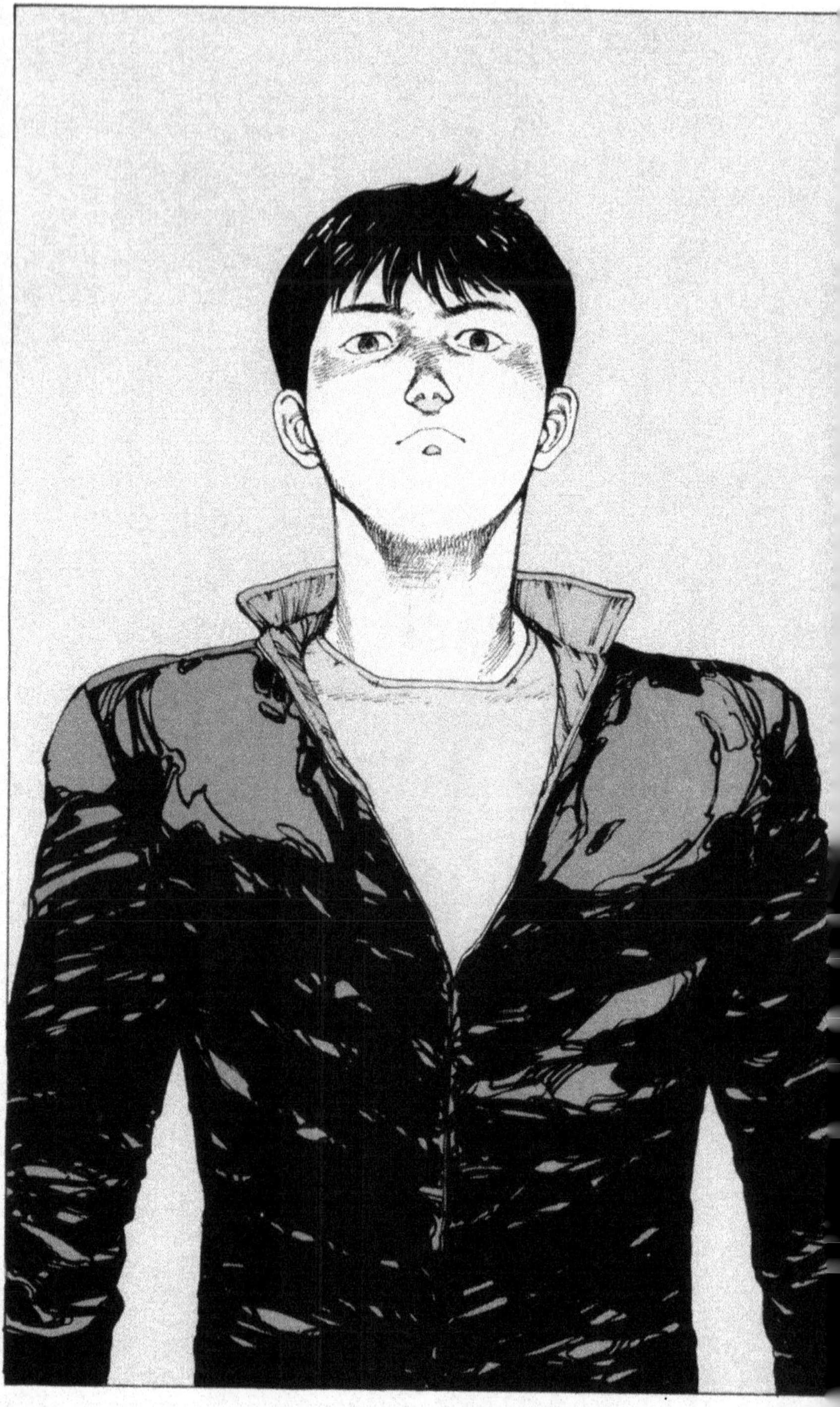

THE ART OF
KATSUHIRO OTOMO

JEREMY MARK ROBINSON

Crescent Moon

First published 2017. Revised 2020.
© Jeremy Mark Robinson 2017, 2020.

Set in Book Antiqua 9 on 12 point.
Designed by Radiance Graphics.

*British Library Cataloguing in Publication data
available for this title.*

ISBN-13 9781861716873 (Hbk)

*Crescent Moon Publishing
P.O. Box 1312, Maidstone, Kent
ME14 5XU, U.K.
www.crmoon.com
cresmopub@yahoo.co.uk*

CONTENTS

PART THREE ✪ CINEMA

PART FOUR: THE *AKIRA* MOVIE

PART FIVE: THE *AKIRA MANGA*

ACKNOWLEDGEMENTS

To the authors and publishers quoted.
To Katsuhiro Otomo and Mash Room.

NOTE

The companion book, *The Akira Book*, contains a complete summary of the story of the *Akira manga* (running over 300 pages).

This revised reprint has corrected the first edition, and updated it to 2020.

AKIRA

TSUHIRO OTOMO

TALIANA
.00
.900
11

PLANET
manga

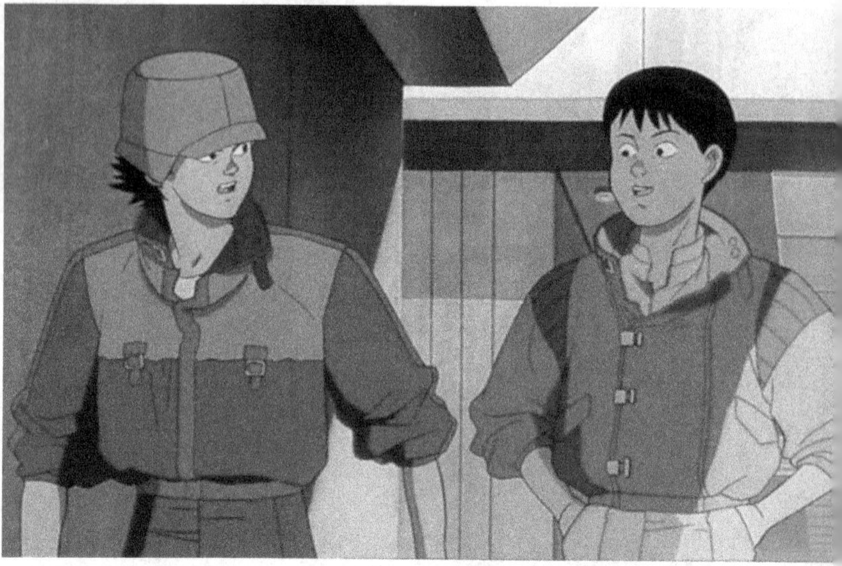

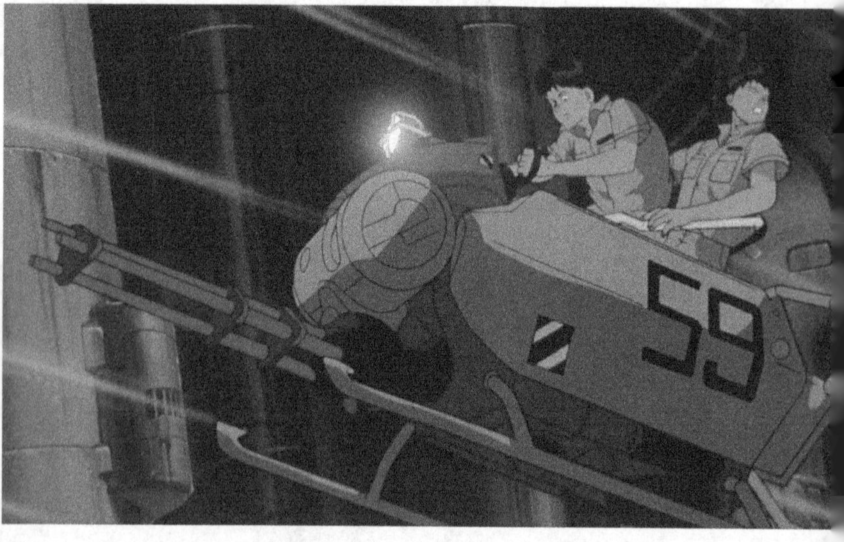
59

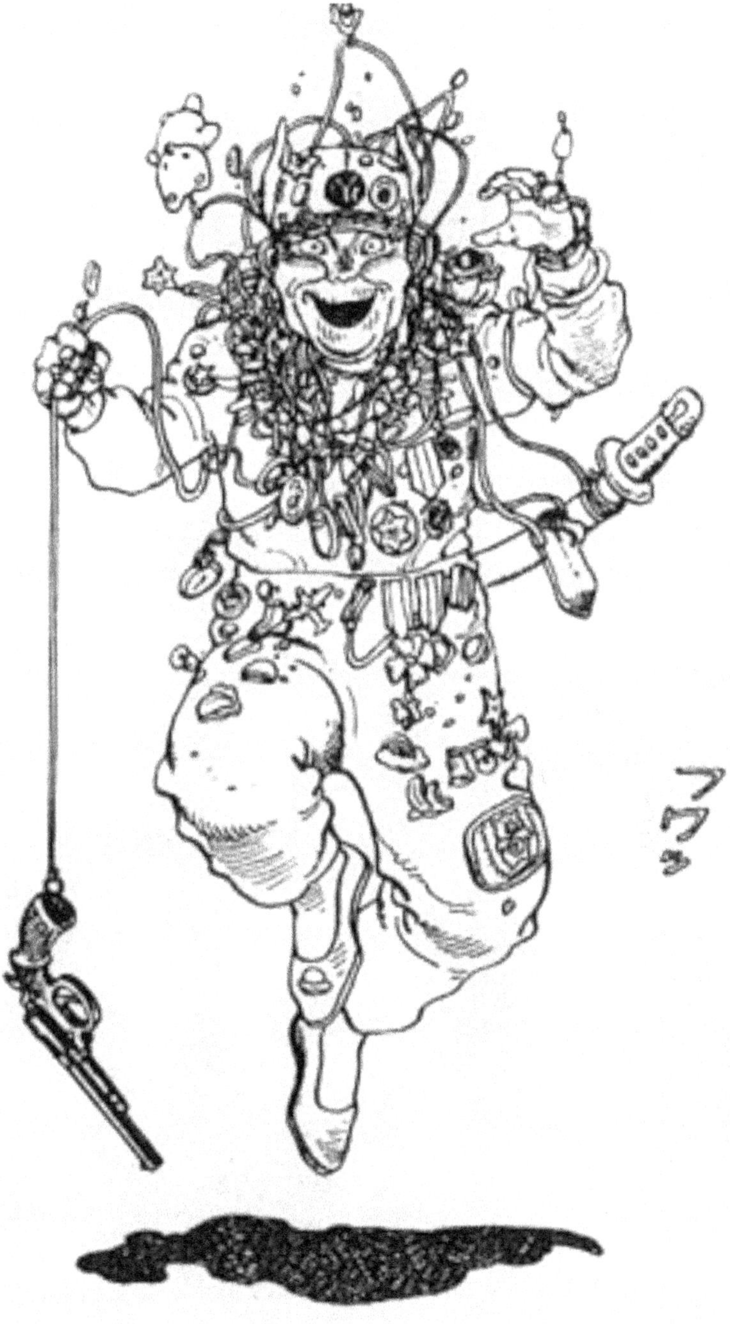
フワッ

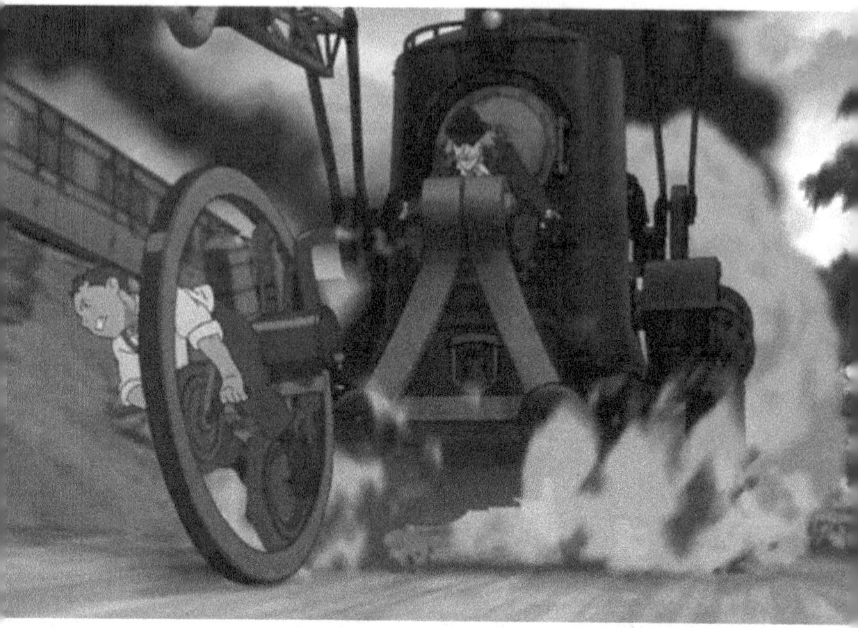

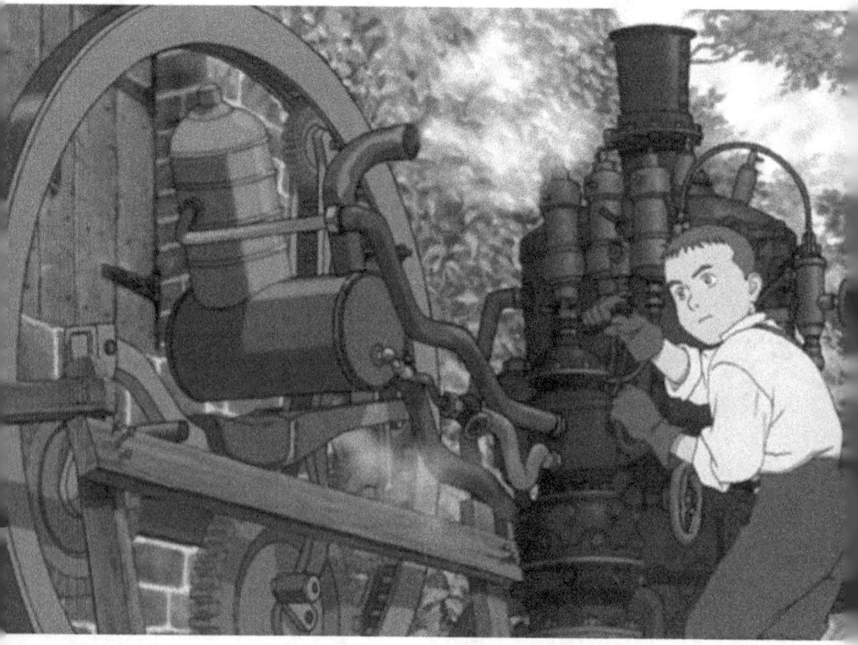

PART ONE

KATSUHIRO OTOMO

01

KATSUHIRO OTOMO

The cinema should always be the discovery of something. I believe that the cinema should be essentially poetic.

Orson Welles[1]

There are very few genuine *auteurs* in Japanese animation: the animation industry, like all filmmaking on a large scale, is truly collaborative. However, you can definitely see elements in the films directed and written and supervised by Katsuhiro Otomo that are auteurist: Otomo has his own style, visually, but also his own concerns, thematically, politically and psychologically (even some animators celebrated for their style and technical wizardry don't have much to offer in terms of themes, issues or psychology. They might be dubbed 'flashy' or visually 'stylish',[2] but aren't great subjects for analysis or discussion.)

However, you can genuinely compare Otomo-sensei with any of the great filmmakers of cinema history, such as F.W. Murnau, D.W. Griffith or Yasujiro Ozu. In animation, only three film directors are in the same league: Hayao Miyazaki, Osamu

---

1 O. Welles, 1995, 39.
2 I hate that word 'stylish'! – everything has a style!

Tezuka and Isao Takahata (there are further contenders, of course, but they are on lower levels: Satoshi Kon, Mamoru Oshii, Yoshiaki Kawajiri, Noriyuki Abe, Kenji Kamiyama, Koji Morimoto, Hideaki Anno, etc).

The world of animation is vast, going back to Géorges Méliès, Winsor McCay and Edwin S. Porter, and taking in experimental and *avant garde* animation, the giants of Eastern Europe (Jan Svankmajer, Karel Zeman, Jiri Trnka, Walerian Borowczyk), to more recent proponents, such as the Quay Brothers, Michel Ocelot, and Henry Selick, or the use of animation in live-action cinema.[3]

The great names of film directors in the history of animation include: Géorges Méliès, Ladislaw Starewicz, Willis O'Brien, Lotte Reiniger, Ray Harryhausen, George Pal, Tex Avery, Chuck Jones, Jiri Trnka, Paul Grimault, Ralph Bakshi, Jan Svankmajer, and Michel Ocelot. The celebrated *auteurs* in *animé* include Hayao Miyazaki, Osamu Tezuka, Isao Takahata, and Mamoru Oshii. You can put Katsuhiro Otomo among them.

BIOGRAPHY.

Katsuhiro Otomo was born on April 14, 1954, in Tome-gun, Miyagi Prefecture (his name is sometimes written Ôtomo or Ohtomo; it's pronounced 'Ohtomo'). He attended Sanuma High School (where he joined the art club). Like many another *mangaka*, Otomo-sensei moved to Tokyo to find work in *manga*. He married his wife Yoko in 1977. Their son Shihoi (b. 1980) is also an artist (his funky, punky art is worth checking out).

The works of Katsuhiro Otomo have been celebrated with awards – he won the Kodansha Comic-Strip Award in 1984 for *Akira*, and the Science Fiction Grand Prix Award in 1983 for *Domu*. Later awards included: the French Ordre des Arts et des

3 To the point where some movies, such as the *Star Wars* prequels or *Avatar*, are virtually animated films with live-action figures added to them.

Lettres (as Chevalier in 2005, and Officer in 2014); the Eisner Award Hall of Fame (2012); the Purple Medal of Honor (2013); the Winsor McCay Award (2014); and the Grand Prix de la ville d'Angoulême (2015). They adore Otomo in France.

Katsuhiro Otomo has cited North American films of the Vietnam War era as artistic influences[4] (such as *Five Easy Pieces, Bonnie & Clyde,* and *Easy Rider,* and Sam Peckinpah. As a youth, Otomo would travel by train for 3 hours just to see a movie in Sendai, so he was a keen movie-goer). Like everyone in Japan who's into cinema, Otomo knows and admires the films of Akira Kurosawa (and directed his own version of a Kurosawan *jidai geki* in *Mushishi*). Other TV and movies that influenced Otomo include *2001: A Space Odyssey, Blade Runner, Metropolis, James Bond, Thunderbirds* (and other Gerry Anderson shows), *Dr Strangelove,* Disney and numerous Japanese animations (with *Astro Boy* and *Tetsujin 28* among the most prominent). He also liked Nikkatsu's erotic films, and *yakuza* movies.

One of the mistaken views of Katsuhiro Otomo is that he hasn't really done that much – in *manga* or in *animé*. As the summary below will demonstrate, Otomo-sensei has achieved *plenty*, and his profess-ional CV is *huge*. The thing is, Otomo prefers to work on short, one-off projects (partly because he says he doesn't like to repeat himself – so he shifts from one subject or form to another rapidly). In the 1970s, for instance, Otomo produced a large number of stories in comicbook form (most were short or one-shots). Maybe if Otomo had focussed his attention on creat-ing two or three more long-form narratives, like he did with *Akira* and *Domu,* he might've had an even greater impact critically (or a wider audience). But Otomo is a *true* pioneer in art, a *true* explorer and adventurer, and going over the same ground isn't gonna to sustain his interest for long.

4 'All the movies were about leaving home, about people with boring lives who wanted to go somewhere else,' Otomo has recalled.

Katsuhiro Otomo is well-regarded in the *manga* and *animé* industries: he is admired, of course, for his immense achievements, but he is also someone that people want to work with, someone who can draw top talent to his projects. There is a lot of good will towards Otomo: everyone knows who he is, and he is an important part of Japanese pop culture.[5]

The big movies (*Akira, Steam-Boy*) and the famous *manga* (*Akira, Domu*) tend to over-shadow everything else that Otomo has done. But his work as *writer* is very important: for example, he wrote *Roujin Z, Memories* and *Metropolis* among movies, and his writing for comics includes the gangster action story *The Sultan's Guard*, the children's book *Hipira-kun,* and the epic *manga* of future colonization, *The Legend of Mother Sarah*.

Katsuhiro Otomo's earliest commission was for *Action* magazine, as a writer, in 1973, when he was 19 years-old (with the publication of *A Gun Report*, an adaptation of Prosper Merimee's novella *Mateo Falcone*). Many *mangaka* start young, and were already published by their early twenties: Masamune Shirow (with *Appleseed* at age 24), Kentaro Miura (the *Berserk* prototype appeared when Miura was 22), Masashi Kishimoto (he created *Naruto* when he was 23), Eiichiro Oda created the biggest comic ever, *One Piece*, when he was 17, and of course Osamu Tezuka, who was a major *manga* star by his early 20s. (And most *mangaka* were and still are self-taught).

Katsuhiro Otomo's subsequent *manga* work for *Action* comic included *Boogie Woogie Waltz* (1974)[6] and *Domu* (1980). *Nippon Sayonara* (1977) was set in New York City (which Otomo had visited in 1977, for his honeymoon with Yoko),[7] about a Japanese martial arts teacher. The signature image of *Nippon Sayonara*

---

5 *The Simpsons* produced a great *hommage* to *Akira* in 2015 (dubbed *Bartkira*).
6 His first work for *Action* was *The Bridge and Them* (*Hashi to Soshite*, 1974).
7 Most Japanese do not travel outside of Japan: altho' many *manga* and *animé* feature locations outside of Japan, most of the *mangaka* and the animators have not visited those places.

depicts a giant, Japanese whale[8] straddling Lower Manhattan. In 1979 Otomo published his *manga* story *Fireball*:[9] this was important in being Otomo's first lengthy exploration of sci-fi, and led towards *Akira* (but *Fireball* was abandoned). *Highway Star* and *Short Piece* were also published in 1979, and the short work *The Water-melon Messiah* in *Manga* (1980-82).

In the late 1970s, Otomo began to explore science fiction in many comics: you can spot the influence of his reading of classic sci-fi authors such as Ray Bradbury, Arthur C. Clarke, Robert Heinlein, A.E. van Vogt *et al*. Otomo's type of science fiction focusses on several themes: the near-future; the colonization of space (many *manga* are set on space stations); 'hard'/ technological science fiction; robots and technology (usually mis-used or going awry); psychics and paranormal phenomena; and post-apocalyptic scenarios (often following catastrophes and wars).

Domu was Katsuhiro Otomo's first big critical and public success; it was published in *Action* comic from 1980 to 1982. Otomo's first full-length movie was *Give Us Guns* (1981),[10] filmed in 16mm.

Akira (*Young Magazine,* Kodansha, 1982-90) was a success in *manga* publishing from the outset: the first *tankobon* sold out (300,000 copies, and it was priced high, at 1,000 Yen = $10). *Young Magazine* was an important outlet for Otomo's work – particularly because he said that they let him do anything (an ideal state for an artist like Otomo, who doesn't need any guidance). *Akira* became a huge hit overseas, with international sales outside Nihon of 7 million copies (the Marvel colour edition sold 2 million copies in the U.S.A.).

As well as *Akira*, Otomo-sensei also published a brilliant parody of fairy tales and famous stories – *Hansel and Gretel* in 1981 (a.k.a *It's a Crazy, Crazy*

8 Otomo-sensei had produced a *manga* of *Moby Dick* as part of his *Hansel and Gretel* collection.
9 One of Otomo's favourite rock acts, Deep Purple, provided the title *Fireball* (and *Highway Star*).
10 Partly based on the classic *À nous la liberté* (René Clair, 1931).

World), including wicked and weird spoofs of *Alice's Adventures In Wonderland, The Wizard of Oz, Snow White, Sleeping Beauty, Cinderella* and *Moby Dick*.

Other *manga* work includes: *Visitors* (1984); *Memories* (*Kanojo No Omoide*, 1980, the basis for the 1995 movie); *Kibun wa Mou Sensou* (*The Mood Is Already of War,* 1982), illustrating stories written by Toshihiko Yahagi; *Zed* (Kodansha, 1994), a *manga* version of the 1991 movie *Roujin Z* (with art by Tai Okada); a story for *Batman* (1996); *Park* (*Kousen/ Slice of Life,* 2006) and *DJ Teck's Morning Attack* (2012). Plus stories for children: *SOS! Tokyo Metro Explorers* (1996, later animated), and *Hipira: The Little Vampire* (2001), a children's story (animated in 2009).

Sultan Boueitai (*The Sultan's Guard,* Kodansha, 1982) was a one-volume *manga* co-written with Haruka Takachiho and illustrated by Akihiko Takadera. *Boogie Woogie Waltz* (1982, Kitansha) was a collection of short stories by Katsuhiro Otomo.

The Legend of Mother Sarah (1990) was one of Otomo's major works in *manga* following *Akira* (but the artwork was by Takumi Nagayasu). It's a kind of re-run of *Akira,* with a woman in the lead role.

Katsuhiro Otomo contributed to a series of books about Go Nagai's *Devilman manga* – *Neo Devilman* (1999, Kodansha), which also included works by Katsuya Terada, Ken Ishikawa, Go Nagai, Akihiko Takadera and Shinobu Kaze.

Kikinosuke Gomen - Giyaman no Sho was an Edo period piece co-written with Yoshihiko Tomizawa and illustrated by Hiroyuki Kaidou. It appeared in 2006 in Kodansha's *Magazine Z.* A follow-up, *Kikinosuke Gomen - Giyaman no Sho,* was published in 2007 in *Dengeki Kuro Maoh* magazine (from Media-Works). In Paris recently, I noticed that Otomo has given his name to a French lifestyle magazine looking at Japanese culture (characters from *Akira* appear on the cover).

Many of Katsuhiro Otomo's *manga* works are one-shots (i.e., stand-alone stories comprising a single chapter – typically 30 pages long, but sometimes only 5, 6, 7 or 8 pages). Otomo's storytelling is often straightforward, but often also deliberately abstract and ambiguous. There are just as many open endings where everything is left unresolved as closed endings, which tie up the strands of plot in the usual manner.

Notice that the *Akira manga* (in collected form) doesn't have chapter titles (like most *manga*), or even chapter breaks (with their customary splash pages and additional artwork). Also, the volumes of *Akira* aren't given titles (many *manga iare*).

A typical *manga* by Otomo will feature either guys in an apartment block in Nihon or a sci-fi setting (a space colony, or a desert planet); extreme scenarios like murder or death are common; the charas are either lower class drop-outs or salarymen (workers); social rebellion and political satire are common issues, with survival ruling supreme; and the comics will revolve around a single gag.

In 2012, Otomo-sensei remarked:

> All you have to do is buckle down while you're young and draw as much as you can, and you'll get really good at it. Manga these days, though, is drawn with symbols — predetermined symbols that people just arrange on the page. That's not really drawing, and I don't think someone can make any real breakthroughs that way. It's important to actually look at things and draw them, I think.

Animé has been only one of many strands in Katsuhiro Otomo's career – design work, commercial commissions, and writing fiction, and of course producing *manga* have been key activities. As well as animation, Otomo has also helmed live-action movies: *World Apartment Horror* (1991), and *Mushishi* (2006). He has directed commercials (for Canon,[11] Honda and Suntory, among others). He has

11 In 1983 Otomo provided material for the Canon T70 camera in the 'Push On' advertizing campaign.

drawn cover art (for Haruka Takachiho and Michio Tsuzuki).

The point to keep in mind is that by the time that Otomo-sensei started animating and directing movies, he was already an established and successful *mangaka*, and had been drawing *manga* for at least ten years before helming his first movies. (His workload, tho', was huge when he was directing *Akira* – directing and writing that movie was plenty to be going on with, one of the most ambitious productions in *animé*, but Otomo was also producing 20 pages of *manga* every 2 weeks. Which is *a lot*! 'I used to finish with the manga, then head to the animation studio – on no sleep – and work on the film. That time in my life has to have been the peak of my physical energy').

Katsuhiro Otomo contributed to a number of anthology *animé* productions, including *Memories* (1995), taken from three *manga* stories by Otomo (*Kanojo No Omoide*, published in 1980/ 1990); *Robot Carnival* (1987) had opening and ending credit sequences directed by Otomo and Atsuko Fukushima; Otomo directed a segment of *Neo-Tokyo* in 1987, entitled *Order To Stop Construction*; and he was linked to *Perfect Blue* (director Satoshi Kon, who went on to become a celebrated filmmaker, was one of Otomo's protegés, as was Enki Bilal, who directed *Le Sommeil du monstre* (*The Dormant Beast*, 1998)).

Other writing credits of Otomo-san's include the 'pink film' *Kôkô Erotopia: Akai seifuku* (*High School Erotopia: Red Uniforms* (Shinichi Shiratori, 1979),[12] *Give Me a Gun Give Me Freedom* (a.k.a. *Give Us Guns*, 1982), and the short films *Shuffle* (1981), *Fushigi Monogatari* (1988) and *So What* (1988).

Katsuhiro Otomo has directed several short animated films. These include: *Gondora* (a.k.a. *Catsuka Player*, 1998); *Gundam: Mission To the Rise* (1998), a short, digitally-animated movie in the *Gundam* franchise; and *Combustible* (2013), a 12-minute

12 This was the first of Otomo's credits as a writer in cinema. It's a low-budget sex comedy.

masterpiece of digital animation (one of 4 short films forming the multi-media project *Short Peace*).

Other credits in animation and movies include the movie of *Crusher Joe* (1983, Studio Nue/ Sunrise), as special guest designer; *Legend of the Millennium Dragon* (*Onigamiden,* Hirotsugu Kawasaki, 2011), as designer; and an episode of *Space Dandy* (2014), as designer. Otomo's children's *manga, Hipira-kun,* was animated as a short (18 min) in 2009.

Katsuhiro Otomo did design work for *Freedom* (2006), written by Dai Saito, Katsuchiko Chiba and Yuichi Nomura, directed by Shuhei Morita, and produced for Sunrise and Bandai. Otomo has story-board, character design and *mecha* design credits. The six 30-minute episodes were made as a commercial for Nissin Cup Noodles.

If Katsuhiro Otomo gets involved with an *animé*, such is his fame he tends to overshadow the other collaborators (and inevitably some of 'em resent Otomo receiving all the accolades. But that's the way of things with superstar film directors: like Tetsuo at the end of *Akira*, they tend to bloat up into giant-size entities that absorb everybody else around them).

I'm sure that Otomo has received many offers over the years for him to join a long-running TV series (maybe in an adviser capacity), or as a high-ranking producer for an animation house. He has never taken up jobs like that – he prefers to work independently, and on short, one-off projects. The factory-style production of long-running *animé* does not suit Otomo.

Two new animation projects were announced by Otomo-sensei at Anime Expo in July, 2019: an animated adaptation of *Akira* (a long time coming), to be produced by Sunrise and others (Otomo had mentioned the project at a French festival in 2016), and a new space movie called *Orbital Era,* which he would write and direct.

Katsuhiro Otomo could've had his own film studio – other filmmakers in *animé* have founded their own studios (including Eiko Tanaka, Koji Morimoto and Yoshiharu Sato with Studio 4°C, Hideaki Anno with Studio Khara, the Clamp collective, the Gainax collective, and of course Isao Takahata and Hayao Miyazaki with Studio Ghibli). Maybe Otomo preferred to focus on filmmaking (like Miyazaki and Mamoru Oshii), rather than running a production facility (his artist's studio is called Mash Room).

Katsuhiro Otomo is known as a perfectionist; this contributed to *Akira* going over-budget.[13] Otomo admitted that he had become obsessed with *Akira*, with getting every single detail right. He would order retakes of shots (which is expensive), as well as projecting the movie again and again in order to polish it up. 'Even after *Akira* was in the can, I kept in getting into trouble over last-minute revisions,' Otomo admitted, 'I'd keep wanting to check it just one more time' (2009, 36). In this case, all of the attention and energy paid off – you can see the sheer amount of work that went into *Akira* up there on the screen.

As many commentators who knew the *animé* business pointed out, *Akira* was not typical of Japanese animation: high budget movies of this kind were very rare. Sure: but such prestige and high budget productions are very important in raising the awareness of *animé* overseas. *Akira* has become one of the key ambassadors for Japanese animation abroad – along with *Pokémon, Naruto,* and Studio Ghibli's movies.

Richard Harrington in the *Washington Post* noted that 'the film moves with such kinetic energy that you'll be hanging on for dear life'. *Akira* may 'the best known and least well understood example of *anime* in America', for Antonia Levi (91).

In the U.S.A., Fred Schodt noted in *Dreamland Japan* of the movie, *Akira* gained

13 'A futuristic thriller by a first-time feature director who ran way over budget by faffing with his color palette', as Jonathan Clements put it (2009, 272).

considerable critical acclaim despite a plot that was too long and muddled. It was violent and graphic, with exquisitely rendered scenes of exploding buildings and transformations, and it was unlike anything American accustomed mainly to Disney-style animation had ever seen. (2002, 314)

AVAILABILITY.

Many of Katsuhiro Otomo's key works are available in the Western world, but some are not so easy to find. One or two of the film works are not widely available (such as *World Apartment Horror*, 1991, and his early short films), and some of the *manga* works have not appeared in official translations in the West (some *manga* works are now out of print). Consequently, I won't include lengthy discussions of those pieces.

KATSUHIRO OTOMO AND THE U.S.A.

Otomo-sensei's work is full of North American cultural influences – which's one reason why his work (including *Akira*) has been so successful in the U.S.A. Not only cinematic influences, but also American comicbook culture:[14] from superhero[15] comics, sci-fi, fantasy and adventure to underground, alternative and satirical comics (Art Spiegelman, *Mad* magazine, Harvey Kurtzman, *Harvard Lampoon*, Robert Crumb *et al*). Further elements which make Otomo's *manga* appealing to U.S. readers include its 'cinematic' style, its photo-realism and emphasis on details, its themes and its characters.

When Katsuhiro Otomo and his wife Yoko went on their honeymoon in 1977, they didn't choose popular destinations for Japanese tourists such as China or Europe, but the U.S.A. Many of Otomo's early *manga* were set in New York City (a depiction of a 'real' New York, rather than the highly exaggerated

14 It would take many pages to consider the relation of Otomo's art to, say, North American comics, or to French comicbooks, or to relate the *animé* of Otomo to, say, Eastern European animation.
15 Otomo was invited to produce a *Batman* comic.

city of most *manga* and *animé* – most Japanese artists have never visited Gotham). However, the ideology of the U.S.A., and its political and foreign affairs, are treated warily and satirically. (Otomo exhibits the familiar love-hate attitude to the U.S.A. of many left-wing artists).

KATSUHIRO OTOMO AND OSAMU TEZUKA.

Among the influences that Katsuhiro Otomo has cited are *Astro Boy*, the *manga* of Shigeru Mizuki, Seishi Yokomizo's novels about 'new breed' humans, and *Tetsujin 28* (a.k.a. *Gigantor*, 1956 to 1966), by Mitsuteru Yokoyama (1934-2004),[16] a forerunner of many famous robots and robot shows. Otomo-sensei acknowledged that in one view *Akira* can be re-garded as a re-telling of *Tetsujin 28*.

Osamu Tezuka has probably had more influence on Japanese animation and *manga* than any other single individual – Fred Schodt reckons that Japanese *manga* and *animé* would be unthinkable without Tezuka, and that *every* major *manga* artist has been inspired by him.

While animators work under the shadow of Walt Disney in the West, in Japan, it's Osamu Tezuka (1928-89). Known as the 'god of *manga*', Tezuka is of course one of the major figures in Japanese *animé*, creator/ director of *Astro Boy, Arabian Nights, Princess Knight, Triton of the Sea, Kimba the White Lion, Buddha, Bix X, Black Jack, Dororo, Jungle Emperor Leo,* and *Phoenix*.[17]

Osamu Tezuka was very successful very quickly: by his early twenties, he was 'the biggest selling *manga* artist in Japan'.[18] And he was immensely prolific, creating thousands of pages of *manga* (as well as developing *animé* and running production comp-anies). Katsuhiro Otomo acknowledged the influence

16 Yokoyama is responsible for an early, influential magical girl *manga*, *Little Witch Sally*.
17 As well as 21 TV series and twelve TV specials, Tezuka also produced 700 stories and around 17,000 *manga* pages (C, 30).
18 H. McCarthy, 1993, 13.

of Tezuka with a dedication that ends the *Akira manga* (and of course Otomo scripted the Tezuka movie version of *Metropolis* released in 2001).

Fred Schodt remarked that Osamu Tezuka was fiercely competitive, and when Katsuhiro Otomo made a big splash with *Akira*, Tezuka was jealous, because 'he had a burning desire to be at the top of the popularity list in all genres for all age groups at all times' (2002, 239).

KATSUHIRO OTOMO AND MOEBIUS.

Katsuhiro Otomo was, like 1000s of others (such as Hayao Miyazaki, Luc Besson and Ridley Scott[19]), a fan of Moebius's art[20] in the French comic *Métal Hurlant* (*Heavy Metal*).[21] Mega-prolific Moebius (Jean Giraud, 1938-2012) designed Alejandro Jodorowsky's abandoned 1976 adaptation of Frank Herbert's *Dune*, the animated *The Orphan From Perdide* (1982), the alien in *The Abyss* (1989), worked on *Tron* (1982), *Little Nemo* (1992), *Les Maîtres du Temps* (1982), *Willow* (1988), *Masters of the Universe* (1986), and designed the spacesuits for 1979's *Alien*.

Moebius was one of a few artists grappling with a 'concentrated city', where *Akira* takes place, a J.G. Ballardian 'metrocosm', the urban sprawl of Isaac Asimov, where a whole planet is a city (other comics dealing with the complex city included *Judge Dredd* and *Ranxerox*).

Katsuhiro Otomo explained the attraction of Moebius's art:

At the time, manga was confined to the real, the

19 Ridley Scott was a big fan of Moebius and *Heavy Metal*, and remarked that *Blade Runner* was an attempt at turning a comicbook into a movie.
20 Moebius's love of depicting the desert (from a visit he made to Mexico to see his parents) possibly influenced Otomo.
21 *Métal Hurlant* was launched in 1975 by Bernard Farkas, Jean-Pierre Dionnet, Jean Giraud and Philippe Druillet. It published mainly French fantasy illustration, and spawned versions and translations in other territories, including a US version, *Heavy Metal*, in 1977. There was also an animated film, *Heavy Metal* (1981), based on the characters and art from the magazine. Fantasy and comicbooks are still hugely popular in France.

everyday, the concrete, the social. Everyone swore only by 'gekiga', the adult version of *manga* which used lots of frames and sombre compositions. The clear yet very expressive and detailed line of Moebius was a real revelation. A fantastical universe like that of *Arzach* pushed us out of our routines. I was far from being the only one to be influenced. Many *manga* authors took it as an invitation to immerse themselves in new worlds, to open up fresh artistic perspectives.

Among Moebius's comic output were the *Jerry Cornelius* stories (from Michael Moorcock), *Arzach, The Long Tomorrow, The Horny Goof, Les Adventures de John Difool* (written by Alejandro Jodorowsky), *The Airtight Garage, The Onyx Overlord, The Fifth Essence* (later filmed by Columbia/ Gaumont/ Patrick Ledoux as *The Fifth Element*, 1997), *The Mysteries of the Incal, Is Man Good?, White Nightmare, Memory of the Future, Crystal Saga, Heavenly Venice, The Blind Citadel, Major's Holiday* and *The Goddess*.

Moebius was a fan (and friend) of Hayao Miyazaki, and *Nausicaä of the Valley of the Wind* was his favourite Miyazaki film (as it is for many Miyazaki fans). *Nausicaä of the Valley of the Wind* is 'a great movie, a masterpiece,' Moebius enthused. 'The work he did after continues at the same level, in the fineness, in the beauty.'

The influence went the other way, too (Miyazaki admired Moebius's comic strip *Arzach*). Miyazaki on Moebius: 'even today, I think he has an awesome sense of space. I directed *Nausicaä* under Moebius' influence.' Miyazaki spoke of Moebius' art:

> Characters are pictured very simply in Moebius' drawings, yet they have a sort of atmosphere around them. And the characters themselves exhale all kinds of things, notably solitude and a great nobleness. For me, it is the greatest quality of Moebius' drawings.

In 2004, Miyazaki and Moebius took part in a joint exhibit of their work (they had met in 1987).

KATSUHIRO OTOMO AS *MANGAKA*.

I think you could put the *manga* of *Akira* beside the great book illustrators of the past, such as, in Europe, George Cruikshank, Arthur Rackham, William Blake, Philip Otto Runge and Randolph Caldecott. And even Gustave Doré, the king of fantasy images of the modern period (Doré (1832-83) is a favourite with filmmakers, such as Walt Disney, Ray Harryhausen, Cecil B. DeMille and Carl-Theodor Dreyer. Many filmmakers have used Doré's marvell-ous art as inspiration).

Katsuhiro Otomo probably wouldn't place himself beside the great artists of printmaking, such as Rembrandt van Rijn or Albrecht Dürer in Europe, or Katsushika Hokusai, Utagawa Kunisada and Kitagawa Utamaro in Japan. However, when you look at the whole of the *manga* of *Akira*, it is certainly as impressive as any of the great illustrations of books in the West – for invention, for scope, for detail, for graphic skill, and for storytelling (as a story, *Akira* has no counterparts anywhere, really: it's a total one-off).

Akira has become one of the great comics of Asia: it's a *manga* that everybody in the industry will know, a classic like the works of Osamu Tezuka, or *Dragon Ball*, or *Lupin III*. Anybody working in the action, sc-fi or fantasy genre will have looked at *Akira*, along with masterpieces such as *Lone Wolf and Cub, Fist of the North Star* and *Cyborg 009*, and later works such as *One Piece, Naruto, Bleach* and *Fairy Tail* (all of which were influenced by *Akira*).

Like all *mangaka*, Otomo has worked to dead-lines throughout his career: 'no matter what I'm writing, I'm always pursued by deadlines', Otomo noted in *Memories*. And he has pushed against them (driving people nuts with *Akira*, for instance, by insisting on working up to the very last minute – just like many filmmakers, such as Tsui Hark, Stanley Kubrick and George Lucas).

Katsuhiro Otomo has produced *manga* using the *Batman* franchise: *Batman: Black and White* (1996)[22] featured Otomo's story *The Third Mask* (there is a subculture of *Batman* stories in Japanese *manga*). Otomo has also written stories about King Arthur, Godzilla, Jesus, jazz in New York, and Asian politics.

Katsuhiro Otomo's first professional *manga*, *A Gun Report* (1973), was published in *Action* magazine. *Fireball* (1979) was the first *manga* that Otomo had serialized (tho' it was not completed. Some ideas were re-cycled in *Akira*).[23] Many of Otomo's early works in *manga* were one-shots, single stories which were not intended to be part of a long-running series (many famous *manga* series started out as one-shots – like *Fullmetal Alchemist* and *One Piece* – or even single illustrations or posters, such as *Naruto*).

The major *manga* artists often publish artbooks of their sketches, paintings, posters, video covers, *manga* covers, special publicity illustrations and the like.[24] *The Akira Club* is a marvellous selection of artwork by Katsuhiro Otomo produced for the *manga* and its many offshoots. If you are a fan of *Akira*, the *Akira Club* artbook is worth looking at: it includes the paintings that Otomo produced for the covers of the many editions of the *manga*, for example (including some that weren't used). There is also an *Akira Archives* book, two *Kaba* books, a *Posters* book, and several other artbooks.

As to style, layouts and the organization of his storytelling in comicbook form, Katsuhiro Otomo favours many apparently 'simple' elements. For

22 Detective Comics (D.C.) and Marvel have experimented with hiring Japanese *manga* artists – sometimes to work on their existing superhero titles such as *Batman, X-Men, Sandman, Thor,* etc (such as Katsuhiro Otomo, Yoshitaka Amano, Kia Asamiya, Akira Yoshida and Makoto Nakatsuka). The North American publishers have also developed hybrids of Japanese and American material.
23 *Manga* artists often re-cycle their ideas and designs.
24 Such books are publishers' concepts, delivering more material to a market that's been established by the artist's work.

example, regular layouts of four, five or six panels per page. Action stays within the frames. There are occasional single-panel pages, and double pages.

Katsuhiro Otomo favours regular black lines (of the same thickness), with lots of white space (within and around the figures). Screen tone increased in some stories (such as *Akira*), but many *manga* by Otomo-sensei are surprisingly free of tone (or even full blacks).

The rounded faces of Katsuhiro Otomo's character designs are famous (and often copied), and his insistence on people who look distinctly 'Japanese' is well-known.[25] (Otomo said he began to draw Japanese people naturalistically when he looked at his friends: 'My style took shape naturally by observing them. I try to draw things as true as possible, without falling into mannerism.') His adherence to forms of 'realism' was notable in his 1970s *manga* (when he was exploring the scuzzier areas of society, including murder and poverty). Critics have drawn attention to the objectivity of Otomo's formal approach to drawing, so that it seems as if Otomo is creating a documentary of his characters. He avoided artificiality – he liked chaotic, messy places. 'Tokyo itself looks like a mess: inharmonious, completely devoid of artificiality', Otomo remarked, *pace Domu*. (Many character designs in Otomo's early works turn up in *Akira* – from *Domu*, from *Sayonara Japan*, from *Kibun*, from *That's Amazing World*, etc).

Katsuhiro Otomo's passion for visual overload in some panels is one of his trademarks. He is particularly fond of dirtying up imagery with cracks in sidewalks and walls, pebbles and debris lying about, and adding textures to drawings which enhance the atmosphere. (He says he goes back over images and adds those elements).

Otomo also regularly puts his characters in

25 Other artists who made their characters look more 'Japanese' included Masakazu Katsura.

tattered clothing – in maybe half of his comics. I can't think of another *mangaka* who has so many people dressed in rags. Beautiful, exquisite clothing is not Otomo's style! (And if they start off chic and primped, they always end up in rags!).

Katsuhiro Otomo is a Japanese artist, and thus works very much in the planar visual tradition of Japanese art, where everything is pushed onto the frontal plane. But when he wants to, Otomo-sensei can execute images of great depth and distance (the *Akira* movie, for example, is full of images of objects or characters moving to or away from the frontal plane, which's one of the trademarks of Japanese *animé*).

Another Otomoan speciality is to create very precise architectural spaces. Out comes the ruler and the graphic artist's ink pen (with a fine nib), as every window and every wall on a skyscraper is carefully delineated, in true (Western) perspective. Otomo's feeling for space and landscape is quite remarkable – he puts the reader into a place completely.

Katsuhiro Otomo is a devotee of drawing. Real drawing, that is, with pens[26] and pencils on pieces of paper. He denounces the over-reliance on computers (and software like Photoshop) to produce comics. For Otomo-sensei, that's not really drawing, it's simply arranging shapes in the digital realm.

Katsuhiro Otomo prefers drawing and observation: looking at the world, and drawing it (Hayao Miyazaki is the same in animation, encouraging his animators all the time to look, look, look). For Otomo, drawing is a way of engaging with the world and with people, it's not separating oneself from the world and inventing things in solitude. (All the time we're struck by how important the *social* and the *political* aspects of life are in Otomo's art: this is not flimsy whimsy, hiding away from the world).

As well as comprising short, self-contained stories, Katsuhiro Otomo's *manga* tends to avoid big,

---

26 Otomo has used map pens and Rotring pens.

climactic scenes to round off the piece. An on-going series demands cliffhangers and climaxes, but Otomo-sensei has only really done that in the *Akira, Mother Srah* and *Domu manga*.

Many of Katsuhiro Otomo's comics are in fact slices of life, depictions of how people live. Even the big horror or fantasy Otomoan outings, such as *Domu* and *Akira*, are full of portrayals of everyday life and domestic details. Which's one of the reasons for their success – you really can believe that people live in that huge, depressing apartment block in *Domu*, or that scavengers are struggling to survive in post-disaster Neo-Tokyo.

One aspect of Katsuhiro Otomo's *manga* is instantly apparent to all of his fans and admirers: there isn't enough of it! Apart from the six-volume, 2,000-page *Akira*, and the long *manga Domu*, and the short stories collected in *Hansel and Gretel, Sayonara Japan* and *Memories,* there is far too little *manga* by Otomo!

Not that we're complaining! – but compared to some *mangaka*, such as Rumiko Takahashi, Masashi Kishimoto, Eiichiro Oda and of course Osamu Tezuka, Otomo-sensei has produced far fewer pages of *manga*.

Because for Katsuhiro Otomo, *manga* is only one of many artistic things that he pursues.

Thus, most of Katsuhiro Otomo's work in *manga* has been self-contained short stories, typically twenty or thirty pages long, but sometimes only 12 pages or less (many of the stories in the fairy tale/ classics collection, *Hansel and Gretel*, are two or three pages).

It takes a lot to maintain Katsuhiro Otomo's interest, perhaps, and we know that he doesn't like to repeat himself. So the idea of becoming embroiled in a long-running *manga* series, like *Naruto,* or *Dr Slump,* or *One Piece*, or *Blade of the Immortal*, doesn't captivate Otomo-sensei (also, he likely doesn't need the dough – his work in other areas, such as commercial work, and animation, might provide enough income for him not to be a slave to the desk like many *mangaka*, who work so hard they don't even take vacations. And if they do, they feel guilty!).

MAKING *AKIRA*.

Manga artists have assistants, though one or two prefer to do all of the work themselves. So Katsuhiro Otomo wouldn't have done *everything* on the *Akira manga*. However, it is still incredibly impressive that Otomo wrote *and* drew the *manga* (many people creating *manga* split the two tasks, like the creators of *Lone Wolf and Cub* and *Death Note*).

Katsuhiro Otomo explained his working methods for *Akira*:

> My method was to completely draw the first page as a warm-up without preparatory sketches, directly on the final board, with no reworking, to get going as quickly as possible. Once that first page was done, an assistant inked the decors and buildings with a Rotring pen and ruler. Meanwhile, I pencilled the following pages, finishing usually two days before the deadline. I then needed half a day to draw all the characters, then I gave a finishing touch to the buildings by trying to instill them with life and expressiveness, with dust, cracks, broken windows. I'd finish the last pencils on Sunday at 5 a.m., the inking of the characters by 7 p.m., and the episode was delivered Monday morning at 8 a.m.

Twenty pages (one chapter) were expected by the publishers every two weeks for *Akira* (for its original magazine serialisation, which put great demands on Otomo. Some *mangaka* have suffered ill-health from the intense workload, like Tite Kubo with *Bleach*).

Katsuhiro Otomo said he had two assistants to produce the *manga* of *Akira*, and a 3rd one who came in to do the screen tone (Otomo's assistants have

included Satoshi Takabatake and Satoshi Kon).
Many of the backgrounds were drawn by the maestro
himself.

Akira was constructed in the usual manner of
comics: scripts and outlines were written (and agreed
with editors), rough sketches of each page were
created (the storyboard or 'name'), and then the
artists got down to drawing, drawing, drawing.
Each stage would be reviewed by Otomo.

Freedom keeps cropping up as a key requirement
for Otomo in creating something. *Just let me get on
with it* is his way of working. Tomohisa Kawasoe,
the manager of *Manga Action*, was an important boss
for Otomo, allowing him a good deal of freedom. In
his foreword to *Fireball*, Otomo remarked: 'I felt
really free when I got to writing *Akira*'.

THEMES IN KATSUHIRO OTOMO'S WORK.

Among the issues that Katsuhiro Otomo tackles
in his art (which are also central to Japanese animation), are: food; killing and eating; murder; death;
war; youth (and youth vs. old age); social rebellion/
anti-authoritarianism; technology; the family; the
city; catastrophes; the baby boomer generation vs. the
postwar generation, etc.

(1) war (the futility of it, but also a fascination
with it), and WWII in particular (Katsuhiro Otomo's
art is entirely a post-WWII art, an art of the Cold
War, of the post-atomic age);

(2) youth (and youth vs. old age, the younger
generation kicking against their parents' generation);
the younger generation grappling with the Sins of the
Fathers; Otomo is one of the baby boomers (born
1946-1964), and his art is very much baby boomer
art;

(3) anti-authoritarianism (again, often embodied
in teenagers); the refusal of authority is absolutely
fundamental to Otomo's life-philosophy (often it's
simply the desire to refuse or negate a situation; a
rebel is someone who says 'no', as Albert Camus put

it; Otomo has a strong contradictory nature – if you're going *that way*, he will automatically go in the *other direction*. He doesn't follow the herd);

(4) technology and science (a perennial issue in Japanese society: Otomo explores the ambiguities and anxieties surrounding technology);

(5) destruction and apocalypse[27] (the emphasis on things falling apart has an æsthetic/ artistic component, because it exposes the nature of things, and creates endless drama; it also chimes with post-war Japanese culture, and the politics of paranoia, desperation and dystopia);

(6) psychic and spiritual issues;

(7) modern Japan (including analyses of politics and institutions); Otomo has also set several stories in the U.S.A., or included N. American charas;

(8) the city, the modern/ futuristic metropolis (and its opposite – not the boring suburb, but the anti-city, the wasteland, the desert);

(9) politics (with an obvious sympathy for left-wing ideology);

(10) utopianism: yes, there must be Something Better, but Katsuhiro Otomo, like 99.99% of artists, can't actually say how a utopian society would work in precise, practical terms, or how it could be achieved;

and (11) society; Katsuhiro Otomo's art is immersed in the complexity, the intricacy and the eccentricity of society; his art charts the failings and flaws of society, but is also alive to its beauties and ecstasies.

❋

Comedy is absolutely fundamental to the art of Katsuhiro Otomo, but too few critics draw attention to it. From his earliest work, however, Otomo-sensei has employed humour. Many of his comic strips are based on humorous gags. Some of his *manga* feature very black humour. And several of Otomo's movies as writer and director are comedies: *Roujin Z*, the

---

27 Ecology and pollution are minor themes.

Stink Bomb section of *Memories,* the *Order To Stop Construction* story in *Neo-Tokyo,* the credit sequences of *Robot Carnival,* and the sex comedy *High School Erotopia: Red Uniforms.*

SURVIVAL.

In the world of Katsuhiro Otomo, the number one issue is survival, which must be protected at all costs. Thus, a weapon is always close at hand in Otomo Land – if you haven't got a gun, a psychic child, or an aircraft carrier – a piece of pipe will do. Failing that, you can find rocks everywhere. Then you can attack anybody who threatens your survival. Otomo's grand theme could be called the politics of survival.

You can call Katsuhiro Otomo's outlook bleak, pessimistic, nihilistic, or just plain realist. In his view, humans have always been and will always be *extremely aggressive.* You can sit and type on a computer, play with a cel phone or a tablet, or you can write clever theoretical essays about consumerism or cyberspace or terrorism or postmodern, post-everything politics, but you'd better make sure there's no one standing on a ledge above you about to smash a rock into your skull.

Food, sex, shelter, pleasure-seeking (drugs, alcohol) – these items are right behind survival and defending it with aggression in the Otomoverse.

CHARACTERS IN KATSUHIRO OTOMO'S ART.

The art of Katsuhiro Otomo is striking in its use of seemingly ordinary people as the main characters. Many of his stories use everyday folk either as the chief charas, or we see events from their perspective. Many of Otomo's protagonists conform to the cliché 'ordinary people in extraordinary circumstances' (the cliché is applied to the cinema of Steven Spielberg, for instance). You see these 'ordinary people' inhabiting the frames of *Sayonara Japan, SOS! Tokyo Metro Explorers, Minor Swing,* etc. And in *Akira,* Kei and Kaneda are not remarkable (at least at first).

Several character designs crop up in many Katsuhiro Otomo's *manga*: one is a young man with a moustache and long hair: he's a regular, working class guy trying to survive; he's one of the brothers in *Fireball*, the guy trying to make it in New York City in *Sayonara Japan*, one of the squad in *A Farewell To Weapons*, and he appears in other 1970s works. Ryu in *Akira* is a modified version of Moustache Man. (One should note that Otomo favours boys or men as his main characters, tho' *Akira* and some of the fairy tales re-dresss the balance).

Another is a portly *otaku* figure with square glasses: this is clearly a humorous self-portrait by Katsuhiro Otomo: Glasses Man turns up in *Domu* (as one o' the victims), in *Fireball*, and in *SOS! Tokyo Metro Explorers*.

You'll see the same types throuhout Katsuhiro Otomo's *manga* among the minor charas: social dissidents/ rebels (who're often hairy guys with moustaches); young, pre-teen girls with their hair in bunches; hapless, repressed salarymen; aggressive cops; scruffy, little toddlers with runny noses who want to go pee-pee (a staple of *manga*); matronly women who're trying to hold families together; and the cop in *Akira*, George Yamada,[28] appears in some of the 1970s *manga*.

Otomo-sensei has made teenagers, and boys in particular, one of his chief character types. Otomo displays a remarkable empathy with young people – how they interact, how they live, what their hopes and fears are. The Otomoan child is idealistic, romantic, rebellious, eccentric, difficult and needy. Otomo's gangs and groups of kids always seem completely convincing. And he captures the often hidden feelings of children – their anger and anxiety as outsiders and loners, their need to be accepted.

---

28 George Yamada appears in the *Akira* movie as one o' the cops in the police interview scene after the riots.

MOTIFS IN KATSUHIRO OTOMO'S ART.

Among Katsuhiro Otomo's motifs are: deserts (sand, beaches); blocky, concrete architecture; skyscrapers (usually wrecked); pebbles; decay; robots; tanks; *mecha* of all kinds; space suits; plants as precious commodities; rock music; Americana, etc.

Narratively, Katsuhiro Otomo is very fond of the twist ending, the 'sting in the tail', the ninety degree turn. Many of his early *manga* stories are (1) short, and (2) feature a twist at the end. Some of the twists are funny (like the hippy who winds up stripped naked and shorn of his locks by a robot), but many are simply weird (for ex, *Minor Swing*, where the fisherman who survived drowning in polluted waters ends up as a sort of pet fish in a tank of oily, black water[29]).

KATSUHIRO OTOMO'S POLITICS.

Katsuhiro Otomo is rare among creators of fantasy, adventure and *animé* shows and *manga* in foregrounding politics – and left-wing politics at that. However, there are a few well-known filmmakers in *animé* who have left-wing views, and put them in their movies: Hayao Miyazaki and Isao Takahata, most obviously, and also Mamoru Oshii and Kenji Kamiyama (in the West, it is extremely rare to find overt political analysis in fantasy, adventure and action cinema, and even rarer to find the exploration of left-wing views. When was the last time you saw a Pixar or Disney or Warner Bros. or Fox or DreamWorks cartoon that explored or endorsed socialism or Marxism? Like, never!).

But the artistic output of Katsuhiro Otomo is genuinely interested in politics, and how individuals interact with politics, and how their political views alter their lives. Otomo is also very interested in exploring society, as well as alternative societies (his futuristic stories, for instance, explore possible societies in great detail). After all, much of the *Akira*

---

29 This kind of gag works only in the visual/ comic medium.

manga (even more than the 1988 animated movie), is all about wondering what it would be like to live in a futuristic society in which right-wing forces are overwhelming Japanese society. And in which resistance takes the form of underground cells of activists as well as big street demonstrations (which're rapidly suppressed by the government).

The political issues tackled by Otomo-sensei include: socialist activism • a left-wing analysis of social systems • a critique of political corruption • terrorism • anti-government movements • second wave feminism • the younger generation vs. the older generation • the exploitation of children • the Sins of the Fathers • and the State's mis-use of technology and science.

The movies, *manga,* O.A.V.s and TV shows of Katsuhiro Otomo are very sophisticated politically and socially; they are far, far, far more sophisticated, subtle and multi-layered than their counterparts in Western pop culture. Otomo-sensei clearly displays a grounding in and understanding of post-WWII politics, in particular the idealistic and utopian optimism and political activism of the 1960s.

Most science fiction movies are pretty simplistic politically (while nearly all of them, like nearly all entertainment in the Westernized world, promulgate a conservative, right-wing ideology). But *Akira* is way more advanced politically than most sci-fi cinema, including many of the celebrated classics, such as *Blade Runner,*[30] *2001: A Space Odyssey, Alien, The Terminator, Star Wars, Close Encounters of the Third Kind,* etc (which are all right-wing). And utopian fictions, which you might expect to have left-wing or socialist elements, also tend to be politically conservative. It seems to be a built-in element of science fiction (certainly all sword and sorcery and dungeons and dragons-style fantasy fiction is right-

---

30 While film critics raved about the visualization of futuristic cities in movies such as *Blade Runner, Akira* went far beyond them. *Akira* was set in a post-apocalyptic Tokyo (called Neo-Tokyo), a city rebuilding itself following World War Three.

wing – some of it bordering on or encouraging
fascism, militarism and white supremacy).

So that, despite the occasionally radical invention of the visuals and of the intricacies of the alternative and futuristic worlds of science fiction, the
ideologies and the politics disseminated are, in the
end, right-wing. *Blade Runner, Iron Man* and *Avatar et
al* may look amazing, but the politics they promote is
still conservative (hell, the hero of *Blade Runner* is a
cop, and you can't get much more establishment than
that!).[31]

KATSUHIRO OTOMO AND *MECHA*.

'I liked machines. It was as simple as that. I *like*
busy, convoluted stuff'. The cinema and *manga* of
Katsuhiro Otomo is as in love with technology, with
mecha, with flying machines, with tanks, with steam-
punk paraphernalia, and with gadgets, as anybody
else in the world of *animé* or *manga*. Yet Otomo's
manga and *animé* is also keener to expose the
problems that technology and science can bring than
many of his contemporaries. Technology and *mecha*
going wrong is a recurring motif in all of Otomo's
work (but of course it's fundamental in drama to
have things going wrong!). And Otomo is also keen to
tie in science and technology to political and social
systems, so that there is always a political critique
built in to his stories, and a social background in
which the issues are explored.

DESERTS.

It's striking just how much of Katsuhiro Otomo's
manga work is set in deserts. Whether it's the deserts
of North America, or of the Middle East, or of China,
they all seem to be post-apocalyptic realms, where the
world becomes one big wasteland. Otomo enjoys the
clean, sparse look of the desert (and the beach), which
suits his preference for lots of white space in his art. A

31 Sure, Deckard's cool, and weary, and cynical, and Harrison Ford
and all, but he's still a *cop*.

desert is also a space which acts as a minimalist stage for his characters, settings and stories, letting them breathe in white, open areas. (As Otomo explained in the *Memories Anthology*, 'stories involving sand and snow are dead easy... can I get away with saying just that?').

ENDINGS.

You have to admit that some of Katsuhiro Otomo's scripts go a little haywire in the last, climactic acts: *Metropolis, Akira* and, most calamitously, *Steam-boy*. Otomo's not the only filmmaker who finds wrapping up a story challenging (Jean-Luc Godard, Andrei Tarkovsky, Stanley Kubrick, Tim Burton, Francis Coppola and Werner Herzog would be others); partly it's Make Your Mind Up time: how do you want this to play? – (A) ambiguous, open-ended, complex, multi-layered (the art cinema option), or (B) romantic, with total narrative resolution on all fronts (the Hollywood option)? Otomo-sensei tends to ask questions[32] rather than provide answers: he is a curious artist, enquiring about the human condition, but he doesn't have all the answers (yet who does?).

It's not a major failing, however, because the significance of endings is overdone by critics (and many fans). That the movie of *Akira* doesn't have a wholly fulfilling ending in narrative and thematic terms doesn't damage the movie too much, because the filmmaking and the experience of the movie is so intense and inspired (but some critics and fans have found the ending dissatisfying). However, in a movie such as *Steam-boy* and *Metropolis*, which're much more conventional in narrative terms, and which conform to the formats of the action-adventure genre, the flaws of the endings injure the movies.

32 Pier Paolo Pasolini said that his films 'asked questions' rather than 'provided answers' or delivered something 'finished'.

Portraits of Katsuhiro Otomo
(left is by Yomiuri Shimbun).

Katsuhiro Otomo in his studio (from Geijutsu Shincho magazine).

Some works influenced by Katsuhiro Otomo

Osamu Tezuka, 'god of manga',
and his signature work, Astro Boy

Tetsujin 28 (a.k.a. Gigantor,
1956 to 1966),
by Mitsuteru Yokoyama

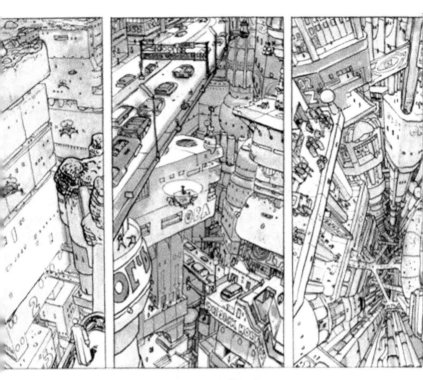

The art of Moebius
(a.k.a. Jean Giraud).

Movies from North America in the late 1960s
have been cited as influences by Otomo.

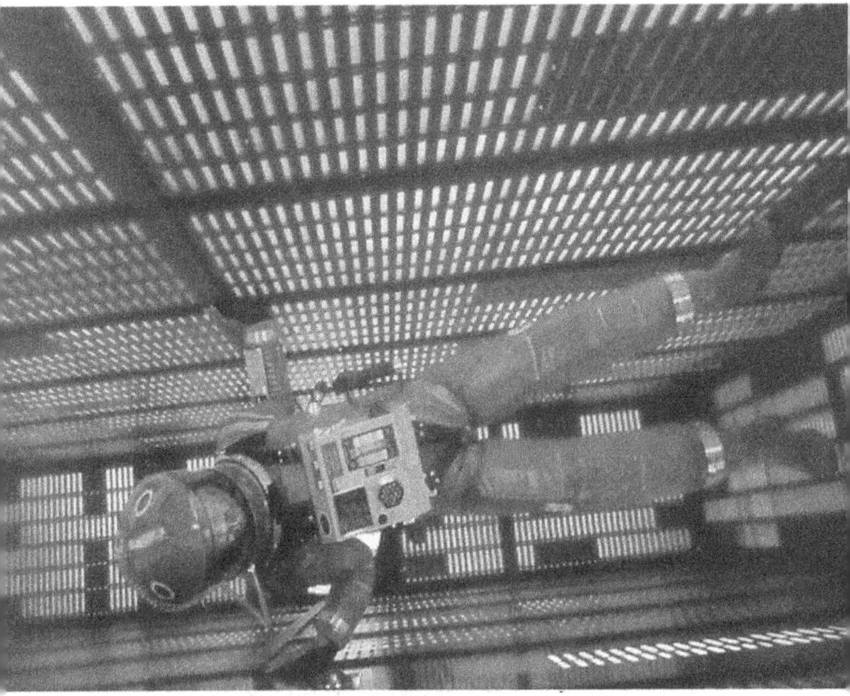

2001: A Space Odyssey

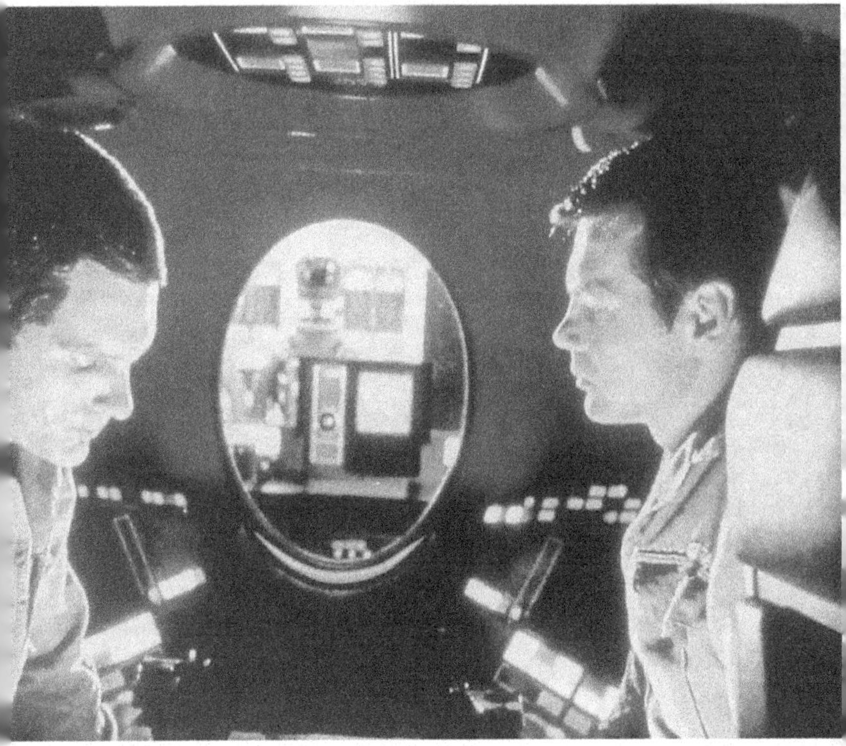

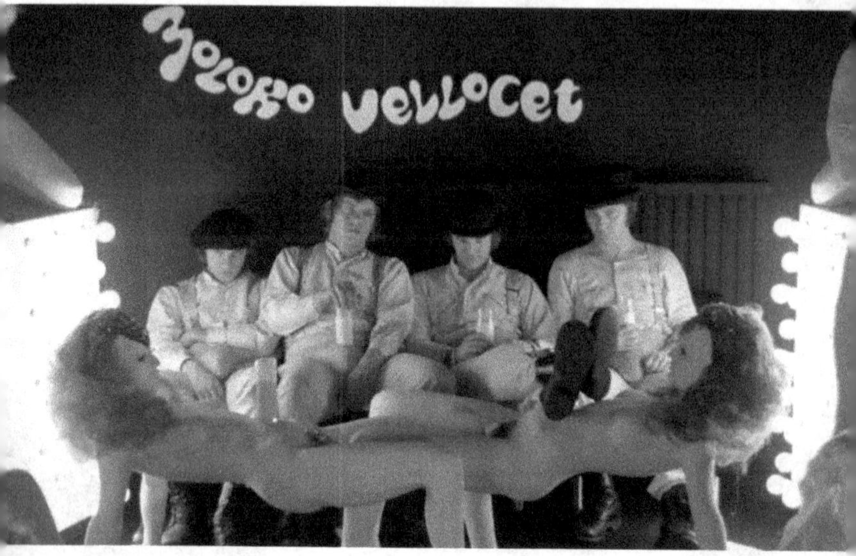
Korova

A Clockwork Orange (1971)

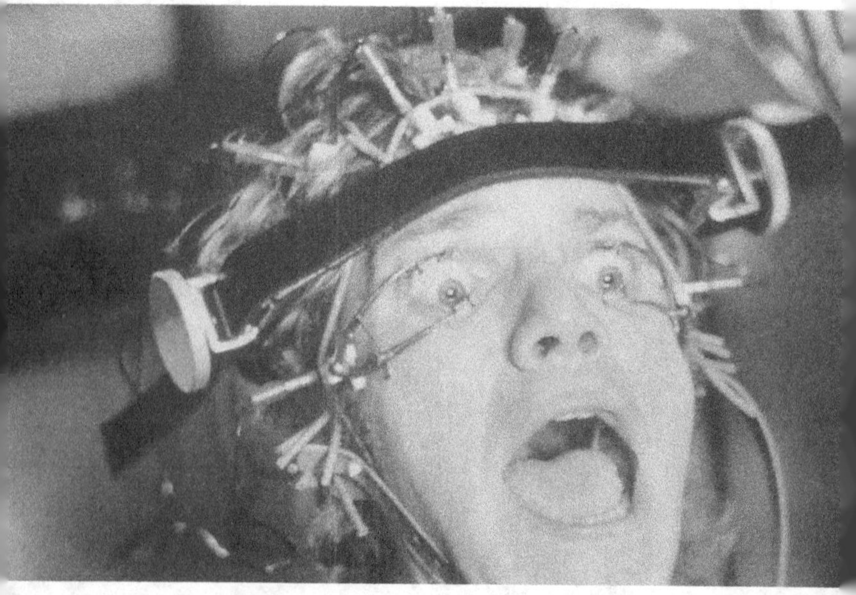

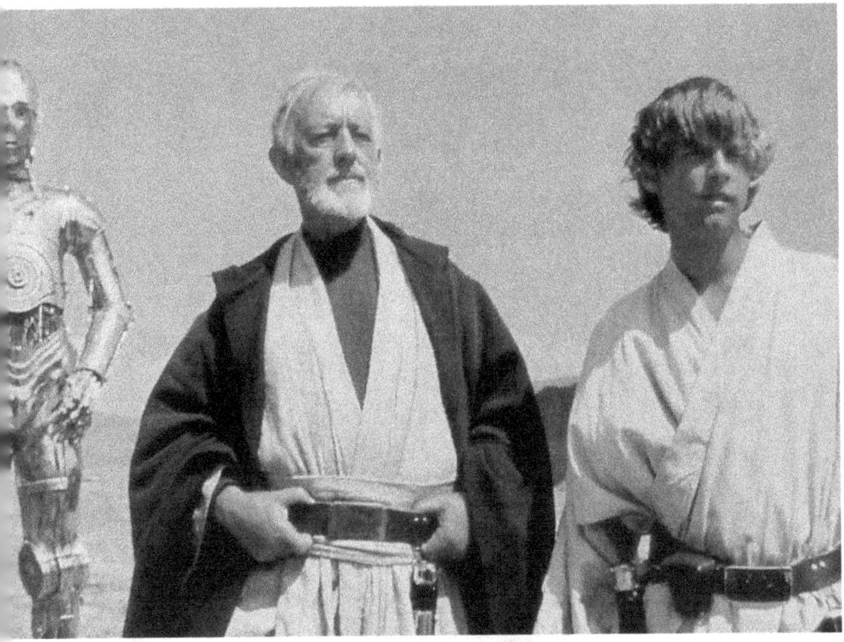

Star Wars

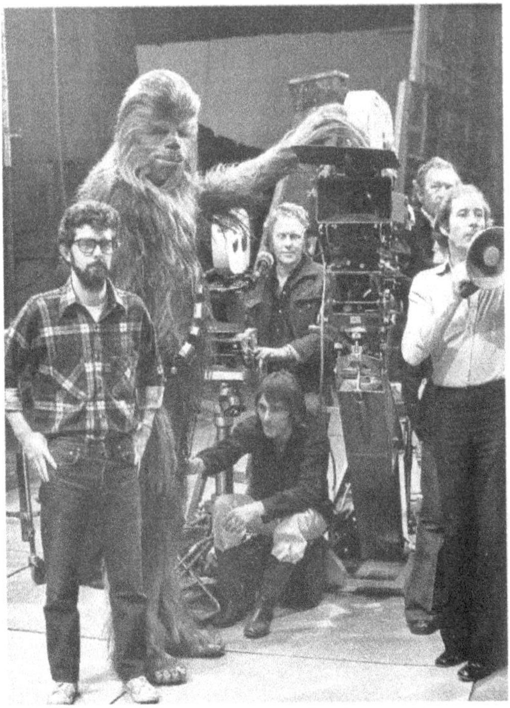

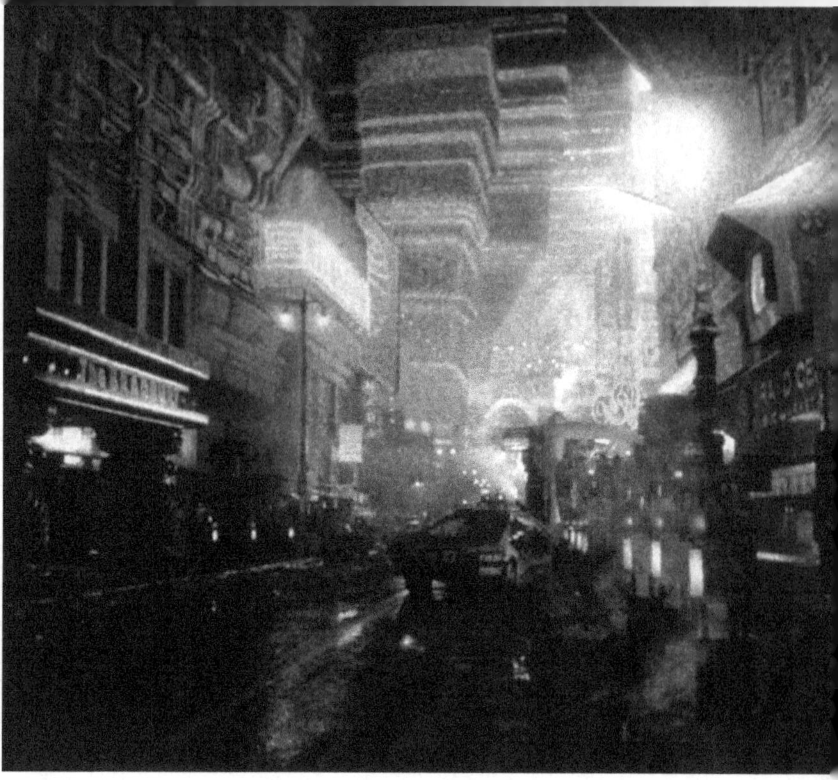

Blade Runner

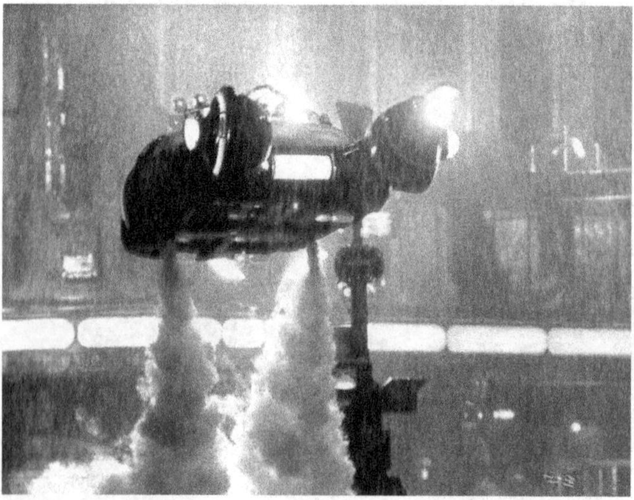

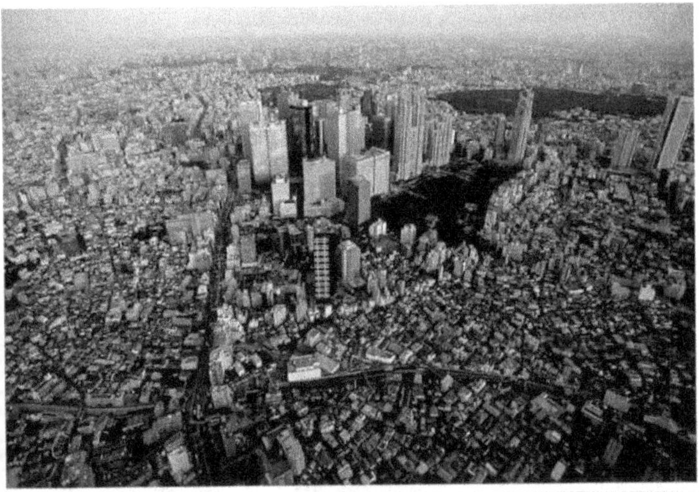

The great city of animé: Tokyo, where nearly all animé is made, and much of it is set.

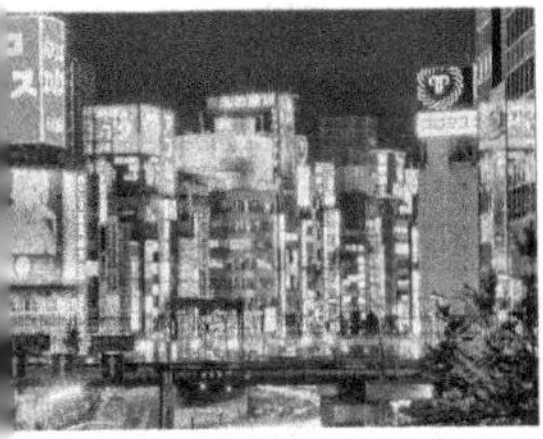

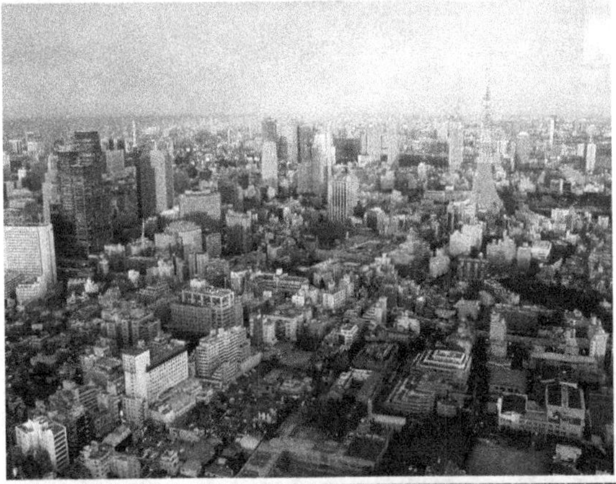

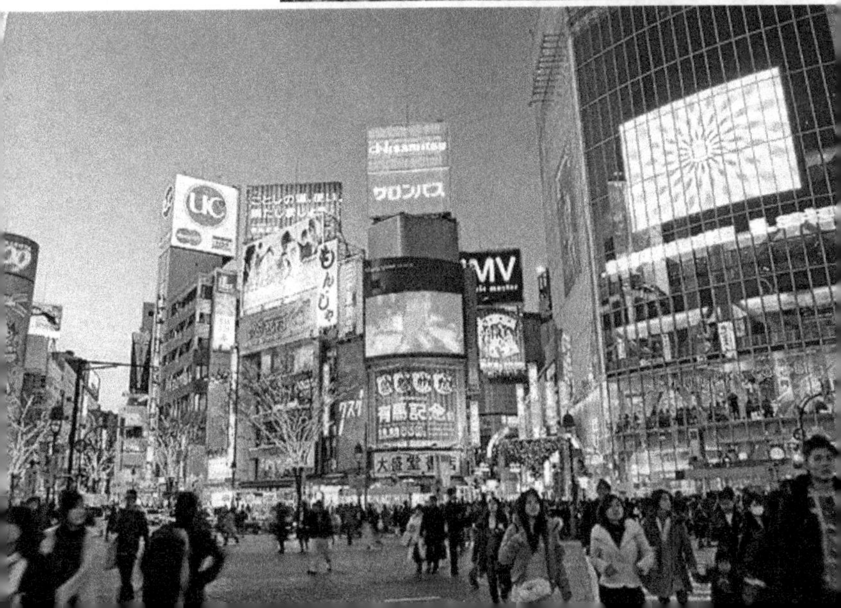
サロンパス
有馬記念

Gotham is a key influence on Otomo's art (Photos: author)

Deserts appear in numerous
works by Otomo.

Mojave Desert, California (left).
Zabriskie Point (below).

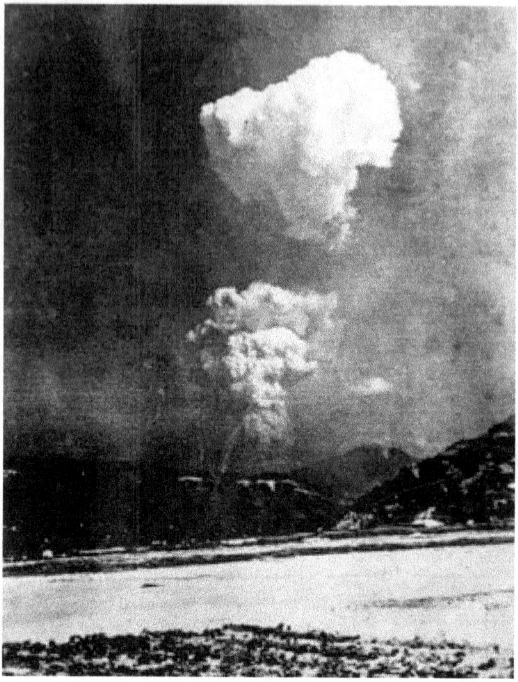

Hiroshima

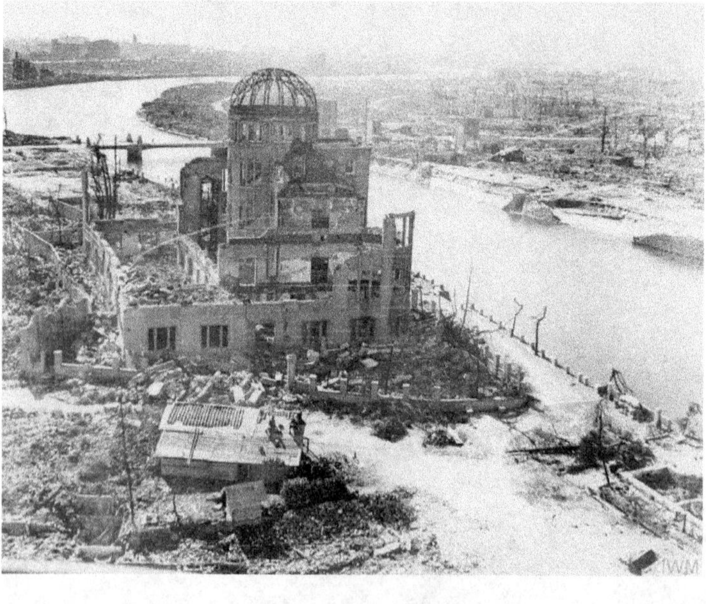
IWM

PART TWO

MANGA

SOME OF KATSUHIRO OTOMO'S *MANGA* WORKS

INTRO.

From his earliest *manga* works onwards, Katsuhiro Otomo has happily worked in the adult, 'R' rated world. Otomo-sensei has no problem depicting sex, drugs, violence, 'bad language', and weirdness of many kinds (yet his *manga* can also be sweet and child-like and aimed at children). Otomo has a mature view of life, which sees right into the poverty, the struggle, the hopes and dreams, the losses and the disappointments of being alive in any era. One word sums up this key theme: survival.

Katsuhiro Otomo comes across as a novelist in the manner of 19th century writers like Charles Dickens or Leo Tolstoy, who aims to portray a large cross-section of human life, coupled with the left-wing, social realist sort of approach to art of Russian culture of the mid-20th century (that Otomo's political views are left-wing is easy to discern if you look at even a few pages of most of his *manga*). And, unlike many left-wing artists who in their works back-pedal, and end up delivering the same conservative, right-wing material that everybody else produces, Otomo has remained a left-wing artist (and an artist who doesn't hide his socialist politics).

BOOGIE WOOGIE WALTZ

In *Boogie Woogie Waltz* (1974), a *nebbish* loner gets involved with a hooker. He's another of the shifty, self-pitying and misanthropic youths that crop up regularly in Katsuhiro Otomo's *manga* work (and in quite a bitta *manga*). The guy works in a jeans store and keeps a gun at home, hidden away. He has murderous, *Taxi Driver*-ish fantasies of using it (as in, 'ugly women should all just die', in ref. to a customer who visited his store, asking for a mini-skirt).

When the guy goes to see the prostitute Mitsuko (who looks like the wonderful Pam Grier, star of many 1970s blaxploitation flicks), he's stunned by the high price of her services (like all first-timers and virgins visiting hookers in comics), and is terrified when her pimp turns up (he keeps insisting that he hasn't got in the bath yet, as if he's in a respectable Soapland in Tokyo, where bathing is a cover for prostitution). Mitsuko says she's pregnant, and that the pimp is the father. Hurrying away from a potential confrontation with someone who's so much tougher and wiser than he is, the guy returns later armed with his pistol. He threatens the prostitute and the pimp with it, but of course he hasn't got the guts to go any further, and is soundly beaten.

Boogie Woogie Waltz is a sad story of disconnection and alienation, with suicide yet again looming on the horizon (in the final pages). But it's an accomplished short chapter, considering that the artist was only 20.

Chuck Check Chicken (1976), from the *Good Weather* collection (Kitansha, 1981), is a ribald comedy set in the Edo period, on the dangerous roads outside of the cities and towns where bandits roam. The hero is a *ronin* samurai, down on his luck, and with a young, hungry child in tow (this is in part a parody of the famous samurai *manga Lone Wolf and Cub* by Kazuo Koike and Goseki Kojima. Koike's *manga* has become *the* samurai *manga* – or, at least, the samurai *manga* which everybody knows, if they know any of them).[1]

Chuck Check Chicken is a comic tale of thieves, peasants, roadside restaurants (*shubuka*), children, vagabonds on the make, hunger and food, sex, dogs, and silly fights. Along the way, it sends up many of the clichés of the *jidai geki* (historical story), and *Lone Wolf and Cub*. There's a charming, road movie, *Canterbury Tales* (Geoffrey Chaucer) aspect to *Chuck Check Chicken:* despite all of the incidents, nobody ends up any wiser or better off (a recurring motif of Katsuhiro Otomo's storytelling is that characters end up where they began). People are met along the road, then they disappear, then we meet them again, in changed circumstances. Everyone's looking for an angle – or, rather, a dupe to rob (and all of the money they find goes on food).

Survival is again a prime theme – the story opens with the samurai and his son trying to kill a stray dog. Not because it's attacking them, but for food. They fail (partly because we can't have doggies being killed, skinned and eaten in a comic, can we? But mainly because they're useless).

There are many swipes at *Lone Wolf and Cub* in *Chuck Check Chicken*, a *manga* that everybody who reads *manga* knows, and that anybody creating action or fantasy *manga* will have studied (any samurai or swordplay *manga* or *animé* made today

1 Kazuo Koike (b. 1936), author of *Lone Wolf and Cub*, also wrote *Lady Snowblood* (illustrated by Kazuo Kamimura, 1940-86), another classic.

or in the past fifty years comes in the wake of *Lone Wolf and Cub*).[2] *Lone Wolf and Cub* is a masterpiece of storytelling, and in every single story, the grim, solemn, never-smiling Itto Ogami triumphs over his adversaries. Ogami is the super-warrior *par excellence* – no matter how many opponents are ranged against him, no matter how enormous the obstacles are, he always manages somehow to emerge victorious. Well, the 22 year-old Otomo overturns that, with a series of comic incidents performed by hapless, useless characters.

The hero of *Chuck Check Chicken* is another of Katsuhiro Otomo's characters who spends most of the story struggling, and never getting what they desire (his design, longish hair and a moustache, was used many times in Otomo-sensei's Seventies comicbooks).[3] The hero becomes angry with his child and thumps him (something that Itto Ogami never does with li'l Daigoro!), fumes about being left by his wife, and lumbered with a kid. The comedy ends with a chaotic scuffle, with the hero discovering that his wife is now working as a hooker.

SHORT PIECE

Short Piece was an early *manga* by Katsuhiro Otomo (Futabasha, 1979). It includes the stories: *Space Patrolman Shigema, Round About Midnight, Schoolboy On Good, Cinema Club, Tai... Kyoo, Whisky Go Go, Nothing Will Be As It Was, Yume no...* and *Okasu.* In one episode, *Space Patrolman Shigema*, a bunch of guys gather during New Year's, and play a kind of truth or dare (when they've run out of *saké*). Turns out they are aliens from Venus, Mars, Mercury, etc (one of them pulls of his human mask to reveal a creature under-

2 Kojima's art in *Lone Wolf* is exceptional – particularly his pen and wash drawings that open each chapter.
3 The guy in his twenties with long hair and a moustache turns up in *Fireball, Hair, A Farewell To Weapons, Sayonara Japan,* and *Akira.*

neath, *Men In Black*-style), while another guy in the group (Shigeru[4]) is space patrolman come to round them up (he even has the spandex suit and helmet, plus a penis-shaped laser pistol). Or are they just a bunch of ordinary guys after all? Shigeru hauls them all to the beach, where he magically raises a flying saucer out of the ocean, Yoda-style (or does he?). *Short Piece* comes over as another of Otomo's depictions of young guys goofing around (that takes up quite a bit of the *Akira manga*).

Another *Short Piece* piece, *Nothing Will Be As It Was* (1977), has a guy murdering a man in his *aparto*, and exploring ways of getting rid of the body. In the end, he buys a big, new refrigerator, cuts up the body, jams it inside, and of course selects tasty parts to eat for dinner each day (it's gory, with plenty of blood sloshing about). It's a minor, black humour episode, and way below Katsuhiro Otomo's talents conceptually. It does have Otomo's grungey, lived-in look, however, and an emphasis on life-or-death scenarios, where mortality and the fragility of being alive is foregrounded. It also features the issue of killing and eating, and the problem of finding food, Otomoan perennials.

VISITORS

Visitors (1984) is a companion piece to *Nothing Will Be As It Was* – it's the same down-at-heel world of suburban apartment blocks, the same desperation seething underneath lives going nowhere, the same barely-repressed anxieties. It's the world of *Domu* and *World Apartment Horror*, which Otomo has depicted many times. And it's all about murder, again.

Visitors employs the visual gimmick of a

4 Possibly a reference to Otomo's regular film producer, Shigeru Watanabe.

subjective viewpoint – the story is told through an observer's eyes as they pay a visit to a student friend, Yukata. The atmosphere becomes grizzly when it's revealed that Yukata killed his landlord when he barged in demanding the week's rent, and then his girlfriend Atsuko when she caught him masturbating (to pictures of Sumo wrestlers, a classic Otomoan twist on porn mags). Yukata's squashed the corpses into the closet, where they tumble out.

Visitors is another of Otomo's black comedy skits about suburban angst, and fantasies of erasing life's many problems with clumsy, impossible solutions (like killing people). Unable to find a suitable image to close this chapter, Otomo opts for a absurd drawing which has nothing to do with the rest of the piece whatsoever: a pleasant, rural scene featuring a bull mounting a cow.

FIREBALL

Fireball[5] (1979) was an abandoned *manga* that was important for Katsuhiro Otomo's career: (1) it was one of his first, serious attempts at science fiction; (2) it featured several elements that were later recycled in *Akira*; and (3) it contained images and scenarios that he would re-use in later works. In his foreword to a re-print of *Fireball*, Otomo-sensei explained that he'd 'had enough' of *Fireball* by page twenty, and his attention was soon taken up with other projects (notably *Domu*).[6]

This is a recurring issue in Katsuhiro Otomo's career: getting bored easily – because, as he explained, the best part is thinking up the story. Once you've done that, writing and drawing is fraught with disappointments (because it's never as good as

5 Deep Purple have provided titles for some of Otomo's works such as *Fireball* and *Highway Star*.
6 *Hair* (1979), with its depictions of hippy rebels vs. the authorities, is a kind of spoof of *Fireball*.

that initial dream). In which case, the subjects of *Domu* and *Akira,* two of Otomo-sensei's longest works, must've really inspired him. (He had the idea for *Domu* while writing *Fireball*).

Fireball includes many ingredients that turned up in *Akira*: the freedom fighters ('those damn pinkos') are involved with an anti-government political movement (which includes violent street demos); a secret department of the State is conducting nefarious experiments on psychics (literally cutting open their heads and chests); the portrayal of the psychics as superheroes (for example, floating in balls of energy above the facility); an action-packed set-piece where the activists infiltrate the psychic facility disguised in uniforms (with gun battles in the corridors), and so on.

In *Fireball*, Katsuhiro Otomo introduced a theme that crops up in several of his later *manga* (such as *Akira* and *Domu*): psychic people. Two brothers have seemingly weak psychic abilities; they are involved with freedom fighters who're trying to expose and possibly over-throw an organization run by a super-computer called A.T.O.M. and a formidable, portly woman known as 'Mama'.[7] A.T.O.M. is conducting experiments into psychic phenomenon (in the usual hi-tech, partly-underground facility).

Fireball plumps for a bigger, more apocalyptic ending than many of Katsuhiro Otomo's previous *manga,* as the brother resurrects on the laboratory operating table as a dead-alive skeleton. This was a famous image, Otomo's nod to *Frankenstein*, one of the key reference points in Japanese horror as well as the horror and science fiction genres the world over. (There are several links to *Frankenstein* in Otomo's œuvre, including in *Akira, Roujin Z* and *Metropolis*).

And then the brother goes on a killing spree. Well, sort of: he targets the facility where the A.T.O.M. computer is based: floating far above it, he attacks it, using heat (and summons his brother, too).

---

7 In *Akira,* Mama becomes the Colonel.

The imagery and the action looks forward to *Akira*, as the whole place goes up in flames.

MAGNETIC ROSE IN *MEMORIES*

Katsuhiro Otomo's *manga* of *Memories* (1980) includes the short, 32-page story that was used as the basis for the truly remarkable *Magnetic Rose* section of the 1995 *Memories* movie (it was the first piece that Otomo wrote for *Young Magazine,* and was published in the West in U.S.A. and G.B. editions in 1992 and 1995).

The *Magnetic Rose manga* is very short, however (like most of Katsuhiro Otomo's *manga*), so there simply isn't space to include many of the details that made the *animé* so spectacular. In the *manga*, for instance, a bunch of robots chase away the astronauts from the ship, firing lasers; that is far less satisfying or gripping than the extraordinary haunted castle *milieu* of the 1995 *animé*. (In the *animé*, there are robotic assistants in the form of little cherubs – Heintz has a running battle with them in a corridor). The *manga* doesn't have the psychological depths of the *animé,* which added back-stories for all three of the main characters (and Heintz doesn't appear in the comic, either).

With the introduction of the opera diva in the animated adaptation of *Magnetic Rose,* and the decision to explode the approach up to the level of grand opera, the comic version was left far behind. The bare bones are there, with the exploration of a rose-shaped vessel in deep space, but the *animé* was something else entirely – a state-of-the-art *tour-de-force* of sound, music and imagery.

OTHER *MANGA* WORKS OF THE LATE 1970s/ EARLY 1980s

GOOD WEATHER.

Good Weather (1981, Kitansha) was another collection of works from the 1970s (1974-80), which Katsuhiro Otomo wrote and illustrated, including: *Chuck Check Chicken, Tokyo Chang Pong, Shincho Senki, Good Weather, Ai no Kaikaku 2 Chome 3, Virgin Shadow, Katsu Kare, So What, Ame Lingo* and *Boogie Woogie Waltz.*

MINOR SWING.

Published in *Manga Action* in Aug, 1977, *Minor Swing* is an atmospheric and eerie meditation on the issue of pollution: a survivor of an accident on a nighttime fishing trip finds himself floating in water which's oily and black, with trash strewn in it (the scenario is repeated in *Akira*, with Kaneda in the sewers). The artwork is dense with dark screentones.

Minor Swing is one of Katsuhiro Otomo's strangest pieces, a story which doesn't seem to go anywhere, which meanders in trackless waters like its abandoned fisherman. Eventually, the guy discovers he's been swimming near an industrial zone (installations loom in the darkness). As daylight comes, he staggers out onto land, covered head-to-toe in black mud too thick to wash off. Locals avoid him, thinking he's a monster/ spirit/ turtle/ shark. The mud won't shift; he tries to hose it off; he stumbles in the hot sun to the beach, and discovers the body of his buddy Hiruma, with the mud dried on him. Some kids find him, wonder if he's an alien, then flee; eventually, a cop is led to the scene by the kids, by which time the survivor is baking in the heat (the beach and sea settings were included because Otomo was writing a story to be published in Summer, altho' it does seem silly that a guy caked in mud, who's survived an ordeal in the water, would end up at the ocean again).

Katsuhiro Otomo said he wanted another weird ending, and *Minor Swing* certainly has that: the fisherman survives, but as a human in a fish tank filled with black, oily water, in an apartment. 'It always feels great to be in the sea!' he says. And he's got all he needs in the room: there's a TV churning out its drivel next to the tank (to soothe the perpetually restless human mind), and medical drips feed the liquids bodies require into the tank.

EAST OF THE SUN, WEST OF THE MOON.

In *East of the Sun, West of the Moon* (from a story by Karibu Marei), an old woman (Lily Matsuhashi) who runs a small, backstreet bar enlists a bunch of no-hoper musos to be her backing band of musicians for a one-off concert revival of her glory days as a torch singer. The guys are stunned to see the woman (who they thought was just another old woman), in her element as a confident vocalist, and the number of high calibre guests from the old days who come to hear her perform (including record company moguls, such as the President of R.C.A.).

The lads have run up a huge tab at Lily's bar (over 3,000 bucks), so they readily agree to be Lily's backing band. They are a wannabe rock act[8] (we see them taking a demo to Island Records), and find playing jazz and reading sheet music on the fly very challenging. They struggle thru the concert, until some of the veteran musicians in the audience take the stage. Lily dozes off towards the end, waking up later in her bar, suggesting that it was all a dream – her wish for a final, reunion gig (however, there's also a photograph commemorating the event). Dream or not, it's the desire that counts.

East of the Sun, West of the Moon is a mood piece, an atmosphere piece; it's about an attitude more even than characters – and the motif of music as the spiritual-social glue which joins people and eras together is pure Otomo.

8 This is the late 1970s.

FLOWER.

In *Flower* (published in *S.F. Hoseki*, Oct, 1979), a 6-page, watercoloured story,[9] a man carries some water in his helmet to a plant that's kept in a smashed glass chamber in what might've been a laboratory. Once again in Katsuhiro Otomo's art, the setting is a desert, and what might be a survey expedition has undergone a catastrophe (there are fresh graves nearby). So, again, it's a story of survival. (The plant is precious – it's a single growth in a glass chamber and, this being a desert, water is a rarity).

Nearby, an alien stalks on thirty-foot tall, spindly, bony legs (clearly evoking the tripods in *The War of the Worlds* by H.G. Wells, which invaded Earth). The man fires his laser pistol at the creature, which (altho' hit) grabs him in a thick, green tentacle, wrapping it round his body, holding him above the laboratory. The alien squeezes like a boa constrictor snake, killing the guy, and his blood rains down (on the plant). The alien-tripod collapses. In the final image of *Flower*, lo and behold, a flower (red, of course), blooms on the plant. (The notion of human bodies literally feeding plants with their blood and flesh crops up in *Mother Sarah*, where potatoes are growing out of humans like they're bags of compost).

SOUND OF SAND.

Sound of Sand comes from *Kisotengai* magazine (Nov, 1979): it's another science fiction tale, and it's once again set in a desert. Poor Kuhl has fallen into the desert in his spacesuit on his own, and it's so unstable, he sinks, and it takes a while for him to be rescued (three days and nights). Kuhl slides into the fine sand once again, just as a two-legged module is hurrying thru the desert to pick him up. When Kuhl's brought back to the shuttle orbiting above, his suit is opened and his body has become replaced by nothing but sand, and the sand… it's moving… it's alive!

9 Katsuhiro Otomo explained that he was inspired to try painting the story because he'd been introduced to the work of Moebius (by his friend Kuromaru).

Sound of Sand is another of Otomo's single gag stories, a variation on the motif in science fiction of bringing back someone on board a spaceship who's been infected. Or maybe it was just an excuse to draw sand and deserts, as Otomo explained in his notes: 'stories involving sand and snow are dead easy'.

HAIR.

Hair (*Young Comic*, 1979.2.28) is one of Katsuhiro Otomo's funniest *manga* (the title is from the *Hair* musical, of course, and it was conceived as a kind of spoof of *Fireball*). It's a wonderful send-up of hippies, long-haired freaks, of musos, and their long-running battle with the straights, the crewcuts, the salarymen. It's the baby boomer and pop music generation versus the WWII and post-war generation.

Set in a world of the future where society has become ruthlessly organized into a uniform whole, where germs have been eradicated, where all is neat and clean, Katsuhiro Otomo's 25-page *Hair* tells the story of a bunch of rebels who're united by their love of long hair and rock music. They wax lyrical about Led Zeppelin, the Rolling Stones and Deep Purple[10] The hippies are portrayed as well-meaning but dim, badly dressed (bare feet, ragged clothes), and rebellious for the sheer hell of it. In one hilarious gag, a guy carrying a prog rock album (*In the Court of the Crimson King* by King Crimson, 1969, with its distinctive red cover of a screaming man by Barry Godber),[11] is being chased by the authorities. As if he's carrying drugs, he ditches the LP in a trash can as he runs away, before he's caught by the fuzz (who beat him up, of course). And the garbage man picks up the can, grumbling, 'it's heavy!' (A reference to the early 70s when rock music was called 'heavy').

10 In this future era, rock albums are now housed in museums (and they're being stolen!).
11 The album cover achieved a certain notoriety when the artist Barry Godber died of a heart attack (aged 24) a few months after *In the Court of the Crimson King* came out. The painting showed a watercolour close-up of a screaming face, in red and blues, clearly in the late stages of a catastrophic madness.

The choice of the first King Crimson album is unusual – you might expect *Fireball* or *Deep Purple In Rock* (Otomo's faves), or *Led Zep II*, or *Dark Side of the Moon*, or *Exile On Main Street*. But the cover of *In the Court of the Crimson King* is very distinctive, and the album had plenty of fans (Genesis, Yes, the Who, etc).

The arch enemy of the hairies is a stern, by-the-book cop who's determined to catch and punish them (particularly as his own son has joined them). *Hair*'s set-piece sees the hippies trying to steal food from a storeroom which's portrayed as a bank heist that goes wrong. (Katsuhiro Otomo enjoys portraying groups of hopeless guys who come up with very dumb schemes, like the bozos in the 'Great Tokyo Empire' in *Akira*).

The long haired hippies represent everything that straight society fears – not least, in this future tale, germs. *Hair* ends with the cop's son developing the first instance of a cold for a hundred years (which freaks everyone out).

ELECTRIC BIRDLAND.

Published in *S.F. Adventure* in July, 1980, *Electric Birdland*[12] is a sister story to *Hair*: it features familiar Katsuhiro Otomo motifs: long-haired (= rebellious) guys, plants as precious commodities in glass containers (called 'p-balls'), police robot tanks (dubbed 'defenders'), the search for food, and conflicts between social dissidents and authoritarian states. We're in another swanky space colony, Otomo's favourite setting in science fiction (the other one being the wasteland or desert following a war or catastrophe).

An older guy and a younger guy[13] are hunting for food (they are the familiar hapless, dishevelled, rags-wearing, bare-footed, long-haired, and not very smart types that Otomo loves to place at the centre of his stories (they're called 'hairies' in *Hair*).) The

12 The title comes from Charlie Parker.
13 The younger one uses the term *anniki*, which means 'older brother'.

notion of a super-sophisticated society running so calm and smug being freaked by the freaks appeals to him. Actually, a *huge* proportion of heroes in the world of *manga* and *animé* are dim – well-meaning, yes, brave, yes, cool, yes, and highly skilled, of course, but also rather stupid – Monkey D. Luffy, Naruto Umuzaki, Natsu Dragneel, Lina Inverse, Keicihi Morisato, Princess Lum, Lala Satalin Deviluke, etc).

Half of the 16-page *Electric Birdland* comic comprises a hunt down alleys and corridors (very much like Kei and Kaneda being chased in *Akira*), as the lads are pursued by the new defender robots, while clutching their booty. Cornered in a dead-end alley, the older guy turns, expecting to be vaporized by the remaining police robot. Instead, he is shorn of all body hair in an instant – because his 'insanitary index' is too high for the law (so he ends up, like Jin in *A Farewell To Weapons*, naked and defenceless, facing a robot tank). That is, shorn of their technology, machines and devices, naked humans can look fairly feeble.

HIGHWAY STAR.

Highway Star (1979, Futabasha) was a collection of short stories from 1975 to 1978, written and illustrated by Katsuhiro Otomo, including: *Kazoku, Suka to Sukkiri, Shusei Sanchi no Yuki Chan, Highway Star, Seisoo, Ashita no Yakusoku* and *Sayonara no Omiyage*.

FAMILY.

The subject matter of this story, *Family* (from *Highway Star*, 1979), is mass suicide (an 'only in Japan' theme). This might be one of Otomo's bitterest stories, but the treatment is full of humorous touches. A Japanese family is in debt, with two kids in tow and one on the way; they are forced to leave home, and decide that death is the only solution.

It's bizarre stuff – it's a Japanese form of escape from a Dickensian poverty trap: *let's all kill ourselves*!

Doesn't turn out like that in *Family*, tho' – little Sachiko vomits up the pills she's wolfed, and mom goes into labour (at a traditional *ryokan*, where they've decided to do the deed[14]). So, still poor and still downtrodden, the family has another mouth to feed.

Again, the humour is black in the extreme (as it often is from Otomo-sensei, particularly in his shorter *manga*), like a modern-day, satirical version of *Hansel and Gretel* (there's the same emphasis on food and hunger), in which the solution to poverty is mass suicide.

The focus is on the relationship between parents and children (as in *Hansel and Gretel*), once again evoked with Otomo's brilliant eye for detail: Sachiko is indulged throughout the family's Last Day: she gets a *bento*, chocolate, juice, ice cream and all on the train;[15] they visit a theme park, where Sachiko and daddy go on all of the rides (daddy feels mighty sick); and it's Sachiko who munches on the pills first in the evening at the inn (she feels very ill afterwards).

A FAREWELL TO WEAPONS.

This story, published in *Young Magazine* in Nov, 1981,[16] was given a lavish animated treatment by Bandai, Dentsu, Sunrise *et al* in the anthology film *Short Peace* (2013) – see the chapter on Otomo's movies.

A Farewell To Weapons is a partially-coloured[17] 'men on a mission' adventure set in, once again, a post-apocalyptic world (and again in a desertified realm, a city in the Middle East). The mission is to nobble some robotic tanks, called 'Gonks'. The comic boils down to men versus a machine (which is ironically a peace-keeping machine, built by humans to police societies).

14 The manager suspects that this might be a family suicide.
15 Once she realizes that she's being spoilt, she keeps asking for more.
16 It was reprinted in a coloured version in the West in April, 1992.
17 Otomo said he used an early video system, 4C, for adding the colours.

Along the way, *A Farewell To Weapons* delivers Otomo-sensei's customary clear, precise and carefully-constructed storytelling, his mastery of inventing striking action set-pieces, his evocations of convincing *mecha*,[18] and his wicked sense of humour. The subtext? Once again, it's man's uneasy relationship with technology. Like a re-run of the Vietnam War, *A Farewell To Weapons* depicts an army kitted out with the latest in military technology (powered suits, unmanned surveillance planes), who're outmatched by an implacable, unstoppable enemy. That the story comprises a whole squadron of soldiers being bested by a single robot tank says everything. They are picked off one by one, until one guy remains.

The guys in the team (Jim, Junkie, Marl, Rhum, and Gimlet) are Otomoan types: Glasses Man, Moustache Man, the Grizzled Veteran, the Chirpy Youngster, etc. They are not differentiated much (apart from some inconsequential banter in the opening pages – about what they'll do when they get home, as in *Magnetic Rose*).

A Farewell To Weapons features the superb men vs. robot tanks material that Otomo recycled for the middle chapters of *Akira*: particle beams, laser beams, grenades, fire-fights, and of course explosions.

The final gag of *A Farewell To Weapons* has the Gonk robot damaged and scurrying off for repairs, while the survivor (Jim the Glasses Man) resorts to that favourite weapon of Otomoan stories, the rock. The robot hands the man a pamphlet proclaiming that its war is justified, and the guy smashes the Gonk with the stone (the familiar evocation of stalemate and the pointlessness of conflict).

A Farewell To Weapons is an ironic, satirical piece, beginning with the title, *A Farewell To Weapons* (humans have never said goodbye to weaponry, they have always been 'weaponized', to use that creepy phrase of contemporary, North American superhero

18 The suits the soldiers wear in *A Farewell To Weapons* are one of the first appearances of powered suits in *manga*.

movies).

Both sides have hi-tech gear to spare, the very existence of which damns them. And yet what they're fighting over is an abandoned, peopleless place.

THE MOOD IS ALREADY OF WAR.

Kibun wa Mou Sensou (*The Mood Is Already of War,* 1982, Futabasha) is a collection of thirteen stories, written by Toshihiko Yahagi (from his novel), and illustrated by Katsuhiro Otomo. The conflicts focus around Chinese-Russian relations, and Soviet-U.S.A. relations, in the Cold War era (with other stories inserted into the main narrative). Many of the tales evoke Soviet politics and militarism (tho' from a sceptical viewpoint). *The Mood Is Already of War* is one of Otomo's longer pieces (working solely as an illustrator here), but is not known much in the West (it lacks an English translation).

This is prime Katsuhiro Otomo, which deserves more recognition. As usual, Otomo doesn't hold back when it comes to portraying the cruder sides of humans – plenty of violence and killing, suffering, drugs, sex, etc. (Some of the violence is completely pointless – a youth play-acting with a gun is shot in the head by soldiers; hippies accidentally fire at each other in a drug haze). In Otomo Land, humans should have nothing to do with guns.

All of Otomo's familiar character types are here, from the snotty, tiresomely energetic kids to the weary, grizzled guys (and of course several itera-tions of Moustache Man, Otomo's all-purpose, go-to characterization). The drawing style is lively and clean, as usual in Otomo's art – his *manga* is always a pleasure to read, there is no confusion about what's going on: Otomo is a master communicator.

The title story, *Kibun wa Mou Sensou,* is a *seinen* military piece, and displays many Otomoan characteristics: tanks (and more tanks!), war, WWII, men in combat, etc.

The Mood Is Already of War displays large

amounts of *mecha* (cars, Harrier jump jets, helicopters, aircraft carriers – and, yes, tanks! Of course, this being Japanese fiction, there are samurai swords, too).

The heroes also perform many of the expected acts in a men-on-a-mission tale – infiltrating an enemy camp at night (and stealing vehicles); befriending locals for intel (in *Monkey Business*); capturing the enemy at a gun emplacement in a cave,*Guns of Navarone*-style (in *Monkey a Go-Go*); and getting involved in enormous land battles with 100s of soldiers (in *Monkey Shine*).

Another story in *The Mood Is Already of War* (*Monkey Suits*) has our heroes in the Central Asian desert, encountering a busload of hippies on the Far Out Trail. Otomo-sensei crams in many references to '60s counter-culture (music, drugs, sex, etc), in a bus jammed with drop-outs, a bald farmer, a sheep, a monkey and a chicken. (This story may have influenced the 2006 *animé* series *Freedom*, which features a similar scene).

Otomo has fun pitting military hawks against loved-up, freaky-deaky people (which he has done several times before – it looks forward to *Mother Sarah*). As the clouds of pot smoke envelope all at an oasis in the desert, there's a very confused fire-fight, in which hippies and soldiers are getting high, and shooting each other by accident (don't give hippies guns – don't give soldiers guns – don't give soldiers or hippies guns when they are high). It's a sort of *Mad* magazine and *National Lampoon* meets *Akira* and a gritty WWII, men-on-a-mission drama.

Other ingredients in *The Mood Is Already of War* include: a story set on a desert island (where the war is still being fought); and a rare evocation in Otomo's art of a *mangaka* at work.

New York City is visited yet again (in *Take the 6 Train*) – the world of downtown bars, weary drinkers, corrupt cops, pimps, hookers – it's the same Big, Bad City of Otomo's *Sayonara Japan manga* (and includes an exciting chase on the subway, with the main character expiring on Brooklyn Bridge).

CHRONICLE OF PLANET TAKO.

Published in *S.F. Adventure* in March, 1981, *Chronicle of the Planet Tako* is a short, comic skit featuring the foolish denizens of the planet Tako.[19] The Takosians are small creatures with octopus heads, who stand on their tentacles (their mouths, in a typical Otomoan gag, are a penis and balls).

Chronicle of the Planet Tako details the origins of the Takosians, their battles with the starfish people and the triangle-heads (Ikans), and their oppression by their rulers – leading to the inevitable political revolutions (led by rebellious firebrands), and the assassinations of kings.

In the sequel, *Chronicle of the Planet Tako: Dawn of Civilization* (J.C.C. Corporation), Katsuhiro Otomo portrays another origins tale of the Takosians, with the octopuses trying to survive in a prehistoric wilderness on Planet Tako. There are more struggles against the starfish people (a gentle, agricultural community), and more assassinations of kings. It seems that if Otomo had his way, political revolution would be mandatory in any society (maybe every five years, instead of elections).

The *Planet Tako* stories are Otomo at his lightest and fluffiest – the stylistic approach comes across as a spoof of Osamu Tezuka (such as his *Buddha* (1972-83) *manga*). As if Otomo is reminding us that Tezuka isn't the only *mangaka* who can draw humorous allegories featuring Disneyesque critters.

APPLE PARADISE.

Apple Paradise (1980) was an unfinished sci-fi story (of six chapters); it hasn't been collected in book form. It opened with a space station on another planet populated by people who just wanna go home to Earth (echoes of *The Legend of Mother Sarah*). In

---

19 In his notes, Otomo says he wrote this story with someone, but can't remember who.

chapter one of *Apple Paradise*, the chief topic of debate is work, workers, work quotas, unions, etc. That is, despite the science fiction settings (all rendered in Otomo's customary hyper-detailed style), these people are really Japanese workers complaining about over-work. There are one or two other elements in chapter one, such as a guy sneaking into a doctor's office (and snitching some pills – echoes of *Akira*), and two guys kissing.

RUN.

Run squeezes a lot of narrative material into its 24 pages. It's the *manga* equivalent of a classic short story in the crime genre – a guy (Koizumi) wanted for the murder of his pregnant girlfriend, the cops who're tailing him, a sleazy Mr Big called Sone (who drugs women then exploits them), and an extended chase on foot thru the back streets (the 'run' of the title).

In 24 pages, Katsuhiro Otomo is able to create rounded characters within a complicated story, and there's even time for flashbacks (Koizumi remembers running at school, and Masuda, the aged cop chasing him, recalls a similar incident chasing a crook, when he ran for miles). Despite shaving his head to disguise himself, changing into a tracksuit and dashing across town (with a desperate detour to a criminal HQ for sanctuary), Koizumi is caught.

Run closes with a scuffle at the police station – the cop Masuda is shot (by Koizumi), and Koizumi comes face to face with the sleazebag Sone. *Run* closes with another of Otomo's open-ended cliffhangers: Koizumi holds his gun to Sone's head: does he shoot? Or is there another misfire (which occurred earlier)?

THE SULTAN'S GUARD.

The Sultan's Guard (*Sultan Boueitai*, Kodansha, 1982, one volume) was co-written by Otomo Katsu-hiro and Haruka Takachiho and illustrated by Akihiko Takadera (Takadera-sensei was one of Otomo's *manga* friends – he helped out with Otomo's

Memories; Takadera includes a portrait of Otomo in the Inspector's assistant, Sakata).

This is a tale of gang warfare among Japan's *yakuza* clans, which comprises a whole sub-genre in *manga* publishing (and 100s of movies). It's the world of tough-talking men, macho posturing, fire-fights, gun fetishism,[20] and fierce battles between rival criminal gangs for supremacy. In short, *The Sultan's Guard* is a Japanese version of *The Godfather*, or the *manga* version of one of 'Beat' Kitano's many crime movies.[21]

The Sultan's Guard has the *yakuza* world down pat (the flashy cars, guns, suits, plush mansions, the samurai swords,[22] etc). *The Sultan's Guard* is rather grim, machismo stuff, as gangster fiction tends to be, with few of Otomo's flashes of humour (it's so manly there's barely a female character in the piece).

Inspector Kanebuchi is the figurehead of justice in *The Sultan's Guard*, a veteran, squat, thick-set and extremely belligerent cop who's determined to bring down the heads and lieutenants of the *yakuza* syndic-ates. Kanebuchi is targetted by the crooks with sever-al physical attacks, but he's so tough he survives being shot at repeatedly.

The artwork in *The Sultan's Guard* by Akihiko Takadera is functional but not arty – it does the job of telling the story, with no frills (and it's not influenced by Otomo, which often happens when Otomo collaborates on a comic that he doesn't illustrate. *Mother Sarah* is the classic example, with artwork that's almost indistinguishable from Otomo).

Katsuhiro Otomo slips in an *Akira* moment in *The Sultan's Guard* when a biker gang buzzes the cops driving on the streets at night, hurling petrol bombs. But that street scene is a mere preamble to the action set-piece of *The Sultan's Guard* – a running fire-fight

20 In the training sequence, weaponry is lovingly evoked.
21 Recent examples in comics include *Black Lagoon* and *Triage-X*.
22 Every *yakuza* story has to include swords, with the gangsters considering themselves as modern samurai. And there's always a scene that pits the sword against the gun.

between the rival gangs, and the platoon that's trained in the hills.

This is a kitchen sink sequence, where the artist and the writers throw in everything they've seen from other comics (and from Hong Kong action cinema in particular): stunts with cars, with motorbikes, with guys crashing thru windows, with grenades, the works. There's red stuff sloshing about everywhere, heads're blown off, arms're sliced, brains're splattered, until both sides seem decimated. The rival crime lord is hurled out of a window, squishng on the street right next to Inspector Kanebuchi.

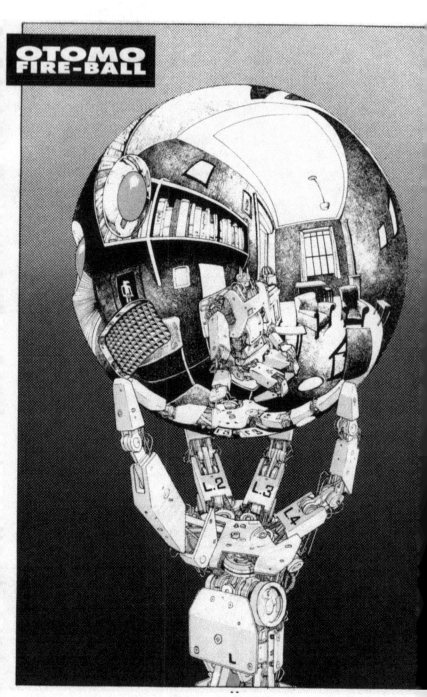

Fireball (this page and over)

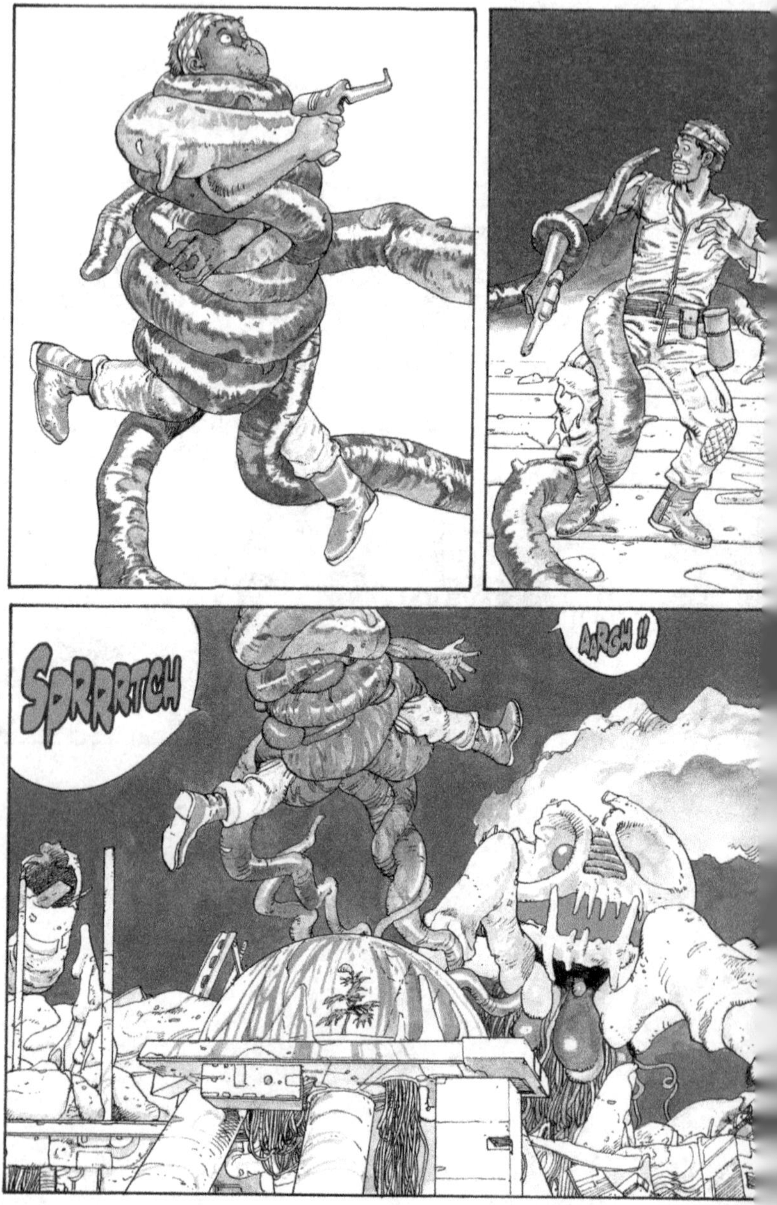
SPRRRTCH
AARGH !!

Boogie Woogie Waltz (this page and over)

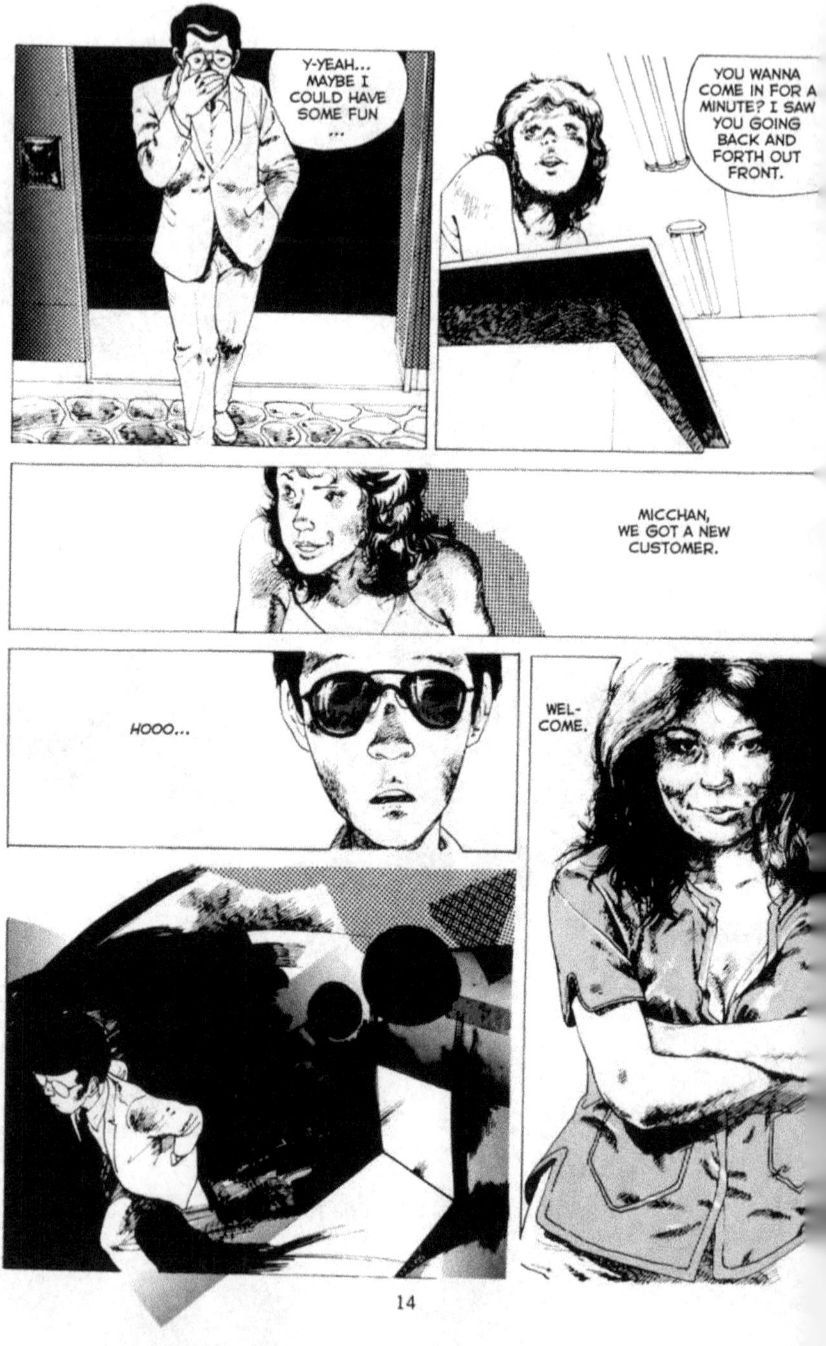
Y-YEAH... MAYBE I COULD HAVE SOME FUN ...
YOU WANNA COME IN FOR A MINUTE? I SAW YOU GOING BACK AND FORTH OUT FRONT.
MICCHAN, WE GOT A NEW CUSTOMER.
HOOO...
WEL-COME.

Chuck Check Chicken
(this page and over)

AND A BOY CALLED DAIGORO!!

FORMER KOUGI KAISHAKUNIN* ?!

SUIOURYUU SWORDMAN-SHIP!?

H-HEY ...

It's the Lone Wolf and Cub!!

THE FUCK DID YOU SAY!? WHY AM I A POOF!? BASTARDS!

WE WON'T FORGET THIS YOU LONE POOF!

* Kaishakunin (介錯人) : appointed second whose duty is to behead one who has committed seppuku. 21
"Kougi kaishakunin" stands for Shōgun's executioner. Look up for "Lone Wolf and Cub" on internet.

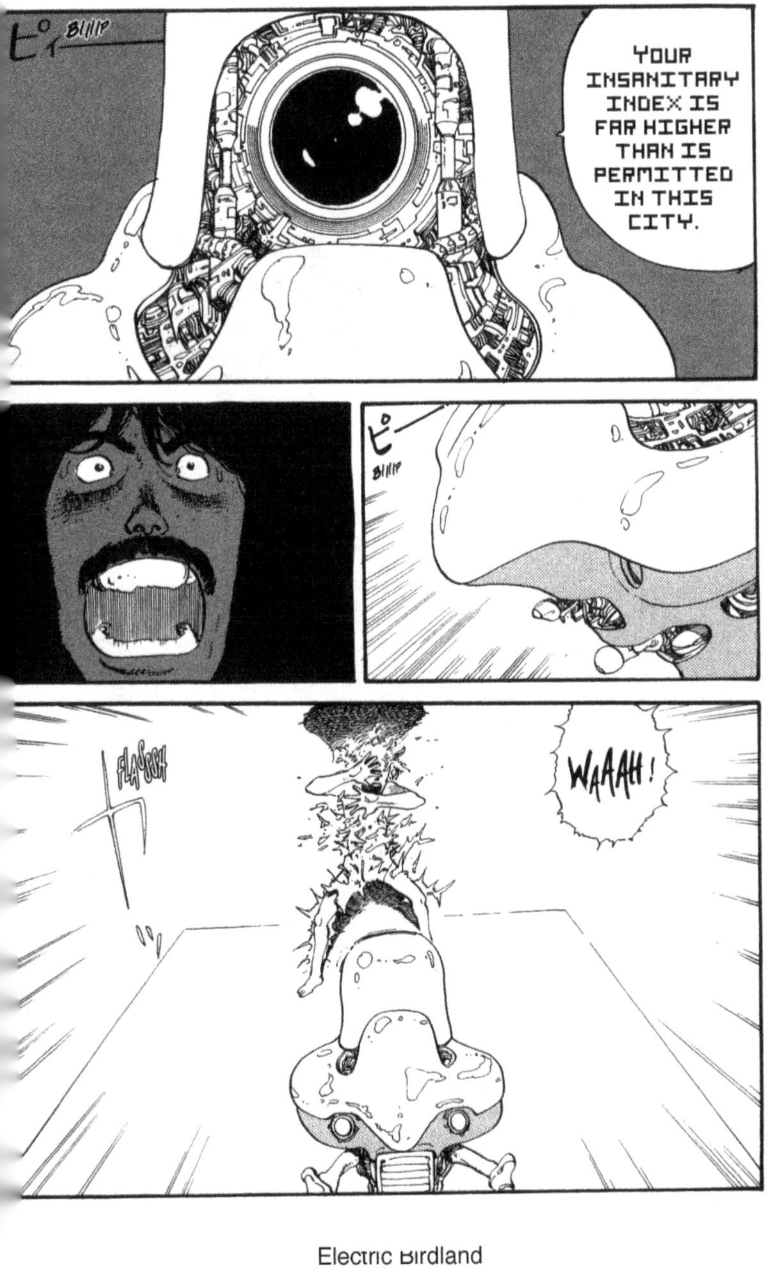
ピィ
BIIIIP
YOUR INSANITARY INDEX IS FAR HIGHER THAN IS PERMITTED IN THIS CITY.
ピー
BIIIIP
FLASSSH
WAAAH!

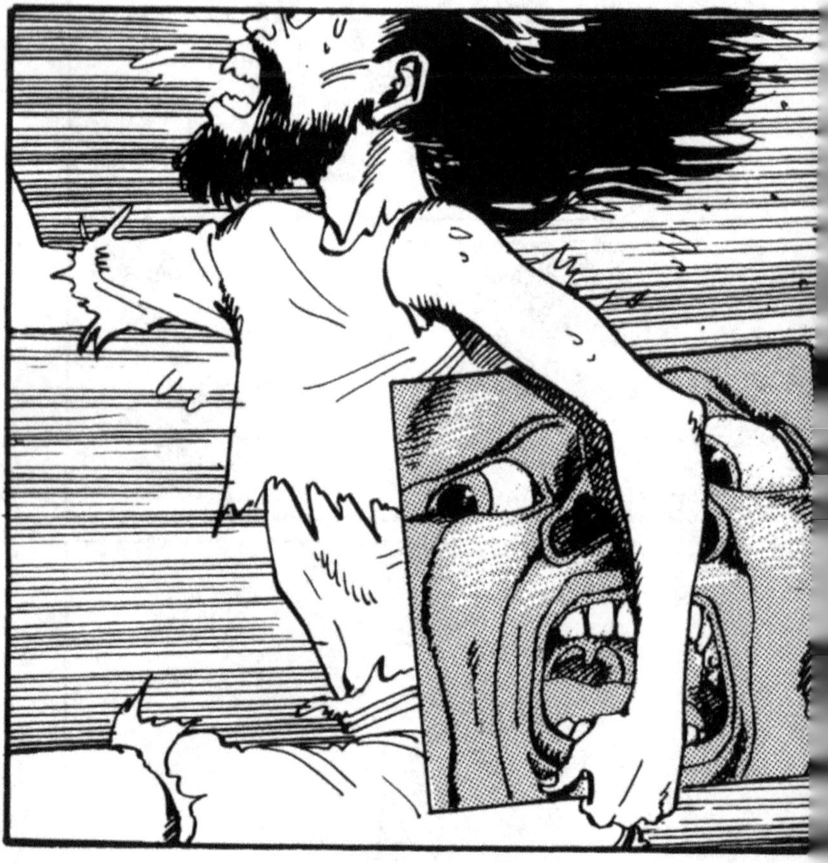

Hair (this page and over)

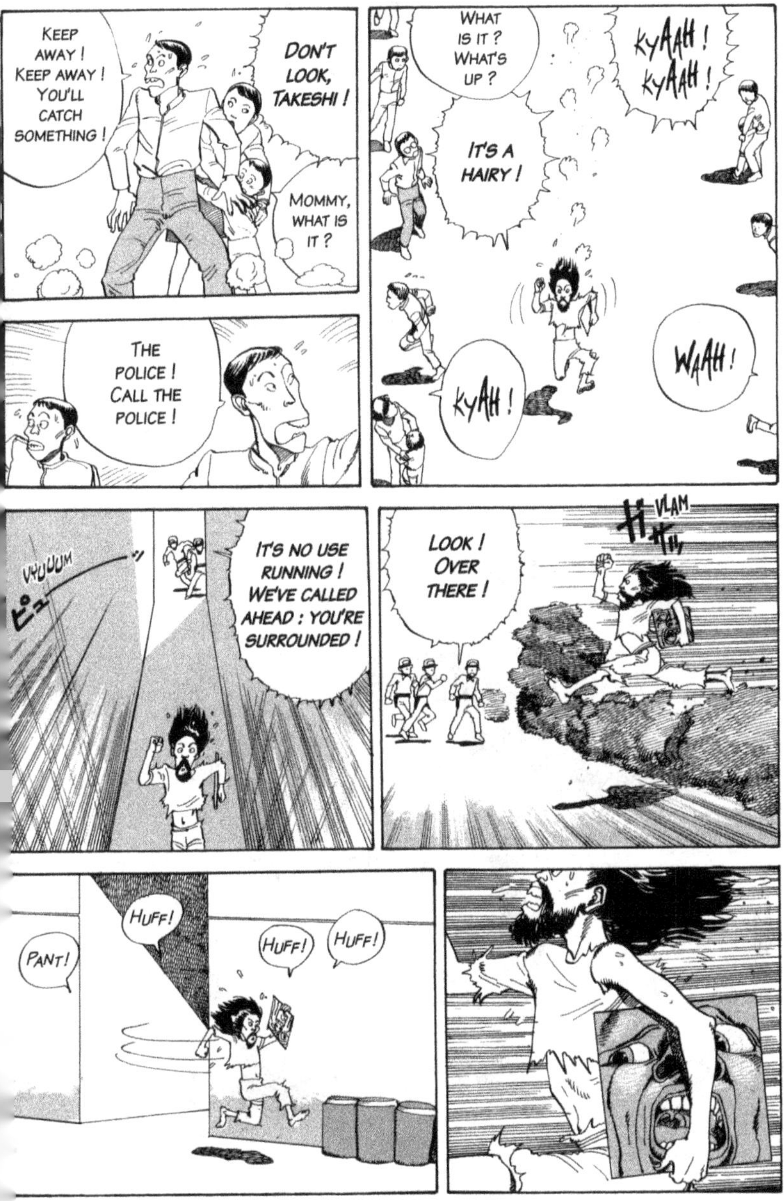

KEEP AWAY ! KEEP AWAY ! YOU'LL CATCH SOMETHING !
DON'T LOOK, TAKESHI !
MOMMY, WHAT IS IT ?
THE POLICE ! CALL THE POLICE !
WHAT IS IT ? WHAT'S UP ?
KYAAH ! KYAAH !
IT'S A HAIRY !
KYAH !
WAAH !
VYUUUM
IT'S NO USE RUNNING ! WE'VE CALLED AHEAD : YOU'RE SURROUNDED !
VLAM
LOOK ! OVER THERE !
PANT!
HUFF!
HUFF!
HUFF!

112

Kibun (this page and over)

ちょっと
いたい

いたいわよ
ここ

いい？

私が上に
なるわ

ねっねっ
いいでしょ

ちょっちょっ
えっおい

すぐだから
我慢しなよ
なっなっ

いてっつてんだろ
このばかどけって

どけよばか

いてて
てて

あっ

いてっいてっ
本当痛ェんだから

おーいて

266

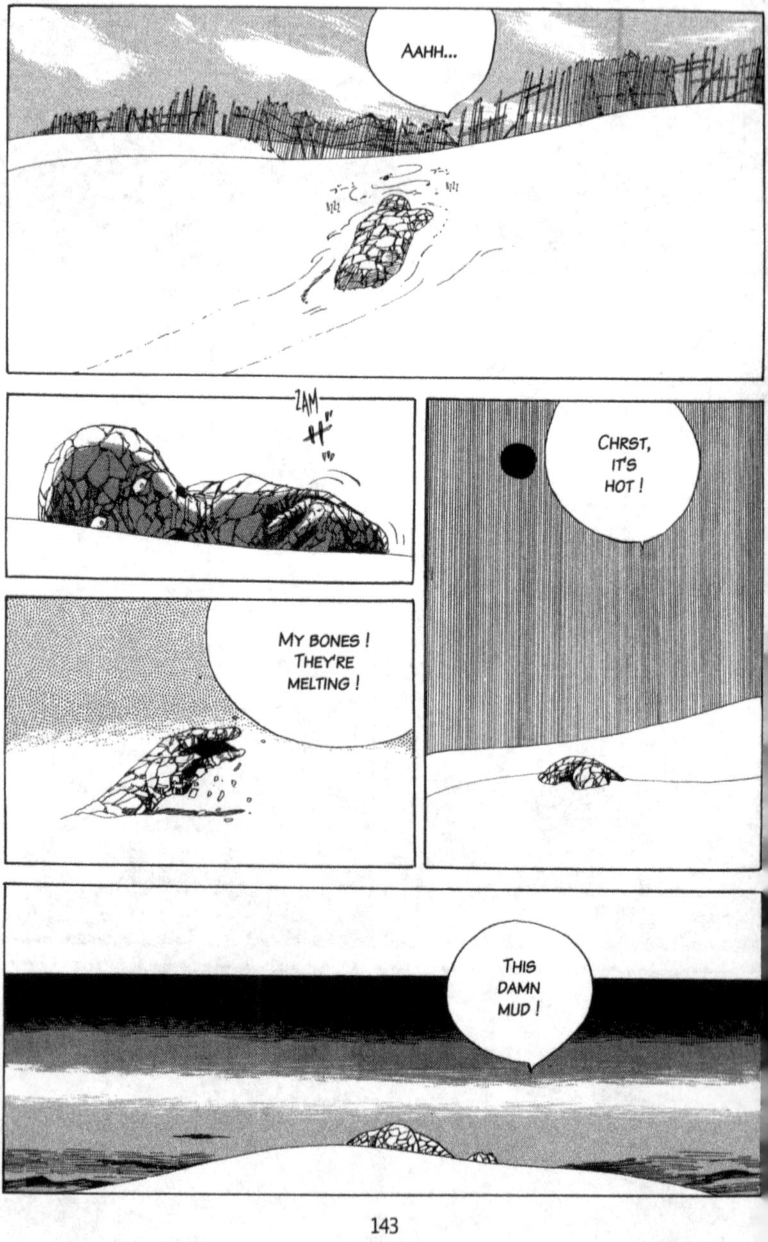
AAHH...
ZAM
CHRST, IT'S HOT !
MY BONES ! THEY'RE MELTING !
THIS DAMN MUD !

Memories (1990)
(This page and over)

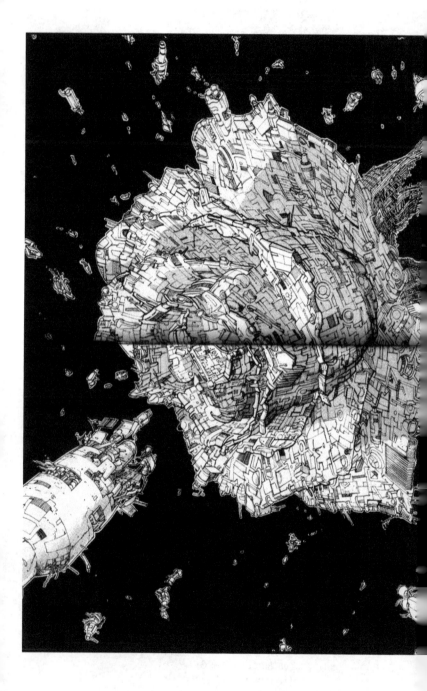

THAT WAS SCARY, EH?

IT'S A BODYGUARD ROBOT, SO THE LADY MUST BE NEARBY.

SHOULD WE OPEN THE DOOR IN ONE KICK?

WAIT A MOMENT.

NYEEEK!

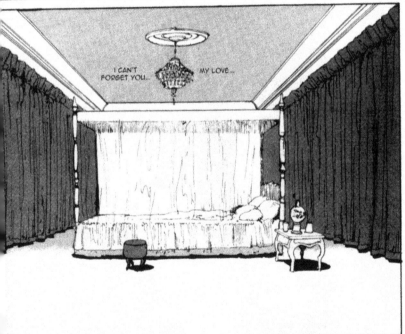

I CAN'T FORGET YOU...

MY LOVE...

THERE'S SOMEONE SLEEPING THERE.

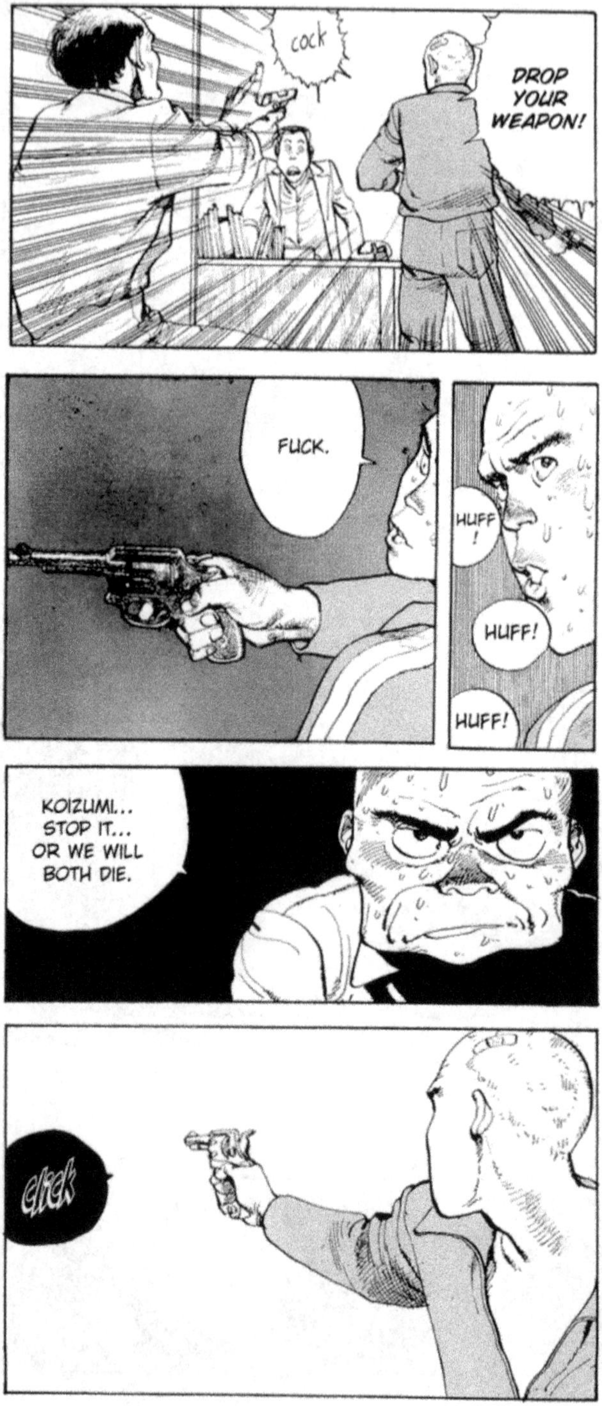
cock
DROP YOUR WEAPON!
FUCK.
HUFF!
HUFF!
HUFF!
KOIZUMI... STOP IT... OR WE WILL BOTH DIE.
click

Run (this page and over)

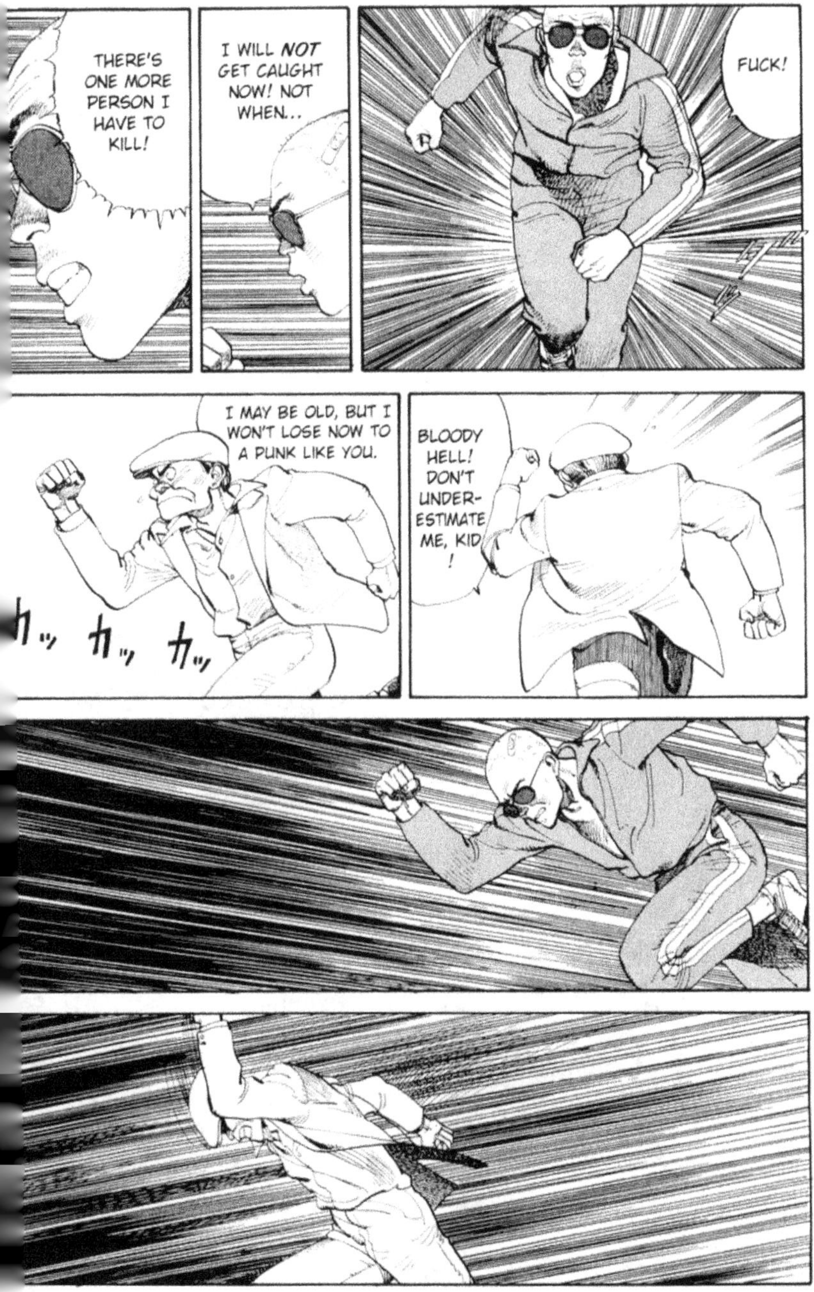
THERE'S ONE MORE PERSON I HAVE TO KILL!
I WILL *NOT* GET CAUGHT NOW! NOT WHEN...
FUCK!
I MAY BE OLD, BUT I WON'T LOSE NOW TO A PUNK LIKE YOU.
カッ カッ カッ
BLOODY HELL! DON'T UNDER-ESTIMATE ME, KID!

I GUESS THIS SHOULD BE ENOUGH.
VWEET
PFFT PFFT
KLANG KLANG
...OR ROAST THIGHS?
Sauté
Liver
Sashimi
Yakitori
Entrails etc.
Stew
MAYBE CHICKEN WINGS...
LET'S SEE... WHAT SHOULD I HAVE TONIGHT?
AND I'LL TOP IT OFF WITH AN EGG.
...I'LL FINISH IT OFF IN TWO WEEKS.

WAIT !
LOOK !

KUHL !!

IT'S
ALIVE !

THE
SAND
...

The Sound of Sand

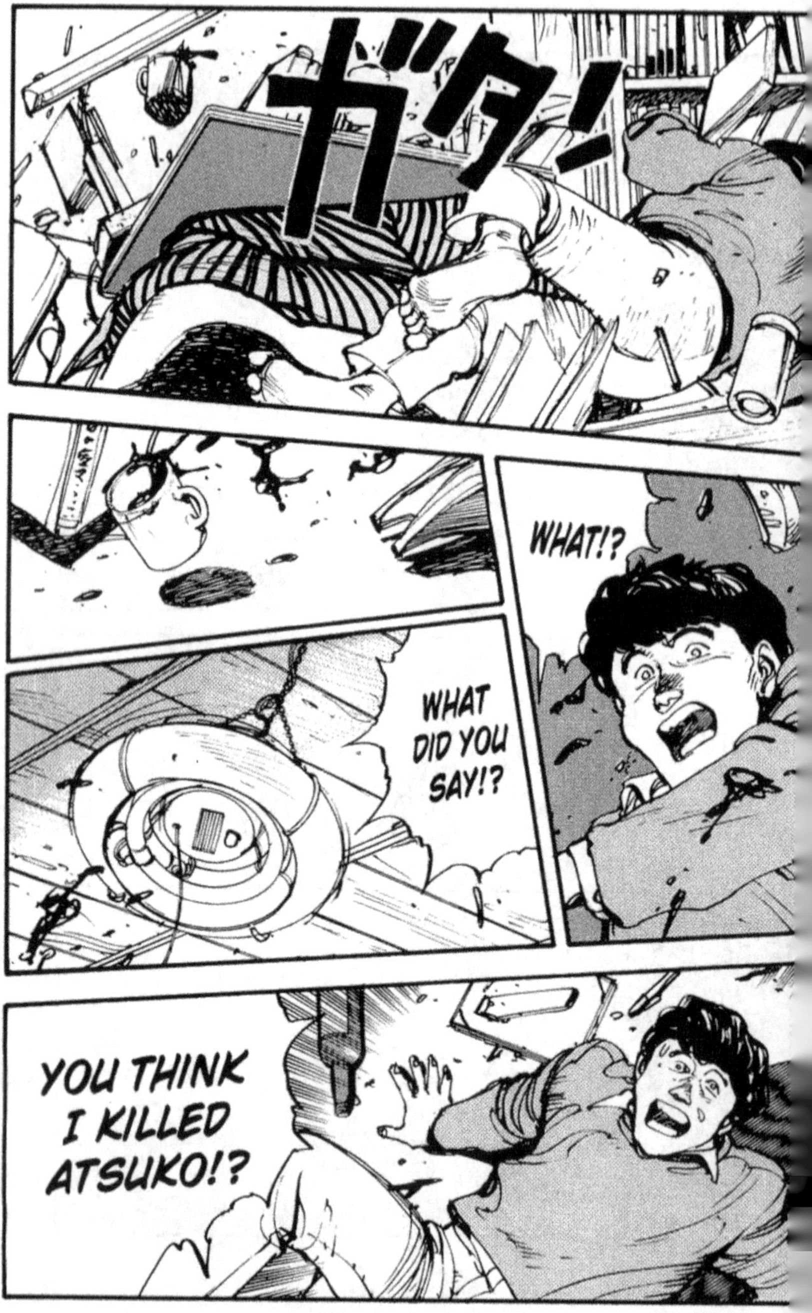
ガタ!
WHAT!?
WHAT DID YOU SAY!?
YOU THINK I KILLED ATSUKO!?

Highway Star (this page and over)

I'M GONNA GO PLAY VIDEO GAMES.

A TALK...?

SACHIKO... WHY DON'T YOU GO PLAY DOWNSTAIRS. PAPA WANTS TO HAVE A LITTLE CHAT WITH MAMA.

PHEW, I'M STUFFED

IT'S OUR FINAL MOMENTS...

YOU CAN'T WHEN I'M IN THIS CONDITION... I...

BABY.

D-DARLING, NO...

!

I NEED MONEY...

S-SA-CHIKO...

MA-MAAA...

AH!

UGH...

AHHH... DARLING... MMM, FASTER...

17

A Farewell To Weapons (this page and over)

ENOUGH BULL-SHIT !
STUPID MACHINE !
IF YOU READ THIS PAMPHLET, YOU WILL UNDERSTAND COMPLE-TELY.
GATCHAK
GATCHAK
YOU'RE NOT GETTING AWAY... OVER MY DEAD BODY !
OUR MILITARY IS ALWAYS LOOKING FOR A FEW GOOD MEN. DON'T HESITATE TO STOP BY OUR ADMINISTRATION OFFICE.
GATCHAK
GATCHAK
GATCHAK
GATCHAK
THE FUTURE IS BUILT BY YOUTH.
GONK !

END

02

SAYONARA JAPAN

GOODBYE JAPAN

In *Sayonara Japan* (*Goodbye Japan*, 1977/ 1981),
Katsuhiro Otomo recreates New York City of the late
1970s, inspired by a visit he made in 1977 (on his
honeymoon, when he was 23). Published in 1981,
Sayonara Japan is the story of several Japanese folk
trying to make it in North America (hence the title –
Goodbye Japan). The focus of *Sayonara Japan* is a young
martial arts teacher, who opens a *dojo* (a martial arts
training school, offering judo and karate) in the Big
Apple (so it's a Japanese-guy-in-North-America story,
a stranger-in-a-strange-land story). It's also a tale of
the struggle to make it in a foreign country, where
money is always tight (a recurring theme in Otomo's
work).

Katsuhiro Otomo lovingly reproduces Gotham
when it was in one of its scuzzy, down-at-heel
periods, before it was cleaned up in the 1990s and by
the 2000s had become Disney-theme-parked in the
areas around Times Square. Otomo's New York is a
place of dirty back streets in the Bowery and Green-

wich Village[1] (with the occasional trek uptown). It looks as if Otomo was busy sketching and taking photographs during his visit in '77 – this is a beautifully observed rendering of N.Y.C., all achieved using black ink on white paper.

Most marked of all in *Sayonara Japan* is the exploration of African American culture – which acts as a mirror to the encounter between Japanese and North American culture. That the hero meets African American characters, and the odd Japanese tourist or visitor, gives *Sayonara Japan* the appearance of a blaxploitation movie of the 1970s. (Tough, down-at-heel Gotham also appears in a story in *Kibun wa Mou Sensou*, with a climactic death set on Brooklyn Bridge).

The *Sayonara Japan* volume opens with our hero eager to recruit new customers to his *dojo*, having spent all of his dough on setting it up. His first pupil is a black kid with an Afro (who becomes his sidekick); the kid's dad, Fuzz, is a giant boxer, a legend in the Village, who takes on the teacher (both're knocked about). A Japanese girl,[2] who lives in the same block, is also introduced: she derides the teacher's crude tactics of promoting his business on the streets, claiming that he's selling out traditional Japanese culture.

In one of the chapters of *Sayonara Japan*, the martial artist gets involved with a bunch of no-goods who're having their wicked way with a young woman in the back streets; they have taken her into the shadows on some wasteland behind a wall. The teacher saves her from gang rape (depicted with a rough and tumble fight scene). Altho' the woman has her hands bound and is gagged, what appeared to a rape scenario isn't what it seems: the woman turns out to be a hooker. Later, when the teacher picks up a

1 The *dojo* is off Bleecker Street.
2 With her long hair and glasses, she resembles a female version of how Otomo caricatures himself in his comics (her friend is almost identical).

black working girl, he runs into the woman (so she wasn't the princess he hoped for, and maybe didn't need saving. The resentment works both ways – she begrudges him for interfering, as do the pimps). The *sensei* has a skinny sidekick with an Afro (Japanese artists seem especially fond of Afro haircuts – *One Piece* puts Luffy in an Afro).

At the end of the chapter, the guys that the hero beat up storm his *dojo*, looking for revenge, and he roughs them up again (but also receives plenty of bruises in the process). The story is reminiscent of the Jet Li movie *The Master* (1989), where director Tsui Hark plops Li down in the mean streets of Los Angeles (and a rival gang busts up Li's uncle's Chinese clinic).

In another story in *Sayonara Japan*, the Japanese teacher is in a park[3] practising martial arts with his colleagues (including his devoted assistant). A group of small kids watches and laughs. There's an encounter with a drifter musician who's hitched from L.A. to Gotham to try his luck as a busker. He takes out his acoustic guitar, playing to a crowd, until a cop tells him to move along. Just then, one of the teacher's *geta* (wooden clogs) flies off during the overenthusiastic demonstration of a high kick, and hits the policeman. In the confusion, the guitarist sneaks away, and meets our hero.

Back at the *dojo*, they bond over the delights of marijuana. Later, the guitarist goes to a musical audition: music, and making it in the pop world, is a recurring motif in Otomo's early stories. For example, the recording studio is full of wannabe punks and rockers (delightfully observed), and the guitarist realizes that there are some really talented musos out there that he has to compete against.

The chapter is a slice of life outing, with characters drifting in and out of the piece (such as the young woman who lives in the same block as the *sensei*, but he's now stoned and drunk).

3 It might be Central Park.

Chapter three introduces one of Katsuhiro Otomo's recurring character types: the clueless, middle-aged Japanese guy or salaryman. This guy is the classic, Asian tourist; he ends up in a predominantly black neighbourhood, unable to communicate, finds everybody intimidating, and is robbed (possibly thru a misunderstanding). The tourist eventually turns up at the *dojo*, seeking a friendly Japanese face (where the martial arts teacher is flying on cocaine). Again, with the tourist being swindled, no one has any money, so they're back to washing dishes in a local restaurant (the teacher's part-time job). At the restaurant, they spot the guys who robbed the tourist, the martial artist dutifully trounces them on the street outside, only to find out that they are under-cover cops.

In another *Sayonara Japan* chapter, there's a comical turf war between a Japanese street vendor of *tai-yaki* and an Italian pretzel stall (yet another manifestation of East-West/ Japanese-American relations). The skit, set on the streets of Gotham, is full of cultural stereotypes: for instance, the guy who runs the *tai-yaki* stall is a caricature Japanese man, with slit eyes, buck teeth, wire rim glasses, a headband (*hachimaki*), and a *banzai* demeanour. (Otomo has never held back from sending up anybody, including his fellow Japanese. The caricature also appears in the *Neo-Tokyo* movie).

The culture clash escalates to all-you-can-eat offers (eat 30 *tai yaki* and you don't pay!), and eventually descends into brawls (the martial artist is roped in as muscle by the disgruntled pretzel guy, but all that the teacher is bothered about is free food). It's a classic Otomoan moment when the rival groups take up the carts and use them as the totems in a procession thru the streets (echoing the *matsuri* of the 'Great Tokyo Empire' in *Akira*).

Murder in Japan's scuzzy suburban apartment blocks is once again the subject of *Sayonara Japan*'s chapter *The 'A' Apartments Murder Case*. Our hero is yet another dim-witted doofus who lives with a bunch of losers[4] in a building of bland apartments (they beg him for some of the dough he received as compensation for an injury, so they can buy *saké* and hit the pachinko parlours). Did our loser kill his neighbour Hiroshi? Seems he might've, but he's forgotten about it after being hit on the head at a building site. *The 'A' Apartments Murder Case* is another of Otomo's black comedies about life in Japan's under-class.

In Otomoville, it's not the motives, the relation-ships between killer and victim, or the forensic details about a murder case that are the focus, but the black humour of dealing with corpses. Hauling bodies into the closet. Chopping bodies up. Mopping up blood. Like, in *The 'A' Apartments Murder Case,* the hero borrows a thermometer from one of the sick tenants and jams in the cadaver's rear, so he can work out when the murder took place. (Our young Sherlock Holmes consults a famous detective book).

The longest entry in *Goodbye Japan* is the double chapter (7): *When the Saints Go Marchin' In*, featuring the adventures of two Japanese record company executives. We're back in Nihon for this story of the dream of making it in the music business coupled with another evocation of the musical past. The wannabe rockers from the *East of the Sun, West of the Moon* plug their latest demo tape to the A. & R. man Tomioka. He hates it – it contains two 30-minute songs and three 10-minute songs (a nightmare for someone from A. & R. to sit thru). The rock act are so poor they never eat, sell their instruments for *gelt,* and they have to run across town to reach the session at the recording studio with their guitars, because they can't afford the train. Tomioka has been handed the project of putting together some material for the teenage daughter (Kiyoko) of the man who bailed out the talent agency Tanaka Productions as a favour, with the rock band hired to be her backing group. The

---

4 One of them is Moustache Man.

girl is dead keen, but this is nepotism – the only reason she has the chance of a shot is because her father has helped out Tanaka Prods. with their debts. (But City Records is suspicious of such deals).

Meanwhile, four veteran jazzers from New Orleans are visiting their friend in Tokyo, Saitou, a production manager at City Records. Katsuhiro Otomo has fun plopping four aged (but energetic) black Americans in the middle of Tokyo (leering over girls, cruising bars to all hours, visiting a brothel, demanding to see geisha girls, etc) – which's why Saitou, knowing they'll be a handful, begs Tomioka to look after them.

The loose, rambling, soap opera-ish format of *When the Saints Go Marchin' In* is charming, piquantly evoking themes such as the older generation versus the younger generation (jazz versus pop music), America and Japan, and amateurs vs. professionals. The jazz musos from New Orleans may be old, but they are professional musicians, and they have several paid, regular gigs; the rock band, by contrast, are young hopefuls but hopeless (they have part-time jobs which have nothing to do with music,[5] and they are even more out-of-step with the current music scene than the jazz guys, who also play disco-inflected jazz. The rock band, though, can't escape the era of twenty-minute guitar solos).

Katsuhiro Otomo has a keen eye for the music industry, how people lean on each other, feel obliged (or guilty) to offer favours, how desperate beginners are for fame, and how music can express what it means to be human.

---

5 One of them digs roads.

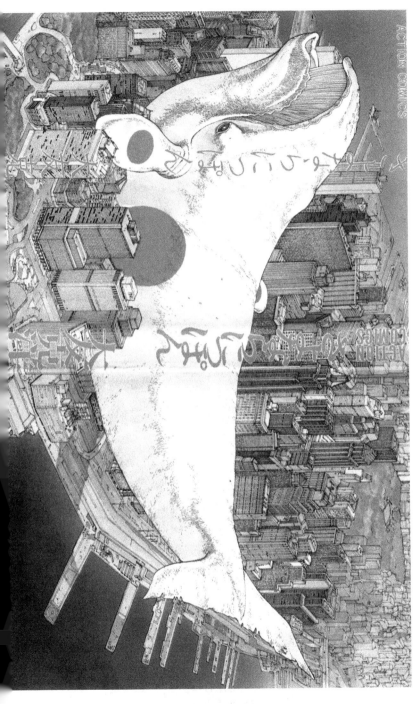

Sayonara Japan
(This page and over)

IT'S BEEN HALF A MONTH... SINCE I CAME TO NY...

ADVERTISEMENT FEE...COST FOR FOOD AND MISCELLANEOUS ...

TRAVEL EXPENSES... ACCOMMODATION FEE... RENTED AN OFFICE THEN CONVERTED INTO A DOJO ...

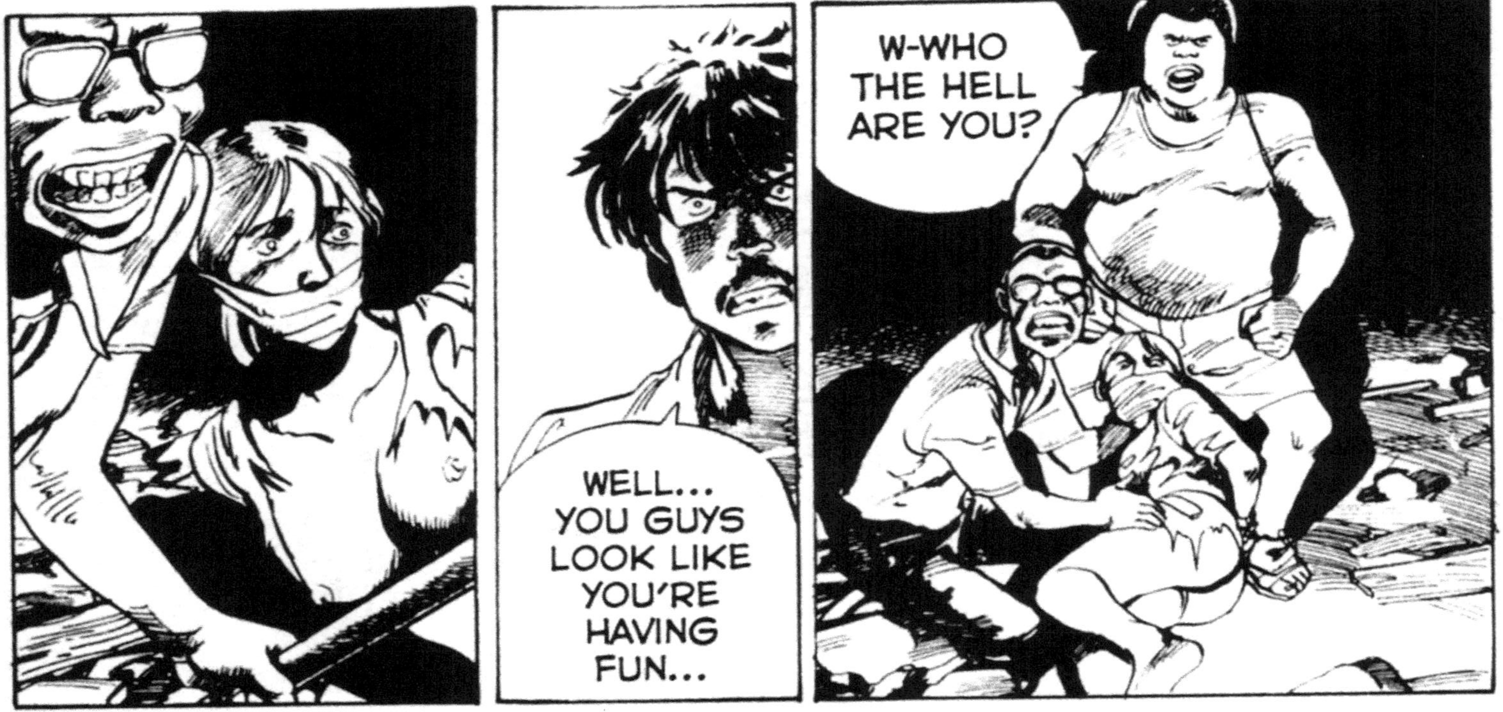
WELL... YOU GUYS LOOK LIKE YOU'RE HAVING FUN...
W-WHO THE HELL ARE YOU?

03

HANSEL AND GRETEL

IT'S A CRAZY, CRAZY WORLD

KATSUHIRO OTOMO'S FAIRY TALES AND CLASSICS

Hansel and Gretel (a.k.a *It's a Crazy, Crazy World,* C.B.S.-Sony Shuppan, 1981) was the 27 year-old Katsuhiro Otomo's thoroughly delightful reworkings of classic fairy tales and children's stories (mainly Western models, apart from the *Arabian Nights*). Published in Sony Magazines in 1981 (the stories were published between 1978 and 1981),[1] *Hansel and Gretel* features many famous fairy tales, including *Little Red Riding Hood, Cinderella, The Little Match Girl, The Boy Who Cried Wolf, Sleeping Beauty, The Bluebird, The Wolf and the Seven Kids, Snow White, The Three Little Pigs* and *Jack and the Beanstalk,* plus

[1] I have also included some of the tales published in the *Memories* collection here.

classic stories such as *Robinson Crusoe, Moby Dick, The Wonderful Wizard of Oz, Don Quixote, Ali Baba* and *Alice's Adventures In Wonderland* (it must mean something that so many of the tales that Otomo-sensei has chosen to adapt feature wolves).

The magic of fairy tales continues unabated in the contemporary world, not only for children but for adults too. It is worth noting that Wilhelm and Jacob Grimms' *Children's and Household Tales* is the highest selling book in the West, after the *Bible*, since its publication in the 19th century.[2] Of the key events in the history of the fairy and folk tale, one of the most significant must surely be the publication in 1812 of the Grimm Brothers' stories. They were translated into English by Edgar Taylor and his family (in 1823), and were illustrated by George Cruikshank, one of the great illustrators of the day. It proved to be a brilliant combination of talents.[3]

The typical fairy tale, or the fairy tale as interpreted today, is usually short (3-5 pages long), usually from a Grimm source (perhaps modified by Disney), concentrating on a character who learns how to use magic and gifts to achieve success, and often involves marriage at the end. Women are beautiful, hard-working, and passive; the men are dashing, brave, and adventurous.[4]

It's important to remember, too, that fairy tales today usually mean a narrow range of ten to fifteen stories – always the same ones: *The Frog Prince, Snow White and the Seven Dwarfs, Cinderella, Rapunzel, Sleeping Beauty, Little Red Riding Hood, Hansel and Gretel, Beauty and the Beast, The Pied Piper, The Snow Queen, The Little Mermaid, Bluebeard, Tom Thumb, The Three Little Pigs, The Twelve Dancing Princesses, Jack and the Beanstalk, Puss In Boots,* etc.

Among the characters in wonder tales were the

2 The celebrated illustrators of fairy tales include George Cruikshank, Gustave Doré, Arthur Rackham, Walter Crane, Kate Greenaway, Charles Folkard, Harry Clarke, Edmund Dulac, Klaus Ensikat, Eric Carle, Lisbeth Zwerger, Raymond Briggs, and Maurice Sendak.
3 This edition has been re-published by Crescent Moon in 2012.
4 J. Zipes, 2000, xxvi.

simple youth, Hans, Pierre, Jack, or Ivan, the youngest brother or son, who seems as if he'll never do well (a favourite character type for Katsuhiro Otomo, of course – indeed, even Kaneda in *Akira* can be regarded as the working class kid from the streets who becomes a hero). Then there's Cinderella, the loyal sister, the faithful bride, the clever thief, the boastful tailor, robbers, ogres, unjust kings, childless queens, princesses who can't laugh, flying horses, talking fish, magic tables or sacks, a sly fox, a kind duck, nasty stepmothers, fools, greedy wolves, brave children, kindly fathers, and a beast as a bridegroom (many of these character types turn up in Otomo's versions of fairy tales).

What is it about fairy tales that so fascinates readers? It is something to do with mythic, primal narratives, obviously, as studied by Vladimir Propp, C.G. Jung and post-Jungians such as Marie-Louise von Franz, Angela Carter and Emma Jung. Early books on the psychological dimension of fairy tales included Charlotte Bühler's *Das Märchen und die Phantasie des Kinders*; Sigmund Freud led the way, and Carl Jung and Géza Roheim aimed to develop Freud's theories; writers such as Marie-Louis von Franz, Emma Jung, Aneila Jaffé, Joseph Campbell, Marina Warner and Mircea Eliade analyzed fairy and folk tales from a post-Freudian and post-Jungian viewpoint; some writers (like Erich Fromm, Julius Heucher and Bruno Bettelheim), concentrated on the œdipal conflicts in the Grimm Brothers' fairy tales; and André Favat employed Charles Piaget's work on children (in *Child and the Tale*).

Often the satire in Otomo-sensei's tales comes from a simple reversal of roles, so that the hunters become the hunted (such as wolves), or cute goats become wolves. Feminist writers, for instance, have got a lotta mileage out of rewriting fairy tales (from the 1970s onwards) by simply reversing the genders. So princesses become heroes, kingdoms're ruled by queens, and men take on women's roles. It's striking just how much satire can be squeezed out of role reversals and gender switches.

There are many film references, too – Katsuhiro Otomo has been influenced by the famous versions of classic books and fairy tales just like everybody else. So you'll find allusions to the Hollywood adaptations of *The Wizard of Oz, Alice's Adventures In Wonderland, Moby Dick, Snow White,* etc. (The output of the Walt Disney Studios, for instance, has had an enormous influence on Japanese popular culture. It's no surprise that the first Disneyland constructed outside of the U.S. of A. was in Japan)[5]

HANSEL AND GRETEL.

The *manga* fairy tale collection opens with a re-telling of *Hansel and Gretel.* Katsuhiro Otomo relishes the prospect, as 100s artists have done, of producing his own version of the very famous fairy tales by the Brothers Grimm in their *Children's and Household Tales* (1812), and the familiar, much-trodden mediæval realm of cottages, castles, farms and of course dark forests.

Most of Katsuhiro Otomo's versions of famous tales, however, are not fully illustrated from start to finish: instead, they comprise two or three pages of *manga*, sometimes several more, and focus on a single gag (so that one joke or one scene has been selected by Otomo-sensei to encapsulate the whole story).

Hansel and Gretel is the one story that is fully illustrated in the 1981 collection, from the beginning to the end (running over 27 pages). With its images of starving children, nasty step-mothers and useless fathers, and its issues of hunger, food, poverty, families, abandonment and violence, the famous Grimms' fairy tale is tailor-made for Katsuhiro Otomo's wicked sense of humour and brilliantly gritty imagery.

In *Hansel and Gretel,* *mangaka* Katsuhiro Otomo

5 In 1990 60 million visited Disney's theme parks in Tokyo, California and Florida.

sticks pretty much to the fundamental outline of the story from the Grimm Brothers. But he adds his own twists, of course, such as the cartoony birds and fish the children encounter in the forest, the fat, layabout, dopey father and the shrewish, witchy mother. (The strange creatures are mysteriously mocking of the hapless family, a sarcastic chorus; for them, this dysfunctional family is simply entertainment that deserves its fate. At the end, they dance in the moon-light in a circle – dances by moonlight are a favourite motif of Maurice Sendak in his children's stories).

In Otomo's version, it's Gretel who eats the breadcrumbs that her brother Hansel drops behind him (the second time they go out), because she is so hungry. And when the magical creatures advise the kids not to take a certain path thru the forest, they pointedly ignore them ('Idiot! Don't take that one!'). The kids' step-mother tells them to chew off their own legs if they're hungry.

The witch in *Hansel and Gretel* (who looks like a grinning scarecrow with a carrot for a nose, a puppet – that is, a character who's empty, without a soul), has a house built in a tree shaped like a sumo wrestler's out-size body (with the entrance between the buttocks, inevitably). Hansel, strung up in a suspended cage like a prisoner left to rot outside a castle, has his feet cut off with a pair of gardening shears (the witch sucks the bloody stumps and decides he's not salty enough). Gretel is fed a frog a day (which she duly crunches – this girl is hungry enough to eat anything). Hansel gets enormously bloated in the cage outside the house, so he that he resembles his father (Gretel is furious: 'ASSHOLE! MAKING FUN OF ME! I'LL FUCKING KILL YOU, BASTARD!'). When the time comes, he's too big to lift into the cauldron which the witch has set up nearby, so the hag climbs up on it to haul him in. Clever Gretel shoves the witch inside with a broom ('Oh just get in already!'), and the kids gorge on her corpse when she's cooked.

The children return to their home chubby and full, waddling up the path (much to their over-weight father's surprise). Hansel stumbles along on crutches (boasting idiotically to his father about his fate of being foot-less). Meanwhile, their step-mom has died from starvation (she's just a wrinkled, shrivelled, naked cadaver on the bed, arms raised, mouth agape in fury, angry to the last). The children study her intently.

Katsuhiro Otomo rewrites *Children's and Household Tales* by the Grimm Brothers with a irreverent sense of humour, recalling Roald Dahl. There's cannibalism as the inevitable result of hunger, there's a no-holds-barred depiction of poverty (the kids're half-naked in hand-me-down rags), and there's an earthy evocation of life at its fiercest and most basic – killing and eating, all delivered with a black humour that's pretty dark even by the standards of contemporary fairy tale parodies.

As Jack Zipes notes in his brilliant study *The Enchanted Screen: The Unknown History of Fairy-tale Film*, *Hansel and Gretel* in the Grimms' version has been celebrated for

> its sanctimonious representation of brotherly and sisterly love, its idolization of a compass- ionate father, who opposes a witch/ wife, and its picture of home sweet home made sweeter by treasures stolen from a cannibalistic witch. (193- 4)

But the Grimm Brothers altered the tale of *Hansel and Gretel* throughout the seven editions of their book *Children's and Household Tales*, culminating in the text of 1857 (which most adaptations of *Hansel and Gretel* employ), which's 'a highly significant, ambiv- alent and memetic fairy tale because it raises more questions than it answers' (194). As they changed the story, the Grimms demonized a stepmother, transformed the children into two pious innocents with cute names who trust in God, and added a silly duck that helps them across a pond to soothe a sobbing father, who does not show any grief about his dead wife, nor does he apologize for abandoning them. (194)

Katsuhiro Otomo's version of *Hansel and Gretel* follows the Brothers Grimms' 1857 text, leaves out elements like the duck[6] and God, and emphasizes the aspects of survival against the odds.

ALI BABA.

In *Ali Baba and the Forty Thieves*, Ali Baba stands outside the cave and yells at the wall of rocks, 'Open, wheat!' Nothing budges. He tries again, 'Open, rice!' Nothing doing. He tries bean, carrot, onion, cucumber, watermelon, tomato, etc. Nothing. He wrenches at the rock wall. Nothing. Eventually, the doors crack open, at the sound of 'Eggplant!' And when the gates are fully open, a giant pile of eggplants tumbles out, smothering Ali Baba. (The cliff is depicted with Otomo's customary obsessive attention to detail – no other *mangaka*, for instance, so loves to draws pebbles, stones and rocks – they are scattered throughout the *Akira manga*, for instance. Except perhaps Masashi Kishimoto in the *Naruto manga*).

NOAH'S ARK.

Katsuhiro Otomo has another run at the *Bible*; this time, it's the story of Noah, the animals, and the Flood.[7] *Noah's Ark* (*Just Comic*, Aug, 1981) centres around one of Otomo's fundamental themes: survival – expressed in the form of the search for food. The

---

6 Turning them into several oddball creatures.

7 The imagery seems to derive from the Dino de Laurentiis-produced movie *The Bible* (1966), a big movie in every respect: an expensive, star-studded, widescreen production, 174 minutes long, in which the main characters of the *Old Testament* are played by Hollywood's leading actors: Richard Harris as Cain, Stephen Boyd as Nimrod, George C. Scott as Abraham, Franco Nero as Abel, Ava Gardner as Sarah, Peter O'Toole as an angel, and John Huston as Noah.

way that Otomo figures it, if the Ark had been at sea for months, they'd have to start eating the animals, right? So, Noah and his sons have already gone through the game birds, and it's roasted monkey for dinns today. All that's left are the snakes and frogs.

Luckily, the dove turns up with the olive branch, land is sighted, and they're saved. As Noah and his lads hop onto the beach, followed by the reptiles, they wonder, 'don't you think we should have brought some women with us?' (And saved the birds for eggs).

ALADDIN'S MAGIC BOTTLE.

Otomo-sensei produced a series of humorous skits called *That's Amazing World*, which ran in Kobunsha Publishing's *Just Comic*. In *Aladdin's Magic Bottle* (*Just Comic*, June, 1981), Katsuhiro Otomo took up the *1,001 Nights* again. This time it's Aladdin and the genie in the magic lamp/ bottle.

So, Aladdin (a grizzled, bearded guy in a turban, not the usual dashing, young thief), finds a bottle washed up on a shore. After opening it (with some difficulty), the genie appears in a puff of smoke (the smoke, inevitably, forms the shape of a mushroom cloud). The big, fat genie is delighted to be released from the bottle, and duly grants Aladdin three wishes. Unfortunately, Aladdin isn't quick on the uptake, and immediately asks the genie to slow down. So the genie does, also announcing that Aladdin now has two wishes left. When Aladdin complains, the genie reduces his offer to one wish. 'No, no. You've got it wrong again!' niggles Aladdin. And while Aladdin rants on (about being a poor man from a village who goes to the beach to collect driftwood), the genie listens, irritated. Then, telling Aladdin he has no more wishes left, he disappears into the blue yonder (leaving a vapour trail like a cruise missile). Alone again on the seashore, Aladdin merely shrugs, says, 'ah well', and carries on picking up firewood. Wishes don't work on adults – they're too cynical, too grumpy, too demanding.

KNIGHTS OF THE ROUND TABLE.

King Arthur and the knights of the round table in myth and pop culture are the target of this November, 1981 story (another *That's Amazing World* tale, published as *Knights of the Round Table* in *Just Comic* by Kodansha).

It's one of Katsuhiro Otomo's squabbling scenes among a group of guys – this time, the knights of legend are only concerned with getting drunk ('Serf! Where's that damned wine?'), women, and 'cutting children into itty-bitty pieces' ('when the little kids cry, that's the best part!'). Some are asleep, or bored, or depressed, or belching. So, not an especially noble and chivalrous bunch of knights, then. It's the Mel Brooks view of history and legend, where heroes are fools.

While King Arthur tries to keep order, and the knights tease him about Lancelot and Guinevere (they're both notably absent), and Merlin noisily practises his magic nearby (dressed in a pantomime wizard costume), in exasperation, the king draws his sword, to exert some authority – and buries it in the round table (and he can't pull it out: 'I pulled it out last time! Shit! Where's my wife?').

THE OLD MAN AND THE SEA.

This five-page send-up of the North American classic *The Old Man and the Sea* by Ernest Hemingway (*Just Comic*, Sept, 1981), ends with a sex scene, as the old fisherman shtupps the swordfish after finally landing it in his boat. The rest of *The Old Man and the Sea* is filled with the guy wrestling with his prey, just like the novella (page after page of fish-hunting). One page contains too-pretty images of starry/ sunset/ sunrise skies, which the old man dismisses thus: 'Shit! Pretentious bitch!'

On the final page of *The Old Man and the Sea* there's one of Katsuhiro Otomo's joke endings:

THE ART OF KATSUHIRO OTOMO ▼ 124

hauling the swordfish into his boat, it turns out to have a human lower half (naked, of course). Whether the half-human-half-fish is male[8] or female doesn't bother the old man, because he has it anyway: 'you're never too old for this! Oooo, this peach skin!'

ALICE'S ADVENTURES IN WONDERLAND.
The work of Lewis Carroll is a huge favourite with *manga* and *animé* artists, as it is with artists the world over. In Katsuhiro Otomo's version of *Alice's Adventures In Wonderland*, we follow the White Rabbit down the rabbit hole, as we have done thousands of times since the publication of *Alice* in 1865. Otomo has fun with optical illusions and visual tricks which depict Alice entering the hall with the tiny door, drinking from a vase and shrinking... Once thru the little door, Alice encounters many of the famous characters from Lewis Carroll's book.

Instead of going thru every scenario in *Alice's Adventures In Wonderland*, Katsuhiro Otomo places them into 32 small, rectangular panels which crowd onto a single page of *Hansel and Gretel*. We see the White Rabbit, the Tea Party, Humpty Dumpty, the Dodo, the Cheshire Cat, and Otomo's additions to the Carrollian, Surrealist menagerie: a Chinese, Imperial Palace plus guards, and what looks like a Hindu deity (Krishna). When Alice encounters Humpty Dumpty, the giant egg spends all of his time laughing, which irritates Alice so much she thumps him (which's classic Otomo!).

A note from the author at the back of *Hansel and Gretel* admits that the *Alice's Adventures In Wonderland* section wasn't quite the whole thing, so there is a reprise of the story (but this time with added translations of the speech bubbles).

The artwork in *Alice* refers to Japanese woodblock prints and artists such as Katsuhika Hokusai (the famous way that Hokusai portrayed the ocean

---

[8] Is it meant to be male, a reference to Ernest Hemingway's homosexuality?

and waves), as well as John Tenniel, the first great illustrator of *Alice's Adventures In Wonderland*.

The *Alice* books of Lewis Carroll (1832-98) – *Alice's Adventures In Wonderland* (1865) and *Through the Looking Glass* (1872) – were hugely popular in the late Victorian era, second only to the *Bible* in Victorian nurseries, according to some critics.[9] Queen Victoria was a fan.

Katsuhiro Otomo's *Alice* is another addition to the 1000s of plays, musicals, songs,[10] school, amateur and professional pantomimes, TV shows, cartoons, posters, operas, books, comicbooks, *manga,* paintings, illustrations, radio versions, fan fictions, sequels, and critical studies of the two Charles Dodgson *Alice* novels (it is a vast industry). Everything in the two *Alice* books is familiar and has become part of popular culture (and not only in the West).

The *Alice* industry began with the books themselves, with artist John Tenniel (and the author) being among the very first to turn the texts into another medium (i.e., illustrations); Katsuhiro Otomo has gone back to Tenniel's drawings (as many artists have done, even tho' literally hundreds of artists have had a run at illustrating *Alice*).

Lewis Carroll also added to the *Alice* mythology with minor, additional publications. Within Carroll's lifetime, dramatic adaptations of the *Alice* books were produced (such as an operetta, for which Carroll added to his texts). Five years after Carroll's death in 1898, the first films of *Alice* were released, and movie adaptations of *Alice* are a minor category in the history of cinema in their own right.

Lewis Carroll's influence is everywhere in popular culture and high art. Among the authors who were influenced by Carroll and *Alice* were Oscar Wilde, J.R.R. Tolkien, Flannery O'Connor, Lawrence Durrell, Jorge Luis Borges, Vladimir Nabokov, Hunter S. Thompson and J.K. Rowling.

9 See J. Zipes, 2002, 10.
10 John Lennon was a huge fan, and *Alice* references abound in the Beatles' output.

SLEEPING BEAUTY.

Sleeping Beauty is another story in K. Otomo's *Hansel and Gretel* collection which relies on a single gag: Sleeping Beauty is sleeping… and sleeping… and sleeping… So the *manga* repeats the same drawing of the princess asleep in her bed. She rolls over, and she continues to sleep. With three images per page, Otomo-sensei shows Sleeping Beauty fast asleep over nine drawings.

But the artwork is beautiful – this is Katsuhiro Otomo in his High Victorian mode, delivering fantastically detailed drawings which are inspired by Gustave Doré, above all, and other great, 19th century book illustrators, such as George Cruickshank and Aubrey Beardsley. Indeed, Doré's interpretations of *Sleeping Beauty* are very similar to Otomo's, so that this goes beyond *hommage* (Doré produced illustrations to many famous fairy tales in the 1867 edition of Charles Perrault).

THE THREE LITTLE PIGS.

In *The Three Little Pigs*, the wolf blows down the straw house and the wooden house with arrogant ease. But when he finds the three little pigs crammed inside the remains, he wonders, 'just how the hell did you guys get inside?' (The visual gag here is that the wily pigs have built the houses as Chinese boxes, one inside the other).

THE WOLF AND THE SEVEN KIDS.

In *The Wolf and the Seven Young Kids*, the wolf arrives first, but the goats' mother is just around the corner, too. The wolf flees. Because the wolf got there first, everything is switched around: now the kids inside aren't convinced that mommy goat is their real mom, because her voice should be rougher, her paws should be pitch black, etc. Once inside, mother goat finds seven wolf cubs who've just eaten her children.

THE WOLF MAN.

Another wolfy story, *The Wolf Man*, has a North American setting (like something out of the stories of Washington Irving or Edgar Allan Poe), with a family man turning into a wolf at the full moon. With drawings that emulate a classic horror movie from the 1950s, Katsuhiro Otomo has the Wolf-Man hiding from his family, who're beating on the door and demanding to know what's wrong. When his wife continues to beg that he open the door and to trust in their love, the final panel reveals that the mother and the daughter have also turned into wolves.

LITTLE RED RIDING HOOD.

The most famous of wolfy fairy tales, *Little Red Riding Hood,* is twisted around pretty much how you'd expect it to be by Katsuhiro Otomo: the wolf's eaten by the grandmother. So, the wolf hurries away to the grandmother's dilapidated hovel ahead of Little Red Riding Hood (who's conceived as a very fat, young maiden, like a German farm girl after months of eating tripe. The wolf, meanwhile, is a scrawny thing with a tongue lolling out).

Granny hasn't been fed for a month – so when Little Red Riding Hood enters the house (despite warnings from her mother), she finds a wide-eyed cannibal that's already eviscerated the wolf, and eaten several humans, too (their skeletons are glimpsed in the background).

While feminists have rewritten fairy tales such as *Little Red Riding Hood* to emphasize the Freudian, sexual subtexts (girls, virginity, pubescent desire, men as wolfish, sexual predators, etc), Katsuhiro Otomo brings it all back to the savage fundamentals of life: killing and eating.

Survival.

THE BOY WHO CRIED WOLF.

In *The Boy Who Cried Wolf*, a youth races into a village at top speed, crying out, 'the wolf is coming!'

Some of the villagers are scared, most are bemused, and some are irritated – because the boy does this every day. Like Bugs Bunny, the youth runs thru the village and out the other side, with the wolf running alongside him (the scene's reminiscent of the main titles sequence that Katsuhiro Otomo and Atsuko Fukushima created for *Robot Carnival*, and of the *Cinderella* spoof, where there's another mad dash thru a village). It's also reminiscent of a gang of bikers roaring through the neighbourhood (as in the *Cinderella* skit below).

CINDERELLA.

In *Cinderella*, the heroine, hurrying away from the castle on the stroke of midnight, is depicted dashing back home riding a coach and whipping the horses in a frenzy. It's another story by Katsuhiro Otomo where a character storms thru a sleepy village creating mayhem (in *Akira*, it was the gang on motor-bikes). With a magical *pop*, the horses turn into pigs, Cinders' fine dress becomes rags, and in subsequent drawings, the coach is now a tiny kids' cart, and the heroine ends up riding a pig.

THE BLUE BIRD.

In *The Blue Bird*, two fairy tale urchins are searching for the 'Blue Bird of Happiness'. It might be a magical creature, but all the boy and the girl are concerned with are catching it, killing it, cooking it and eating it (Katsuhiro Otomo recognizes that hunger and the search for food – i.e., the issue of survival – plays a huge role in fairy tale culture – as it does in his *Akira manga*). Forget about admiring the bird, or discovering its magic – how about *eating it*?! (Similarly, the animals in *Noah's Ark* are eaten, Don Quixote spears the tiny dragon out of disgust, and the woodcutter accidentally kills the Lady of the Lake in *The Honest Woodcutter*).

ROBINSON CRUSOE.

In Katsuhiro Otomo's take on the old Daniel Defoe favourite, *Robinson Crusoe*, the hero discovers he is not alone on the desert island. He duly names the native he meets Friday. But when another guy materializes from the undergrowth, he needs a name too: so he's Saturday. A third one appears: 'I am Robinson Crusoe. You are fucking Sunday'. Soon Crusoe is surrounded by a host of guys, goofing around, and he can't control them. (In the portrayal of the island's locals, as gross caricatures of black men, this is one of Otomo's very un-PC strips).

JACK AND THE BEANSTALK.

In *Jack and the Beanstalk*, the boy Jack dutifully goes off to market to sell the cow. Despite his mom's warnings about doing 'something stupid like swapping our cow for a bean', of course Jack does just that. Jack hurries home with his prize – and it's a colossal bean, twice as big as he is (which he carries hoisted on his back). The joke is simply that – a bean the size of a pig.

THE LITTLE MATCH GIRL.

In the Christmas favourite *The Little Match Girl* (by Hans Christian Andersen, 1805-75), the poor family trying to sell matches in a town thinks of ways of making the image of matches less depressing and more appealing to the passers-by on the street. So the father spends all night working on a display for the match girl: it's a match costume, like the ones that performers wear at Disneyland (so the Match Girl literally becomes 'Match Girl', in a match suit; and of course, it's round about now that she wants to go pee-pee!).

SNOW WHITE.

Katsuhiro Otomo's take on that old fairy tale favourite *Snow White* focusses on the dwarfs and on Snow White. As with *The Wizard of Oz*, this version of

Snow White refers to the famous Hollywood movie. *Snow White* is only two pages long (9 panels). It's based around the single gag of counting and numbers: the dwarfs are returning home (singing the familiar 'Heigh Ho' song from Walt Disney's 1937 animation), and they halt to take a roll call. '1, 2, 3, 4, 5, 6'. Eh? Only *six*?! So the seven dwarfs have become the six dwarfs, much to their consternation. Because every time they count themselves up, the counter forgets to include himself.

Meanwhile, back at the dwarfs' home, Snow White is also having trouble working out how many places to set at the table for supper. 'Now there are twice three... So there's only one left... Twice three and one once...' And in the final panel of *Snow White*, the witch is also having trouble with her poisoned apples – is it *this* apple? Or maybe *that* apple?

In *Snow White* Katsuhiro Otomo has fun (as all artists do) with differentiating the dwarfs, creating an individual look for each one. He also conceives them as *very* small dwarfs – so they are not three or foot feet tall, but lilliputian.

THE HONEST WOODCUTTER.

The Honest Woodcutter is another take by Katsuhiro Otomo on a fairy tale which has slapstick violence added. Our young woodcutter is out in the forest, doing what woodcutter do – cutting trees. Yes. And – whoops! – out flies the boy's axe into the lake, and right into the skull of the Lady of the Lake. She is a plump, old maid with angel's wings, who rises impressively from the lake in wreaths of smoke. She has an axe buried in her head (and in her chest), so she's very miffed. The woodcutter apologizes, but at that moment the tree he was chopping falls down... on the Lady of the Lake's head. Blood spurts from her skull. It's another death (sort of accidental) of a fairy tale figure. In Katsuhiro Otomo's fairy tale world, the hero/ines can't help injuring or killing the special creatures they're supposed to be seeking or exalting.

They are clumsy oafs who accidentally (or with evil intent) bash or kill the magical beings.

MOBY DICK.

In Katsuhiro Otomo's take on *Moby Dick*, while Captain Ahab spouts his religious invective about battling the behemoth from the oceans in his boat, another whale appears. 'Oh, merciful God!' he cries, 'there are two white whales!' Then more whales appear. The beasts are utterly oblivious of the titanic struggle the humans in their vessels are undertaking on the surging waves: the whales chat amongst themselves, waiting for the rest of the family to arrive. The whales decide to go to the Indian Ocean, leaving behind the crew in the water, their boats capsized. It's another tale of the complete indifference of the natural world to humanity.

DON QUIXOTE.

Miguel de Cervantes' *Don Quixote* is another of the great classic works of Western literature which Katsuhiro Otomo has spoofed, along with *Moby Dick*, *Robinson Crusoe* and *Alice*. Instead of tilting at windmills, Otomo-sensei imagines Don Quixote as an ageing biker in the Californian desert, a former Hell's Angel on a hog (with Sancho Panza riding in a sidecar). Quixote sports goggles, a long beard and a cape; Sancho is the usual hapless sidekick of adventure yarns (with a cooking pot for a crash helmet).

The Ingenuous Gentleman Don Quixote of La Mancha is conceived as a road movie in the desert (harking back to favourite Otomo movies such as *Easy Rider*). The odd couple refuel their motorcycle at a Middle Eastern-looking settlement (mud buildings, market stalls), where they spot a carpet on sale designed with the image of a knight on horseback fighting a dragon (the Don is fascinated). Quixote and Panza leave, following directions from a tradesman to find the dragons' run. Soon they're out in the deep desert, and passing the remains of warriors (their skulls and their swords), presumably former heroes who've attempted to slay the dragon/s.

An enormous skeleton looms above the adventurers – the remains of the beast (but framed as if it's still alive, breathing fire and just about to attack our heroes). It happens to look like the bones of a stegosaurus (as if this is a graveyard of dinosaur remains). Don Quixote has his lance at the ready as he rides in on his motorcycle. The travellers examine the relic, the bones towering over them; Sancho Panza finds a huge egg. It hatches. Out pops a tiny lizard, which breathes a tiny plume of fire. Disgusted, disappointed, the knight simply spears it with his lance, then leaves in a huff.

The Ingenuous Gentleman Don Quixote of La Mancha is partly about the gap between dream (art) and reality, about the dreams that old warriors have and the real world they have to deal with. Like Japanese samurai, the ageing soldiers in *Don Quixote* find themselves living in a society in which their services were no longer required.

THE WIZARD OF OZ.

Giant genitals are the joke in Katsuhiro Otomo's take on L. Frank Baum's *The Wizard of Oz*. Japanese erotic art (going back to the Edo period) features plenty of out-size genitals, which're given to the three guys in the story – the Tin Man, the Scarecrow, and the Lion. *The Wonderful Wizard of Oz* is a send-up of the 1939 Hollywood movie more than Baum's famous, much-loved *Oz* books.

Impossibly nice, 12 year-old Dorothy skips along the yellow brick road singing a happy song, *hmm hmm, over the rainbow*. The Scarecrow is encountered first, sitting beside the road like a bum, and off they go together on the yellow brick road to see the Wizard. Dorothy spots a squashy sack being dragged along the ground between the Scarecrow's legs; the Scarecrow yelps when she accidentally treads on it. The Scarecrow tells Dorothy to ignore it. Dorothy, curious, lifts her dress to show the Scarecrow that she doesn't have anything like that dangling down there. *Bang!* The Scarecrow gets an instant erection which whacks him in the face. The Scarecrow tells Dorothy not to worry about it, and he carries on walking, clutching his erection to him like a bean bag.

Soon the travellers meet the Tin Man, another goofy dude lurking at the roadside (he's designed like a Japanese robot, with a rocket attached to his back, as if he's just walked out of a 1960s Japanese comic). Like the Scarecrow, the Tin Man also has a mysterious appendage sticking out from between his legs. Dorothy points at it and lifts her dress: 'how come I don't have one attached?' *Creak, crash!* The Tin Man's member bloats and whacks into his face from one look at *kawaii* Dorothy's white panties. And it continues to creak as the Tin Man walks, joining the travellers on the yellow brick road. While the guys struggle with their unwanted but persistent erections, Dorothy continues to skip and sing, oblivious.

They meet the Lion next: he looks like a circus performer crossed with a relic from a glam rock band of the 1970s (he has knee-high, stacked boots, a star painted over his eye, a circus strongman's leotard, and a mane of shaggy hair). 'I'll ask for some courage!' the Lion yells. But Dorothy isn't listening – she peers down at the Lion's package (which has eyes and a mouth drawn on it, to match his costume – and when it's erect, it gives the Lion a smiley mouth, a great detail).

'Everyone has one, how come I don't?' Dorothy wonders about the wieners. Again, she gives the three men a glimpse of her underwear, and once again the three giant weenies slam into the guys' faces.

When the Scarecrow asks Dorothy what she is going to see the Wizard of Oz for, she replies, 'Me? Well, you see... I want to have a cute baby.' The Scarecrow, the Tin Man and Lion look delighted: they lead Dorothy off the yellow brick road and into the trees: 'We can give you a nice baby'.

Sexualizing fairy tales is a common tactic when modernizing and updating and satirizing them. The eroticism is already there in fairy tales, of course – to a super-intense degree (fairy tales are all about desire and temptation and romance – plus the prohibitions and taboos and rule-breaking which sometimes results in violence and death). But contemporary authors can't resist making some of the relationships more graphically explicit. Giving the characters in *The Wizard of Oz* enormous genitals and flirting with a girl is in the tradition of the satirical cartoon art of Robert Crumb and Ralph Bakshi. That Dorothy is clearly a prepubescent girl, with an undeveloped body, adds to the scandal – and it's a girl with three middle-aged men, too, not with a single boy of her own age.

Hansel and Gretel, Katsuhiro Otomo's versions
of classic stories and fairy tales (this page and
following pages).
Above – Ali Baba and Robinson Crusoe

Hansel and Gretel, frontispiece

Alice's Adventures In Wonderland

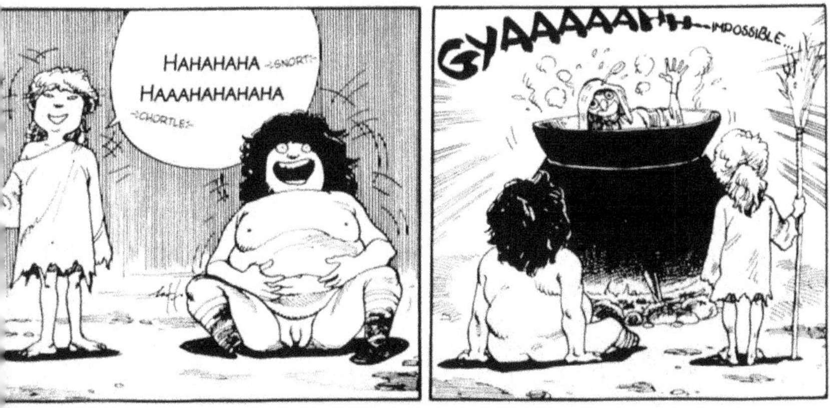
HAHAHAHA -SNORT-
HAAAHAHAHAHA
-CHORTLE-
GYAAAAAHH
IMPOSSIBLE...

20

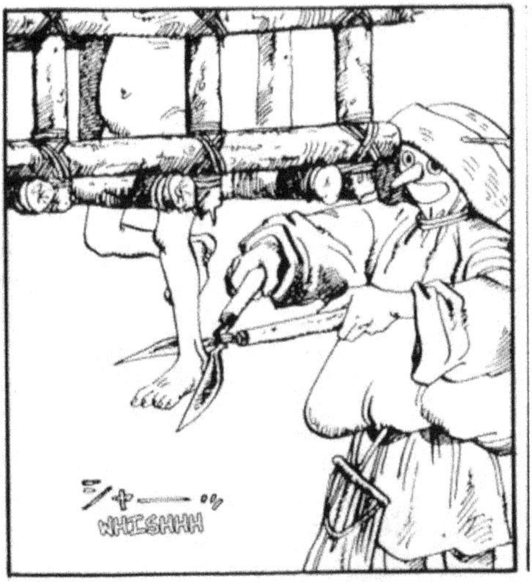
WHISHHH

Hansel and Gretel

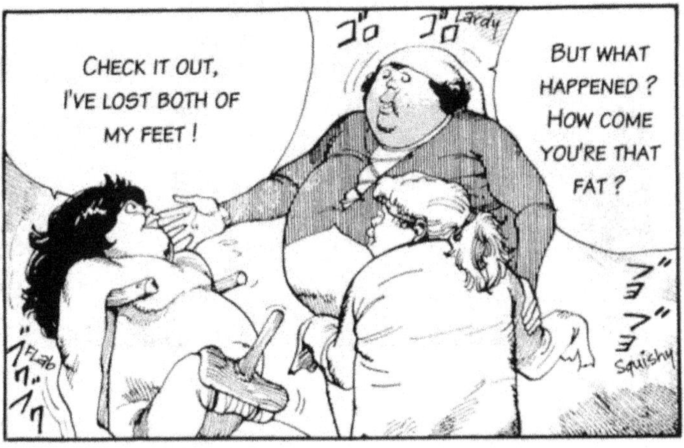
CHECK IT OUT, I'VE LOST BOTH OF MY FEET!
ゴロ ゴロ Lardy
BUT WHAT HAPPENED? HOW COME YOU'RE THAT FAT?
Flab
Squishy

In the deepest depths
of an ever dark forest...
A single castle was
buried there... In the
deepest depths of an
ever dark forest...

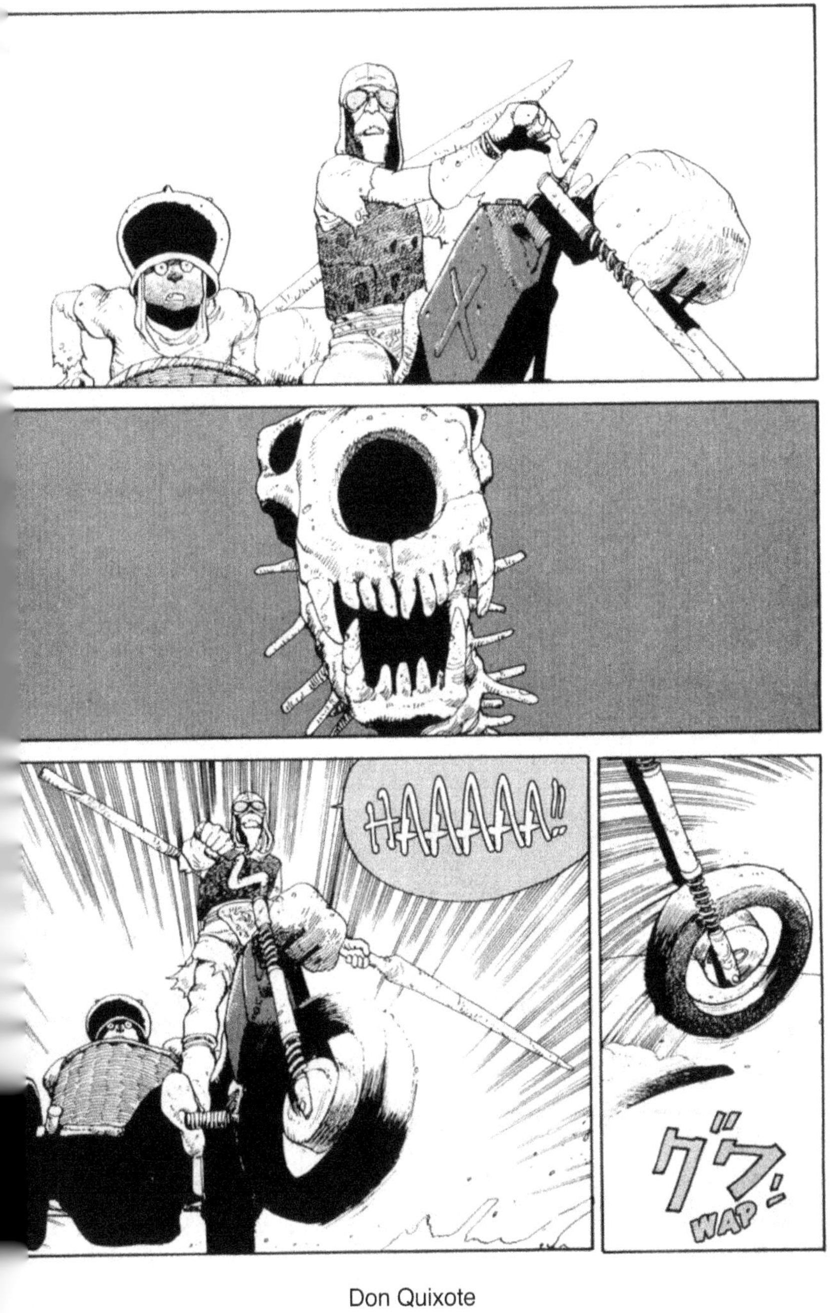
HAAAAAA!!
グワ!
WAP!

Don Quixote

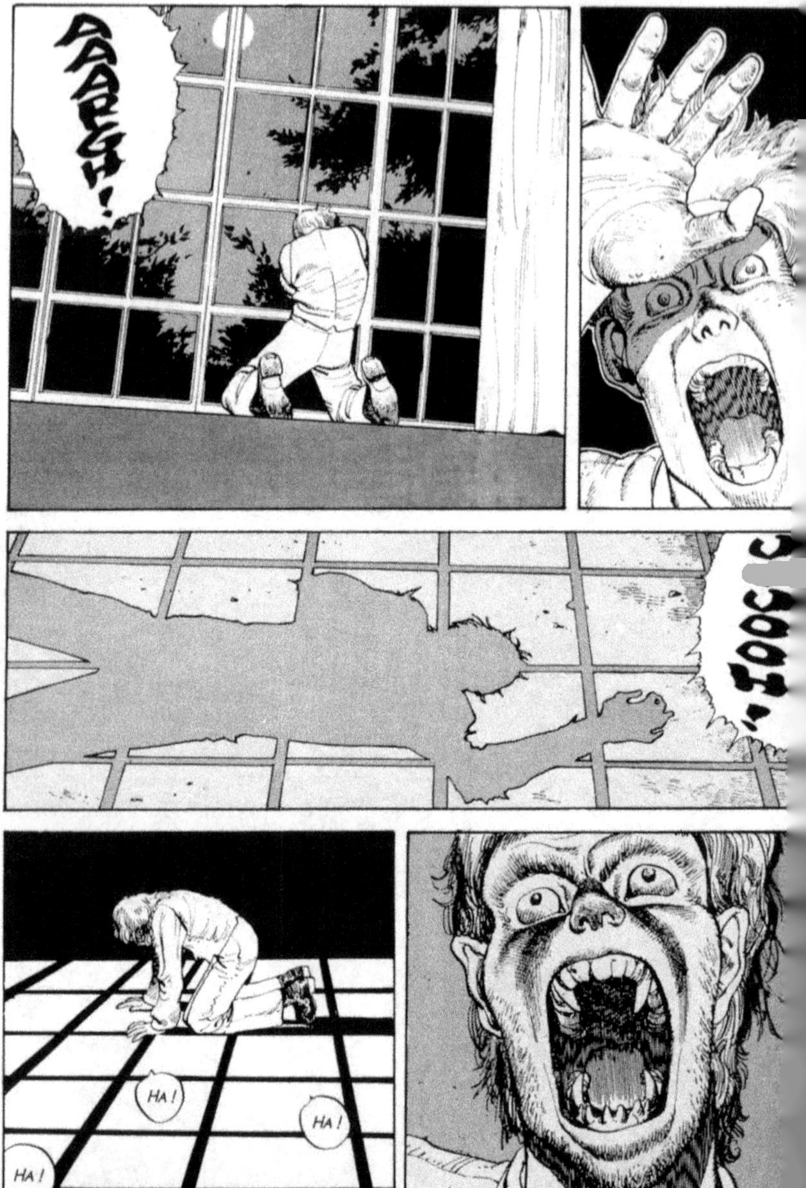
AAARGH!
HA!
HA!
HA!

Katsuhiro Otomo takes on The Wizard of Oz

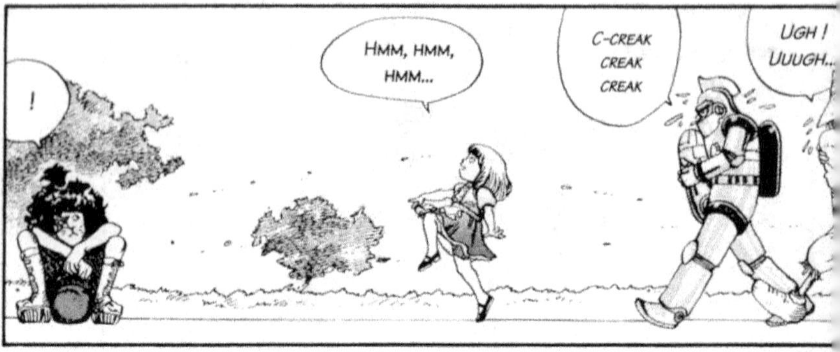
UGH! UUUGH...
C-CREAK CREAK CREAK
HMM, HMM, HMM...
!

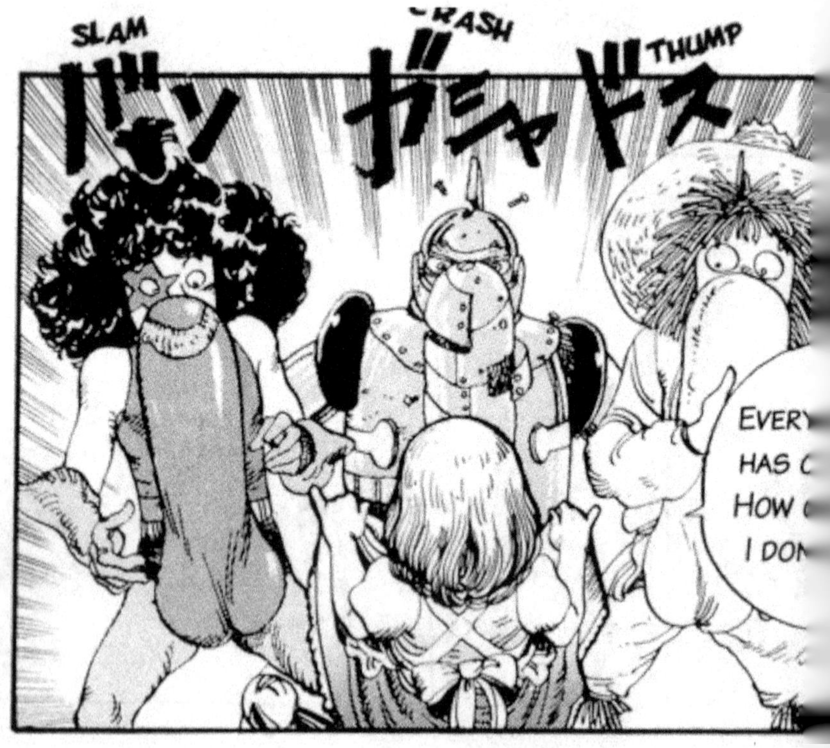
THUMP ドス
CRASH ガシャ
SLAM バン
EVERY
HAS
HOW
I DON

The Old Man and the Sea, from That's Amazing World

Aladdin, from That's Amazing World

King Arthur's court in That's Amazing World

Noah and his family in That's Amazing World

04

INRI

The most outrageous work that Katsuhiro Otomo has created, and one which would have many religious groups going apoplectic (if they knew about it, that is), is without question *Inri*[1] (1980, part of the *Hansel and Gretel* collection), Otomo-sensei's incredible, self-consciously sensationalist rewriting of the story of Jesus. Few major publishers in the West would publish it, and very few major Western artists would bother to create it – knowing that it would be highly unlikely to see the light of day. But the 26 year-old Otomo-sensei just steamed ahead!

In just twelve pages, *Inri* manages to cover a huge slice of the life of Christ, delivering a savage, no-holds-barred send-up of Biblical stories, of the *Gospels*, of 2,000 years of Christian art, and of the fundamental concepts in Xianity.

Inri is the Christian story as you've never seen it before – which is a major accomplishment, as it's been the subject of millions of artworks over two thousand years.

The subject of *Inri* is the pornography of religion, how religious beliefs can become perverted over time,

1 The word INRI stands for the initial letters of *Ieusus Nazarenus Rex Judaeorum* ('Jesus of Nazareth, King of the Jews'), from the *Gospel of John* (19: 19). It's often placed in paintings on the Cross, as here (Pontius Pilate ordered the plaque to be put on the Cross).

how religions contain – or try to contain – and control – powerful forces, of violence and aggression, of sexuality and desire, of fear and horror.

I'm sure that Katsuhiro Otomo did not sit down and think, *how can I wind up Christians, moral guardians, religionists and educators?* (Has Otomo-sensei received death threats because of this *manga*?) But in this work, he parodies what millions of people regard as sacred – Jesus, his birth, his mother and father, his divine status, his disciples, his philosophy, his Ministry, and his legacy.

Christianity for Japanese artists is something exotic, other-worldly, *different*, and sometimes creepy and dangerous. The pretty visuals of Catholicism – angels, crosses, nuns, churches, stained glass – appear in many *manga* and *animé* (usually as superficial, skin-deep motifs without the symbolic, theological and philosophical weight they have in the West).

Christianity comes from overseas for Japanese – it is automatically and irrevocably *foreign* (yet for Westerners, too, Xianity is *not* Western: it is a Middle Eastern religion). To the sinister view of Christianity in Japanese pop culture, Otomo-sensei adds violence, bloodshed, sex, torture, perversity and cannibalism!

❖

It's a short (but explosive) work, short enough so we can look at each individual page of *Inri*:

Page 1. A wide view of a rocky desert at night, with the Three Wise Men looking out over the plain and the town of Bethlehem. While not an image that could appear on a Christmas greetings card (too 'realistic'), there's nothing that could trouble anybody about the opening page of *Inri* (hell, Otomo-sensei's even included the Star of Bethlehem).

Page 2. That cute-cute beginning, however, lasts only one page! Because on page two of *Inri* – wow! – here comes the outrageous, in-your-face rebellion of Katsuhiro Otomo! The first panel is a ramshackle hovel underneath gaunt, twisted trees (a setting for a witch or an ogre, not the romanticized stables of Xian mythology). The second drawing depicts the Three Kings (Caspar, Balthazar and Melchior) as you've never seen 'em before – three gap-toothed, old coots, they look like bandits from a 1960s Spaghetti Western who've come to steal what they can, rather than to bear gifts to the Son of God.

The third image of page one of *Inri* is a reverse angle, revealing what the Magi are looking at: the Virgin Mary, Joseph and Jesus. The drawing is a brutal assault on the beloved iconography of Western religion: this single image contains a *ton* of elements which maul Christian theology: the Madonna is a skinny, exhausted figure who looks mournfully at the viewer; Joseph is dead, his internal organs are spilling out from his belly – it seems as if Christ has been ripped from inside him, *Alien*-style. Joseph is naked from the waist down, with his legs spread as if in childbirth. (And on the right, there's a dead cow with an axe buried in it, and more internal organs falling out).

A dead St Joseph who's given birth to Jesus! And a grotesque birth, too, which means instant death – stomach, bowels and the like bursting open. But even that horrific image is not the end of it – because the Anti-christ himself (or 'it'-self), is a human baby in the form of an alien, with a huge, domed, bald head, and eyes glowering at the viewer in malevolence. (Recalling the way that Tetsuo glares out at you in *Akira*). The child sits in a halo of light, but there is no halo above him/ it (and none in the rest of *Inri*).

❖

The third page of *Inri* depicts the youth of Jesus/ the Anti-Christ. In the top drawing, the babe is apparently being baptized with blood (this crops up on the fourth page). In the six small drawings below, Jesus attacks a boy (who's been innocently picking flowers) with his scythe, beside a tree, stripping the body of its clothes after death. When they meet, Jesus shows no emotion, but glowers at the boy (this is a version of the Massacre of the Innocents, perhaps). So, by the age of six, he's a murderer! And for no reason or motive! This is, simply, a *very* nasty child.

The fourth page of *Inri* introduces the grown-up Christ in a truly grotesque scene: the Baptism. But this is not St John the Baptist as you've ever seen him! And not the Baptism as you've ever seen it! The Baptist is a pug-ugly lout with a squashed boxer's nose (inspired by figures in the art of Hieronymous Bosch, as the profile drawing shows). Instead of the usual sunny setting beside a river or a lake, the Baptist is conducting black magic rituals at night: a naked woman is laid out on the ground as a sacrifice; above her, the Baptist holds a naked baby by its legs, gripping a knife in his hand. It is a baptism with the blood of a newborn babe, plus a naked virgin, lit by wood fires, with the onlookers gathered in a circle.

Into this over-the-top scene of death and blood and ritual sacrifice, Jesus stalks: he is dressed in the usual Biblical clothing, with sandals, long hair and a grim expression. He is, like many Christs in modern art and movies, very much like a hippy in appearance, and he could fit in with the turned-on, spaced-out crowds and flower children in California *circa* 1967 with no problem. Jesus is also very *Japanese*, while some of the other charas appear Middle Eastern. Jesus kneels, and the Baptist slices open the baby and anoints Christ with blood.

Still on page five of *Inri*, Jesus begins to gather followers around him (in a hi-key drawing, lambs – no, devils with tails – gambol around him in Disney-esque jollity as he begins his Ministry). When two women hurry along a forest path after him, kneeling before Jesus and begging him to let them be his disciples, we can guess what's gonna happen! Especially when the two women're young, attractive and heavily made-up, with one tanned, in the *ganguro* style (and thus they're probably hookers, so one is presumably Mary Magdalene. It's typical of Otomo to give Jesus not one but two prostitutes!).

Yes – you guessed right! On page six, Katsuhiro

Otomo delivers what for millions of people would be a blasphemous image: Christ having sex. And with two women, not one (so one rides him, while he licks the other one straddling his head). As she tups Jesus, the woman gasps, 'You are the son of our living God'.

Many artists have explored the links between Christianity and sexuality, tho' few have been as brazen as this, putting Jesus into explicit sexual scenes. Artists such as Eric Gill have depicted Jesus making love, for instance, and Auguste Rodin drew images of Jesus with Mary Magdalene. But the approach of Otomo-sensei is not reverential in the slightest (as Gill, Rodin, Félicien Rops *et al* still were, despite their graphic approach), but satirical and iconoclastic.

The disciple Peter appears behind a tree (having spied on the holy threesome), asking to be another follower of Jesus (we're still on page six of *Inri* here). Peter is stunned to see Jesus naked, legs splayed, with two cherubs hovering over where his phallus would be – the drawing suggests that Christ is an androgynous being, with both male and female genitals, and also that the cherubs are hanging onto Christ's erection (the genitals being airbrushed out, in the manner of censored *manga*). Jesus pulls Peter down (by his ear – looking forward to the Garden of Gethsemane and the moment when the ear is cut off). They tup, while the naked women watch (yes, it's gay sex as well as group sex in Otomo-sensei's reworking of the Christian story).

❖

We are now halfway thru *Inri* – on page seven (and by page 7 Otomo-sensei has already portrayed enough blasphemy and heresy to have him tortured for millennia). The Messiah is collecting around him a large crowd as he marches thru the desert. Katsuhiro Otomo cruelly satirizes the followers of Christ as toothless, ugly, lame, disturbed roughnecks, all clad in rags (some are *very* ugly). Judas is portrayed as a grinning, stuttering idiot who looks like he's just escaped from a lunatic asylum. They are going to Jerusalem.

The key image of page eight of *Inri*, taking up half the page, depicts the court of Christ on Earth, as imagined by Katsuhiro Otomo in 1980: in a temple setting (presumably it's Jerusalem), a horde of followers are enjoying themselves (cackling and grimacing), while teasing and torturing naked women. Peter is the Master of Ceremonies. While Jesus looks on, bored (sprawled in an anachronistically modern armchair, a great touch), the victims're man-handled into the area. Some women lie on the floor, either already dead or just raped. There's a woman's severed head, and a dog sniffing at remains.

Compositionally, the drawing is reminiscent of the paintings of artists such as Nicholas Poussin, Tintoretto and Raphael, where a large group of people are spread out in an elegant setting – it might be a Renaissance or Baroque picture of a feast in Ancient Rome, the trial of a saint, or Salomé dancing before Herod.

The three, small drawings at the bottom of page eight depict a woman about to be decapitated, with Christ looking terminally jaded, and Peter grimacing as the blood spurts. (Even mass orgies, gory slaughter and black magic rites get boring after a while).

❖

You want more? Oh, there is more! How much sacrilege and satire has Katsuhiro Otomo packed into these twelve outrageous pages of the *Inri manga*?! The Last Supper in the mind of naughty Otomo-sensei is another grotesque circus: the long, wooden table is piled up with food… food that includes unidentifiable organs (from Lord knows what animal!), plus a dead child. Jesus's disciples raise their goblets in a toast to their Overlord, crying, 'This is my flesh, this is my blood!' (That they are drinking blood instead of wine is made clear in the following panels).

The Last Supper leads to a mass orgy – or at

THE ART OF KATSUHIRO OTOMO ▼ 154

least a pile of naked bodies (the sort of mound of corpses seen on a battlefield, with a superhero like Conan (from Robert E. Howard) standing on the top). Some are dead, and some are alive – the followers are clambering over the corpses, arms raised, as if they're drugged or insane.

It's a baptism in blood again – blood from a goblet is poured over the nude corpse of a young lad, and over the body of a naked suppliant, who throws her head back in ecstasy.

At the bottom of page nine of *Inri*, the Passion story kicks in again, with the mentally retarded Judas Iscariot receiving his thirty pieces of silver, and the Roman guards rushing in to capture Jesus.

The trial of Christ is depicted by Katsuhiro Otomo as a farce. Pontius Pilate is portrayed as a glum dimwit who whinges that he's against the death penalty (!), and that crucifixion is mighty painful for everyone involved (a wet liberal Pilate is a blackly humorous twist, instead of the usual weary statesman who'd much rather be back in Roma). Jesus stands there, sullen and withdrawn, not uttering a word in his defence (this Messiah speaks nary a word in *Inri*, except 'No', right at the end).

❖

The last page of Katsuhiro Otomo's frontal assault on organized, Western religion depicts the Crucifixion. It is the largest image in *Inri*, apart from the first one (of the landscape setting). It's typically eccentric of Katsuhiro Otomo to draw Jesus nailed up *facing* the Cross, his face on the wooden beams, not looking outwards.

One of the Pharisees or the Jewish elders urges Jesus to repent, as he carries the Cross. The Messiah cries, 'NO!' This is the only word he says in the whole of *Inri*. Yep, the last word of *Inri* is one of defiance, of rebellion: 'NO!'

Typically for Katsuhiro Otomo, there are no overt signs that this Jesus in this 1980 portrayal is divine. Some of the iconography, however, suggests that – the use of light, the hints at haloes, etc. And the image of the Crucifixion features a wide band of light descending from the heavens (it's a thunderously gloomy sky, with beams of God-rays piercing the clouds,[2] a favourite Otomoan motif, which appears throughout the *Akira manga*. In *Akira,* of course, the column of heavenly light also came from man-made satellites).

But this is not a Christ who preaches (there are no quotes from the *Gospels*, the *Parables* or sayings of Jesus). There are no miracles, of course. No Sermon on the Mount. There are few indications that this guy will be the founder of a worldwide religion (his followers're depicted as idiots or losers or insane).

With its images of children and babies being murdered, its blood rites and black magic, its scenes of rape and group sex and gay sex and torture, *Inri* is among the most outrageous of the works of Katsuhiro Otomo (from a Western viewpoint, at least).

It's savage partly because Katsuhiro Otomo doesn't offer understandable motives for the aggression and the violence. When Jesus kills a boy aged six, no reason is given. It seems to be killing for the sake of it. Meanwhile, the followers of the adult Jesus are mercilessly satirized, and the cult of Christ is founded on the basest instincts of rape, murder, blood rituals, sex and coercion.

---

2 Reminiscent of Rembrandt van Rijn's etchings.

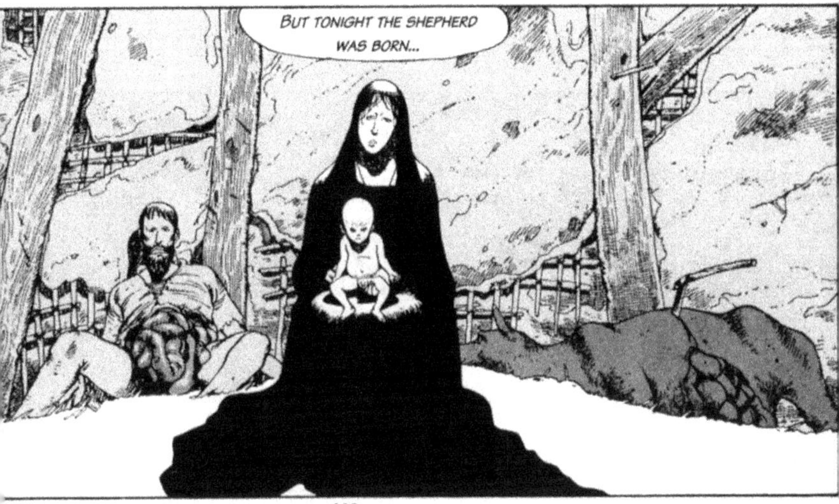
BUT TONIGHT THE SHEPHERD
WAS BORN...

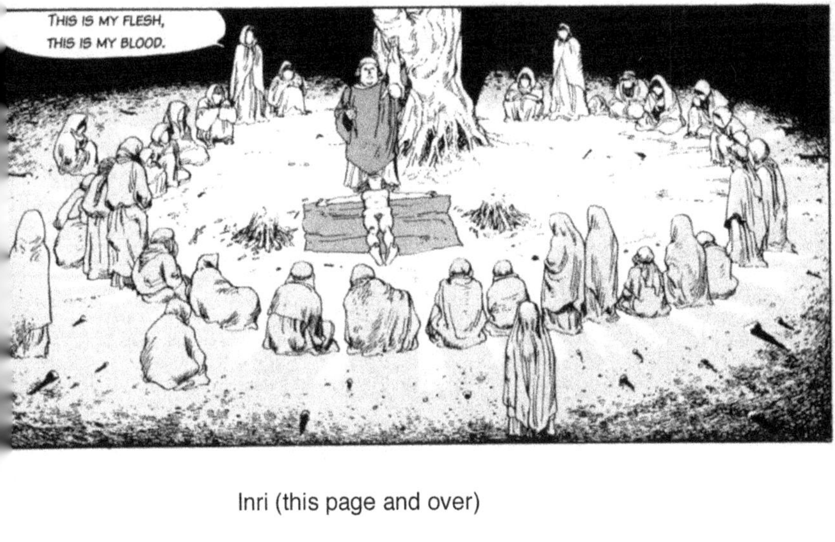
THIS IS MY FLESH,
THIS IS MY BLOOD.

Inri (this page and over)

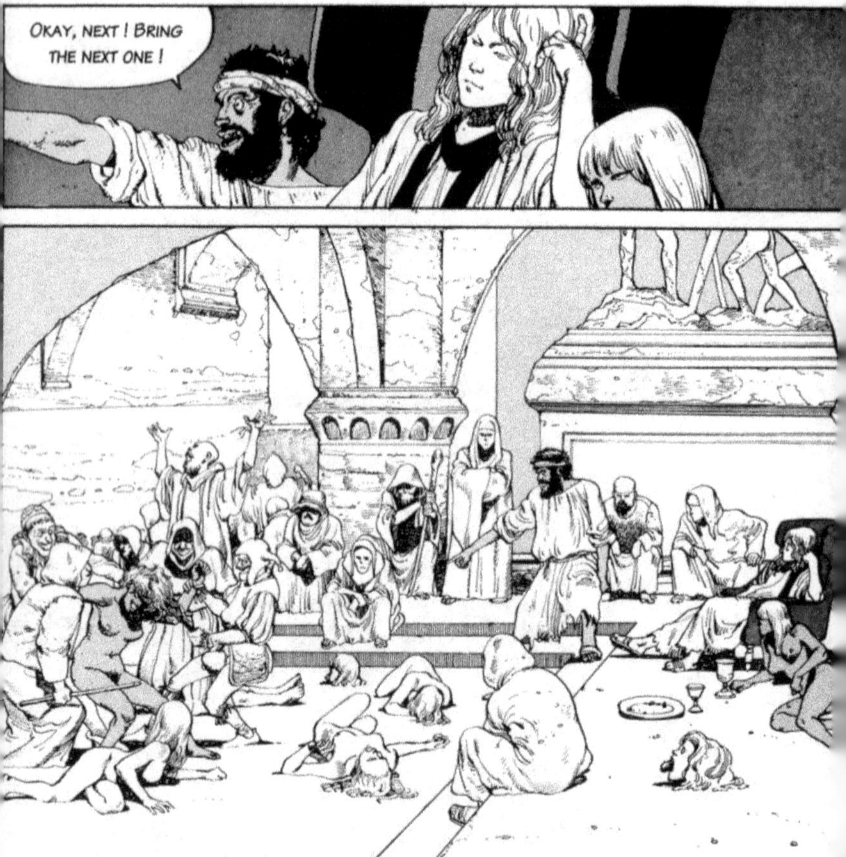
OKAY, NEXT ! BRING THE NEXT ONE !

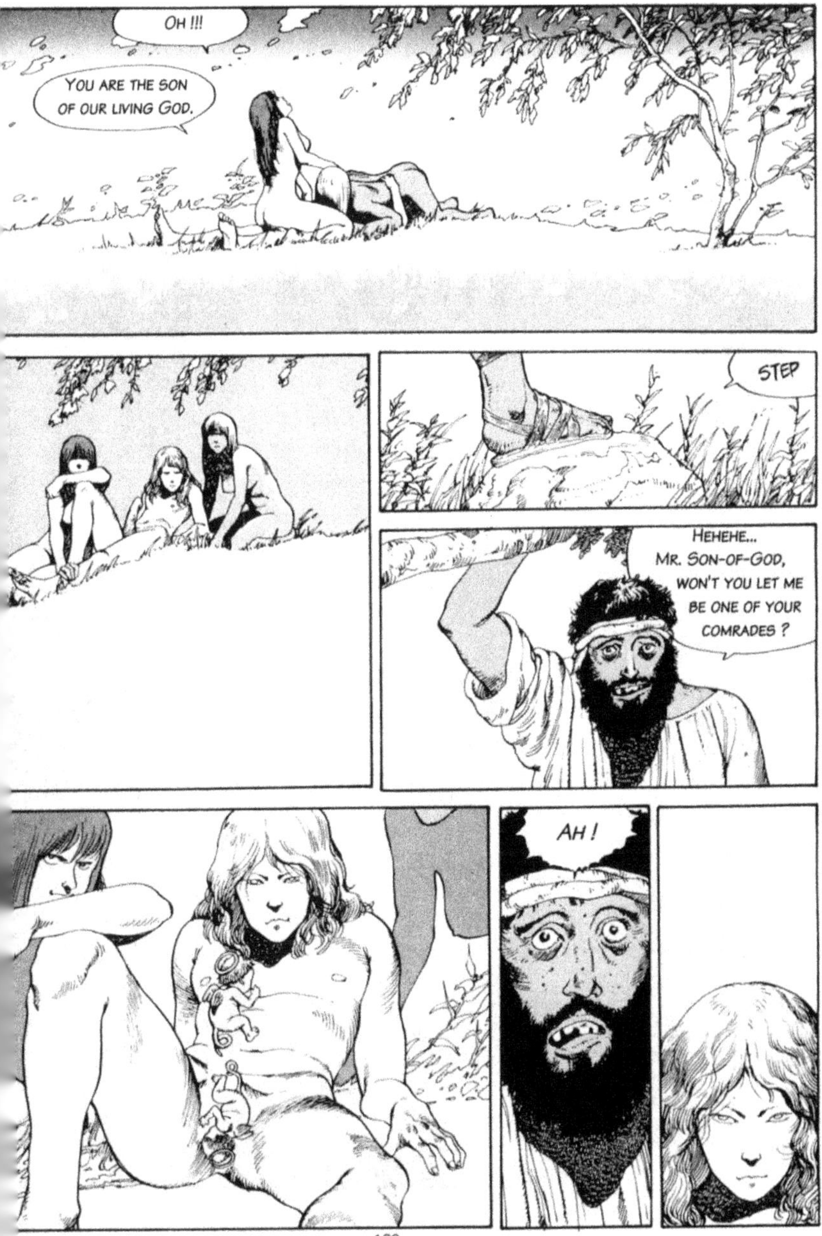
OH !!!
YOU ARE THE SON OF OUR LIVING GOD.
STEP
HEHEHE... MR. SON-OF-GOD, WON'T YOU LET ME BE ONE OF YOUR COMRADES ?
AH !

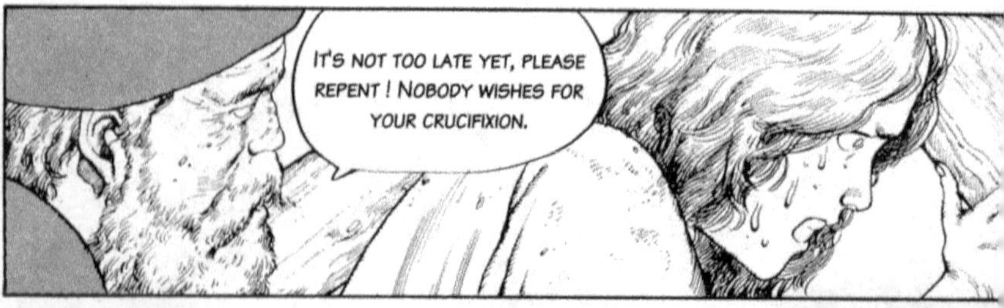
IT'S NOT TOO LATE YET, PLEASE REPENT ! NOBODY WISHES FOR YOUR CRUCIFIXION.

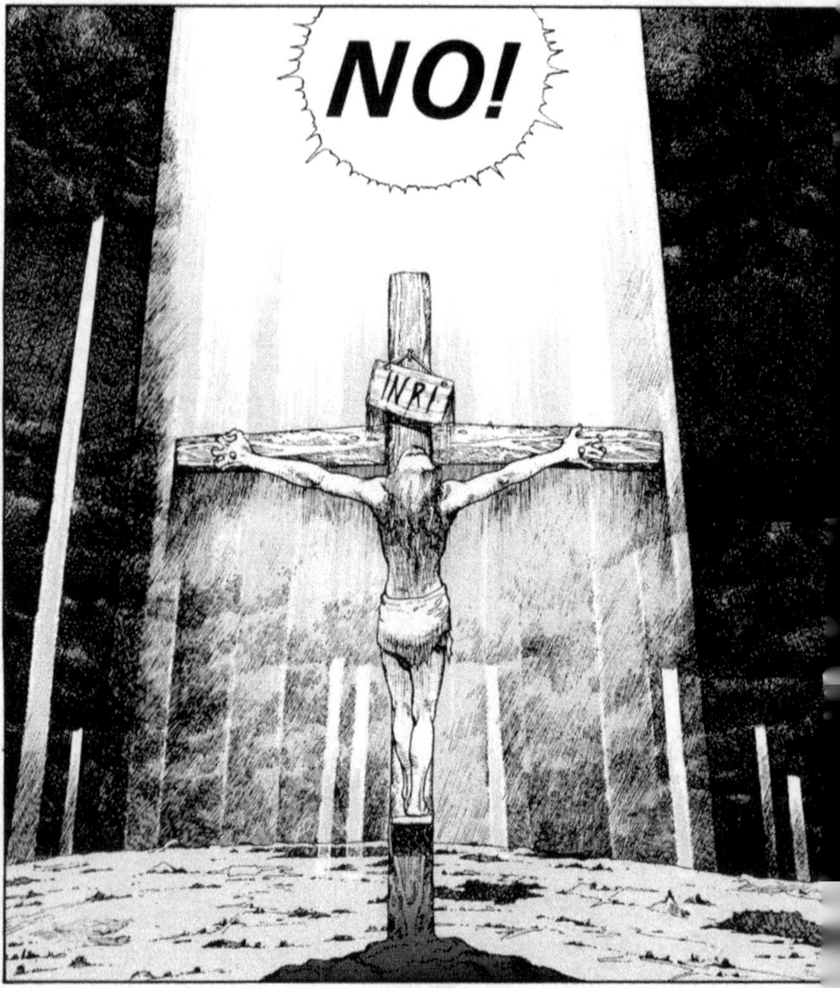
NO!
INRI

05

DOMU

In 1980, Katsuhiro Otomo published one of his early *manga* works, *Domu: A Child's Dream* (1980-83, in *Manga Action Deluxe*, from Futabasha). It won awards (including the Science Fiction Grand Prix Award and a Seiun Award in 1983), and was a big critical success: *Domu* raised Otomo-sensei's profile hugely in the *manga* world (it sold half a million copies).

  Domu was in part a reworking of *Sarutobi Etchan* (*Monkey-jump Etsuko*, 1971), written by Shotaro Ishinomori (1938-98), author of *Kamen Rider, 009 Cyborg, Himitsu Sentai, The Legend of Zelda, Kikmaider Code 02* and *The Skull Man*. Otomo's live-action film *World Apartment Horror* can be regarded as an adaptation or reworking of *Domu*.

  Domu is an urban thriller with supernatural elements: it's the story of psychic warfare in a Tokyo suburb, between an old coot (Mr Cho, a.k.a. Mr Chojiro Uchida) and a bunch of children (led by Etsuko), while the cops observe, unable to find out exactly what's going on, or how to stop it. (*Domu* was inspired by a newspaper report of a series of suicides in a housing project in Takashima-daira Danchi, Tokyo).

  Domu was translated in the West by Studio

Proteus,[1] overseen by Toren Smith: 'arguably one of the finest Japanese manga rendered', according to Fred Schodt (2002, 319). 'Otomo's art is beautifully detailed and fine-lined; his characters are realistic, and the omnipresent apartment complex is imbued with mundane hostility', noted Jason Thompson in *Manga: The Complete Guide* (85).

No doubt the production of an animated version of *Domu* has been discussed many times over the years; the film rights were with Guillermo Del Toro (*Hell-Boy*, *Pan's Labyrinth*) for some time. But of course, as with *Akira*, *Domu* is so vivid, and already so cinematic, an animated or live-action version is pointless. *Domu* is a masterpiece that doesn't need (or want) adaptation.

Domu is very sophisticated storytelling: Katsuhiro Otomo produced this *manga* in 1980, when he was 26. Yet he already had a very subtle and penetrating insight into what makes people tick – and not only people of his own age (like the long-haired cop Takamura, a clear author alter-ego), but also the ageing inspectors (Yamagawa and Takayama), and the crusty, old Uchida himself.

And the children – let's not forget that Katsuhiro Otomo has a magical knack of reproducing the lives of kids – their sense of play and delight – and of fear, of anxiety. It's a skill on a par, I would claim, with the great children's authors, such as Maurice Sendak and Roald Dahl (Otomo certainly shares their wicked sense of humour!).[2] Little Etsuko is a forerunner of the psychic children in *Akira*, of course – and also *Akira*'s Kei (look at the way that Etsuko stands up squarely to Uchida on the roof, her head lowered, her eyes fixed firmly on the quivering,

---

1 Studio Proteus is one of the prominent translators and packagers of *manga* in the United States of America. Among their translations are *Legend of Kamui* and *Nausicaä*. Studio Proteus has translated most of Masamune Shirow's key works, including *Ghost In the Shell*, *Orion*, *Dominion* and *Appleseed*.

2 Katsuhiro Otomo also has a naughty sense of humour, which comes over strongly in *manga* such as *Domu* and *Akira*. Twisted, you might call it at times!

sweating, old man).

Katsuhiro Otomo has a *manga* style all of his own. There is simply nobody in the world of comic art who has the same skewed vision of the world, and the same highly originally way of translating that vision into pencil sketches and inked and screentoned *manga* drawings.[3]

Domu follows many of the rules of making *manga*, Otomo-style:

- Rule one: create a compelling concept[4]
- Rule two: create a strong villain to run amok.
- Rule three: develop unlikely heroes.
- Rule four: build in twists and turns in the story.
- Rule five: place the characters in a fascinating setting.
- Rule six: let the characters go – let *them* tell the story.
- Rule seven: let the action escalate up to the finale.

Certainly Mr Chojiro Uchida is a creepy, weird, powerful and formidable villain – this is, after all, a sick serial killer story, too. A bald, 65 year-old guy who lives alone in an *aparto* that's empty one minute and stuffed with children's toys and bric-a-brac the next. Uchida is fundamentally a trickster figure, the trickster god of ancient mythology, someone who specializes in turning the world upside-down. Unfortunately, he's also a psychotic deviant who delights in brutality. He's one of those villains in Japanese fantasy *manga* and *animé* who has no idea how revoltingly painful his acts can be. For him it's a bunch of fun.

> What is immediately striking about *Domu* is its sophisticated treatment of the subject matter, very impressive in a young author who had only entered the professional world of *manga* a few years earlier. (*1001 Comics You Must Read Before You Die*, 427)

3 *E-Chan the Ninja* crops up in *Domu*.
4 This is the most difficult part.

Once again, Katsuhiro Otomo demonstrates in *Domu* his genius for gradually escalating violence and madness. It begins with simple things like playing ball in a park, or someone sitting on a park bench, or kids playing games, and then builds and builds over the course of the *manga*, until the place is exploding with aggression and duels between psychics. The gas mains are switched on, rooms blow up, the psychics crumple metal and concrete, glass explodes with shards spinning across the drawings. The emergency services arrive, but still nobody can prevent the horrors from unfurling.

Katsuhiro Otomo is a master at depicting the aggression, the existential unease, the resentments and the fears that simmer underneath life in the city, and how they accelerate and finally explode.[5] The way that the *Domu* manga screws up the tension like a tourniquet until it's biting deep is masterful: Otomo certainly has a handle on how communities of people that don't always get along survive. Until the cracks get too big, and the social network crumples.

Domu is very much a tale of what it means to live in a close-knit community, and in the suburbs, and in tower blocks and apartment blocks built in the 1960s, all concrete and glass, stairwells and walkways, with a children's park down below. Everybody is crowded in together (there are many scenes where the neighbours come outside and discuss what's happening.)[6]

The powerlesness of the authorities to deal with something as indefinable and amorphous as the wave of malice that's flowing thru the apartments is emphasized throughout *Domu*. No matter what the police try, nothing seems to work. And people are dying regularly. Can the authorities protect a

5 'The weirdness that lurks in the seemingly peaceful living environment of a huge housing complex symbolizes the precariousness hidden at the bottom of today's living conditions in Japan', noted the newspaper *Yomiuri* of *Domu*.

6 There are modest domestic scenes, too – such as the neighbours gathering to gossip in the open area below the tower blocks.

community? No. Can they protect a community from itself? No. Instead, the cops, inspectors and social services can only offer crude, short-term and ultimately useless solutions. When it comes to psychological deterioration, there is no one to blame, and no way of fixing things. Which's the beauty of an artwork – because in *Domu* there *is* someone to blame, there is a single person who's behind it all: Mr Uchida. Ah, if only life were as easy to fix as art!

Domu pits, like *Akira* and *Steam-boy*, youth against age, one of Katsuhiro Otomo's recurring themes. And the public against the police (and the authorities). Quite a bit of *Domu* takes the viewpoint of the authorities, however, as a group of police, led by veteran Inspector Yamagawa, investigate the paranormal occurrences in the housing complex (but the amount of time spent with the authorities is also part of the genre – investigating a mysterious occurrence often involves detectives or experts).

Domu is exceptionally violent – another of Katsuhiro Otomo's specialities. Nope, Otomo never holds back when it comes to creating scenes of widespread mayhem and bone-crunching nastiness. In *Domu*, he includes scenes where a young girl is threatened in an elevator by a guy and then is forced to witness his suicide when he slices open his throat with a knife. In another scene, a young boy is shot at point blank range by a psychopath. In another, the same psycho shoots at his own son.

The violence builds and builds in *Domu*, and it takes quite some time before our saviour appears to counter the catastrophe: little Etsuko-chan. A plucky, stubborn, determined child, Etsuko faces up to Uchida with calm and bravery. She stands there, facing him, while admonishing him over his cruel acts. Luckily, Etsuko is also gifted with præternatural powers, and the duel that ensues prefigures the Tetsuo/ Kei/ Kaneda battles in *Akira*: they're on the roof of the apartment block, hurling psychic waves at each other, they're blowing up stuff around them, and they're flying thru the night sky.

The *otaku* in his twenties who spends all his time building plastic model kits of aircraft and war machines is possibly a wry, eccentric self-portrait: the appearance of Tsutomu Sasaki in his square glasses and rather non-descript features is reminiscent of the appearance of Katsuhiro Otomo in the early Eighties. Even odder is the way that Sasaki-san is taken over by the psychic powers, and commits suicide right in front of Etsuko, by slicing open his neck with his modelling knife! Ouch!

Visually and thematically, there are many aspects of *Domu* that're forerunners of *Akira* – from the psychic warfare to the escalation of violence, to the use of speed lines in larger panels, and the emphasis on visual storytelling (the dialogue is minimal in *Domu*). And Katsuhiro Otomo knows how to tell a story visually – many of the sequences unfurl without dialogue at all. Yet with the use of angles, frame size, shadow and light, speed lines, and the flow of one picture to the next, Otomo can tell the story, while also delivering the sheer pleasure of consuming images.

Domu is a slice o' black humour, to be sure: it depicts an urban community sliding into dissolution, beginning with an (unexplained) suicide (a middle-aged man, Ueno,[7] falls or jumps from the roof of the apartment block, tho' the police aren't sure how he got there thru a locked door). To the cops' exasperation, the suicide is merely one of many recent unexplained deaths in the tenements.

It's one of the most disturbing themes in contemporary Japanese culture: suicide haunts many *manga* and *animé*. In *Domu*, the psychological disintegration is explained by the psychic phenomena unleashed by the trickster figure of Mr Uchida. Sometimes Uchida directly causes the horrors, but in some instances it appears that Uchida is contributing towards the

---

7 Ueno sports a cap with wings, a coveted object in the tenements. Unfortunately, the wings don't help Ueno fly, and he becomes an angel the old-fashioned way – by falling off a building and dying.

malaise which helps to drive people to jumping off the roofs of the apartment blocks.

Every day Uchida-san is down on the park bench, in his default position, sitting there right under the noses of the cops, with nobody apparently suspecting that he's the cause of the mayhem (before Uchida is revealed as the villain, he is depicted lurking in the background).

Except for li'l Etsuko. *She* knows he's up to no good (at one point, Uchida has a baby falling from a balcony, but it's saved (by Etsuko). No, even Katsuhiro Otomo draws the line at the bad taste of having a baby slam into the tarmac from seven stories up!).

It's Etsuko who leads her fellow kids in finally vanquishing Mr Uchida in *Domu*'s finale. It comes two weeks after the catastrophic events of the crazy night when all hell broke loose. Uchida is sitting on his favourite bench, a criminal who haunts the scene of a crime. Etsuko is there: she sits on a swing and stares at Uchida. He is pinned to the spot, he can't move, he sweats, he trembles… Etsuko continues to glower at him, and she has enormous powers! Other kids move closer, watching, watching. Uchida quivers, and Etsuko stares, and the detective, Takayama, who's nearby, knows something is going on, but hasn't a clue what it is.

Eventually, Mr Uchida simply expires from the force of Etsuko's and the children's psychic energy. The ending of *Domu* satisfies on a number of levels – not least that Etsuko and her generation are not going to let old folk mess up *their* lives. They – children – are the future.

The message of *Domu* is clear: you can mess with people of your own generation, and drive them to acts of desperation or even suicide, but don't you DARE try that with children!

THE STORY OF *DOMU*

The genre of *Domu* is a supernatural urban thriller; it's a murder mystery, which starts with a death, and continues (with more deaths) until the case is re-solved. It's also a portrait of urban decay and alien-ation, of a modern, post-war housing scheme, of a community (and several generations) in decline.

First, the suicide of Mr Ueno: two pages feature mysterious images – of piles of toys in a dark room, and a disembodied voice. Later, we discover that this is Chojiro Uchida, Old Cho, the villain of the piece, who collects trophies from the people he kills (with a particular fascination for toys and bric-a-brac). Thus, the mysterious presence seems to be directing Ueno to his death, by walking up to the roof and diving off.

Next day, we're introduced to several characters, such as Inspector Yamagawa, the *otaku* Tsutomu Sasaki, the local kids, the gossipers (who discuss Ueno's suicide), and Mr Uchida himself (a bald dude sitting on a bench. Uchida is glimpsed in several of the early scenes – and that bench is also where he sits in the finale of *Domu*. No one suspects that the senile old man is actually the mass murderer terrorizing the tenements).

Notice that Otomo-sensei puts his self-portrait, Tsutomu Sasaki, on that bench, sitting next to the Uchida (this is the first time that we see Uchida). It's like the cameos of Alfred Hitchcock, who's seen next to the hero or the villain in his films. (Little does Sasaki realize that the seemingly harmless. old guy will command him to slit his throat and die in front of a little girl).

Next is the exposition scene of *Domu*, in the local police station, where Inspector Yamagawa, Detective Takayama and others discuss the case (multiple un-explained deaths in the Tsutsumi housing complex).

When Inspector Yamagawa visits the site later, he sits with the complex's manager, talking about what to do; we're introduced to more residents: a simple-minded giant (Yoshio Fujiyama, a.k.a. 'Little Yo'), a forlorn woman (Mrs Tezuka)[8] who lost her baby in a miscarriage and pushes a symbolically empty buggy (she's disturbing the residents), and the violent drunk and deadbeat dad Yoshikawa. These characters play key roles later on.

The *Domu manga* continues with the cops investigating the death of Ueno-san (interviewing neighbours who saw him last, and Ueno's widow). We now get the picture that the Tsutsumi housing complex is 'really creepy', as a tenant puts it. (Nobody wants to live there, but nobody's got the *gelt* to move out).

Another death occurs when two cops are on the beat at night in the neighbourhood. The death (or murder) itself occurs off-screen (as with Ueno's suicide), and again there is an inscrutable entity nearby (the cop hears a voice saying it wants to see the cop's gun, echoing the children who annoyed the cop from earlier in the day. Again, these are trophies that Mr Uchida collects from his victims).

Inspector Yamagawa and the cops're getting desperate: Yamagawa-san visits the tenements at night, on his own, and sits on a bench. Now follows a suspenseful sequence which leads Yamagawa from the bench down below all the way up the stairs (twelve floors) to the roof, where he suicides.

Katsuhiro Otomo again employs shadows and offscreen space, suggesting that someone or something is out there. Objects such as a ball[9] and the telephone pager become sinister; the presence seems child-like – it covets the electronic pager, but then decides it doesn't want it (instead, the pager explodes).

Inspector Yamagawa pursues the presence, but never reaches it; he is taunted repeatedly by a voice (which might be in his head) – that's he's gonna be retired, about his mother, his daughter, etc (the voice

8 The name is likely a reference to Osamu Tezuka.
9 A reference to *The Shining* perhaps, when a ball is rolled in the Overlook Hotel when Danny is exploring it.

exploits the victim's weaknesses and guilt). We follow Yamagawa to the roof, where we meet, for the first time, the villain of *Domu*, Mr Uchida, in his killer regalia (Yamagawa recognizes him).

This is one of Katsuhiro Otomo's iconic drawings: Uchida's jacket and pants are decorated with badges, jewellery, keyrings, toys and trophies from his victims; he wears the winged baseball cap (of Ueno's son); his fingers're covered in rings; the dead cop's gun dangles on a string; he floats above the ground, grinning and cackling at Yamagawa.

Again, we don't see Inspector Yamagawa's demise, but the encounter with Uchida forms the climax of the chapter (tho' Takayama has a vision of the suicide later).

In the next chapter, Katsuhiro Otomo introduces the heroine of *Domu*, the delightful, intrepid, strong-willed Etsuko (a ten year-old Japanese girl, wearing a padded vest with her black hair in bunches). Etsuko has supernatural powers, too, as *Domu* immediately demonstrates.

Etsuko-chan is moving into the Tsutsumi tenements with her family: they are just arriving in a removal truck with all their belongings. Uchida is nearby, sitting in his customary position on a park bench. His target this time is a toddler, playing on a balcony way up high. The baby climbs onto a parapet, and throws itself off – while Uchida simply hums happily to himself.[10]

But Etsuko (and the removal guys) see what's happening: Etsuko saves the child (by levitating it before it hits the ground). Old Cho has met his match here: Etsuko strides up him, all huffy and stern, and asks him what he was thinking of: 'What do you mean, 'ripe tomato'? You could have *killed* that baby!' (Uchida, in his mind, told the kid it would be like a ripe tomato when it splattered on the ground).

Mr Uchida is shocked to encounter li'l Etsuko-

10 That Uchida is now conducting murders in daylight with plenty of people about is either (1) unconvincing, or (2) expresses his self-confidence, that he thinks he can get away with it.

chan – she is the first person who's offered a serious challenge to his reign of terror. Etsuko immediately takes on the persona of a strict parent or teacher with Uchida, recognizing that he is really a weak, infantile personality.

As Etsuko angrily storms off, Uchida retaliates, hurling some stones at her. But Etsuko is easily able to deflect them. The chapter closes with images of Uchida bent over, sweating, stunned (this is the pose in which he dies – following the final confrontation with pint-sized, psychic genius Etsuko, in this same spot).

A new inspector is introduced next, Okamura, taking over the case from poor Yamagawa (Okamura is the same age, and is essentially the same weary, beaten-down character). Katsuhiro Otomo cleverly intertwines scenes here, so they occur in parallel action: for instance, when the baby was falling from the parapet, the cops Takayama and co. were seen discussing the case (Takayama, in a nice detail, is laying a bunch of flowers at the spot where Yamagawa died). And when Okamura is introduced, he walks past the local children (with Etsuko among them).

These modest but delightful scenes explore Etsuko's characterization a little – how she fits in right away with the kids in the area (they're talking about playing a new video game), and how she is aware of outsider figures, such as Hiroshi Yoshikawa, the son of the drunk dad. Etsuko represents making connections, forming relationships, and not excluding scary or threatening people, like Little Yo and Hiroshi.

So Inspector Okamura ploddingly pursues the case of the mysterious deaths in the Tsutsumi complex (now up to 29 victims). He visits Yamagawa's widow, but discovers nothing of use (it's out of character for Yamagawa to jump off a building). He sits, as Yamagawa did, on a bench, and hears a taunting voice in his head warning him away from the tenements (and he also thinks he sees the ghost of Yamagawa on a nearby seat).

Katsuhiro Otomo sends himself (and his friends) up in the next section of *Domu*, with a biting satire on *otaku* culture: Tsutomu Sasaki sits in his bedroom, doted on by his mom, building plastic models of jets and planes (his shelves are stuffed with 'em), and listening to a radio show about mathematics while he studies.

Porky, speccy, lonely Tsutomu is focussed intently on his latest purchase (a model of a Japanese Zero fighter from WWII), when Mr Uchida material-izes out of thin air, and perches on the *otaku*'s swivel chair. Uchida teases Sasaki (spinning the propellers on the model planes, for instance). Elsewhere in the apartment complex, Etsuko is awake, her psi powers attuned to Uchida's appearance; she knows he's up to mischief.

More scenes of the police investigation follow – Inspector Okamura chats to his troops, is brought up to date with the case, and talks to Takayama on the roof (the notion of ghosts or the supernatural is again considered; Okamura recently saw Yamagawa's ghost).

Next: some sweet scenes of Etsuko bonding with the outsiders in the *apartos* – silent giant Little Yo and troubled loner Hiroshi. Now we see that Etsuko-chan is a friendly intermediary between the groups of characters in *Domu*; she is the conscience, the heart, of *Domu*. That Katsuhiro Otomo should choose a ten year-old girl as his hero is typical of his idiosyncratic approach to comicbook stories (the heroine might be a young girl, but *Domu* is as far away from *shojo manga* as possible!).

Poor Hiroshi goes home,[11] stepping gingerly past his loser dad, who's collapsed in a drunken stupor next to the fridge. Bottles and cans everywhere, an overflowing ashtray. Hiroshi-kun eats his dinner squatted on the floor in front of that most magical

11 His homecoming is contrasted with that of Etsuko.

object, where billions worship every single night – the television set. (His pa calls out drunkenly for more beer).

Old Cho continues to act the trickster demon in the tenements – appearing on the table of Yoshikawa (just his head), haunting the childless mother Mrs Tezuka, and spinning the propellers of the *otaku* Sasaki's models in his bedroom.

Indeed, it's Tsutomu Sasaki who is the next victim of the thoroughly evil Mr Uchida, when the model-making geek, controlled by Uchida, threatens poor Etsuko with a modelling knife, then turns it on himself, and slits his own throat. This is one of the most grotesque scenes in all of Katsuhiro Otomo's output – a no-holds-barred depiction of self-loathing and mind control taken to the point of suicide.

It begins when Etsuko has popped out to fetch some cigs for her folks: she encounters Tsutomu Sasaki looking very strange by the elevator (a half-page drawing depicts a spaced-out Sasaki). After cutting his neck, Sasaki looms over little Etsuko (in a worm's-eye-view angle):[12] the girl is terrified, and manages to slip away.

Breaking up the page into into small panels (7 or 8 per page), Katsuhiro Otomo portrays the hypnot-ized Sasaki cutting his throat from ear to ear, while Etsuko watches in horror (she begs him not to do it). The shifts to Mr Uchida in his den, surrounded by his toys, grinning evilly as he manipulates Sasaki from afar, underline what we already know: that Sasaki is Old Cho's latest victim.

The scene is excessively bloody (the blood is reproduced as full black tones), bringing the horror right under the audience's nose, and putting the heroine in maximum jeopardy. This scene has a huge dramatic impact partly because Katsuhiro Otomo has chosen to withhold showing the actual murders or suicides in detail thus far: but this one is right in your face – there's no ignoring it.

12 The composition recalls a scene in *The Shining*.

The aftermath scenes depict the cops at the crime scene, the locals gossiping, and poor Etsuko in bed in the medical wing of the Tsutsumi complex. Detective Takayama thinks he sees Inspector Yamagawa's ghost looking forlornly down from a balcony. Mr Uchida is back in his usual spot, sitting on a bench and watching the world go by; Little Yo and Hiroshi are playing catch with a ball nearby.

There is no let-up in the action of *Domu*, because the next dramatic sequence occurs very soon: it involves the drunken dad Yoshikawa, his son Hiroshi, and Little Yo (plus one of the boys from the neighbourhood): Yoshikawa is taunted by a voice in his head about alcohol, as he wanders alone at night in the park below the apartments, and offers him something better: a gun hovers in the air, like the knife before Macbeth in William Shakespeare's play (it's the gun that was stolen from the cop).

The police continue their investigation: they are now getting desperate, as the deaths mount up and they still have no decent clues[13] So Detective Takayama goes to visit a professor about shamanic practices, who puts him onto a psychic (who turns out to be an over-acting charlatan, in a scene out of a Woody Allen movie).

The second shaman that Detective Takayama meets is a middle-aged woman, Noriko Nonomura: she turns out to be more amenable to Takayama's problems, and agrees to visit the Tsutsumi housing complex. When she arrives, however, she finds the place overwhelming and oppressive, and hurries away. Nonomura reacts very badly, and agitatedly implores Takayama to leave, because there'll be more deaths. 'The children! *You must watch out for the children!*' Nonomura begs Takayama as she flees (unfortunately, Nonomura visited the place just as Etsuko was glaring at Old Cho, resuming their battle of wills. That, coupled with the general atmosphere of

13 A cop visits Mr Uchida's *aparto* with the complex's manager, and finds it empty except for a shattered window.

unease, scares the shaman away).

Yes, the battle of wills in the Tsutsumi housing complex continues between Etsuko and Mr Uchida: in her pyjamas (which she wears for much of the subsequent scenes), Etsuko stands at the window of the medical centre, looking out over the park, and at Uchida on his bench in the far distance. She glares; he whimpers: Uchida is wilting under the strong psychic waves emitted by Etsuko (it is partly this enormous psychic energy that the shaman Nonomura reacts to). This is also how *Domu* ends (when Etsuko defeats Uchida).

The *Domu manga* shifts to another nighttime scene, the start of an incredible supernatural horror sequence in Katsuhiro Otomo's œuvre. Again, it begins in the area between the apartments (where most of the action of *Domu* takes place). A kid walking home at night is waylaid by Yoshikawa and, for no apparent reason, shot at point blank range and killed with the gun that Yoshikawa found.

Yoshikawa is completely under Mr Uchida's psychic control, and his mission is to find and nobble Etsuko, Uchida's nemesis. Yoshikawa staggers over to the medical centre, but Etsuko is already out of bed and waiting for him in the foyer. She stands there, glaring straight ahead (as she often does in *Domu*), out-facing her opponents by sheer force of will. Yoshikawa raises the pistol to shoot, but of course Etsuko is too powerful for him, and his arm is painfully twisted and broken. (Etsuko has the most powerful will in *Domu*: she might be 10 years-old, but has a stronger life-force than any other character).

Domu orchestrates several scenes of parallel action here: the residents gather around the body of the dead kid, the cops examine the victim, and Hiroshi and Little Yo meet up, and hurry around to the back of the medical centre, where they discover Mr Uchida lurking (he's dressed in his killer's outfit).

Bringing the giant Little Yo and Yoshikawa's son Hiroshi into the picture escalates the horror, as

Yoshikawa, still under Uchida's sway and out of control, fires first upon Little Yo, and later his own son. Etsuko responds to Yoshikawa's attack by hurling him thirty yards thru the air, down the corridor, where he smashes against the wall.

Etsuko realizes that Mr Uchida is up on the roof, and she hurries off to confront him. Once again, Etsuko uses a stern tone with Uchida, as if she's addressing a naughty child. She wags her finger at him, hand on hip, like an strict teacher, telling him off for being a horrible, little boy.

For this section of *Domu*, which stages a superhero-style battle between two psychics flying thru the night air, Katsuhiro Otomo employs many visual tricks: tilting the frame, using upside-down imagery, extremes of scale (tiny figures against enormous structures), plenty of dark screen tone, and of course speed lines. Plus his customary successive symmetrical compositions as well as off-centre designs, and several double-page drawings. (One of Otomo's favourite devices is to employ giant close-ups in the centre of a rectangular panel, when he's portraying two people confronting each other).

This is not your usual superhero battle! – a 65 year-old, bald coot versus a feisty, ten year-old girl! A psychotic, child-like mass murderer vs. the next generation. (Otomo keeps them far apart all the time – Uchida never get shis hands on Etsuko – and when the girl defeats the man at the end, it is from a distance).

From the outset, Etsuko acts unafraid of Mr Chojiro Uchida: she stands on the very edge of the building, ten stories up (on the other side of the railings), while Uchida teeters on a railing. Uchida puts himself immediately in the inferior position – he flees, becoming the hunted, with Etsuko as the hunter. By not dealing with Etsuko straight away, Uchida seals his fate (which was announced as soon as Etsuko showed up).

The flying chase in *Domu* is a superb piece of

Otomoan action, with bold, cinematic angles, vertiginous compositions to accentuate the feeling of three-dimensional space, and some bits of psychic power as the protagonists fly past (bending railings, lifting paving stones from the ground, smashing windows, and hurling rubble).

But Mr Uchida is not cornered and caught yet – in the midst of the pursuit, he manages to force Yoshikawa to shoot his own son, Hiroshi (so now Uchida via Yoshikawa has shot at two young boys). Up in the night sky above the Tsutsumi complex, Etsuko senses Hiroshi's agony nearby. Uchida thinks he's won, launching loose bricks at Etsuko. But no, she's able to deflect them. As Uchida looks round, he sees children standing outside their *apartos*, attracted by the noise, and glaring at him accusingly – a great touch (which's reprised in the final scene, when Uchida expires under the hard stares of the local children).

Meanwhile, in the corridor of the medical centre, the silent giant Little Yo has staggered to his feet; despite Yoshikawa shooting him again (at point blank range), Little Yo is able to grab the guy and smash him against the wall, repeatedly, until he dies (or appears to). Another gory death (Katsuhiro Otomo relishes depicting them!). A macabre flourish has Mrs Tezuka (the woman who had the miscarriage), materializing like a lost spirit, singing crazily to the corpse: 'sleep tight, little boy'.

Outside the medical centre, the cops have convened, aided by a squad with riot shields and batons. Inside the building, Little Yo is on the rampage, unstoppable, chucking policemen around like rag dolls. Even the tear gas fired at him doesn't slow him down.

Up on another roof, below a tower, the Etsuko versus Mr Uchida duel has reached a stalemate – Uchida won't back down, and neither will Etsuko (for a ten year-old girl, she is very tenacious!). Uchida acts like a spoilt, needy brat, sticking his tongue out at

Etsuko and regaling her with childish taunts (as if it's all a game, as if he's in the playground at school).

'I HATE YOU!' screams Mr Uchida, hurling a bolt of energy at Etsuko; she is blown about, and her cheek is cut, but she stays her ground (true heroes never give up! Etsuko looks forward to Kaneda in *Akira,* who keeps on coming on).

So now Etsuko reveals some of her wilder psychic powers: Katsuhiro Otomo employs a simple but effective visual device here, to indicate the altered state of reality – a tonal reverse, so blacks are whites and vice versa (so the sky's white, the roof is black). Head down, floating in the air, with her clothes flapping in the high energy release, Etsuko is a formidable opponent for Old Cho (everything he tries is countered or bested by this little girl).

Sudden, explosive releases of energy (or just plain, old bombs) are one of Katsuhiro Otomo's specialities as a *mangaka.* So we have hurricane winds, flashes of light, with energy pouring thru the Tsutsumi tower blocks, and everyone diving for cover, arms protecting their heads, grimacing, eyes squeezed shut. It's a loud, busy scene.

Mr Uchida gloats when he turns on the gas taps of the ovens in the apartments, thinking he's finally got the better of the girl; Etsuko can sense him doing that, but she doesn't know which buildings and which apartments. So what does Etsuko do? Only smash open the windows of the kitchens of the *apartos,* to let the gas out and prevent explosions (a dangerous plan, tho', which sends splinters of glass everywhere).

The two super-psychics face each other (they stand on the edge of separate buildings), scowling. Etsuko is able to deflect/ defeat everything that Old Cho attempts.

Meanwhile, in another apartment block, Takayama and some cops are investigating Mr Uchida's dwelling again.[14] This time, it's jammed with toys and trinkets, which weren't there before (each time the toys and curios are shown, it's in a shadowy mid-tone, emphasizing the unreality of the drawing).

In a corridor not far away, the police encounter the simple-minded giant Little Yo, staggering along with a bloody chest wound. In a tussle, Little Yo throws a cop over the wall, to his death. Takayama whips out his pistol, yelling at Little Yo not to move (the giant seems to be making his way to Etsuko – to join up with her? or to kill her? Presumably, as he's killing cops, he's now being controlled by Mr Uchida, so his target is Etsuko. Indeed, one reason why Uchida is being trounced by Etsuko is because he is using some of his powers to control first Yoshikawa then Little Yo).

The following chapter of *Domu* opens with a spectacular series of explosions, as the gas in several apartments ignites. Uchida-san taunts Etsuko-chan again – that she wasn't able to prevent the gas blasts: 'Nya ha ha ha ha! Fooled ya!' And, oh, Etsuko is even more furious: concentrating hard, the girl launches another blast of energy at Mr Uchida, hurling him back, and cracking the roof with waves of psychic power. Uchida flees, at high speed – running, leaping, and flying away from Etsuko's wrath.

We return to Little Yo in the corridor: he's amazed to see Mrs Tezuka arrive, pushing her buggy as usual – except now she's lugged Hiroshi into it (Little Yo's new friend), altho' Hiroshi looks dead. Mr Uchida is flying thru the air nearby, and now it appears as if he's using Mrs Tezuka as his medium of mayhem (judging by the evil grin she gives Little Yo). Another blast of energy crashes into the building, taking out several floors (whether this comes from Uchida via Tezuka, or from Etsuko, watching from above, and aiming for Uchida, isn't quite clear). Anyway, the place's collapsing, and Hiroshi falls from

14 A telling detail has the sign outside the apartment with the names of Uchida's family crossed out (they've left him).

the buggy: Little Yo throws himself into the air, to catch and save the boy. Mrs Tezuka cackles like a witch, and is promptly flattened under a falling concrete pillar (a typical Otomoan demise – sudden, unforeseen, accidental and gory).

Now Etsuko is creating surges of force which demolish the building near Mr Uchida, so it's as if he's being hunted down by falling debris (waves of rubble pursue him). Uchida is picked up and slammed against a wall by Etsuko. Weeping, she is in a heightened, hysterical state (suffering from all of the horror she's witnessed), and Uchida experiences the full force of her torment. So fierce is Etsuko's agony that Uchida is squished into the wall, which crumples and eventually breaks.

Moral/ poetic justice at this point might have Mr Uchida expiring. Certainly, as a mass murderer, and in this form of comicbook, he should be punished. Being pummelled by psychic energy so strong it forces him thru a wall would probably be enough to kill anyone. But Old Cho survives – and he flees once more.

And, instead of Mr Uchida being killed by Etsuko, it's a fireman who takes the brunt of Etsuko's disturbed state (he tries to console her, but she can't control her psychic power, and kills him). She walks out of the unstable building, still pursuing Mr Uchida, who's fleeing as fast as his old legs can carry him.

So strong is Etsuko's energy that she destroys several floors of the building around the entrance as she emerges, a tiny figure in her pyjamas. Mr Uchida is pushing his way through the crowds of emergency services personnel, crying out for help, being yelled at by the firemen for being in the way, and he's trampled as everyone flees.

Now, just as Etsuko is closing on Mr Uchida, who crouches and whimpers on the ground, Esuko's mother appears. This saves Uchida, and Etsuko's mom is probably the only person who can truly console the girl. They embrace fiercely; Etsuko weeps. Uchida is thus let off the hook, and the finale is put back.

Three large drawings depict Mr Uchida on the ground, hands over his head, cowering, expecting the killing blow to come from Etsuko at any moment. The views of the site move further away – now there's no one in the vicinity (it's been evacuated), except for the tiny figure of Old Cho.

✳

Thus, after this climactic and chaotic sequence, the Tsutsumi murder case remains unsolved, and Mr Uchida, the serial killer, goes unpunished (he's being questioned in the police station). To contrast the scenes of mayhem and destruction, Katsuhiro Otomo reverts to simple, modest scenes – children playing, and Inspector Okamura sitting on a bench, glum and fed up, because the case remains frustratingly un-resolved. It's two weeks later.

With his head bent low in defeat, Inspector Okamura reluctantly goes to a press conference (passing the destroyed tenements that are being re-built on the way). The TV and the newspapers are out in force. Detective Takayama, his head bandaged, turns up; he goes thru some of the evidence with a buddy. There are some objects in amongst the piles of junk on the tables that hint at Uchida's guilt – a fount-ain pen top found in Uchida's *aparto* (belonging to Inspector Yamagawa), and Ueno's baseball cap with wings.

At this point, the police seem to have concluded that Mr Uchida is a senile, old man who can't have committed the twenty-some murders and un-explained deaths (plus the further deaths caused by the gas explosions). Inspector Okamura has quest-ioned him at length, and got nowhere. Takayama begs for the chance to interview the suspect too. Okamura, going to lunch with the rest of the cops, agrees.

At the threshold of the interrogation room,

Takayama is beset by nightmare-like visions of Inspector Yamagawa committing suicide on the roof – Yamagawa falls, and Takayama is unable to stop him. Yoshikawa also appears in the vision, taunting him. And then Takayama is suddenly back in the police station, confronting Mr Uchida (the obvious cause of these nightmares), who pretends to be innocent and unaware (he's playing with a toy car like a child). Katsuhiro Otomo again uses reversed tones, to indicate Takayama flashing back to the scene where the shaman Noriko Nonomura warned him about looking out for the children.

Mr Uchida is led away and taken back to the Tsutsumi housing complex, where he will stay while waiting for a place in a home for the elderly. So, is Katsuhiro Otomo going to allow mass murderer Uchida to go free? And what's happened with little Etsuko? (Inspector Okamura says she's staying with her relatives in Kyoto).

The *Domu manga* takes a breather while we wait to see What Happens Next. Again, Detective Takayama is our link to the case, when he pleads with his boss Okamura to be allowed to watch over Mr Uchida.

The *manga* switches back to the Tsutsumi housing complex on what appears to be a beautiful, Spring day. Detective Takayama and his buddy are relaxing in the sun on a bench, while children play nearby. It might be an idyllic scene in a soap opera (in between melodramatic scenes of tears and screaming).

And over there is Mr Uchida, in his customary spot on a bench, apparently dozing off (Takayama is watching over him). Thus, nothing seems to have changed in the weeks since the *Domu manga* began: we are back in the park area between the apartment blocks, where the *manga* opened, with old Uchida snoozing on a bench, and the sun shining.

The climax of *Domu* takes place on an ordinary day in the Tsutsumi housing complex: kids're playing, women're gossiping, etc (we hear snatches of

their everyday conversations throughout the sequence, reminding us that life goes on, and people still
do what people do: 'hey, I'm over here!', 'you stop
that *right* now, young man!', 'the block association
meets tomorrow night', etc).

And now comes the final episode in *Domu*, the
pay-off and the climax: it's introduced with a close-
up of a pair of sneakers walking in the park, followed
by two angles – high above, and from the back – of
our heroine, Etsuko (she passes by Takayama's
buddy as he leaves).

Yep, Etsuko-chan is back! And she is of course the
right character to deal with Mr Uchida – and
Uchida's knows it! (Indeed, she's the only one who
really can deal with him). Because the next page of
Domu features a huge close-up image across two
pages of Old Cho, wide-eyed in total fear, as he
realizes that his nemesis has arrived on the scene.

The drawing, in pencil, is superbly creepy,
evoking all of Mr Uchida's past deeds coming back
to haunt him. Katsuhiro Otomo is a master artist –
this sketch recalls the art of Chuck Close, Richard
Estes and the Photorealists (very popular in the
1970s), where much was made of rendering faces and
bodies in extreme detail (partly in reaction against
the too-cool, dry abstract art and Minimalism of the
1960s).

The final confrontation between the two psychic
powers in *Domu* is wonderfully under-stated, and all
the more powerful for that. Katsuhiro Otomo employs his beloved vertical symmetry and centralized
compositions, and a selection of carefully chosen
angles (high, low), plus some subjective views.

This is a very dramatic scene, and yet nothing
appears to be 'happening'. For instance, Etsuko-chan
doesn't go up to Mr Uchida on the bench and confront
him (as she did when we first met her). Instead, she
walks to a swing in the playground,[15] like any child,

---

15 A similar play area appeared in the childhood flashbacks in
Akira.

and sits on it. The drama is thus occurring between two people who're sitting down, far apart from each other (200 yards, perhaps).

Yet it's riveting: the intensity stems largely from two elements: (1) Etsuko glaring at Mr Uchida constantly. She doesn't look away, she doesn't even blink. She keeps staring at Old Cho all the time, concentrating all of her energy on him (as if she's already decided, before arriving, that this is what she's going to do); Etsuko means business: she is calm but unstoppable, a true force of nature.

Meanwhile, (2) Mr Uchida reacts very badly (his reaction illustrates how strong Etsuko's attack is). He rapidly becomes a quivering wreck: he's unable to flee, unable to fight back. He's cowering on the bench, sweating, head lowered, grimacing in pain. To evoke just how strong Etsuko's psychic assault is, Katsuhiro Otomo allows himself some speed lines, and a ripple of energy wafting over Uchida.

When Mr Uchida drops his cane, and a window breaks in the apartment block above, Detective Takayama is alerted that Something Might Be Going On. Etsuko's psychic energy is so high now, it's buckling the steel supports of the swings in the park (but only a boy notices), and snapping the metal chains holding up the swings. The wind gets up, stones bump along the ground (and hover, a classic Otomoan motif of high energy), and Uchida is crumpling.

All of this occurs within the seemingly 'normal' setting of just another day at the Tsutsumi housing complex – Katsuhiro Otomo intercuts the psychic combat between Etsuko and Old Cho with modest panels of children playing and neighbours chatting (the snippets of their conversation illustrate how completely oblivious they are).

But as the titanic struggle continues – Etsuko attacking, Uchida defending – Katsuhiro Otomo introduces a marvellous touch: the children in the area become aware that Something Is Happening.

They walk out of their apartments up above and look down on the park area; they stop playing for a moment, and turn to see; four kids gather near Uchida, to watch him squirm.

Mr Uchida makes a last attempt to stand and flee; finally, he gives up; a last close-up depicts Old Cho staring imploringly, pitifully. Then he dies (or seems to). The children watch solemnly, then they run off to play. To them, it's just an old man who looks tired. Detective Takayama approaches Uchida, and realizes he's gone. For the last drawing of *Domu*, Katsuhiro Otomo switches back to Etsuko on the swing – but she's vanished.

Does Etsuko kill Old Cho? Is our ten year-old heroine a killer? You can interpret what Etsuko does in several ways. Maybe she forces him to recognize what he's done, and the horror of it consumes him. Maybe she just wants the chance to confront Uchida one last time, and show him that he won't get away with his evil acts.

Thus *Domu* depicts the uneasy relation between the older and the younger generation (with the children rightly triumphing when the adults exploit them), the quest for survival in a densely-populated community, the problematic issues arising from living in such conditions (alienation, misunderstanding, resentment, distrust, intolerance, emerging in violence), the inability of the authorities to deal with such deep-seated issues, and how young people have to rely on their own resilience to survive.

These issues (among others) are still very relevant today. The political critique in *Domu* is glaringly obvious (a socialist, humanist attack on poor living conditions and the socio-political structures behind them).

KATSUHIRO OTOMO'S

DOMU

A CHILD'S DREAM

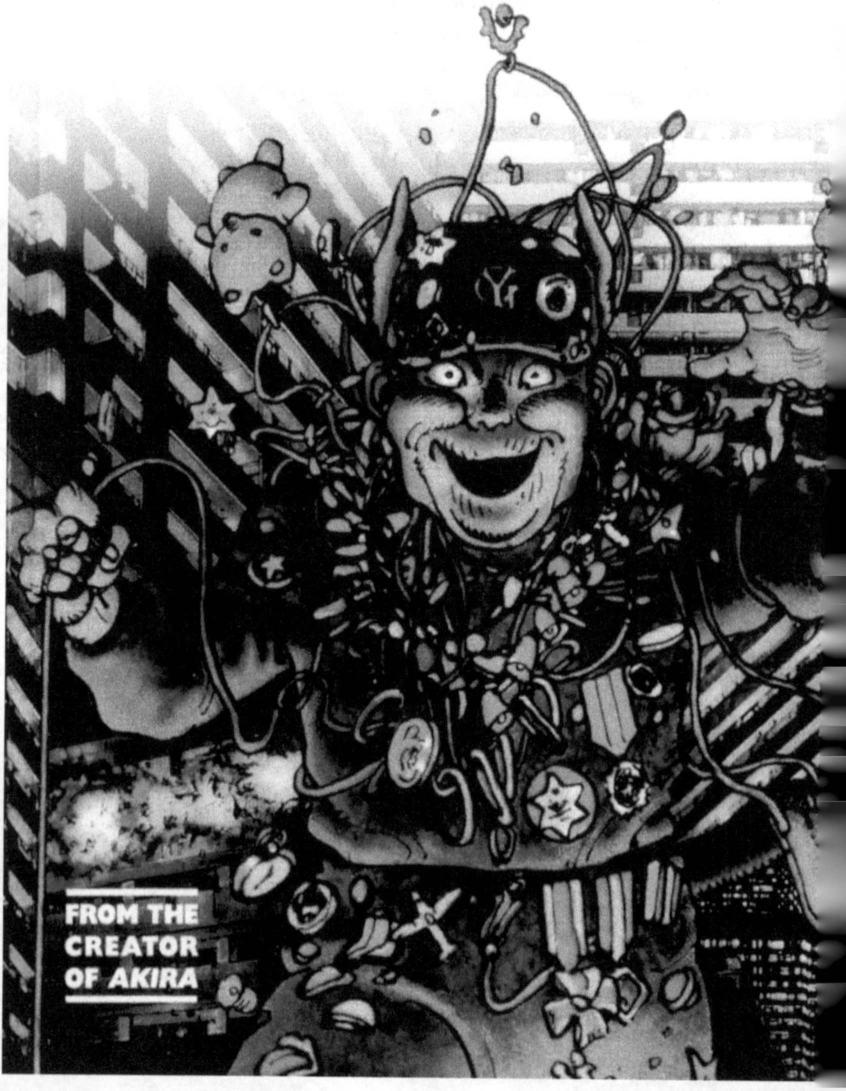

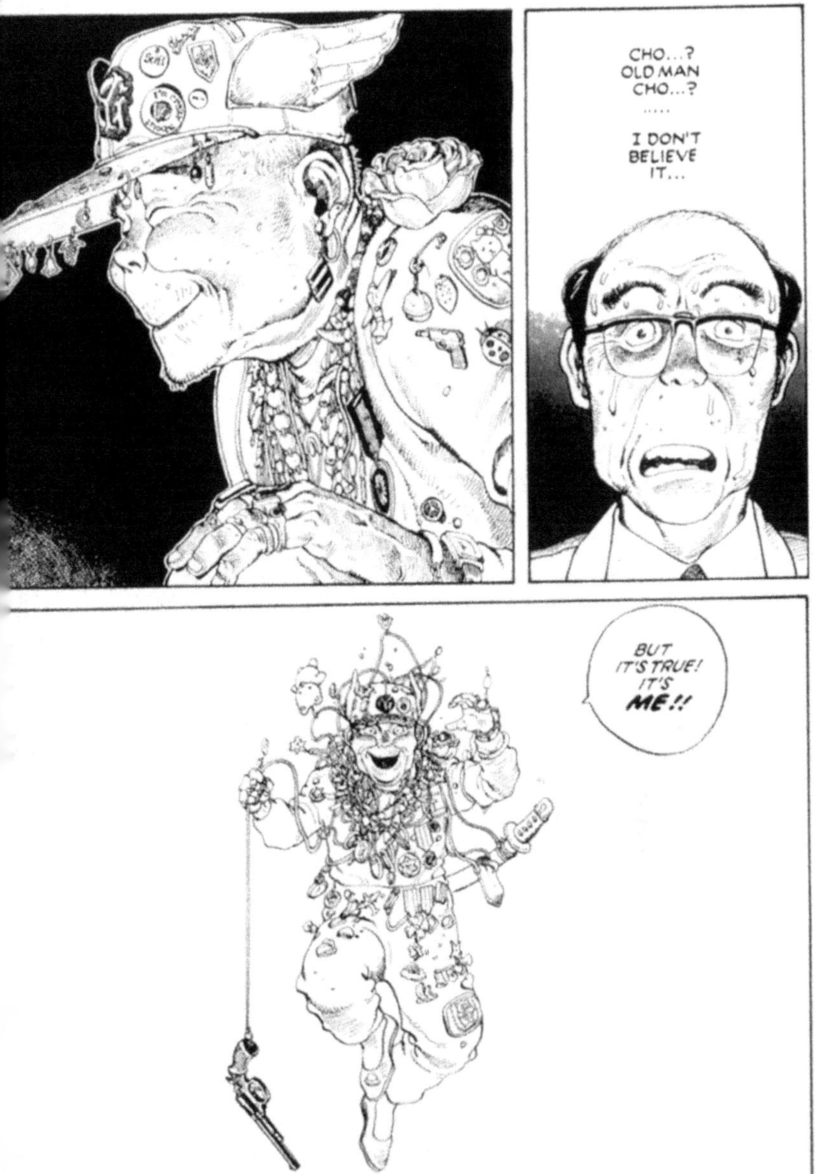
CHO...? OLD MAN CHO...? ..... I DON'T BELIEVE IT...
BUT IT'S TRUE! IT'S ME!!

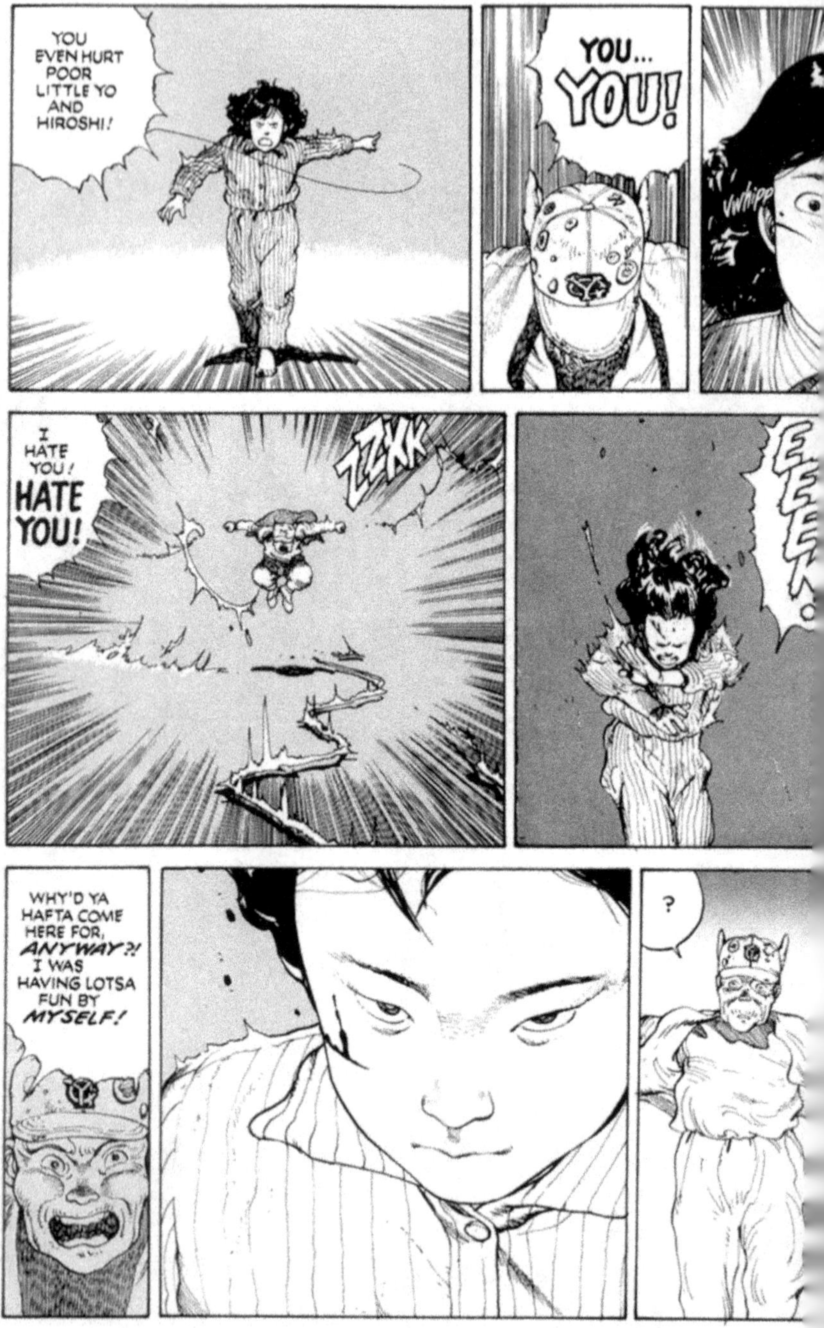

YOU EVEN HURT POOR LITTLE YO AND HIROSHI!
YOU... YOU!
I HATE YOU! HATE YOU!
ZZZKK
EEEEK!
WHY'D YA HAFTA COME HERE FOR, ANYWAY?! I WAS HAVING LOTSA FUN BY MYSELF!
?

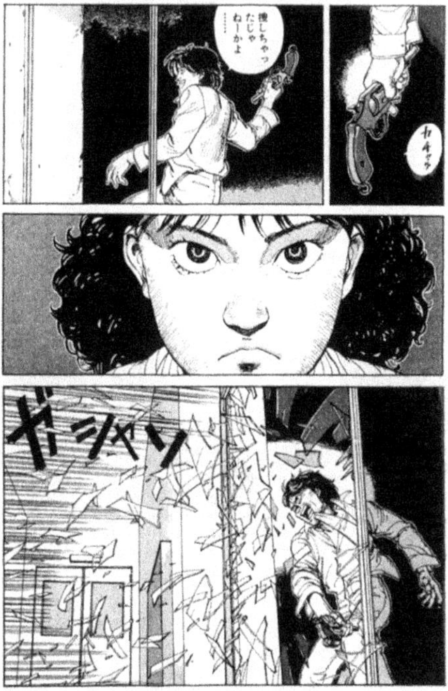

カチャッ
捜しちゃったじゃねーかよ……
ガシャン

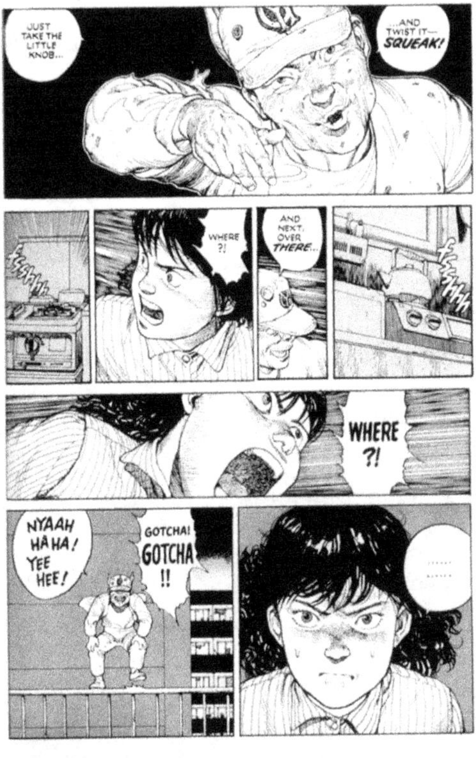

JUST TAKE THE LITTLE KNOB...
...AND TWIST IT— SQUEAK!
WHERE ?!
AND NEXT, OVER THERE...
WHERE ?!
NYAAH HA HA! YEE HEE!
GOTCHA! GOTCHA !!

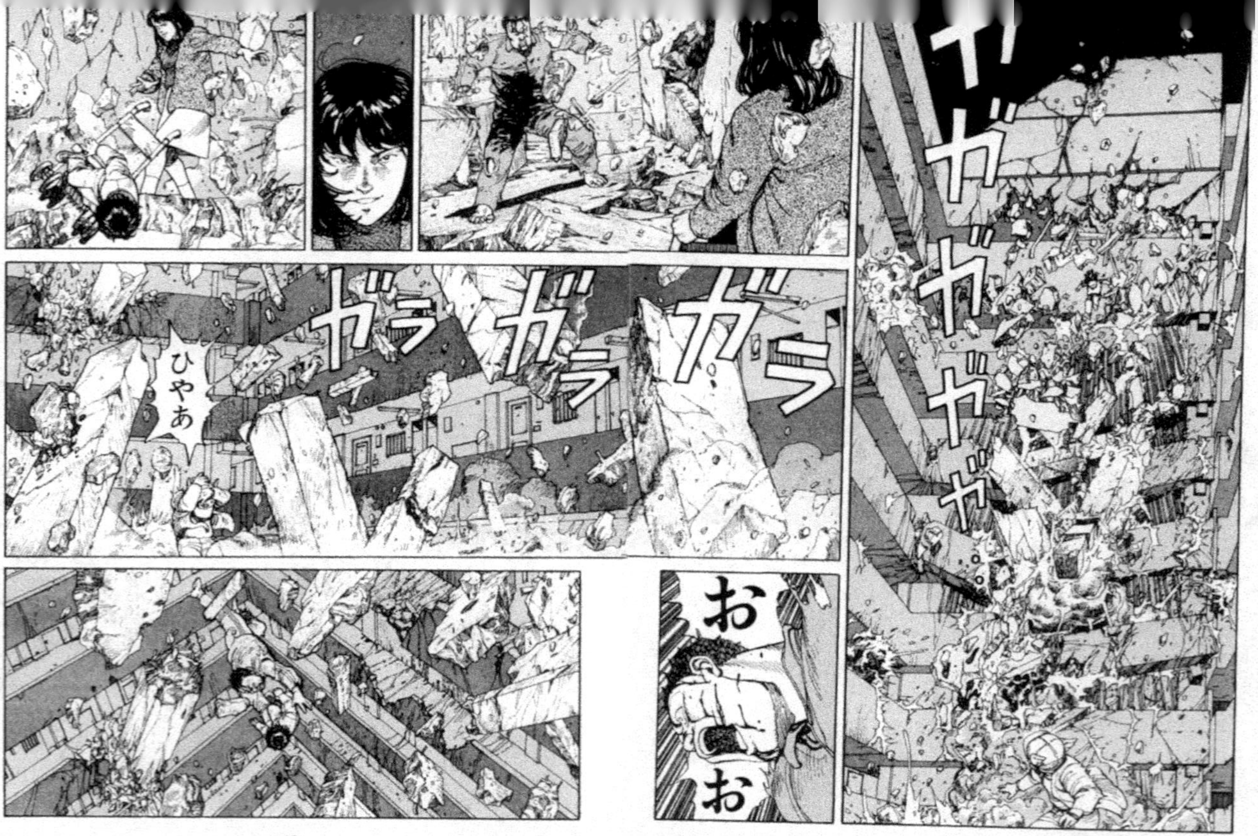
ガガガガ。。
おお
ガラ
ガラ
ガラ
ひやあ

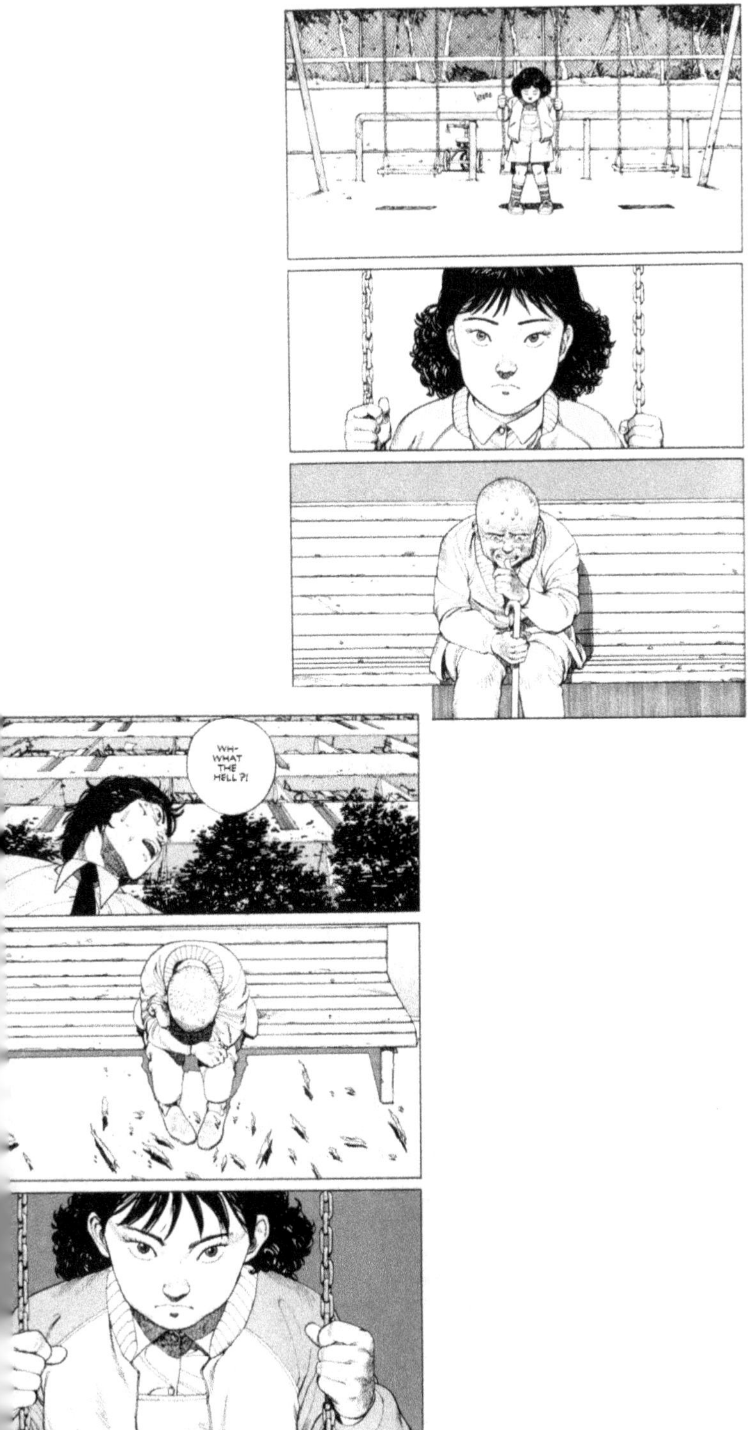
WH- WHAT THE HELL ?!

06

THE LEGEND
OF MOTHER SARAH

SHARYURA

The Legend of Mother Sarah: Tunnel Town (*Sara/ Sharyura* = "Sand, Current, Silk", 1990-97, *Young Magazine,* published by Kodansha), was an epic action-adventure, seven-volume *manga* set in the future, written by Katsuhiro Otomo with artwork by Takumi Nagayasu (b. 1949). Instantly recognizable as an Otomoan story, with its evocation of a difficult, desperate life in a post-apocalyptic future, as the survivors struggle to pull through on the stricken Planet Earth (Otomo is returning to colonies in space with his new film),[1] *The Legend of Mother Sarah* was also remarkable for its art by Nagayasu, which more than lived up to the ambition and scope of the story. Just as striking was how Otomoan the art was[2] – if you didn't know that Otomo hadn't created the

1 Colonies orbiting the Earth have been used in other *manga* and *animé* – famously in the *Gundam* series, for instance (where there's a civil war between the colonies and Earth, which also crops up in *Sarah*).
2 'Sarah is a memorable heroine, and Nagayasu's art is a near-perfect imitation of Otomo's hyper-detailed art style', noted Jason Thompson (189).

artwork, you'd assume this was drawn by Otomo. The wide views with meticulously crafted, architectural perspectives, the rocks and rubble drawn in detail, the flapping cloaks, the grizzled, weather-beaten characters, the junked technology, and the whole, near-wasteland look of *Mother Sarah* – this was all very much in the Otomoan vein. Except in one key area: the character designs. Here, the famous, round, Otomoan faces were not employed (except in a few instances).

It's possible that Katsuhiro Otomo also contributed towards the artwork in terms of sketching ideas. Some comic writers produce storyboards/ layouts for each page (called the 'name'). Creating storyboards would entail a lot more work for Otomo (maybe he drew them for some key chapters). Some of the layouts and the progression of the panels do suggest Otomo's influence.

One reason that *Mother Sarah* features so many over-the-top scenarios is that Katsuhiro Otomo knew that someone else was going to have to work out how to draw them.

What a story! *The Legend of Mother Sarah* is certainly a gripping, hugely imaginative science fiction extravaganza. The background and set-up combines conventional, futuristic, post-apocalyptic scenarios (which, admittedly, we have all seen 100s of times before), with a uniquely Otomoan vision of politics, revolution and political activism that becomes terrorism. Katsuhiro Otomo turns the future, as in *Akira*, into a highly politicized world, reflecting, of course, the politics of contemporary Japan, and Otomo's own left-wing political views.

Thus, *The Legend of Mother Sarah* comes across as both a sequel to *Akira* in many respects, and also a version of *Akira* replayed in a post-Bubble Economy Japan (or Japan's post-Bubble Economy society seen as a futuristic, post-apocalytic fantasy adventure). The political factions portrayed in *The Legend of Mother Sarah* are at once simplistic (left vs. right, liberalism vs. militarism, socialism vs. fascism), and sophisticated. Which's one of the really compelling things about the work of Katsuhiro Otomo. This guy does *not* deliver dumb, politically uninformed, uneducated material. There's a level of political analysis and ideological exploration that's rare in the action-adventure genre or the sci-fi and fantasy genre in any format.

In *manga*, *The Legend of Mother Sarah* has affinities with *Gunnm* (*Ganmu* = 'Gun Dream', a.k.a. *Battle Angel Alita*, 1991-95), created by Yukito Kishiro (a very accomplished slice of futuristic adventure *manga*, centring on a cyborg girl), *Berserk* (1989-), the truly astonishing, high fantasy adventure *manga* by Kentaro Miura (still not finished!),[3] and Masamune Shirow's *Appleseed* (1985, where warrior girl Deunan Knute and her cyborg boyfriend Briareos are living in the post-apocalyptic 'Badlands').

Mother Sarah portrays a rough-and-ready, post-catastrophe environment of extremely oppressive and violent communities. The heroine is attacked many times (and raped). We're in the tough world of *manga* such as *Fist of the North Star, Lone Wolf and Cub* and *Berserk*, the gritty, macho realms of artists such as Go Nagai and Buronson. If you are feeling delicate or vulnerable or hanker after some hearts and flowers *shojo manga*, do *not* read this comic!

The themes of *Mother Sarah* are the very familiar one of Japanese pop culture: war/ peace, military/ science, domination/ empathy, technology/ spirit, us/ them, etc.

✻

Out of the desert, cloak flapping in the high wind, appears a solitary figure: it's our hero, Sarah. A woman. Yep, no Tetsuo or Kaneda this time, no teenage street punks, no grizzled soldiers, but a woman in her thirties. Of course, she's slim, attract-ive, athletic, self-confident, independent, brave, smart, sensitive and possesses a million other positive attri-

---

3 Miura-sensei, please finish *Berserk*!

butes. She is Kei from *Akira* grown up, combined with a little of big, burly Chiyoko's talent for fist fights and survival in tough circumstances.

That the heroine Sarah's a *mother* is vital. Yep, our heroine's a mom in her thirties. Thus, what do Katsuhiro Otomo and Takumi Nagayasu do in the prologue? They separate the mother from her three children, and in doing so give themselves one of the most powerful emotional and psychological engines in all of drama and art: a mother's love for her off-spring.

Mother love – it drives the central quest of *The Legend of Mother Sarah*: for a mother to recover her children, Harato, Satoko and Tsumuri (remember those names, we will meet them later – a *lot* later).

The Big Separation set up in the prologue is staged on a space station orbiting the Earth. The back-story has our blue-green planet being polluted and ravaged (by, yes, you guessed it, humans and their insane devotion to Very Dangerous Technology. It's *Akira* all over again! If anyone's going to wreck the planet, it's *us humans*, not chickens or hamsters!).

So humanity exoduses to space. Bombs are part of the tale, as many folk want to use a new type of bomb, to tilt the Earth on its axis, to make it re-inhabitable (yes, I know, it's mightily ironic that a weapon of mass destruction will be the item that rights wrongs and renews the Earth).

Society in space splits in two familiar camps: the liberal, ecological, right-on types, and the right-wing, aggressive, intolerant, military types. It's the hippies and the hawks, the wimps and the bullies, the liberal rebels and the oppressive authorities all over again in Otomo Katsuhiro's *œuvre* (they're dubbed the followers of 'Mother Earth' and 'Epoch'). It's H.G. Wells' *The Time Machine*, the Morlocks and the Elois.

Terrorism, a key element in *Akira*, crops up again in *The Legend of Mother Sarah*, with Sarah's husband Bard being hunted down by the authorities. This occurs in the prologue in a border control set-up, just as the crowds are queuing up to board one of the many spaceships heading to Earth, to re-colonize it. In the chaos, as the crowds panic when the soldiers guarding the spaceships fire on them, Sarah is separated from her children, and her husband. (We meet them all again, much later on in this 7-volume comic. Characters disappearing for a *long* time is typical of long-running *manga*).

By the time the story of *The Legend of Mother Sarah* starts up, on Earth, with Sarah in the desert, the big blocks of the drama are in place: separation, loss, a quest, an oppressive, militarized society, and survival in challenging circumstances. (We are maybe 8 or 10 years after the Big Separation in the prologue).

Sounds gloomy? It is! But no, wait, Katsuhiro Otomo does have a sense of humour! (Otherwise works like *Akira* would be harder to take). So Otomo pairs Sarah up with Tsue, a gnarled, world-weary trader, a cynical (but also naïve) capitalist who's out for what he can get in this dog-eat-dog world. Tsue's quips, the sniping banter between Sarah and Tsue, and Tsue's comic antics are absolutely necessary to lighten up the story of *The Legend of Mother Sarah* (Tsue's appearance helps with the humour, too: a cock-eyed, short, scrawny guy with a flak jacket and a motorcycle helmet – he'd fit in to the 'Great Tokyo Empire' mob in *Akira*). Tsue has a large, customized truck that he trades out of, setting up his stall in towns he visits; Sarah likes to ride on the roof (cloak flapping in the breeze, a'course, a futuristic, female Lawrence of Arabia – she's a bit like a female version of the Colonel in *Akira* after the Akira-explosion).

Some exposition scenes follow, watering-hole scenes, as Katsuhiro Otomo and Takumi Nagayasu set out the world they've created for us. Before we get into slambang action and unbridled aggression, there are some moments of calm. For ex, one of the first family groups that Sarah encounters is a teenage girl (Lucia) and her grandfather, working their farm (i.e., it's a cute, homely set-up, common in *manga*). It is, of course, also a reminder of what Sarah has lost, and what she's searching for (she shows Lucia her family photo, explaining that she's looking for her lost children).

In *The Legend of Mother Sarah*'s first volume, the story features Sarah and Tsue turning up at a city built in a crater, to trade (there are many echoes of *Akira*). They encounter the first of many despotic regimes in the *Legend of Mother Sarah* saga (these consist of guys with guns who put them to hard, physical work). The imagery evokes a persecuted society with prisoners being herded at gunpoint and then executed *en masse*.

The politics are polarized in an exaggerated manner: there are essentially two sides, the hawks and the hippies, the war-mongers and the peacekeepers. It's simplistic, ideologically, at first, to get the story up and running. Later, the explorations of politics and ideology are more shaded.

Sarah acts as a kind of messiah figure, literally bringing water to the desert in a giant flood.[4] Katsuhiro Otomo and Takumi Nagayasu orchestrate a bunch of action-adventure genre clichés – subterranean realms, treasure (gold bars), greedy officials, firing squads, betrayals, and of course big fights.

At first, however, Sarah is our observer figure in *The Legend of Mother Sarah*: we see the world thru her eyes and she travels around with the trader Tsue. Sarah doesn't take decisive actions in the first chapters of *Mother Sarah*, as Otomo and Nagayasu set out the realm they've created for us.

Sarah and Tsue also encounter a couple of rather dim, naïve but well-meaning kids; they offer scenes of companionship (as well as delivering exposition). Toki and Lucia also embody the future of Earth: they are the next generation. Sarah, importantly, is adept at befriending people: she doesn't pose a potential threat in the same way that a male character like

4 A motif that crops up in *manga* like *One Piece*.

Indiana Jones or James Bond would (that is, until people have seen her fight! Then they change their opinion of her rapidly!).

Katsuhiro Otomo certainly likes underground spaces. Even better if they're decayed or post-apocalyptic urban areas. They occur throughout his fictions. Here there's a sunken pool and a colossal circular door which protects a former bank (Sarah discovers it after taking a dip in the mine). But behind the rows of gold bars is a build-up of water (tunnels and water and floods appear in the *Akira manga*).

Once all of the chess pieces have been placed in their starting positions, and the relationships have been set, and the conflicting motives and goals have been announced, the action can kick in, as we know it must and will in a comic like this.

Thus, the second half of the first book of *The Legend of Mother Sarah* erupts into a series of intense action sequences, featuring Sarah, Toki, Lucia, the Colonel and many soldiers. They are fighting over different things: Otomo-sensei uses the gold bars[5] as a way of getting the action started, but pride, survival and other issues are at stake.

This is one of those treasure hunt scenarios, escalating in desperation and betrayal, with rival groups tussling over the gold, people brandishing guns and yelling threats. Sarah is quickly revealed to be a fantastic warrior, smashing guys in the face, wrestling them down, and even taking direct hits from a machine gun (this is a girl who wears a breastplate).

*

We next travel to a snow realm, a gloomy, industrial environment of falling snow, extreme cold, paranoia and grizzled, unwelcoming inhabitants. In *manga*, a snow world usually means Hokkaido in the North; sometimes it also means the territories disputed with Russia; or it's Russia itself (the snowy,

---

5 What use would gold be as a trading token in this post-apocalyptic world?

industrialized North appears in *animé* such as *Cowboy Bebop, Wolf's Rain* and *Ghost In the Shell: Stand Alone Complex*, and in comics such as *Fullmetal Alchemist*).

In *The Legend of Mother Sarah*'s subsequent volumes, we see Sarah undergoing numerous torments. In the second volume, she's captured as a spy and imprisoned, and she's ordered to work for another violent, militarized community, this time a regime set up at a former nuclear power station. The prisoners are ordered to dig up barrels of radioactive waste (which the authorities are going to use, some-how. Seems crazy? It is!).

There is an extended flashback inserted into the prison sequence: now we see what happened after the spaceship crashlanded on Earth – how the survivors plodded thru the desert until they were set upon by a bunch of insanely vicious scavengers. It seems ridiculous that these gun-toting freaks would shoot and kill the exhausted survivors – who pose no threat to them (they can barely stand). So silly, because they possess only a few crummy belongings. If this was *Planet of the Apes*,[6] the gorillas would have rounded up the humans and used them as slaves. Simply to slay a bunch of people is Katsuhiro Otomo at his most pessimistic: he reckons that people, armed with guns, will kill civilians purely for pleasure, if they can get away with it. Anyhoo, in the midst of the chaos of the nighttime murders, all hell breaks loose among the spaceship's survivors, and they flee.

There are further degradations in the early volumes of *The Legend of Mother Sarah* for our hero-ine, some of which are pretty repulsive. One is a gang rape at gunpoint – still in the extended flashback. Well, in this ultra-violent sort of *manga*, and in this extremely savage, post-apocalyptic world, a rape might be expected. Or at least, *threatened*. In *Akira*, Kei was nearly raped (before help arrived, in the

6 There are several links to the *Planet of the Apes* franchise – such as the worship of an atomic bomb in *Beneath the Planes of the Apes* (1970).

THE ART OF KATSUHIRO OTOMO ▼ 199

figure of the burly Chiyoko). In *The Legend of Mother Sarah*, Katsuhiro Otomo has decided to deliver on the threat. (That Sarah chooses to work topless, as she slaves away in a quarry, when she's surrounded by men and armed guards, seems incredibly dumb. Yeah, she's doing hot, tough work, but you only strip down if you're Kirk Douglas or Charlton Heston in an ancient world epic movie! The idea that Sophia Loren or Katherine Hepburn would go topless in a similar action-adventure tale is ridiculous. And there's a very good reason why people cover up entirely in the Middle East and in deserts! It's hot! Rule No. 1: keep bare skin out of direct sunlight!).

The second slice of nastiness has Katsuhiro Otomo going too far: he depicts Sarah shoving a spiky piece of wood thru her own breasts![7] To stop them leaking milk! Because she's in agony over losing her baby! Oh, *come on*! If I had been Otomo's editor at the time, I would've told him, *no way*; you may be the punk genius who created *Akira*, but do you really wanna see your main star mutilating herself? And like that?! It's preposterous!

And you want to say to Sarah: jeez, put a shirt on, girl! It's only a bit of milk! Fashion yourself a maternity bra out of dead leaves and some string! It turns Sarah into someone not just agonized but mentally ill; it loses empathy for the heroine; and it loses the audience: who can care for or root for a character who does something so incredibly stupid?! g, you wanna show that your heroine is getting so desperate and is suffering so much, but not like that, for ¥$¥$'s sake! (Of course, it might not have been Katsuhiro Otomo who came up with this idiotic idea – but, knowing that Otomo also wrote *Akira* and *Inri*, it probably was!).

Tsue and Sarah are put to work clearing up the radioactive waste (much to Tsue's horror), and pretty soon another fight's broken out (yes, it involves

---

7 Try pitching this at a story meeting: then, right, she stabs herself with a piece of wood! After suffocating her baby so she won't be discovered!

Sarah). The heroine is slammed around a good deal –
if you don't like seeing women being beaten, smashed
with rifle butts, shot at and punched, don't read this
comic!

The community in the snowbound, one-time
power plant is presided over by two psychotic
characters (stereotyped as villains by their shocks of
white/ blond hair, staring eyes and imperious
attitudes. They might have wandered out of a 1960s/
70s retro movie about the Nazis such as *The Damned*
or *Cabaret*). Katsuhiro Otomo is certainly adept at
portraying evil characters – that is, not ambiguous
characters who might be better termed 'rivals'
(Japanese *manga* and *animé* don't have simple heroes
and villains types of Western literature; often their
villains are actually rivals, and sometimes anti-
heroes).

But Zarh and his mom in the second and third
volumes of *The Legend of Mother Sarah* are definitely
villains! In the finale, they stage a Roman gladiat-
orial-syle show for the assembled guards (who loll
about drinking[8] on top of a mass of radioactive waste
– a terrifically O.T.T. image of decadence). Our heroine Sarah is pitted against a bundle of giant Neander-
thals who've been pumped with drugs (exactly like
the bodyguards in the 'Great Tokyo Empire' in
Akira). The action is fierce, intense, and bone-
crunchingly brutal. We know for sure that the heroine
is not going to be sacrificed, but she is certainly beaten
up plenty!

In a twisted take on the motherhood theme,
Zarh's mom is regarded as the 'mother' by the
soldiers: she is the 'bad mother' to Sarah's 'good
mother' in *The Legend of Mother Sarah*. In the climax,
there are fights and killings like the end of an Ancient
Greek or Shakespearean tragedy. Katsuhiro Otomo is
brilliant at portraying super-creepy, vicious children,
and Zarh, with his glaring eyes and *Village of the
Damned* blond locks, is another psycho *à la* Tetsuo

---

8 Tsue provides the alcohol.

Shima in *Akira*. Zarh is a formidable opponent
– because he can control people's minds to a degree.

Zarh's mind control inaugurates another
flashback for Sarah: this time, it reveals further
elements of her life before the exodus, and more
details about what happened after the spacecraft
crashlanded on Earth (thus, each time the *manga* uses
a flashback, it reveals more of the back-story).

Now it seems that Sarah apparently killed her
baby Kazuki so she won't be detected by a gang of
murderous scavengers. Once again, Otomo-sensei has
taken things too far, especially for such a devoted
mother like Sarah.

✻

In the fourth and fifth *tankobons*, the *manga* of *The
Legend of Mother Sarah* takes a different approach to
the saga, with a World War Two scenario[9] of a town
in wartime, not far from a battle zone. We might be in
France, Russia, Italy or Spain in the 1930s and 1940s.
Yet, altho' the tanks rumble thru the town, and there's
a distant battle, the enemy isn't depicted at all (rather
like the *Cannon Fodder* episode in the movie *Memories*). Nor are the reasons for the war explored. It's just
war, that's all we need to know. (Only later is it
revealed that the two sides in the re-colonization of
Earth debate are at war – the hawks and the hippies.
However, the liberals are armed to the teeth just like
the right-wingers, and apart from their occasional
arguments (in dialogue), there's not much difference
between them!).

Tanks! Oh yeah – it can't be a Katsuhiro Otomo
manga or *animé* unless there are big, heavy, metal,
military tanks in there somewhere! And *The Legend
of Mother Sarah* includes many examples, lovingly
drawn by Takumi Nagayasu. In this episode of *The
Legend of Mother Sarah*, however, the tanks, and
soldiers, and the military machine are a mere side-
show: this section is about Sarah once again, and her
quest to find her children. And – thank the Buddha's

9 It might also be Korea or Vietnam, or Bosnia in the 1990s.

golden socks! – in this part of the *manga,* Sarah *does* find one of her offspring. Phew! At last! And there are hugs and reunions, which're *much* needed after so much debasement and downright nastiness in this extraordinary Japanese *manga* (which, needless to say, doesn't have any humorous *omake,* no jokey 4-*koma* strips showing Sarah creating a fashion craze for wooden stakes stuck thru the breasts. *Hey, Sakura-chan, is that a cute new swim suit? No, it's a coupla pieces of wood where my breasts used to be!*).

✳

After the Nazi psychos and their twisted regime in the previous episode in vol. 3 in *The Legend of Mother Sarah,* we are introduced to a much more routine scenario in vol 4: *Sacrifices*: nuns who're looking after abandoned children in a church outside the town (they also help out in the military hospital in the town – and sell their bodies in return for food – nuns and hookers, virgins and whores. Catholic nuns fascinate Japanese writers – and they use them exactly how you'd expect!). Of course, this being Katsuhiro Otomo's take on action-adventure and war genre staples, it's not an ordinary bunch of Catholic nuns, but young girls (one of whom is Sarah's daughter Satoko). And of course, the mother superior here, Mother Theresa, is a squat, pug-nosed and formidable woman (who was rumoured to have run a bordello in a former life).

We know that Japanese *animé* and *manga* artists tend to employ foreign religions such as Christianity as exotic and often sinister cults. However, Katsuhiro Otomo and Takumi Nagayasu are rather restrained in *The Legend of Mother Sarah,* and the weirdness that so often accompanies depictions of Christianity in Japanese popular culture is in the main avoided here. A church, a life-size statue of Jesus on the Cross, nuns praying, nuns helping in the medical tents... It's all fairly straightforward.

However, there is the undercurrent of exploit-ation, with the nuns using sex to buy *meshi* (and some of them are not of legal age, adding to the abuse). And we are in the midst of a war: Katsuhiro Otomo employs the famous image of Tiananmen Square (which occurred at the time of the comic), placing the nuns right in front of the path of a convoy of tanks driving to battle. And when Sarah scurries out of the crowds looking on to snatch up one of the nuns out of the way of a tank as it swerves to avoid her, everybody thinks it's a religious miracle that Sarah manages to stop the vehicle in time (Sarah insists it was the brakes, altho' it does look as if she was able to halt the tank).

The finale of book 4: *Sacrifices* involves the town being shelled by the unseen and unknown enemy. The imagery is truly horrific, as if making up for the talkiness and slowness of the previous 120 pages. We see children being killed, not something anybody wants to see at any time ever. (One of them survives but is badly injured; Sarah, Satoko and the nuns rush into town to save the child, but it's too late, and the girl expires. Otomo shamelessly piles on the melodrama – with heartache after set-back after calamity. Like *Akira*, *Mother Sarah* is the closest thing in the Otomo-world to a long-running soap opera).

In the following installments in *The Legend of Mother Sarah*, we are still in the town, the nearby church and its environs, with scenes that involve plenty of running around as the *mangaka* put their chess pieces in their starting positions for the finale, when the adventure plays out with another big action finale that combines Shakespearean tragedy (multiple deaths) with WW2 battles and action.

On the night before the bust-up, Sarah saves some of the nuns when she halts a gang rape conducted by the troops. This is another very hysterical scene, as only Japanese pop culture can produce, it seems: Mother Theresa is screaming that children should not be brought in this mad world (*pace* Satoko's admission that she's pregnant), the commander shoots an underling in the head who dares to argue with him (note to self: never talk back to an officer!), Sarah

affirms that she'll fight evil (but is smashed in the face
for her trouble), and everybody is having a Very
Horrible Time (which is what the *Mother Sarah manga*
amounts to for most of its run).

For some reason, the insane commander of the
army orders the nuns, Mother Theresa and Sarah to
join the soldiers in the trenches, as they prepare for
battle. It's mad! In the spectacular bombardment
scenes, in which both sides're shelling each other with
tanks and guns, Mother Theresa loses her mind. She
hurtles off into the chaos, muttering about atoning for
her sins (as a brothel madame, she killed not only the
children of her hookers in abortions, but also her own
children). In her hysteria, the squat, eccentric nun
wanders off into a mine field, with predictable
results. (Sarah bravely hurries after Mother Theresa,
trying to persuade her to return to the safety of the
trenches, but to no avail).

Back at the trenches, the psycho, Nazi-like
kommandant has also descended into insanity. He
has already killed the youngest of the nuns, Sheila
(after selecting her the night before), so he's a pædo-
phile and a child-murderer on top of everything else.
Why he orders the nuns out of the trenches is bizarre:
he wants the nuns to form a line to stop the approaching tanks. Talk about losing it! He shoots at Sarah for
no particular reason, other than being miffed that
most of his soldiers are dead or injured (which's
what can happen to soldiers if you send them out into
battle). He's one of those characters that you hope
someone – anyone! please! – is going to kill. Handily,
Yukito, Satoko's lover, is on hand to waste the guy
(unfortunately, Yukito is shot to pieces, too, by an
irate officer).

So this installment of *The Legend of Mother Sarah*
is also pretty grim: it begins when an injured child
dies in the arms of a nun, and it closes with multiple
deaths, as well as the widespread carnage of the
battle for the town. However, Satoko is pregnant, and
there's a birth scene, to offer some hope in this post-

apocalytic nightmare. Babies! Children! Yes, thankfully, people are still giving birth, having kids, starting families (even tho' Mother Theresa voices the familiar gripe of pessimists: why bring children into this horrible world? Because, *duh*, if you don't, humans will die out, within one generation! And three million years of evolution, from the savannahs of Africa in prehistory to war-torn Japan, would be wiped out!).

᪄

Here they come! Here come the bikers, the teenage rebels, the gun-totin' gang of misfits! It's not a Katsuhiro Otomo *manga* unless there's a motorcycle gang (or summat like it)! In *The Legend of Mother Sarah*, Harato (Sarah's long-lost son) turns out to be the long-haired, bandana-wearing Che Guevara leader of a bunch of politically-active, right-on rebels. They have a clutch of stolen military vehicles, plus some trucks, and some motorbikes (*en masse* they look like a scene out of *The Road Warrior/ Mad Max*). And a'course they have plenty of weaponry (including the mandatory rocket launchers – do you think that Otomo is a weapons nut like Steven Spielberg,[10] Brian de Palma and John Milius, and has built up a collection of grenades, machine guns and rocket launchers?! Many *animé* and *manga* artists are weapons fanatics – Kohta Hirano (*Hellsing*), Kentaro Miura (*Berserk*), Hiroaki Samura (*Blade of the Immortal*), Mamoru Oshii (*Ghost In the Shell*), Hayao Miyazaki, etc. And some, such as Masamune Shirow (*Appleseed, Ghost In the Shell*), fetishize arms to a scary degree).

The rebels (they're regarded as terrorists by the two armies of 'Epoch' and 'Mother Earth'), are a collective intent on Doing The Right Thing (as they see

---

10 Steven Spielberg went on shooting parties with John Milius and others in the 'New Hollywood' bratpack; Spielberg had a large collection of guns, something he kept quiet about, perhaps because possessing firearms was not in keeping with his media image. Spielberg would hang out with Milius at the Oak Tree Gun Club in L.A.'s Newhall Pass district. On *Jaws* Spielberg wanted to liven up the hours of waiting around with some skeet shooting, one of his favourite sports.

it), and putting a spanner in the works of the peace talks in the town of Byron. They are first introduced in a giant ambush and fire-fight sequence, in which they steal a tanker of fuel (very *Road Warrior*!). They hole up in a makeshift camp of tents in a graveyard for sea tankers in the sand (an image right out of *Close Encounters of the Third Kind*, of the ship beached in the Gobi desert).[11] Being a collective, they aren't supposed to have a leader, altho' Harato has lent his name to the whole group (they have it sprayed on the side of their trucks, as in *Akira*). But there are inevitable conflicts among the upper echelons of the group – Mordon argues with Harato about the leadership issue[12] (meanwhile, the girls grouse about always schlepping from uncomfortable desert hole to uncomfortable desert hole. They don't wanna play Lawrence of Arabia anymore!).

The authorities are caricatures: President Hans is a bald, stern-looking, muscular, old gent who resembles Dracula in his black cloak. And Commander Hamed, leader of the Epoch army, is a send-up of a pompous, military man who might've come out of Japan in the 1930s (with his olde worlde military uniform and medals). Then there's General Bates, another military cliché, a shrewder, caluculating leader.

The authorities deride the populace, are only interested in their own goals, are always angling for the deal which will give them the upper hand, and make secret agreements behind closed doors (as anti-democratic as possible!). They are the last people you'd want in charge of any community. They have no compassion, empathy, sensitivity or morality. They are empty souls, either bland civil servants or

11 In *Close Encounters*, the vessel was supposedly lost in the Bermuda Triangle, one of Steven Spielberg's 'Hitchcock moments' (the scene was shot in the California desert, with a model of the ship in the foreground, without needing mattes or visual effects).
12 They have a knife fight later – the time-honoured manner of solving macho, testosterone conflicts in macho, testosterone action stories. Mordon emerges victorious (and Harato rushes away to help his 'brother', Claus/ Tsumuri).

sadomasochistic militia.

The second Big Action Sequence for Harato and his band of merry men in *The Legend of Mother Sarah* is to storm the peace talks in Byron and force the authorities to look at a slideshow they've brought along, depicting a giant bomb discovered in a trench. Some of the staging here, tho' spectacular and action-packed, does stretch credulity a tad. There are a hundred soldiers in the audience in the old-style theatre venue, and there are even more lined up outside, complete with tanks and weapons, yet the 20-some Harato rebels manage to run rampant, and get clean away, too (one of their guys gets shot in the arm – that's all! – even when soldiers are spraying 'em with a hail of bullets).

But such gripes are minor quibbles, because Katsuhiro Otomo likes to create a scenario in which the younger generation can stick it to the older generation, in which the kids can take the stage and whup the butts of the oldsters. The concept that a bunch of idealistic, and, importantly, *not yet* cynical, youths can storm peace talks and make a stand for what they believe in is very appealing (even if it's highly unlikely they would get past security – especially when there are rows of tanks parked outside!).

Well, with the narrative switching over to Harato and the gang, there is less time spent with Mother Sarah. So Katsuhiro Otomo and Takumi Nagayasu do what many authors do when they're not sure what to do with their characters: they put Sarah in prison. If you've got a powerful main character, a hero who always has to be in motion and *doing something* (preferably Something Important or Exciting), and doing stuff linked to the main narrative spine, you have to keep the situations fresh and challenging. When in doubt, stick your hero in the slammer, to allow events to develop around them (in *Akira*, Otomo used an extreme version of this ruse – having Kanade being whisked away to a whole other dimension!). In this case, Otomo and Takumi Nagayasu have a lot of charas – Harato and his chums, plus the kid Tsumuri and his friendship with the crusty, old aviator Maggy (a very Hayao Miyazakian character), plus the scheming amongst the corrupt leaders of the two armies, so there's far less time to spend with Sarah.

However, there is time in the middle chapters of the *manga* of *The Legend of Mother Sarah* for Sarah to encounter Harato (and her other son, Tsumuri – but he turns out to be someone else, Claus, a boy that Harato rescued and pretended he was his brother, who died). In time-honoured fashion, Katsuhiro Otomo orchestrates a moment of high drama for our heroine to meet her long-lost children: on the perimeter wall, just as they're fleeing the peace talks.

The mid-volume action sequence features Claus/ Tsumuri visiting Maggy and co. at the aerodrome (now Tsue is helping out Maggy). But the Epoch army is closing in: the heroes escape in a fabulous machine, a kind of a drag racer combined with a dune buggy (and lovingly rendered down to every nut and bolt by Nagayasu-sensei).

This action sequence is shamelessly recycled, when our heroes meet the enemy at the aerodrome to trade Sarah and Claus/ Tsumuri. The handover swiftly escalates to all-out action (as usual in *Mother Sarah*), with our heroes careening about in Maggy's drag racer while being chased by tanks, motorcycles and soldiers on foot (even when 50 guys are strafing them with machine guns, they can drive straight thru and survive).

The violence of the *manga* of *The Legend of Mother Sarah* is simply mind-boggling in terms of sheer numbers. The end of the Harato-rebels-peace-talks sequence climaxes with yet another Big Battle. This time Claus/ Tsumuri has turned traitor, and sold out the rebels to the Epoch army, who storm the camp and slaughter everybody there. Yep, even down to rounding them up and wasting them in a hail of bullets. Nobody survives. The guy who helped Claus/ Tsumuri wire the rebels' tanks to blow gets shot, as does Claus/ Tsumuri himself, and the grandpa scientist figure, Maggy. And Harato's rival, Mordon.

For some foolish reason, the Epoch army orders all of its forces, including all of its main battle tanks, to rendezvous at the atomic bomb (now, that's just asking for trouble!). Regroup, search for stragglers, take prisoners, bury the dead, confiscate supplies – do all the usual things of a victorious army, but don't command everybody to drive over to a valley containing a deadly bomb!

And then, in a giant, climactic gesture typical of Katsuhiro Otomo – Maggy manages to trigger the enormous bomb that's been excavated (with only a prod of a button! Yep, it's that easy! You press one li'l button and you can set off an atomic bomb! *Duh!*). And here comes the customary bang, the mushroom cloud, the hemisphere of white light, and the colossal destruction.

So… everybody's slaughtered, and only three folks survive: Sarah (of course), Tsue (thankfully – he's great value!), and the wannabe Che Guevara rebel leader, Harato (they were on their way to the Harato HQ, from the aerodrome, when the bomb exploded. So they survived. (Again, there's another far-fetched piece of foolishness – Hirako, Sarah and Tsue walk right into a mass of atomic radiation – ground zero of the bomb site. They're looking for survivors, but there are other ways of doing that).

Anyway, Hirako finally tells his mother about how the real Tsumuri expired: he was ill, quarantined in a hellhole of a hospital, where he died.

And just when you thought the story of *The Legend of Mother Sarah* might be flagging, with Sarah re-united with one son, one daughter, and the other son long dead, Katsuhiro Otomo and Takumi Nagayasu wheel in another *deus ex machina*: one of the gigantic space stations landing near the peace talks.

✽

Thus the re-colonization of Earth plot strand is re-activated (this was how *The Legend of Mother Sarah* started, after all). The Biblical/ religious aspects of people travelling to a new land to start life afresh are emphasized by the costumes of the faithful who gather to welcome the colonizers. The colony is led by a bunch of twelve leaders who dress like Biblical prophets. Assyre is the wily, old coot who out-manœuvres the armed forces of 'Epoch' and 'Mother Earth' until he's slain in the final battle.

Harato is tormented by guilt over the people he's wronged or killed. Good! – finally someone ex-presses some remorse in this ultra-violent, mega-death comic. Someone aside from Mother Sarah is needed ethically to embody the torment of surviving in a world where human life is close to worthless.

Harato is soon left behind, and the *manga* of *The Legend of Mother Sarah* focusses on the returned colony ship, landed in the desert. We go back, also, to Sarah. A new chara is introduced – returning to her apartment: Laila, a striking young woman given a look that includes a mini-skirt, blonde hair and a cleavage (she's a hooker).

Harato, however, does have a side-story of his own: he becomes an embittered rebel, taking desper-ate measures, such as trying to assassinate the town of Byron's leaders as they enter their limos. Having walked away from his mom in despair, and with all of his followers immolated in the attack on their camp, Harato is a shell of his former self. The depths to which he has sunk are expressed in the arguments he has with his former girlfriend, Laila: he hits her. He's captured by the authorities in Byron and tortured after failing to shoot the generals by their limo. There is a redemption of sorts for Harato: he joins the new model army at the end of the *manga*. (He might also be the guy who tries to assassinate General Bates at the assembly).

Certainly the story of *The Legend of Mother Sarah*

takes unusual turns in its final chapters. For instance, the people on the colony spaceship have become so devoted to the idea of re-colonizing the Earth with crops and plants, they have used their *own bodies* for growing them! So when Sarah explores the space station on her own, and enters one of the forbidden laboratories of science fiction, she doesn't find clones, or aliens, or the usual sci-fi guff, but rows of plants such as potatoes in pods. And below them, nourishing the roots… are dead people! *I see dead people… and they are feeding the plants!* It's an out-there concept, certainly, as is Sarah's husband's admission that they are also allowing plants to be planted in their own bodies, while they're alive!

Yes – there is a hug, *finally*, something positive and heart-warming, *finally*, for our heroine Sarah in *The Legend of Mother Sarah*, when she is re-united with her estranged and long-lost husband Bard. However, the reunion doesn't stay jolly for long, because Bard has become another of the manically idealistic, Mother Earth types, the zealous hippies who are so devoted to re-establishing plantlife on the planet, they have taken to cutting open their torsos and sticking plants in there!

So Bard isn't the husband that Sarah once knew, or the father to her children that she so loved. There are tearful scenes in their old apartment, but soon Bard departs, and Sarah is left to her own devices.

The plant-in-the-body motif is Katsuhiro Otomo's extreme, melodramatic version of the ecological view that humanity will wreck the planet, that they will suffer the consequences of their selfish actions. So the eco-friendly types repay the debt to Mother Earth by allowing plants to be literally, physically part of them.

The motif can be found in Otomo's early comics, such as *Flower* (1979), where a plant in a desert is watered with human blood, when an alien squishes a guy above it.

Otomo is fond of using very crude, literal motifs

from time to time to get over his ideological messages, like the 'Great Tokyo Empire' mob in *Akira*, literally drugging their followers, or Tetsuo literally regressing to the form of a baby (but a Baby Monster, a Freudian Godzilla).

Plants have been around for hundreds of millions of years, and it's unlikely that humans could create a disaster to kill them all off, and to turn all of the soil completely lifeless. The planet has bounced back from all sorts of catastrophes. Also, note that water is absent in *Mother Sarah* – no rivers, lakes or seas.

The storytelling in *The Legend of Mother Sarah* shifts from Sarah and Bard to the leaders of the spaceship colony, and their battles with the two sides, the 'Epoch' people and the 'Mother Earth' people. There are talks round a table, and polite visits to the colony, but these aren't enough to stave off disaster. Wily politicos like these guys can pretend to be deferential and courteous when the occasion demands it. Then they'll return to their headquarters and order up a bombardment! Inevitably, this being a Katsuhiro Otomo story, there is a giant battle, with widespread destruction and death. (You know the formula by now: every new character that's introduced will be killed off! Get used to it!).

✻

The finale of the *manga* of *The Legend of Mother Sarah* is spectacular and unusual, though also a little predictable and by-numbers. There is, for a start, a Big Battle – the Epoch forces are hurling every missile in their armoury at the colony;[13] the colony defends itself with lasers, but some missiles get through; the colony is breaking apart; in the chaos, Sarah is separated from her husband Bard; a vigilante team armed with machine guns shoots the evacuees from the colony, including Bard; they are also burning the bodies of anybody from the colony (dead or alive),

13 The conflict begins partly as an accident, with the leaders out of contact with the troops, who open hostilities.

because they reckon they're infected; Sarah witnesses Bard being shot; in fury, she snatches up a gun and wastes a whole bunch of soldiers – at least 15 of them.

The climax of *Mother Sarah* plays out pretty much as one would expect, after having slogged thru this lengthy, epic and astonishingly brutal *manga*, and seen what is on offer, and what the struggle has been about. There is a long and underwhelming *dénouement* scene involving a trial back at the peace talks theatre location in Byron. A new army is formed (with Harato now re-established as one of the soldiers), as if, hell, the first thing you've gotta do in this vicious world is to form an army! Of all the things the trial could discuss or formulate, they choose to create a new army! But there's nobody to fight! And the survivors are starving! Nobody poses any threat! No one's got the strength to even lift a gun! Yet there is President Hans presiding over the court case and creating a new army! (Otomo's message seems to be: *human beings are a bunch of idiots!*).

So the trial is very boring, and a complete let-down after everything that's gone on before in *The Legend of Mother Sarah*. It is also far too long. But the real *dénouement* comes with the re-establishment of the odd couple pairing of Sarah and Tsue, as they set out on another journey. There are scenes at the new cemetery (for the numerous colony survivors, who perished in the battle), now knee-deep with vegetation (the potato plants have taken well). The new growths of plants are a classic motif of post-apocalyptic stories which depict the rejuvenation of the Earth (altho' most stories don't have 'em growing out of human bodies). And then our heroes set off into the sunset, in Tsue's new truck. The final gag of *The Legend of Mother Sarah* is, of all things, a fart joke!

❉

In the end, the character of Sarah in *The Legend of Mother Sarah* doesn't compel the reader as deeply as some of Katsuhiro Otomo's other characters. Sarah is a far less appealing or interesting character than the principals of *Akira*, for instance. I mean, she's an assured combatant and warrior, a compassionate soul, brave, fierce, independent, and smart. And her predicament – of finding and re-uniting with her lost children – is certainly a terrifically powerful emotional place to start any story.

But for much of the plot of *Mother Sarah*, the heroine is an observer figure, only occasionally intervening (particularly in the second half). Sarah is not driving the narrative for much of the time; instead, she's our audience identification character – she's there to witness the events for us, and we also see things through her eyes.

Similarly, apart from Tsue, Satoko and Harato, most of the characters in *The Legend of Mother Sarah* are not particularly gripping. And Tsue disappears from the story for too long (he has even to do less than Sarah in the final chapters). As for the many commanders, generals, soldiers and presidents, they don't make much of an impression beyond being a bunch of nasty, embittered, unsympathetic and vindictive old men.

Somehow, though, *The Legend of Mother Sarah* story loses steam towards the end (not uncommon in long-running *manga* series). All of the points that the artist and the writer want to make have been made. All of the spectacles they can cook up have already been dished out. The later installments of *The Legend of Mother Sarah* do tend to repeat earlier scenarios (again, very common in lengthy comics). And the dogged insistence on the savagery of humans does become wearing (as it does in 'real life'!).

Also, Sarah has far less to do, and her quests and goals fall into the background, in the final section of *The Legend of Mother Sarah*, when it becomes much more about the colony and the battle for the planet between the Epoch/ Mother Earth people and the colony survivors. That is, in the earlier episodes, Sarah was driving the plot along, and we followed her story closely, rooting for her to escape the horrific snakepit situations and be re-united with her kids. But in the later chapters of *The Legend of Mother Sarah*, the focus of the story shifts away from Sarah (really, from the split between Sarah and Harato and the arrival of the colony space station onwards).

✳

There is a feeling of desperation and negativity running throughout *The Legend of Mother Sarah*, resulting in some incredibly cruel moments. But it is especially prominent in the final chapters. It seems as if the forces of violence, oppression, ignorance and militarism win out every time. It's a depressing view of humanity that Katsuhiro Otomo and Takumi Nagayasu deliver in *The Legend of Mother Sarah*: there are some good people trying to do good things here (our heroine Sarah most obviously), but they are vastly out-numbered. In *The Legend of Mother Sarah*, one armed force attacks another, and the notion of 'peace talks' are laughable. A token, merely.

The spaceship colony, for example, is full of ageing hippies (presided over by Assyre), who're so dedicated to the cause of re-populating the Earth with crops, they use cadavers as soil. They have lasers and assorted weaponry, but they are out-matched in the end by the combined forces of Epoch. The planet needs those plants, but what do the armies below do?: they attack with missiles!

In *The Legend of Mother Sarah*, people have long forgotten what they're fighting for: when a group of humans appear, they are naturally assumed to be enemies that must be taken on and defeated. In the world of *The Legend of Mother Sarah*, everybody is potentially a threat, and the only means of negot-iation is the use of armed force. What's so depressing about *The Legend of Mother Sarah* is that it depicts humans as savages, intent on beating the •••• out of each other. Everyone reaches for their guns at the drop of a hat! No one wants to listen, and no one's got anything interesting to say anyway!

THE ART OF KATSUHIRO OTOMO ▼ 216

Meanwhile, the heroine, Sarah, undergoes extraordinary hardship. People die around her. And if she's not experiencing the agony herself, she witnesses horrors on every side being enacted on other people. Yet she battles through it all. She remains optimistic and compassionate to the end. *The Legend of Mother Sarah* is a horror show, with little redemption or tranquillity in sight.

The ending of *Mother Sarah* doesn't possess a grand, cathartic impulse, and is far less satisfying than the ending of many other long-running *manga* series. One imagines that Otomo-sensei had an idea of where he was heading, but didn't have it all mapped out. You get the feeling with Otomo's longer stories that the endings are up for grabs, that he doesn't like to have everything set in stone; instead, he prefers to discover it along the way.

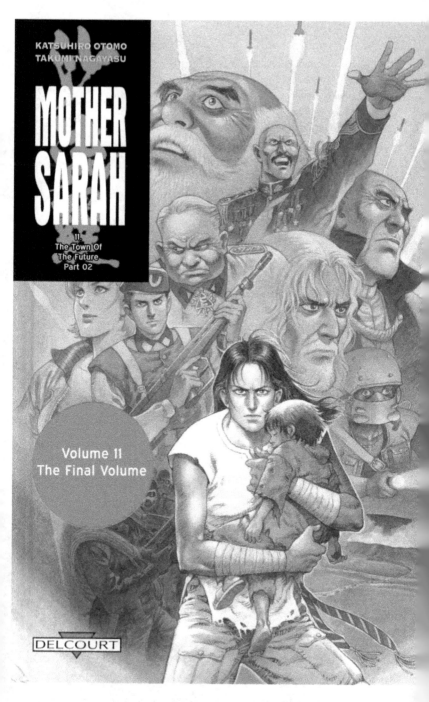

The Legend of Mother Sarah
(this page and over)

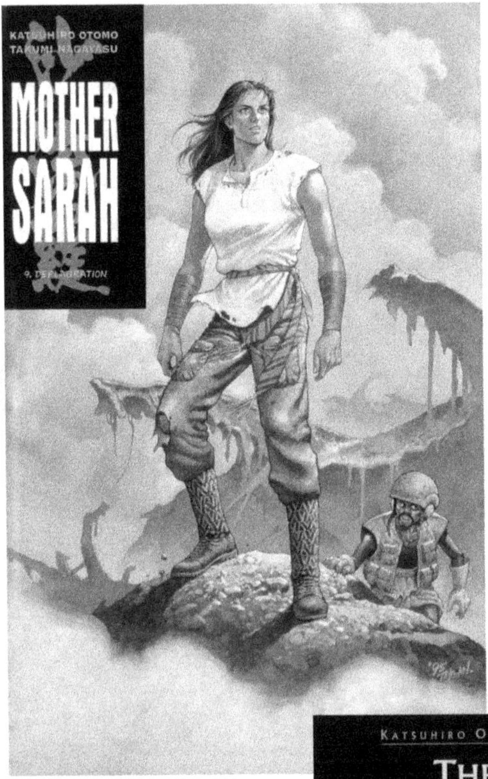
KATSUHIRO OTOMO
TAKUMI NAGAYASU
MOTHER SARAH

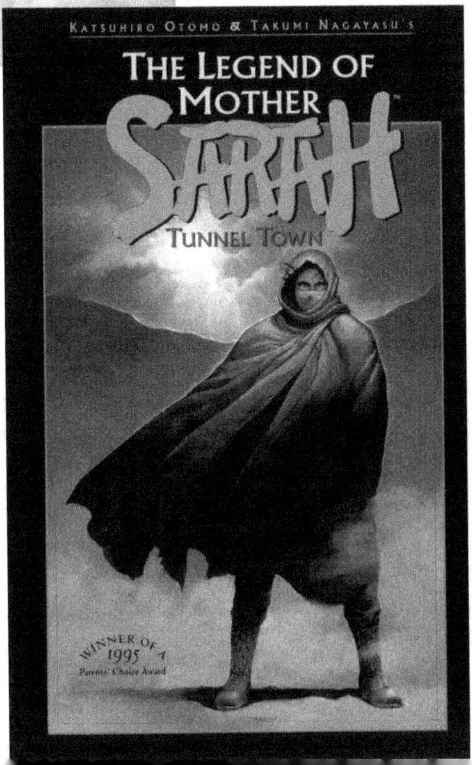
KATSUHIRO OTOMO & TAKUMI NAGAYASU'S
THE LEGEND OF MOTHER SARAH™
TUNNEL TOWN
WINNER OF A 1995 Parents' Choice Award

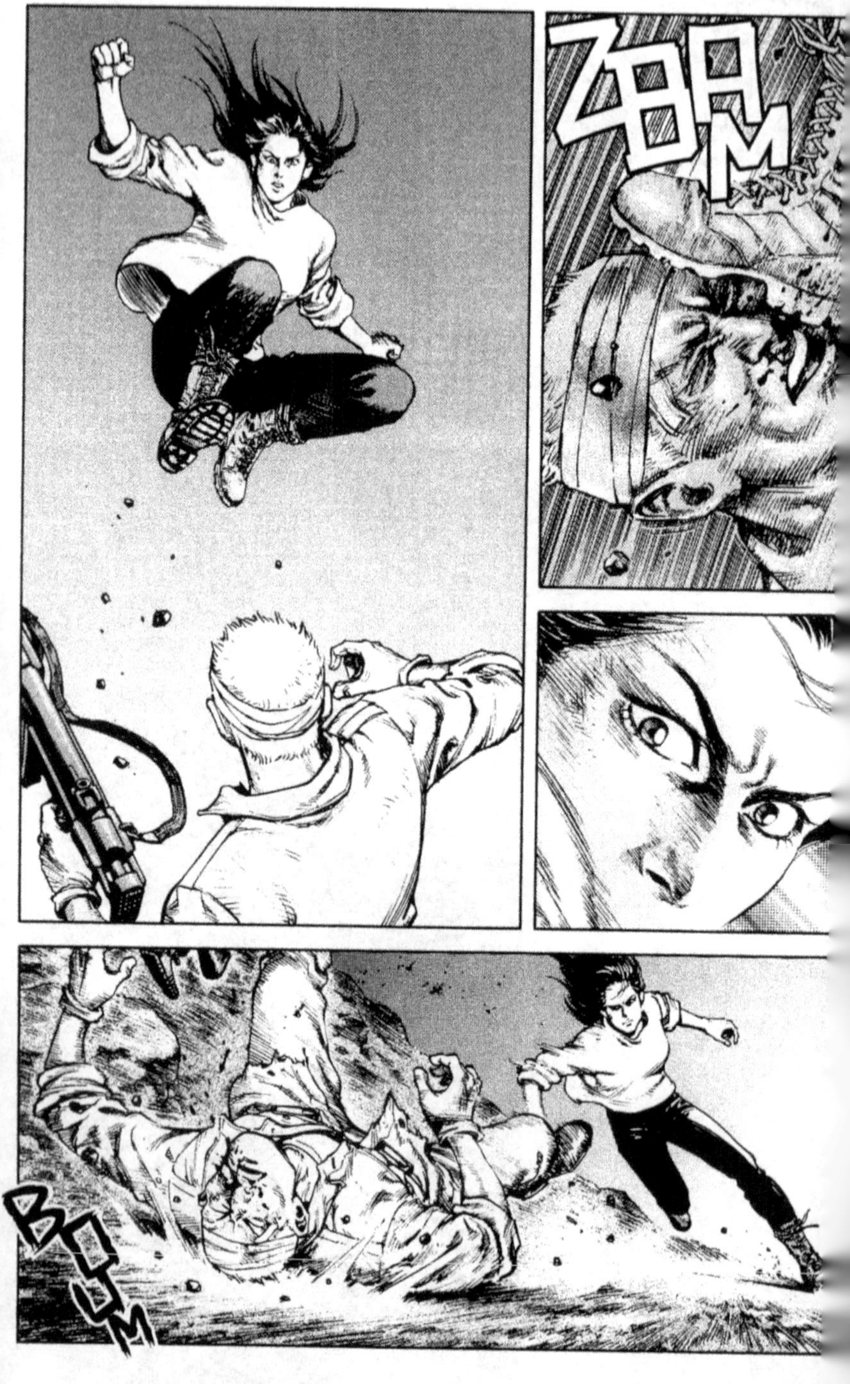
ZBAM
BOUM

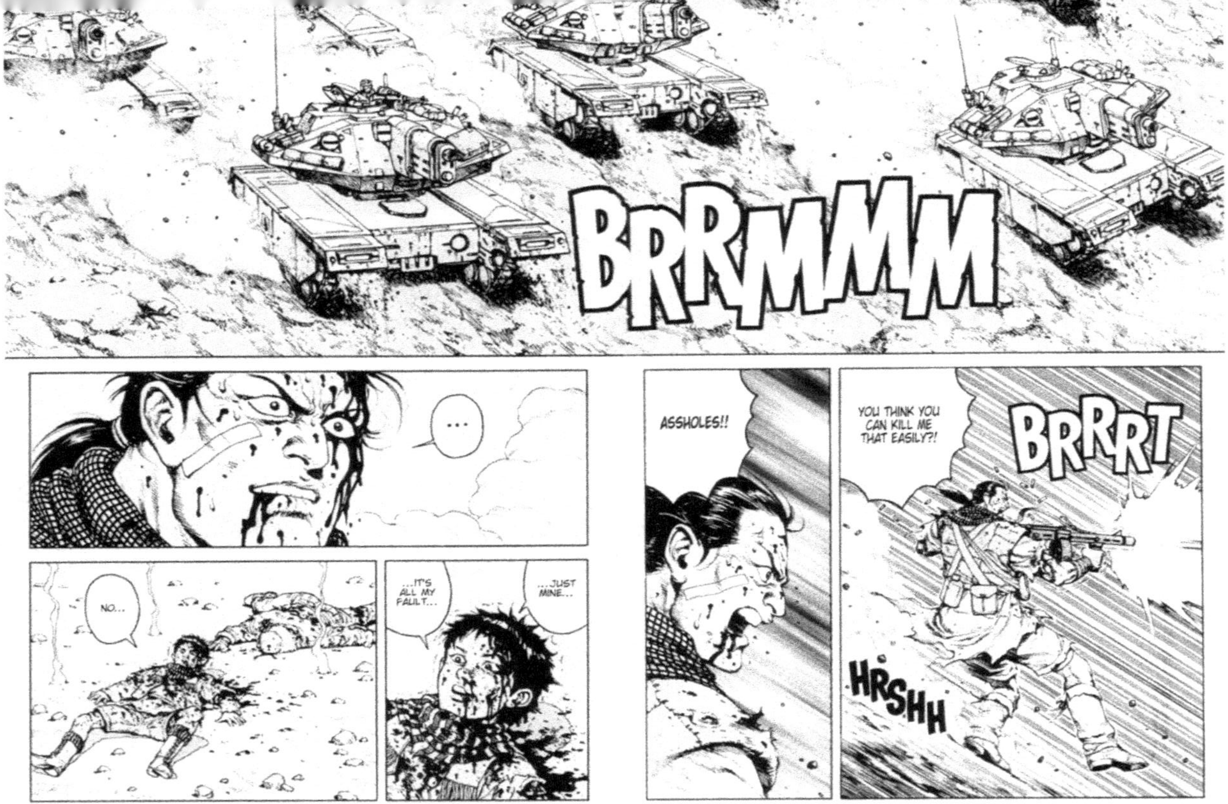
BRRMMM
...
NO...
...IT'S ALL MY FAULT...
...JUST MINE...
ASSHOLES!!
YOU THINK YOU CAN KILL ME THAT EASILY?!
BRRRRT
HRSHH

07

LATER *MANGA* WORKS BY KATSUHIRO OTOMO

WORLD APARTMENT HORROR.
A *manga* was published by Kodansha in 1991 based
on the Otomo-directed movie *World Apartment
Horror,* with art by Satoshi Kon. The story *Joyful Bell*,
about a guy lumped with a lost, young girl at
Christmastime, looks forward to *Tokyo Godfathers*
(2003), directed by Kon and scripted by Keiko
Nobumoto, who also co-wrote *World Apartment
Horror*. *Joyful Bell* is a sweet tale of bonding btn a
(reluctant) father and an (eager) daughter, plus some
subtext about an estranged husband and wife. The
setting – of suburban Japan in the snow – is a delight,
as are the clever ways in which the hero, dressed in a
Santa Claus outfit, gets to act like Father Christmas
(by climbing up onto a roof to fetch the toy bell of the
title. He's spotted by kids nearby, who're awaiting
the arrival of Santa).

BATMAN.
Katsuhiro Otomo's *The Third Mask* was a short
story for the *Batman: Black and White* book of 1996.
The Third Mask is only ten or so pages long, but it has
Otomo-san's stamp on it. Using the style of the

THE ART OF KATSUHIRO OTOMO ▼ 222

square-jawed Batman of the older comics, Otomo explores the theme of split personality (which the 1989 *Batman* movie had focussed on). As in other *Batman* stories, the superhero is contrasted with his targets – in this case, an insane serial killer. Is Batman as mad as his opponents? Is he Batman or Bruce Wayne? Which is dominant? (Alas, Otomo-sensei's take on *Batman* doesn't answer the fundamental question of the entire *Batman* franchise: why would anybody dress up as a bat to fight crime?!).

HIPIRA.

Hipira: The Little Vampire (2001) is a charming children's book that Katsuhiro Otomo wrote and Shinji Kimura illustrated (Kimura worked as art director for *Steam-boy*). *Hipira* tells the adventures of a young vampire and his chum Soul, a spirit. The story is delightful, told in short chapters, and the illustrations are stunning, revealing a clear inspiration from Tim Burton (in Burton's graphic art as well as his movies). The jokey, Hallowe'en approach to the horror genre is common in publishing for children.

Hipira depicts a magical realm of olde worlde, Gothic, Mittel Europa, with spindly, curly designs in blues, blacks and reds of acrylic paint. You can practically see the animated version (in which case, there's no need to animate it. But of course it *was* animated (in 2009, by Sunrise, directed by Shinj Kimura, for a Christmas broadcast), with Otomo receiving story credit).

SLICE OF LIFE.

In *Kouen* (*Slice of Life*, 2007, in *Brutus*), three teenage kids (On, Hanaken and Shinta), visit a local town park in the present day and sit around and talk. That is pretty much it for *Slice of Life*, as far as spectacle and action is concerned. What do the youths talk about? School > girls > politics > money > astrology > their hopes and dreams. (How can you convert

youth and free time into money? one of them asks.
When you're young, you've got time and youth, but no
money).

Towards the end of *Slice of Life*, there's some
cross-generational tension, when the kids litter the
park, and the old volunteer guys cleaning it up get
angry. They argue, admonishing the kids for being
negligent and disrespectful of 'Earthship Space' (as
they call it, instead of 'Spaceship Earth').

The issue of environmentalism takes an unusual
turn when, at the end of *Slice of Life*, a swarm of
parrots fly over the park, and the old park cleaners
disappear. The inconsequential and minimal form of
the story recalls the short stories of Raymond Carver.

STEAM-BOY.

The *Steam-Boy* movie was mangafied – published
in 2005 in 2 vols, it was written by Katsuhiro Otomo,
with illustrations by Yuu Kinutani. A side-story (of
18 pages), *Another Story of Steam-Boy*, co-written and
illustrated with Tony Takezaki, was published by
Kodansha.

DJ TECK'S MORNING ATTACK.

In Shinchousha's one-shot, full-colour *manga DJ
Teck's Morning Attack* (2012), Katsuhiro Otomo
revisits another post-apocalyptic world, this time set
in a Middle Eastern country. It's the familiar, ruined
city of *Akira*, with the streets full of mud and debris.
A robot is sent from the Goodwill Defence Service to
help the survivors of the Govinda district. To the
astonishment of the people on the streets, the little, red
mecha splits open its spherical head to reveal Sancho
inside (the husband of one of the women there).
Unfortunately, the robot self-destructs in an
explosion.

The *manga* then cuts to new charas, a grandfather
and a child, sitting around an open fire in the hills
outside the city; another ambassador robot appears,
and again it explodes.

DJ Teck's Morning Attack depicts a post-war world in which any attempts by authorities to help the citizens with charitable aid result in mayhem and destruction. The same sort of thing happens in *Akira*, when the United Nations relief forces arrive – nobody really wants to be helped, and the do-gooders end up being resented and even attacked. (And dumb, annoying and plain murderous robots acting for welfare or public services crop up in *A Farewell To Weapons* and *Electric Birdland*).

TOKYO METRO EXPLORERS.

S.O.S. Daitoukyou Tankentai (1996, Kodansha) was a collection of stories such as *Run, Speed, Sukiyaki, Night Flames, Visitors* and *Eiyoo Manten.* Some of them were animated (in 2007).

Many writers have created adventures involving a group of young kids – Philip Pullman, Enid Blyton, and C.S. Lewis, etc. Katsuhiro Otomo's own contribution to this young teens/ tweens market was *S.O.S.! Tokyo Metro Explorers* (1996), in which a group of boys explores the Tokyo subway system (which of course featured prominently in the *Akira manga,* as well as many, many other *manga* – in Japan, millions ride the commuter trains every day). One of the goals is to find a mysterious, lost, abandoned subway line.

As with many tales involving a young gang, it's the interaction among the individuals that provides much of the entertainment, rather than the mysteries they're investigating or the adventures they're undertaking. Shou is the leader of the group, a boy wearing a baseball cap who's well-prepared, determined and decisive. The others include the nerdy kid in glasses (Jun), and a tubby kid (Hiro); Shou's younger brother Sasuke tags along. The boys bring weapons, too – a B.B. gun, a baseball bat, and a nunchuk.

S.O.S.! Tokyo Metro Explorers is Otomo-sensei in his charming, storyteller persona, with the cynicism and political analysis put aside. With 6, 7 and 8 panels per page, the layout is neat and rapidly-paced. *S.O.S.! Tokyo Metro Explorers* is full of Otomo's compassionate observations of everyday life: how children interact, and how families work. This is an innocent, simplified adventure yarn, but the characters are totally convincing.

S.O.S.! Tokyo Metro Explorers was animated in 2007 by Sunrise and Bandai Visual, with Katsuhiro Otomo credited for the story and creation. (See the chapter on Otomo's cinema).

SOS! Tokyo Metro Explorers (this page and over)

Katsuhiro Otomo

TOKYO METRO EXPLORERS

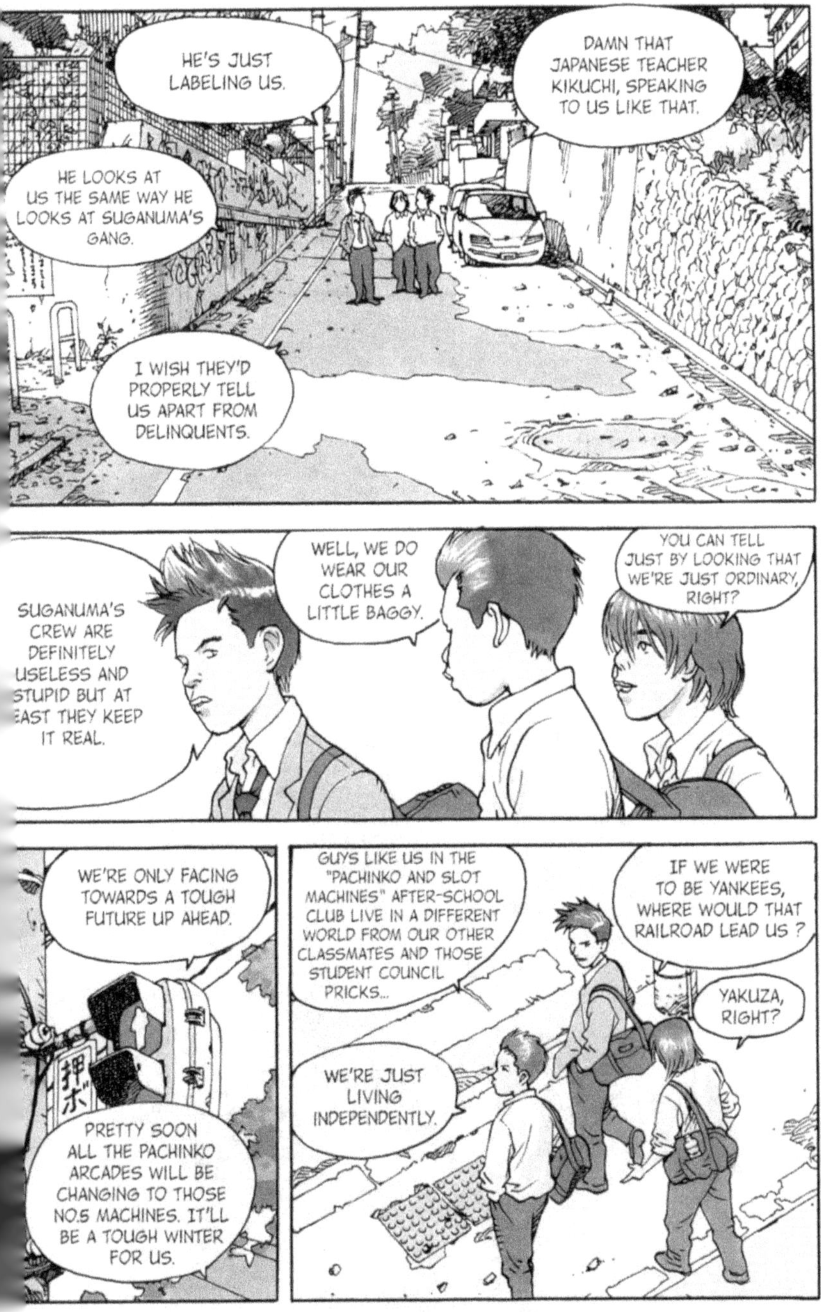
DAMN THAT JAPANESE TEACHER KIKUCHI, SPEAKING TO US LIKE THAT.
HE'S JUST LABELING US.
HE LOOKS AT US THE SAME WAY HE LOOKS AT SUGANUMA'S GANG.
I WISH THEY'D PROPERLY TELL US APART FROM DELINQUENTS.
YOU CAN TELL JUST BY LOOKING THAT WE'RE JUST ORDINARY, RIGHT?
WELL, WE DO WEAR OUR CLOTHES A LITTLE BAGGY.
SUGANUMA'S CREW ARE DEFINITELY USELESS AND STUPID BUT AT EAST THEY KEEP IT REAL.
IF WE WERE TO BE YANKEES, WHERE WOULD THAT RAILROAD LEAD US ?
YAKUZA, RIGHT?
GUYS LIKE US IN THE "PACHINKO AND SLOT MACHINES" AFTER-SCHOOL CLUB LIVE IN A DIFFERENT WORLD FROM OUR OTHER CLASSMATES AND THOSE STUDENT COUNCIL PRICKS...
WE'RE JUST LIVING INDEPENDENTLY.
WE'RE ONLY FACING TOWARDS A TOUGH FUTURE UP AHEAD.
PRETTY SOON ALL THE PACHINKO ARCADES WILL BE CHANGING TO THOSE NO.5 MACHINES. IT'LL BE A TOUGH WINTER FOR US.
押ボ

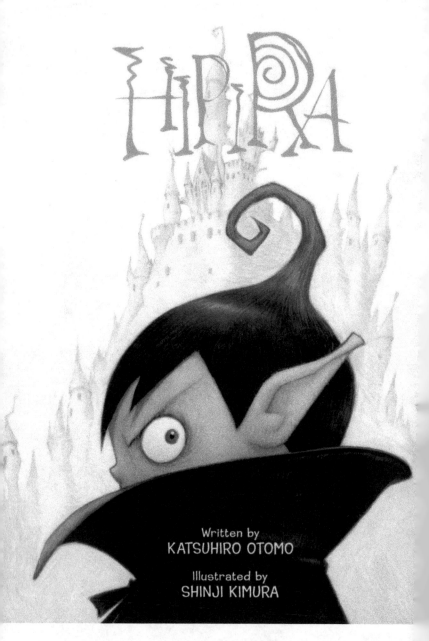

Written by
KATSUHIRO OTOMO

Illustrated by
SHINJI KIMURA

Hipira (this page and over)

Hi, my name's Soul.
Pleased to meet you!

But after that,
Hipira and Soul...

...became best friends.

My name is Hipira.
The truth is, I'm a vampire!
Everybody had better be really afraid of me!

D.J. Teck's Morning Attack

PART THREE

CINEMA

01

SOME OF KATSUHIRO OTOMO'S WORKS IN CINEMA

HARMAGEDDON

Harmageddon (Rintaro, 1983) was the first feature in animation which Katsuhiro Otomo designed. *Harmageddon* was produced by Madhouse[1] / Magic Capsule/ Kodokawa Shoten; Keith Emerson (of rock group Emerson, Lake & Palmer) and Nozomu Aoki provided the music; animation directors were Takuo Noda, Mukuo Takamura, Yoshitaki Kawajiri,[2] Takashi Nakamura[3] and Iwao Yamaki; and it was written by Chiho Katsura, Makoto Naito and Masaki Mori (adapted from *Gemma Wars*, a *manga* by

[1] Madhouse, founded in 1972, has produced *Ninja Scroll, Wicked City, Barefoot Gen, Lensman, Metropolis, Paranoia Agent,* and films by Rintaro, Yoshitaki Kawajiri and Satoshi Kon (*Perfect Blue* and *Millennium Actress*).
[2] Director Yoshiaki Kawajiri (b. 1950) helmed the incredible *Ninja Scroll, Demon City Shinjuku, Wicked City, Cyber City Oedo 808, Midnight Eye Goku* and *Vampire Hunter*, among others. Kawajiri also worked on *Neo-Tokyo, Memories, Future Boy Conan* (for Hayao Miyazaki), *Cleopatra* (for Osamu Tezuka), *Harmageddon* and *Dagger of Kamui* (both for Rintaro).
[3] Takashi Nakamura worked with Katsuhiro Otomo many times (he was the chief animation director on *Akira*), and was a director in his own right, often in children's animation (*Catnapped!*, 1995 and *Tree of Palme*, 2001).

Kazumasa Hirai and Shotaro Ishinomori, in turn
adapted from the novels of Hirai). 131 minutes.

However, Katsuhiro Otomo hadn't been happy
working on *Harmageddon* (tho' he did collaborate
with some of the team again – such as director
Rintaro, who helmed the 2001 version of *Metropolis*,
animators Yoshitaki Kawajiri and Takashi Nakamura, and the studio Madhouse, who co-produced
Neo-Tokyo and *Metropolis*, among others[4]).

NEO-TOKYO

Neo-Tokyo (*Manie Manie Meikyu Monogatari*, a.k.a.
Labyrinth Tales, 1987) was a 50-minute Original
Video Animation featuring shorts by directors
Rintaro, Yoshitaki Kawajiri and Katsuhiro Otomo.
Each story was based on Taku Maruyama's fiction. It
was produced by Project Team Argus/ Madhouse/
Kadokawa (distributed in Japan by Toho/ Kado-
kawa Shoten). Haruki Kadokawa was executive
producer, Masao Maruyama and Rintaro were
producers. Released: Sept 25, 1987.

Katsuhiro Otomo's segment was titled *Order To
Stop Construction* (*Koji Chushi Meirei*, a.k.a. *Construction Cancellation Order*). Otomo has design,
director and script credits. The animators included
Takashi Nakamura, Atsuko Fukushima, Koji
Morimoto and Kunihiko Sakurai (these are enormously talented animators). Micky Yoshino composed
the music,[5] art dir. by Takamura Mukuo, Kinichi
Ishikawa was DP, and editing by Harutoshi Ogata.
18 minutes.

Order To Stop Construction is another classic
Katsuhiro Otomo tale of the troubled issue of humans
vs. technology, society vs. science, as hapless construction manager Tsutomo Sugioka (Yuu

4 *Harmageddon* was thus important for Otomo in meeting some of the
collaborators of his later works.
5 Hikaru Ishikawa was music producer.

Mizushima) travels to a flooded Amazon to salvage and shut down a colossal building site. Clad in a safari suit like an explorer in an old, Hollywood, adventure serial *circa* 1935, the entry of Sugioka into the construction site (which is, really, Neo-Tokyo from *Akira* again), is at first depicted as an awe-inspiring trip into a post-apocalyptic wonderland (the journey by hovercraft starts in jungly bayous *à la* Mississippi or Florida). But soon, as Sugioka discovers he's the only human around, and is surrounded by idiotic but domineering robots, who keep him shut in a room like a prisoner, the trip turns into a nightmare. (Sugioka is in essence another spoof of a Japanese salaryman – uptight, a stickler for rules, a loyal worker. He's also a gross caricature of a Japanese guy – he's got the buck teeth and the slanted eyes).

Katsuhiro Otomo's segment of *Neo-Tokyo* is stuffed with familiar Otomoan concerns and motifs, such as technology going wrong, humanity's uneasy relation with technology, and the use of technology in advanced capitalism. The setting – of a flooded, modern industrial zone that resembles a city – of course prefigures *Akira*, and *Neo-Tokyo* has the same lovingly crafted depictions of skyscrapers (Otomo might've had an alternate career as a visionary architect. *No one* in *animé* can match him for visualizing futuristic cities). And of course there are not only plenty of robots but machines of all kinds (bulldozers, diggers, drills, cranes, tractors – *Order To Stop Construction* looks as if the research team have spent a few days wearing hard hats on giant construction sites, studying the heavy duty machinery that's employed these days to build the great cities of the capitalist era. Tokyo, like any other big city, ancient or modern, is continually being re-built).

The animation style of *Order To Stop Construction*, meanwhile, is bright, clear, and endlessly inventive – it is very much of its era in the mid-Eighties, but it is also a style of animation that hasn't dated at all (which's one of the reasons for Otomo-san's continuing influence and importance in the world of animation).[6] The colours are again striking – bright oranges, reds and yellows, and exaggerated colours for the jungle skies: bright pink, and buttercup yellow (emphasizing the unreality of the site).

Musically, there are repetitions of simple motifs on piano from Micky Yoshino (to evoke the robotic activity, but also the repetition of one day following another. The deliberately crude piano riffs might also be a spoof of serial/ minimalist music). For each breakfast scene, the *Peer Gynt Suite* (1875) by Edvard Grieg, a piece of pastoral classicism, becomes increasingly ironic.

And it all goes wrong – hell, it can't be a Katsuhiro Otomo movie unless things are going into decline and ending in chaos! The robots're falling apart (some explode, of course), the machines sink into layers of mud, and the trays of food the robot brings to Sugioka in his little room get worse every day (eventually becoming nuts and bolts and bits of smoking *mecha*. Terrible food being offered to guests is a staple of *manga* and *animé*).

> Sugioka's cartoonish intransigence is funny and endearing, especially in contrast to the mad, uncontrollable push of the machines around him relentlessly performing their functions, even as the waters of the Amazon seep in and obliterate their efforts. It's Otomo's most focused effort and one of his most enjoyable

summed up Brian Camp in *Zettai* (244).

Ironically, Sugioka doesn't hear that the con-struction site has been given the green light again – he had travelled there to shut everything down (while the robots, as diligent workers, insist that they keep

---

6 Jonathan Clements pointed out in 2002 that *Akira* was old news now: the *manga* and the movie had been supplanted by many newer products (2009, 271). You could say that: but still no movie apart from those directed by Hayao Miyazaki or Isao Takahata has reached *Akira*'s heights.

working, to make crunch time).

ROBOT CARNIVAL

Robot Carnival (Another Push Pin Planning, 1987), which preceded *Akira* by a year, was an anthology movie in nine parts, with opening and closing scenes directed by Katsuhiro Otomo and Atsuko Fukushima. The other directors involved were: Lamdo Mao, Hiroyuki Kitazume, Yasuomi Umetsu, Manabu Ôhashi, Hidetoshi Ômori, Koji Morimoto (who directed part of *Memories, The Animatrix* and *Tomorrow's Joe*, as well as animating *Akira*), Hiroyuki Kitakubo[7] (who directed *Roujin Z* and *Black Magic*), and Takashi Nakamura (director of *Catnapped* and *Tree of Palme*, and a regular collaborator with Otomo). Most of the directors also have design, script and animation credits. The executive producer was Kazufumi Nomura. Joe Hisaishi (Hayao Miyazaki's regular composer), Isaku Fujita and Masahisa Takeshi scored the movie, and A.P.P.P. produced. 90 minutes.

The cast included: Hikaru Kotono, Kei Tomi-yama, Kouji Moritsugu, Chisa Yokoyama, James R. Bowers, Kaneto Shiozawa, Katsue Miwa, Toku Nishio, Aya Murata, Hideyuki Umezu, Keiko Hanagata and Kumiko Takizawa.

The brief for *Robot Carnival* was, according to producer Kazufumi Nomura, 'to show robots in some manner' – well, that's about the easiest brief you could give animators in Japan! (One of the key creative decisions was to reduce dialogue to a minimum in *Robot Carnival*, so most of the episodes play thru with only music and sound effects).

The opening credits of *Robot Carnival* offer a typical Otomoan scenario, as a quiet, desert village (it

---

7 Hiroyuki Kitakubo's other credits include *Blood: The Boring Vampire, JoJo's Bizarre Adventure* and *Golden Boy*.

might be a setting for his *The Legend of Mother Sarah manga*), is invaded by a colossal machine[8] bearing olde worlde robots and the title of the movie in giant letters. This being Katsuhiro Otomo, there are of course many explosions, unusual camera angles, and much mayhem. The ballerina automata emerging from the upper levels of the machine (plus the fireworks) look forward to the Steam Tower in *Steamboy* (which has a funfair attached to it).

A guy running thru a quiet town is a recurring scenario in the Otomoworld (it occurs in his fairy tales, for instance). Sometimes the populace reacts to the messenger with indifference and scorn – or, as here, with mass panic. The Circus Coming To Town means widespread carnage, so everybody battens down the hatches. In the end credits, the Robot Carnival machine grinds to a halt on a sand dune and – of course! – explodes.

Another motif of Otomo's early *manga* is an apparently friendly emissary or robot visiting a locale which turns out to be malicious (sometimes unintentionally so). *Manga* such as *A Farewell To Weapons* and *Electric Birdland* depict robots which start out programmed to be helpful to the community, but it doesn't work out like that in the end. The colossal machine in the *Robot Carnival* credits promises to bring entertainment to the masses in the out-lying regions of the desert, but ends up destroying stuff (the populace hurry to the hills).

In the end credits, a guy brings back a sphere from the wreckage of the Robot Carnival machine; at first, his family is enchanted by the ballerina automata who emerges from it and pirouettes; but then, in true Otomoan style, it explodes, along with the house (presumably killing the whole family).

In Otomomania, the rule is: never trust a machine. Along with: never build a complicated machine with weapons. And: never allow a machine

8 It resembles the castle in *Howl's Moving Castle,* and the sand crawler in *Star Wars.*

to operate unattended by humans. And: never give humans guns. Otomo himself of course breaks all of these rules.

The tongue-in-cheek humour and the celebration of *mecha* in all its forms are typical of Otomo-sensei (there are nods, too, to *Monty Python* and *Star Wars*. Meanwhile, Tetsuo and Akira have a cameo in the first episode of *Robot Carnival*, *Starlight Angel*).

❋

Starlight Angel was the first entry in *Robot Carnival*. It was directed by Hiroyuki Kitazume, a romantic tale set in a classic *animé* environment: a Disneyesque theme park at night (since 1987 many more theme parks have opened in Nihon; this one draws heavily on Disneyland Tokyo).

A theme park is Date Destination Number One in Japanese *manga* and *animé* – closely followed by a shopping mall, an ice cream parlour, and a cherry blossom-strewn park.

Starlight Angel was a rather twee, mawkish *shojo* tale, complete with a cheesy synthesizer score (which contrasts vividly with the explosive carnage of the opening credit sequence). Two girls visit a theme park at night, with one of them experiencing a fantasy romance which include numerous favourite motifs in Japanese *animé* (a flight in the sky *à la Superman*, robots becoming human, and of course a battle with a giant robot).

Cloud (dir. by Mao Lamdo a.k.a. Manabu Ôhashi) is a wistful piece of animation-as-art, or arty animation. It depicts a small robot in a series of walk cycles (one of the basic motifs of all animation. Japanese *animé* is very fond of using walk cycles for the opening/ closing credits in TV shows).

Cloud has our forlorn robo-boy walking in different-sized cinematic frames against back-grounds that include Miyazakian clouds, thunder clouds, quotations from art (such as the Sistine Chapel), and favourite motifs in Japanese animation (angels, moons, rain, etc).

Deprive (dir. by Hidetoshi Omori) is a routine robot and superhero outing: it's a simple boy plus villain plus girl format: a boy has to save a girl who's captured by a villain. Cue lots of fighting, laser bolts, and explosions. The characters turn into robots (and giant robots, too), so we get our superhero battles plus our robot battles. The style of the art is pedestrian – this might be any robot show from 1964 to 1987.

Franken's Gears (helmed by superstar director Koji Morimoto – he directed *Magnetic Rose* from Otomo's story) is one of the outstanding sequences in *Robot Carnival*: it's another re-run of the famous laboratory scene in the 1931 Universal *Frankenstein* movie which is one of the two or three key scenes in *all* science fiction and fantasy cinema.[9]

Very much in keeping with Katsuhiro Otomo's passionate love affair with machinery of all kinds, and destruction and explosions of all kinds, *Franken's Gears* delivers a battery of cogs, wheels, cables, pipes, electrical gadgets and versions of the celebrated apparatus in *Frankenstein* (which was supplied by Ken Strickfaden),[10] achieved via some extraordinary visual effects animation (it's like a Japanese version of a Disney *Silly Symphony* from the Thirties; *Robot Carnival* has been compared to *Fantasia*).

Here, the birth of the robot on the slab in the scientist's laboratory is a noisy, chaotic scene of things falling apart – it's birth out of chaos, or chaos as birth. Beginning with the customary lightning storm, *Franken's Gears* conjures a steam-punk version of the creation of artificial life, the foundational scene of all cyborg and robot stories.

The sound effects editor (Kazutoshi Satô) added

9 The Frankenstein myth is a primal myth for the whole process of animation – and of cinema.

10 The flashing lights of the machinery in the famous 1931 *Frankenstein* movie, the Van der Graaf generators, Tesla coils, and an assembly of weird machines, were created by designer Kenneth Strickfaden, who dubbed them 'bariton generator', 'nucleus analyser' and 'vacuum electrolyser'. Yet they weren't really in the novel, but were added for the dramatizations, starting with the theatrical versions of *Frankenstein* in the late 19th century.

every variation in the sound library of crunching, grinding, clanking, scraping sounds to accompany the shuddering, toppling, smashing pieces of metal, tubes, cogs and wires. Every item in the laboratory explodes or crumbles, all in order to bring the over-size robot to life.

It works, but only for a few moments before the robot apparently attacks the scientist (or falls on top of him), providing the customary punishment for the *hubris* of the inventor.

The wonderful designs of the *mecha* in the laboratory and the collapsing objects in *Franken's Gears* look forward to *Steam-boy*, achieving an abstraction of stuttering metalwork, reminiscent of a Jean Tinguely[11] machine that runs well for a few minutes then falls to pieces.

In *Presence* (directed by Yasuomi Umezu), an inventor has a romantic relationship with the robot he's created to keep him company in his loneliness. It's a staple of science fiction, of course – it's *Pinocchio* (and *Blade Runner*) all over again. *Presence* stages the ambiguous, yearning relationship between the lonely scientist and his creation in a wistful, gentle manner (where the score, by Joe Hisaishi, does much of the emotional and psychological work).[12]

Presence imagines someone who can only relate at a deep level with a robot, a recurring notion in Japanese *animé* (her/ its appearance evokes a maid). Though she or it expires in a traumatic scene where the inventor seems to destroy his creation, she/ it returns to haunt him. This occurs twice, with the aged scientist now retired to the countryside – the repetition has *Presence* running on a little too long (the

11 The master of kinetic sculpture is the rebellious Jean Tinguely, whose motorized sculptures mischievously create chaos. Tinguely's sculptures don't just move – in all directions – they are very noisy, with clatterings, bangs, pants, grinds and wheezes. The most famous, *Hommage à New York* of 1960, was a sculpture 'created for self-destruction'. The artwork was intended to perform many bizarre actions.

12 'It's a contemplative, sad, and visually beautiful piece of animation, and the highlight of the anthology', summarized Brian Camp (314).

point had already been made the first time).

The penultimate tale of *Robot Carnival*, *The Tale of Two Robots*, directed by Hiroyuki Kitakubo, is an over-the-top battle between two giant, homemade, steam-punk-style robots in late 19th century Japan. This being Japanese animation about robots, there is a good deal of carnage (tho' we've already seen plenty in this 1987 movie!), with good, ol' Japanese technology (and character types) defending their nation against nasty, white foreigners (again, the robots looming over the clusters of houses and canals Godzilla-style looks forward to the Steam Tower climax of *Steam-boy*).

Watching giant monsters wading through cities and waging titanic battles with each other, while the populace below run for their lives, is something that Japanese audiences never seem to get tired of. Even when the motif is revived in clever, postmodern spoofs, it's still the same thing: monsters, cites and carnage.

Nightmare (dir. by Takashi Nakamura) was a wild evocation of robot pandemonium, as the city is overtaken by artificial life erupting everywhere. *Nightmare* was a kitchen sink outing, where the animators throw in everything they've got. A hapless salaryman rides a moped thru the mayhem and explosions, trying to escape (and failing). The amazing robot designs evoke the demon parades of Japanese folklore, the night festivals where *yokai* and spirits emerge from the shadows and process thru the streets.[13]

'Whimsical, frightening, hilarious, breathtaking, and quixotic by turns, *Robot Carnival* is like having your own in-home animation art festival', as Trish Ledoux and Doug Ranney put it in *The Complete Anime Guide* (54). The anthology format in Japanese animation, as in *Robot Carnival*, *Neo-Tokyo* and *Memories*, is very satisfying (in contrast to many

[13] See the extraordinary *manga* and *animé Nura: Rise of the Yokai Clan* (*Nurarihyon's Grandson,* 2008-2012) by Hiroshi Shibashi.

anthology movies in the West. Why? Because live-action anthologies of short films tend to look like cut-price versions of feature film ideas, and they're always producer-dominated movies, packaged and marketed, and the filmmakers forget/ ignore the beauty of the short film form. A typical anthology film is hit-and-miss, with often only one decent entry). Some of the episodes in *Robot Carnival,* however, are a little Saturday morning TV-ish, with superhero action[14] and giant robot antics and rather routine plot developments.

GUNDAM

Gundam: Mission To the Rise (1998) was a short film of 2-3 minutes animated digitally. Directed and written by Katsuhiro Otomo, prod. by Sunrise/ Bandai/ Bandai Visual, by producers Masuo Ueda and Hironobu Osaki,[15] *Gundam: Mission To the Rise* features a battle in deep space, with the usual displays of *mecha* and technology that the *Gundam* universe makes a trademark. Amusing enough, and slickly produced and very spectacular – tho' well below the talents of an artist like Otomo-sensei.

GONDORA

Gondora (a.k.a. *Catsuka Player,* 1998) was Otomo in his funky, punky guise: a boy (drawing on the son in *Cannon Fodder* in *Memories*) stands in a room with a WWII plane as a helmet, and then moves along a city street. Story-wise, that's it – because *Gondora* about

14 There's yet another lift from the romantic flying sequence in the *Superman* movie, for instance (a popular scene in Japanese animation), as well as *Peter Pan.* (It crops up in *Akira,* too, when Tetsuo and Kei fly up to the satellites).
15 On the show were some high-calibre talents, such as Shinji Aramaki.

the look, the design, the attitude and the music. The boy wears a pilot's helmet under the (American) plane, and a bomber jacket.

The film is very short, and ends with a classic Otomoan device – the twist ending, when someone else turns up with wacky headgear (a guy with a steaming kettle as a helmet). Technically, *Gondora* emphasizes drawing, colour, and a fidgety approach (the outlines of the figures are constantly quivering). The street is filmed with partial pixillation, and hand-tinting.

S.O.S.: TOKYO METRO EXPLORERS

The *animé* version of *S.O.S.: Tokyo Metro Explorers: The Next* (2007), based on Katsuhiro Otomo's 1996 *manga*, was produced by Sunrise and Bandai Visual, distributed by Shochiku, written by Sadayuki Murai (co-writer with Otomo of *Steam-boy* and *Mushishi*), music by Yoshihiro Ike, and directed by Shinji Takagi. It's a charming *Boys' Own* adventure yarn (with a token girl added), as a gang of pre-teens dive into the subterranean world of Ye Olde Tokyo (armed with only a flashlight, a video camera to record their adventures, and plenty of bravado). While the animation has a bit of a cheapo, digital look, you are won over by the light-hearted tone, the comedy, and the interactions between the boys (really, it's another team show, and in *sentai* formats, the relationships within the group provide much of the entertainment).

And, this being a Katsuhiro Otomo-inspired piece, there are many Otomoan motifs in *S.O.S.: Tokyo Metro Explorers*, such as fights using metal pipes, a big, military tank-on-the-loose scene, and an underground community of down-and-outs (who might easily be denizens of Neo-Tokyo in *Akira*).

In the *manga* of *S.O.S.: Tokyo Metro Explorers*,

there's a teenage youth with very Otomoan features
(long, bowl-shaped hair and square glasses); in the
animé, he's turned into an adult character, but retains
the familiar features of the young Otomo.

HIPIRA-KUN

Hipira-kun (2009) was animated by Sunrise, with
Otomo taking story credit. It was broadcast on N.H.K
at Christmas, 2009, dir.by Shinji Kimura. *Hipira-kun*
was a short (18m) film based on Otomo's children's
book (*Hipira-kun,* 2001), which he wrote with Shinji
Kimura drawing the art. Yumiko Kobayashi was
Hipira.

The animation of *Hipira-kun* was, like the
children's book, aimed at pre-teens (though with a
layer of knowing humour aimed at adults, in the
Disney model). Cuteness abounded – in every scene,
every chara design, every piece of business.

Stylistically, *Hipira-kun* employed *chibi*-style
digital animation in broad strokes, with bright
colours. In *animé* form, *Hipira-kun* is even more like
Tim Burton meets the *Addams Family* meets Universal
horror flicks of the Thirties (the title sequence features
a gradual move towards Hipira's town of vampires,
and has him wake up, like Bela Lugosi, in a coffin).

The *animé* of *Hipira-kun* expanded on the
children's book considerably, but retained the key
narrative beats. For ex, the town is much bigger (and
rather over-designed by the Sunrise team, drawing
on the ability of digital animation to jam visuals with
detail), many scenes were added (such as Hipira at
school, joshing with his chums, etc).

OTHER MOVIES

Some of Katsuhiro Otomo's early films are not easily available in the West, and are relatively unknown in his *œuvre.*

• Otomo-sensei provided the script for the sex comedy *Kôkô Erotopia: Akai seifuku* (= *High School Erotopia: Red Uniforms,* Shinichi Shiratori, 1979), a low budget 'pink film'. Shiratori co-wrote the script. The cast included: Jun Takahashi, Kanji Kume, Hiroshi Fujino, Etsuko Hara, Moeko Ezawa and Tayori Hinatsu. The plot of *High School Erotopia: Red Uniforms* is a porn version of that high school staple in *manga: hey kids, let's make a movie!* So the after-school film club decide they're gonna make a porn flick for their end-of-year project. A sort of sexed-up spin on the *Ichigo 100% manga* by Mizuki Kawashita.

• *Give Me a Gun Give Me Freedom* (a.k.a. *Give Us Guns,* a.k.a. *Freedom For Us = Jiyû o warera ni,* 1982) was wr. and dir. by Katsuhiro Otomo. Filmed in 16mm, it was partly based on *Liberty Is Ours (À nous la liberté,* René Clair, 1931). So it was in part a remake – of a movie regarded as an early sound era classic, a musical-comedy which explores economic depression and industrialization, themes which Otomo would address in *Akira* and *Steam-boy. Liberty Is Ours* also chimes with *Metropolis,* and influenced *Modern Times* (Charlie Chaplin, 1936).

02

WORLD APARTMENT
HORROR

WARUDO APATOMENTO
HORA

In 1991, Katsuhiro Otomo directed the live-action
movie *World Apartment Horror*. It was produced by
Yoshihiro Kato and Yasuhisa Kazama, scripted by
Otomo and Keiko Nobumoto from a story by Satoshi
Kon, Noboru Shinoda was DP, with art dir. by
Terumi Hosoishi. In the cast were Sabu (Hiroki
Tanaka – he went on to become a film director), Jazz
Cutz, Mohammed Abdul Sahib, Hiroshi Shimizu and
Hua Rong Weng.

World Apartment Horror is a curious, little-
known and seldom-discussed entry in the life and art
of Katsuhiro Otomo (in 1991, *Akira* was still over-
shadowing much of Otomo's career; it was released
in the West on video in 1991). And the much better-
known movie *Roujin Z* was released in 1991.

The production of *World Apartment Horror* was
based on an idea by one of Katsuhiro Otomo's

protegés, Satoshi Kon (one of his assistants on the *Akira manga*), who went on to become a superstar *animé* director: *Millennium Actress, Paprika, Paranoia Agent, Tokyo Godfathers,* etc. Kon is known for creating classy, intelligent and quirky *animé* which explore contemporary Japan and popular culture from a distinctive and individual perspective. Kon is highly influential in *animé* circles – many shows are Kon Lite, versions of Kon without Kon's genuinely idiosyncratic touches: *Serial Experiments Lain, Gantz, Elfen Lied, East of Eden, Hack/ Sign,* etc. However, sometimes it seemed that Kon found it tricky to find forms or material that suited his particular gifts (the same can be said of Stanley Kubrick, Donald Cammell, Andrei Tarkovsky and Orson Welles).

World Apartment Horror was co-written by Katsuhiro Otomo and the very wonderful Keiko Nobumoto (b. 1964), the chief writer of the sublime *Cowboy Bebop* series. Nobumoto was born in Hokkaido in North Japan, and has also written novels. Nobumoto was a protegé of Takao Koyama's writing school. Among Nobumoto's writing credits are *animé* such as *Macross Plus* (1995), *Wolf's Rain* (2003) and the enjoyable *Tokyo Godfathers*, a stunning 2003 *animé* comedy (written for Satoshi Kon), and live-action such as *Give Me Good Love, Nurse Call* and *LxIxVxE*.

□

Anyway, let's look at *World Apartment Horror*: it is set in the present day, in a built-up area of Japan: the setting – a run-down apartment block – automatically brings to mind Katsuhiro Otomo's many *manga* about living in down-at-heel apartments, and in particular, *Domu*, Otomo's first mega-hit as a *mangaka*. We have the same atmosphere of humanity in close proximity, of unease and anxiety, of seething resentments behind closed doors. *World Apartment Horror* might be seen as a live-action version of *Domu* and Otomo's many early comics which explored living in similar tenements.

The story – a *yakuza* (Ita) is sent to clear out the tenants of an apartment block – is not what *World Apartment Horror* is about. It's about the hothouse environment of humans living side by side and on top of each other; it's about the people at the edges of society, the workers, the have-nots, the people struggling to survive (key Otoman themes).

And an ethnic undercurrent is part of the mix of *World Apartment Horror*: many of the tenants are not Japanese, and are part of a group of mobile, overseas workers (they are all male, mainly in their 20s and 30s). Ita, being a nationalistic *yakuza,* seizes on this aspect of the tenants like a wolf and won't let go: he's like a guard dog sent in by his bosses to rout the whole place.

The way that Sabu (Hiroki Tanaka) plays Ita enhances the violence and resentment seething under the surface: if he had his way, no one would be allowed into Japan, and certainly not Chinese, Taiwanese or Koreans. (He mercilessly derides the tenants' attempts to speak Japanese, for instance).

As a character, Ita embodies a contemporary version of the nationalist attitude of the Japanese in early decades of the 20th century, when the isolationist ideology of the Edo period was revived. In *Akira*, the 'Great Tokyo Empire' are emissaries of the same ideology, which rejected 'foreign' influences, and foreigners themselves.

Racial stereotyping is all over *manga* (and *animé*): foreigners are often portrayed as foreign in a clichéd manner: Chinese and Korean characters, for instance, will have slanted eyes and buck teeth. Westerners are depicted as hairy hulks, altho' Japanese characters will be given Caucasian features. (Remember that only one per cent of the Japanese nation are from other territories: Japan remains very much an isolated island in that respect).

Ironically, the subtext of nationalism and racial intolerance in *World Apartment Horror* is shifted 180 degrees later – now Ita stands in between the tenants

THE ART OF KATSUHIRO OTOMO ❋ 250

and the *yakuza* and his brother; he has now come round to seeing them as fellow citizens, not as foreigners. The moral message of *World Apartment Horror* is the simple, liberal one of: 'let's all just get along with each other'.

☐

In *World Apartment Horror*, Ita tries all sorts of ways of dislodging the residents – loud noise, smoking them out, and even making love to his girlfriend in view of the central upstairs corridor (everybody comes out to watch). Everything bar assaulting them physically.

In the final act (of three acts), the situation escalates to Ita himself becoming possessed – by something in the building. An exorcist is called in to go to work; which he does, roping in the tenants to chant and prayer alongside him. (They, in turn, don't quite understand what's going on, and insist that they aren't religious).

World Apartment Horror is not a re-run of demonic possession narratives such as *Poltergeist, The Omen* or the mega-hit movie *The Exorcist. World Apartment Horror* is of the psychological kind: it's the effects of the mysterious forces on humans (on Ita and the tenants) that the film is concerned with, not the origins of the unrest.

The finale of *World Apartment Horror* is one of those all-hell-breaks-loose climaxes, similar to *Poltergeist, The Exorcist, Ghostbusters,* etc. We've got lightning flashes, thunder rumbles, loud noises, bright light and sudden darkness, people yelling, special effects and action erupting in several places.

The finale brings together all of the characters, and to make things more intense of course it's in the middle of a storm (like the endings of *Akira, Spriggan, Steam-boy*, etc).

Ita's *yakuza* brethren turn up (his brother wields a samurai sword – mandatory in any *yakuza* movie. Yes, in Nihon, the samurai of the Edo period became officers in the Army, or part of the Japan Self-Defence

Force, or *yakuza*). The brother is baying for blood, swinging the sword and roaring, launching himself at the damn foreigners still clinging onto the tenement.

☐

As a piece of filmmaking, *World Apartment Horror* is confident and polished:[16] it represents a career path that Otomo-sensei might've pursued – live-action movies, or live-action television. A man as talented as Otomo might've had a successful career directing high profile TV shows. But maintaining his interest after the pilot episode would be tricky – Otomo is the sort of artist who would likely bore of the factory-like schedules of television production. Live-action television also operates under the close scrutiny of many producers and department bosses, which might stifle an artist like Otomo. TV is a giant machine for churning out material, whereas Otomo has preferred the one-off approach – hand-made, personal, individual.

If it was anybody else, and not Katsuhiro Otomo, a producer might've looked at *World Apartment Horror* and immediately signed him up for a multi-picture deal, or put him to work on a much bigger budget production. *World Apartment Horror* might've been a stepping stone for Otomo to much bigger things in live-action cinema or television. Instead, Otomo opted to oversee movies like *Roujin Z* and *Memories*.

16 The cinematography is pretty dark and murky in the final act – something that television doesn't like.

03

ROUJIN Z

OLD MAN Z

Katsuhiro Otomo provided the screenplay and *mecha* designs for the wonderful, broad comedy of 1991, *Roujin Z* (= *Old Man Z*), produced by Another Push Pin Planning, the Television, Tokyo Theater, M.O.V.I.C., TV Asahi and Sony.[17] Executive producers were: Masayoshi Yoshida, Shugo Matsuo, Tsuguhiko Kadokawa and Yutaka Takahashi. Directed by Hiroyuki Kitakubo. Other designers on *Roujin Z* included character designer Hisashi Eguchi,[18] Satoshi Kon (Otomo's regular collaborator), and Mituso Iso. Fumi Iida was animation director. The music was by Bun Itakura. The *seiyu* included: Shinji Ogawa, Chie Satou, Chisa Yokoyama, Hikojiro Matsumu, Masa Saito, Kouji Tsujitani and Rica Matsumoto.

The central relationship in *Roujin Z* was between the aged invalid Kijuro Takazawa and his young

17 There is a depressing amount of product placement of Japanese electronics giant Sony in *Roujin Z*.
18 Hisashi Eguchi's credits include *Perfect Blue, Spriggan, Steam-Boy, Ghost In the Shell, Naruto* and *Dragon Ball Z*.

nurse, Haruko.[19] Also involved was the group of young friends surrounding Haruko (a much nicer bunch that the biker gang in *Akira*), including goofy, wimpy, possible boyfriend (to Haruko), Maeda,[20] nerdy, concerned Nobuko, and feisty, sexy, ginger-haired Norie, plus a coterie of old coots in the hospital where Haruko works who band together to help her out.

Many of Katsuhiro Otomo's concerns were to the fore again in *Roujin Z* – technology, the misuse of technology by the military (in this case, linked to the North American war machine at the Pentagon),[21] how technology is fought over (here, between Japan's medical profession and the military), Japan's ageing population, and the conflicts between humans and technology.

Roujin Z sends up institutions like the health service, medicine,[22] the military, the police and the government. (The issue of Japan's ageing population has been taken up in many *animé* – by the films of Katsuhiro Otomo's *protegé* Satoshi Kon, for example, and *Ghost In the Shell: Stand Alone Complex*).

And you can see Katsuhiro Otomo's influence on the designs of the characters (Haruko and her chums have the familiar round, Otomoan eyes[23]), and the penchant for group scenes where every individual is animated independently (*Roujin Z* is another ensemble piece).

The action gets bigger and wilder in *Roujin Z*, escalating from Takazawa in the hospital bed escaping from the hospital (aided by the four youths), to

19 Which may have influenced *Real Drive*, the 2008 TV series inspired by Masamune Shirow.

20 I wonder if the name Maeda is a joke about Toshio Maeda, the well-known erotic *manga* artist, whose *Legend of the Overfiend* was at the time of *Roujin Z* (1991) very popular. However, there are plenty of Maedas in Japan!

21 *Roujin Z* thus yet again explores the uneasy political and military relationship between Japan and the U.S.A.

22 Terada, from the Ministry of Public Welfare, has an over-zealous reliance on modern science to aid Japan's ageing population, as if a new-fangled apparatus like a mechanized hospital bed can replace a carer.

23 With some Satoshi Kon in there.

outstanding confrontations on the streets and in a shopping mall,[24] to the helicopter chase, to the road block outside the tunnel, to the duels between the hospital bed and the military's tank (it's not an Otomo script unless there's a scene with a tank!), and to the finale on the road next to the beach.

Katsuhiro Otomo has scripted tons of action in *Roujin Z*, with Kijuro Takazawa and his robotic bed facing off against the police with bulldozers, or smashing thru buildings (including a *pachinko* parlour, in the shopping mall sequence), or clambering along a monorail (in a spectacular helicopter-and-monorail chase), and in the climax going head-to-head with the combat versions of the super-computer installed in the bed (you could intercut the climactic scenes from *Roujin Z* with *Akira* and not know the difference. Except that Haruko is a much sweeter and kinder heroine than the heroes in *Akira* (she recalls *Akira*'s Kei, including in her design), and *Roujin Z* is a send-up of *Akira*.

In *Roujin Z*, the new technological marvel of the hospital bed that looks after Kijuro Takazawa automatically runs amok, its computer is taken over by Kijuro's dead wife, Haru, and it becomes essentially another mobile power suit (but this time with a wrinkly, old man inside it, who's barely conscious for much of the movie, a great joke on the usual pilots of mobile suits, who're gung-ho, pretty boy youths, or attractive, young women like Deunan Knute in *Appleseed* or Asuka in *Evangelion*).

Haruko is an endearing heroine, kind and caring, putting others before herself first, plucky, and brave: Haruko is the heart of the 1991 movie, as Kaneda and Kei were the heart of *Akira*, and Ray Steam was the heart of *Steam-boy*. Haruko transcends being a function of the plot, and manages to stand out from the big action sequences.

It is Haruko's concern for Takazawa, for

---

24 This scene recalls a beat in the *Akira manga*, where Kaneda & co. are in a tank.

instance, that is crucial to the film's narrative set-up in the first act. Halfway through act one, for instance – in the usual place for a dramatic turning point – there is a distress call from Takazawa to Haruko, which pops up on the computers in the hospital. This is the inciting incident in *Roujin Z*, and Haruko responds just like a hero: she answers the call with action, and soon she and her chums are busting into the facility at night which houses Takazawa in his robot bed. (Act one is rather over-written in the over-long scene where the fancy hospital bed is presented to the press. Here Takashi Terada has a very lengthy speech which explains everything about the hospital bed. Yes, the audience does need to know some of this – such as the ability of the machine to update itself automatically – because it plays into the rest of the film. But not as much as this!).[25]

In *Roujin Z*, Haru assumes a powerful motherly role for Takazawa, as Antonia Levi explains in *Samurai From Outer Space*:

> she is not only strong but gentle, patient, and self-sacrificing in her misguided attempt to fulfil her dying, confused husband's wish to spend a day with her on the beach at Kamakura. (119)

The humorous elements in Katsuhiro Otomo's cinema are often overlooked (there are even more in his *manga*), because the screen is often packed with action, amazing visuals, explosions and fetishized hardware. But comedy is definitely one of Otomo's chief concerns, and it's even present in *Akira*, in amongst the psychic warfare and buildings being blown to bits.

In *Roujin Z*, the humour is broad and sometimes coarse (bed-wetting, defecation, erections, vomiting, boob jokes and sneaking looks up girls' skirts), but also sweet and emotional. The core of it all is Nurse Haruko's loving concern for the aged Kijuro (like a

25 The traitor in the midst, Yoshihiko Hasegawa, has sold out to the Yanks (there's always one in Japanese stories of this kind).

daughter for a father), and the affection that he shares with his dead wife Haru. Without that emotion at the core, *Roujin Z* might fly off into a series of farcical effects and scenes.[26] (There are gratuitous scenes featuring views up the skirts of young women in the first minutes of *Roujin Z* (Haruko works in a restaurant where the waitresses wear red mini-skirts), Haruko is eroticized, one of the girls presses her breasts into Takazawa's face, and Norie is seen partially naked).

As many comedians and writers of screen comedy have stressed (such as Mel Brooks), if there isn't an emotional foundation for the comedy, it won't work. The escalation of mayhem from modest beginnings to something epic in *Roujin Z*, involving helicopters, tanks, police and officials, is a format that Katsuhiro Otomo uses elsewhere – in the *Stink Bomb* episode in *Memories*, for instance (which *Roujin Z* resembles – a guy just wants to travel to Tokyo, or to go to the beach).

But the comedy doesn't detract from *Roujin Z* having plenty of observations to make about life in contemporary Japan: indeed, the comedy allows the filmmakers to slip all sorts of political statements past the audience. Yet *Roujin Z* never feels like you're being preached to, because the political material comes directly out of the narrative and the characters, and the way that the 1991 movie pulls the audience along, allowing them to enjoy this explosive, hi-tech romp (*Roujin Z* essentially boils down to a road movie – with Takazawa in the hospital bed and Haru in the computer as the fugitives trying to reach Shangri-La, while the authorities do their darnedest to stop them, and Haruko tries to mediate and intervene).

There is plenty of social observation in *Roujin Z*, too: the group of old guys in the ward in the hospital are wonderfully depicted (they hack into the super-

26 Even the Ministry of Public Welfare representative, Terada, recognizes the value of familial relations.

computer[27] and help Haruko remotely, as Haru and Kijuro and the hospital bed head to the beach). Katsuhiro Otomo is great at portraying older characters, the sort that usually get shunted to one side when the story hots up and the action begins. True, the old coots haven't left their hospital ward, but they are shown having a great time in fooling the military and getting their own back against the Japanese government (and they directly affect the narrative a number of times – such as connecting Haruko to Takazawa-san initially, so that she is able to talk to him via the computer. Cleverly, Haruko speaks to Takazawa in the voice of his dead wife Haru,[28] and soon the super-computer controlling the hospital bed takes on Haru's voice, and her person-ality. Later, the old guys tell Haruko how to nullify the military's robot).

The threesome of kids centred around Haruko (comprising two girls and one guy), fellow workers/ volunteers at the hospital, is also wittily observed – in one scene they get drunk at a karaoke bar (a regular occurrence in *manga* and *animé*), with the animators adding all sorts of comic gags (after all, animators know bars very well!). Young masculinity is satirized as the young women berate Maeda for being a wimp and not being a man (in the end, it's Norie who dates Maeda, although Maeda is still trying to win over Haruko by playing the knight in shining armour, with disastrous results – as he drives a van thru the tunnel, and also launches himself at the cops on a bike in order to save Haruko from being arrested. It doesn't work, and he ends up vomiting. In this film, the girls are *way* ahead of the guys!).

The finale ends as expected – *Roujin Z*, for all its black humour, is a light-hearted comedy with a soft centre. The hospital bed, now being run by the spirit

---

27 They've already hacked into the computer of the Tyrell corporation (another reference to *Blade Runner*).
28 It's contrived, but more appealing filmically than words typed out on a computer screen.

of Haru (kindly but firmly), goes up against the Z-001 robot/ tank, which Yoshihiko Hasegawa has wheeled in to stop the hospital bed (at a road block outside a hill tunnel, recalling a similar scene in *Stink Bomb* in *Memories*). So the filmmakers get to stage a favourite *animé* moment: two robots beating the hell out of each other. That there's an old man at the centre, barely conscious, is a great joke on the usual young, gung-ho, hotshot pilots of mobile suits in *manga* and *animé*.

Our heroine, Haruko, is also given several things to do in the finale of *Old Man Z* – one is to pursue the hospital bed into the tunnel, where the fight continues (with an aircraft, rendered in sepia tones), another is to help rescue Takazawa from the bed and get him into the ambulance, and another is to stop the Z-001 taking over the hospital bed by crunching its brain with an oxygen tank (which then of course explodes). Meanwhile, Yoshihiko Hasegawa is trying to stop Haruko, chasing her. (An additional complication has the ambulance containing Terada and Takazawa collapsing[29]). Meanwhile, the old guys back at the hospital are helping by operating the hospital bed remotely. The finale of *Roujin Z* is thus stuffed with as many action beats, countdowns and set-backs as a blockbuster action movie, tho' played for out-size comedy.

In the destruction of both the Z-001 and the hospital bed, the brain, containing Haru (in a heating unit), bounces onto the beach. Terada carries old man Takazawa onto the beach, and we have our Happy Ending, where the old man and his dead wife get to go to the beach for the last time.

Haru says that Takazawa will be joining her (in death) soon. But not yet – cries Haruko – no, because the filmmakers add a short, twist coda (reminiscent of the twist endings of Otomo's early gag *manga*), where Haru returns one more time in robotic form. Now, she's commandeered a giant, stone statue of the

---

29 Maeda continues to be useless, after driving the ambulance – he's caught up in a mass of tentacles (like the author of *Overfiend*).

Buddha,[30] which stomps into the hospital grounds like Godzilla, providing our comic ending (the characters take their curtain call gawping at the statue and praying).[31]

30 A snapshot showed the couple on vacation visiting a Buddha statue in China.
31 Other plot strands are tied up – such as the arrest of Hasegawa, the old coots celebrating, Terada facing the press, etc.

04

MEMORIES

KANOJO NO OMOIDE

Memories (1995) is a top-of-the-line, 100 per cent
animé masterpiece. It is a must-see in animation.
Memories was overseen by Katsuhiro Otomo (he
receives a 'Katsuhiro Otomo Presents' credit), and
was based on three of his *manga* stories (remember
that the director is often billed above the voice actors
or other collaborators in Japanese animation). Otomo
also wrote the scripts, alongside regular collaborator
Satoshi Kon.

The three segments in *Memories* were *Magnetic
Rose*, directed by Koji Morimoto (from Katsuhiro
Otomo's 1980 *manga*, 32 pages long), *Stink Bomb*,
directed by Tensai Okamura[32] and *Cannon Fodder*,
helmed by Katsuhiro Otomo.

Madhouse and Studio 4°C produced the animat-
ion (the links between Madhouse and Katsuhiro
Otomo include *Harmageddon* and *Metropolis*), with
Bandai Visual, Kodansha and Shochiku handling

32 Tensai Okamura directed *Wolf's Rain, Medabots, Naruto* and
Kikaider. Okamura's credits include *Samurai Champloo, Spriggan,
Fullmetal Alchemist, Jin-Roh, Ghost In the Shell, Evangelion, Ninja
Scroll, Wings of Honneamise,* and *Cowboy Bebop.*

production, Shigeru Watanabe (one of Otomo's regular producers),[33] Makoto Yamashina, Shoji Yakigaya, Teruo Miyahara and Otomo executive produced, along with Atsushi Sugita, Eiko Tanaka, Fumio Samejima, Hiroaki Inoue and Yoshimasa Mizu as producers, Toho distributed (in Japan) and Sony (in the U.S.A.), the animator director was Yoshitaki Kawajiri, designers included Toshiyuki Inoue, Takashi Watanabe, Hirotsuge Kawasaki and Hidekazu Ohara, sound producer was Masakatsu Aida, sound director was Sadayoshi Fujino, sound production by Tetsuo Ono, editing by Takeshi Seyama, and music[34] was by Takuya Ishino,[35] Jun Miyake (*Stink Bomb*), Hiroyuki Nagashima (*Cannon Fodder*) and *animé* super-composer Yoko Kanno (for *Magnetic Rose*). Many in the *Memories* team (one of the finest crews ever in *animé*) had worked with Otomo on *Akira*.[36] Released Dec 23, 1995. 113 minutes.

Originally planned as a video project, *Memories* evolved over time into a theatrical release (the budget and schedule subsequently expanded). The title came from the first episode, *Kanojo no Omoide = Her Memories* (this was subsequently titled *Magnetic Rose*). The other two stories were *Stink Bomb* (*Saishu-heiki*) and *Cannon Fodder* (*Taiho no Machi*).

Generously, Katsuhiro Otomo allowed the *Magnetic Rose* episode to go first (the obvious sequencing of the movie would have either the third or second parts going first, with *Magnetic Rose* providing the Big Finale. Although, each of the three movies is pretty spectacular).

MAGNETIC ROSE.

Magnetic Rose is an *animé* masterpiece, 43 or so minutes of pure genius. The opulence of the animation

---

33 And a key producer in the *Ghost In the Shell* franchise.
34 Music producers were Masao Itou and Shiro Sasaki.
35 Ishino composed the theme music 'In Her Memory'.
36 The DVD release of *Memories* includes an insightful video documentary about the making of the movie.

and imagery is rarely equalled in filmmaking, West
or East. The filmmakers have thrown *everything* into
the mix, and it works. This is hyper-dense, mega-
layered animation, where every cut is crammed with
incident, movement, colour, texture, light, shadow,
visual effects and pure imagination.

'Running only forty-five minutes, it can still be
compared with the greatest anime productions in
every single aspect from animation to storyline.'
(Anime Academy). 'A science fiction marvel' (Mark
McPherson, Homemademech). 'One of the triumphs of
anime', as J. Clements and H. McCarthy put it (2006,
409).

Magnetic Rose like watching an entire history of
animation (like the *Pierrot le Fou* episode in *Cowboy
Bebop*). It contains everything, and then some.

On the basis of *Magnetic Rose* alone, 36 year-old
Koji Morimoto enters the highest echelons of *animé*
directors (another of Morimoto's finest moments was
the super-spectacular concert sequences in*Macross
Plus*).[37]

Koji Morimoto (b. 1959, Wakayama Prefecture)
studied at Osaka School of Design, and first worked
on animations such as *Tomorrow's Joe*, *Dirty Pair,
Macross*, *Space Adventure Cobra*, and *Neo-Tokyo*. Later
works included *Macross Plus*, *Fly Peek* and *Genius
Party Beyond*. He directed segments of *Robot Carnival*
and *The Animatrix* (2002), and short films such as
Eternal Family and *Noiseman* (both 1997). Morimoto
was one of the founders of Studio 4°C in 1986 along
with Yoshiharu Sato and Eiko Tanaka (Studio 4°C
co-produced *Steam-boy* and *Spriggan*). Morimoto has
also made pop promos (for the Bluetones, Utada

37 The colossal pop concert at the beginning of the second O.A.V. is
one of the stand-out sequences in*Macross Plus* – and in all *animé* –
with the filmmakers letting rip with wild, trippy visuals. The concert
footage in *Macross Plus* is extraordinary – and some of the most
impressive aspects of it is the way that the filmmakers have portrayed the audience. For the pop concert alone, *Macross Plus* is worth
the price of admission. It really is a stand-out sequence that can hold
its own with any of the celebrated sequences in animation – in Japan
or anywhere. The invention, the colours, the use of silhouettes and
black, the mickey mousing with the music – it's marvellous.

Hikaru and Ishii Ken).

The *animé* of *Memories* expanded the *manga* by the maestro to an enormous degree, altho' it retained most of the elements of the story: the visit to the rose-shaped vessel, the luxurious, olde worlde interior, the approaching magnetic storm, the music on the comm-unications link (tho' it's Glenn Miller not opera – opera is a *much* better choice), the talk about pay, the necessity of answering a distress signal, the joshing between the crew (tho' the personalities were changed, and there's no one like Heintz among the crew), and the cadaver of the owner in a four-poster bed.

Magnetic Rose is basically a haunted house or ghost ship scenario, like something out of a TV sci-fi or horror show from the 1960s (*Twilight Zone*, *Outer Limits* or *Star Trek*), at the level of the premise of the outer shell of its narrative.

A more literary comparison would be ghost stories going back to Edgar Allan Poe and E.T.A. Hoffmann.[38] Is it that good? Oh yes (and you can imagine Poe or Hoffmann or Novalis or Mary *Frankenstein* Shelley loving *Magnetic Rose*).

Plot-wise, *Magnetic Rose* is fairly simple (or at least, the initial set-up is): a bunch of space salvagers heading home[39] after their shift's done intercept an S.O.S. call and investigate, finding more than the loot they bargained for.[40] The colossal spaceship, big as an asteroid (with a giant magnetic storm approaching),

38 Brian Camp notes the echoes of *Solaris* (Stanislav Lem) and *The Martian Chronicles* (Ray Bradbury) in "Magnetic Rose" (212). Stanislav Lem's 1961 book was the story of a man who can't escape his past, who regrets what he's done, and wants to relive his life in order to make amends for it. The major motif is the implacable but conscious and intelligent planet, with its vast sea which produces 'mimoids', solid phantasms. The dichotomies in *Solaris* are between the present and the past, the past as it really was and the past as one'd like it to be, the human and non-human, age and youth, reality and wishes/ dreams, inside the station and outside, the individ-ual's unconscious and the Ocean, Earth and Solaris.

39 The date for the events is October 12, 2092 – the 600th annivers-ary of Christopher Columbus.

40 The filmmakers explained in the 'making of' documentary that the script wasn't quite full enough at first, and the characters and plot needed to be fleshed out.

is in the shape of an enormous, red rose, and is now the mausoleum of an opera diva, Eva Friedel (clearly drawing on Maria Callas). Now dead, the singer's life comes alive via automata, robots, holograms, and all sorts of tricks and hallucinations.

Maria Callas (1923-77, born and raised in the U.S.A., but of Greek descent), was a true superstar, blessed with a divine voice. On stage, she out-shone (and out-sang) everybody else. She was born in Gotham (Dec 2, 1923), went to Greece aged 13 to study at the Athens Conservatory (her early studies and career were all in Europe). She debuted in Italia in 1947, as Gioconda (in Verona), and made her professional debut in 1941 in Athens, in Giacomo Puccini's *Tosca*. Callas appeared at La Scala, Covent Garden, the Met in New York, Chicago, etc, playing roles such as Lady Macbeth, Aida, Tosca, Imogene, Elvira, Amina, Isolde, Brunhilde, Lucia, Anna Bolena and Violetta (in works by Verdi, Spontini, Wagner, Donizetti, Bellini, etc). The word 'diva' (and 'prima donna') might've been invented for Callas.

Maria Callas was very well-known – not least as a celebrity, pursued by *paparazzi* (she had an affair, for instance, with Aristotle Onassis, and married G.B. Meneghini, an Italian industrialist, in 1949).

Heintz Beckner and Miguel enter the seemingly deserted spacecraft, while their buddies Ivanov (the tech and communications guy) and Aoshima (their burly, bearded boss and pilot), stay on board their *Corona* ship and monitor their progress.

It's fairy tale time, too – it's Sleeping Beauty and her castle under a spell, with the astronauts as the heroic princes come to wake her up (which they do). And it's *Bluebeard*, and *Dracula*, and every haunted house in cinema (Susan Napier has compared the scenario in *Magnetic Rose* to *Rebecca*, with its Manderley manor house ruled over by Mrs Danvers in the Daphne du Maurier story [2006, 27]).

Magnetic Rose's opening scenes portray the salvagers at work, and also include issues which will play into the second part, set inside the *Magnetic Rose* spaceship. One is that Heintz, the rather buttoned-up and terse hero, has a daughter (we see her picture in his wallet). The other is that Miguel is a guy who likes women and has a couple of girlfriends waiting for him back home (notice how the narcissistic Miguel floats around the salvage vessel naked but for his underwear).

The opening scenes in *Magnetic Rose* are standard science fiction, with recognizable types among the crew. But the filmmaking is anything but ordinary: if *Magnetic Rose* was simply a routine sci-fi story, set entirely on the salvage vessel, it would still be marvellous (the filmmakers play inventively with weightlessness and which-way-is-up in outer space).

What's so impressive is the number of levels that *Magnetic Rose* is operating on, and the sheer joy of watching it. The lavishness of the visuals swamps the viewer: the filmmakers and designers have conjured up a vast Xanadu out of *Citizen Kane*, a Dracula's or Bluebeard's Castle, the palace of enchanted princesses of fairy tales, and the mansions of millionaires with too much time and money on their hands. It's European opulence in the French and Italian, 18th century mode, the kind of imagery that Jean Cocteau, Luchino Visconti, Mickey Powell and Walerian Borowczyk loved to explore in cinema.

And it's also an Opera Theme Park, a diva's private Disneyland, a Las Vegas for classical music buffs, with robots, automata, holograms, video screens and other technology bringing the theme park to life (it's a theme park that can operate for decades after everyone's left). And, like a theme park, the spaceship features several theatres, with 3-D recreations of events from the past, some of them presided over by animatronic or holographic characters.

All of this is intensely *Japanese* – *animé* and *manga* adore to recreate life as a theme park,[41] and to evoke mazes within labyrinths within puzzles within

---

41 The number one date in *manga* is a theme park.

entertainment complexes.

Pillars in scarlet marble, ornate chandeliers, candelabra, huge drapes, a stage set, an enormous painting (and many Old Master canvases), a grand piano in a Greek temple (which plays music from dripping oil), an Italian garden, an opera house (the first set to be encountered), carpeted corridors, four poster beds, chaise longues – and then more chandeliers, candelabra, statuary... The designers (who included Toshiyuki Inoue, Takashi Watanabe, Hirotsuge Kawasaki and Hidekazu Ohara), have concocted a fantastically over-ripe setting inside the spaceship. (It draws on Baroque, Rococo, 18th and 19th century art, furnishings and architecture, chiefly from Europe).

From the visuals and designs in *Memories*, one moves onto the powerful imaginations at work in the animation: the filmmakers have really let themselves rip: *Magnetic Rose* is not only packed with enough visual and thematic material for ten movies, it is also a visual effects extravaganza. As with *Akira*, director Koji Morimoto and his team have stuffed tricks and effects into every corner of *Magnetic Rose*. It really is breathtakingly imaginative cinema. (The past for instance is evoked in several types of reality and memory).

As the *Magnetic Rose* episode develops and the dramatic countdown of the magnetic storm accelerates, the scenes become thick with swirling, spinning images and colours, and startling metamorphoses (the filmmakers conjure numerous striking dissolves and superimpositions, layering the past onto the present – the glowing, flamboyant past which becomes decayed and dusty in the present. It seems that each transition employs a different technique). There is a layering to the visuals, too, with multiple planes that mesh together, sometimes one fading away, to reveal something decayed and broken underneath. This movie has been worked over and over, with more and more layers being added to it.

In your usual ancient civilization story, there might be only one transition from the past to the present (showing Ancient Rome as it was, say, and moving into the present tense). In *Magnetic Rose*, the present is continually being subverted by the past (and vice versa). This is all beautifully worked out visually and thru the staging.

There are scenes in *Magnetic Rose* that simply overwhelm the viewer – like the moment when Miguel moves up to the grand piano (which magic-ally plays a soft, plangent tune on broken keys, from oil dripping above); he touches the keyboard, and the camera moves thru rapid 360° moves, and the decay-ing basement flooded with oil transmutes into a beautiful garden in full Summer (with richly satur-ated colours). Miguel is now dressed as Carlo Rambaldi,[42] and Eva Friedel swoops in from screen right to kiss him passionately on the lips. (Flowers – in particular, red roses – are everywhere in *Magnetic Rose* – even floating inside Heintz's helmet, in the final shot, as he breathes his last breath).[43]

The use of subjective camerawork is very fine in *Magnetic Rose*, as we see many of the rooms in the spaceship explored from the p.o.v. of Heintz or Miguel. The mobile shots, filmed continuously without cuts, are a hallmark of Katsuhiro Otomo's cinema. Screens, too, feature prominently, as the film cuts back and forth between the *Corona* ship nearby and the *Magnetic Rose* (and the video monitors which Aoshima watches carefully, a movie within a movie). As the magnetic storm closes in, the images become more degraded and shakier.

Inside the spaceship, Heintz Beckner is swept back to his family home, with his wife and daughter, and his guilt and agony over seeming to abandon them for months on end (Emily's death is an exagger-ation of the guilt and yearning that Heintz already

---

42 Is the name Carlo Rambaldi an allusion to the famous film magician who designed the puppets of E.T., the 1976 King Kong, the worms in *Dune* and the aliens in *Close Encounters of the Third Kind*? 43 There is always going to be a Last Breath.

experiences. The child's demise is kept ambiguous). The filmmakers magically intertwine the present tense of the spacecraft and the idealized past – they have the diva Eva replacing Heintz's wife, for instance. But Eva Friedel is a far sterner incarnation of Heintz's wife: she is Eva, not Heintz's wife. She is accusing, unforgiving. The unreality of the scene in *Magnetic Rose* is marvellous: Heintz's wooden house materializes inside the spaceship, and the hues darken to dark browns out of Gothic romances, lit with German Expressionist side lighting and shadows, like a scene from 1927's *Sunrise* (to contrast with the 'real' memories that Heintz has of being with his wife and daughter back on Earth, which're in full colour). The topic of conversation at the initially idyllic table scene swiftly hits the crux of the matter: Heintz as the absent father and husband.

Heintz Beckner is doomed to replay his guilt not only over Emily's death (or her imagined death – same thing in this movie), but of being away from home so much. *Magnetic Rose* conjures numerous tricks, playing with perception and reality (which's one of co-writer Satoshi Kon's beloved themes – it's in all of his *animé*). So Emily falls from the roof repeatedly, but becomes an animatronic figure, and then semi-transparent, a hologram that Heintz can't hug; then she's a paper puppet that crumbles thru age. Eva takes the place of Heintz's wife, accusing and implacable; Heintz fires a gun at her, she becomes both a hologram and an animatronic creature underneath.

On the set, now on a stage in a small theatre (in another run through Heintz's former life), Heintz's wife, daughter, the table and everything else (from the kitchen scene) is now nothing but papery, grey dust, as if the humans figures become plants that withered to ash, that crumble at the slightest touch. (Otomo has explored this notion several times, of the frozen, memorialized past, and how it haunts the present, and how the present can never break with the past.

The protagonist of his *Mother Sarah* comic, for ex, is haunted by the death of her children).

Meanwhile, the vain womanizer Miguel finds himself cast in the role of Eva's dead lover Carlo Rambaldi (who jilted her, and whom she may have murdered). Here Eva becomes a *femme fatale*, a demonic presence (recalling late 19th century, *fin-de-siècle* culture which depicted women in their negative aspects as demons, sphinxes or vampires). Miguel will never escape – because his desires have doomed him. In *Magnetic Rose*, no one can escape what they desire. And the desires portrayed in *Magnetic Rose* – for sex/ romantic love and for family – are two of the strongest in human life.

Among the numerous impressive sequences in *Magnetic Rose* was the montage exploring the opera singer's life – snippets of video, of live performances, of TV chat shows, newspaper articles, magazine photographs, etc, which were seen on the monitors and computers in the salvaging ship. (The montage recalled the famous 'News On the March' scene in *Citizen Kane*, an oft-copied sequence).

The thematic layers of *Magnetic Rose* are striking, too, with poignant explorations of time and memory, of recreating the past, or keeping the past alive long beyond its use-by date. Everything in the *Magnetic Rose* spaceship is an extension of Eva Friedel and her life: the spaceship becomes filled with her memories. Eva has god-like powers: the memories and desires of the visitors become interpreted thru *her* life: she colonizes their lives, so that even their memories aren't their own. Or she is a vampire, absorbing them. (The cut, late in the piece, to the corpse of Eva on her deluxe bed, is really startling and really creepy: the skull, the sunken eye sockets, the dry, grey hair: this is the End of Everything in life, when you become naught but a skeleton and a skull). But as the two spacemen enter the vessel, they also interact with the ship, so it takes on their pasts, too.

☐

Yet another layer of *Magnetic Rose* is the music: this is a masterpiece of music editing, music arrangement, music selection, and music production. The music is handled with a *genuine* sensitivity towards its function within the piece. This is rare. Even the greatest film composers have had their work cut up into itty bits, or awkwardly repeated, or plastered everywhere in movies and television. Music spotting (placement) and editing can be so clumsy, it not only harms the music (treating it as just another effect), it damages the movie or TV show, too.

As it's all about an opera singer, of course there is plenty of opera in *Magnetic Rose*: *Madame Butterfly* (1904) and *Tosca* (1900) by Giacomo Puccini, for example. But Yoko Kanno and Hajime Mizoguchi also scored *Magnetic Rose* (with music production by Victor Entertainment), adding unexpected music cues as well as more obvious ghost story cues (for instance, Kanno & co. deliver a saxophone solo on top of a choir, very reminiscent of Jan Gabarek's work, in the opening scenes). And Puccini's opera music is also treated electronically, and skewed, so the familiar refrains come out muffled or echoey.[44] It's very effective. There is also music box music (*animé* adores music boxes!), harp music (for the first, shimmering reveal of the opera house set), grand, orchestral themes in the 19th century mode, and eerie piano cues. *Magnetic Rose* has one of the great scores in *animé*.

Yoko Kanno (b. March 19, 1964, Miyagi, Japan) is a superstar of *animé*. Make no mistake, Kanno may look (and sound) like a little pixie, but she is one of the great talents of film music, the equal not only of *any* of the great composers for the screen thru cinema history, but also most contemporary classical and new music composers.

For Helen McCarthy, writing in *500 Essential Anime Movies*, Yoko Kanno 'is the best composer working in anime today' (18). She might well be:

---

44 The S.O.S. message to the salvage ship contains snatches of *Madame Butterfly*.

simply on the basis of two TV series, *Cowboy Bebop* and *Ghost In the Shell: Stand Alone Complex,* Kanno is up there with the finest. But she has also composed soundtracks to *animé* TV and movies such as *Escaflowne, Macross Plus, Record of Lodoss War, Wolf's Rain, Gundam, Earth Maiden Arjuna, Genesis of Aquarion, Sakamichi no Apollon* and *Brain Powerd.* Kanno also produced her own albums, as well as composed and arranged songs for other artists, wrote for television, for movies, and made music for video games.[45] Have a look at Kanno's CV: it's hugely impressive (how Kanno finds time to sleep in the midst of producing all that music, arrangements, and lyrics is incredible. And it's the *quality,* so high, as well as the sheer volume of scoring).

The sound mixing and production is state of the art in *Memories,* too – much greater care was taken over the soundtrack than your average television show (sound production was by Tetsuo Ono, sound producer was Masakatsu Aida, and sound director was Sadayoshi Fujino). A good of attention was paid, for instance, to the physical and emotional context of the sounds in *Magnetic Rose*: the sound is helping to tell the multi-layered story, which evokes several types of scene in the past and the present.

❑

Critics have noted the affinities of *Magnetic Rose* with *2001: A Space Odyssey* and *Solaris* (Andrei Tarkovsky, 1972)[46] – and of course there's *Alien* and *Blade Runner* in there (as ever in Japanese animation, and especially science fiction *animé*). Other obvious reference points include *Citizen Kane, Metropolis, La*

---

45 Yoko Kanno's other film soundtracks include: *Tokyo: Sora, Mizu no onna, Say Hello!, Surely Someday, Honey and Clover, Asalto, Su-ki-da* and *Elegant World (The Show Must Go On).* Her TV work includes: *Chichi ni Kanaderu Merodi, Camouflage, Kaze ni Mai Agaru Vinyl Sheet* and *Mayonaka Betsu no Kao (The Other Side of Midnight).* Yoko Kanno has composed and arranged music for numerous Japanese pop and rock acts, including: Maya Sakamoto, Akino Arai, Kyoko Koizumi, Miki Imai, Akino Arai, Chiyono Yoshino, Crystal Kay and Kyoko Endo.

46 The haunted-by-the-past theme while in deep space recalls *Solaris,* which also has long-lost lovers returning to spook the hero.

Belle et La Bête (Jean Cocteau, 1946), *The Leopard* (Luchino Visconti, 1963), and the Edgar Allan Poe adaptations produced by Roger Corman. And also the whole of the Gothic and Romantic literary movement, where the concept of the*unheimlich* (the uncanny) is venerated.

It's one of those horror or ghost story scenarios where the visitors see aspects of themselves and their lives coming alive in a disturbing and creepy manner (for Heintz, it's his family life and the death of his young daughter Emily, for Miguel, it is *les femmes*).

Magnetic Rose is also about desire leading to death, about how desires can damn you, about the dangers of nostalgia, hanging onto the past, and about escaping desire. In this story, desire is *not* what you want, whether it's Miguel's desire for Eva, for Heintz's desire for his dead daughter, or Eva's desire for a past that's dead and gone (like she is herself).

Rarely in cinema have those Big Themes been tied to such grandiose visuals in such a convincing and poetic manner. Comparisons with *bona fide* classics from the history of cinema such as *Citizen Kane* or *La Belle et La Bête* or *Vertigo* or *Sunrise* are not over-the-top:*Memories* really is that good.

It all collapses: everything falls to pieces: *Magnetic Rose* is a movie where everybody dies,[47] and yet the ending is completely satisfying: the magnetic storm closes in (with some brilliantly achieved visual effects – now every instrument on the *Corona* ship is fizzling with arcing, electrical discharges). Back on the salvage vessel, boss Aoshima and Ivanov are struggling to stay free of the storm. Eventually, they lose contact with Miguel and Heintz. In desperation, they fire a cannon at the*Magnetic Rose* spaceship, which blows a hole in it, but they still can't fly free; their ship is torn to pieces (by debris – achieved in long shot).

In the maelstrom, as the *Magnetic Rose* ship is ripped apart inside, Heintz Beckner is sucked out

47 Altho' there is a suggestion that Miguel possibly isn't dead.

with the air into open space (along with some of Eva's former victims). There are some rose petals floating in his helmet in the final image of the 1995 movie, as he drifts in space, his oxygen running out. (Yet, incredibly, the *Magnetic Rose* vessel survives – a final pull-up shot reveals its shape (in a dissolve from a rose) to be rose-shaped – taken from a double-pager in the *Memories manga*).

How can you follow that? You can't! Yet there are two more segments in *Memories*, each one exceptional, to come!

✻

STINK BOMB.

The middle episode of *Memories*, *Stink Bomb* (*Saishu-heiki*), directed by Tensai Okamura, was a comic extravaganza based on a single gag: a hapless, average salaryman who's been infected by a military experiment (which makes him emit a caustic stink), becomes an unstoppable force. He's Fart Man in this send-up of disaster movies, monster movies, and superhero movies: instead of Godzilla bestriding Tokyo, we have a skinny dweeb on a bicycle.

Much of the fun of *Stink Bomb* derived from the filmmakers piling on scenes that topped the ones before, as the whole of the Japan Self Defence Force is unleashed, yet remains completely unable to stop a guy on a scooter from making his way to Tokyo.[48]

The comedy in *Stink Bomb* is broad, and very over-the-top, and also black – it draws upon satires such as *Dr Strangelove* (there's a War Room with a giant wall of monitors and images – which every military HQ in a movie has to have since Ken Adam designed the War Room with its enormous world map for the 1963 Columbia movie). The out-size acting in the War Room scenes also recalls George C. Scott and Peter Sellers in *Dr Strangelove* (which was also referenced in *Akira*).

---

48 There are obvious affinities with *Roujin Z*, with characters who try to get somewhere or find something, and never give up until they achieve it. Indeed, some sequences are virtually replays of *Roujin Z* – such as the road block at the end of the tunnel thru a hill.

Heroes who accidentally and comically cause devastation wherever they go is a staple of *animé* – *Slayers, Dirty Pair, Dominion: Tank Police, Cowboy Bebop* and *One Piece*. That the hero in *Stink Bomb* is completely oblivious is reminiscent of the Leslie Nielsen cop character in the *Naked Gun* movies.

Stink Bomb has a great script, worked out in every detail. Altho' the premise is simple (and ridiculous!), it's elegantly presented to the viewer (in the exposition scene where Nobuo Tanaka talks to the head of development (Nirasaki) at the pharmaceuticals company thru a bank of video monitors (after the alarm has been sounded).)

What's wonderful here is how everybody reacts hysterically (as in the terrific scene where Tanaka's boss goes absolutely apopleptic when he discovers that Tanaka has taken some of the forbidden pills. No one can animate out-of-control hysteria like Japanese filmmakers!). But *not* Tanaka: nope, this guy is so dumb, so casually oblivious, he *under*-reacts to everything. Even when he's bombarded by the massed attacks of the Japan Self-Defence Force, he simply keeps riding that battered scooter.

Tanaka has a cold, he goes to the doctor, receives a shot in the arm for it, and goes to work (trudging through snow – *Stink Bomb* is set up in the mountains of Japan. The background art is especially fine, re-creating the mountainous regions of Nihon after heavy snow). And, to be fair to all-time loser Tanaka, he isn't to blame for swallowing the wrong pills – it's one of his co-workers who suggests he try one of them (but wait, was it the blue pills in the red bottle, or the red pills in the blue bottle...?).

The *Sleeping Beauty* scene, where Tanaka wakes up to find everybody unconscious in the chemicals factory is a terrific dramatic set-up: *Stink Bomb* gets the tone dead-on, and it's very funny. From that point, the events escalate in grandeur and carnage – from Tanaka on a bike, to a moped, to the tunnel road block, and so on. (That the effects of Tanaka's stench increase when he perspires is a clever twist – he has to be kept calm).

Director Tensai Okamura and the team also enhance the mystery and poetry of Tanaka being a one-man weapon of mass destruction. For example, as he cycles thru the (eerily quiet) mountain roads, suddenly flowers are erupting everywhere, and cherry blossom fills the air. This part of *Stink Bomb* is surreal and beautiful, and the screen is full of pink and white. It's a 'last man alive' scenario (there are crashed cars, the occupants all asleep or unconscious). Animals collapse, and whole towns're strewn with overgrown flowers (revealed in a superb helicopter sequence, which skilfully combines exposition with action).

Stink Bomb also allows the filmmakers at Madhouse and Studio 4°C to unleash every fetish they have for weaponry, military vehicles, helicopters, jets, destroyers, tanks, and of course guns (there's also the familiar uneasy relationship with the U.S.A., when it's discovered that the Yanks have been secretly pushing along the bio-weaponry experiment – again, a recurring theme in *animé*, which also crops up in *Spriggan* and *Akira,* and is part of *Roujin Z*, too, with Yoshihiko Hasegawa secretly working for Uncle Sam in developing the computerized hospital bed).

It's all played for laffs in *Stink Bomb* – like > the moment when Tanaka, riding his moped, emerges from a tunnel into white light, which fades to reveal the sky filled with helicopters and planes, all with their missiles trained on Tanaka. Like > Tanaka riding along roads with streaks of yellow-green gas emerging from his body. Like > a whole traffic jam of tanks piling into each other, setting off their guns, and they're still unable to nobble Tanaka on a distant bridge (a very Otomoan scene! If there's a chance to include tanks, Otomo will do so! And *Stink Bomb* certainly provides plenty of opportunities). Like > groups of helicopters firing missiles, and a cluster of jet fighters unleashing rockets, and destroyer ships off

the coast also firing shells at the guy on the moped.
All to no avail!

Take away the hapless salaryman riding thru
Japan on a moped, and you have a superb war
scenario, with each section of the Japan Self Defence
Force doing their job (there are similar scenes of
mechanized attacks in the *Ghost In the Shell* TV
series, and in *Patlabor*). But when you put Tanaka into
the mix, somehow managing to avoid every pounding shell and exploding missile, it's very funny.

Marvellously-imaged carnage, widespread
devastation and stuff blowing up – *Stink Bomb* is very
Otomoan, in the spirit of *Akira*. There's a deliciously
childish thrill in blowing stuff up, in smashing things,
in seeing the whole fabric of society falling to pieces
in the space of a few minutes. (Yes, animators in Japan
love to blow up Japan – preferrably with Japan's own
military forces! If anyone's going to blow up Japan,
it's going to be the Japanese!).

That the salaryman Nobuo Tanaka keeps coming
on and never stopping is wonderful – he's as unstoppable as a Terminator or giant robot, but he's just a
weedy, little guy! (It's a send-up of technology going
A.W.O.L. scenario, which Japanese *manga* and *anime*
have dined out on for decades). That he's the guy that
nobody notices in the company (and hasn't got a
girlfriend). That he's incredibly stupid, too, and
doesn't realize that the clouds of yellow-green smoke
surrounding him are streaming out of his body,
enhances the comedy. That he doesn't understand
why his grandmother is yelling at him out of a
helicopter to head back to the mountains. That he is
dutiful to the point of obsession, and brings the
suitcase containing industrial information all the
way to Tokyo, and right up to the head of department
in his company, to their total disbelief, is wonderful
(and a humorous comment on capitalist labour,
devotion to work and doing your duty as ordered
(no matter what the cost), and salarymen). In any
other circumstances, Tanaka would be the ideal

employee, going through hell and high water to fulfil the task given him by his employer!

But *Stink Bomb* is also, like the rest of *Memories*, a *tour-de-force* of visual effects animation, coupled with forays into abstraction and vivid colouration (the rippling reds and purples in the final tunnel scenes, for instance,with smoke effects reminiscent of *Akira*).

As with *Roujin Z*, there is a comic coda to *Stink Bomb*: once again, the North Americans are in on the act (much to the fury of the Japanese generals), with their new space suits that can withstand anything. But not Tanaka-san! Oh no – the tunnel scene features a terrific face-off, with Tanaka reacting badly (unconsciously). But the outcome is left hanging in the (very smelly) air – until the scene cuts to the military HQ in Tokyo, where a visitor, presumed to be one of the Yanks who saved the situation, enters. Except of course it's not a beefy foreigner, it's Tanaka! He hands the briefcase to his boss, Nirasaki, just as he promised to do, then he struggles to take off the helmet. Meanwhile, everybody is fleeing for their lives.

What a stink! (the final words of *Stink Bomb*). A terrific piece of animation and comedy, with a silly premise exploited to the max by a team of dedicated souls (who, under the pretext of creating a cartoon comedy, have once again snuck in the images they *really* wanted to animate – tanks, jets, helicopters, ships, missiles, and multiple explosions!).

CANNON FODDER.

'I did it because I wanted to', Katsuhiro Otomo commented (2009, 37) of *Cannon Fodder* (*Taiho no Machi*), a comedy directed by Otomo, the final segment of *Memories*. It's another of Otomo's steampunk outings, beginning life as a five-minute short, but expanding to 23 minutes (it can also be regarded as a dry-run for *Steam-boy*).[49]

---

49 The designs in the Otomo short *Gondora* (a.k.a. *Catsuka Player*, 1998) have affinities with *Cannon Fodder*.

Cannon Fodder explores an unnamed city fighting an unnamed foe in an endless war somewhere in the 20th century, somewhere in between Japan and Europe. It's a steam-punk vision which takes in WWI and WWII and the Thirties, the Forties and the Fifties, mixing historical periods with different places, like Hayao Miyazaki and Studio Ghibli did with *Laputa: Castle In the Sky, Kiki's Delivery Service* and *Howl's Moving Castle.*

Cannon Fodder is fundamentally a comic, satirical piece: it's about the futility and surrealism of war (and, by extension, any industrial society). The script, the designs, the animation, the characterizations, and the plot all support the view that war is a bizarre, wasteful and ultimately pointless activity for humans to be engaged in.

On every roof of the crowded, European-looking city, for instance, gun turrets and cannons are mounted (revealed in a hilarious wide shot as father and son descend in an elevator); the television (which probably has only one, government-sponsored, heavily-censored channel) exhorts the populace to shoot well at the enemy (at the end of the day, the TV news[50] relates how many weapons were fired in a series of meaningless statistics, and promises victory soon);[51] the area between the city and the unseen enemy is a flat, barren strip of bomb craters; the mother[52] in the family works in a munitions factory (where lunch breaks're cut down to a minimum – because the enemy doesn't take breaks); the father's part of a huge, regimented team that shoots a colossal cannon (number 17); and the main protagonist of the piece, a young boy, goes to school to learn about wars and weaponry.

---

50 The weather mentions the wind speed – because this is a society of cannon-firing folk, where the wind is a key factor in judging trajectories.

51 There's also a snatch of a soap opera about a Cannon Family (which the son thinks is 'baka'). We don't see much of this soap, but it almost certainly features a family of dutiful citizens who do their bit for the State's war effort.

52 A great touch has mom wearing a Germanic helmet.

In his downtime, the kid draws himself as the pompous officer who fires the Big Cannon, going to war (the child's sketch becomes a mini cartoon in its own right, as he dreams of militarized exploits in a child-like manner. He doesn't wanta become a cannon loader, like his father – he wants to be the self-important guy who fires the gun). But nobody has seen the enemy, and no one explains why the war is being fought: the giant cannon fires black shells bigger than houses into the distance (but the impact isn't seen or heard).[53] The war, we can guess from the dogged, downbeaten appearance of the citizens, has already dragged on for years (with no end in sight).

Meanwhile, every character in *Cannon Fodder* is portrayed with stylized lined, pinched and puffy (and discoloured) faces as if they're terminally ill.[54] Everybody looks beaten down and depressed and near-death (with green or grey skin). The father is a picture of a hopeless, down-trodden man who's had his soul beaten out of him by mind-numbing routine and pointless labour. When the boy asks his father about the enemy, dad doesn't really know (he hasn't seen them; his father says the boy'll understand when he's older. That is, when there's nothing he can do about it! And he becomes just another cog in the societal machine). The boy, meanwhile, attends a school where the pupils (who all look the same, with the same round helmets), listen to a wizened, old teacher talking incomprehensibly about the technology of cannons.

The design of the city in *Cannon Fodder* is an amalgam of Berlin, London, Moscow, Paris, Rome, Stockholm, Prague, Vienna and numerous European cities. Lettering and graphics evoke Soviet art of the 1920s, Communist propaganda, fascist propaganda, and of course Nazism (every double 's' is in the form of the Nazis' 'SS'). Propaganda posters are everywhere, exhorting the workers to work harder (and to

53 Though the women in the factory cheer after firing.
54 Or as if they're the victims of nuclear fall-out.

'K.O. the Enemy'). Victory is always just around the corner.

When the father and the son go to work and school, there is a brilliant reveal of their society: it's a vista of the city, with roofs, walls and every nook and cranny festooned with round gun turrets. That shot alone encapsulates the one-note satire of *Cannon Fodder* (so there isn't any need to see more of the episode); but it's a terrifically powerful dig at how real, modern societies in our world are armed to the teeth. How there are real, armed conflicts occurring all over the globe all the time. How the populace of real, particular nations or communities are kept in the dark about the motives, the causes and even the enemies of wars (because all they know about the wars in distant lands is from the media. And who controls the media – and most especially in a time of war? Governments. The global media, in any form, is never more than the communications department of governments and big business).

Well, it's true that the political satire in *Cannon Fodder* is simple (political satirists such as John Heartfield (1891-1968) did it all in a single, Dadaist collage sending up Adolf Hitler), but it's so skilfully and wittily achieved, so technically spectacular, it doesn't matter. '*Cannon Fodder* is a jewel of twenty-three minutes that fascinates with its atypical æsthetics and language', Stefano Gariglio noted.[55]

As if he wanted to be extra challenging for himself and his animation team, Katsuhiro Otomo opted to use continuous, mobile shots in *Cannon Fodder* – as if they were tracking the camera about with the ease of an Orson Welles, Jean-Luc Godard or Theo Angelopoulos. The result was technically startling, with smooth sweeps of the camera through 2-D illusions of three-dimensional space (including a number of 360° pans): 'a masterpiece from Otomo, planned as a single, continuous tracking shot'.[56]

55 In C. Chatrian, 159.
56 J. Clements, 2006, 410.

(*Cannon Fodder* isn't one, single continuous shot, tho'
– there are devices used to hide shifts between shots,
such as dissolves, or moving in very close, or wipes
with objects like smoke in front of the camera, etc, all
familiar techniques used to mask the joins in shots.
However, creating a film in a single, continuous shot
has been a dream of many filmmakers – Orson
Welles, Alfred Hitchcock, Bernardo Bertolucci and
Andrei Tarkovsky come to mind).

Was it difficult? Katsuhiro Otomo was asked in
the interview in the 'making of' documentary for
Cannon Fodder: 'ask the camera team!' he replied. You
bet it was! There is a shot in the documentary of
background artwork stretching all over the floor of
the film studio. The approach required quite a few
retakes, Otomo explained (I bet it did – not only
because it was technically mind-boggling, but also
because of Otomo's perfectionism. Look at the
opening shot of *Cannon Fodder*, with the perspective,
the image size, the backgrounds and all the rest
shifting throughout the continuous take. That opening
shot moves from the boy's alarm clock,[57] to the boy, to
the boy getting dressed, to the boy moving down a
corridor into the kitchen, and to the breakfast scene.
And it continues going, on and on).

The look of *Cannon Fodder* is a highly stylized
take on self-consciously child-like designs which
include thick outlines, cross-hatching, and squat,
deformed shapes (evoking comicbook art of the 1940s
through 1960s, plus some satirical Robert Crumb and
Fritz the Cat-era Ralph Bakshi[58]). The colour scheme
exploits reds and greens (as *Akira* did), but this time
a rusty, ugly red, not a proud, shiny scarlet; and a
very sickly green, not the green of Spring, trees and
growth (the combination of the two delivers a look
that unnerves with its suggestions of perpetual
decay).

The family home is a very funny send-up of the

57 A great prop – a cannon shell bashes a wooden castle to bits
when it chimes the hour.
58 Alluded to in Otomo's comics.

famous steam-punk look – the kitchen looks like the interior of a submarine (with pipes everywhere and machines that do God knows what); the living room window comes from a bomber plane; and the boy's bedroom spoofs quaint, storybook Victoriana.

Scenes in *Cannon Fodder* of the boy at school are contrasted with the father at work, and the mother in the munitions factory (as if school is simply another form of labour, as well as a preparation for a working life). That is, in a war-mongering society, everybody must work, must do their bit. (That we too live in a war-ready, war-hungry, war-working world hardly needs to be said. The country that *you* live in right now has police, security services, spies, intelligence organizations, armies and military institutions that *you* pay for with *your* taxes. And they are training and working *all the time. Cannon Fodder* isn't a crazy, fantasy cartoon, it's a documentary!).

The scene of the preparations to fire the super-cannon is brilliant in its evocation of showy, regimented activity within a rigidly hierarchical and intimidating power structure. The slightest mistake is loudly castigated.[59] Even in the control room the operators wear gas masks (as if they are always just about to be attacked, or the whole contraption is going to explode). The pride in the giant, red, phallic cannon and its function within the society is contrasted with the hopelessness of the complicated and dangerous enterprise of preparing it and firing it. When the cannon fires, the women in the factory nearby salute and cheer (however, during their lunch break, they're gossiping).

As a portrait of humans as mere cogs in a machine, *Cannon Fodder* looks back to classic movies such as *Modern Times* (Charlie Chaplin, 1936) and *Metropolis* (Fritz Lang, 1927). Certainly, *Cannon Fodder* displays that gritty, smoky and rather grim approach of silent movies to evoking the world of

---

59 When the father slips and falls onto the metal floor, there is no sympathy whatsoever from his superior.

boring, repetitive (and ultimately pointless) work, and of people existing in near-poverty conditions. (That the war effort is bankrupting the nation in *Cannon Fodder* goes without saying. There are no glimpses of the rich and the wealthy, as in *Metropolis*).

05

SPRIGGAN

STRIKER

Katsuhiro Otomo acted as story supervisor and producer[60] for 1998's *Spriggan* (a.k.a *Striker*), a hugely enjoyable action-adventure movie (though *Spriggan* was co-written by Hirotsuge Kawasaki (designer on *Memories*), Yasuaka Ito and Otomo), adapted from the 1988 *manga* by Hiroshi Takashige and artist Ryoji Minagawa (b. 1964, creator of *Project Arms*, 1997-2002, story by Kyoichi Nanatsuki).[61] *Spriggan* was directed by Hirotsuge Kawasaki, designer and animation director was Hisashi Eguchi, the editor was Takeshi Seyama (Otomo's regular editor), backgrounds were by Hajime Matsuoka (*Shamanic Princess*), with music by Kuniaki Haishima. *Sprigan* was produced by Tokyo Broadcasting System, Toho, Bandai, Shogakukan-Shueisha Productions and Studio 4°C.[62] The producers were Ayao Ueda, Eiko Tanaka, Haruo Sai, Katsuhiro Otomo, Kazuhiko Ikeguchi and Kazuya

---

60 Otomo also contributed the design of Noah's Ark.
61 Initially, the movie was going to adapt the 'Beserker' chapters of the *Spriggan manga*. The *manga*, which is excellent, appeared in *Weekly Shonen Sunday* in 1988.
62 Studio 4°C also produced *Steam-boy* and *Memories*.

Hamana. The exec. producers were Akito Yamashita, Hiroo Takimoto, Masamichi Fujiwara and Shigeru Watanabe.

In the cast: Showtaro Morikubo was Yu Ominae, Ryuji Aigase was Colonel MacDougall, Takehito Koyasu was Jean Jacques Mondo, Katsumi Suzuki was Little Boy, Kenji Takano was Fat Man, Ken Shiroyama was Dr Meisel and Sakiko Tamagawa was Margaret.

(Some commentators, such as Jonathan Clements (2009, 351), have suggested that Otomo was the director of *Spriggan* in all but name – you can see Otomo's influence in the design of Noah's Ark, for instance, or the night scenes, or the child psychic General MacDougall. And notice just how many long takes and complex camera moves there are in *Spriggan* – from *Memories* onwards, Otomo pursued the concept of the continuous shot. The timing is also right – Otomo had recently helmed *Memories*, and was into the pre-production of *Steam-boy*. He also directed the *Gundam* short in 1998).

The *manga* of *Spriggan* (1988-96), by Hiroshi Takashige and Ryoji Minagawa, is a terrific fantasy adventure romp, highly recommended if you enjoy *manga* like *Akira, Ghost In the Shell* or *Nausicaä* (tho' it can be hard to get hold of).[63]

The elements featured in *Spriggan* comprise familiar Otomoan ingredients: giant action sequences, stuff blowing up, futuristic settings, the military, children old b4 their time with supernatural powers, hi-tech *mecha*, weapon fetishism,[64] power suits, eccentric scientists, bully-boy soldiers, and truckloads of visual effects.

Spriggan is a highly entertaining mix of elements – fantastic action, imaginative animation and staging, rich textures and settings (modern-day Turkey), appealing characters, ancient mythology, a memor-

---

63 Viz produced a translation, which's sadly O.P.
64 There's a scene where Yu takes apart his gun and cleans it (on the plane to Turkey). As every good superhero should do. Hell, I clean my gun every day. Doesn't everybody?

able super-villain, and a ballsy score of electronica.

The hero Yu Ominae is a Spriggan (a Celtic term for a magical being like an elf or fairy), basically a 17 year-old, Japanese kid and superhero (a youth with enhanced powers – and further enhanced by a hi-tech suit).[65] There's a helper scientist figure (Doctor Meisel), and his assistant, Margaret (who's about the only woman in the whole show – *Spriggan* is *very* boysy). Yu works for A.R.C.A.M., a Japanese organization dedicated to protecting ancient artefacts and cultures. What've they got this time? Only Noah's Ark. The *real* Noah's Ark.

Forerunners of *Spriggan* included *Giant Corg* (1984), a Sunrise/ TV Tokyo show with ancient artefacts, and *High School Agent* (1988) with its *James Bond* adventures (the first act contains a scene of Yu at a high school, which includes a scene where a fellow student is wired with bombs, attempting to nobble Yu on the roof). Later *animé* with affinities with *Spriggan* include *Gilgamesh* (2003). Ancient civilizations also crop up in *The Big O* (1999), *Nadia* (1990) and *Escaflowne* (1996), and two Hayao Miyazaki films (*Laputa: Castle In the Sky*, 1986, and *The Castle of Cagliostro*, 1979), and *manga* like *Immortal Rain* (Kaori Ozaki, 1999), *Offered* (Kazuo Koike and Ryoichi Ikegami, 1989-90) and *O-Parts Hunter* (Seishi Kishimoto, 2002).

The *manga* of *Spriggan*, by Hiroshi Takashige and Ryoji Minagawa, had the first adventure set in Japan, not Turkey, with Mount Fuji as the mountain where the action occurs (here, it's an ancient magical device for controlling volcanoes). Yu battles against Russians, as well as Americans (the Russian agents are technologically enhanced like Yu).

The Noah's Ark section of the *Spriggan* comic moves to Turkey, with another mountain (Ararat) which contains super-weaponry. The movie greatly expanded on the *manga* (where the Noah's Ark story

65 In the *manga* of *Spriggan* (1988), the hero was older; the hero's nephew was made the hero because the story was sold to an anthology magazine for boys (J. Clements, 2009, 350).

is only four chapters). For some other elements, *Spriggan* used sections of other chapters (such as for the back-story of Yu's training in the jungle).

The 1998 *animé* added several back-stories to the comic, including having Fat Man working with Yu (so they have a history, expressed during the big action scene), and a scene depicting Fat Man and Little Boy at work, in battle.

In the *manga*, Jean Jacques Mondo has an attitude, a bickering relationship with Yu, and transforms into a berserker warrior. Also, Jean accompanies Yu into the Ark (but then Yu orders him to carry off the doctor and his assistant to safety, leaving Yu to confront MacDougall). The finale of the movie is inevitably a much bigger, more complicated deal than in the four chapters of the comic. The dinosaurs, for example, come alive (then crumble).

Spriggan's setting is interesting, and not your usual location in Japanese animation: it's Turkey[66] (where Noah's Ark ended up – on Mount Ararat).[67] The early scenes look as if the filmmakers took a research trip to Istanbul[68] and Turkey (only big budget productions can afford research jaunts for the core team), because it's jammed with wonderful, real-life details (seen at their best in the out-size car 'n' foot chase in downtown Istanbul, thru the covered *souks* and alleys).

And who're the Japanese up against this time? The Yanks, yet again: the Pentagon wants to get its hands on Noah's Ark, to harness its power (it's the reverse of *Raiders of the Lost Ark*, with the North Americans this time cast as the bad guys (the influence of the *Indiana Jones* flicks on *Spriggan* is obvious,[69] as well as affinities with *The X Files* and Erich Von Däniken's books – the lost/ ancient

66 The exciting chase in Istanbul isn't in the comic.
67 *Spriggan* opens with a long shot of Mount Ararat, and a short and dynamic prologue scene where a bunch of explorers uncover the alien-looking Noah's Ark down a crevasse.
68 Istanbul crops up in *Cowboy Bebop*.
69 The *manga* was more anti-American; the translation into English, called *Striker*, played down the critique of the U.S.A.

civilization and alien-influenced civilization theme). But history has shown that when nations become too powerful for their own good they shift all too easily towards right-wing politics and even fascism – and not only Germany and North America, but also Japan in the first half of the 20th century. And Communist states, too – Russia and China. A recurring theme for Otomo – *Akira* is Otomo's uncompromising deconstruction of the ideological aspects of super-powers.

The action scenes in *Spriggan* are really rocking – bodies are slammed about with a child-like viciousness, the fire-fights're loud and brutal, and there is an extraordinary amount of bloodshed and gore.[70] The cat-and-mouse chase on the freeway when Yu reaches Istanbul is wonderful, and the on-foot pursuit thru the *souks* is marvellous (*Spriggan* takes the hero Yu from high school in Japan[71] thru a rapid sequence of events, as he commandeers one of A.R.C.A.M.'s planes to travel to Turkey on his own).

The chases in Istanbul evoke *Lupin III* (inevitably), *James Bond,* Jackie Chan[72] and the masterpiece animation made the same year as *Spriggan* (1998): *Cowboy Bebop* (which also drew heavily on *Lupin III*). All of the expected gags occur in the *souks* (heavies crashing into stalls, passers-by scattering, Yu hiding in the roof, plus the mandatory sword-wielding henchman. No Japanese action film is complete without swords).

Meanwhile, the sequence following the *souk* chase, where Yu travels in a jeep across the desert and up into the snowy mountains, is remarkable for its length. No Western movie would slow the picture down so much (and in the first act, too), and include so many wide angle shots of mountains, rocks and narrow passes. There is no voiceover, no dialogue, no

---

70 The cutting has a 'breakneck pace worthy of Tsui Hark', remarked Helen McCarthy and Jonathan Clements (2001, 372).
71 A daydream when Yu's in class reveals his true nature – he's in combat in a jungle (with temple ruins reminiscent of Cambodia or Central America), against overwhelming odds.
72 The Jackie Chan movie *The Accidental Spy* (2001) also features a *souk* chase.

exposition, and virtually no sound effects – only the culture-clash music provided by Kuniaki Haishima.[73]

Arriving at Mount Ararat,[74] in his one-man mission to wreak vengeance on the villains who rigged his school chum with explosives, Yu Ominae is captured. The short scene with Dr Meisel and Margaret is long enough for the hero to be given his new battle suit. It's the usual wizard/ helper scene, where veterans/ father figures hand the hero useful stuff or info, but it includes just the right amount information. (The scene explaining the new weapons and devices of the spriggans was added to the comic.)

Every scene in *Spriggan* is like this: very rapidly-paced, yet it doesn't feel rushed. Short scenes, but each contains all the info you need. Yet this is a film which features a two-minute drive in the desert with nothing happening except a car driving thru a series of pretty background art.

The first big action sequence in *Spriggan* climaxes the first act: here the Machine Corps (from the Pentagon) stage an assault on the Mount Ararat facility. There are so many gags, stunts, explosions, bits of business and incidents, enough for the finale of many a movie. Another spriggan's introduced – Jean Jacques Mondo (who helps Yu), and two of the chief bad guys – Fat Man,[75] the giant, partial cyborg, an *animé* staple (and Yu's former boss), who wields an enormous machine gun, and Little Boy, a cackling, demonic psycho (a very Otomoan characterization, with hints of the old man Mr Uchida in *Domu,* as well as the freaks in *Overfiend*). Little Boy's weapon of choice is that scary ninja staple, razor wire (with which he dices multiple victims into pieces). The

---

73 Not all of Kuniaki Haishima's score is successful: some of it is a little hackneyed. However, there are enough unusual choices, such as the world music for the driving scene, as well as the use of silence, which makes up for that. (On subsequent viewings, the score gets better). Music producer was Shin Shibata, orchestral co-ordination by Yoshitaka Ono and the orchestral score was by Muneo Teruya.
74 The approach up the mountain is much expanded from the comic.
75 No prizes for knowing where the names 'Fat Man' and 'Little Boy' come from.

animé doesn't stint on depicting bodies splurging into bloody shreds when Little Boy yanks on the wires.

As with *Memories, Spriggan*'s action is big, broad, violent and very rapidly-paced (it is edited by the greatest editor in *animé*: Takeshi Seyama – *Akira, Steam-boy, Patlabor, Little Nemo* and most of Hayao Miyazaki's movies). The stand-out action is the fight between Yu and Fat Man (Yu triumphs). Like *Akira, Spriggan* hurtles from one action set-piece to another, yet always has time to slow down and think.

The filmmakers have created one of those scenes where they've aimed to include all of the gags and stunts they've loved. The setting is vividly rendered (a snowbound A.R.C.A.M. compound at night). The use of props, vehicles and bits of the location, is inspired (recalling Hong Kong action cinema). When Yu first enters the fray, for instance, he dives down at Little Boy (who's hiding atop a truck) from above, misses him, but slices through the entire vehicle. Machine guns, handguns, shotguns, knives, razor wire – the sequence has the lot (the only thing missing, with Katsuhiro Otomo as story supervisor, is a tank!).

The central act of *Spriggan* (it's a three-act movie of around 85 minutes, minus the credits), introduces the fearsome General MacDougall.[76] He's a diminutive, psychic child-man. With a baseball cap and loose-fitting, casual clothes, MacDougall at first appears as a regular, twelve year-old kid – uhh, except for his pale blue skin and odd-coloured eyes, and his manic villain's cackle, and his psychotic behaviour, and his ambitions to become a new god.

In his first important scene, MacDougall issues the prime directive of every super-villain to his minions: don't get in my way and you won't get killed! Every white-coated lackey in the Pentagon gives MacDougall a wide berth ('cept for the minder in a suit who injects MacDougall with the mandatory

---

76 The name is likely a reference to General Douglas MacArthur, the Occupation commander in Japan after WW2.

pharmaceuticals to maintain the psi-child's balance).
So MacDougall exhibits numerous links to the *Akira
manga.*

Such as when General MacDougall arrives at
Mount Ararat: in a sphere of energy which protects
him from the chilly elements of the snowbound slopes
(and the weaponry of the A.R.C.A.M. agents). When
MacDougall clicks his fingers, he expects everyone to
jump. It takes some time (and many deaths) before the
crew in the Ararat compound understand that. But
MacDougall needs one thing – the knowledge of Dr
Meisel, because even this fearsomely powerful tyke
can't work out how to enter Noah's Ark.

The scenes at the entrance to the Ark[7] are intercut
with both Yu and Jean battling the remaining
spriggster, Little Boy. A vicious maniac who's
another of those impossible-to-kill (or wound)
opponents, it takes many action beats before Little
Boy expires in a truck hanging off a cliff.

These are gloriously rendered action scenes, with
a vivid use of space and very rapid movement,
orchestrated by razor-sharp editing. The storyboards
(by director Hirotsugu Kawasaki) keep things lively
with angles and compositions that perfectly match
the flow of the action. And the scenes receive a welter
of swishing, smoky visual effects enhancing the
textures of a battle in the snow at night.

The finale of *Spriggan* doesn't disappoint: it's
another face-off between two super-beings (with
obvious echoes of *Akira*, only this time both Yu and
MacDougall resemble Tetsuo). The imagery in the
climax in *Spriggan* is astonishing, and the visual
effects are truly extraordinary.[78] The filmmakers have
thrown everything into the mix, with some very wild
vfx animation – swirling smoke and clouds, vivid
colours, lightning bolts, falling debris, the works. The

77 There is a 'time lock' on the doors, so that inside the Ark there is a
different dimension of space-time. And light doesn't enter the door.
78 Helen McCarthy and Jonathan Clements complain in their
encyclopaedia that the animation in *Spriggan* looks too much like
summat made for video enhanced with additional money (2001,
372). No: *Spriggan* is top-o'-the-line animation.

use of giant video screens which shift around the hemispherical interior of Noah's Ark is unusual and very effective (and hasn't been done better, really). The screens show what's happening in the outside world, and within the Ark, and also more abstract imagery (which's constantly sliding around, and the screens themselves don't stay put, either).

Wild too is the soundtrack in the finale,[79] which makes striking use of sudden cuts to silence (no Western, action blockbuster would employ so many reductions of the soundtrack to silence). However, Kuniaki Haishima and the music team also provide the customary 19th century choral cues of action-adventure climaxes, and a full-bodied orchestral cue for the final moments, over a pull-back shot from Mt Ararat to Turkey to the Middle East and finally Planet Earth.

By this time, pint-sized super-villain General MacDougall has delusions of grandeur, and is think-ing of himself as a god (or God), with the ability – using Noah's Ark's alien technology – to create new lifeforms. So it's the familiar action-adventure genre finale of the Crazy Villain Intent On Taking Over the World, but with the added cosmic dimensions of creating life itself. (Naturally, the hero Yu scorns MacDougall's deific ambitions – 'what kind of god is made by humans?' he quips. But of course, all gods are human-made).

Yet although General MacDougall is a powerful villain, he spends quite a bit of time viciously and repeatedly attacking Yu, but he's somehow unable to kill him. The fight between the two enhanced youths goes on and on, with MacDougall always getting the better of Yu, but Yu always managing to struggle to his feet again (meanwhile, MacDougall is wreaking havoc on the world, melting ice caps and deluging cities – we see floods in Venice and London, for instance).

Until, in a rage, Yu Ominae hurtles at General

---

79 Sound design was by Shoji Hata.

MacDougall and knifes him (with the customary samurai duel freeze). That's not the end of the villain, tho', in a movie like this: MacDougall recovers and sails off into the distance riding a flying rock (leaving room for a sequel – or you could go read Hiroshi Takashige and Ryoji Minagawa's *manga*! But for sheer amount of life he's taken, MacDougall really deserves, in movie-movie terms, a suitably brutal death).

The finale expanded the duel between Yu and MacDougall greatly from the comic, tho' Yu still uses his knife to stab the boy. At the end, MacDougall expires in the wreckage, but in the movie (with an eye to sequels), he's allowed to float away.

More interesting, tho', is in the insertion of a flashback sequence, where we see that Yu Ominae was part of a North American scheme training children for military use (there're many echoes of *Akira* here, as throughout *Spriggan*). The imagery is again very violent, with Yu rebelling against the indoctrination and the harsh military regime, turning on his commanders, and killing them, including what appear to be civilians. (There is also an older flash-back depicting Yu seeing his parents killed. The rage, confusion and sorrow in Yu conflates the two). Thus, both MacDougall and Yu are the victims of government-sponsored scientific experiments, which turn children into weapons, the same issue in *Akira*.

The efforts of the filmmakers in *Spriggan's* climax are especially effective in the evocation of the interior of Noah's Ark as existing in an alternative dimension. It's a familiar trope in science fiction, but in *Spriggan* the combination of visual effects, move-ment, colour, scale, distance, music, sound effects and silence is unique: there isn't a climactic battle quite like this one in *animé*. I don't mean the duels between Yu Ominae and General MacDougall (although the filmmakers come up with some really inventive beats), but the setting and the interaction of the charas with the environment. For example, when Yu prowls thru the inside of Noah's Ark looking for Doctor Meisel and Margaret, it's in total darkness, so that all that can be seen is the flashlight on his rifle. But that's not all: the filmmakers also include vivid special effects imagery, reminiscent of solarization and infra-red photography, and ultra-violet lighting (but in a blue-and-white colour scheme). And the scene where Yu encounters dinosaurs, but frozen like a giant, stuffed animal zoo, is really imaginative (as if Noah's Ark has collected not only two of every animal from 4,000 years ago, but every species of every animal that ever existed on Earth. Later, MacDougall tells the Doctor that Noah's Ark is actually a crucible or laboratory for manufacturing life. Of course, in the climactic escape from the Ark, the dinosaurs come alive – that's too irresistible for the filmmakers (with shades of *Jurassic Park*) – but then they disintegrate rapidly).

MacDougall is a sore loser – he hits the self-destruct button of the Ark (every giant machine in sci-fi has a destruct mechanism built-in. Well, *of course* – so we can have the colossal devastation we expect from a flick like *Spriggan*. As if there hasn't been enough already! *Spriggan* is jammed with scenes of buildings, machines, vehicles, mountains – and people – being blown to pieces). Anyway, it's written into Otomo's every film contract that Stuff Must Blow Up – explosions and catastrophes occur in three-quarters of Otomo's output in film and TV as director and writer. (Even *Combustible*, a historical drama which starts with cutie scenes of kids playing in a garden and lovers trysting, ends with Ye Olde Grande Apocalypse).

Kôkô Erotopia: Akai seifuku
(Shinichi Shiratori,
High School Erotopia:
Red Uniforms, 1979),

Robot Carnival (this page and over)

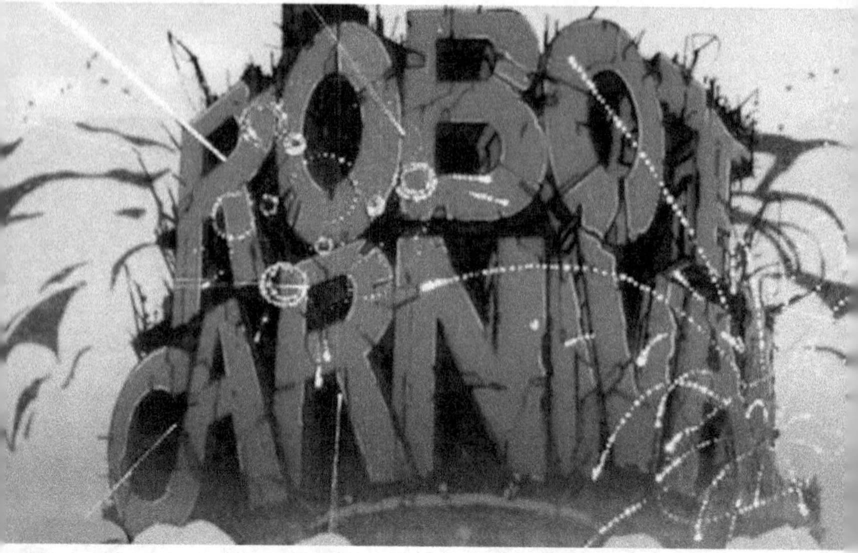
ROBOT
CARNIVAL

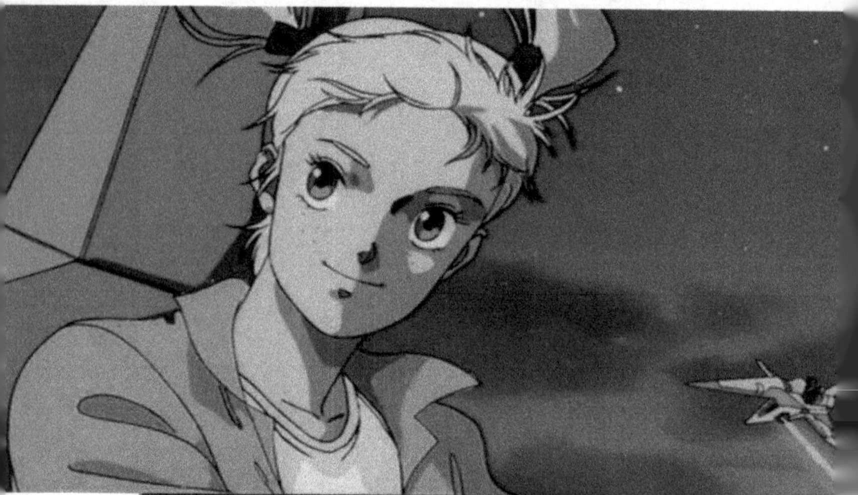

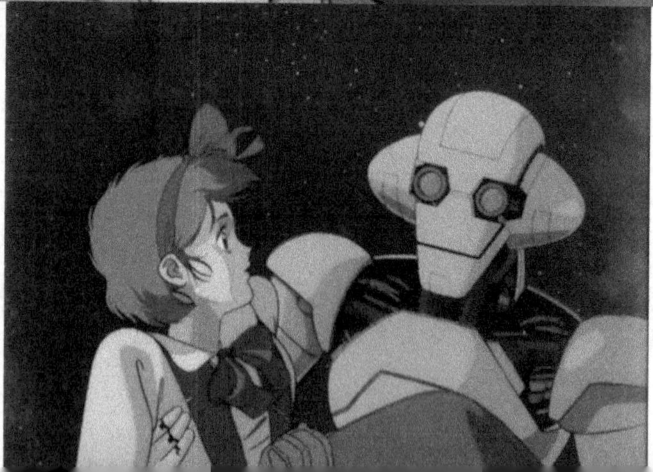

Neo-Tokyo, 1987 (this page and following)

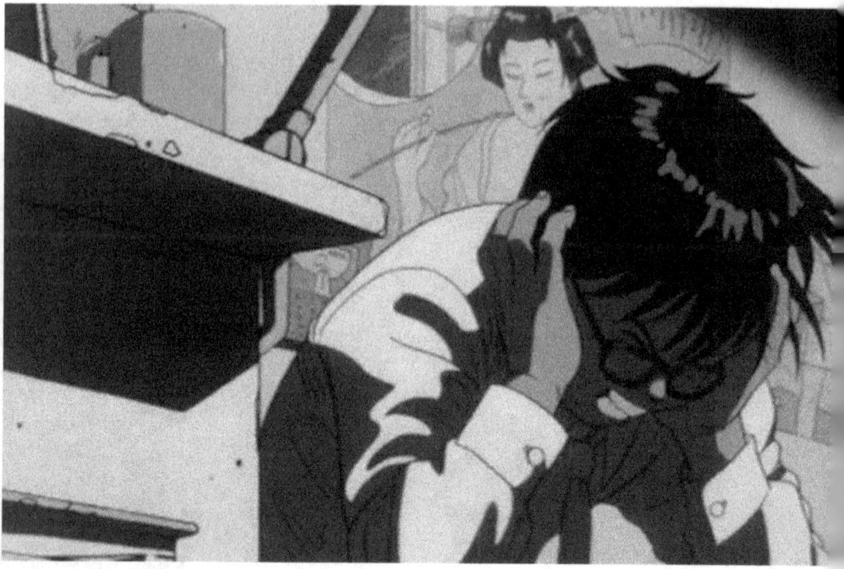

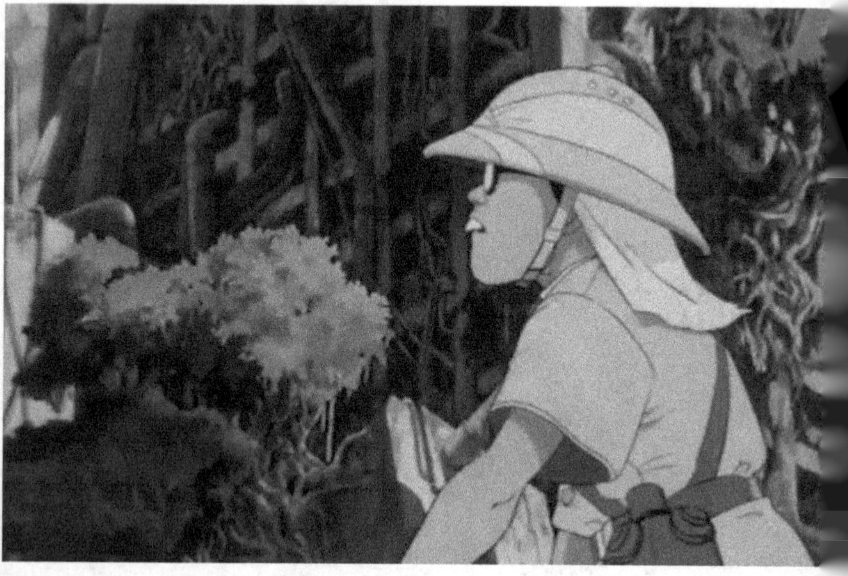

Roujin Z (Hiroyuki Kitakubo, 1991).
(This page and over).

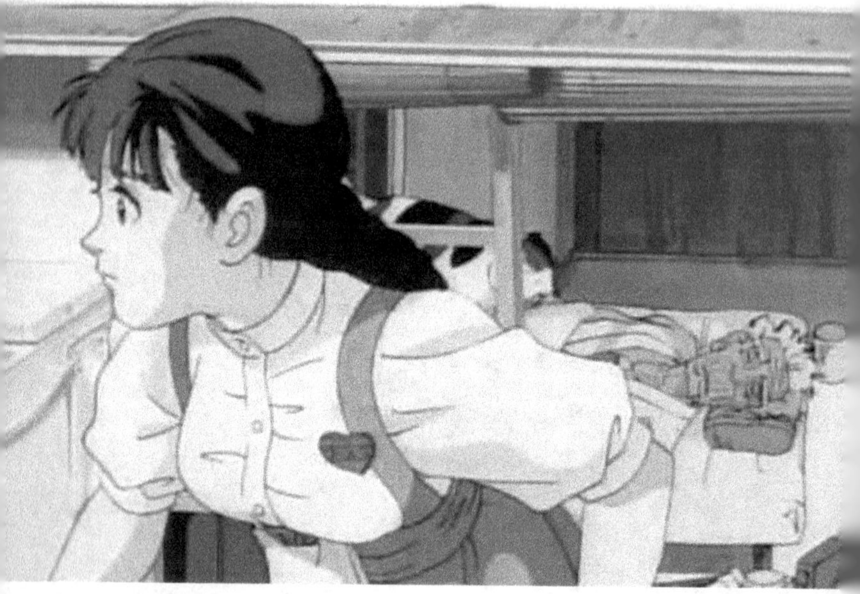

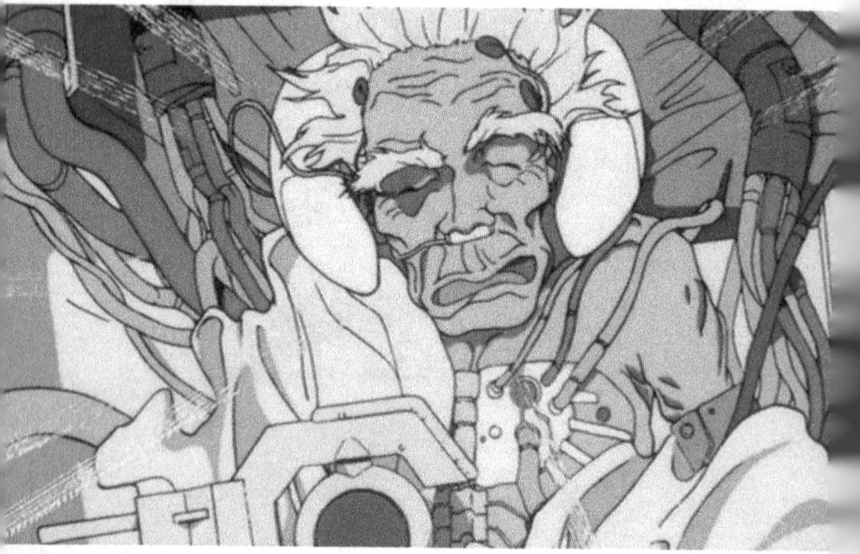

World Apartment Horror (1990)

Memories, 1995 (this page and over)

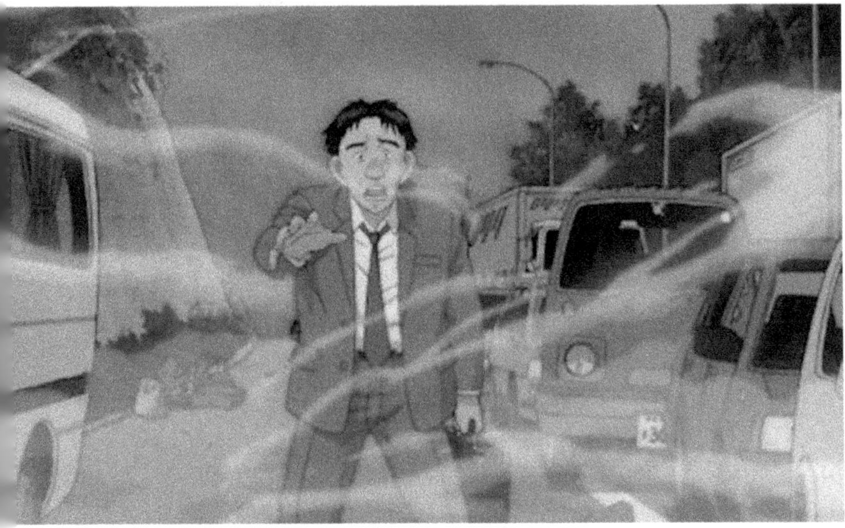

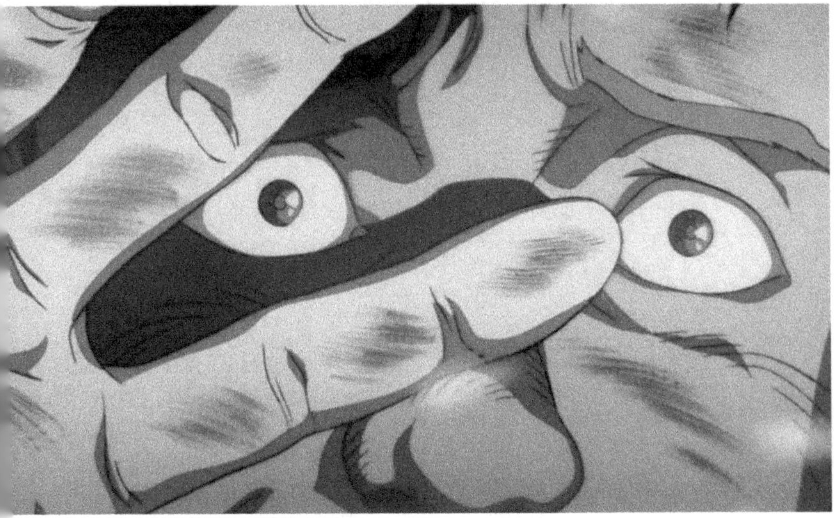

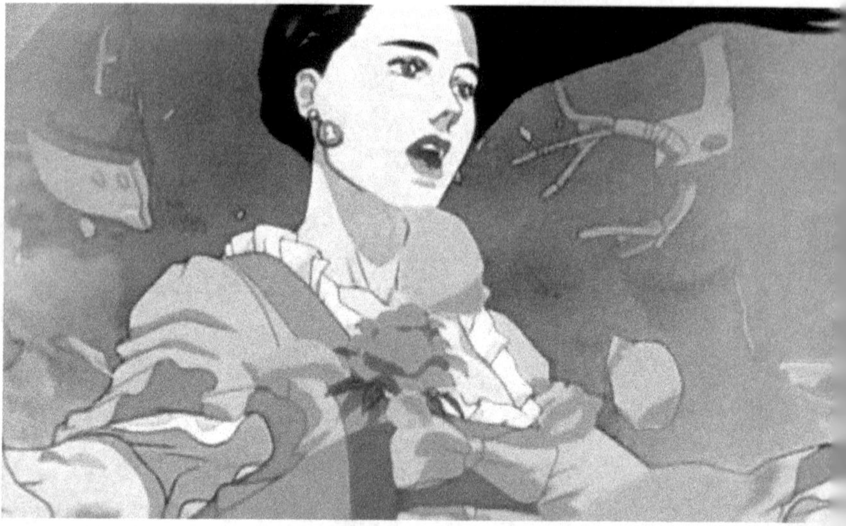

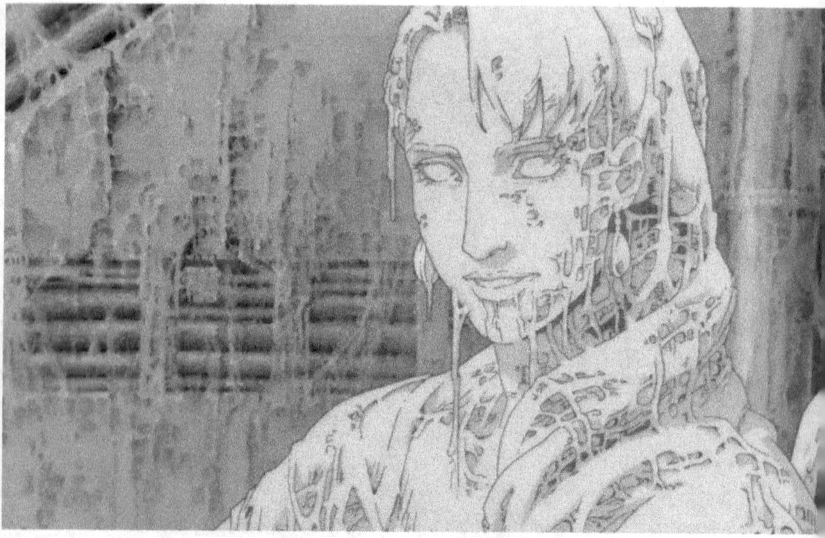

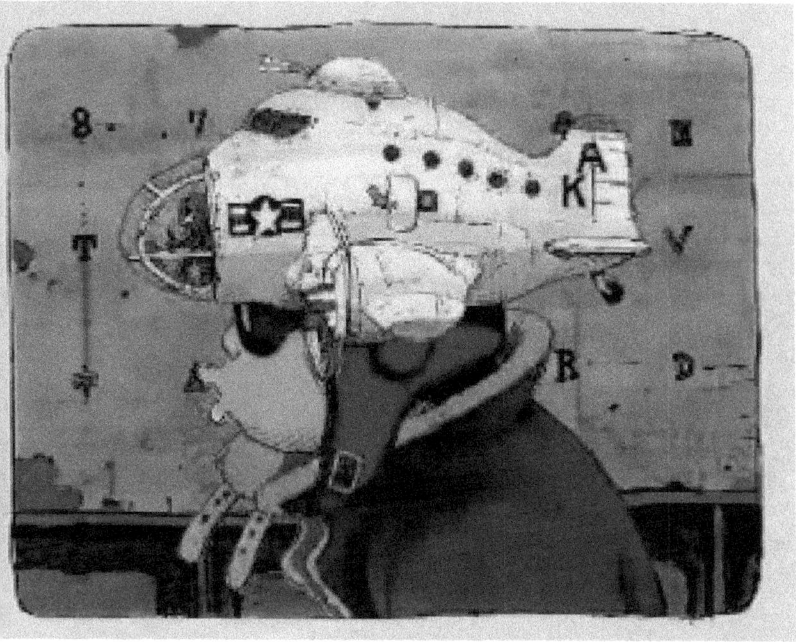
8
7
A
K
T
V
B
D

Catsuka Player

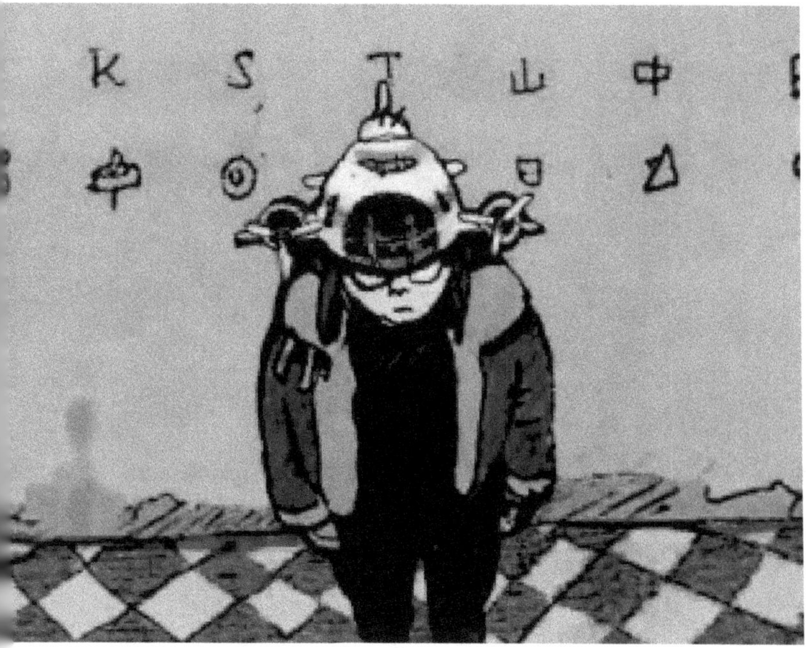
K
S
T
山
中

Gundam: Mission To the Rise

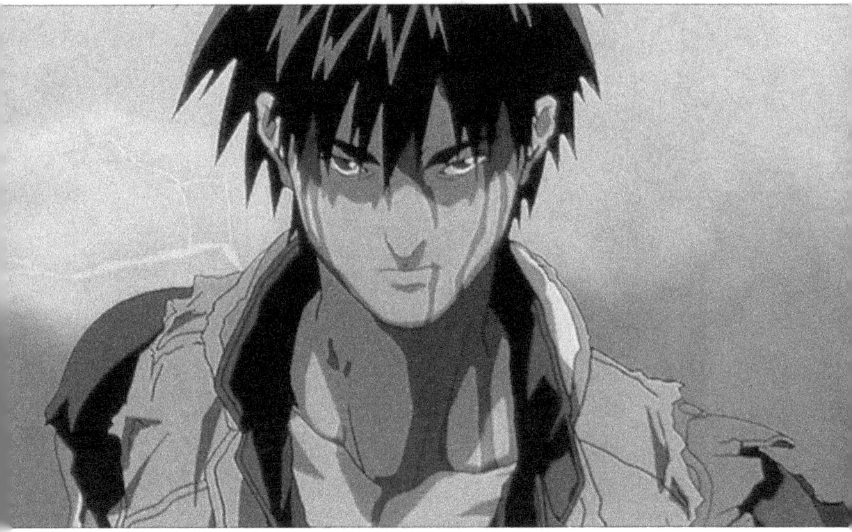

Spriggan (1998)

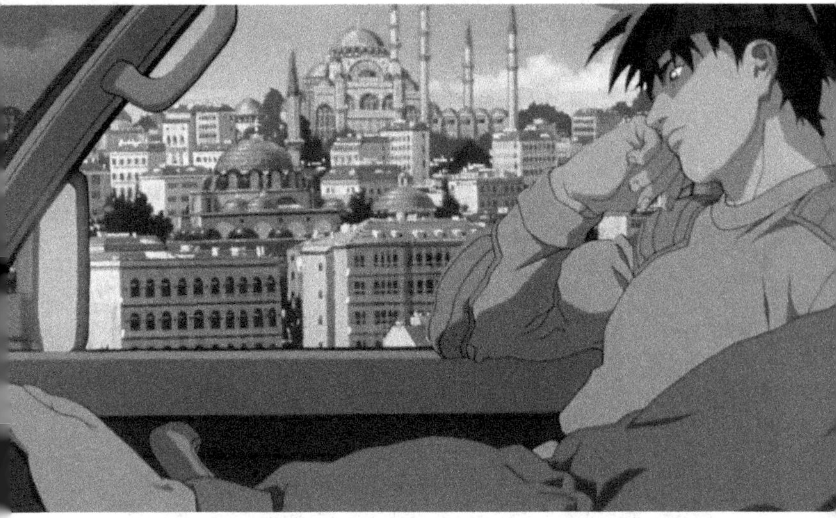

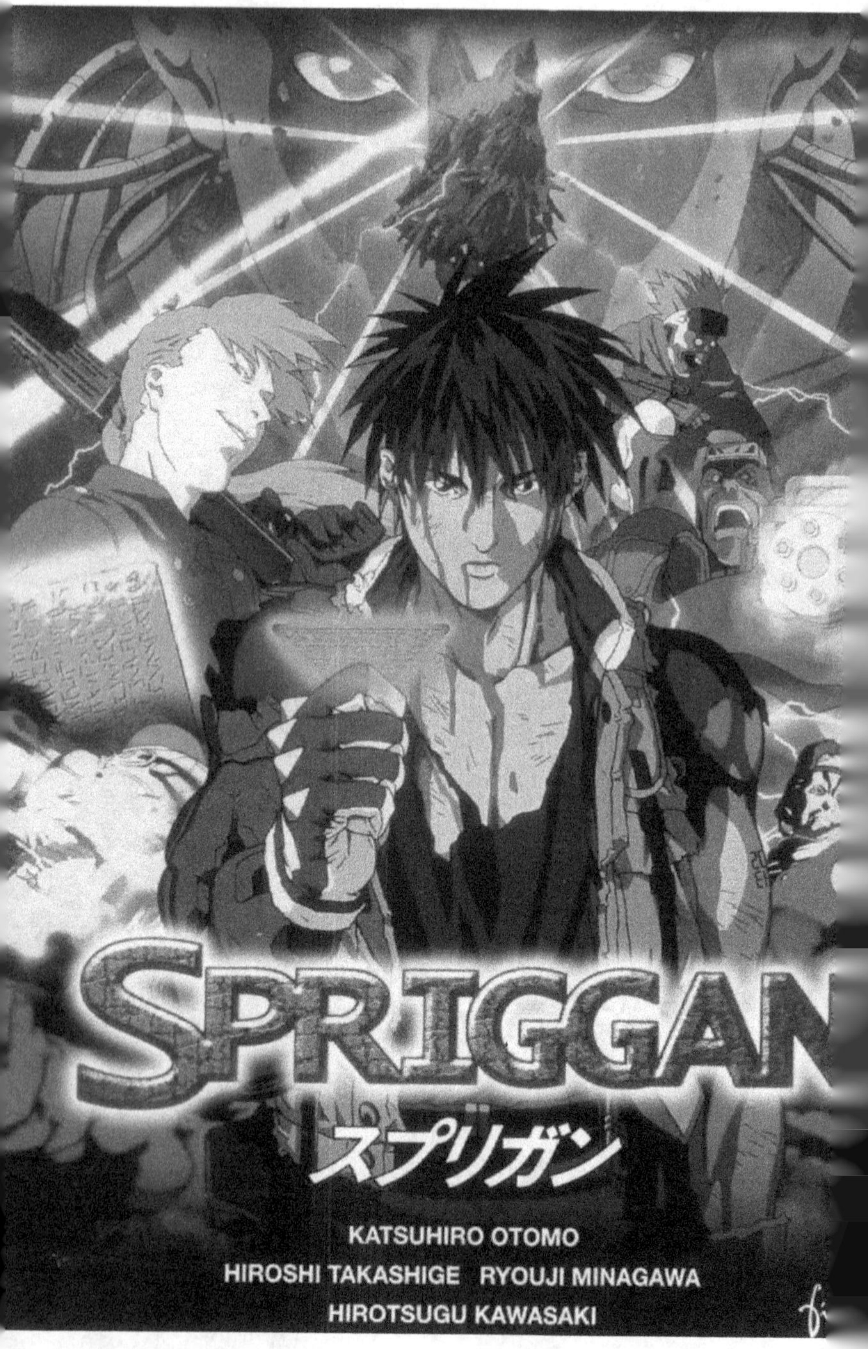
SPRIGGAN
スプリガン
KATSUHIRO OTOMO
HIROSHI TAKASHIGE RYOUJI MINAGAWA
HIROTSUGU KAWASAKI

Metropolis, 2001 (This page and over).

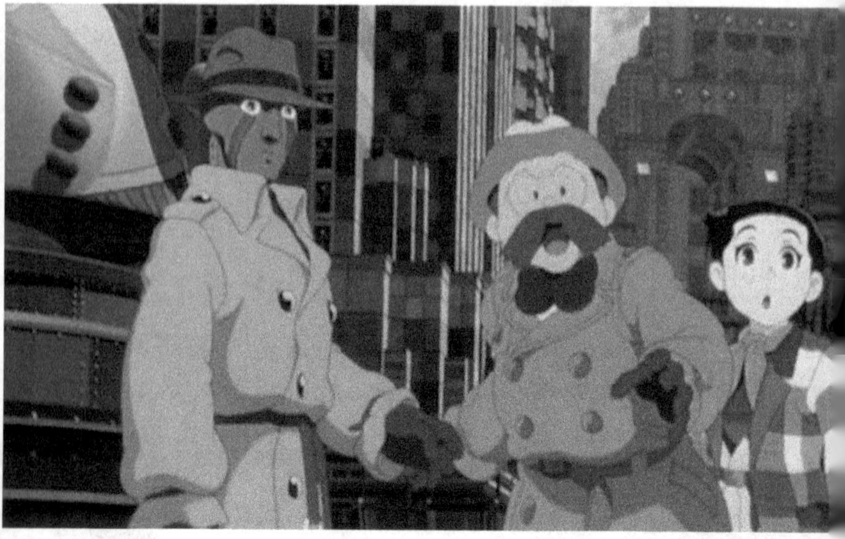

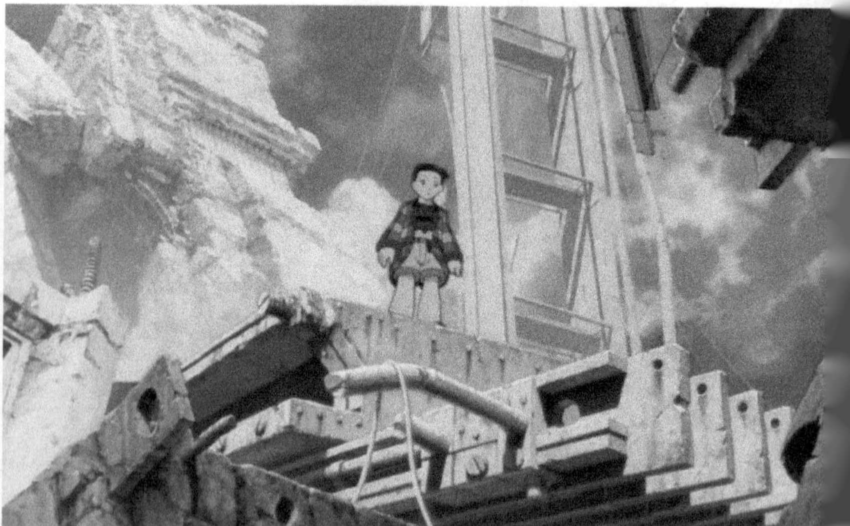

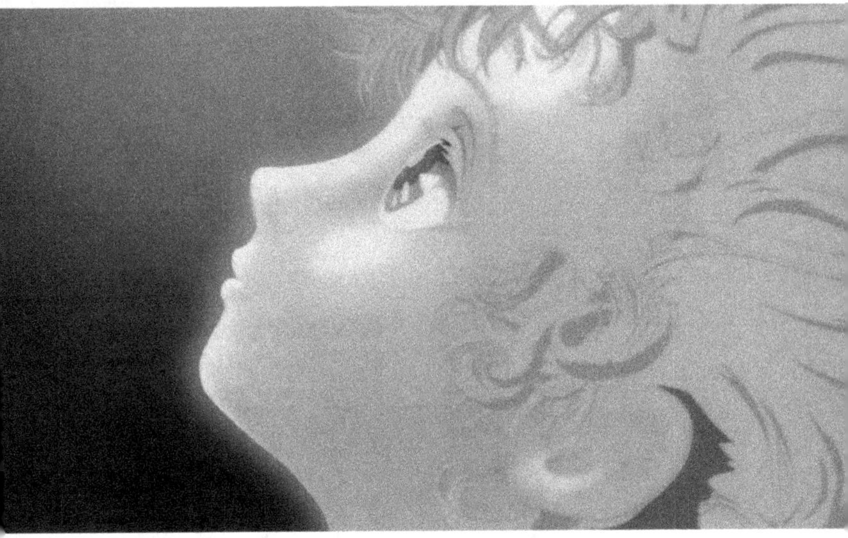
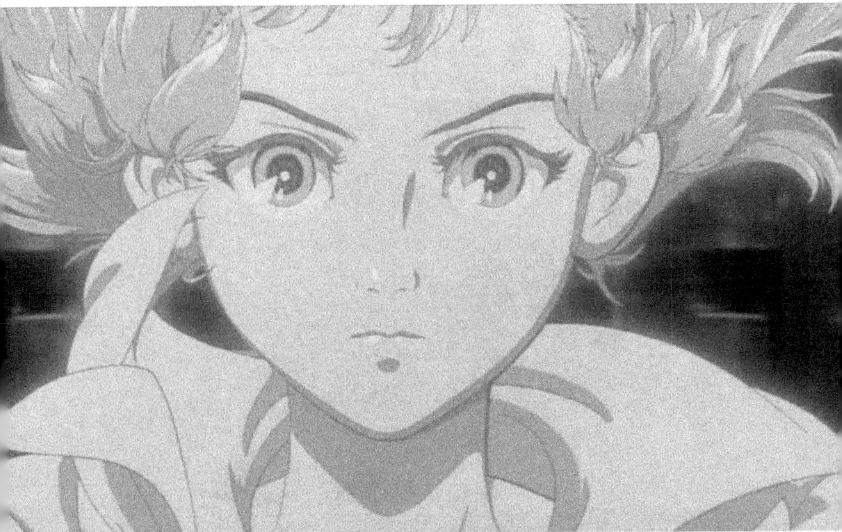
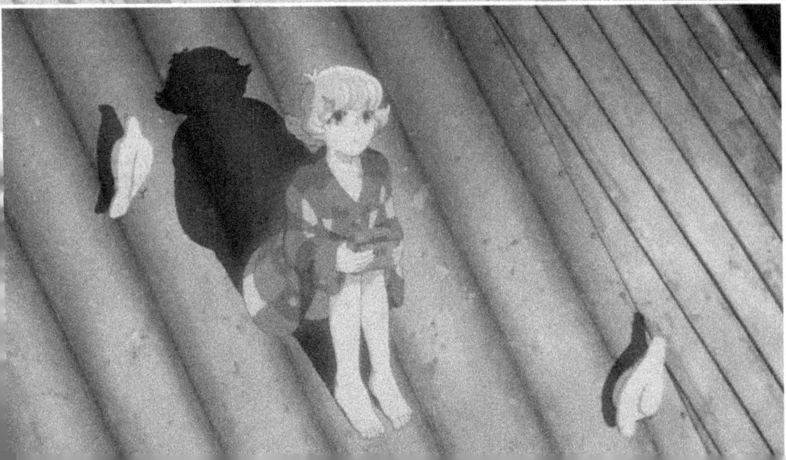

Osamu Tezuka's Metropolis manga

06

METROPOLIS

METOROPORISU

Metropolis – produced by Madhouse/ Bandai
Visual/ Dentsu/ Imagica/ Kadokawa Shoten/
Toho/ Sony/ Metropolis Production Partners/ Starchild Records/ Tezuka Production – was a 2001
animated movie with a script by Katsuhiro Otomo,
directed by Rintaro (who had helmed *Harmageddon*,
Otomo's first movie), based on the comic by the god
of *manga* and *animé*, Osamu Tezuka (Rintaro was a
Tezuka *protegé*). *Metropolis* was a 'double homage' –
to Tezuka, and also to the German movie of the 1920s
(directed by Fritz Lang in 1927). *Metropolis* was
conceived by Tezuka Production as another installment in the continuation of Osamu Tezuka's legacy
(*Astro Boy* and *Black Jack* have also been re-made).

    Like *Heat Guy Japanese* and *Full Metal Panic*,
Metropolis was affected by the political climate
following 9/11 (its story of terrorism in a Gotham-
like city inevitably making it socially sensitive).[1]

    Osamu Tezuka had written the *manga* back in

1 100 Japanese had died during 9/11. Following the terrorist
attacks, the Japanese government persuaded its citizens to say at
home. The destruction in the finale recalls the Twin Towers.

1949, when he was 19 years-old; he hadn't seen *Metropolis* – his *manga* was based on a magazine article about the movie[2] (as well as the *Metropolis manga*, the script also used Tezuka's 1951 *Nextworld manga*, a Cold War thriller). Tezuka's *Metropolis* was part of a series of sci-fi adventures, which also included *Lost World* (1948).

Metropolis in Tezuka-sensei's interpretation focusses on the robot created by Dr Lawson (not a girl or a boy, but both, and called Michi. Its gender can be changed via a button in its mouth). Duke Red reveals his scheming early on, and much of the first half of the Tezuka *Metropolis* comprises tussles over who gets Michi (instead of Duke Red's henchmen, the movie has trigger-happy Rock).

As well as gender confusion, the 2001 film dropped many other elements of Tezuka's comic – like giant rats in the form of Mickey Mouse (not something Disney would be happy with); the pre-historic prologue; a museum scene; a conference of scientists; Michi and Kenichi going to school, etc.

Osamu Tezuka's *Metropolis* is a much smaller-scale story than the 2001 adaptation: Katsuhiro Otomo tends to write big (and expensive!); thus, the *manga* was greatly exaggerated.

Part of the charm of the 2001 *Metropolis* is the combination of character designs in the famous Osamu Tezuka mold[3] with hi-tech digital animation (which delivers awesome visions of the grand cities of the 1920s/ 1930s).

Katsuhiro Otomo, as the screenwriter of *Metropolis*, was taking on one of the most prominent figures of German pre-sound cinema: Thea von Harbou, the superstar screenwriter and wife of Fritz Lang. Thea Gabriele von Harbou (1888-1954) was one of the giants of German silent cinema, the writer of *Metropolis, Die Niebelungen, M, Spiione, Faust, Dr Mabuse, The Testament of Dr Mabuse, Phantom* and *Das*

2 But Tezuka's so talented, he could make a *manga* out of anything!
3 Everyone, not only Duke Red, has a huge nose.

Wandere Bild (some of those movies, such as *Die Niebelungen* and *Faust*, are colossal productions). Von Harbou wrote for Carl Dreyer, E.A. Dupont and F.W. Murnau[4] as well as Lang.

Director Rintaro (Shigeyuki/ Masayuki Hayashi, b. 1941, Tokyo) is one of Japanese animation's veterans, who has done pretty much everything: he directed or worked on episodes of *Astro Boy, Kimba the White Lion, Captain Harlock, Galaxy Express 999, Neo-Tokyo, Doomed Megalopolis, Harmageddon, Final Fantasy, The Endless Odyssey, Dagger of Kamui, X: The Movie,* and *Yona Yona Penguin.* Rintaro began his career (like so many others) at Toei Animation (in 1958). In *animé*, only figures such as Isao Takahata or Hayao Miyazaki have had similarly long and consistently successful careers.

The 2001 *Metropolis* is one of those prestige Japanese animated productions, where no expense, it seems, is spared. Everybody in the contemporary *animé* business seems to be involved in *Metropolis*. The veteran talent included director Rintaro and writer Katsuhiro Otomo, the Tezuka/ Madhouse team, Yasuhiro Nakura[5] (chief animation and character design), animators Kunihiko Sakurai (*Final Fantasy*), Yoshitaki Kawajiri (*Ninja Scroll*), Toshio Hirata (*Barefoot Gen, Catnapped*), and Horiyuki Okiura (*Jin-Roh*), Toshiyuki Honda (music),[6] DP Hitoshi Yamaguchi, art director Shûichi Hirata, sound director Masafumi Mima, and Go Nagai (*Devilman, Cutey Honey, Mazinger Z*) provides a voice. The executive producers were: Akihiko Terajima, Fumio Nagase, Ken Munekata, Ryohei Tsunoda, Tadamichi Abe, Hisanori Hiranuma, Takayuki Matsutan, and Toru Shiobara. Budget: ¥1,500,000,000 ($15 million). Released May 26, 2001. 107/ 113 minutes.

4 For Murnau, von Harbou wrote *Burning Soil, Driven From Home, The Finances of the Grand Duke* and *Phantom.*
5 Yasuhiro Nakura's credits include *Angel's Egg, Laputa: Castle In the Sky, Cyborg 009, Galaxy Express 999, Honey Honey, Tale of Genji, Ghost In the Shell 2,* and *The Girl Who Leapt Through Time.*
6

The voice cast included: Yuka Imoto as Tima, Kei Kobayashi as Kenichi, Kôki Okada as Rock, Tarô Ishida as Duke Red, Kousei Tomita as Shunsaku Ban, Norio Wakamoto as Pero, Junpei Takiguchi as Dr. Laughton, Takeshi Aono as Ponkotz and Masaru Ikeda as President Boon. Mami Koyama, who played Kei in *Akira*, was Enmy.

Metropolis is the sort of classy production that goes over well at film festivals, with its high profile contributors (Tezuka, Otomo, Rintaro), exalted source material (Tezuka and a classic German movie), and its exquisite look. It's the sort of movie that *animé* fans in Spain, Italy and France adore, with its amazing retro, steam-punk designs.

But despite all of that talent seething around the collective of *animé* houses that produced *Metropolis* and despite the skilful blending of digital 3-D animation and conventional 2-D animation, at times it's all too much. *Metropolis* is one of those movies that's jammed with detail and colour, with design and spectacle, which in the end dwarfs the story and the characters. The real stars here are the background artists, the layout artists, the colour designers, the lighting technicians, the *mecha* designers, the cinematographers, etc. You can admire the look of *Metropolis*, and how the filmmakers've updated the classic Tezukan design of charas, but it doesn't really engage the audience at the level of emotion and drama.

Yet the most intriguing element in the Japanese *Metropolis* may be its jazz score by Toshiyuki Honda (rather than the expected electronic and/ or orchestral soundtrack for this type of movie. Kozue Okada was music producer). It was a brave decision by the producers not to go the usual route for the score, so we hear Jazz Age clarinets, bassoons, and drums, instead of synthesizers or classical orchestras. And it works, when combined with the visions of the future imagined back in the Twenties and Thirties.

The jazz score for *Metropolis* includes "St. James

Infirmary Blues", covered by Atsuki Kimura, and Ray Charles, "I Can't Stop Loving You" (as the ziggurat collapses). Minako 'Mooki' Obata provided the ending theme, "There'll Never Be Good-Bye".

It could be that the famous Universum Film Aktiengesellschaft production of 1927 towers over the 2001 animated movie as it does over all science fiction cinema.[7] The 1927 *Metropolis* is one of the two or three most influential sci-fi movies. Once seen, never forgotten (*Metropolis* has been of course a *huge* influence on science fiction animation in Japan).

For all its digitally-rendered spectacle and its visual density,[8] the 2001 *Metropolis* can't crawl out from the shadow of the 1927 production. But if you can forget about the colossal zeppelin that is the 1920s German movie casting a shadow over the 2001 animated film, and appreciate the 2001 production on its own terms, it is still a not wholly satisfying piece.

But if you set aside the story – and also the fact that Katsuhiro Otomo wrote the script – *Metropolis* comes across as a masterpiece of design. I can't think of another movie which presents such a variety of levels, spaces, walkways, corridors, interiors, tunnels, gantries and towers. This really is the city as a multi-level labyrinth (with verticality a significant feature, as it was in the 1927 movie). Equally marvellous is the fusion of digital technology with bolt-and-rivets, steam-punk technology (Japanese animators are the kings of technological fusions of all kinds).

All of this looks forward to *Steam-boy* (as if *Metropolis* is a dry run for *Steam-boy*, or as if *Steam-boy* is a sequel to *Metropolis*). But you can spot the influence of Katsuhiro Otomo's entry to *Memories*, *Cannon Fodder*, with its depiction of a community lost in the middle of an alternative twentieth century.

One of the striking elements of the 1927 U.F.A.

---

7 The 2001 movie opens with a black-and-white sequence, made to look like ye olde filme with scratches, in *hommage* to the 1927 movie.
8 *Metropolis* employs many silent era filmic devices, such as irises-in, and fades.

Metropolis was its depiction of the social strata of the city: no movie b4 that had created such a distinctive social structure, which has been copied numerous times since (altho' the politics of *Metropolis* has been often criticized since). The 2001 Japanese *Metropolis* doesn't have quite the same sophistication of characterization and stratification of society, but it does possess a large cast of characters – from the despot at the top of the pile, Duke Red, his stepson, the Premier, the twisted, tough, wannabe fascist Rock, the bumbling scientist Dr Laughton, his creation, angelic girl robot Tima,[9] and the audience identification figures of crusty, old detective Shunsaku Ban and his assistant, the regular, teen kid, Kenichi (that collection of charas is typical of *animé* – most of them have correspondences in the 1927 *Metropolis*, and in Tezuka's comic).

In this version of *Metropolis*, Ban and Kenichi are visitors from Japan, come to see the city of the future of Metropolis, where robots and humans co-exist. (So it's Japanese visitors landing in a pseudo-Europa – which is ultimately, as always, Japan).

The emotional heart of *Metropolis* was Tima, the robot who wants to be human – the beloved *Pinocchio* theme of *animé*. Well, hell, it's worked 10,471 times b4, why not now? True, the scenes btn Tima and Kenichi were tender, and they make a cute early teen couple on the run (but those btn Uncle Ban and Kenichi were actually more convincing and more affecting (any scenes featuring either Ban or Kenichi are the most satisfying in *Metropolis*, and Shunsaku Ban (Kousei Tomita) is by far the most compelling character).[10] Tima was a forerunner of Astro Boy, and in the comic Michi looks quite like Astro Boy).[11]

9 In a clever scene, Tima stands in the sunlight, and a bird lands on her shoulder: from down below, with the bird's wing and the glow of light, she looks like an angel.
10 But not as compelling as similar scenes between Sheeta and Pazu in *Laputa: Castle In the Sky* (which some of the team of *Metropolis* worked on).
11 Otomo's *Fireball* included a computer based on the one in *Astro Boy*.

As to Katsuhiro Otomo's creative input in *Metropolis* – you can see that in a number of elements: the political machinations, for instance, pitting the anti-robot faction against the authorities (with radicals making protests), or in the relation of the levels of social hierarchy to each other (which the 1927 German movie made so vivid), or the fireworks and celebrations (seen in *Robot Carnival* and *Steam-boy*), or in the anxiety over new technology (of course there's yet another scientist, yet another robot creation), or in the scientific experiments conducted by the scientist, or in the conflict between youth and age (and the working class and the rulers), or the over-reliance of the ruling class on the military-industrial complex, or in the portrayal of a complex, future city, or in the action set-pieces, in which stuff blows up (as in every project that Otomo's associated with. Yes, even before Otomo-sensei makes a mark on a piece of paper, a building explodes).

There are several *hommages* to *Akira* in *Metropolis*: as Kenichi and Tima flee Rock (in the second act), some youths ride by on a bright, red motorcycle (more like a trike); the big crowd scene at the top of the show; the view down some steps to a scuzzy zone (recalling the Harukiya bar); the signage and graffiti on the streets; the owner of an ice cream stall evokes Joker, leader of the Clowns; a leap into the sewers (and 100s of subterranean spaces, an Otomoan speciality); and of course the futuristic setting of multi-levels and soaring skyscrapers (*Akira* was also influenced by *Metropolis*, because *Metropolis* has had a colossal influence on science fiction and fantasy in many media).

The colour design seems especially Otomoan – it is built from reds, golds, yellows and sepias. *Metropolis* is a marvel of colour design (colour setting was by Osamu Mikasa, with chara colour design by Shuichi Hirata). In some scenes, everything is scarlet – the people, the faces, the walls, the ceiling, the doors, with just one or two areas of other colours.

Metropolis, story-wise, plays out all too predict-ably, especially in its final act: it is like *Steam-boy* in this respect. The heroes and villains are clearly defined, and all receive the usual rewards or punish-ments. One or two of the big confrontation scenes between the major charas – like between Kenichi, Tima, Rock, Ban and Duke Red in the snow on the steps outside a building, or the face-off in the throne room of the weapons system at the top of the Ziggurat skyscraper – played slightly different from expect-ations (or from the Western/ Hollywood model). (In the snow/ stairs scene, for instance, Rock acts, as he usually does, as a seething, chip-on-the-soulder villain, in the Tetsuo Shima mold: he shoots Ban, beats up Kenichi, and seems about to get away with kidnapping or killing Tima (he has a pathological jealousy of being Number One[12] in Duke Red's affect-ions, as an orphan). But then the Duke materializes, reprimands Rock, and takes Tima under his wing).

Tima is one of the treasures or what's at stake in *Metropolis* – she's conceived as a beautiful innocent, yet she is, ironically, a robot (tho' every character treats her primarily as a young girl). So, as in the central portion of the *Akira manga*, where several sets of characters are chasing and capturing Akira, and the boy is being dragged or carried this way and that, in the middle acts of *Metropolis*, Tima is being hunted down by different groups (such as Duke Red and Rock, while Kenichi is trying to elude every-body).

Much more interesting, thematically, than the cat-and-mouse chases and escapes, are the scenes of an uprising by the working class and the repressed masses in *Metropolis*. Kenichi and Tima are found by Atlas and his chums, radicals intent on revolution (Atlas is a would-be Che Guevara).[13] This political

12 Is this a swipe at Tezuka himself? He liked to be number one in every category of *manga*. Remember, when *Akira* was so successful, Tezuka regarded Otomo as a rival.
13 And there's even a picture of Che Guevara on the wall at Atlas's place, just in case we don't make the connection!

plot gains speed in the second part of act two, along with the test of the ziggurat; the first part of act two is a classic Couple On The Run plot, as Kenichi and Tima flee from Rock and his lackeys via bicycles and robots.

The scenes of the street demonstrations are some of the finest parts of the 2001 version of *Metropolis* (and are a fitting tribute to the 1927 U.F.A. movie). As in the *Appleseed manga* by Masamune Shirow,[14] there are uneasy relations between humans and robots. So the first victim of the face-off between the activists and the robots is the robot Pero (who has been a kindly guide for Ban and Kenichi). And we've already seen Rock shooting a robot anarchist in the first minutes.

The action is slambang spectacular in the climax of *Metropolis*, where everything plus a coupla kitchen sinks were hurled into the maelstrom. As one cliff-hanger moment followed yet another, as yet more of the sets exploded and fell to bits, *Metropolis* delivers the expected cataclysmic ending of a Katsuhiro Otomo script. The destruction was foreshadowed in the testing of the ziggurat scene. If it's a cliché of this sort of pricey production, the finale is certainly spectacular.

Tima is a robot who becomes a tyrant – she is the familiar girl robot as a key to a weapons system.[15] Once in place on the throne, however, she initiates a catastrophe, setting off the armaments which start blowing everything up (without any commands from Duke Red or the humans). Why? Is it because she's not human, altho' she's convinced she is? (The Duke tells her she's a robot). Is it revenge on humans? Is it simply what she was designed to do? And why do humans build giant cannons in the ziggurat, in the middle of the city? (The movie draws on the creation of the false, robot Maria in the 1927 movie, and its destructive nature).

14 Which were also given the pricey, digital make-over around this time, with *Appleseed* movies in 2004 and 2007.
15 Which also appears in *Appleseed*.

In *Metropolis*, the story doesn't convince at the level of motivations and goals for the characters, even tho' the action plays out according to genre and thematic concerns. In the finale of an action-adventure movie, yes, the heroes and the villains battle it out, yes, stuff blows up, yes, some people die, yes, the heroes to save their comrades... But in *Metropolis*, exactly what some of the characters want or plan or hope for is confused or not clear. (Also, the movie declines to resolve the fates of several key charas).

Duke Red talks about how the ziggurat is going to build a new world, but why are so many weapons required, which can only smash things and people to bits? It's the usual vilainous plot in *animé* – build a new world by destroying the old world first. (Meanwhile, Ban talks darkly about the Tower of Babel[16] in the *Bible*. The ancient world motifs, part of Thea von Harbou's script for the 1920s *Metropolis*, occur elsewhere in Otomo's output – such as Noah's Ark in *Spriggan*). Rock we understand clearly – he's the possessive, jealous youth who wants to rid the world o' robots, and have his surrogate father rule the world (not a robot like Tima). Ban and Kenichi, representing 'ordinary' people, are there as observers (at first), but get drawn in, so they're helping Tima.

Poor Kenichi doesn't get the girl: robot Tima falls away from him to disappear 100s of feet below, at the end of a series of over-complicated cliffhanger scenes, as Tima gradually wakes from her tyrant mode. (Kenichi searches for her remains, and finds another robot, Fifi, instead. But he opts to stay in Metropolis a little longer, while old Ban flies back to the Land of the Rising Sun. Kenichi, note, decides to spend time with the friendly, oppressed under-class in the city).

Tima is the mystery in *Metropolis*: what she wants is abstract, spiritual, impossible: the *Pinocchio* yearning, to become human. A robot as a super-computer who's just another pawn or machine for

16 It appears in *Nadia* (1990).

humans to exploit. Yes, but why do those same humans create machines and technology they can't control, and why do those humans construct colossal weaponry which ends up going haywire and destroying the whole ziggurat?

Oh yes, *I see,* it's because of the perennial, sci-fi moral themes of the ethical uses of technology, how humans can't stop exploiting everything they come into contact with (all of the robots are slaves in *Metropolis,* for instance – there are many images of robots cleaning the streets). I get it: humans are toxic, venal, paranoid, insane, blah blah blah.

STEAM-BOY

SUCHIMUBOI

Steam-boy (Suchimuboi, 2004)[17] was the first full-length feature movie that Katsuhiro Otomo directed after Akira. Of course, Otomo hadn't spent the intervening sixteen years sitting on the couch eating potato chips and watching re-runs of Cheers. He had done loads, including contributing to multi-part movies such as Memories and Robot Carnival, written screenplays such as Spriggan, Roujin Z and Metropolis, put on exhibitions, made commercials, and also published more of his manga.[18] (Marketed as the long-awaited 'follow-up' to Akira, Steam-boy wasn't: Roujin Z is the feature-length follow-up to Akira, released 3 years after Akira – in fact, Roujin Z is virtually a send-up of all the things that Akira took so seriously.[19] But Steam-boy does contain numerous affinities with Akira, and its astonishing finale is what Akira would look like if it had been produced in 2004. Howl's Moving Castle (Studio Ghibli), which shares a similar devotion to mecha and steam-punk,

17 It was released on March 18, 2005 in the U.S.A.
18 Manga is time-consuming: there's no quick, easy way of drawing those panels: you have to slog your way thru them.
19 Metropolis is also a sort of sequel to Akira.

and with a mobile castle that resembles the Steam Tower, was also released in 2004. Also, the incredible *Fullmetal Alchemist*, a steam-punk outing *par excellence*, was released in 2003-04).

Steam-boy was produced by Shinji Komori, Hideyuki Tomioka and Shigeru Watanabe (executive producer)[20] for Studio 4°C,[21] Sunrise[22] and Mash Room; the production companies were: Bandai, Bandai Visual, Culture Publishers, Dentsu, Imagica, Sony, Studio 4°C, Sunrise, Tokyo Broadcasting System and Toho; distributed by Toho; the budget was $20.2 million (which's very high for Japanese animation, but every single Yen is up there on the screen); Steve Jablonsky wrote the music;[23] the screenplay was by Katsuhiro Otomo and Sadayki Murai;[24] Takeshi Seyama was editor; art director was Shinji Kimura; character designs were by Atsushi Irie and Katsumi Matsuda; *mecha* designer was Makoto Kobayashi; Keiichi Momose was sound director; the 100s of animators included Tatsuya Tomaru (chief animation supervisor), Shinji Takagi, Atsushi Irie, Katsumi Matsuda, Tsutomu Awada, Yasuyuki Shimizu, Hisashi Eguchi and Hirotsugu Kawasaki (the latter directed *Spriggan*, which Otomo wrote); Otomo also designed the film. Virtually every animator and animation studio in Tokyo seems to have worked on *Steam-boy* (as often seems to happen with giant productions). Of course, many would be attracted by the prospect of working on a prestige project – and one helmed by the legendary Otomo.

20 The other executive producers were: Atsuhiko Chino, Chikara Takano, Hiroo Murakami, Kazuya Enna, Kenji Uchida, Kiyoshi Watanabe, Masao Seyama, and Ryohei Tsunoda.
21 Studio 4°C, who also produced *Spriggan* and *Memories*, was founded by Koji Morimoto (director of *Magnetic Rose*), Yoshiharu Sato and Eiko Tanaka (in 1986), a big name in Japanese *animé* (she had been a producer on *My Neighbor Totoro* and *Kiki's Delivery Service*). Studio 4°C's output includes *Mind Game* and *The Animatrix*.
22 Sunrise, founded in 1972, and now owned by Namco Bandai, produced shows such as *Cowboy Bebop, Escaflowne, Mobile Suit Gundam* and *Inuyasha*.
23 Alan Meyerson and Keiichi Momose were music producers.
24 Sadayuki Murai (b. 1964, Nara) has credits which include *Millennium Actress, Boogiepop Phantom, Perfect Blue, Kino's Journey, The Dimension Travellers, Ultraman Nexus*, and the updated *Astro Boy*.

Among the *seiyu* of *Steam-boy* were: Anne Suzuki as Ray Steam, Katsuo Nakamura as Lloyd Steam, Masane Tsukayama as Eddie Steam, Manami Konishi as Scarlett O'Hara, Kiyoshi Kodama as Robert Stephenson, Sanae Kobayashi as Emma, Satoru Sato as Archibald Simon, Osamu Saka as the Admiral, Ikki Sawamura as David, and Keiko Aizawa as Ray's mother.

The production of the boy-of-steam movie was rumoured to have run on for 10 years (it was due to be released in 1998-1999). That can't be true, at least not for the full production of the animation.[25] Rather, it would mean that money had been allocated for pre-production (prep includes developing the script, animation tests, creating designs, casting, etc). Also, Katsuhiro Otomo's perfectionism is well-known, so I imagine there were halts and re-thinks of what had already been produced.[26] In a 2004 interview, Otomo said they had started production on *Steam-boy* about 7 years ago (i.e., 1997), and that he had begun work on *Steam-boy* in 1994, around the time of the production of *Memories* (and the experiments with computer animation in *Memories* had led towards *Steam-boy*. Some of the crew from *Memories* were hired for *Steam-boy*. Another reason offered for the long production cycle was that the computer systems and the way of working (called the pipeline) had to be set up from scratch. The late 1990s and the early 2000s was a period when many in the animation industry – all over the world – were getting to grips with digital animation. Which meant buying and learning new software (or creating it from scratch), getting used to new and computer systems, hiring new people, trying out tests, etc).

I first saw *Steam-boy* in the English dub (released by Sony). Although it featured name actors such as

25 A five-minute pilot of *Steam-boy* had been produced in 1995, with a view to attracting backers.
26 Again, Katsuhiro Otomo's perfectionism was partly responsible for the delays. Using computers meant that 16.7 million colours are available to filmmakers – too many for Otomo, who would ask for re-takes.

Alfred Molina and Ian McKellen (with Anna Paquin as the hero James),[27] I always prefer the original language (for any movie). *Steam-boy* comes over far, far more satisfyingly in the Japanese cut. *Steam-boy*, despite its English settings and characters, is *wholly* Japanese (England here is employed as exotic other-world. Yes, it's England, yes it's Europe, but, actually, it's *always* Japan. *Always*).[28]

Clearly Ian McKellen and Alfred Molina and the others in the cast of the English dub are fine actors (McKellen is a god among actors – understandable if you've seen him on stage). And McKellen and Molina (and others) do employ a (reasonably accurate) Northern British/ Mancunian accent (which probably makes it even more unintelligible for U.S.A. audiences). But even with the finest cast, the original soundtrack is still the best way and the most appropriate way and the most accurate way to view *Steam-boy*. (Otomo and sound director Keiichi Momose did not direct the English-speaking actors).

The North American and European versions of *Steam-boy* also had about 15 minutes (some said 20 minutes) cut from them (chiefly in the early, Manchester scenes). *Steam-boy*'s listed as 104 minutes in the international edition, and 126m in the Japanese version by *The Anime Encyclopedia*.[29] The DVD of *Steam-boy* has it running at 126 minutes. The so-called 'director's cut' is 126 minutes, and happily has the original Japanese language dub on it.

This being a *thoroughly* Japanese movie, it demands to be viewed in the original language. The longer cut of *Steam-boy* certainly plays better in the early scenes, where more time is spent establishing Ray's character, and also his family: his mom, his friend Emma, her younger brother Thomas, and his

27 Like the Japanese original, which featured Anne Suzuki as James, the English dub also cast a woman (a common practice in *animé* – *Naruto, One Piece, Fullmetal Alchemist*, etc).
28 Take minor details, like the way the characters interact, for instance. Or how characters politely introduce themselves. Or that Ray Steam reads a book backwards.
29 J. Clements, 2006, 616.

pals. (Additions to the longer cut of *Steam-boy* include a beat where Ray, walking home from school, goofs around for the sake of a girl he's sweet on, a little more of Ray's relationship with his brother and sister, more of Ray in his laboratory (with its pulley inventions for altering the room), more of Ray watching trains in some sidings (this's what *mecha otaku* did in 1866!), and more atmosphere and texture of mid-19th century Manchester).

Most of *Steam-boy* concerns three people, a trinity of 13 year-old son (Ray – James in the English dub), middle-aged father (Eddie) and grandfather in his seventies (Lloyd). Then there's Scarlett O'Hara, the unlikely companion/ love interest, and Robert Stephenson as an ambiguous rival. And a host of secondary characters, such as Stephenson's aide David, and Archibald Simon, the unctuous business manager of the O'Hara Foundation and the Steam Tower.

Ray Steam is on a father quest, and has not one but two father figures to contend with – his dad, Eddie, and his grandfather Lloyd. The prologue of *Steam-boy* establishes both of 'em as adventurous scientist-inventor types, familiar from many other Victorian fantasy outings (and also the accident which scars Eddie). There's some Captain Nemo (*20,000 Leagues Under the Sea*) and some Polar explorers in the characterizations. (Splitting the father into two, into father and grandpa, enables them to embody opposing ideological issues, such as science vs. politics, science and capitalism, technology and weaponry, etc).

Thus, *Steam-boy* takes from *Akira* the anxiety-laden relationship that the younger generation has with the older generation (and vice versa). The psychological and emotional subtext of *Steam-boy* is about fathers and sons and the Sins of the Fathers (this was very much in Katsuhiro Otomo's mind). How they don't really understand each other. The political and societal aspects are as significant for the movie and the director as the personal and psychological ones.

Actually, there are multiple father figures in *Steam-boy* – this world is full of powerful, mystifying, complicated men – the ambiguous, avuncular (wary, distant) figure of Robert Stephenson, for instance (Stephenson is a good expression of a representative of Imperial ideology and institutions – he's the equivalent of General Shikishima in *Akira*), and his equally untrustworthy assistant, David (both Stephenson and David appear at first as allies, until they take the steam ball and use it to power one of their own military vehicles. Ray steals it back). Stephenson has several sombre dialogues with the Admiral about politics and the state of the nation.[30]

Then there are heavies, O'Hara's Foundation, the police, the British government, the military – *Steam-boy* is stuffed with stern, patriarchal figures (and Ray has to negotiate his way through this multi-layered moral maze).

Ray Steam wants to look up to both his father and grandfather: they are great men to him, men of science and discovery. But it turns out that his returned father Eddie is a changed man, now zealously enamoured of transforming the world thru science by developing weapons (half his face covered by a black mask and goggle for one eye, and he has partial cyborgization, so it's the visual expression of his new ambiguity and duality). The links to Frankenstein's monster are obvious (he has the clumpy boots of Boris Karloff in the 1931 movie). The off-balance psychology of Captain Nemo is another reference point. And late in the piece, David also becomes somewhat obsessive and manic, launching into a villainous monologue about becoming famous scientists if Ray teams up with him (he also hits Ray when they're arguing over the steam ball). *Steam-boy* is a portrait of

30 While the police raid the Steam Tower, the Admiral takes tea with Stephenson on their ship. Yes, even in the midst of pandemonium, upper-class Brits still sip at their blasted cups of (Asian) tea!

men who lose sight of their humanity, of what it means to be human, and of the place of science in the modern world. It is a cautionary tale.

And Ray's grandfather Lloyd has become a wild, crazy man (who spends most of the 2004 movie near-naked, clad in nowt but tattered pants, a not entirely successful creative choice (even if it has a thematic point, reducing humans to their 'primitive' origins). It automatically weakens your authority figure, doesn't it?, when you look like Robinson Crusoe. What Lloyd needs to do is stop running around and yelling for a moment and find a dark suit and shades, so he can look like the Colonel in *Akira*).

As well as all of the familiar steam-punk outings in *manga*, movies, TV or novels, and action-adventure films like *Indiana Jones, Nadia: Secret of the Blue Water, Soul Eater, Black Butler, Fullmetal Alchemist,* the animations of Hayao Miyazaki and *Star Wars, Steamboy* also draws on Victorian adventures such as *Treasure Island* (Robert Louis Stevenson), *Journey To the Centre of the Earth* and *20,000 Leagues Under the Sea* (Jules Verne is a forerunner of plenty of steampunkania, and Miyazaki, like the Walt Disney corporation, has also drawn on Verne repeatedly).

We're introduced first to the figure of the grandfather, Lloyd, just a little obsessed with steam and power, and his son, Eddie. We see mines (in Iceland),[31] a submarine, and all sorts of intricate machinery (the 2004 movie spreads these prologues over different times and places). The scientists are searching for a special liquid which'll help create the power of the steam ball. There's a huge laboratory (in Alaska) where Lloyd is presiding over a steampowered experiment involving the steam ball (which's the much-used MacGuffin of the 2004 piece – and another equivalent for atomic power). It's night, and there's a storm. Of course, Lloyd is the crazy scientist who is pushing things to the limit, while

---

31 Iceland – maybe that's a nod to *Journey To the Centre of the Earth*.

Eddie is the voice of caution (later that will be reversed, as Eddie becomes the Nietzschean Superman campaigning for eternal glory in the name of science). Meanwhile, a bunch of businessman and politicos (from the O'Hara Foundation, we find out later) watch from an upper walkway. Of course, the experiment flies off the handle, causing a huge explosion, and injuring Eddie in the process (the scenario is revisited in the finale, when Archibald Simon is trying to sell new weapons technology to prospective customers from Prussia, France, Arabia, India, etc).

Thus, as soon as the technology of steam is introduced in the first scenes of *Steam-boy*, it is going wrong. Scientists are trying to grasp for energy sources and technology which's powerful and perhaps untameable (it's certainly dangerous and injures people). Which announces one of the key themes of *Steam-boy*: humans and technology.

The following sequence in *Steam-boy* introduces us to Ray Steam: he's working in a factory in Manchester in 1866: another immense, steam-powered machine goes awry, and nobody can seem to stop it. The manager of the factory is depicted as a ruthless capitalist (they crop up throughout the 2004 movie), who prefers to save his machinery than prevent injury. He's a cowardly bully, pushing his workers and machines onward, and prattling non-stop about how much every machine costs and how they mustn't be damaged. In the end, it's our Ray who saves the day (thus establishing his personality as a tech-head, who can also survive potentially dangerous situations, who doesn't mind getting his hands dirty, and who doesn't see what all the fuss was about).[32]

But the opening scenes of *Steam-boy* are also introducing us to the world of this expensive animated movie, which's the most richly, densely complex vision of the Age of Steam in recent

32 There's a classic *animé* reverse angle shot when Ray emerges from underneath the machine, to see everybody gawping at him.

animation. Pretty much every shot is wall-to-wall machinery, so that the human figures can appear refreshingly simple, with their classic, Otomoan round faces, wide foreheads, and round eyes.

🖥

Set in 1866 in Manchester and London, among the most curious aspects of *Steam-boy* was its Englishness seen thru Japanese eyes (especially if you're looking at *Steam-boy* in Britain!). There's a similar oddness about watching some of Hayao Miyazaki's movies set in Europe or in a European-influenced setting – such as *The Castle of Cagliostro*, with its French Riviera *milieu,* or *Laputa: Castle In the Sky*, with its Welsh mining town in a valley, or *Kiki's Delivery Service* (which drew on Lisbon, Naples, Stockholm, Paris, and San Francisco).[33] Or when *animé* shows like *Hellsing, Black Butler* and *Ghost In the Shell: Stand Alone Complex* visit London (which they manage to make look truly exotic and other-worldly – as well as completely deserted! But London in the 19th century was the biggest metro-polis on the planet!).

Certainly Katsuhiro Otomo, art director Shinji Kimura, and the team had the look and feel of Victorian England down to minute detail[34] (Otomo's perfectionism paid off handsomely). Otomo said they had looked at *Sherlock Hound* (1981),[35] a TV show part-directed by Hayao Miyazaki: 'not an exact copy, but we want to recreate the same sense of English-ness' (2009, 37), and also the British television soap opera *Coronation Street* (there's a nod to the *Rover's*

---

33 Stockholm was a key influence on *Kiki's Delivery Service* – the filmmakers visited it, and took a large number of photos for refer-ence). It was a Mediterranean coastal town on one side, and a Scandinavian city on the other.

34 The 1851 Great Exhibition in London at Crystal Palace inspired part of *Steam-Boy* (it was also an influence on the museum at the end of the first *Ghost In the Shell* movie).

35 In 1981 Hayao Miyazaki directed the TV series *Great Detective Holmes* (a.k.a. *Sherlock Hound the Detective),* made as a co-production with R.A.I. TV in Italy. It featured Sherlock Holmes-style capers in a dog world (a world populated only by dog characters). On *Great Detective Holmes* Miyazaki worked with Italian animators, including his friend Marco Pagott.

Return pub).

There's no doubt that the Britain of the Victorian era on show here is as detailed, as meticulously researched, and as lovingly recreated as any live-action, Public Broadcasting Service, British Broadcasting Corporation, or Merchant-Ivory costume drama (*Steam-boy* certainly looks as if Katsuhiro Otomo and the key designers took a research trip to London and Manchester. The high budget of *Steam-boy* would've meant that the filmmakers could make some research trips. Usually there isn't the money (or the time!) for research jaunts in the Japanese animation industry).

In some scenes in *Steam-boy*, awash with browns, beiges, ochres and greys (in a palette markedly different from *Akira*, tho' with thematic links), it's as if you're looking at old photographs by Julia Margaret Cameron, or paintings by John Everett Millais or Holman Hunt. It's true that the level of detail and intricacy in *Steam-boy* is astonishing, and beyond obsessive, and goes far beyond the requirements of the narrative. (It is also, incredibly, a vision of London that has never been put on screen before: you have never seen London portrayed quite like this. *Steam-boy* certainly captures the grandeur of London in its Victorian, Imperial heyday, when it really was an extraordinary, flourishing metropolis, as well, of course, as being filled with poverty and problems. There's a remarkable feeling of grandeur in the architecture and the public spaces, especially in the way that the designers and background artists have portrayed the River Thames and the riverside areas – they have taken regions such as Tower Bridge, the Southbank, St Katharine Docks and Greenwich and enlarged them with a feeling for Ancient, Imperial Japan. Evoking scale (especially enormous scale), is of course one of Japanese animation's specialities. Much of *Steam-boy* in London is set either in Greenwich or in the City, around Tower Bridge, London, Southwark and Bermondsey).

Steam-boy should be commended too for attempting to portray a vision of Great Britain that *isn't* solely occupied by upper-class twits drinking tea. When Japanese *animé* visits Victorian Britain (or a variation on it), the chief charas are always aristos and nobles – *Black Butler, Trinity Blood, Hellsing*, etc (plus the odd working class oik). By contrast, *Steam-boy* depicts people actually working (at looms, in factories), and working class communities (and the famous terraced houses of Manchester). However, the Steam family are *not* working class – they are scientists, explorers and entrepreneurs (and they're self-taught – versions of Victorian autodidacts).

The score for *Steam-boy* (by Steve Jablonsky) is a thoroughly Westernized, orchestral creation, very much in the mold of Joe Hisaishi's scores for the films of Hayao Miyazaki. Thus, there are jaunty themes for the early, happier scenes, big, broad, brassy adventure cues for the *Indiana Jonesian* chases, and, most impressively, epic choral cues for the grandiose moments (such as Eddie revealing his idealistic ambitions for steam power, or the first appearance of the armoured soldiers). There is, however, too much music in *Steam-boy* – it falls for the Hollywood approach to filling out scenes with music which don't need or want it.

▾

The key issue of *Steam-boy* is: what is science for? Or: how should science be used practically in modern society? Or: what is the relation between science and politics, and in particular, national security? These issues concern Japanese animators deeply – you can find them in the *Ghost In the Shell* series, for instance, or in Hayao Miyazaki's works (and in much sci-fi and fantasy in Japan).

Ray Steam is the questioner, the seeker, the character who asks these questions (or, instead of asking them, the boy who comes into contact with situations and characters that embody the issues). In *Steam-boy*, though, the *link* between the *story* and the *issues* is not as elegantly and convincingly made as it is in similar fare, such as *Laputa: Castle In the Sky,* or *Ghost In the Shell,* or Katsuhiro Otomo's own *Akira.*

Or put it like this: in *Steam-boy*, the story and the characters do not quite express or embody the issues, and the issues are not fully explored or embodied by the story or the characters (one reason is that the movie bloats itself up for too long with action sequences, and bogs itself down too much with details, losing sight of the bigger picture).

One of the problems with *Steam-boy* is that the three main characters are somewhat under-written, and their psychologies don't quite do justice to the gargantuan scale of the story (and the background context). By comparison, *Akira* managed to create multi-dimensional characters in the figures of Kaneda, Tetsuo and Kei, that also linked up more satisfyingly to the themes and the issues. (Also, the three generations of Steams are not completely compelling as characters: the movie lacks the bunch of pirates in *Laputa: Castle In the Sky*, for instance, or the force of nature that is Kaneda in *Akira.* In short, it is in the areas of characterization and story that *Steam-boy* stumbles, and isn't as rich as it might be).

After *Akira*, anything is going to seem an anti-climax, and *Steam-boy,* for all its spectacle and invention, was. Had nothing else appeared in the time between *Akira* (1988) and *Steam-boy* (2004), then *Steam-boy* would have seemed incredibly impressive. But by 2004, many movies had delivered similar spectacles.[36] And, besides, as I have pointed out many times, Katsuhiro Otomo had been busy with numer-ous projects between the two flicks.

Steam-boy is less than satisfying, if you compare it to *Akira.* But then, almost *anything* in *animé* – or live-action – is disappointing after *Akira*! *Steam-boy,* though, had been built up by the marketing teams as

---

36 The ending of the *Appleseed* digital remake (2004), for example, or the ill-fated *Wild, Wild West* (Barry Sonnenfeld, 1999).

Katsuhiro Otomo's big movie to follow *Akira*: as with filmmakers such as Orson Welles and Francis Coppola, there was a tendency in *animé* circles to compare Otomo's later works always in relation (often negatively) to *Akira*. (Welles has this problem with people's perceptions in relation to *Citizen Kane*, and Coppola with *The Godfather*. As in, 'oh, it's not as good as *Citizen Kane*', or: 'Coppola's latest movie is another let-down from the director of *The Godfather*').

On its own terms, *Steam-boy* is staggeringly inventive, imaginative, and visually spectacular. But...

...*Steam-boy* is let-down partly by its characters, partly by its story, and partly by some awkward pacing, in the international cut (even tho' it was edited by the finest editor in Japanese *animé*, Takeshi Seyama. For the pacing, the longer cut is far more engrossing). The movie is over-burdened by a too-fussy, too-action-filled final act. Contrary to popular opinion that 'more is better', that longer films are 'better', or that a director's cut is more satisfying, the opposite is true with *Steam-boy*: the international cut, at 104m, is a more suitable running time for this sort o' action-adventure movie, rather than the 126m of the Japanese cut (even tho' the 126m is a more satisfying movie in some areas).

A good solution would be to keep the early scenes of the Japanese cut, which flesh out the characters, and lose 10-15 minutes from the final act (5m from the police & Navy vs. O'Hara steam troopers battle, and 10m from the climactic Steam Tower vs. London sequence). The final act of *Steam-boy* adds too many cliffhangers, too many climaxes, too many moments of jeopardy, and too many obstacles. The final act over-balances the movie and the characters.

The hero, Ray Steam, the Steam-boy of the title, is a young, English kid, a wannabe inventor, but ultimately he's rather unengaging. He has the oval eyes, the high forehead and the rather solemn demeanour of Katsuhiro Otomo's other characters – like a younger Tetsuo from *Akira* (and there's a little of Tetsuo's resentment and aggression, too: in an early scene, where the local kids tease Ray,[37] he whacks one of 'em. There's a nice jokey reference to *Akira* when Ray's mom tells him you can't go around hitting people on the head with pipes. There was, of course, no mom – or dad – to tell the kids in *Akira* they couldn't do that!).

Ray Steam's characterization errs too far towards playing the sullen anti-hero, or the unlikable hero (like Shinji in *Evangelion*). When these anti-hero characterizations don't work (as in *Evangelion, Paranoia Agent* and *Eden of the East*), it can unbalance the stories. But it can work – as in *Death Note* and *Berserk*. (I wonder if the 'fault' lies partly with the direction of *seiyu* Anne Suzuki (by sound director Keiichi Momose), who plays Ray very intense in most scenes). Ray lacks humour, and is played too straight (which, for an Otomoan hero, is a mistake: look at Otomo's early *manga*, which are full of humorous bits for the heroes). It seems as if Otomo and Murai said, let's *not* do the usual plucky boy hero of action-adventure flicks, let's try something else.

Part of the problem with *Steam-boy* is that there is no subtext, no theme, and no psychology, so that the drama lacks an emotional (or spiritual) impact. *Steam-boy* is too empty, and too predictable (maybe, in the end – and ironically – too Westernized).

Well, that's not quite true: there *is* a subtext about fathers and families in *Steam-boy*, tho', and the sins of the fathers, and the antagonisms between the generations, and about the corruption of science by political interests, but somehow it isn't sufficient to render the 2004 movie as compelling as it wants to be. And the primary theme is the abuse of science by

---

37 Notice that the other lads taunt Ray about his family, and his father and grandfather – people that Ray reveres.

money and political power.

Steam-boy features a trinity of male characters, linked by blood and family: a grandfather, father and son. This generational masculinism enhances the patriarchal flavour of Steam-boy: it's wholly a movie about boys' stuff, about boys being boys, about boys' adventures.

The key female character, Scarlett O'Hara, heir to the O'Hara empire, is meant to be an irritating spoilt brat of a girl;[38] unfortunately, she remains that way for too much of the picture (she's a little less irritating in the Japanese cut, as played by Manami Konishi). She whacks her pet dog (so in movie terms, she's a vile villain!), gets on Ray's nerves a lot, and her snub, up-turned nose and snotty manner simply becomes tiresome after a while. Placing Scarlett in amongst the world of macho men, heavy industry and later in the midst of warfare, is a conventional ploy offering dramatic contrast. However, it isn't wholly success-ful, and is a minor flaw in Steam-boy; partly because the humour doesn't work too well, and her design is so eccentric, and you resent Scarlett's uppity inter-jections after a while (as Ray does!). Scarlett is a character no one would want to be around for long, except for the hangers-on eager for her inherited wealth, like Archibald Simon. (I kinda wish that Scarlett wasn't part of Steam-boy at all).

But there isn't a female character like Kei from Akira here (or even any of the sassy biker gang girlfriends), or like the lovely Haruko from Roujin Z. Instead, only Ray's mom and sister Emma make an impression (and there's a brief cameo from Queen Victoria, tho' she's chiefly a figurehead). Ray's sister is modelled visually on Alice in John Tenniel's famous illustrations to Alice's Adventures In Wonder-land. It's a pity that Emma (Sanae Kobayashi) dips out of the movie early on – she is much preferrable to

---

38 The dubbed voice, by Kari Wahlgren, enhances her aggravating characterization.

the bratty Yank Scarlett O'Hara. (Note that Scarlett is the main significant North American figure in *Steam-boy*, and is sent up mercilessly. As with the *manga* of *Akira*, *Steam-boy* takes a very dim view of North Americans, altho' of course Scarlett isn't represent-ative of anyone but herself).

Ray Steam is caught between two father figures who represent two poles of the uses of science: Lloyd with his talk about the philosophy and ideals of science (a machine without a philosophy behind it worthless for Lloyd). Lloyd's idealized, utopian vision of science is contrasted with Eddie's prag-matic, practical view, in which science and the technology it creates must have a physical application in the real world. And that means dealing with capitalists, and with weaponry, and with events such as armed conflict.

For Lloyd, Eddie has sold out to the capitalist West, with their power-mongering and coercion of people by the use of arms. For Eddie, Lloyd is a crazy dreamer who clings to out-dated, idealistic beliefs. The key scene where all of this is discussed occurs mid-way in *Steam-boy*, when Ray discovers his grandfather Lloyd lurking in the shadows, having escaped from being held captive. There is a *lot* of argument, back and forth, as Lloyd tries to make Ray see the light, that his father has become twisted and debased in his views and acts. It's a *lot* for Ray to take in (because he still idolizes his pa, and is helping him run the giant Tower, which he thinks is marvell-ous. When Ray sees the weaponry and military vehicles lined up in the hold of the Steam Tower, he gasps, *sugoi!* Lloyd has to persuade him, no, not 'sugoi!' – these are machines created to kill people). So Ray has to shift his emotional and psychological position in the space of a few minutes (and Lloyd is played at hysterical levels at times, grabbing Ray repeatedly by the labels and shaking him).

Meanwhile, as the pros and cons of the uses of

science argument are explored by Lloyd, Ray and Eddie, the characters are moving all around the Steam Tower (handily giving us a tour of the place, which sets up the finale, as with the scene where Eddie shows off the control room of the Tower. The interior is very reminiscent of the underground facility in *Akira*).[39] Forerunners of the Steam Tower include the giant machine in *Robot Carnival* (which also had things popping outta the sides and roof), the hospital bed at the end of *Roujin Z,* and another 2004 movie, *Howl's Moving Castle.*

Lloyd Steam is on a mission: to shut down the workings of the Steam Tower (he is forever depicted turning steels wheels to close off valves or open valves), and to capture the steam ball which he developed. Eddie, meanwhile, is also trying to make Ray see things *his* way, and also to prevent his father Lloyd snaffling the steam ball.

So it goes on and on – until the action kicks in, and Lloyd passes the ball to Ray, who, after plenty of action-adventure chases, gags and beats, eludes the henchmen and escapes into the River Thames (there is a terrific use of the river here, with Robert Stephenson's vessel looming out of the fog, and Ray trying to evade the O'Hara heavies who're shooting at him. This part of *Steam-boy* is very reminiscent of the *Akira manga*, with its many scenes in tunnels and water – Katsuhiro Otomo likes to put his heroes in water).[40]

No one can miss that the 2004 movie evokes several political conflicts: between North America and Britain, for instance (the O'Hara Foundation is North American, and the Steams are Brits). The O'Hara Foundation is out-and-out capitalism eager

---

39 For all its use of historical research, *Steam-boy* is a wholly fantastical outing. For instance, the Steam Tower would require 100s and 100s of people to run it, rather than the few guys in overalls we see (there would be guys – 'trimmers' doing nothing but hauling coal to the boilers on trolleys; there would be workers stoking the fires, others cleaning out the ashes, and so on).
40 Ray manages to stay afloat with the steam ball – and that thing's gotta weigh a ton!

to sell to any schmuck who'll buy their products, while the Brits are portrayed as proud nationalists, keen to protect their national sovereignity.

In Japanese animation, however, the heroes are always actually Japanese. So, if we see the Steam family as Japanese (as in other Japanese animations set in Britain or starring Brits, such as *Hellsing* with its Integra family and Alucard the vampire), then *Steam-boy* is once again rolling out the Japan vs. North America political tussles which have been a big part of Katsuhiro Otomo's output (as well as a recurring antagonism in *animé* – *Ghost In the Shell*, *Legend of the Overfiend*, *Death Note*, etc).

So the Japanese characters in *Steam-boy* – the Steam family – are brave scientists and explorers, that're pitted against the crude capitalists and exploiters of the North American O'Hara Foundation (who enter their country first as merchants, selling technology, but rapidly move into aggression).

There's no question that *Steam-boy* is *the* animated movie when it comes to steam and steam-punk[41] – even more so than *Laputa: Castle In the Sky*, *Fullmetal Alchemist*, *Trinity Blood*, *Nadia: Secret of the Blue Water* or the 2001 *Metropolis*. That is, if we're talking a compulsive passion for steam-power and its numerous manifestations in a million an' one machines, which goes beyond any of the characters. The real Steam Boy is of course Katsuhiro Otomo! Whose love of all things steam-powered rivals that of the chief hero of the Age of Steam (at least in Albion): Izambard Kingdom Brunel.

As a movie featuring *mecha*, *Steam-boy* has no rivals – for sheer quantity, at least. *Steam-boy* is jammed, rammed and crammed with *mecha* of every variety, every size, every possibility. It is *Mecha* Heaven – aircraft, airships, tractors, trains, tanks, ships, giant cannons, cranes, Ray's bike (the 1866

41 Other steam-punk outings, apart from the films of Hayao Miyazaki, include *Steam Detectives* (1994).

version of Kaneda's red motorcycle) and 'steam troopers' (steam-powered men in suits of armour). Absolutely *everything* has been squeezed into *Steam-boy* (and it cheats, like all steam-*animé* do – set in 1866, it includes vehicles and designs from the 1910s up thru the 1940s). It's the *James Bond* movie of steam, the *Star Wars* movie of steam. (You could mount a huge exhibition in a museum of images and models from *Steam-boy*).

And visually, *Steam-boy* is extraordinary: the filmmakers are totally confident about what cinema can do. Seen as entertainment as a machine, as a whirling, smoking, steaming, hi-tech extravaganza, *Steam-boy* is superlative (there's even a funfair which erupts across the Steam Tower during the climax). If the story doesn't have the same density as the visuals, or the characters that much depth, or the themes are hackneyed and obvious, it doesn't matter if you only consider *Steam-boy* as an experience, or a sensation, or a look.

Steam-boy is visually daring in many respects (this is, after all, a Katsuhiro Otomo-directed and designed movie! And with twenty million dollars to spend, Otomo can be relied upon to come with something distinctive!). The colour palette of *Steam-boy* is unusual,[42] taking the movie into the expected reds and oranges of an Otomo movie (Otomo-sensei is *very* fond of reds and oranges!), yet also skewing them into darker and browner versions of the bright scarlets that Otomo and co. used in *Akira*. You can see the impact of digital inking in *Steam-boy* (compared to the more opaque ink and paint of *Akira*): now the filmmakers can use blurred colours, foggy colours, and 16 million variations of beige, brown,[43] grey and black. (There are more varieties of the colour brown than in any other movie ever made).

42 As one might expect from the director of *Akira*, the colour scheme in *Steam-boy* is not what you'd expect. A striking amount of *Steam-boy* is lit with reds and pinks (including the skies). Interior design includes reds flattened and dirtied – these are not the neon-bright reds of *Akira*.
43 Everybody in the Steam Tower is clad in a uniform of dull brown.

Daring indeed is *Steam-boy* when it takes the colour palette right down to so many *very* dark greys, blacks and browns, so the frames are printed with few lights. Yet the result isn't muddy, or like a badly-exposed piece of celluloid: the filmmakers manage to keep the compositions readable. For instance, many of the scenes in the engine rooms of the O'Hara Castle are extremely dim, as if we're in the bowels of hell, not a steam room. Giant, industrial interiors are of course one of Katsuhiro Otomo's specialities (they crop up in *Akira, Spriggan, Memories* and *Robot Carnival*).

The continuous camera shots of *Cannon Fodder* were employed again in *Steam-boy* (the test for *Steam-boy* goes back to the time of *Cannon Fodder* in *Memories*). So, once again, Katsuhiro Otomo indulges his taste for continuous takes with a dollying camera *à la* Orson Welles or Akira Kurosawa. Yet, because these shots are so extravagant, they call attention to themselves (tho' in a spectacular production like *Steam-boy*, that's isn't a problem: pretty much everything in this extraordinary (tho' flawed) movie demands attention).

Roger Ebert noted that the third act of *Steam-boy* over-balances the 2004 movie: in the North American version (the 104m cut), with some of the early scenes dropped, the third act (or the fourth act in the 126m cut) does loom too large. (The 126m cut is a four-act movie – and acts 3 and 4 – a whole hour! – constitute a continuous climax).

Even though the action (its timing, its invention, its staging) is stupendous, even though the visuals are magnificent, even though the filmmakers exploit every nook and cranny of the Steam Tower, the final act simply drags on for too long, and, fatally, it's too samey in tone and content. It becomes a case of one thing blowing up after another, one thing crashing into another after another, one set-piece after another. Normally, this would be plenty to be going on with in a movie (we know, watching a Katsuhiro Otomo movie, we are gonna see stuff blow up! And if we're Otomo fans, we enjoy seeing stuff blow up!). But in *Steam-boy* it gets wearisome.

You do get a little tired of seeing yet another wheel being turned to shut off or open something (every time summat goes wrong, someone – usually Lloyd or Ray – hurries to a wheel or valve to turn it), yet another vehicle hurtling thru the air, yet another scene of Ray or Grandpa Lloyd yelling at someone, and yet another pipe bulging and spraying steam (the phallic connotations are vividly obvious – *Steam-boy* contains more vibrating, pulsing, throbbing and exploding pipes than any other movie in the history of cinema).[44]

Even multi-million-dollar movie-making like this can be repetitive and can out-stay its welcome. Which seems a dumb, complaining view, considering just how extraordinary the combination of digital imagery[45] and 2-D animation is in the final act of *Steam-boy*. One of the problems is with the script: there is never a true feeling of jeopardy, because the audience knows that a movie like this will *never* sacrifice the hero (whom we are not especially fond of – Ray is too one-note and under-written to really care about or root for). Tetsuo may die, even Kaneda or Kei may die in *Akira,* but a young hero like Ray will *never* die.

The other characters, such as the grandfather Lloyd, will not be sacrificed either. The father, Eddie, may die, and Robert Stephenson or David might die, and who cares if the irritating, snooty Scarlett dies? (In the end, none of 'em die. Lloyd shoots a gun at his son, but Eddie survives). *Steam-boy* wants to have villains, but then it abstracts them into forces or

44 The Steam Tower as a giant erection – and, in the end, the father and the grandfather can't keep it up!

45 About a quarter of the shots in *Steam-boy* used CGI, Katsuhiro Otomo said, or some 400 shots. As Otomo noted in 2004, 'the U.S. prefer super-realism. Since Japan is a country that prefers plane vision, I don't think we will leave 2D and substitute hand-drawing with CGI entirely.'

issues such as 'war', or 'science', or 'war vs. peace'. If *Steam-boy* is about the Sins of the Fathers, the Fathers are not punished, or even seem to learn the errors of their ways (in movie-movie terms, Eddie should die or receive some punishment. Why? Because the Steam Tower freezes and crashing into London must've killed thousands of people! But we don't see that, do we? No – the movie includes people watching (a family from a smashed house), but no one among the civilians is seen injured or expiring).

The influence of the heavily industrialized look of 2001's *Metropolis* is apparent in *Steam-boy*: you could swop many shots (and many scenes) without anyone realizing it. Some commentators (H. McCarthy & J. Clements) have wondered whether *Steam-boy* used some shots or digital imagery from *Metropolis* (maybe not actual shots, but certainly some compositions – like humans standing next to enormous, rotating cogs[46]).

Another problem with the final act (or two acts) of *Steam-boy* is the lack of twists, turns and reversals: the drama plays out all too linearly. There are no surprises, and nothing is held back for a revelation. There is no emotional, subtextual or psychological material to be explored (apart from the œdipal antagonisms between the fathers and the sons). The only goal is to stop the Steam Tower exploding over London (despite that it already seems to have destroyed most of the City area of London, between St Paul's and Bank; and, anyway, it *does* explode[47]). This is the humanity vs. technology issue; the other is the 'sins of the fathers' issue, with the uneasy relations between the trinity of son-father-grand-father.

Consequently, the perpetual fireworks of *Steam-boy* don't carry as much weight or impact as they might do if some more work had been put into the screenplay (compare with the rich subtext in the

46 Maybe, but big steam engines do include immense wheels.
47 How can it *not* explode?!

rivalry btn Kaneda and Tetsuo in *Akira*, for instance, or the powerful political satire of *Cannon Fodder* in *Memories*).

An off-shoot of this is the samey *tone* of the final act of *Steam-boy*: the movie careens from noisy, kinetic set-piece to set-piece as characters struggle to achieve this or that short-term goal (twisting a wheel, finding a way out, fleeing a murderous machine). But there is no let-up, no change of tone (how about some 'pillow moments'? a break in the headlong rush? some flash-backs or back-story?). The moral and psychological issues get lost in the cacophony of pipes bursting and buildings collapsing.

Steam-boy struggles to find summat for Scarlett O'Hara to do in the finale, so that, for much of the time, she storms about in a perpetual huff, yelling 'Simon!' Oh, yes, the screenwriters *do* give Scarlett summat do – yep, you guessed it! – she pulls some levers (in the control room)! Which's what everybody does in *Steam-boy* – turns a wheel, or closes a valve! *Here* is where a sub-plot involving Scarlett would pay off, and give the bratty heroine something to contribute.

The end credits of *Steam-Boy* include stills and partially-animated images which take a leaf out of Hayao Miyazaki's *Book of Cinema*, and include the story continuing into the future: so we see images of the older[48] Ray Steam (and an older Scarlett[49])… Ray at the graveside of his Grandpa Lloyd (who appears momentarily then fades away)… Ray and co. next to a plane called *Scarlett*… World War One (the trenches)… and, best of all, Ray as a kind of super-hero,[50] complete with cloak…

Part of the problem with *Steam-boy* is that the screenwriting (by Katsuhiro Otomo and Sadayki

---

48 Not looking much older, though – Ray in World War Two would be 60.
49 Now she's a pilot.
50 Flying about in his steam-powered jet-pack, Ray is a steam-punk version of Astro Boy.

Murai) isn't quite up to scratch; or perhaps the storyline changed quite a bit during production (and maybe there wasn't a locked script in the first place). The lengthy pre-production, usually all to the good on a movie, might this time have worked against the filmmakers, as they thought of adding more an' more items to the script, as the years went by.

A good illustration of this are the quieter, character-based scenes, where the movie really should fix itself in the audience's minds, with character-led scenes which will establish these people. The 2004 movie is so obsessed with its own technical amazingness (it *is* amazing), the characters get lost in the state-of-the-art visuals. The strength of *animé* and *manga*, according to many commentators (including Fred Schodt and Helen McCarthy), is their *characters* (*not* its stories). We root for Naruto (in *Naruto*), for Ed and Al (in *Fullmetal Alchemist*), and for Yuki in *Lady Snowblood*. Well, of course, both run together, fusing at every point, but what I mean is that the depth of characterization in *animé* and *manga* is a large part of what makes it so successful, and what makes its storytelling so compelling.

In the end, Ray Steam, Eddie Steam and Lloyd Steam simply *don't* compel as characters as they should. And if they did, *Steam-boy* would be hailed as a masterpiece. It's a *technical* masterpiece, but emotionally it's rather soulless (rather like the 2001 *Metropolis*, which Katsuhiro Otomo also scripted). By contrast, *Roujin Z, Memories, Akira* and *manga* such as *The Legend of Mother Sarah* have done the necessary work to establish the characters. However, I can watch *Steam-boy* any time; this is a movie of a genius working at full force.

08

BUGMASTER

MUSHISHI

I've always been interested in *jidai geki* and in making one. As a Japanese, you grow up watching *jidai geki*. Every filmmaker probably wants to direct one – to be like Akira Kurosawa. But not everybody can be Kurosawa.

Katsuhiro Otomo

2006's *Mushishi* (a.k.a. *Bugmaster*) was a live-action adaptation of the *manga* by Yuki Urushibara (b. 1973), published in *Afternoon Season* magazine in Japan (from 1999 onwards).[51] Sunmin Park, Kiyoshi Inoue and Satoru Ogura produced for Ogura Jimusyo Inc.; Sadayuki Murai[52] and Otomo-sensei wrote the script; Kuniaki Haishima composed the music; Takahide Shibanushi was DP; Noriyushi Ikeya was prod. des., costumes by Keisuke Chiyoda, sound was

---

51 *Mushishi* was published in the West by Del Rey (part of Random House, established in 2004).
52 Murai had also co-written *Steam-boy*.

by Yoshiya Obara; and Soichi Ueno was editor. The budget was US $8.5 million. It was released in Japan on Mch 24, 2007 (tho' the premiere was in Sept, 2006 in Venice). 131 minutes.

Katsuhiro Otomo didn't originate the project. Otomo explained that producer Satoru Ogura had come to him hoping to make a period piece in conjunction with the team behind *Crouching Tiger, Hidden Dragon*. Otomo didn't feel confident directing something that big (even tho' Otomo had helmed two of the biggest, most complex *animé* ever), so he suggested adapting the *Mushishi manga*.

There was also an *animé* version of *Mushishi* (Hiroshi Nagahama, 2005-06), which has rightly become a favourite with *animé* fans. (For a note on the *animé* of *Mushishi*, see the appendix.)

The hero, Ginko, the *mushishi* or bugmaster of the title, was played by Joe Odagiri.[53] Makiki Esumi (as Nui), Nao Ômori (as Koro), Yû Aoi (as Tanyu), Makiko Kuno (as Ginko's mother), Hideyuki Inada (as Yoki, the young Ginko), Baku Numata (as Nui's husband), Reisen Lee (as Tama) and Reia Moriyama (as Maho) were also in the cast.

Mushishi adapted chapters 2, 7, 9, and 15 of Urushibara-sensei's *manga:* the chapters from the *Mushishi manga* were not simply strung together, one after another, but were combined (for instance, the sequence where the man Koro is chasing rainbows from the *manga* became couched in a format of buddies travelling together – which departs from Urushibara's *manga*, which isn't in a buddy format). Murai and Otomo's script also mixed in flashbacks to the hero's childhood (including the loss of his mother in a landslide, his relationship with the troubled *mushishi* Nui (portrayed as a witch by Makiko Esumi), and how he became a one-eyed, grey-haired youth). Part of the flashback structure included

53 Pretty boy actor Odagiri was best-known for *Kamen Rider Cougar* (2000); the 'Odagiri Effect' referred to the extra audience for children's shows of mothers attracted by handsome, young heroes. Who knows what Odagiri's female audience made of *Mushishi*.

the lengthy and crucial origins story for Ginko (this was inserted throughout the movie, and formed the final sequence, too).

Not only that, writers Sadayuki Murai and Katsuhiro Otomo invented many sequences in *Mushishi* (having chosen the chapters from the *manga* by Yuki Urushibara, the 2006 movie then proceeded to link them together with invented scenes – a standard practice in film adaptation: you pick your fave bits and make a story from them, joining them together, inventing links as necessary, and dropping all of the rest. The script also took characters such as Nui and had her narrating sequences in flashback. Otomo-sensei sent the script to *mangaka* Urushibara, and she gave him free rein).

The live-action version of *Mushishi* dropped plenty of elements from the *manga* by Urushibara-sensei: Ginko is a somewhat different characterization in the live-action film – he seems more deferential, more troubled, and much sadder than the Ginko in the *manga* (or the *animé*), who has a stoic, occasionally nonchalant feeling for survival (and a reverence for all living things); the movie-Ginko droops his head a lot, as if he's depressed or guilty; Ginko smokes a little, but in the *manga* he has a cigarette permanently taped to his mouth, like Sanji in *One Piece*.

Structurally, the 2006 *Mushishi* is episodic (as is Urushibara-sensei's *manga*): that can weaken a feature film. Thus, the flashbacks supply a dramatic structure that develops Ginko's characterization. So that the sub-plot of *Mushishi* is about Ginko finding out who he is. This isn't really the structure of the *manga*, which focusses on Ginko as a healer in the present tense, travelling around Japan, and meeting a new scenario in each chapter. (The *manga* only occasionally dips into Ginko's origins).

Katsuhiro Otomo said he had always wanted to do a *jidai geki*, a Japanese historical movie, the kind that Akira Kurosawa did (*Mushishi* is full of Kurosawan imagery, from rivers and mountains to Shinto shrines and, of course, rain storms. No *hommage* to Kurosawa is complete without plenty of rain, the *sensei* being well-known for liking all sorts of natural world effects. The scene where the characters shelter from the rain is likely a reference to *Rashomon*, a hit with international audiences. And the film opens with heavy rainfall, which perhaps causes the landslide).

Mushishi has a grainy, dirty feel (it looks like it was filmed on video). Shooting up in the mountains and lakes and rivers of Japan ensures the movie looks tremendous and lived-in (no green screen backdrops here. But there are plenty of digital effects, as well as the usual practical effects of historical films – fire, smoke, fog, rain, wind, etc). The music by Kuniaki Haishima included much digeridoo, lending a familiar 'tribal' / 'ethnic' lilt to the score; jangling bells and drones with strings are almost mandatory in a score for this kind of slow-moving, spiritual picture. The sound team (Yoshiya Obara and Masaya Kitada) added plenty of abstract, whooshing sounds and bass rumbles for the appearances of the *mushi* (but much of the movie is actually fairly quiet, including the delivery of the dialogue – editor Soichi Ueno allows *lots* of air between exchanges of lines, which helps to create the stately pace of *Mushishi*).

Mushishi boasts a truly spectacular look in terms of the production design (by Noriyushi Ikeya), the cinematography (by Takahide Shibanushi) and the costumes (by Keisuke Chiyoda). *Mushishi* fashions a unique look that's part-Japanese *jidai-geki*, part-fantasy and part-Otomoania. It's an archaic, exotic Nippon out of mythology and legends.

Mushishi is a curious slice of Japanese folklore and mythology, and definitely one for the dedicated. *Mushishi* resembles the *slow*, restrained, muted (and very Japanese) movies of Yasujiro Ozu and Kenji Mizoguchi, pictures from the 1940s and 1950s where Very Little Happens (but these are classics of Japanese cinema). There *are* magical elements in *Mushishi* (characters, including the hero, who sport white wigs[54] which irritatingly cover one eye,[55] children who grow horns, sprites and monsters), and visual effects (the bugs/ *mushi* themselves, rainbows, intricate special make-up, etc), but if you come to *Mushishi* expecting summat resembling Katsuhiro Otomo's other works, such as *Akira, Steam-boy* or *Roujin Z,* you will be disappointed. *Mushishi* is the kind of flick that quite a few people, I'm sure, would watch for ten minutes and exclaim, 'what the hell is this?! I don't get it!' It's quite some ways from the late-night-beer-and-pizza appeal of *Akira.* If the boys are coming back to yours at 2 a.m., don't put on *Mushishi*!

However, if you stick with *Mushishi*, it does re-pay your investment: ultimately, it's a pæan to the beautiful Japanese countryside and the energies of the natural world, as if Katsuhiro Otomo and the team decided they were going to visit their favourite mountains, lakes, rivers, streams, forests, wayside shrines, trails and fields in Japan (the influence of a movie like *Princess Mononoke* is plain to see, as it is on the *manga*). Thus turning the experience of making the movie itself into a vacation (the location scouts for *Mushishi* deserve every Yen of their fee, for discovering so many extraordinary places in Japan. They must've driven thousands of miles scouting these to-die-for locations!).

And the buddy relationship of the main character – Ginko (Joe Odagiri) and a fellow traveller on life's highway, the simple-minded Koro (Nao Ômori) – was appealing (a friendship added for this movie; the *Mushishi manga* comprises stand-alone episodes, with very few recurring characters – Ginko is nearly always travelling alone).[56] If you've seen and enjoyed

---

54 Watch any live-action Japanese film, and you'll see wigs every-where. Japanese pop culture is very fond of crazy hair, maybe stemming from *Kabuki* theatre (which *manga* has exploited).
55 The *manga* makes more of this, as does the *animé* series.
56 The *animé* of *Mushishi*, like the *manga*, didn't include any buddies on the road for Ginko (instead, he has a new colleague or patient in every episode).

Akira Kurosawa's movies, which are especially strong on friendships between men (like *Akira* itself), you'll enjoy *Mushishi* (it recalls movies of Kurosawa's such as *The Hidden Fortress*). Koro is looking for a special rainbow that has haunted him since childhood (it's linked to his father, with an œdipal subtext) – this was episode 7, *Raindrops and Rainbows*, in the *animé*. Of course, the rainbow was yet another *mushi* (as Ginko explains to Koro as they travel).

In cinema, Katsuhiro Otomo's province is animation – but many animators in the Japanese film industry say they would rather be making live-action cinema. Otomo-sensei hasn't produced as much live-action as animation: he expressed some lack of confidence going in to *Mushishi*, that he wasn't sure if he could pull off a *jidai geki* picture. No need for that doubt – Otomo is as natural a filmmaker as any director in the history of cinema!

Mushishi is a formidable piece of cinema: it seems modest and nostalgic, with its evocations of the Meiji period[57] and the back-waters of rural Japan. But there is a lot more going on, from the folklore aspects, the natural world aspects, the depictions of life in the countryside, to the spiritual and supernatural elements, and the visual effects. (And not forgetting a lovingly crafted rendition of life in pre-modern Japan, which, it seems, so many artists, filmmakers and writers long for in contemporary Japan. This is the Nihon that didn't exist, but *should* have existed).

Once again, one wishes that Katsuhiro Otomo was given hundreds of millions of dollars to shoot any movie he likes! On video, on film, in animation, anything!

The insects/ life-forms/ *mushi* themselves are

---

57 'The film is a kind of fable, so it needs a setting that is a bit otherworldly. It wouldn't really work in the Edo period, and the Taisho and Showa eras are already too modern', Otomo-sensei remarked in 2006.

simply a multi-purpose analogue or metaphor for whatever you want – in the end, like the child Akira in *Akira*, for life itself. The images of the bugs crawling everywhere, including over hands and faces, are certainly memorable. Most intriguing was the evocation of a direct relation between the bugs and creativity and writing: Tanyu writes with her finger directly on a paper scroll (she is infected with *mushi* (which results in her damaged leg), and the bugs provide the ink, turning into *kanji* by magic (as if the cost of being an artist or writer is to literally use up your body/ energy/ *chi*/ spirit/ soul. So that in the end you waste away, your body turning to brown mush).)

The scene where Ginko encounters his fellow *mushishi* somewhere on the road was added to the *manga*. Here, Ginko catches up on news, and on his messages (sent in insect cocoons). The joshing among the *mushishi* is very Kurosawan (the guys exude a weary but friendly machismo, drinking *saké*, eating, and talking about women). This is not the quiet, reserved Ginko of the *manga* or the *animé*, but this interpretation of Ginko fits right in.

It's here that Ginko meets Koro, the man who's searching for a rainbow. Ginko is intrigued by this guy, who carries a huge, empty vessel on his back (a send-up of the backpacks that *mushishi* carry), in which he hopes to catch something and take back, maybe the rainbow itself. Koro is a drifter, someone permanently on the road, looking for something, a mirror of Ginko himself.

Ginko also introduces the character of Tanyu (whom he's just heard from): the film cuts to Tanyu in her home making records on a scroll (Urushibara-sensei's magical version of the Japanese art of calligraphy). We hear Ginko in voiceover explaining the fate of Tanyu, but it's not until much later, in act three, that we visit Tanyu.

✿

Among the themes explored in *Mushishi* are the

troubled relationship between the younger generation and the older generation (it's the Sins of the Mothers here, not the Sins of the Fathers), the search for identity, and the encounter with mysterious, non-human forces.

A recurring theme in Otomo-sensei's work is the problematic relationship between humans and technology (it's perhaps the key theme in science fiction in Japanese culture): here, the unknowable, inscrutable *mushi* form the other side in that relationship. In part it's *Frankenstein* again, humans meddling with the powers of the universe which they don't fully understand. Like the technologies represented in *Akira* and *Steam-boy*, the *mushi* are mysterious, implacable, and some of them are very dangerous. There's always a price to pay (here embodied in eyes and premature ageing, or, in the case of Nui, turning into a crippled mud-creature). You thought that life was 'free'? It's not.

The search for identity for Ginko is a traditional theme presented in a conventional manner: Ginko is troubled by dreams and reads stories of his youth. The question of whether you are defined by your origins or by your destination is raised once again.

The 2006 adaptation of *Mushishi* weaves together the stories of Ginko, of Nui, and of Tanyu (which doesn't occur in the comic), to create a *Bildungsroman*, the story of Ginko's journey to self-realization. *Mushishi* is thus a conventional film, structurally and thematically, tho' it uses new technologies like digital animation to tell its story.

What's at stake is the hero's well-being (or soul) – which is echoed in the fates of Nui, Tanyu, little Maho, etc. Ginko, Tanyu and Nui are the battle-grounds of *Mushishi*, their psyches, their well-being, with the conflicts with the *mushi* being the colourful fantasy/ supernatural expressions of what is essentially an internal struggle.

The first act of *Mushishi* introduced the back-story of Ginko, when he was a child[58] (Hideyuki Inada) travelling with his mom, and was known as Yoki. In a landslide[59] (one of numerous evocations of earthquakes in Japanese cinema), he lost his mother, and was found by an enigmatic figure, Nui. *Mushishi* revisits Ginko's childhood at several points: so we see Yoki recovering from his ordeal in Nui's home; talking with Nui; visiting the mysterious lake with its one-eyed, white fish, hoping to stay longer because he has nowhere else to go, etc.

The flashbacks are inserted without preamble in *Mushishi*, and without the usual cinematic indicators of moving into the past (one of the clues is that the flashbacks are filmed in bright sunlight, and often outdoors. Sometimes there's a visual rhyme linking past and present).

In the present tense of *Mushishi*, the first act features the story from the *manga* (*The Tender Horns* – episode three of the *animé*), which explores the links between snow and silence and sound: the villagers are losing their hearing in one ear (it's a snowbound valley in the mountains, a favourite locale in the *Mushishi* franchise. *Mangaka* Urushibara is mad about snow). Well, Ginko solves that malady pretty swiftly, by halfway thru act one (as he always does – *Mushishi* is an upbeat, optimistic movie, despite its slow, meditative and somewhat melancholy feel). But one young child of around six, Maho (Reia Moriyama – she's adorable), has four small horns growing out of her head (it was a boy in the *manga*), the result of a more serious infection of *mushi* (there're two kinds, 'Un' and 'Ah'), and a bigger challenge for Mushishi Master Ginko (he uses smoke, a mosquito net, and the shock for Maho of seeing him crumble one of her mother's horns).

The section comprises the second half of act one

---

58 We could guess that Otomo would be a great director of children – his comics feature some of the most convincing portrayals of young people in all *manga*. In *Mushishi*, Otomo directs several child actors, including Hideyuki Inada and Reia Moriyama.
59 Yet again a Katsuhiro Otomo movie opens with a catastrophe!

of *Mushishi*: at the climax, with Maho healed, the second act begins, with another flashback, to Ginko's childhood (there's a clever dramatic link here, btn Ginko smoking in the present tense, and Nui smoking in the past tense. Yes, there is a *lot* of smoking in the *Mushishi* universe!).

The subtext of this section of *Mushishi* is the familiar one of the relationship between parents and children, a mother and a daughter (such psycho-dynamic subtexts are the dramatic meat of the *manga* version of *Mushishi*. Ginko is a healer of psycho-logical wounds as well as physical injuries). Here, the child Maho can't let go of the mother (she's built an elaborate shrine to her mom in a tree near the family home).

The impact of the past impinging on the present and preventing Maho from living her life is mani-fested in the striking scene of Maho being terrorized by sound. The movie adds layers of loud, abrasive noises and plonks poor Maho in the middle of it, sitting on the floor, while *mushishi* swirl around her like an audio blizzard. It's the abrupt cut into cacophony that hits home, evoking Maho's torment, even more than the visuals (reminiscent of the cuts on sound, from silence to noise, that Otomo deployed in *Akira*, in the finale).

✿

The stand-out and central sequence in *Mushishi* in the present tense (comprising act 3 of 4 acts) was where Ginko visits Tanyu (Yu Aoi) and her grand-mother Tama (Reisen Ri) in a lengthy spiritual exorcism[60] episode: Tanyu is infected with the bugs, but when Ginko helps to release her from their grip (aided by some blood-letting in a bath), he himself is overcome by them – a recurring motif in the *Mushishi manga*. The 2006 movie combines two people in danger, Ginko and Tanyu, so that saving Tanyu (in the bath) is necessary in order that Ginko be rescued.

---

60 The build-up to the exorcism is played a higher pitch than the rest of the movie (and more hysterically than most o' the *manga*).

(This sequence appeared in the 2005-2006 *animé* in the episode *Sea of Writings*).

In a clever piece of writing, it's when Ginko reads the story that Tanyu was reading when she collapsed that the trouble starts (bugmasters activate *mushi*, as we know, by simply being who they are, and in this version of *Mushishi*, they attract special forms of *mushi*). Here, in Tanyu's archive room, Ginko reads the story of Nui and the young boy, Yoki (which he realizes must be himself). Earlier, speaking to Koro, Ginko reveals that he couldn't remember anything about his childhood (writing and story-telling is of course one of humans' primary methods of recording memories).

The Tanyu sequence in *Mushishi* depicts the origins story of Ginko (a flashback within a flash-back) and that of the witch Nui: Nui, now blind, turns up at Tanyu-sama's home. Nui relates (in voiceover) the story of the *mushi*. (No doubt this section of *Mushishi*, with its layers of memories and stories, helped to confuse some critics. If you haven't grasped what *mushi* are, and how dangerous some *mushi* can be, like the *Tokoyami*, just what happened to Nui and her husband (Baku Numata) and son, and to Yoki/Ginko, could seem bewildering).

For example, in Nui's story is a sequence not in the comic by Yuki Urushibara, which portrays Nui having a husband and a son (in the *manga* she's alone). We go back to the early days of Nui's life, when her husband and son encountered the *Tokoyami* in the pool (the motif of irrigating rice fields, a common plot in Japanese folklore, is also introduced). This explains why Nui's husband was injured to the point where he can't speak.

Further ties between the back-story and the present tense occurred with Tanyu recognizing that Ginko remained in darkness after the dispersal of the *Tokoyami* – the darkness of his childhood (Ginko remains in a near-catatonic state for quite some time, until he gradually revives).[61]

We see further flashbacks which depict the aftermath of the underworld experience of Yoki's, when he followed Nui into the pool. Now Nui is reduced to a hysterical figure lost in the dark mud in the centre of the drained pool, while Yoki, now transformed into his grey-haired, shell-shocked Ginko persona, walks away. Nui begs him to stay – it's a moving, scary depiction of a person in total despair. Nui completely loses it here.

The method that Tanyu employs to capture all of the wayward *Tokoyami* letters that're swarming around the archive room is novel: she has a pair of long, steel chopsticks[62] which she plunges into the end of the line of *kanji*. With a flourish, Tanyu, now in a shamanic, wizardly mode, whips the strings of words in loops, and onto the paper scroll which Tama holds ready on the floor. (As an image of literally whipping words into shape, it's terrific; ah, if only getting words to do what you want were that easy!).

With its evocations of underworlds, and shadowy presences materializing in the darkness, and metaphysical abstractions like letters created from darkness, *Mushishi* resembles Japanese ghost stories, with their very peculiar twist on the supernatural (there's a superb horror movie moment when the *Tokoyami mushi* coalesce into a hooded figure that rises from the floor and shuffles towards the petrified Ginko. Of course the *Tokoyami* begin to take the form of the wounded Nui). That, after all, was one of the appeals of the *Mushishi manga* by Yuki Urushibara – the reworking of Japanese folktales, giving them a contemporary, ecological, New Age-spiritual tweak.

The Tanyu-Tama episode also includes a mildly

---

61 To signal his return to health, Ginko is now back healing people. In one scene with a clear Christian slant, he heals a man who's blind (via a form of acupuncture, inserting a needle in the third eye. A white *mushi* wriggles out. It's taken from *Sea of Writings* chapter in the *manga*).
62 With the rings at the end, they resemble the staffs that magicians wield in Asian folklore.

flirtatious relationship for Ginko and Tanyu: a fellow *mushi*, Tanyu stands by Ginko's bedside as he sleeps. When she reaches out to touch his hand, he wakes from his sleep to mutter summat about the moon. In a happier moment (another flashback), Ginko carries [63] the lame Tanyu up to the hills [64] where they can view the ocean. Ginko sums up why a romance wouldn't work: she stays in one place all the time, while he never stays still.

Notice how the film includes Koro in the Tanyu episode, as the audience's stand-in: told to wait outside by the imperious Tama, Koro subsequently sheepishly enters the grand house looking for Ginko-san. He then becomes our audience reaction figure for the supernatural happenings involving *mushi* and occult infections and blood-letting.

✿

Comparing the Tanyu episode in *Mushishi* to the *manga* by Urushibara-sensei – it's from the chapter entitled *The Sea of Brushes* – we can see that the filmmakers included many of the same beats in the story, and many of the same images, but they altered them, combined them, and left out some.

In the *Mushishi manga*, the setting is different – there's a tunnel to the library, which's now far underground (as a house in a cave, a terrific image). The movie possibly altered that because it would be expensive (the interior of the library is also much bigger in the comic strip).

There are flashbacks to Tanyu's origins in the comic, not included in the 2006 movie (such as the baby with the black leg), and the generations of *mushishi* transcribers. There's a long conversation with the young Tanyu about what she is going thru (where Tama explains about the *mushi*), which the film dropped. (Because the movie delved into Ginko's back-story, there wasn't time to explore Tanyu's

---

63 Girls being carried piggyback by boys suggests flirtation in *manga*.
64 There are two scenes in the *manga* where Ginko carries Tanyu up onto the hills (including the hint of romance).

youth as well). Also, the blood-letting ritual and putting Tanyu in the bath aren't in the *manga*.

Oddly, the live-action movie dropped the notion of Tama telling Tanyu stories, which Tanyu writes down. This would be perfect for storytellers like Katsuhiro Otomo: instead, the texts in the library in the movie are records from visiting *mushishi*.

The *manga* doesn't link Ginko's back-story to the texts in the library unravelling, as the movie does (which cleverly connects up Nui's story with Tanyu recording it and Ginko later reading it). But the movie does retain the scenes of the *mushi* running all over the walls and ceiling of the room, and Tanyu collecting them with the giant chopsticks.

✿

In the *animé* version of *Mushishi*, episode 12: *One-Eyed Fish* was an origins story for Ginko: the live-action version (unlike the *animé*), alters much of the *Mushishi manga*, but keeps to the principal themes of Nui as the haunted *mushishi*, Yoki/ Ginko as her ten year-old shadow, and their encounter with the dangerous, mysterious *Tokoyami* (darkness) *mushi*. In the *Mushishi manga* as in the *animé*, the *Tokoyami* are ambiguous at best and lethal at worst (i.e., like the universe itself). When Nui decides 'to finish it at last', and descends into the pool in the forest (in the live-action film), Yoki follows her, wading into the water. As in the *animé*, the visuals are abstract and foggy, taking the viewer into the heart of whatever is at the foundation of life in this world – it's a world of darkness and endless space, with Nui and Yoki glimpsed in shadowy close-up, their clothes billowing around them as if underwater (Japanese *animé* is especially adept at portraying abstract spiritual/ psychological realms – far, far in advance of anything in Western animation).

The descent into the *Tokoyami mushi* episode is very impressive, portraying the central theme of the *Mushishi manga* – humanity's encounter with the natural world – as something potentially life-threatening as well as life-giving. It's here that Yoki pays the price of visiting the shadow world of the *mushi*, as in a folk tale, by losing both his eye and his memory of his former life (Nui plucks out his eye as payment for escaping the *Tokoyami*). For author Yuki Urushibara, you can't go out and confront the mysteries of life and natural forces blithely or without considering the consequences. After this trauma, Yoki becomes Ginko, prematurely aged with grey hair, a one-eyed fish living on Earth as a perpetual loner and outsider.

The subtext of this sequence resembles the*mushi* themselves – a metaphor or equivalence for anything you like. Whatever you think the*mushi* are, or what they represent, or what they point towards, the key dramatic element of this episode is *payment*. In short, the costs of being alive. Nothing comes for free in the world of *Mushishi*, in any of its adaptations.

Nui the witch is all too aware of the dangers, and continually pushes Yoki away. At one point, she takes him to a town where a *mushishi* offers him work as his assistant (and Nui slips away, abandoning him without looking back). But Yoki won't let go of Nui, isn't ready to step out into the world, and hurries back to join her.

Nui and Yoki make for one of the oddest couples in recent Japanese cinema, and certainly one of the most intriguing relationships in all of Otomo-sensei's work (remember that one of his longest comics, *The Legend of Mother Sarah*, focussed on a mother searching for her offspring).

But mother and child relations (and parents and orphans), are only the start of it, because Nui is a complicated personality, superbly played by Makiko Esumi, suggesting at all sorts of hidden depths and withheld secrets. And Hideyuki Inada is terrific as Yoki, the young Ginko, a vulnerable, confused child who's overwhelmed by life.

The script is minimal in terms of dialogue for Nui and Yoki in this key sequence in act two of

Mushishi, but many layers are evoked through the storytelling and the performances. As he does in his *manga*, Katsuhiro Otomo stages scenes where the psychological subtext is rushing with energy (reminiscent of *Domu*, with its evocations of barely-suppressed and very negative emotions just under the surface).

As well as Sarah in *Mother Sarah*, one also thinks, as a comparison with the relationship between Nui and Yoki in *Mushishi,* of Lady Miyako and Tetsuo in *Akira*. Remember when Tetsuo appeared at Miyako's temple, demanding answers, and Miyako responded by sternly reprimanding him, and then telling him things he didn't want to hear.

❖

As Otomo-sensei admitted, *Mushishi* doesn't really have a typical ending for a movie: the ending is like life, Otomo asserted, it keeps going on, calmly. That's a rather lame explanation for the episodic nature of the movie which also doesn't have a satis-fying close (and neither does the *animé* of 2005-2006 – that, too, sort of peters out. And the *manga* does, too. Why? Because the *manga* is episodic, with a chapter-by-chapter structure. So there's no over-arching plot).

Well, anyhoo, the ending of the live-action version of *Mushishi* comprises two sequences (dealing with two of the main sub-plots): in the first, Koro gets to finally see his rainbow. It's an impress-ive encounter with nature as super-nature – a rainbow as an enormous serpent in the sky, rainbow-hued, made up of millions of flying *mushi*. This is the Big Finish from the visual effects team on *Mushishi*, which delivers a spectacular 'wow' sequence (there are two appearances by the rainbow-serpent: the first scene, staged during the day in a low valley of tall plants, and it soon vanishes, is far less wonder-inducing than the second, set at night).

The second ending of *Mushishi* closes the origins story which involves Nui and her consumption by the *Tokoyami. Mushishi* has given us glimpses of Nui and her husband from time to time (in one scene they are part of a troupe of travelling puppeteers and players, a delightful evocation of Ye Olde Japan).

Ginko follows his instinct for seeking out *mushi* to a ramshackle hut in a forest where he discovers Nui in an extremely degenerated state. The brilliant special make-up job (by Akiteru Nakada) turns actress Makiko Esumi into a grotesque demon of mud, growths and darkness, while the visual effects crew add black smoke rising from Nui's body.

Note the corpse dragged out of the hut by the husband as Ginko approaches (tho' he doesn't see it), suggesting something vampiric is going on (another addition to Urushibara's *Mushishi* comic).

Note too how the husband is clad in rags: this is actually one of Katsuhiro Otomo's favourite costumes for any of his characters! Probably half of Otomo's output in *manga* has people in rags. (In Otomo's world, if you don't start out in rags, you will end up in rags!).

Nui, recognizing Yoki (Ginko), launches herself at him, pleading. There's not much that Ginko thinks he can do for her now she is in such a far-gone place, almost eaten alive by the *Tokoyami mushi* (but Ginko does remember her name and, presumably, more about her now, thanks to the accounts of Tanyu).

The final scene involving Ginko and Nui is once again abstract and ambiguous (and, for those critics who found *Mushishi* confusing in its storyline, it must've been irritating and dissatisfying). Ginko carries Nui on his back to a *mushi*-rich spot in the forest (another gold star for the location scouts in finding all of these unusual places in Nippon). He pours some liquid which attracts *mushi* over her as she squats there silently. He leaves. Nui's husband (now reduced to a hoarsely-screaming wreck), watches as *mushi* fly towards Nui, settling on her and glowing.

What this means and what happens next isn't depicted or explained. Presumably it means some sorta transformation for Nui – from human into *mushi*, or into *Tokoyami*, or back into the darkness which she struggled out of, or maybe the *mushi* will draw off the *Tokoyami* and purify Nui. (Maybe Ginko's thinking, if it was caused by *mushi*, maybe it can only be cured by *mushi*. Certainly Nui is a state beyond the help of Ginko's medicine).

Needless to say, very little of this part of the Nui and Ginko story is in Urushibara-sensei's *manga*, but is an invention by the filmmakers. It rounds off Ginko's back-story and origins story, but remains enigmatic to the end.

On a much-easier-to-understand note, and with a more audience-pleasing flourish, Ginko and Koro part company (at – where else? – a crossroads!). By now the two men are fond of each other, and after walking some way, Koro turns as if to go back and re-join Ginko. Instead, he shouts his blessings, and Ginko continues to walk away. (Again, this isn't in the *Mushishi manga*, but there are many scenes where Ginko is leaving yet another village or house or family which he has helped with his *mushishi* know-ledge). So *Mushishi* doesn't end – it stops (over a wide shot of Ginko walking beside a river).

Maybe other endings were considered for *Mushishi*. Bringing back Nui for the last time seems essential, as the Ginko-Nui plot has been woven throughout the movie. A more spectacular finale seems in order, though, with Ginko saving Nui (as he does here), but with an action sequence (perhaps involving the 'river of light', the streams of *mushi* running thru the Earth, Urushibara-sensei's version of Chinese 'dragon lines' or ley lines. This was not employed in the movie (except briefly as a fish-form), but it's a key element in the *manga* and the animated series).

SIDENOTE ON AKIRA KUROSAWA.
More than any other director, Akira Kurosawa

defined the image of Japan before the modern era for Western audiences. Many of Kurosawa's films were set in mediæval or pre-1900 Japan: *The Hidden Fortress, Kagemusha, Ran, Rashomon, The Seven Samurai, Throne of Blood* and *Yojimbo*. Kurosawa's pre-modern Japan was a world of rainswept landscapes, distant mountain ranges, deserted temples, elegant palaces, rural villages, wooden forts, forests and streams.

Akira Kurosawa created a phenomenal body of work, a series of films which have become classics: *The Hidden Fortress, Kagemusha, Rashomon, Stray Dog, Dersu Uzala,*[65] *Ikuru, The Bad Sleep Well, The Seven Samurai, Throne of Blood, Red Beard, Ran, Yojimbo* and *Sanjuro*.

Akira Kurosawa's influence has been immense on world cinema. Paul Verhoeven said he put on *Rashomon* or *The Seven Samurai* from time to time to remind himself that films could be art. Terry Gilliam spoke highly of *Rashomon*. John Woo said he watched the last reel of *The Seven Samurai* before making his films, for inspiration on action. Bernardo Bertolucci remarked that Kurosawa (with Federico Fellini) was one of the reasons he wanted to become a film director.

There are Akira Kurosawa moments in the work of Francis Coppola (the extravagant machine gun death of Sonny Corleone in *The Godfather* recalling Macbeth's demise by arrows in *Throne of Blood*, or the mythical soldiers in *Apocalypse Now*); Paul Verhoeven (the battles with bugs in *Starship Troopers*); George Lucas raided Kurosawa's mediæval *samurai* for the Jedi knights in the *Star Wars* saga; the *samurai* warriors also popped up in *Brazil* (Terry Gilliam), the elaborate gun battles in John Woo's Hong Kong action cinema, and the *bushido* warrior ethic also

65 I wonder if Katsuhiro Otomo and Sadayuki Murai looked at *Dersu Uzala* (1975), in researching *Mushishi*, the *sensei's* Russian-Japanese co-production and the deserved winner of the foreign film Oscar. *Dersu Uzala* is a stupendous, adventure film portraying the friendship between an old, Chinese, Goldi hunter, Dersu Uzala, and a Soviet Army captain in the early years of the 20th century.

appears in John Milius's films; Andrei Tarkovsky *hommaged* Kurosawa in films such as *Andrei Rublyev* and *Mirror;* and Bertolucci made his own version of a Kurosawan epic in *The Last Emperor*. Kurosawa was one of Ingmar Bergman's favourites. Bergman said he had studied *Rashomon* dozens of times (one can detect the influence of Kurosawa on films such as *The Virgin Spring* and *The Seventh Seal*).

09

FREEDOM

FURIDAMU PUROJEKUTO

Freedom (*Furidamu Purojekuto* a.k.a. *Freedom Project*, 2006) was written by Dai Saito, Katsuchiko Chiba and Yuichi Nomura, directed by Shuhei Morita, and comprised seven[66] eps. x 30m (half an *animé* season). It was produced by Sunrise, Dentsu, Freedom Committee and Bandai Visual. Executive producers were: Atsushi Sugita, Katsuji Umizawa, Kenji Uchida and Wataru Tanaka; the producers were: Hideo Matsushita, Motoki Mukaichi, Shinjiro Yokoyama and Yasumasa Tsuchiya. Music – Yoshihiro Ike, char. des. – Atsushi Irie, Daisuke Sanbu and Katsuhiro Otomo. *Freedom* was conceived as a commercial for Nishin Noodles[67] – thus, charas scarf a pot o' noodles from time to time (the boy characters mainly, of course – because they are the target audience).

The voice cast included Daisuke Namikawa as Takeru, Showtaro Morikubo as Kazuma, Sanae Kobayashi as Ao, Seizo Katou as Alan, and superstar

---

66 Really it's eight shows – the final episode is a double episode.
67 Even in jail!

Kappei Yamaguchi[68] as Biz.

❖

Freedom (2006) is a kind of *Akira Lite*, a riff on many of *Akira*'s famous elements – biker gangs and races, disaffected youths (headed up by Takeru), a group of boys, the younger generation versus the older, science fiction, a post-apocalyptic narrative, etc. (Takeru is a Kaneda lookalike, while the other two in the trio, Kazuma and Biz, recall Yamagata and Kai, and Ao plays the Kei role).

Katsuhiro Otomo's epic *manga* of space colonies, *Mother Sarah,* is another obvious reference, with its themes of space colonization, a damaged Earth, and starting again (one of the mantras of *Freedom* is: 'it's never too late to start', symbolized by colonizing new territory, and planting crops).

Freedom contains numerous Otomoan motifs – kids street racing motorbikes to alleviate boredom (shades of *Initial D, The Fast and the Furious, The Phantom Menace* and *Sky Blue* here); being dressed down by the authorities and anti-authoritarianism; age vs. youth; the past and the present; police robot spheres; fetishizing *mecha;* chases on bikes; a girl who's out of reach; a post-catastrophe world; fights echoing Tetsuo and Kaneda; the hero and heroine in jail (like Kaneda and Kei); and design elements such as circles, the Moon, pop (and kitsch) Americana, astronauts,[69] bright orange, tunnels, the desert, and retro-stylzed *mecha.*[70]

Freedom includes an intensively designed, hyper-detailed space colony, a vast Moon-base of tunnels,

---

68 The wonderful Kappei Yamaguchi (b. May 23, 1965) is allowed to whinge and whine a little too much as Biz (but it's amazing that Yamaguchi, then 41, can completely convince as a mid-teen). Kappei Yamaguchi has appeared in just about every modern *animé,* it seems, including many classics: 'L' in *Death Note,* Usopp in *One Piece,* Rhint in *Cowboy Bebop,* Tombo in *Kiki's Delivery Service,* Inuyasha in *Inuyasha,* Hugo in *Battle Angel Alita,* Ranma Saotome in *Ranma 1/2,* Feitan in *Hunter x Hunter,* Shesta in *Escaflowne,* Hikozaru in *Pokémon,* and Nin-nin in *La Blue Girl* (!).
69 The Apollo Moon shots, the 'right stuff', and the U.S.A.'s space programme are referenced many times, and the helper grandfather figure on the Moon, Alan, is modelled on the Apollo astronauts.
70 Several environments in *Freedom* are direct *hommages* to *Akira.*

platforms, walkways, gates, towers, domes and roads; many of the designs are Otomoan. (Like *Metropolis* and *Steam-Boy*, the cities in *Freedom* have been worked over to an obsessive degree. Thousands of sketches must have been produced for the background art. And it's no surprise that the futuristic domes just happen to look a lot like contemporary Tokyo).

The style of *Freedom* combines flat, 2-D animation with digital, 3-D simulations (very prominent in the vehicles and racing scenes). The settings are intricate and detailed, a vision of a community on the Moon which has extended for miles (with service tunnels allowing for the youths to explore the literal edges of society).

The context of *Freedom* is clichéd science fiction – a colony on the Moon, a ruined Earth, a rigorously policed environment of survivors, etc. And the narrative, every single beat of it, is thoroughly predictable (had Otomo scripted *Freedom*, it surely would've taken more twists and turns story-wise).

However, Otomo-sensei has explored the notion of space colonies many times – including in his long-running comic *The Legend of Mother Sarah,* and many of his early *manga.* And in 2019 Otomo announced a new film project – about space colonization.

The topic fascinates Otomo – it's the next step that humans will take (and might have to take). *Freedom* evokes the familiar thematic oppositions of colony stories: here and there, the homeland and the new territory, the past and the old life and the present and the new life.

Let's remember, though, that Otomo did *not* conceive *Freedom,* did *not* write the script, and did *not* produce the show. But he is the most well-known name behind the scenes.

Freedom fetishes the space race, and the North American space programme and N.A.S.A. in particular. Alan, the old adviser/ helper figure, is modelled on astronauts such as Buzz Aldrin. The ambiguous attitude towards North America that's part of Otomo's work (and many Japanese *animé*), is not part of *Freedom* (it's the authorities who run Eden on the Moon who are the monolithic, oppressive powers here).

Takeru is our main character – enthusiastic, cocky, rebellious, and vulnerable and sweet underneath. Like Kaneda in *Akira,* Takeru's attitude sets the tone of *Freedom.* (Like many teenage boys who are the principal character, such as Naruto Uzumaki or Monkey D. Luffy, Takeru is boundlessly energetic, wearing out everyone around him).

The kids are mid-teens, not late teens: they attend school, and have to work (following an accident, they are ordered to perform boring volunteer chores). Their days are structured by the authorities, and when they step out of line, the system is quick to control them (they wear bracelets which monitor their movements).

Notice that parents are absent – instead, the group of boys encounter many parental substitutes and authority figures (and Alan the astronaut is a kindly grandfather figure).

❖

The first half of *Freedom* is a biker gangs on the Moon adventure, the second half is an Earth-based drama exploring several issues (age vs. youth, the past and the present, different utopias and ways of life, etc). When it returns to the Moon, it's all about 'freedom' and rebellion, sticking it to The Man and striking out on your own.

Freedom's first episodes are indulgently enjoyable and boysy – street racing outings have been roaring away around the corners of pop culture for decades (and some speed movie franchises, such as the *Fast and the Furious* series, are very lucrative).

Freedom happily and shamelessly revives every cliché of the street race genre, including the all-important rivalries (between individuals and between gangs), the tinkering with engines, the girls[71] the crashes, etc. It's filmmaking on autopilot (no production team anywhere on Earth could deliver a bad or boring race scene), but it's fun.

The photo of the cute Earth girl and her friends, which Takeru on the Moon discovers, leads to one quest which leads to another: first, Takeru wants to find the girl in Eden. This takes up much of ep. 2, with Takeru racing around Eden on his trike, looking for the Mystery Girl. This romantic quest merges with the larger, thematic quest – for Planet Earth. Takeru and Kazuma head out of the Moon-base (helped by Alan the astronaut) just to get a glimpse of Earth (the sequence develops into an exciting chase, with the authorities crab-like security robots pursuing them[72]).

The chase continues in episode 3 (along tunnels, a reprise of the street racing scenes in ep. 1 – and handily using some of the same digitally-created material). Finally, with the help of Alan (and Taira), the lads whoosh away from the Moon in a rocket, bound for Earth (Kazuma is in the control room, operating the countdown, so it's Biz instead who gets to travel to Earth with the unstoppable Takeru).

The second half of *Freedom* does get bogged down too much (way too much for only a 7-episode run, where every second of running time is precious), in arguments between the teenagers and the adult and parental figures (such as the sceptical Blue Earth). They disagree about returning to the Moon, for example. In the event (and inevitably), Takeru does travel back to the Moon – though accompanied by Ao, not Biz (he opts to stay behind). It's wish-fulfilment time, as what are depicted as trailer trash folk manage to re-build a Saturn V Apollo Moon rocket, no less – and launch it!

❖

So the lads head to Earth, crashlanding in, of all places, Las Vegas (right on the Strip, of course,

71 The design of Taira's girlfriend (and her twin) seems to be an *hommage* to Satoshi Kon, Otomo's former assistant.
72 The robots are the all-purpose henchmen in *Freedom*.

between the New York Casino, the Luxor and the M.G.M. Grand). They were aiming for Florida (the centre of the space race): thus, ep. 4 entails an extended *hommage* to the Great American Dream, as the boys head for Cape Canaveral – cruising along Route 66, camping out at the Grand Canyon, and the stand-out scene: an encounter with a band of hippies on a road trip across the U.S. of A. in a beat-up bus, an amusing sequence right out of Katsuhiro Otomo's early *manga*.[73] (Composer Yoshihiro Ike provides some spoofs of Country & Western and blues music).

The inspiration for the bus scene may have come from *The Mood Is Already of War*, which Katsuhiro Otomo illustrated for author Toshihiko Yahagi in 1982 (from the story *Monkey Suits*). There's a Jimi Hendrix lookalike (as there was in *The Mood Is Already of War*), an ape from *Planet of the Apes*, baseball players, and other bozos (alcohol and pop music are employed in *Freedom*, but not the sex and drugs from the *manga*).

As Otomo didn't write or originate *Freedom*, one wonders who in the team suggested using an idea from one of Otomo's early comics. (Maybe it was Dai Saito, one of the writers; it's the kind of material that Saito might go for).

The hippy bus isn't a one-off gag – our heroes travel with them for a while, culminating in an unusual and bizarre sequence: a sort of theatre show round the campfire, with dancing and fooling about. It's cute seeing the uptight Biz wearing a tie, hippy fashion (around his head). Takeru is loving it: several times he exclaims, 'I love Earth!' A great touch has the freaks giving some Hallowe'en costumes of spacesuits to Takeru and Biz as a parting gift (in silver and gold) which, incredibly, they happily wear (so now they really do look like spacemen).

Teen romance is a subplot of *Freedom* – between

73 There are some fun jokes in *Freedom* – about the reserved Japanese charas encountering brash Americana, and the cultural differences (the boys recoil in horror at the sight of an octopus, for instance, a creature that Japanese eat by the ton).

Takeru and Ao, the girl he travelled from the Moon to see (Ao is ethnically either meant to be Native American or Latino). Takeru's first crush, Chiyo, turns out to have a boyfriend already (Takeru is miffed). *Freedom* includes some cute comedy in the Takeru-and-Ao scenes, where Takeru is much more bashful than his cocky exterior suggests.

Some of the action is artificially added in *Freedom*: for instance, the yearly festival of sending off a rocket into the ether filled with messages from the community is used as the focus of the action climax of episode five. A tornado hits the coast, and one of the boys in the village (Ricky) hopes to save the rocket on its launchpad. The goal is thus to rescue Ricky in the storm.

Episode six of *Freedom* takes a very different narrative approach to the material: first, the story jumps forward 2.5 years, and then skitters between that and the story so far. Second, it has Biz narrating the show (helping to explain the time shifts). Plus it adds some back-story for Ao, going back maybe ten years.

When we land two and a half years into the future from when the boys arrived on Earth, we are in the middle of a launch sequence for a Saturn Five rocket no less. The destination? The Moon, of course.

To reach this point, the community pulls together to make it possible. There's a side trip to Washington, D.C. for the lads, to meet a rocket scientist (in the national space museum).

Biz opts to remain on Earth, instead of travelling back to the Moon with Takeru and Ao (he's formed a friendship with Anna, the music DJ that he listened to while they crossed the U.S.A.). Biz, however, is instrumental in overseeing the build and the launch of the Saturn V rocket. Blue Earth, Anna's brother, helps out with the launch (after repeatedly opposing it. Turns out that Blue Earth was supposed to pilot an earlier mission with Ao's father).

Ao's back-story types her as another father complex girl (like every girl in sci-fi, fantasy and adventure material): she lost her daddy during a space rocket launch that went wrong about ten years before (a reference to several disasters in the space race, including the *Challenger*). Ao's flashbacks add some motivation for her character, and thicken the emotional content of the relationships in the community a little.

❖

Freedom has a dissatisfying ending: the youths travel to the Earth, yes, using the 'Freedom' rockets (which were designed to terraform Mars), after they have beaten the oppressive regime of Eden, on the Moon, yes – yet the hero, Takeru, opts to stay behind on the Moon and sort out unresolved business with the Council and with Alan (and is thus separated from his chums, and Ao). But the issues didn't need resolving, within this format and this sorta story (tho' Alan receives a death scene). Then we switch to a coda – 'two years later' – and Takeru finally lands on Earth (resulting in the expected joyful reunions among the principal cast), but he instantly announces they're off again – this time to Mars!

But for action and *mecha* fans, the finale of *Freedom* is certainly exciting and spectacular, with multiple events occurring at the same time: chases down tunnels, clashes with robots, the launching of the 'Freedom' rockets, speeches from Alan and Ao, and a fist fight between Takeru and Kazuma (evoking Tetsuo and Kaneda in *Akira*).

10

SHORT PEACE: COMBUSTIBLE

SHOTO PISU: HI NO YOJIN

In 2013, Katsuhiro Otomo wrote and directed *Combustible* (*Hi no Yojin*), a twelve-minute movie, one of four short films forming *Short Peace* (*Shoto Pisu*). *Short Peace* was conceived as a multi-media project using the theme of Japan, which included a Play-Station video game, *Ranko Tsukigime's Longest Day*.

Otomo-sensei scripted and directed *Combustible*; David Del Rio, John Ledford and Eiichi Takahashi produced; Tatsuya Tomaru was animation director; the production companies were Bandai Visual, Dentsu Inc., Lantis, Bandai Namco Games, Shochiku Co., Ltd., Short Peace Committee and Sunrise. Music by Makoto Kubota, character design by Hidekazu Ohara, and CGI direction by Shiji Shinoda.

The other directors of *Short Peace* were Hiroaki Ando (*Gambo*), Shuhei Morita (*Possessions*), and Hajime Katoki (*A Farewell To Weapons*). Released July 20, 2013.

Combustible is a *tour-de-force* animation of a doomed love affair in Edo period Japan. There are two central characters in this *Romeo and Juliet* story, Owaka (Saori Hayami) and Matsuki (Seiichi Morita), which ends in catastrophe when the famous fire that destroyed half of Edo (the former Tokyo)[74] is caused by Owaka, and the lovers perish (along with thousands of others).

When you watch *Combustible* you think, why isn't someone – anyone! *please!* – giving Katsuhiro Otomo any amount of money he wants, to make any sort of movie he wants?!

Please give that man $10 billion! $50 billion!

Can someone please cancel the ten Hollywood tentpole movies for next year, each one costing $80-200 million, and give all of that $$$$$ to Katsuhiro Otomo, and let's watch him fly!

We know what Otomo wants: complete creative control; no studio interference; no censorship; and no limits on subject matter (i.e., what all filmmakers want!).

Film producers should be lining up to get down on their knees to beg Otomo-sensei with ever-more lucrative deals. Come on, guys, film directors like Otomo are very rare! There are only one or two Otomos in each generation.

The quality of filmmaking in *Combustible* is staggering – it's yet another example of Otomo-sensei delivering something unlike anything else in Japanese animation.

No one can miss the fact that, in a mere 12 minutes, Katsuhiro Otomo has woven in some of his key themes: the modern city (once again, it's the Great City of *Anime*, Tokyo); the interaction between the individual and the city (the community); the relation between the individual and big events (the individual and fate); star-crossed lovers; night scenes; and of course a gigantic apocalypse (yes, once again Otomo-sensei is wreaking havoc in downtown Tokyo!). It's not a war this time, or exploding psychic children,

---

74 *Combustible* alludes to the Great Kanto Earthquake of 1923, which appeared in *Urotsukidoji* (1989) and *The Wind Rises* in 2013.

but an elemental disaster (an out-of-control fire), which's linked to doomed love – a new twist on old Otomoan themes.

Owaka and Matsuki are friends from childhood – he hops over the wall to play in Owaka's garden (she is from a wealthier family – it's the difference of class, the poor man and the lady theme). Katsuhiro Otomo is a genius at depicting children at play, and *Combustible* is no different: there are charming scenes of the kids in the garden (thru lap dissolves, we see several days).

The viewpoint is with Owaka thru most of *Combustible*[75] (tho' we cut away to see Matsuki, too). Matsuki is cast out of his family, in a big, emotional scene, by his stern father (his mother weeps nearby). Thus, Matsuki has added impediments why he can't wed Owaka, his childhood sweetheart. Owaka is betrothed in an arranged marriage – hence her despondency. She mopes alone in her room, where a bridal kimono takes pride of place (the kimono becomes one of the symbolic objects in *Combustible* – it is the last thing we see, flying above the flames, towards the camera).

Combustible hints at suicide for the lovers: Owaka, bored, resentful, sulking, is throwing fans across her room. One lands in a lamp and catches fire. At first, Owaka hurries for help, but then she closes the screen door, deliberately allowing the blaze to flourish (she is to be married in a few days).

Combustible cuts away from the Owaka scene, to show images of panicking crowds and guards racing to the site: wow! shots reveal the enormous extent of the fire – from the rooftops, we see that it's engulfing much of Edo. Here the music (by Makoto Kubota) is introduced: a stunning piece of loud percussion on drums.

The fire is seemingly unstoppable – until the officials decide to pull down some houses to form a fire-break. Towards the end of the piece, the lovers

---

75 She is the first character to be introduced.

spy each other on the roofs, but're unable to be re-united (flames roll in between them with roars like monsters). Owaka can't hear Matsuki, and goes the wrong way. Owaka climbs a tower,[76] but perishes in a final explosion of fire.

Combustible is another of those prestige animations which self-consciously draw on and update 18th and 19th century Japanese art – in particular, woodblock art and prints (from time to time, Japanese animation will go back to its origins in woodblock prints and revive it for a contemporary audience).[77] The filmmakers have looked at the great artists of the pre-modern era again: Katsushika Hokusai, Utagawa Kunisada, Nishikawa Sukenobu, Torii Kiyonobu and Kitagawa Utamaro.

Combustible is a celebration (and a history) of Japanese art, exploring the famous 'floating world', and emphasizing planar vision. Using long lenses (*à la* Akira Kurosawa), the filmmakers flatten every-thing onto the frontal plane (Katsuhiro Otomo has often spoken of the emphasis on planar vision in contrast to the penchant for 'realism' and naturalism and Renaissance perspective in Western cinema). There are images of Japanese gardens, kimonos, lamps, fans, sliding doors, moons, etc, conjuring up the very familiar Ye Olde Japan.

As well as flattening the world into a single plane of form and shape, *Combustible* is also a highly individual exploration of colour, with softly muted reds, very dark grays, and moon-like yellows (much of the film is set at night). Katsuhiro Otomo estab-lished his very own colour palette with *Akira*, of course – a film of colour like no other in the whole history of cinema (just the way that Otomo-sensei uses red, for instance, marks his work out from any others in animation or live-action; you can find the idiosyncratic deployment of red throughout Otomo's career, along with his signature orange and yellow).

76 It's a rule in movies: never climb the tower! In *Akira*, Miyako opts to do that.
77 But *Combustible* doesn't feel like a history lesson.

THE ART OF KATSUHIRO OTOMO ✖ 381

In later movies such as *Cannon Fodder* and *Steam-boy*, Otomo-sensei delved further into unusual colour schemes (favouring dirtied colours, beaten-out colours, and once again setting scenes at night with colours mixed with black and gray).

There is also a decorative border at the top and bottom of the frame in *Combustible*, making a pretty change from the usual black bars of widescreen formats (the border alters as the movie plays, to match the images). *Combustible* is a major visual effects piece, with the filmmakers exploring fire effects in numerous shots (and, for obvious reasons, the film is set mostly at night).

And the camerawork too is a Katsuhiro Otomo speciality in *Combustible*, with his customary, very lengthy mobile shots (which refuse the tendency everywhere in contemporary cinema to compose and cut in staccato rhythms), and rapid pans using long lenses (often employing high angles). No one else in animation uses the camera like this. Like Orson Welles or F.W. Murnau, two masters of the moving camera over lengthy takes, Otomo-sensei has his own, instantly recognizable style. (Most animations *don't* use this technique for obvious reasons: it's *very* fiddly, requires immense skill, consumes resources, and drives up costs).

The opening shot of *Combustible*, for instance, is a very long (and expensive) pan from right to left (the direction of Japanese writing) – beginning on some scrolls and written texts, the camera pans over a 19th century-style illustration of Edo… and keeps going and going, getting progressively closer to the houses, until it rests on the home of the main character, Owaka.[78] The shot continues Otomo-sensei's experiments with continuous, mobile takes in *Memories*, and also recalls the elaborate multi-plane camera shots of the Walt Disney (like the famous opening to *Pinocchio*, which Uncle Walt ordered to be re-shot, at a cost of $45,000 – at 1940 prices).

---

78 Bringing the scrolls to life.

The music (by Makoto Kubota) should also be mentioned – *Combustible* opens with a traditional, Japanese song, which fades as the characters are introduced. Once the fire starts up, and the camera trucks into a close-up of Owaka's wedding kimono, there is a pounding percussive cue (plus skirling whistle), which continues throughout much of the second half of *Combustible* (rising to a crescendo at the end).

❖

The other three movies in *Short Peace* are state-of-the-art animations which also explore very Japanese stories.

Possessions (*Tsukumo*) was written and directed by Shuhei Morita (from a story by Keisuke Kishi), with music by Reiji Kitazato, char. des. by Daisuke Sajiki, art dir. by Goki Nakamura, and ani. dir. by Hiroyuki Horiuchi.

In *Possessions*, a guy, Kaeru Hebisakka (Takeshi Kusao), finds shelter in a wayside shrine in a forest in a storm at night (the story starts exactly like the traditional opener for a tale: 'it was a dark and stormy night'). Pretty soon a great many spirits emerge: a small frog (played by the very wonderful Koichi Yamadera) that might've hopped out of *Spirited Away* (2001), leads a song and dance featuring colourful umbrellas. But the umbrellas are broken, so the hero offers to fix them up. Which he does (using materials that magically appear in his backpack). Then come streams of kimonos flying thru the air, which also need sewing.

Possessions is a superbly-realized *hommage* to traditional Japanese art and religion, setting the scene for the three excursions into the past of *Short Peace* (the final installment, *A Farewell To Weapons*, is set in the future).

Gambo was written by Katsuhito Ishii and Kensuke Yamamoto, directed by Hiroaki Ando, music by Hikaru Nanase, char. des. by Yoshiyuki Sadamoto and Yusuke Yoshigaki, and art dir. by

Yoshiaki Honm.

In *Gambo*, traditional Japanese mythology and legend provides the context for a story of fire-red ogres terrorizing rural communities, wandering samurai, guardian spirits in the form of polar bears, and young heroines. Part *Kabuki* play, part horror movie, part gory fairy tale, and part supernatural *manga, Gambo* is a marvellous yarn, which doesn't explain everything, and allows mystery to flourish. It also doesn't hold back on the portrayal of violence and bloodshed – this is more gruesome than Western equivalents such as *Jack and the Beanstalk* or *Jack the Giant Killer*. Ogres (*oni*) are a Japanese speciality, of course, popping up in *Legend of the Overfiend, Bleach, Berserk, One Piece, Ogre Slayer*, etc.

Short Peace's last entry, *A Farewell To Weapons* (*Buki yo Saraba*), was written and directed by Hajime Katoki (from Otomo-sensei's *manga* of 1979), music by Tomohisa Ishikawa, char. des. by Tatsuyuki Tanaka, art. dir. by Hiromasa Ogura, and editing by Takeshi Seyama.

A Farewell To Weapons is a wholly boys' own story, a 'men on a mission' tale, a men with guns, robots and tanks outing. *A Farewell To Weapons* is set in the near-future when Europeand the Middle East have been destroyed, and desertification is rife (this is a very Otomoan *milieu* – familiar from *Akira* and *The Legend of Mother Sarah*).

Narratively, *A Farewell To Weapons* owes plenty to Masamune Shirow (*Ghost In the Shell, Appleseed*) as well as Katsuhiro Otomo: the scenario – a bunch of guys have to take out tanks driven by A.I. – is completely Shirowian.

A Farewell To Weapons is a wild, video game-style piece where Mecha Rules OK, where firearms and grenades are exploding all over, where remote planes drop missiles, where guys set up sniping positions and flee as soon as they've fired, where tanks roll along trash-strewn streets, and where buildings are crumbling and our heroes're leaping to save themselves.

The 'Gonk' tank is a savage and clever beastie that our heroes find very difficult to trounce. Along the way, the wild geese are picked off one by one by the tank (in the manner of the usual 'men on a mission' genre).

A Farewell To Weapons closes with a moment that comes right out of Katsuhiro Otomo's 1979 *manga*.[79] Here, the second tank rises from the ruins (caused by a nuclear missile on a train, which explodes!), to confront the survivor, Jin (Akio Ohtsuka).[80] The tank scans the hapless, cowering Jin, and decides he offers no threat anymore (he popped out of his military suit).

There's a great gag when the robot tank prints a brochure about non-violence for Jin to peruse at his leisure (having only just killed his commander!). And then the tank strips Jin of his clothes[81] when he picks up a boulder and smashes the tank with it (a very Otomoan moment). That the robot tank shifts from being a vicious killing machine to a peacenik civil servant, politely taking care of business, and handing out leaflets, then ignoring the angry human Jin, is terrific.

Thus, *Short Peace*, despite the mayhem of the entries, closes on a *Mad* magazine kind of gag – the naked soldier chasing the snooty robot tank with rocks through the ruins of Tokyo, as the camera pulls back and back. (Otomo's *manga Hair* also closed with a guy stripped by a robot tank).

79 It also recalls the short *manga DJ Teck's Morning Attack* (published in 2012 – the same period as *Short Peace*).
80 Akio Otsuka plays Batou in *Ghost In the Shell*, and has appeared in some Studio Ghibli and Hayao Miyazaki films.
81 The 1979 *manga* opened with an image of a naked soldier with a small bomb or grenade over his genitals.

PAR LE R ALISATEUR DE AKIRA

STEAMBOY

Steam-Boy (2004).
(This page and over).

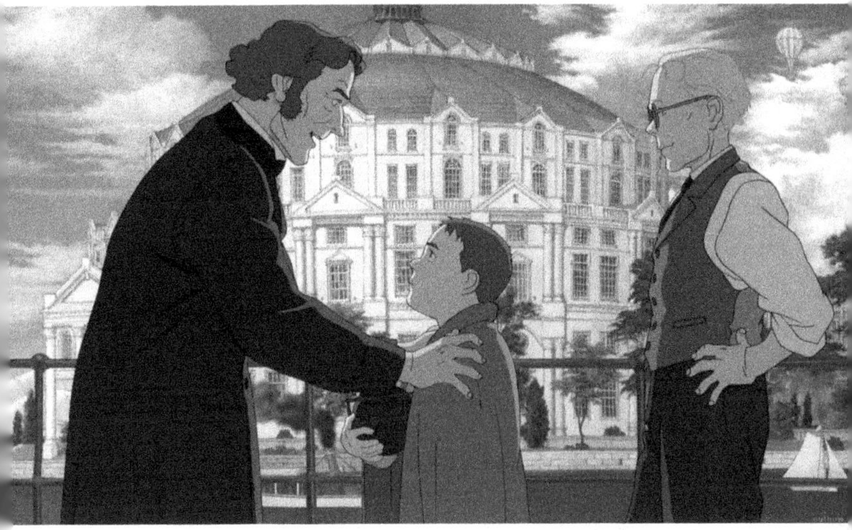

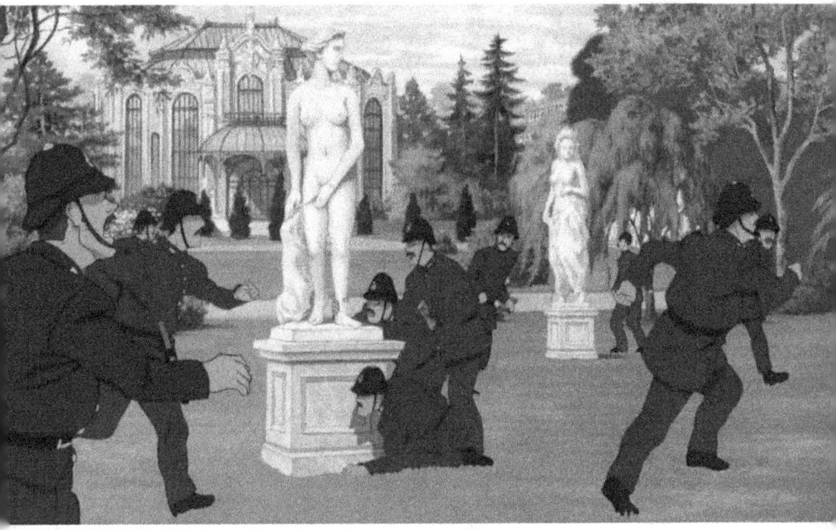

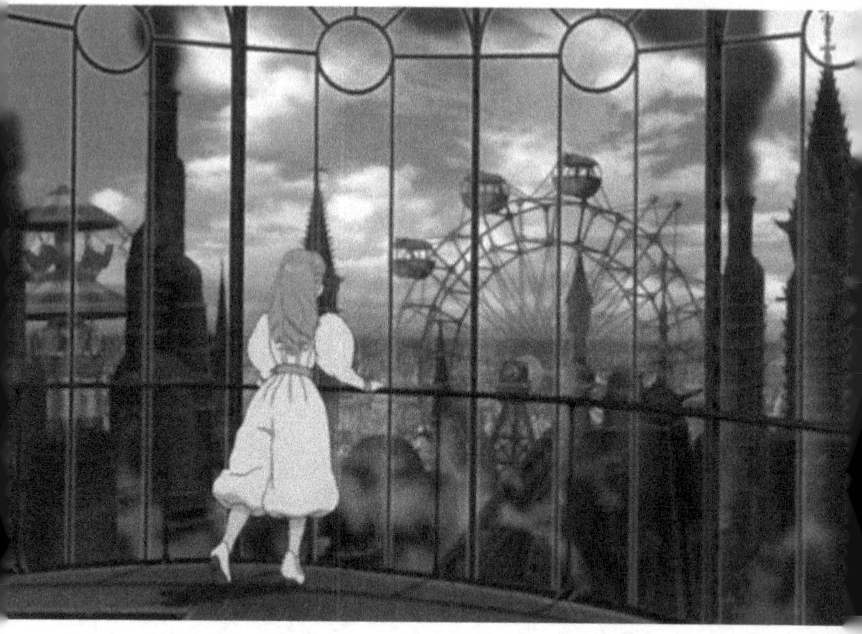

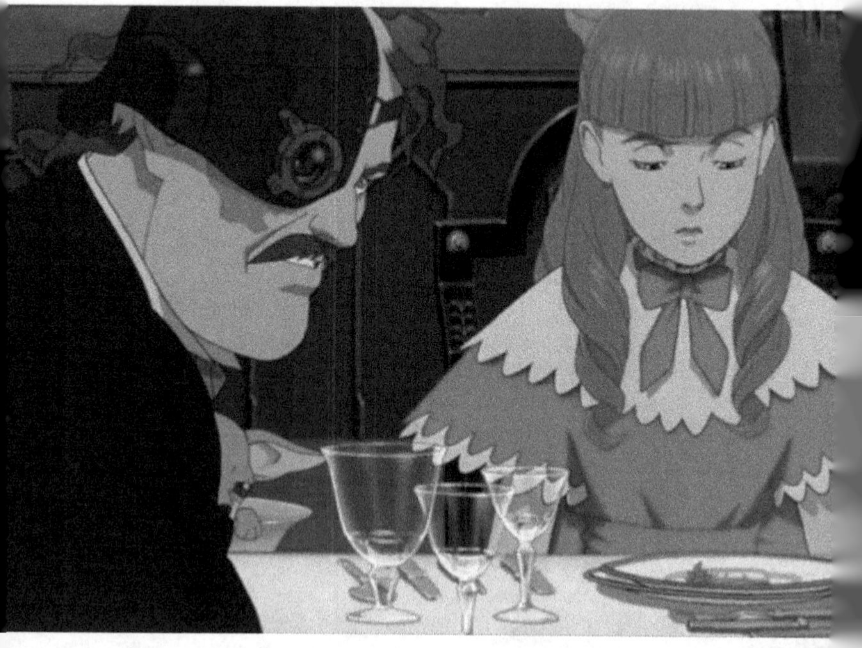

Steam-Boy computer game (below).

FROM THE DIRECTOR OF AKIRA

MUSHISHI

"ASTONISHING"
VARIETY

15

Mushishi (2006)
(This page and over)

蟲を感じたらお知らせください。

蟲師
むしし

2006年ヴェネチア国際映画祭コンペティション部門出品最新作

監督・脚本：大友克洋

オダギリジョー
大森南朋
蒼井優
江角マキコ

企画・製作プロダクション／小学館制作／楢山節考 ／ビームエンタテインメント／東京テアトル／バンダイビジュアル／ぴあ／バップ／日本出版販売／電通 配給：東宝 宣伝：東宝エンタテインメント

それとも、幽霊でも物の怪でもない、奇妙な存在たち……「蟲」
百年前の日本、もとには、"蟲"が棲む壮大な世界が広がっていた
「蟲」と「ヒト」をめぐるファンタジー

v.mushishi-movie.jp

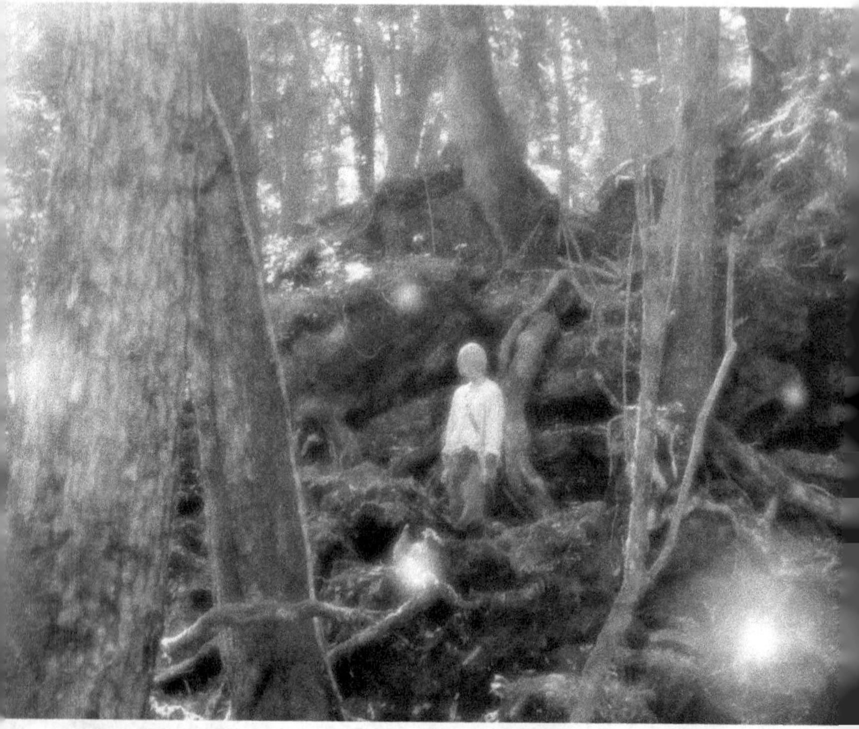

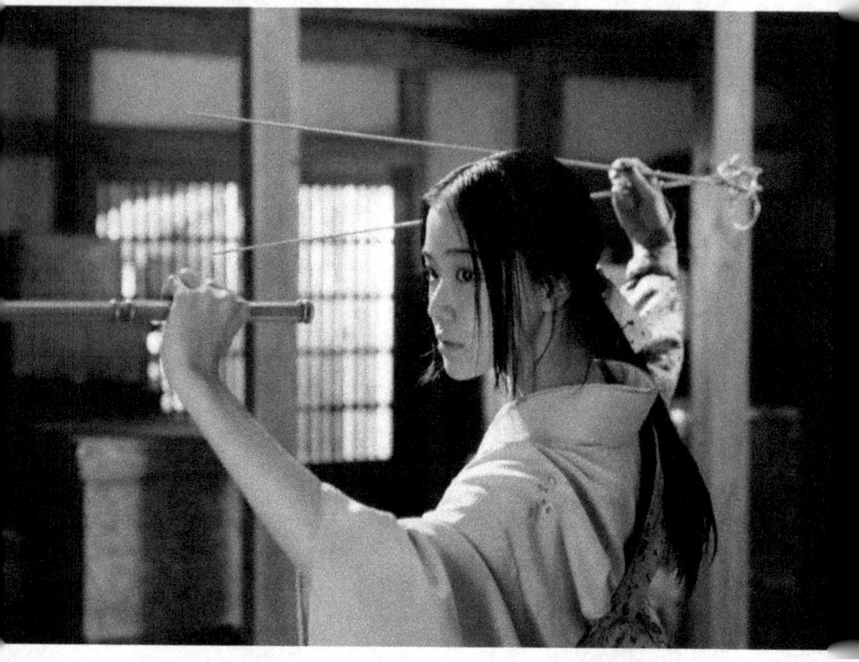

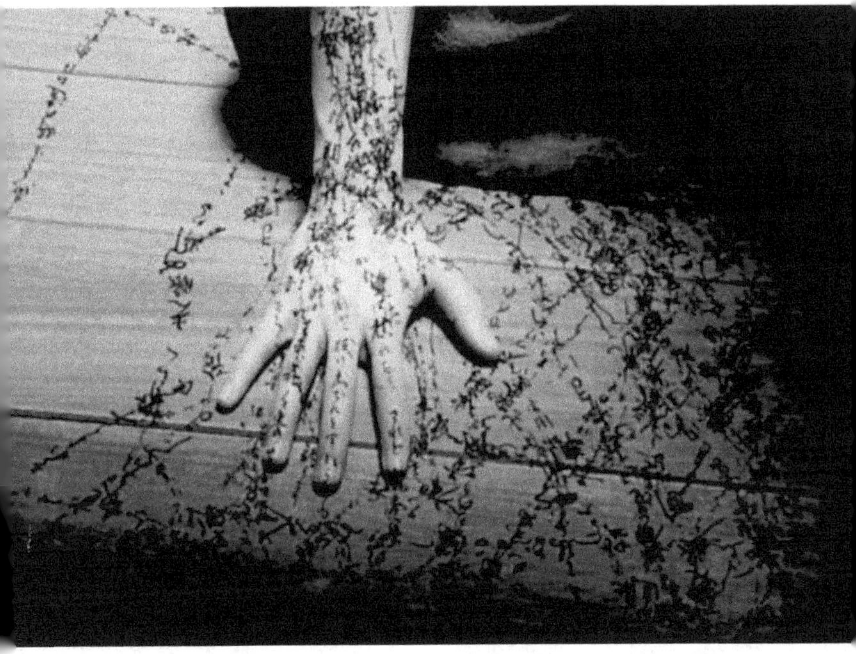

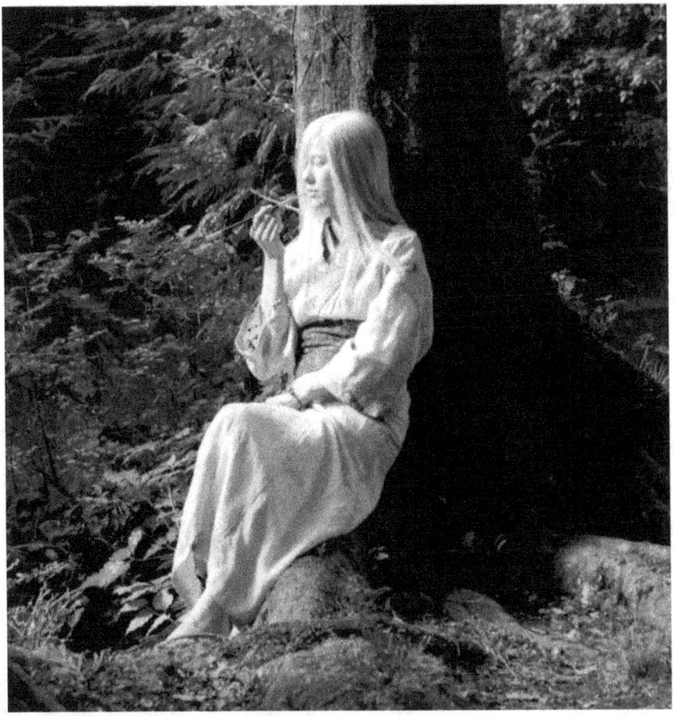

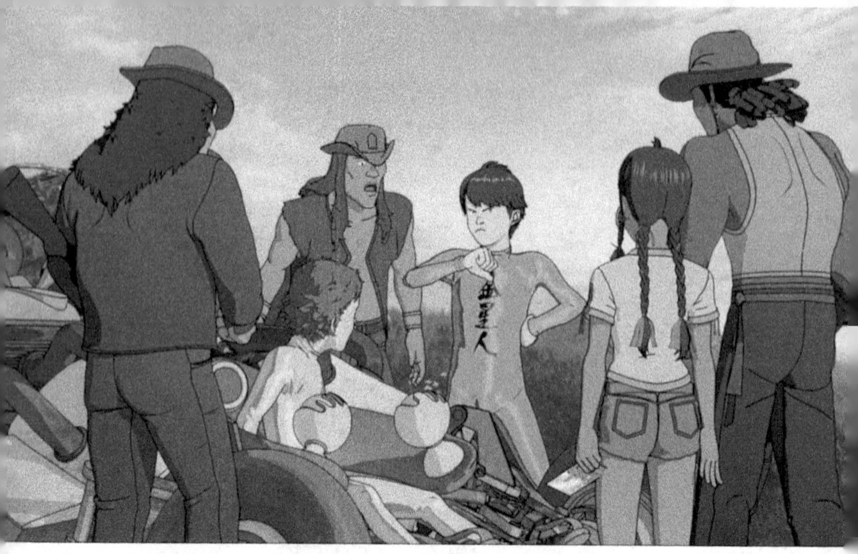

Freedom (2006)

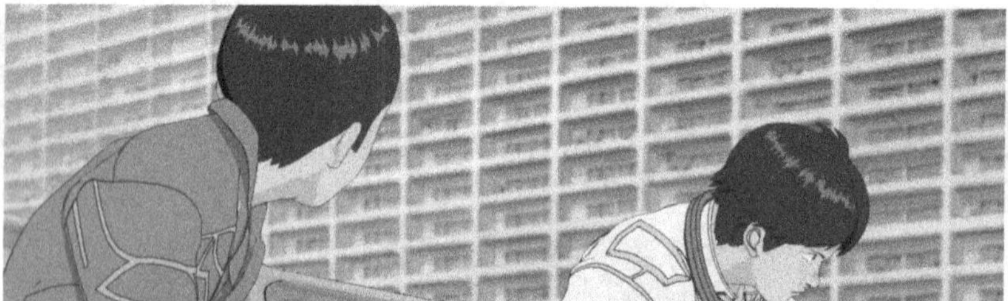

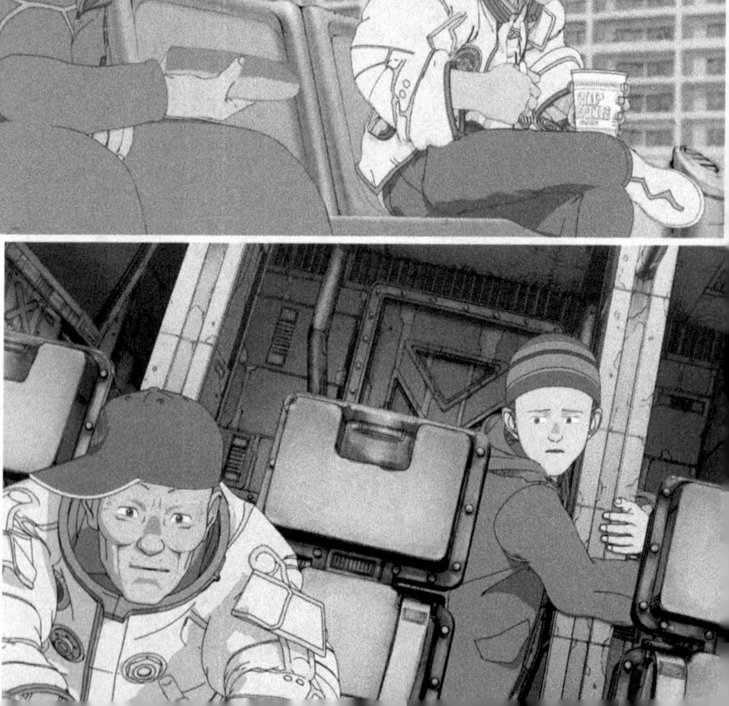

Combustible, from Short Peace (2013)
(This page and over)

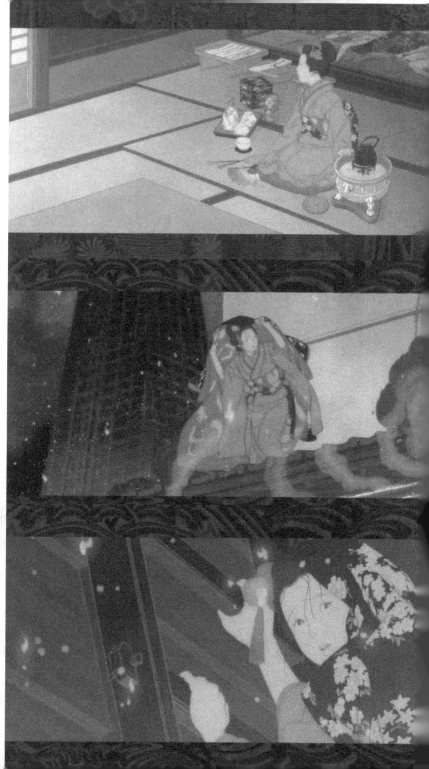

PART FOUR

THE *AKIRA* MOVIE

01

INTRODUCTION

SOME REASONS WHY *AKIRA* IS A MASTERWORK

(1) *Akira* is one of those movies you watch in a state of awe, like *Intolerance*, *The Magnificent Ambersons*, *The Seventh Seal*, *Close Encounters of the Third Kind*, *Ran*, *The Gospel According To Matthew*, *Vampyr*, *Princess Mononoke* or the 1967 *War and Peace*. You simply cannot believe that someone conceived it, imagined it and led the creation of it. It seems almost impossible.

(2) *Akira* is one of those magical, magnetic movies: if you start watching *Akira*, you can't look away: it compels the viewer with total authority, like *2001: A Space Odyssey* or *Citizen Kane* or *The Devils* or *Apocalypse Now*. You can't switch it off. *Akira* gets under your skin. This is high voltage filmmaking.

Akira possess a raw power, an elemental force, which very few movies have.

The energy is literally burning off the screen in *Akira*.

If ever there was a movie that was 'on fire', *Akira* is it.

KATSUHIRO OTOMO! – is he a hero or what?!

To have written what many regarded as the finest *manga* ever (as well as one of the longer ones), is an astonishing achievement.[1] To have *also* directed (and co-written) what many acknowledge as the greatest *animé* movie is beyond belief. Only Hayao Miyazaki and Osamu Tezuka among *all animé* filmmakers and *all manga* artists can be placed in that heavenly category.

(3) *Akira* isn't a movie – it's 20 or 30 movies. There're enough ideas, characters, plots and situations for 30 movies. One of *Akira*'s action scenes alone would do for a movie, but in *Akira* they just keep coming.

(4) If you watch *Akira* after looking at other *animé*, you are struck by the level of *detail* and *intricacy*. The *density* of visual layering is astounding. This is a movie that's been storyboarded[2] by a genius: look at the framing, the camera angles, the blocking of the characters within the frame, the use of perspective and distance, the variations in image size, and the variety of lenses.

There's no section of *Akira*, either, that's slapdash, no area that looks as if the filmmakers looked at the first takes and agreed they would be just fine. No, the sequences have been worked over and polished, again and again – to a striking degree.[3] Which gives *Akira* a solid foundation of accomplishment: if there's one thing that won't crumble or let

---

1 On the *Akira* show, Katsuhiro Otomo was aided by a huge crew that included veterans of the animation industry as well as many newbies. Look at the credits of *Akira*, and you'll find many talents that went on to create many of the *animé* you know and love. *Akira* is one of those animated productions, like *Bleach* or *One Piece*, where it seems as if everybody in Tokyo was working on it.

2 Katsuhiro Otomo drew 738 storyboards for *Akira* (and that was on top of drawing the epic *manga*!). He said he had produced 2,000 pages of notebooks.

3 I would imagine that the animation team would quickly realize that Katsuhiro Otomo wasn't going to accept a first take, that he was a perfectionist who would encourage the team to go back again and again to get it right.

Akira down, it's the animation. And when you combine first-rate animation with first-rate story-telling, themes and characters, you have a master-piece.

(5) Like many celebrated movies in cinema, *Akira* operates on a number of levels at the same time. As an action-adventure movie, a science fiction movie, a futuristic movie, and as pure entertainment, it works like gangbusters. As a visual feast, as a *tour-de-force* of animation and technical brilliance, it soars, with hardly any peers. And on the thematic level, it is deeply satisfying.

The big themes are very familiar: *Akira* is *Frankenstein*, it's science creating monsters, and the monsters rebelling and turning on their masters; it's *Faust* (and the myth of Prometheus), with science (and society) making a pact with the Devil; it's capitalism and the military machine expanding unchecked (including exploiting humans in grotesque experiments); and it's any number of anxieties – about technology, science, militarism, nationalism, youth vs. age, and modern Japan.

The *ambition* of *Akira* is very high: the movie reaches for the skies. (Again, this is also why *Akira* is unusual among any movie-making, not only animation: its *ambition* really is genuinely enormous.)

(6) *Akira* is among the most *sophisticated* movies of its kind *politically*. Indeed, by comparison you find that nearly all action/ adventure/ fantasy/ horror/ sci-fi movies are Neanderthal and/ or offensive in their politics (which, in the West, boil down to this: U.S.A. = good, everybody else = bad). Most big, Western blockbuster movies don't get beyond a cretinous adherence to right-wing, pro-military ideology (yup, even the celebrated genre movies such as *Blade Runner, 2001: A Space Odyssey, Alien, The Terminator, Avatar, Superman, Harry Potter, James Bond, Avengers, X-Men, Star Trek, Star Wars*, every

superhero and comicbook movie, etc). They are all right-wing, all pro-military (and, among Western movies, all pro-American, as if the only lifeforms blessed by Gawd, or the only lifeforms worth endorsing or following, are Yanks).

(7) *Akira* is one of those movies of youth, rebellion and urban style that become cult movies for a generation: in the 1950s it was *The Wild One, Jailhouse Rock* and *Rebel Without a Cause*; in the late 1960s/ early 1970s, it was *A Clockwork Orange, Performance, Easy Rider* and the Beatles' films; in the early 1990s, it was *Pulp Fiction* and *GoodFellas*. But you know what? *Akira* is a finer movie, more complex and more imaginative, than any of those pictures.

(8) *Akira* was produced in the mid-to-late 1980s, and was released in 1988 – 1988.07.16 (with the *Akira manga* being published in *Young* magazine from 1982 onwards, up until 1990): it was the height of the 1980s, then, with its nuclear paranoia, its capitalist greed and personal excess, and its postmodern superficiality. And 1988, one should note, was but a year or so before the Bubble Economy in Japan burst (which had a big impact on Japanese animation).

Akira is thus right on the edge of the apocalypse, the economic, cultural and political catastrophe, a movie so much of its time (within a year or two came a global recession in the early 1990s – which would've made *Akira*'s high budget less likely, for instance).

And that timeliness is perhaps something that keeps *Akira* feeling so contemporary – as if our time, or any time, is always on the verge of collapse, is always apocalyptic, is always an era of unease and confusion and yearning and despair… as if there never has been a time of harmony and tranquility (but we like to think there was. When would it have been? 1900, before the First World War? No! 1780, before the French Revolution and Napoleon? No! 2,000 B.C., before the Roman Empire? No! You can search and search, but the Golden Age *never existed*, folks. Yet, like the Garden of Eden, like any Paradise, it's the *idea* of it that's important, and needed).

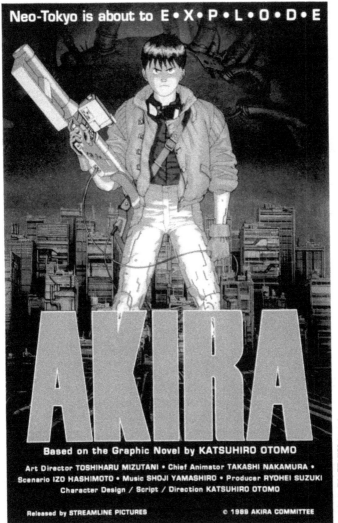

Artwork for Western release, 1989

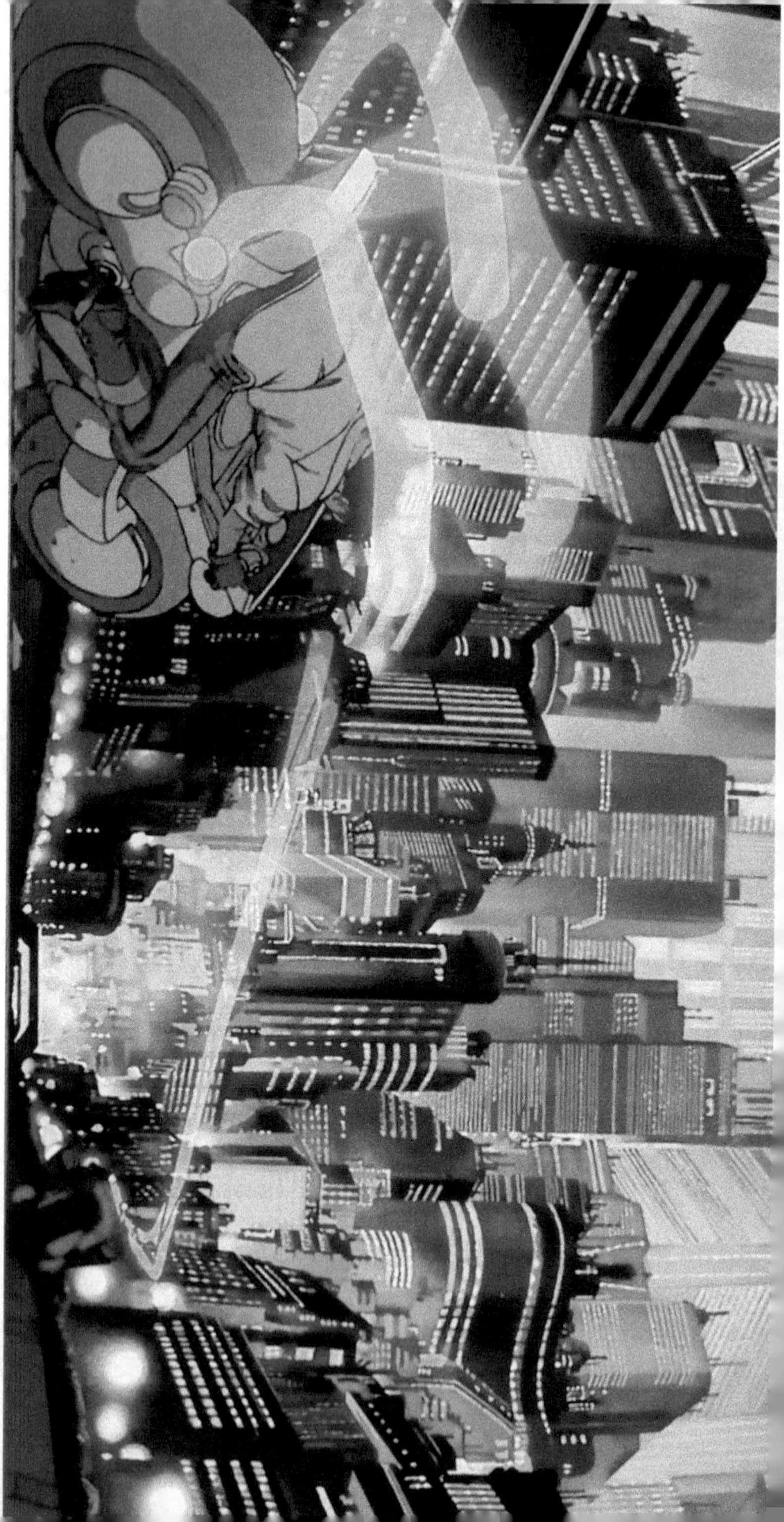

02

AKIRA AND THE JAPANESE ANIMATION INDUSTRY

The world of Japanese animation is instantly recognizable: characters with spiky hair, red hair, purple hair, long hair • hair blowin' in the breeze • giant eyes • tiny mouths • snub, pointy noses • women with pneumatic bodies and big breasts • guys with muscle-bound bodies • superheroes • grimaces showing lots of teeth • elfin ears • cat-girls (*nya!*) • angels, crosses, churches • feathers • grizzled, old guys who smoke • child-like *shojo* figures • tall, skinny villains • high schools • people who can fly • grotesque transformations • excessive violence • technofetishism • robots • *mecha* • more robots • more *mecha* • mobile power suits • explosions • spaceships • jets • helicopters • motorbikes • guns, guns and more guns • characters holding guns at every opportunity • samurai swords • swordplay • swords vs. guns • cloaks • teams, gangs, clans, harems, after-school clubs • lightning storms • the ocean • expressions of awe and joy: *sugoi! subarashi!* • noisy disbelief (*eeeeeeeeh?!*) • hysterical reactions to *everything* • girls in swimwear • flashes of underwear • the colours green and silver and red • headbands • silly hats • comic sidekicks like dogs or cute critters • stuffed toys • evil villains • nerds (*otaku*) • festivals • kimonos • cherry blossom pillow moments • *saké* • Tokyo • futuristic cities, gloomy cities • always skyscrapers and mean streets (always with the skyscrapers!) • theme parks • giant moons • neon signs • tentacles • monsters • demons • blood and guts • masochism • suicide• and last but not least: the atomic bombs dropped on Japan by the United States of North America.

Needless to say, *Akira* exhibits many of those features (and some of 'em were defined irrevocably by *Akira*: motorcycles… atomic bombs… extreme violence… Frankensteinian experiments… hi-tech cities, etc).

THE JAPANESE *ANIMÉ* INDUSTRY

Japan has the biggest animation industry in the world,[1] and many would agree with me that it's also the finest. That Japan is one of the richest nations on Earth plays a part (at the height of the Bubble Economy in the 1980s, Japan had 16% of the global economic power, and 60% of real estate wealth). The famous TV shows, O.A.V.s, specials, videos, and movies in *animé* include: *Digimon, Pokémon, One Piece, Dr Slump, Star Blazers, Dragon Ball, Sailor Moon, Legend of the Overfiend, Evangelion, Gunbuster, Gundam, Lupin III, Fullmetal Alchemist, Patlabor, Bleach, Naruto, Cowboy Bebop, Astro Boy, Ghost In the Shell*, Studio Ghibli's output, and of course *Akira*. According to Helen McCarthy, animation in Japan accounted for 6% of films released in late 1998, 25-30% of videos, and 3-6% of television shows made in Japan. The *animé* market was worth about ¥20 billion ($200m) in 2004.

In 2013, a 13-episode TV *animé* (= one season) cost about $2 million, with a 26-episode series

1 The U.S.A. is next, then Korea.

costing up to 4 million (with around $100,000-300,000 spent per episode).

In 2005, there were 430 *animé* production studios in Japan, and most of them were in Tokyo. (And that's one of the reasons why so many *animé* shows are set in Tokyo, including many of Katsuhiro Otomo's films and *manga*).

Animation studios themselves become the centre of attention for *animé* fans, and fans will follow particular animation houses and their work (as well as filmmakers like Katsuhiro Otomo and Hayao Miyazaki). The famous ones include Production I.G., Pierrot, Sunrise/ Bandai, Studio 4°C, Gainax, Madhouse, Pioneer, Tezuka, Gonzo, Clamp, Bones, Toei, and of course Studio Ghibli. *Akira* used well-known *animé* studios (see filmography).

There are many links to the Japanese *animé* tradition in *Akira* and Katsuhiro Otomo's work. For instance, young heroes, youth vs. old age, *mecha*, the ambiguous treatment of technology, Tokyo settings, Japanese mythology, war (and the two World Wars), the atomic bomb, the military machine, and science fiction. And the motifs that crop up in thousands of *animé* products are also found in *Akira* (indeed, *Akira* created some of them, and defined others better than any other *animé*).

An important thing to remember about Japanese *animé* is that it is an industry that can sustain itself by producing movies and TV shows for a *domestic* audience: it doesn't need television syndication or releases overseas (but it will always take them up if available). In other words, one of the reasons that the Japanese animation industry is the biggest in the world is because there is such a large market in Japan itself for animation.

That also means that Japanese *animé* filmmakers can make their films and TV shows for a *homegrown* market, and don't need to pander to an international (or an American) audience. *Akira*, and other films by Katsuhiro Otomo, are very much *Japanese* movies,

movies that are made primarily for the *Japanese* market (and *Akira* was a hit at the box office). As Otomo-sensei's *manga* are very Japanese comics. So the O.A.V.s and TV series can reflect and explore local or national culture, and don't need to build in elements that will appeal to a global audience (no need to shift the action to, say, Ohio or Chicago, and turn their characters into, *duh*, Americans).

Some of Katsuhiro Otomo's movies have been high profile and costly productions, so there is even more incentive to recoup the negative costs. Otomo hasn't been as financially successful as some other *animé* filmmakers, but his reputation has ensured some pretty big budget shows (*Akira* was very successful in Japan). It's an envious position to be in for a filmmaker. European filmmakers, for instance, can similarly make movies only for their own national audience, but they tend to be much smaller (or cheaper) movies (which's why much of *animé* comprises lower budget TV series and O.A.V.s; very few *animés* cost as much as *Akira* did – $11 million – not only in 1988, but even today).

A country such as France can sustain a huge production of movies per year because it has the largest film industry in Europe (that's one of the reasons why French movies travel outside France). And it means that France can make much bigger movies (it has more government investment than many other countries).[2] And it can attract more co-productions than other European countries.

The *animé* industry in Japan has been, in the main, a *television* industry. Although the prestige *animé* movies, TV shows and O.A.V.s receive much of the media's attention (especially outside Japan), most of animation in Japan is produced for television (as well as commercial and corporate work – Otomo-sensei has produced commercials). A movie is 80, 90 or maybe 120 minutes of animation (at most), but a

---

2 And the French love animated movies, as they love comics and fantasy art.

big *animé* series on television runs to large numbers of 22-minute episodes. Look at the numbers of shows: *Doraemon* (over 2,000 episodes by 2004), *Astro Boy* (193 episodes x 30m – first series), *Dragon Ball* (153 episodes), *Dragon Ball Z* (291 episodes), *Galaxy Express* (114 episodes), *Mazinger Z* (92 episodes),[3] *Gatchomon* (105 episodes), *Legend of Galactic Heroes* (110 episodes), *Maison Ikkoku* (96 episodes), *Naruto* (720 episodes), *One Piece* (800+), *Digimon* (205 episodes), *Pokemon* (550 episodes and counting), and *Sailor Moon* (200 episodes).

Lonely Planet's travel guide to Japan makes some useful points about contemporary Japan:

> First, Japan is an island nation. Second, until WWII, Japan was never conquered by an outside power, nor was it heavily influenced by Christian missionaries. Third, until the beginning of last century, the majority of Japanese lived in close-knit rural farming communities. Fourth, most of Japan is covered in steep mountains, so the few flat areas of the country are quite crowded – people literally live on top of each other. Finally, for almost all of its history, Japan has been a strictly hierarchical place, with something approximating a caste system during the Edo period. (C. Rowthorn, 2007)

WWII and the Occupation had enormous effects on the Japanese movie industry, which still resonate today (and you can also see the effects in Katsuhiro Otomo's output). In *A History of Narrative Film*, still the finest single book on cinema (if you need to buy one book on cinema, this is the one), David Cook set the scene:

> When World War II ended on August 14, 1945, much of Japan lay in ruins. The massive fire-bombing of its sixty cities from March through June 1945 and the dropping of atomic bombs on

3 The first power suit with a pilot was introduced in *Mazinger Z* by Go Nagai.

Hiroshima and Nagasaki had resulted in some 900,000 casualties and the nearly total paralysis of civilian life. On the morning of August 15, when Emperor Hirohito broadcast to his subjects the news that the war had ended and that Japan had lost, there was widespread disbelief. Never in their history had the Japanese people been defeated or the nation occupied, and so the circumstances of the American Occupation, 1945-52, were utterly unique. (783)

Following WW2, North American military bases remained in Japan (as in many parts of the world, including Europe), and the North Americans stationed in Japan had an influence on Japanese culture.

One of the first animated TV series in Japan, *Astro Boy* (1963), had a science fiction and *Pinocchio* theme.[4] *Astro Boy*, from Osamu Tezuka's *manga Ambassador Atom* (*Atom Taishi*, 1951-68), introduced themes which have resonated in *animé* ever since (including *Akira*): the son of a scientist dies in a car crash and is recreated as a robot; and the robot wants to become real. It's the 'doll with a soul' theme (in Japanese folklore, 'dolls loved and cared for could develop an actual soul', noted Gilles Poitras [2001, 19]).

Another early *animé* series has themes which still crop up in Japanese animation (including *Ghost In the Shell* and *Akira*): in *Eighth Man* (or *8 Man*, Haruyuki Kawajima, 1963, Eiken/ T.B.S.),[5] policeman Hachiro Azuma (Peter Brady) has his memories inserted into a robot following his murder by a crime gang. Based on a *manga* by Kazumasa Hirai (illustrated by Jiro Kuwata), the concept predated *RoboCop* and *Cyborg 009* by decades.

⊖

Gilles Poitras defined *animé* in his excellent

---

4 Actually, *Manga Calendar*, from the Otagi company, was the first series, running from 1962 to 1964, but *Astro Boy* is usually taken as the breakthrough *animé* series.

5 *Eighth Man* was remade in *animé* in 1993 (as *Eight Man After*), and also re-cut and dubbed for the U.S.A. (as *Tobor the Eighth Man*).

> anime is not to be confused with cartoons. Anime uses animation to tell stories and entertain, but it does so in ways that have barely been touched on in Western animation. While the U.S. continues to pump out cartoons with gag stories, musicals with cute animals, animated sitcoms, and testosterone-laced TV fare, the Japanese have been using anime to cover every literary and cinematic genre imaginable in a highly competitive market that encourages new story ideas and the creative reworking of older ideas and themes. (vii)

The genres of Japanese animation include pretty much all of those in live-action, as well as some genres particular to *animé*: comedy; romance; crime; action-adventure; horror; historical drama; science fiction[6] (including *mecha*, cyberpunk, war, epics); fantasy (including comics; supernatural tales; myths and legends; and superheroes); animal stories; martial arts; children's stories; epics; erotica; porn; and sports stories.[7] Gilles Poitras noted in *The Anime Companion* that *animé* has more genres than exist in Western cinema (43).

In live-action, genres are divided into *jidai-geki* = period movies (typically in the feudal age), and *gendai-geki* = set in the contemporary era.[8] There are further categories within the two genres. Fantasy and science fiction are two key genres of Katsuhiro Otomo's cinema (as well as the youth picture). There's also a strain of social satire and overt political commentary in Otomo's cinema that you don't find in many other Japanese *auteurs*.

In *manga*, Otomo-sensei took on fairy tales, fantasy, horror, thrillers (including the urban

---

6 More people consume science fiction in Japan than anywhere else.
7 Although it is regarded as popular culture, Japanese *animé* draws on high culture, including woodblock prints, *ukiyo-e*, *Kabuki* theatre, painting, and classical music.
8 See G. Mast, 1992b, 410.

thriller), children's adventures, and the samurai genre (plus many satires).

The Japanese film industry has been one of the most prolific historically, producing over 400 movies a year. The Japanese movie business has been dominated by studio conglomerates, just like the North American system, since the 1920s (the big guns are Nikkatsu, Shochiku, Toho,[9] Toei, Shintoho and Daiei). Although the independent film sector has grown since the 1980s, the major studios continue to take up most of film production. And most Japanese film directors work for the major studios in some form or another, or for television.

Like the films of Yasujiro Ozu or Kenji Mizoguchi or Akira Kurosawa, the movies of Katsuhiro Otomo are very *Japanese* – they are set in Japan, draw on Japanese history and culture, and are about Japanese subjects. But they are also – like the movies of Yasuojiro Ozu, Kenji Mizoguchi and Akira Kurosawa – films which can and do travel around the world. Most films don't. Most movies *don't* get released or shown outside their country of origin. (Or put it this way: even if you are adventurous and have gone out of your way to see movies from many other countries, you will not actually be able to see most of the movies produced by any country, unless you live there).

Other notable filmmakers in Japanese cinema, apart from the *sensei* himself (Akira Kurosawa), include: Yasujiro Ozu, Kenji Mizoguchi, and Ichikawa Kon, and Japanese New Wave directors, such as Nagisa Oshima, Hiroshi Teshigahara, Masashiro Shinoda, Takeshi Kitano and Yoshishige Yoshida.

Among the classic films of Japanese cinema are: *Tokyo Story, The Flavour of Green Tea Over Rice, The Life of Oharu, Ohayu, Sansho Dayu, Kwaidan, Early Summer, Woman of the Dunes, Ugetsu Monogatari,* and

9 Toho, founded in the 1930s from a number of smaller companies, is best known as the studio of *Godzilla,* Hayao Miyazaki and Akira Kurosawa.

THE ART OF KATSUHIRO OTOMO ◆ 412

Ai No Corrida (*In the Realm of the Senses*). And of course, *anything* by Akira Kurosawa (even one of Kurosawa's minor films is finer than many film-makers' best efforts).

In Japan, the director is king of the movie-making industry, rather than the star or producer; the director will often appear above the title, and is often used in marketing more than stars. The director is 'the paternalistic head of his own production "family"', as Gerald Mast and Bruce Kawin explain in *A Short History of the Movies*, a social structure which echoes Japanese society (1992b, 409). Needless to say, Katsuhiro Otomo's name is often used in the marketing of the movies and shows he directs or is involved with. (Otomo-sensei is always placed next to *Akira* in advertizing, for instance, rather than the names of the producers, the voice cast, the chief animators, or even his co-writer, Izô Hashimoto).

In Japanese animation, terms like 'director' and 'designer' don't have the same meaning as in the Western film industry. 'Director' might refer to a 'wide range' of different jobs (H. McCarthy, 1996, 9). It's customary, for instance, for designers to have a speciality, and to be brought onto a production to exploit that gift.

Japan is one of the major film markets in the world – for North American movies, yes, but also for movies from everywhere. And when it comes to animation, there is a huge appetite for it in Japan. That helps to sustain *animé*. Without that large, national market, and that enthusiastic response to animated movies and television, it would be more difficult for Katsuhiro Otomo to make the kind of pictures he wants to make; similarly, the home market for comics has largely sustained Otomo-sensei's career as a *mangaka* (as with every other *mangaka*). *Akira, Domu, The Legend of Mother Sarah* and *SOS! Tokyo Metro Explorers* exist because readers in Japan want to read them.

You can see this operating in blockbuster North

American movies, which consciously target a range of audiences (casting actors from different countries, for instance). Those ultra-high budget, North American movies have to generate half their money back from international sales (since the Nineties), so the films have to be able to play in Italy or Israel or Argentina as well as in North America. (Japan is one of the key markets for North American movies).

Japanese *animé* sells in the Western world via O.A.V.s,[10] streaming, videos and DVDs, TV shows, and related *manga* comicbooks. Animated series and movies are prepared for the Western market[11] with English language dubs (nearly always using North American actors and American-style English), as happened with *Akira,* and also subtitles (there is also a subculture of fans subtitling shows, and fans translating *manga*).

In Japanese animation, there are many differences between the English subtitles – which one might expect to presumably translate the Japanese dialogue (though not all of it) – and the English dubbed versions. There are lines in the English subtitles which don't appear in the English dubbed version – and vice versa. Background sounds and additional lines of dialogue are also added (ruining the emphasis on silence or near-silence which's found throughout Japanese cinema). This means that *Akira* has a slightly different impact in its Japanese subtitled and English dubbed versions. I would urge fans who have seen *Akira* enough times to get the story to watch it in Japanese (and without subtitles).

---

10 O.A.V. means Original Video Animation (a.k.a. O.A.V. = Original Animé/ Animation Video) – referring to sell-through videos, which may be linked to TV shows or movies, and, of course, *manga*.
11 In the West, the markets for *animé* 'n' *manga* are mainly male.

Manga are certainly huge in Japan, and more so than in any other country (though they are on the increase in some regions). North America doesn't have a comic tradition anything like *manga* culture in Japan (few countries do!): in Japan, a *manga* like *Shonen Jump* has sold 6 million copies a week, enormous numbers.[12] (And even when sales of *manga* have declined, the amounts involved are still colossal).

Japan has the most sophisticated, the most varied, the funniest, the most entertaining, and by far the most imaginative comic culture in the world. Yes, we know that France, Germany, Spain, Italy, China, Korea, Britain and the U.S.A. (among others) have thriving comic industries, but none of them come anywhere near Japan.

In Japan, the audience for *manga* is pretty much everybody: the stigma in the West attached to comics and comicbooks simply doesn't exist:[13] everyone reads *manga*. The Japanese *manga* market is bigger than the *animé* market. *Manga* also requires far fewer personnel to create, and is cheaper to disseminate.

In 2000 in Japan there were 15 monthly magazines, 10 twice-weekly magazines, and 12 weeklies. Some have print runs of over a million copies. *Manga* accounted for about a quarter of all publishing sales (about 550 billion Yen/ $5.5 billion). *Manga* absorbed around 40% of Japan's printed matter. The average spend on *manga* was 4,500 Yen ($45) for everybody living in Japan. According to VIZ Media, the *manga* market in Japan in 2006 was worth $4.28 billion (and $250m in the U.S.A.).

Manga and *animé* are closely aligned commerc-

---

12 In a 1994 speech, Hayao Miyazaki compared that 6 million with the video sales of *Beauty and the Beast* in the U.S.A.: 20 million, for a nation with twice the population of Japan. Selling 20 million in America would be like selling 10 million in Japan, Miyazaki suggested, and *Shonen Jump* sells 6 million *manga* a week!
13 The marketing term 'graphic novel' has been applied to comics in an effort to raise their cultural profile.

ially as well as culturally.[14] Many *anime* shows are based on *manga* (and some of the big shows have their own *manga* spin-offs). *Manga* can be a cheaper means of testing out if a story will work with an audience. There are many more *manga* stories than *anime* stories. Thus, *anime* has a huge source of stories to draw on, alongside novels, plays, TV shows, video games[15] and all the other products than can be adapted.

Manga magazines and books read right to left; some translations in the West (such as from Dark Horse and Viz in North America), have tried to maintain the right-to-left format, without flopping the artwork. Unfortunately, the *Akira manga* is flipped, which's very irritating! (In both the Marvel colour and the Dark Horse editions). And especially annoying because we're talking about a masterpiece! Would you flip Leonardo da Vinci's *Last Supper*? No!

Manga in translation are often published as *tankobon*, collected *manga* stories (partly because, as in Japan, there is more money in *tankobon* than in *manga* magazines).[16] Famous *manga* works such as *Ghost In the Shell*, *Nausicaä of the Valley of the Wind* and *Fullmetal Alchemist* are republished as *tankobon*. *Tankobon* have a longer shelf life than throwaway magazines, and usually stay in print much longer than magazines.

Akira comes in 6 *tankobons* (in one of its key versions; there is also a colourized edition from Marvel). Some publishers in the West (or, like Viz, with a Western division), have brought out translated versions of magazines such as *Shonen Jump*.

Certainly *manga* and *anime* have been important in depicting Japanese culture overseas – and it will be

14 The crossover between *manga* and *anime* is well-known (many animations are *manga* first, and *manga* are in turn produced from movies and TV series). There is also a crossover into computer games, board games, card games, pop music and online gaming.
15 Among the well-known *manga* and *anime* that were based on computer games were *Final Fantasy*, *Pokémon*, and *Sakura Wars*. And in the *Akira manga*, Kaneda quips that driving the tank is 'probably just like a video game!' (vol. 3, 169).
16 G. Poitras, 2001, 66.

for many folk their first encounter with Japanese culture.[17] *Manga* and *animé* are popular in many Western markets, including France, Britain, Italy, Spain, Germany, and into Hong Kong, South America, and South-East Asia.[18] The U.S.A. is the primary market outside Japan. In Europe, *animé* is most popular in France (and France has a substantial animation industry). Sci-fi, cyber-punk and steam-punk are also much-loved in France, as are comic-books and graphic novels.

Manga has become more popular in North America and Europe in the 21st century, with new *manga* magazines being launched by the big Japanese publishers (such as *Daisuki, Banzai* and *Manga Power* in Germany, *Shonen* in France, and *Shonen Jump* in the U.S.A.). In the mid-2000s, the *manga* market in the U.S.A, was $40-50 million, and the *animé* market was $400-500 million.

ANIMATION IN PRODUCTION

In *Akira*, the *sheer pleasure* of making cinema comes thru. You really can tell when a filmmaker is having a great time making their film: you can see it in *Citizen Kane*, in *The Music Lovers*, in *An American In Paris*, in *Once Upon a Time In China*. You can see the film-makers letting their imaginations unfurl, and that helps to inspire the rest of the creative team to do better work.[19]

Animation is a long, hard slog – *very* labour intensive, with projects like feature films sometimes taking up to three or four years complete. It takes a particular kind of individual, then, to maintain a high level of enthusiasm and interest, to stay focussed

17 See G. Poitras, 2001, 8.

18 H. McCarthy, 1996, 7.

19 'Those who join in the work of animation are people who dream more than others and who wish to convey those dreams to others. After a while they realize how incredibly difficult it is to entertain others.' (Hayao Miyazaki, 2009, 25)

on the project and not be distracted into other things. Stanley Kubrick spoke of keeping hold of his initial inspiration for making a movie all the way through the long process of development, pre-production, shooting, post-production and distribution. You have to hang on to whatever it was that really excited you about doing the project in the first place (a production that doesn't have that initial spark of excitement and fascination can all too easily lose its momentum and energy).

I haven't visited an animation studio in Tokyo, but in every 'making of' *animé* documentary, in every photo, and in every account, every animation house is a shabby building of messy desks and work stations in which animators, ink-and-paint women, in-betweeners, *mecha* designers, character designers, CG technicians and the rest of the staff, slave away at all hours. There are no plush, front office buildings, as at the Disney Studios in Burbank or Pixar in Northern California. The new Studio Ghibli building among Tokyo animation houses is about the only one with an upmarket, front office feel (and on the main floors of Ghibli, it's animators and their desks and shelves crammed into small spaces again – look at the 'making of' documentary about *Spirited Away*).

It is commonplace for animators and staff to sleep under their desks in animation houses in Tokyo.[20] Visitors from the West to companies such as Production I.G. have been surprised by that, and by the tiny working spaces that even high-ranking animators have: just a desk and a few shelves. Cables run over the floor, DVDs, posters, books, toys and photocopied timing sheets are packed in everywhere, and there's not much space btn the workers and their chairs. Look at a photo of any animation house in

[20] Sleeping on the floor in the studio was more common in Japanese animation in the 1970s and 1980s than one would think: it wasn't unknown for animators to stay at work all day, and sleep there too, getting up to carry on. I would imagine that today the intensive, workaholic nature of animation in Tokyo is still prevalent, despite unions, labour laws and all the rest (yep, and animators still sleep under their desks).

Tokyo, and you'll see every nook is crammed with stuff. Staff eat their *bento* boxes at their desks (taking less than an hour for lunch). They often have multiple jobs, not just one (i.e., dealing with other aspects of the production company, not only animation). And it's not unknown for staff to have nervous breakdowns due to the heavy work-load (as with director Hideaki Anno on *The End of Evangelion*, and Tomomi Mochizuki after working on Ghibli's *Ocean Waves*).

If you dream of flying to Tokyo and working at Studio Ghibli, Sunrise or Toei or one of the other 450 *animé* houses, be prepared to work very hard, and for long hours (12-14 hours a day, plus every other Saturday), to eat your lunch at your desk (and sometimes sleep there), to enjoy few perks and benefits, to do many tasks (photocopying, say, or website design), and make barely enough to live.[21]

Animation is hard work for little pay.

In 1987, at the time of the production of *Akira*, Hayao Miyazaki described the typical animator as young, good-natured, and poor. They made less than ¥100,000 a month (= $1,000). They were paid ¥400 ($4) a page for theatrical movies and ¥150 ($1.50) a page for TV animation. Miyazaki reckoned there were about 2,500 in animators Japan (2009, 135). There were around 3,000 *manga* artists working in Japan in 2000 (not including assistants or contributors to anthologies). In 2001 a typical salary in *animé* was estimated at $15,000-20,000; many workers still lived with their parents, or supplemented their income elsewhere. In 2015, the average pay was $27,700.

Everybody who works in animation knows about the sheer struggle of production. It is an industry for workaholics ('without workaholics, Japan's animation could never be sustained', Hayao Miyazaki remarked [ib., 187]). It is hard work all the way, and there is no way of creating it without

---

21 You'll have to speak Japanese, too.

months of labour. 'Works of art are created by those who are prepared to go to the limit,' asserted Miyazaki (1991). *Akira* is certainly one of those workaholic, going-to-the-limit productions!

For the *auteurs* of Japanese animation, and that definitely includes Katsuhiro Otomo, pursuing animation means pursing perfection – or something as good as one can produce. Otomo-sensei has a famous reputation as a perfectionist.

But $11 million for *Akira* is still a lot cheaper than the North American equivalent: in 1985, the Mouse House's *Black Cauldron* cost $25 million (it was a troubled production, and a very disappointing movie for everybody concerned). The animated Disney and Pixar movies of recent times have included the following budgets: *Tarzan* $115m (or $142m or $150m, depending on sources); *Treasure Planet* $140m; *Ratatouille* $150m; and *Home On the Range* $110m.

These figures aren't really helpful, because movie budgets are notoriously difficult to check accurately: no one wants to admit how much money something *really* cost, or *exactly* how much they're earning (and Hollywood studios routinely exaggerate figures like budgets and grosses). But you know that if the budgets are one hundred million dollars or more, then *somebody somewhere* is making a lot of money.[22]

It's hard to believe that movies like *Home On the Range* or *Tarzan* from the Mouse House could have cost over $110 million or $115 million (or *The Black Cauldron* costing $25m), but there are all sorts of economic factors to consider. The piece-work labour of Japanese *animé* is going to be cheaper than hiring staff on a permanent basis that occurs more in North

---

22 As William Goldman noted, there's a lot of money to be had in simply *making* a film, regardless of whether it's released or seen or not. And some people make a living out of producing movies, including existing on development deals and other deals, and many of those films aren't shot, and some that *are* filmed aren't released.

American animation.[23] Living costs, unions and working conditions in Japan and North America are further factors. The much longer production schedules of North American animated movies must contribute to the higher costs too: Disney and Pixar movies can take 3 or more years. However, the large crews of hundreds of workers aren't hired for all of those years, but it's safe to say that the production teams in North American (and Western) feature animation can be larger than those in the Japanese animation industry, and that they are hired for longer periods. All of which drives costs up (at the same time, Western animation companies farm out work to outfits in countries such as Korea, China, Thailand and India, just as the Japanese animation industry increasingly does. And they are paid less).

THE ANIMATION PROCESS.

In the Japanese animation industry, the script comes first. Storyboards and image boards are drawn when the script is completed (but sometimes before then). The storyboards are called *e-conte* (a combination of *ei*, picture, and continuity). On a Katsuhiro Otomo show, it would be Otomo who'd be drawing the storyboards (directors like to do that – if they have time) – drawing the storyboards is very labour intensive, there's no easy way of doing them.

Once the film is complete as far as the storyboard stage, plus indications of frames, timing, dialogue and sound effects, it goes to the key animators: they put the movie together in terms of the key animation (the animation at the beginning and the end of an action).[24] In-between work means animating the movements between the key frames which the key

23 Hayao Miyazaki often complained about the piecework system of producing animation in Japan, which turned out work like an assembly line, instead of the hand-crafted and personal, artistic approach that Miyazaki favoured.
24 Keyframes or main poses are drawn by the animators or animation directors; assistant animators will usually draw the halfway poses between the keyframes; in-betweeners are animators (often trainees) who draw the frames in between the keyframes.

animators have drawn, using time sheets. (Sometimes storyboards are collated with dialogue, music and sound fx, as animatics ('line tests'),[25] and sometimes pencil tests of animation are produced. Animators have said that pencil tests and animation tests – before everything else is added – is their favourite part of the process).

At the same time, the drawings are cleaned up (one single outline will be chosen, for example, from a mass of pencil lines). Throughout this and all stages of animation, drawings and artwork are being tweaked and adjusted (each stage is reviewed, and directors often oversee each process. No doubt Otomo-sensei opted to redraw some of the animation himself – Otomo is one of those filmmakers in animation who can actually do much of the work himself. Not every animator can, and some directors of animation can't even draw!).

Once the drawings have been completed, they are transferred to cels (celluloid), and inked and painted. In digital animation, some stages of the process today are achieved with the aid of computers or tablets,[26] such as colour, photography, 3-D simulations, etc. Software can streamline the in-between animation process, for example, though key animators still have to oversee the work. Colour is one obvious area of difference between digital animation and ink and paint animation. There are millions of colours available in the digital realm, existing only in the computer. For *Akira*, to paint those 160,000 cels, gallons of real paint would be required – especially for the signature colours of Otomo's art, red and orange.

Finally, they are photographed (a whole complex process in itself). Photographic and special effects may be added at this stage. (However, animation doesn't always use 24 frames per second, called 'ones' or 'singles': it often goes to 'twos' or 'doubles'

25 Sometimes using the Quick Action Recorder.
26 Tablets are often used for drawing.

(12 frames a second) or 'threes' (8 frames per second). Even the most sophisticated and expensive movies use those frame rates).

CELS VERSUS COMPUTERS

Most Japanese animation is still basically 2-D/ cel animation in its style and approach, but computers and computer-generated effects and devices are increasingly employed. *Akira* used both, though most of its 160,000 cels were achieved with traditional techniques.

Cel animation in movies is already as supremely *technological* and *industrial* as computers or digital technology. *Everything* in movies is *technological*, everything is fake, everything is a highly sophist-icated cultural form created by humans for mass entertainment, to be screened with sophisticated machines in very particular cultural environments. So whether it's done with machines and tools like cameras or pencils or paintbrushes or computers isn't really the point. (And audiences don't care: they want a good story, they want to be entertained.)

A common gripe is that digital additions to scenes don't really mesh with traditional, 2-D anima-tion. For instance, Disney's *Treasure Planet, Atlantis, The Rescuers Down Under* and Warner Bros' *The Iron Man* have used computer-generated (so-called 3-D) elements placed into hand-drawn (but probably computer-inked) 2-D animation. The digital elements often look floaty and disconnected to the rest of the scenes (*Steam-boy* looked more like that, but *Akira*, being mostly hand-drawn, doesn't).

However, using computers is just another tool out of many that animation employs: a common view, still being voiced by critics who should know better, is that:

cel animation = good, computer animation = bad.

Rubbish – *all* animation is *already* highly technological.[27]

If you visited an animation house in Tokyo, Paris, or Hollywood (or the many out-sourced centres in, say, India or Korea), you'd find tons of technology and machines, with computers being just one among multitudes. For instance, the cameras employed to photograph the cels are very sophisticated. And they always have been: have a look at the famous multi-plane camera designed by William Garity at the Walt Disney Studio in Burbank in the 1930s, which required a group of technicians to operate it. The cel vs. CGI argument merely trots out the ancient oppositions between old and new, or tradition and modernism.

Altho' Otomo-sensei has embraced digital animation right back to *Akira*, he noted that there isn't that much difference btn cel animation and computer animation: 'it is not that I prefer it over the other, as there is very little difference between the two in terms of an approach' (2004).

27 Film critics really should visit film studios from time to time, to dispel the falsehoods that they perpetuate. For instance, that some movie sets look made out of cardboard: actually, *all* movie sets are constructed from bits of wood or foam or cardboard and painted, then they're torn down as soon as shooting stops on them.

The voice actors in Akira
(this page and over).

Naomu Sasaki,
the voice of Tetsuo

Mitsuo Iwata, the voice of Kaneda

Mami Koyama,
the voice of Kei

Publicity material for the Akira movie

Akira toys and merchandize

03

PRODUCTION

THE PRODUCTION OF *AKIRA*.

Akira was produced by Akira Committee Company Ltd, Kodansha Ltd,[1] Mainichi Broadcasting System, Inc., Bandai Co., Ltd,[2] Hakuhodo Incorporated, Toho Studios, Laserdisc Corporation, Sumtomo Corporation and Tokyo Movie Shinsha Co.[3]

 Akira was distributed by Toho (in Japan), and Manga Entertainment, Madman and Bandai overseas (among others). Bandai also distributed the video release (1988), and later the DVD (2001) and the Blu-Ray (2009), with Pioneer releasing the

---

1 Kodansha is one of the three big *manga* publishers in Japan. The other two are: Shogakkan, and Shueisha (Kodansha published *Akira*, of course).

2 Bandai was originally a toy company (founded in 1950), that moved into *animé* via the sponsorship of kids' shows. Among Bandai's productions were *Gundam, Transformers, Brave Saga* and *Mighty Morphin Power Rangers* (all shows with strong links to toys). Sunrise is one of Bandai's subsidiaries (others include Asahi Pro and Happinet). Sunrise was founded in 1972 (as Sotueisha), and is now owned by Namco Bandai. Sunrise produced shows such as *Escaflowne, Mobile Suit Gundam, Dirty Pair, City Hunter, Outlaw Star, Mai-Hime, Gasaraki, Inuyasha* and *Cowboy Bebop*. In 2005, Bandai merged with Manco (another toy manufacturer, founded in 1955).

3 One of the production companies behind *Akira* was T.M.S. – Tokyo Movie Shinsha. Founded in 1964 by puppeteer Yutaka Fujioka (as T.M.S. Entertainment, it was founded in 1946), T.M.S. was based in the Suginami district of N.W. Tokyo, where Madhouse and Sunrise are also based. T.M.S. worked on *Rose of Versailles, Moomin, Treasure Island, Case Closed, Lupin III, Golgo 13,* and *Monster Rancher*.

Japanese laserdisc (1988). In the U.S.A., Streamline distributed the film (1989); Criterion produced a laserdisc (1992); Fox released the DVD.

Akira was produced by Haruyo Kanesaku, Shunzo Kato, Yutaka Maseba, Yoshimasa Mizuo, Ryohei Suzuki, Hiroe Tsukamoto, and Sawako Noma and James Yosuke Kobayashi were executive producers.

Music for *Akira* was by Shoji Yamashiro; Katsuji Misawa was DP; Takeshi Seyama was editor; production design was by Kazuo Ebisawa, Yuji Ikehata and Koji Ono; art direction was by Toshiharu Mizutani; Susumu Akitagawa was sound recording director; Michiko Ikeuchi, Setsuko Tanaka and Kimie Yamana were key colour stylists; Takashi Maekawa and Noriko Takaya supervised the special effects. The number of animators who worked on *Akira* are too many to list (see filmography).

Companies involved in producing the animation for *Akira* included a huge proportion of *animé* houses in Tokyo (it seems as if everybody was working on it). They included High Tech Labs and Telecom Company (visual effects), Asahi Production and Toms Photo (camera dept), Dragon Production, Telecom Animation Film Co. and Nakamura Production (in-between animation), and background art by Baku Production, Studio Fuga, Studio Uni, Koyabashi Production and Ishigaki Production.

The production of *Akira* also acknowledged a group of animation studios in the credits,[4] including many famous studios: Anime R, Gainax, Kyoto Animation, Magic Bus, Mook Animation, Oh Production, Shindo Production, Tezuka Productions, Studio Deen, Studio Kuma, Studio Musashi, Tamazawa Animation, Tiger Production, etc (see filmography). You will have seen many productions from

4 The usual practice in Japanese animation was to hire staff on a piece-work basis, for individual projects. Staff would leave when their work was done. Producer Toshio Suzuki (Studio Ghibli) reckoned that animators were making only about ten thousand dollars a year (in some (smaller) studios it might be a lot less, maybe 500 bucks a month).

those companies, as well as the companies that backed *Akira* – Mainichi, T.M.S., Toho, Hakuhodo, Sumtomo and Bandai.

Akira was made in 70mm (but prints were struck in regular 35mm),[5] and employed about 160,000 cels in 783 scenes over 124 minutes (that means 783 shots – in Japanese animation, shots are also called scenes or cuts). For a fast-paced, action-adventure movie, 783 shots is fewer than later *animé* movies (such as *Princess Mononoke*, with around 1,600 shots, or *Spirited Away*, with 1415 shots), and some Hollywood actioners go to 2,500-plus.[6]

160,000 cels is a very large number. As a guide, for *Black Magic* (Hiroyuki Kitakubo,[7] 1987), the famous *manga* artist Masamune Shirow (*Ghost In the Shell*) wanted to employ 20,000 animation cels for an O.A.V. running 48 minutes, which was deemed too many. But he wasn't allowed to (Shirow eventually left the production, and didn't direct again). And for *Akira*, a bunch of people had to paint all of those cels, in the days before computerized ink and paint.

Although Katsuhiro Otomo is celebrated as the key force behind *Akira*, he didn't do everything in this 1.1 billion Yen ($11m) production on his own (though I imagine Otomo is the kind of filmmaker – like Andrei Tarkovsky, Walerian Borowczyk and Stanley Kubrick – who would if he could!). Animation of this kind is entirely a collaborative process that involves 100s of people working together for years (look at the credits for the movie – and there were probably many other people who worked uncredited).

Katsuhiro Otomo is credited with direction, co-

5 70mm is more expensive and only rarely employed in animation (or any movies these days). The 70mm gauge goes back, of course, to the super-productions of Hollywood's heyday, the roadshow movies and Biblical spectaculars.

6 If you're interested in how movies use shots, and how average shot lengths change over time, and with fashion, the work of David Bordwell is excellent. His 2006 book *The Way Hollywood Tells It*, is a good starting point.

7 Hiroyuki Kitakubo (b. 1963) had impressed Otomo-sensei with his entry in *Robot Carnival*, and he was invited to contribute to *Akira*. Kitakubo went on to work on *Blood* and *Roujin Z*.

writing and character design. His co-writer, in turning the *Akira manga* into a two-hour film script, was Izo Hashimoto. Thus, Hashimoto-san is a hugely significant figure in the production of *Akira*, alongside Otomo-sensei. (Born in 1954, the same year as Otomo, Hashimoto's credits as a writer include *Black Jack, Shamo, Geisha Detective, The Guys From Paradise, Gentlemen Mugen* and *Spirit Warrior*, and as a director: *CF Girl, Evil Dead Trap 2, Driving High* and *Kagero 2*).

Akira cost ¥1,100,000,000 (which is about USD $11 million). For an *animé* feature, including one made in 1987-88, that is a very high budget (but compared to a Western animation, it's low). Even today, $11m for animation is still a high budget (even after decades of inflation and rising costs!). The domestic (Japanese) box office for *Akira* was around $80 million, according to some sources (whether that's gross or rentals, that's great business for a Japanese movie in 1988 – and only matched by Studio Ghibli). As well as merchandizing, there were also video games tied to the movie.

It's unusual, too, that Katsuhiro Otomo, then aged 34, was given the control of this huge animation project: he hadn't directed a feature movie at this point (altho' he had contributed sections, among others, to *Neo-Tokyo* and *Robot Carnival*, which would show anybody that this guy was hugely talented). Young directors are sometimes hired to direct ultra-high budget productions (for a no. of reasons), but Otomo-sensei certainly wasn't your average director-for-hire! (and certainly not in the North American studio system!). Of course, he was also a supremely accomplished *manga* creator (with several hits under his belt, including *Domu*).

That is, young directors are hired partly because they are (1) cheap, (2) eager to please and enthusiastic, (3) easier to control than veterans, (4) don't bring in so much baggage (they're not cynical and bitter – yet!), (5) they don't (usually) come with an entourage,

(6) they aren't usually prima donnas (!), (7) they don't usually have personnel that they insist on using (and will accept the studio's choices), (8) they might be more suited to the material, and to the target audience, than older directors, (9) they are probably less tied to other projects and schedules, and (10) they have the energy and stamina to see the project through.

Katsuhiro Otomo inevitably proved a director nobody could really control, tho' he is so incredibly talented, and was delivering such astonishing material, that I guess the producers preferred to back him up and let him finish the movie. (Once a production starts, it becomes much more difficult to cancel: 100s of Hollywood productions, for example, continue to completion even tho' many involved would have preferred it if they were halted. And replacing a film director is something everybody tries to avoid at all costs).

Not a frame is wasted. One of the beauties of animation for the viewer is that because it's so expensive and so labour-intensive, animated movies are rarely too long. It's a vital element of *Akira*'s success. Compare, for instance, with so many Hollywood films of the same period – 1980s-2000s – and you'll find movies that drag on and on, that have every dramatic highpoint s-t-r-e-t-c-h-e-d o-u-t mercilessly l---o---n---g, each plot point will be hammered home bluntly, and the films out-stay their welcome by twenty, thirty or forty minutes (movies that in the 1960-1970s would have been 1h 40m are in the 1990s and 2000s running to 2h 10m or more. Why? Value for money? Maybe. Because the stories are richer or more complex? Nah. And certainly not for more showings per day).

Instead of including meanderings and atmospheric incidents, the best Japanese films focus on the main theme ruthlessly, as Bruce Kawin and Gerald Mast explain in *A Short History of the Movies*:

the great Japanese films seem to rivet every incident of the plot, every character, every visual image, and every line of dialogue to the film's central thematic question or dominant mood. (1992b, 410)

KATSUHIRO OTOMO AS WRITER AND DIRECTOR.

Katsuhiro Otomo spoke of 'just letting the characters go' in the *animé* movie of *Akira*, from the *manga*. However, like other filmmakers who have produced *manga* as well as *animé* (including Hayao Miyazaki), Otomo noted that it wasn't wholly successful adapting his own *manga*. The fact that he hadn't finished the *manga*, either, didn't help (2009, 36). You can see the conflicts between Otomo the Film Director and Otomo the Writer (you can also see this in other writer-directors such as Ingmar Bergman or Woody Allen, where the Director wants to do one thing, and the Writer in them wants something else), and also Otomo the Director and Otomo the *Manga* Artist (we are also talking about *very* talented people – to be enormously successful as a *manga* artist, like Otomo or Miyazaki are, is achievement enough, but to do that *and* write and direct movies is sensational).

However, Katsuhiro Otomo was not working alone – Izo Hashimoto was his co-writer on *Akira*, and clearly added many ingredients. The producers (Haruyo Kanesaku, Shunzo Kato, Yutaka Maseba, Yoshimasa Mizuo, Ryohei Suzuki, Hiroe Tsukamoto, Sawako Noma and James Yosuke Kobayashi) would also probably have had their own contributions to make (as producers often tend to do – you gotta justify your producer status). So those 8 producers, the production committee and a co-writer would have contributed many ideas, not to mention the huge team of animators, designers, background artists, etc.

It must have been difficult for the crew working on a Katsuhiro Otomo production, because of his

well-known drive for perfection[8] (and if his perfectionist reputation wasn't well-known before *Akira*, it
certainly was afterwards!). Perfectionist filmmakers
have included Akira Kurosawa, Jackie Chan and
Charlie Chaplin (who have all driven some of their
crews nuts), and in *animé*, Hayao Miyazaki and
Otomo-sensei.

There must have been times during the production of *Akira* when some in the crew were frustrated.
The demands that Katsuhiro Otomo made from his
team were probably high, and that can be tough
(particularly towards the end of production, when
the work schedule goes crazy). On the other hand, if
the production team looked at the rushes, they
must've known they were working on something very
special.

THE *AKIRA* TEAM.

Akira is one of those productions in Japanese
animation, like *Fullmetal Alchemist* or *Lupin III*,
which seems to have involved pretty much everyone
in Tokyo. The chief animator on *Akira* was Takashi
Nakamura (b. 1955, Yamanashi Prefecture); he
directed *Catnapped* and *Tree of Palme*, and worked on
Robot Carnival, *Fantastic Children*, *Peter Pan* and
Nausicaä of the Valley of the Wind.

Hiroyuki Okiura (b. 1966) was another animator
on *Akira*: his credits include *Roujin Z*, *Memories*,
Ghost In the Shell, *Metropolis*, *Paranoia Agent*, *Paprika*,
and he directed *Jin-Roh*. Kitaro Kosaka has credits on
Angel's Egg, *Metropolis*, *Grave of the Fireflies*, *Nasu*,
Pon Poko, and Hayao Miyazaki's movies. Animator
Shinji Otsuka's credits include most of Studio
Ghibli's works, plus *Tokyo Godfathers*, *Millennium
Actress*, *Jin-Roh*, *Blood*, *Golgo 13* and *The Wings of
Honneamise*. And most of the other animators on
Akira will have similarly numerous credits.

Editor Takeshi Seyama has more formidable

8 One of the biggest challenges for the animators was that so many
scenes were set at night (traditionally more difficult to achieve). Was
Katsuhiro Otomo going to budge on that issue? I doubt it!

credits than any other film editor in Japanese animation, which makes him the most significant editor in animation in Japan, and around the world: look at these credits! – they include many masterpieces and celebrated works: Studio Ghibli movies such as *Whisper of the Heart, Tales from Earthsea, From Up On Poppy Hill, Grave of the Fireflies, My Neighbors the Yamadas, Only Yesterday, Arrietty, Pom Poko* and *Ocean Waves,* all of Hayao Miyazaki's movies, the Katsuhiro Otomo movies *Akira, Steamboy, Stink Bomb, SOS! Tokyo Metro Explorers, Magnetic Rose* and *Cannon Fodder* – plus *Votoms, Conan, Adventures of Tom Sawyer, Devilman, Dirty Pair Flash, On Your Mark, Gintama, Himawari!, Magic User's Club, Beelzebub, Lupin III, Mahoromatic, Mobile Suit SD Gundam, Paprika, Paranoia Agent, Patlabor WXIII, Serial Experiments Lain, Shamanic Princess, Sherlock Hound, Sakura Wars, Golgo 13, Rurouni Kenshin (Samurai X), Tegami Bachi, Space Pirate Mito, Elfen Lied, Starship Troopers, Tokyo Godfathers, Ultimate Girls, Ultra Nyan, The Whale Hunt, Wizard Barristers, You and Me, Tetsujin 28* and *Little Nemo.* One of the chief reasons why *Akira* is such a powerful piece of storytelling is down to Seyama's rock-solid editing and the pacing.

VOICES IN *AKIRA*

The voice cast (*seiyu*) for *Akira* is very impressive. Highest honours of course go to the voices for Tetsuo Shima – Nozomu Sasaki – and Shotaro Kaneda – Mitsuo Iwata. Sasaki and Iwata, both veterans of numerous *animé* (and video game) outings, are just sensational as the childhood buddies who become (uneasy) friends and (unfortunate) rivals (they are slightly too old for the roles, though, as is usually the case with voice acting, though at 21 they can get away with being 15 (Mami Koyama as Kei was older – 33 playing 16).[9] It's the usual case of

9 This isn't always the case: older women tend to be much more successful at playing girls in voice work for *animé* than older men playing boys (*Naruto* and *One Piece* are good examples).

finding a 15 year-old who is right for the role, and can act, and who wants to do it. Also, I would imagine that this high budget production would've required many recording sessions – not least because of Otomo-sensei's perfectionism, which would mean coming in to re-record dialogue tracks that on most other movies or TV shows would be deemed adequate, plus of course rewrites).

Nozomu Sasaki was born on Jan 25, 1967 in Hiroshima. Sasaki's credits include: Mello in *Death Note*, *YuYu Hakusho*, *Rurouni Kenshin*, *Monster*, *Revolutionary Girl Utena*, *Bubblegum Crisis*, *Cardcaptor Sakura*, *Yu-Gi-Oh!*, *Inuyasha*, *Darkside Blues*, *Naruto*, *Blood +*, *Please Save My Earth*, *Earthian*, and *Heroic Legend of Arslan* (many of his roles are as *bishonen*). Like many voice actors, Sasaki has also recorded albums and singles as a singer.[10]

Mitsuo Iawata was born July 31, 1967 in Tokorosawa, Saitama. Iwata has appeared in *Cyborg 009*, *Urusei Yatsura*, *Dragon Ball Super*, *Inuyasha*, *One Piece*, *Time Stranger*, *Shakugan no Shana*, *Sonic the Hedgehog*, *Detective Conan*, *Shana-tan*, *Please Teacher!*, *Paprika*, *Golden Boy*, *Here is Greenwood* and *Initial D* (a car racing *animé* that's perfect for *Akira*!).

Mami Koyama, who played Kei, was born on January 17, 1955 in Aichi, Japan. Koyama's credits include: *Sailor Moon*, *Detective Conan*, *Black Lagoon*, *Rainbow*, *Dragon Ball* (playing Lunch), *Ayakashi – Samurai Horror Tales*, *Appleseed* (as Athena), *Metropolis*, *Gundam*, *Millennium Actress*, *Magical Princess Minky Momo* (the lead role), *Lupin III* (playing Fujiko, of course), *X*, *Gunnm*, *Goku Midnight Eye*, *Case Closed*, *Shaman King*, *Ninja Scroll* (TV), *Fullmetal Alchemist* (as Pinako), *Silent Möbius*, *Riding Bean*, *Urusei Yatsura*, *Vampire Princess Miyu*, *City Hunter*, *The Dagger of Kamui*, *Doraemon*, *Lensman*, *Harmageddon* and *Dr Slump*. (This is only a small selection of Koyama's credits: by the time she was

<hr>

10 Sasaki was part of the first boy band in Japan made up of voice actors, NG5.

cast as Kei in *Akira,* when she was 33, she was already a veteran of at least 53 movies, TV shows and O.A.V.s!).

Among the other voices in *Akira* were: Yuriko Fuchizaki was Kaori, Tesshô Genda was Ryûsaku, Hiroshi Ohtake was Nezu, Masaaki Ôkura was Yamagata, Tarô Arakawa was Eiichi Watanabe, Takeshi Kusao was Kai, Kazuhiro Kamifuji was Masaru, Tatsuhiko Nakamura was Takashi, Fukue Itô was Kiyoko, Kôichi Kitamura was Priestess Miyako, Tarô Ishida was Colonel Shikishima, and Mizuho Suzuki was Doctor Ônishi (the scientist).

A good deal of credit should also go to Susumu Akitagawa, sound recording director: in the Japanese *animé* industry, the sound director oversees the direction of the voice actors in the recording studio (liaising with the director in the control booth), and can often have a significant impact on the overall sound for the movie. Akitagawa would be in the studio, in amongst the actors, directing them (and also involved in the casting).

It is standard procedure in Japanese animation to record the voice tracks after the animation has been completed (rather as European movies and Chinese movies dub on the voices later, as was Federico Fellini's habit). It's the other way around in the Western animation tradition, with animators using pre-recorded voice tracks for part of their inspiration (it is common for animators to employ video recordings of the actors performing the script, and also to draw on the actors in other work). *Akira* used the Western approach. The dialogue was pre-recorded, in the Western manner (and, as the 'making of' documentary shows, mouth movements in sketch form were checked against the sound recordings).

MUSIC.

The music for *Akira* – by Shoji Yamashiro[11] (Keiji Muraki and Shiro Sasaki were music recording directors, Hiruhiko Ono was musical editor, and Shoji Yamashiro was conductor and musical director) – is unusual: although rock music is quoted within the movie visually (such as on the juke box in the Harukiya Bar), the soundtrack is not rock music but predominantly electronica. Sometimes it recalls dance music, sometimes an updated, digital version of Japanese folk music (with simple, repeated motifs on percussion and glockenspiels, which recall minimalists like Steve Reich), and sometimes it's low, choral cues, as when Akira's evoked (particularly striking in the apocalyptic final scenes, countering the carnage visible on screen). Very effective are the single, loud, echoey drum beats (used much more often in movies since 1988). Perhaps the least effective cue is the big church organ sound for the Akira messiah scenes: using a church organ here comes over as a little too obvious.

The soundtrack album of *Akira* included tracks with the following titles: 'Kaneda', 'Battle Against Clown', 'Winds Over Neo-Tokyo', 'Tetsuo', 'Dolls Polyphony', 'Shohmyeh', 'Mutation', 'Exodus From the Underground Fortress', 'Illusion' and 'Requiem'. Shoji Yamashiro later used the music as the middle section of trilogy of symphonies, which opened with *Reincarnated Orchestra* and closed with *Echophony Rinne*.

Shotaro Kaneda is first glimpsed in the dive bar, at the juke box (note the rock music on display: the Doors, Cream, and of course the giants of hard rock, Led Zeppelin. It's the kinda macho, testosterone, all-out rock music that's been dubbed 'wargasm' music, music to go to war to). As the bike chase begins, the movie cuts back to brief shots of the juke box repeatedly, as if Kaneda & co. are going out to play to

11 Yamashiro was part of the Yamashiro Arts Group (Geino Yamashiro-gumi); their works include *Reincarnated Orchestra*.

the sounds that Kaneda's selected on the juke box
(except that the music for this sequence is much
stranger, and more contemporary than classic rock
music: a fidgety, itchy electronica. But it should be
'Immigrant Song' (Led Zep), 'Layla' (Eric Clapton),
or 'Riders On the Storm' (the Doors). It 'should be',
but actually it's much better for the movie in the end
that the producers *didn't* ask for and obtain the rights
to summat by the Stones, say, or Otomo's faves, Deep
Purple).

MARKETING AND RELEASES.

Akira (1988) was one of the best-selling of
Japanese *animé* films overseas (that and *Legend of the
Overfiend*). If you've seen an *animé,* it's probably
Akira. The first time audiences in the West will have
seen *Akira* will probably be in the dubbed version
(they are favoured by TV broadcasters, for instance:
if there's a choice, a broadcaster will always go with
a dubbed version). *Akira*, as *animé* expert Helen
McCarthy put it in *500 Essential Anime Movies*, is
'still the only anime many people have ever seen,
thanks to its widespread TV and movie distribution'
(12).

The poster of *Akira*, and the image used to sell the
movie in many outlets, was a full body image of
Kaneda standing, legs apart, and wielding a big gun
(from the scene where he takes on Tetsuo in the
climax). He looks like he means business. He's
looking at the viewer (in the movie, he's confronting
Tetsuo in a point-of-view shot). An arresting image,
and in line with many action-adventure movies
which feature a man with a gun, but it doesn't
accurately represent the 1988 movie (still today so
many action movies have that dull, uninspired image
on their advertizing[12]).

Subsequent publicity for the July 16, 1988 movie
focussed on Kaneda, rather than Tetsuo, Kei or Akira.

12 Drive along Sunset Boulevard any time, and you can't miss the
giant billboards of middle-aged, white stars waving phallic-substitute
guns about.

Because Kaneda is the hero of the piece, obviously, he is the audience identification figure, he is our way in to the movie (but if *Akira* was live-action, Tetsuo might have something to say about Kaneda stealing all of the limelight!). So there are many marketing images which focus on Kaneda and his bike – perfect images of teenage, of rebellion, but not so representative, really, of the story, the futuristic setting, or of just what *Akira* is *about*. But Kaneda is an idealized portrait of the target audience, however – in the West, at least, the chief audience for *manga* and *animé* is young males. (Other images used to market the movie have included the atom bomb from the opening pages, and Kaneda and a gun. Tetsuo appeared in a few marketing images, but very few of the other characters).

1988, the year of *Akira*, was a great year for Japanese animation: *My Neighbor Totoro*, for many the finest *animé* ever made, was released on April 16, 1988;[13] *Grave of the Fireflies*[14] (*Hotaru no Haka*), another extraordinary *animé* (and another haunted story by the horrors of WW2), was also released in 1988, plus the classic *Gunbuster* TV series (a fan

---

13 For Helen McCarthy and Jonathan Clements, two of the most informative commentators on Japanese *animé* in the West, *My Neighbor Totoro* is 'Hayao Miyazaki's greatest work, and hence probably the best anime ever made' (2001, 265). For McCarthy, *Totoro* was Miyazaki's masterpiece, 'and my favourite film': in *The Anime Movie Guide*, McCarthy commented: 'I think this film is perfect. It is also my favourite movie, of any kind, in any genre, ever' (78). 'It's like revisiting the happiest summer of your childhood. Oh, and it's technically as near-perfect a piece of animation as you could wish for' (28).

14 *Grave of the Fireflies* (1988) is an absolutely stunning movie, a masterpiece of animation. It is undoubtedly one of the great war pictures – in this case, a passionate anti-war movie. *Grave of the Fireflies* takes its place with the great war movies, such as *All Quiet On the Western Front*, *Paths of Glory*, *Apocalypse Now* or the *Kanal* trilogy (Andrzej Wajda). Roger Ebert was a big fan of the film, and it has also been compared with *Schindler's List* (in some respects, it is superior to the 1993 Universal flick, partly because it doesn't stoop to sentimentality). For Ebert, '*Grave of the Fireflies* is an emotional experience so powerful that it forces a rethinking of animation'.

favourite),[15] the *Appleseed* O.A.V., the *Dominion Tank Police* O.A.V.,[16] the *Patlabor* series,[17] *Vampire Princess Miyu*, and *Legend of the Overfiend II*. A miracle year, then: *Akira*, *Gunbuster*, *Patlabor*, *Overfiend*, *Totoro*, *Appleseed*, *Dominion*, *Patlabor* and *Grave of the Fireflies* (the 1980s is often regarded as the golden age of *animé*. Yes – but the Nineties offers strong competition. Though for some, the 2000s and the 2010s is the golden age, with many amazing shows, and *animé* has a higher profile globally than ever before).

Akira was first seen by many Westerners in an English (i.e., North American) dub. Thankfully, releases on home entertainment formats have included the original Japanese dub (always the one to watch in *anime*, for many, many reasons: *Akira* is a *very* Japanese movie – why would you want to watch it with North American actors speaking English? By voice actors *not* cast and directed by Otomo and sound director Susumu Akitagawa?).

Akira hit the West in December, 1989, when it played in arthouse theatres. As Gilles Poitras put it in *Anime Essentials*, *Akira*'s 'impact was so huge that for the entire decade it was probably the single anime most familiar to adult non-fans in North America since the 1960s' (24). For some commentators (such as Helen McCarthy), *Akira*'s success in the West was too much of a one-off and it unbalanced expectations: nothing could follow *Akira*. Well, yes, *Akira* is impossible to top – or follow. There has also been a

---

15 *Gunbuster, Aim For the Top!* (Hideaki Anno, 1988) was a classic *animé* O.A.V. series (of only 6 30-minute episodes) that has become a favourite with many fans and critics. Produced by the Gainax Studio (following up their influential *Wings of Honneamise*), and released by Bandai/ Victor in Japan, *Gunbuster* was written by Toshio Okada.
16 The first *Dominion: Tank Police anime* was released in 1988. It was written and directed by Koichi Mashimo and produced by Agent 21 (4 x 40m episodes). It was based on Masamune Shirow's *manga* which was first published in *Comi-Comi* in 1984-85.
17 The *Patlabor anime* TV series began in 1987; this was Mamoru Oshii's first big success as a director. Also on the production of *Patlabor* were Kazunori Ito, screenwriter, Masami Yuki, *manga* artist, Yutaka Izubuchi, mechanical designer, and Akemi Takada, character designer (Oshii, Yuki, Izubuchi, Takada and Ito were collectively known as Headgear).

THE ART OF KATSUHIRO OTOMO ◆ 443

suggestion that *Akira* was too unusual or individual in its themes and look, so it gave Western audiences a skewed idea about animation. Maybe: but you never know how audiences're going to interpret anything, or how they relate one movie to another. Personally, I'm glad it was *Akira* that broke thru big time rather than, say, *Pokémon* (which dominated the following decade). And besides, the films of Studio Ghibli have become some of the most well-known examples of *animé* overseas, and nobody could complain that Hayao Miyazaki, Isao Takahata and Ghibli offer a skewed vision of *animé*. Indeed, you could hardly choose finer ambassadors of *animé* than the cinema of Miyazaki and Takahata.

In *Anime Essentials*, Gilles Poitras defines each *animé* generation (the '*Astro Boy* generation', the '*Sailor Moon* generation', etc), and reckoned that the '*Akira* generation' didn't move on to other *animé* shows, but stalled at *Akira*, seeing it as an isolated, unrepeatable work. Thus, the '*Akira* generation' missed the wider context of *animé* and *manga* which *Akira* drew on (31).

Akira's number one place among Western audience's perception of *animé*, until the output of Miyazaki-sensei grew to colossal proportions, has been both beneficial and problematic, according to Helen McCarthy and Jonathan Clements. Because it raised the bar so high that almost no subsequent filmmakers could reach it. Because it stamped *animé* in the West with a particular genre and type of movie – and nothing can follow *Akira*. But that's just defeatist – it's like saying, darn, I wish Orson Welles and his Mercury Theatre team and the R.K.O. production crew hadn't made *Citizen Kane*, because nobody can top it!

Helen McCarthy noted in *Anime! A Beginner's Guide To Japanese Animation* how *Akira* seemed to raise the profile of Japanese animation in the West when it was shown in 1990:

in the eyes of most British critics, Japanese animation arrived from outer darkness in one cataclysmic explosion at the beginning of the nineties with the first British showing of Otomo Katsuhiro's film of the manga *Akira*. (23)

For Brian Camp in *Zettai: Anime Classics, Akira* was perhaps the most influential of all of the animations which broke thru in the West:

a film that almost single-handedly directed the world's attention to anime as an innovative art form capable of entrancing adult audiences with complex stories and breathtaking visual detail. (9)

In the U.S.A., *Akira* grossed just under $1 million when it was released in December, 1989 by Streamline.[18] On video, Streamline released *Akira* (in December, 1990) as a 'Video Comics' tape (designed for the comic store market). *Akira* has been a bestseller on home entertainment formats, and has crossed over into the mainstream, selling to consumers who aren't *animé* fans.

In Great Britain, *Akira* was released on video in 1991 by Island World Communications (the company which later became Manga Entertainment). The limited theatrical release of *Akira* meant that it really reached audiences, like so much of *animé*, thru home entertainment video releases (indeed, *animé* is above all a television form, which leads into home video, home DVD/ Blu-ray, cable/ satellite channel and the internet, rather than a theatrical form. It's only Studio Ghibli's movies, and the odd movie like *Evangelion, Oh! My Goddess*, and of course *Pokémon*, which makes a big impression in theatres. How many *animés* did you see in theatres between 1980 and 2010?).

18 Streamline, run by Carl Macek and Jerry Beck in Hollywood, were one of key distributors of *animé* in the West. Streamline brought *Robotech, Nausicaä* and *My Neighbor Totoro* to the U.S.A.

Akira has had two English language dubs – in 1988 (by Streamline) and 2001 (by Animaze/ Pioneer).[19] There was a film restoration in 2009.

In *cinemas* in Japan and the U.S.A., the financial performance of *animé* is relatively small, compared to the big American and international live-action movies, and compared to Disney's animations. In the U.S.A., the *Pokémon* movies have generated the biggest ticket sales ($85 million gross in 1999), while Ghibli's *Spirited Away* made around $10m in North America. And in Japan, the big sellers at the box office are Ghibli's movies, and of course *Pokémon*, plus others such as *Evangelion* and *Oh! My Goddess*. That is, it's on TV, video and DVD that *animé* really sells. For instance, the first *Ghost In the Shell* movie (a masterpiece) only played for 2 weeks in cinemas in Tokyo.

As J. Clements and H. McCarthy put it:

> Its success abroad, greeted with elation and bewilderment by its own over-stretched producers, ushered in the age of Japanese video exports – the beginning of "anime" as we know it. (2006, 205)

In *The Complete Anime Guide,* Trish Ledoux and Doug Ranney remarked of *Akira* that

> its technical and artistic credentials were unassailable, it was "as good as Disney" (or even better), and the subject was definitely *not* for kids. (1997, 47)

The overall effect of *Akira* was 'stunning and masterful, despite the inexplicable ending, and [it] truly deserves to be called a masterpiece' (73). 'A virtuoso piece of speculative fiction, a violent adventure tale, a head-bending sci-fi morality play,'

19 Pioneer restored, re-dubbed and re-translated *Akira* for a 2001 release (tho' some fans prefer the original dub and translation. You can buy editions of *Akira* which have both versions).

Time magazine called *Akira*.

The reception in the tabloid press in the West of the two most well-known movies *Akira* and *Legend of the Overfiend* may have damaged the reception of other *animé*, Jonathan Clements argued. Because they gave the wrong impression about *animé*: the sensationalism and violence damns other *animé* by association.[20] That may've been true in the late Nineties, but not now, I don't think, not after the high profile of *Spirited Away* (winning an Oscar) and other Studio Ghibli products, or *Pokemon*, which are not 'tits 'n' tentacles' or extreme fantasy.

THE LIVE-ACTION REMAKE: DON'T BOTHER.

Live-action versions of *animé* and *manga* are occasionally produced in Japan, though seldom in the West. Inevitably, rumours of a Western live-action version of *Akira* have circulated from time to time (for instance, with James Cameron as director; or with Leonardo DiCaprio starring; or with Ruairi Robinson directing and Gary Whitta writing; or the Hughes brothers; or with James Robinson scripting and Stephen Norrington directing (*circa* 2002);[21] Cameron and Steven Spielberg were also linked to a live-action remake of *Ghost In the Shell*, and DiCaprio to *Ninja Scroll*). The rumours have persisted, and it seemed as if, *circa* 2010-2011, Warner Brothers had picked up the rights[22] to produce a live-action version.

One idea for the live-action *Akira* would shift the story to New-Manhattan (how predictable), with two movies adapting all six of the *manga* books. The Americanization of a very Japanese story led to accusations of 'white-washing' (white Westerners playing Asian charas). The budget is a key issue: *Akira* is a $200-300 million movie if ever there was

20 In H. McCarthy, 1998, 82.
21 Or with Jaume Collet-Serra directing and Garrett Hedlund, Kristen Stewart, Ken Watanabe and Helena Bonham Carter starring (2012); or with Marco J. Ramirez writing (2015).
22 In 2008; some said 2002.

one, but Warners, meanwhile, wanted something much cheaper.

Otomo-sensei had a clause in his contract which stipulated that he could review the scripts of the live-action adaptation of *Akira*. This is the familiar legal means of giving away the material while retaining control of by far the most important element: the script.

Otomo-sensei said in 2017 in *Forbes* that he had already been there, done that – he'd written the comic, made the movie, so didn't need to go there again. His chief concern was over the script – he would have to agree to the script. But sticking to the *manga* wouldn't be a good idea – better, Otomo said, to try something very different. If was he was re-making *Akira*, he would 'much rather do something entirely new and separate'.

For myself, I have no interest in it: it's a pointless exercise, cynical and money-grabbing. Anyway, the *Akira manga* is *already* a giant, blockbuster movie – you can hear the music pounding all the way thru, you can see the brilliant colours, enjoy the slamming action, and you can hear Tetsuo yelling 'KAAANNNEEEDA!'

The *Akira* comic is *already a movie*, and the animated film of 1988 *already is* a masterpiece movie! So why bother to tackle it yet again in live-action? (On the plus side, it would mean more money, kudos and influence for Otomo, it would raise his profile overseas, and attract more people to his work).

In fact, the comic of *Akira* is so movie-like, even the animated version of 1988 is somewhat redund-ant (and even tho' Katsuhiro Otomo was involved with it). Storytelling as compelling as the *Akira manga* simply doesn't not require (or want) to be adapted into any other medium.

My advice on remakes of classic films is simple: go make your *own* movie instead! Think up your *own* story! How can you remake a classic movie? (There are *thousands* of stories aching to be told all over this little planet – and millions more from unpublished and new writers! Give them a chance instead of remaking an existing movie, and a masterpiece!).

What would Kaneda or Tetsuo think of a live-action remake of *Akira*?! Yes! You got that right! Replacing their animated selves in *Akira* with some Hollywood jerk actor? Gimme a break!

Here's my idea: if you can't think up a story like *Akira* (and, let's face it, not everybody can), then don't waste 150 million dollars remaking it in live-action: give 150 new filmmakers a million dollars each, to make a movie from an original concept. Instead of a rubbish remake, you'd have 150 new movies! Wow – think of that – 150 new movies by 150 new film-makers! Another idea: spend $150 million on P. & A. and marketing for a global re-release of *Akira*, and let's see a restored print in 10,000 theatres (if all you want is to bring *Akira* to new audiences, do that; you don't need to 'update' *Akira* to make it appealing or 'new'). Or give the money to Otomo-sensei to make something *he* wants to make. Or give the money to a film school. Or give the money to charity.

Anyway, forget about the live-action movie – why hasn't the *Akira manga* been adapted as an animated series in Japan? Good question. Many reasons are possible: the rights (above all), costs, scheduling, etc. In July, 2019, Otomo announced a new adaption in animation of *Akira*, to be produced by Sunrise (among others).

04

CHARACTERS

There is typically one main character embodying each of the main groups in *Akira*'s universe: Colonel Shikishima for the military, Doctor Ônishi for the scientists, Nezu for the corrupt politicians, Ryusaku (and Kei) for the activists/ terrorists, Kaneda (and Tetsuo) for the biker gangs,[23] and so on.

Akira is clichéd, of course, on so many levels. The *bosozoku* gang is cool, rebellious, good-looking, cocky, and rides fantastic machines.[24] Colonel Shikishima (Taro Ishida) really is a giant of man, with a big, shaved head, pencil moustache and a crew cut (Kaneda dubs him Skinhead). Yes, the Colonel does stalk about grimly as if he owns the world (well, he *is* running/ safeguarding Japan's capital). Yes, it's true, the scientist, Doctor Onishi (Mizuho Suzuki), is a wacky, old coot with white hair and a crazed attitude. He may warn of the dangers of the scientific paranormal experiment, but he also can't help himself: he'll go ahead and explore the unknown realms

23 Japanese movies are often about communities and families rather than individuals, and Katsuhiro Otomo's cinema (including *Akira*) presents many ensembles and groups, with multiple charas 'who make different choices, take different paths in life, and thereby come to different ends', but are united by a common theme, as Gerald Mast and Bruce Kawin note of the typical Japanese film.
24 Where did they get those bikes? The movie doesn't explain it; probably stolen. The *manga* asks Kaneda where he got the new bike, and Kaneda replies he found it on the street.

of science. There is a small, rat-like politician, Nezu, who does deals with the activists, but ends up having a heart attack as he flees the city with a suitcase stuffed with goodies (Nezu is the mole in the government – and he really does look like a mole and a rat, with over-large front teeth and whiskers).

KANEDA.

The animators – too many to name each one – looked like they had a great time with Shotaro Kaneda. They give him out-size animation, in the Walt Disney mode, with a restless dynamism, and exaggerated gestures and movements (he might be placed into a Fleischer or Disney animation from the 1930s and fit right in – he'd have to lose the red biker leathers, tho', which he wouldn't like at all!).

Kaneda is wonderfully alive, goofing around, pulling faces, waving his arms about, pleading, joking, cajoling, yelling, running all over the place; he's a personality that can't keep still for more than 5 seconds (but then, *Akira* the movie is like that: it won't let anybody or anything stay still for more than 100 frames).

Irrepressible, all-energy charas in *manga* and *animé* include Luffy in *One Piece*, Lupin in *Lupin III*, Natsu in *Fairy Tail*, Naruto in *Naruto*, Nausicaä in *Nausicaä of the Valley of the Wind*, Ed Elric in *Fullmetal Alchemist*, and Ichigo in *Bleach*. They are brave, loyal, determined, kind, rather dim, and they exhaust everyone around them.

I don't know who did which piece of animation with Kaneda in *Akira*, but the producers and director will know: in animation, an animator will typically be given a scene, or part of a scene, to animate, and then hand over to another animator; in Japanese animation, however, animators will sometimes oversee several scenes; they also animate all of the charas in that scene, rather than, in the Disney system, focussing on one chara.

The personalities of the animators comes thru

very strongly: some animators will use more hand gestures, for instance, and other animators will incorporate more facial expressions, or use the eyes (one animator is clearly responsible for the scenes when Kaneda is wheedling or making excuses, like an apologetic Woody Allen character).

Shotaro Kaneda is the spirit of life in its optimistic, laid-back, devil-may-care, don't-give-up attitude: Kaneda's a guy who bounces back from obstacles and barriers, who looks for a way around them, and who fights for the people he cares about.

Shima Tetsuo is the polar opposite in many respects. Certainly he is a fairly downbeat guy – he barely smiles or laughs, except to laugh evilly (that is a staple of Japanese animation: watch more than one or two shows, and you'll see the villains chuckling to themselves rather than reply to someone. The laugh – with their back to the camera, or after a pause when a normal spoken reply would come from an ordinary human – is one of the hallmarks of the *animé* villain).

The more you look at *Akira*, the more you appreciate the significance of Shotaro Kaneda as a character, and how he works within the *Akira* story. He is highly exaggerated – more rebellious, brash, more aggressive and more violent than he needs to be – but he is also, with Tetsuo, one of the key ways-in for the audience. Kaneda is also a very switched-on and dynamic character: like Bugs Bunny or Road Runner, he won't keep still, and he won't lay down and not fight for his friend Tetsuo. It's always Kaneda for instance, who stands up to the cops or the military first, before the rest of the gang. Kaneda, for all his rebellious, laid-back, who cares? attitude, has standards and a sense of honour (in the scene beside the canal, he 'sends Yamagata his wheels', by crashing his bike into a wall – much to Kai's astonishment. Waste of a good bike!, you can see Kai thinking).

In splitting the narrative into two strands – (1) Tetsuo and the scientific experiments and (2) Kaneda (and Kei) and the bid to help Tetsuo (and find out what's happening), and avenge Tetsuo's suffering – the filmmakers create a strong, unusual story. You could leave out Kaneda, and have *Akira* be all about Tetsuo and his experiences with the telepathy experiments, meeting the other mutants, and going up against the military-industrial complex, Colonel Shikishima, and all the rest of it (or you could reverse it, and have Kaneda carry the story – which some viewers might prefer, as Tetsuo is a pain in the ass for much of the time). But including Kaneda means there is always a connection for the story back to the gangs, to the kids on the street, to something close to 'normality' (although Kaneda's life is heightened, and not particularly 'normal'. There is no home life depicted anywhere in *Akira* – the closest thing the kids have to 'home' is their local dive, the Harukiya Bar. But the bar tender is no caring 'parent' – he sells them drugs! Kaneda, and the other kids, never speak about their parents or guardians; they're not shown – and not in the *manga*.[25] Because *Akira* isn't interested in them, at all. Instead, there are many other characters to stand in for the teenagers' parents, who are the same age as their parents. Tetsuo's folks *are* shown, however, but only in flashbacks, and only in scenes where they seem to abandon him).

Thus, Kaneda's quest is to rescue Tetsuo – that is, the best parts of himself that reside in Tetsuo. And vice versa. Except that Tetsuo is most concerned with saving himself, and bugger anybody else (does he ever ask how Kaneda is, or how Kaori is? No).

KEI.

Kei, in her short-sleeved, Michael Jackson jacket and shorts, is designed and drawn so much like Kaneda that they look like twins (or brother and sister – especially in their bright orange utility uniforms. Which fits their relationship, which, in the movie at least, doesn't blossom into romance. In the

---

25 You might assume that Kaneda's folks are dead or have left him with foster parents, or simply let the juvenile school deal with him.

manga, thankfully, it does – they become a couple). Kei also sports a cap, which gives her a vaguely military appearance, and is something of a tomboy type, and a little of the girl next door type (her clothes become sexier in the *manga*). With her short, black hair in a bob, she reminds me of Anna Karina in the early-to-mid 1960s films of Jean-Luc Godard (*Vivre Sa Vie* and *Une Femme Est Une Femme* in particular. Kei even has the curl on her cheek, *à la* Anna Karina or Liza Minnelli in *Cabaret* – look at pages 160-1 of volume one of *Akira*).

It's significant, however, that Kei isn't like the other girls who hang around the *bosozoku* gang or at high school (who tend to be working class and straight-talking, and dress more flashily than Kei): Kei is of a different social class (a higher class), and probably slightly older, so that the Kaneda-Kei romance employs the conventions of the poor man and the lady, the peasant and the princess relationship. (We don't see Kei's home life, in either the movie or the *manga*, but we can assume that she comes from a middle-class background, until she became a political radical and activist).

Kei is also cool as can be, not especially romantic (or girlie), and rarely reacts to Kaneda's wisecracks or come-ons. That Kei should *not* respond to Kaneda's cocky attitude is classic writing, but it also works, it fits. Kei is not going to be girlie and all over Kaneda (notice how Kaneda reacted to his girlfriend in the earlier scene in the *Akira* movie, when the boys emerge from school, complaining loudly and swearing revenge on their brutal teachers. Kaneda's girlfriend, dressed in red, with spiky hair and a headband, gives Kaneda a cigarette, links her arm with his, and fawns over him. He tells her angrily to quit flirting. Kei is portrayed as a very different sort of woman. She doesn't react strongly to Kaneda's romantic overtures, she simply quietly ignores them, deflecting them, as if she's got more important things to think about).

Kei also represents for Kaneda something more complex and ambiguous: the activist/ terrorist cell (from the government's p.o.v., they're terrorists, but activists is a more accurate name in this oppressive, martial law regime in Japan's capital). In hooking up with Kei, Kaneda encounters a bunch of people who're in another close-knit group, like his Capsules gang, but they're not hare-ing around the city fighting other biker gangs. They have a higher purpose, with a clearly-defined target: the military-industrial complex and martial law. When Kaneda tags along with the activists, he is somewhat out of his depth: he becomes part of the group, which has a leader of its own (Ryu). Kaneda wisely defers to Ryu, while also pointedly ignoring him (he also regards Ryu as a rival for Kei's affections).

Kaneda is eager to find out if there's anything romantic going on between Kei and Ryu, the leader of the activists: notice, for example, when Ryusaku and co. first encounter Kaneda, the kid immediately launches into a jokey/ scared defence of his relationship with Kei ('we haven't done anything physical yet'). That, though, is Kaneda's default position when he runs into adults (to weasel his way out!). Again, age plays into this scene – Ryu[26] (who's late twenties or early thirties, perhaps), is considerably older than Kei (and we have to remember that Kaneda is only 15!). Plus, in the movie, in the scene in the corridor at the activists' lair, there are more of them, and they have guns! So Kaneda's naturally gonna be defensive!

THE TEEN ROMANCE IN *AKIRA*.

There are three main characters in the *Akira manga*: Kaneda, Kei and Tetsuo. Really, it's the story of three teenagers, and the amazing adventures they have when they stumble upon a secret government military experiment which has the power to unleash

26 Ryu is a version of the Moustache Man from Otomo's early comics.

city-wide devastation, and to launch World War Three.

Notice that altho' much of *Akira* is about three teenagers – Tetsuo, Kaneda and Kei – Katsuhiro Otomo doesn't take the easy option of putting Kei in between Kaneda and Tetsuo romantically, to enhance the rivalry. That perhaps gives the Tetsuo-Kaneda relationship even more fire, because these two guys are definitely sublimating some of their erotic attraction for each other into other areas of their lives. Not that Kaneda and Tetsuo are gay, or secretly homosexual (though Tetsuo certainly displays some clichéd elements according to pop culture of repressed homosexuality),[27] but the bond between them is deeper and more powerful than mere friendship or teen brotherhood.

The romance in *Akira* – between Kaneda Shotaro and Kei – is more than simply a sub-plot. It directly affects the primary plot – of the magical children-Akira experiment in the Japanese capital – a number of times. Most spectacularly in the climactic scene of the whole *manga*'s six volumes, when Kei appears to Kaneda in spirit-form when he's about to be absorbed by the Akira-power. She tells him that he must come back: she doesn't say for her (unselfishly), she says there are people who need him (of course, she is included in those people). You could say that Kei saves Kaneda's life here. (It's a pity that the movie of *Akira* didn't include some of this moment; it is in there, when Kei calls out to Kaneda, but not in this form).

And Kei is not simply the Girlfriend of the Hero, relegated to waiting on the sidelines while the hero Dispatches the Villain and Saves the World, as in the conventional action-adventure tale. No: Kei becomes the primary character in many sequences, and is

---

27 Is Tetsuo Shima gay? Maybe. Camp certainly. Look at the cover of *Book Two* of the *Akira manga*, and you see Tetsuo dressed in lilac pants, and a red jacket with a fake fur collar: he might be on stage with the Village People. However, dressing up is common among villains in Japanese *manga* (many are narcissists and dandies).

elevated, via the long distance, telekinetic help of the magical children and Miyako, to superhero status. Kei becomes a kick-ass action hero, affecting the primary plot on numerous occasions.

TETSUO AS ANTI-HERO.

Shima Tetsuo is envisaged as an anti-hero, and also a rather weak personality: which makes him, as James Clarke put it in his book on animation, 'never really likeable and even in his most intense moments, where his mindset is besieged by terrifying visions, he does not really inspire the audience's sympathy' (141). But he's also not meant to: an anti-hero is a deliberately ambiguous, often unlikeable figure in literature and cinema. And often, when an audience finds itself spending a lot of time with an anti-hero, they discover that they are empathizing with her/him too much, which's uncomfortable. Especially when the anti-hero takes to committing negative, violent or even murderous acts.

Characters from classic literature such as Macbeth or Othello, or Michael Corleone (*The Godfather*) and other gangsters in cinema, are useful to contemplate as examples of characters who're the main protagonist but who're also anti-heroes and ambiguous. The audience becomes drawn in, whether they like it or not – sometimes because they have no other option, because the movie features only that main protagonist in many scenes, or that main protagonist is the chief character in the whole story. Cinema and literature are full of such characters – criminals, robbers, brigands, pirates, vampires, bad boys, despots – who though they may possess some fine qualities like decisiveness, determination, energy, nobility and integrity ('honour among thieves', say), they're also murderers, betrayers, crooks, and often violent and nasty. Michael Corleone kills his own brother in order to protect the family business in *The Godfather II*, and Othello strangles his new wife in William Shakespeare's play ('I kissed thee ere I killed thee' [V.2.357]).

In *manga* and *animé,* examples of anti-heroes include Vicious in *Cowboy Bebop*, Guts in *Berserk*, Alucard in *Hellsing*, Sasuke in *Naruto* (consciously modelled on *Akira*'s Tetsuo), Ciel in *Black Butler*, Manji in *Blade of the Immortal,* Revy in *Black Lagoon*, Yuki in *Lady Snowblood,* and Raito Yamagi in *Death Note.* (However, some of those characters – such as Guts and Sasuke – are also portrayed as heroes at times).

In foregrounding Tetsuo and the anti-heroic, anti-social elements of his personality, *Akira* goes against the prevailing trend in Western storytelling (though not in Japanese comicbooks and animation). For instance, Hayao Miyazaki, the Number One Filmmaker in *animé,* has been determined to portray characters who are 'life-affirming and have clear hopes and goals'; Miyazaki is keen to send out positive, life-affirming views when it comes to his lead characters and their hopes and dreams. Miyazaki would never, and has never, created an anti-hero as his main character, as in *Akira,* or featured characters who are nihilistic or even pessimistic. Miyazaki's characters might be subject to bouts of depression (like Kiki in *Kiki's Delivery Service*), or might be 'cursed' by the gods (like Ashitaka in *Princess Mononoke* – the closest character to an anti-hero in Miyazaki's universe), but they are not pessimists or nihilists. (However, they might be anarchistic, and rebellious – but usually that's part of their bid for independence and individuality.) By contrast, Tetsuo is not only a manic depressive and incredibly angry and resentful, he is nihilistic and negative. And Kaneda is a rebel and bad boy (but not thoroughly nasty, as Tetsuo rapidly becomes).

✳

Tetsuo is helluva diva, isn't he? Oh yeah, it's true, he's had his brain invaded by a sinister government scientific experiment, but what a prima donna he is once he gets going! He is reminiscent of the demons in the *Legend of the Overfiend* series, who are similarly diva-like, such pouters and poseurs, such cry babies and sulkers. They are highly neurotic and vulnerable, sensitive to the slightest slight against their dignity or manhood – and they over-react to the teensiest insult with expressions of colossal violence. That's Tetsuo[28] – a neurotic over-reacting to everything; Tetsuo speeds from zero to fury in 3 seconds. (Tetsuo is a classic case of a youth heading towards suicide, a recurring theme in Japanese pop culture).

Tetsuo is every lonely kid, every introverted nerd, every kid who got beat up at school, every boy who was teased and scorned, every kid who found it hard to make friends.

Kaneda, meanwhile, is the popular kid, the jock, the football player,[29] the kid who's the centre of attention, the boy who gets the cool bike and the babe girlfriend. He has a wise-ass remark for every occasion – nobody gets one over on Kaneda (the police station scene[30] is the funniest in *Akira*, and also includes some of the broadest animation of characters in the 1988 movie). Dressed all in bright red for much of the movie (and much of the *manga*), so he pops out of any background or layout (including the predominantly red layouts – and his bike is bright red, too),[31] Kaneda is a fantastically dynamic character, one of the most pro-active and in-your-face personalities in all *animé*. Nothing seems to daunt Kaneda, and he will even snatch up a laser rifle so he can kill his childhood buddy, Tetsuo.

But there's also an enormous amount of rebellion and kicking against the pricks in Shotaro Kaneda (though not with the self-loathing and angst that proves to be Tetsuo's weakest points, that brings Tetsuo down in the end). It's Kaneda, after all, who leads the *bosozoku* gang the Capsules, and anybody

28 And Edward Elric in *Fullmetal Alchemist*.
29 He's depicted playing soccer (quite well, too) as a child.
30 You can see George Yamada, the Japanese-American soldier from the *Akira manga*, as one o' the background charas here.
31 At school, the filmmakers put Kaneda in an unusual colour: pink (he wears a pink shirt).

who exerts authority is in the gang's sights as an enemy and an obstacle: teachers, cops, soldiers, politicians, they detest them all.

✳

That Tetsuo is a murderer there is no mistake: in the movie, he kills the Harukiya Bar owner, and fellow gang member Yamagata; he fries the soldiers in the tank; he kills plenty of civilians when the bridge collapses; he slays the doctor and orderlies in the hospital corridor; he kills some soldiers at a toll-booth (off-screen, but their corpses're seen); and he kills some guards in the underground facility corridor. Tetsuo is thus a mass murderer: some of those deaths occurred when Tetsuo was lost in one of his hysterical fits, but some – most significantly Yamagata – were in cold blood – he knew what he was doing (he's not in a rage when he kills Yamagata – he's sitting in the bar, laughing coldly. Yeah, he's taken some pills – but they don't have the same effect on him they used to have!).

That's partly why Kaneda fires at Tetsuo with the laser rifle point blank, with no warning – too many people have died (Kaneda has been in amongst some of the people that Tetsuo has killed – at the tollbooth, for instance).

TETSUO AND KANEDA.

When I think of Tetsuo, it's of the youth with his head tilted down, black hair spiked-up, eyes blazing ahead, and yelling, 'KANEDA!!!' Tetsuo's normal state is simply not relaxed and laid-back at all.

Many scenes in *Akira* depict Tetsuo going over the edge into psychosis and vehemence. Tetsuo is an astonishingly *angry* personality; most every scene involving him encountering other characters, after his fateful crash with the paranormal child, has him going from sulky and moody to angry and violent. Tetsuo is like the rage of every post-WWII generation in Japan compressed into one persona: Tetsuo is a soul literally crumbling inside and at the edges. He is a soul for whom the ground is cracking underneath his feet. Those amazing fantasy sequences in *Akira*, where the sidewalk splits open, serve to illustrate just how shaky and volatile Tetsuo's mind is. (We've seen many scenes portraying the tortured mindscreens of characters in cinema, but the ones in *Akira* are some of the most impressive in depicting a personality splitting apart).

Talk about unstable! One of Tetsuo's many fiendish acts is to kill one of the gang members, Yamagata (Masaaki Ôkura). As far as any gang's concerned, that is a major and unforgivable betrayal. On his way to the Olympic Stadium, Tetsuo calls in at the seedy Harukiya Bar where the gang hang out at the beginning of *Akira* (yes, the structure of the movie is a little odd here: it's towards the end of the second act – or the middle of the third act, if you use the four-act model for a 4-act movie, which I prefer. So it seems odd that the movie should scale down here, rather than following Tetsuo straight to the Stadium).

Tetsuo demands pills of the unfortunate bartender. More is made of the pill-popping of the youth gang by critics than necessary: it's not that big a deal (it's more significant in the *manga*, where there's a minor subplot relating how Kaneda scores pharmaceuticals off the school nurse, with whom he has a fling). They're like mods of the 1960s in Britain, where the links between taking pills and gangs and rivalry with other gangs was part of the culture (as manifested in movies such as *Quadrophenia* and *A Clockwork Orange*, and the music of the Who, the Kinks and the Small Faces).

One of the creepiest appearances by Tetsuo occurs when the camera slowly tilts up from the carnage in the Harukiya Bar to reveal Tetsuo hunkered down, laughing evilly. Yamagata quickly realizes what's happened, and stands up to Tetsuo, and climbs up to him to do something about it. Tetsuo kills Yamagata: it is this evil, senseless act, perhaps more than any of the (many) others that Tetsuo performs, that incenses

Kaneda when he hears about it (the murder itself is not shown, as it is in the *manga* – it's recounted in dialogue by Kai at the river, to Kei and Kaneda).

For a member of the gang to turn on another member and kill them is too much for Kaneda. In the fascinating and beautifully-written scene by the canal (with a switch to daylight), involving Kaneda, Kei and Kai, Kaneda's anguish is vividly, movingly expressed. The scene where he smashes a motorcycle into the nearby wall might be mis-read on first viewing: Kaneda is not going to commit suicide (though the framing and cutting partially suggests that), and he's not smashing up *Tetsuo's* bike, either, to punish him. No, Kaneda hurls *Yamagata's* motorcycle into the wall, where it explodes. He says he is sending Yamagata's wheels to him, wherever he is: he is dead, so his motorbike must die, too. That is, it's a moment where warrior/ *bushido* ethics are honoured. It's a send-off for Yamagata from the band of brothers (it's very emotional at the very end of the six volume *manga* series of *Akira* that both Yamagata and Tetsuo appear as ghosts, riding motorcycles. Yamagata, after all, hasn't been a part of the story for a *long* time, but he duly appears in the coda).

When Takashi, the psychic child, appears (walking on water – a nice touch – and Kaneda's pal Kei does, too), Kaneda is further enraged. Kaneda's fury is boiling – he accuses the E.S.P. kids of starting all this trouble (Kiyoko talks to him as a dis-embodied, off-screen voice). The animation is brilliant, employing all of the skills of the animator for pure performance to depict Kaneda's outrage. The staging, too, is marvellous, with Kaneda hurling himself into the water, and yelling in the middle of the waist-deep canal for Takashi to come back.[32] (Takashi and Kei have simply vanished into thin air on the other side of the canal). One of the best lines in *Akira* is Kaneda's retort to Kiyoko's assertion that Tetsuo must be stopped: if anybody's going to kill

32 They're a striking no. of scenes of characters waist-deep in water.

Tetsuo, it's going to be us, he's our friend!

And from this point onwards, that is what Shotaro Kaneda resolves to do. The more you consider *Akira*, the more it appears that it's the *script* that's as impressive as the visuals or the concepts or the animation or the voices or the music. It's the rock-solid, psychological relationship of the two main characters, Tetsuo and Kaneda, and their fraught friendship, that helps to create the overall impact of *Akira*: you are rooting for Tetsuo to be saved from the hell of his paranormal agony, to be back to being the kid he was b4 it all went wrong, even though you suspect and fear that Tetsuo can't be saved, that he has a death-wish, that he is doomed, and is dooming himself, and you're rooting for Kaneda to save his friend Tetsuo (and maybe to get the girl, Kei).

The script in *Akira* also gives the three psi-kids something to do: they have a plan to use Kei to reach Tetsuo (a better choice than Kaneda, seeing as the mere sight of Kaneda winds Tetsuo up! And vice versa, when Kaneda finds out what Tetsuo's done!). When that doesn't work, the psychic children are brave enough to enter the dome of white light at the end to save Tetsuo (notice how Takashi goes in first – because he was the one whom Tetsuo crashed into, so maybe his sacrifice will make good that accident; Masaru and Kiyoko make a pact to sacrifice themselves to save the boy – but they might mean Kaneda, not Tetsuo). In the *manga*, there are multiple attempts to nobble Tetsuo, which run on for chapter after chapter.

The three psychic children sacrifice themselves to help Tetsuo – and Akira. Takashi goes first, walking into the white globe that is Akira's power (in the *manga*, he is shot by Nezu). Kiyoko and Masaru agree to help. They don't come back: like Tetsuo and Akira, they are not seen again (but Kiyoko and Masaru are heard in voiceover, hinting at a rebirth). The sequence differs from the *manga* of *Akira*, though the theme of sacrifice and brotherhood, as the psychic children work together to help, is retained (the *manga* is even more graphically apocalyptic, for example – if that's possible).

HEROES AND ANTI-HEROES.

Nobody would suggest that the brotherly rivalry and friendship between Tetsuo and Kaneda is of a Shakespearean stature – it's not at the high art level of Othello and Iago (in *Othello*), or Macbeth and Banquo (in *Macbeth*). But it is way, way richer and subtler than many comparable rivalries and friendships in movies (and certainly in action and fantasy movies). One of the reasons that *Akira* really works, I reckon, is because the psychology of the relation between Kaneda and Tetsuo is convincingly and elegantly portrayed. The *manga* spends more time with the characters, true, but the movie delivers sufficient characterizations to make the central relationship pay off (and this is absolutely vital to the impact of *Akira*).

Another reason for *Akira*'s success is that the characters're given compelling motivations. Why, for instance, does Kaneda do what he does?, why does he follow Kei and save her?, and why does he join the activists' cell? For at least three reasons: one is erotic desire for Kei (the ♥ story is a primary motive in most movies – love is the prime theme in cinema for Jean-Luc Godard); the second reason is to help Tetsuo, his blood brother since childhood; a third reason is for the spirit of adventure (from the opening scene of the Capsules bikers rumbling with the Clowns gang, we see that Kaneda is up for action and fights. He is not a boy to sit at home playing video games! – he *is* a video game!).

The motives of Shima Tetsuo include some that're questionable: first off, and most importantly, Tetsuo wants the agonizing head trip to cease; secondly, he has a bunch of issues stemming from childhood to work through (being the picked-on kid, his vulnerability, instability and over-sensitivity, his neediness, masochism and depression, not being the gang's leader, and so on); third, as the 1988 movie progresses, and Tetsuo realizes that he has accidentally been granted (or has rediscovered) extraordinary powers, his motives change: now he can assume power over others.

Splitting the hero into two, into a hero and an anti-hero, makes for a fascinating psychological dynamic in *Akira*. Making both characters sympathetic and rounded helps enormously. Shotaro Kaneda, after all, is no pure-as-pure hero: he's no Disney prince or lovable boy-next-door or flawless superhero. He's the rebel without a cause, a delinquent, hates cops and teachers, steals bikes, causes trouble, and resents authority. Yet he's a smart kid: in the scene in the lecture hall, while his fellow students're goofing around, he's reading a book, and he comes up with ideas for the gang.

THE MOTORCYCLE GANGS AND THE GROUPS OF KIDS.

Who are those kids? the Colonel asks when he first meets them, landing in his helicopter.[33] Just an ordinary biker gang[34] a soldier replies. Which's how the authorities think of Kaneda, Tetsuo, Kai, Yamagata and the gang: they're just a bunch of ordinary kids. 'Ordinary', that is, for an epic, apocalyptic action movie set in the future. That is, not 'ordinary' at all.

The gang in *Akira* is known as a *bosozoku* gang, made up of *yanki*. *Bosozoku* (= wild speed tribe) are biker gangs, known for their bad boy ways; they emerged in the mid-1970s, wore headbands, 'punch perms' hair, and surgical masks, took speed, and

---

33 The appearance of the helicopters in the opening act, much to Kaneda and his friends' astonishment, might allude to *Close Encounters of the Third Kind*, where the UFOs send beams of light onto the ground silently.
34 Bikes appear throughout *anime*, including *Bubblegum Crisis, Oh My Goddess!, Ghost In the Shell, Bomber Bikers of Shonan, 5 CM a Second, Megazone 23, Bakuman, Dominion, Macross Plus* and the *Lupin III* flicks.

often moved in processions, waving flags; they drove the straight world nuts racing about all night; *yanki* are groups of kids who hang out, with a striking emphasis on fashion.[35] *Akira* is certainly a marvellous movie of fashion and image, with each gang and group of kids having its own identity. In this respect, *Akira* is a terrific youth movie, and a subculture movie (a movie which celebrates the subcultures of fashion, music and image), taking its place alongside classic, Western movies such as *The Wild One, Easy Rider, Gimme Shelter, Tommy* and *A Clockwork Orange*.

The costumes are sometimes unusual in *Akira*: shirts, Tee shirts, short jackets and jeans for the youths are expected, yes, and are part of the youth/ rebellion/ gang genre (though some of the gear the biker gangs wear is odder: gas masks, pilots' masks, and clown[36] make-up, reflecting Katsuhiro Otomo's genius for funky design). Poor Tetsuo has to play large chunks of the movie of *Akira* in hospital clothes (if a live-action version is made, that'll definitely change! And if it was Kaneda, he'd be sure to snaffle some new clothes immediately!).[37] For Kei, the costumes range from tomboyish (shorts and a fitted jacket), to the more conventionally 'feminine' (skirts and tight tops). Well, this is 1982 (for the first draw-ings of the *manga*), and *Akira* reflects its cultural context of the early Eighties vividly. Later in the *manga*, Kei sports sexier clothing, such as a tight Tee shirt, and skintight, shiny pants.

Some of the most enjoyable images in *Akira* are the group shots, framed like group portraits, one of Otomo's signature shots, which involve a number of characters each with their own animated gestures and movements (these cuts take a lot of time to animate). You can see them at the police station and,

---

35 G. Poitras, 1999, 14, 146.

36 No one dares to make fun of Clown in his bizarre clown get-up: if you did, he'd nut you!

37 Which he does as soon as he lands from the spirit world in the later chapters of *Akira*.

one of the best examples, as the kids emerge from the 8th District Youth Vocational Training School, hooking up with the girls (who've been waiting for them).

The biker gang is wittily and skilfully individualized – Kaneda, Tetsuo, Kai, Yamagata *et al.* Each gang member is different, but their loyalty is fierce. In common with many *animés*, which reflect Japanese society, the group is valued more than the individual.

For instance, apart from Kaneda and Tetsuo, there is Yamagata, who appears to be second-in-command in the gang (he arrives with news of Joker's mob at the bar, and he emerges first with Kaneda from the bar). And the smaller, more emotional, less self-assured Kai (sometimes called Kaisuke in the *manga*), who makes it to the end (he's in the*dénouement* scene, talking to Kaneda, and he survives in the *manga*, too).

The motorcycles always have to do wheelies in *Akira* (even Kei lifts the stolen scooter's front wheel as she speeds away). *Akira*, in both printed and painted cel form, exploits motorcycles (and motorcycle culture) to a striking degree. Certainly, in *animé*, despite some strong competition, *Akira* is *the* Motorcycle Movie. Motorcyles're way more than simply a means of getting characters from A to B: they become a way of life for the kids of the Japanese capital (and in the *manga*, even Kei gets her own Motorcycle Moment, though it's riding a more modest scooter; however, at the end of the whole series, Kei becomes a Motorcycle Girl as she hurtles into the scene, picking up Kaneda and speeding away for the finale).

There are *hommages* to the red motorcycle in *Ghost In the Shell: Arise* (and Motoko's clad in red leathers), *Sky Blue* and *Macross Plus* (which features a prominent red motorcycle). And Kaneda is a popular character in cosplay (costume play), including among women (in his red leathers, of course, not in his school gear!).

Product placement features in *Akira*: the amazing, iconic red motorcycle that Shotaro Kaneda rides, for instance, has Canon and B.M.W. stickers on it (as well as Shoei, Citizen, and an American insignia). And you can bet Kaneda's heavily fetishized motorcycle sold quite a few garage kits! (And it cropped up again in some *animé* rip-offs). But it was too big and expensive to be a same-scale piece of merchandizing!

THE PSYCHIC CHILDREN.

E.S.P. – extra sensory perception – paranormal – supernatural – psi/ psychic – telepathic – the terms become interchangeable. Magical children, prematurely aged children, mutants, freaks – sci-fi literature and cinema is full of such beings. In *Akira* they – Kiyoko, Takashi and Masaru – are all small, old before their time (they are invalids, significantly, apart from Takashi), each given their own personality (there are more psychics in the *Akira manga*, including three who go up against the heroic trio).

The paranormal kids are also versions of *espers*, psychics popular in the 1970s and early 1980s. The kids also have affinities with *newtype*, which refers to characters with supernatural powers, with a genius for technology.[38] As Jason Thompson noted, 'by far the most influential portrayal of psychic powers in manga' are the works of Katsuhiro Otomo (284). *Manga* featuring psychic characters include *Overfiend, Silent Möbius, 3 x 3 Eyes, Berserk, Basilisk, Hellsing* and *Nausicaä of the Valley of the Wind.*

Each psychic child in *Akira* has a number (usually on their hands): Takashi, for instance, is number 26. The climax of the first *manga tankobon* has Tetsuo being assigned his own number (which's 41).

Kiyoko (voiced by Fukue Itô) is pinked out in the *Akira* movie (did anybody reading the *manga* b4 seeing the movie think she was going to be *so pink*?!) – she wears a pink nightie, sleeps in a bright pink crib, has crude make-up (blue eye shadow), and evokes a Hollywood, child starlet from the 1930s – Shirley Temple or Judy Garland, say, aged up forty years but

---

38 The term *chônôryoku* is sometimes used.

remaining four feet tall. Masaru floats around in a spherical chair (it's also on wheels in the *Akira manga*); with his side parting in his hair and suit, he recalls a spy master from a 1960s flick, or the puppets in Gerry and Sylvia Anderson's celebrated fantasy adventure shows of the 1960s (*Thunderbirds, Joe 90, Stingray*), which influenced *animé* (including Katsuhiro Otomo).[39] *Village of the Damned* (Wolf Rilla, 1960), with its kids with glowing eyes and white-blond hair, is a link to the psychic children in *Akira*. *Altered States* (Ken Russell, 1980) is another touchstone for *Akira,* for the trippy visions.

Takashi is clad in more regular, casual clothing, and might be the kid you used to play with on the block, but prematurely aged thirty years (he's the only child able to move around under his own power). Takashi is the gentler of the two boys, with Masaru acting more mature and sterner. But it's Kiyoko who is the heart of the three magical children – they are often gathered around her bed.

The psychic children use Kei to intervene remotely – to talk to Kaneda thru Kei, for instance (to deliver exposition about Akira in the police cell). Later, when they abduct Kei (to Kaneda's intense frustration – he's just met a girl he likes a lot!), she's employed in the fight against Tetsuo (to the point where Kei-Kiyoko goes head to head with Tetsuo in a superhero duel). In the *manga* of *Akira*, there is plenty more of Kei as the messenger and action heroine of the psychic children, including lengthy scenes with Lady Miyako, one of the chief fighters in the war against Tetsuo.

The psychics in *Akira* reflect, like the cyborgs, wizards, and aliens of science fiction in *manga* and *animé*, the new generation of Japanese kids of the

39 The 1960s puppet TV show *Thunderbirds* (and others created by Gerry and Sylvia Anderson) was a big hit in Japan (you can spot its influence in shows such as *Nadia, Patlabor* and *Macross* as well as *Akira*). The focus on the team in *Thunderbirds* would be one of the chief ingredients to appeal to Japanese television audiences (*animé* is stuffed with team shows), as well as, obviously, all of that *mecha* on display. Puppets, too, are a big deal in Japanese pop culture.

1960s onwards (the baby boomer generation – Katsuhiro Otomo is a classic baby boomer ('new breed' in Japan) filmmaker, like the 'New Hollywood' film directors). As Jonathan Clements noted (in *Schoolgirl Milky Crisis*), the 'new breed' of Japanese children were jokingly regarded as aliens by the older generation, becoming more Westernized, less 'Japanese' (2009, 304). The aliens, telepaths and cyborgs as the expressions in the sci-fi genre of Japan's younger generation also reflect the widespread Americanization of Japan and Japanese culture. As Jean-Luc Godard often remarked, when the Nazis lost the war, North America was able to fill the vacuum in Europe culturally. The same happened in Japan. Godard reckoned that while the Allies in Europa had won the war against Germany, they lost the cultural war with Amerika.

WHAT OR WHO IS AKIRA?

Katsuhiro Otomo would have preferred it if Akira hadn't appeared at all in *Akira*: it was about Kaneda and Tetsuo, not Akira.[40] But anyhoo, Akira doesn't make that much of an impression in *Akira* – and he doesn't, really, in the *manga* series, either, even though he has more to do, and is seen more often. Indeed, in the 1988 animation, Akira is more a narrative device or a function of the plot, than a character or a personality (and, again, in the *manga*, Akira has very little personality, and is actually a rather dull, bland child. Compared to the three magical children, for instance, Akira barely registers. Who would you rather spend an evening with – Akira or Kaneda?!).

In Japanese, 'Akira' means intelligent, bright, clear, ideal. What is 'Akira' in the movie? A character, yes (at one point – visualized as a young boy), but more a force, an energy, a metaphor. Akira is life itself: as Kei/ Kiyoko puts it, 'Akira is ultimate energy'. Akira is one of those multi-purpose elements

40 J. Clements, 2009, 271.

in a movie which can mean or be whatever you like.

In both the movie and the *manga,* Akira is not really a character, more a figure who embodies certain issues, such as the military-industrial complex's experiments in warfare, the uneasy alliance between science and politics, and the misuses of technology. Akira is whatever the warring factions in the story want him to be: (1) to the dispossessed, down-trodden people of Neo-Tokyo, he is a potential messiah and saviour; (2) to Nezu and his crew, Akira is the vehicle to political power and money; (3) to Ryu, Kei and the activists, Akira is the means to 'blackmail and bring down the Japanese government; (4) to the Colonel he is unstoppable destruction; (5) to the Scientist he is the scientific experiment of a lifetime; and (6) to Tetsuo he or it is something or someone that might be able to give him some answers.

Akira is the Grail or McGuffin that everybody is jostling to get hold of and exploit. The whole of *Book 3* of the *manga*, for instance, is a (rather silly) cat-and-mouse hunt for Akira, who's stolen, then taken, then stolen back from this or that group.

Only later does Tetsuo realize the truth: he tells Kaori that Akira is just the name of some long-gone weapon. His disappointment that his quest for Akira has come to nothing, to just a bunch of glass jars with liquid in 'em, like a science class, feeds his frustration (in the movie). In the *manga*, Kaneda taunts Tetsuo by calling him a king of a heap of junk: Tetsuo flies off the handle at the suggestion, even tho' he knows it's the truth (Tetsuo is a guy, especially at his worst, drug-addled moments, who won't or can't face the truth).

Notice that Akira hardly speaks, and barely expresses anything; yet that doesn't give the little boy an air of mystery. Rather, as a child, li'l Akira is dull and unresponsive, and possibly autistic (his favourite line seems to be 'the moon'. *Uhh*, yeah). Akira never expresses desire, or what he wants. He remains blank – a void.

The fact that Akira is so unemotive, so neutral, aids the fact that the warring factions make of him what they will. It also renders the final apocalypse, at the end of *Book 3* (and the end of the 1988 movie), all the more shocking. In the *manga*, Akira goes nuts and explodes in rage or frustration or sadness (or whatever) when he sees Takashi being shot right next to him (seeing someone die is traumatic – yet, let's also remember that Akira has little or no conscious or emotional link with Takashi or the other two children in that scene, that he's been in cryogenic sleep for 30 years, so Takashi doesn't seem to mean that much to him (altho' in later *tankobon*, Akira seems to remember the other kids – as kids – and a former relationship is established). Takashi is not a best friend, a brother, a relative, etc, which might make the bond btn them much stronger – and more convincing).

The 1988 animated movie is more ambiguous as to exactly what sets Akira off (but it's primarily the three psychic children). Even so, not everybody you know gets so upset when someone is shot next to them that they explode with the force of an atomic bomb and kill thousands of people and lay waste to the whole of a vast city!

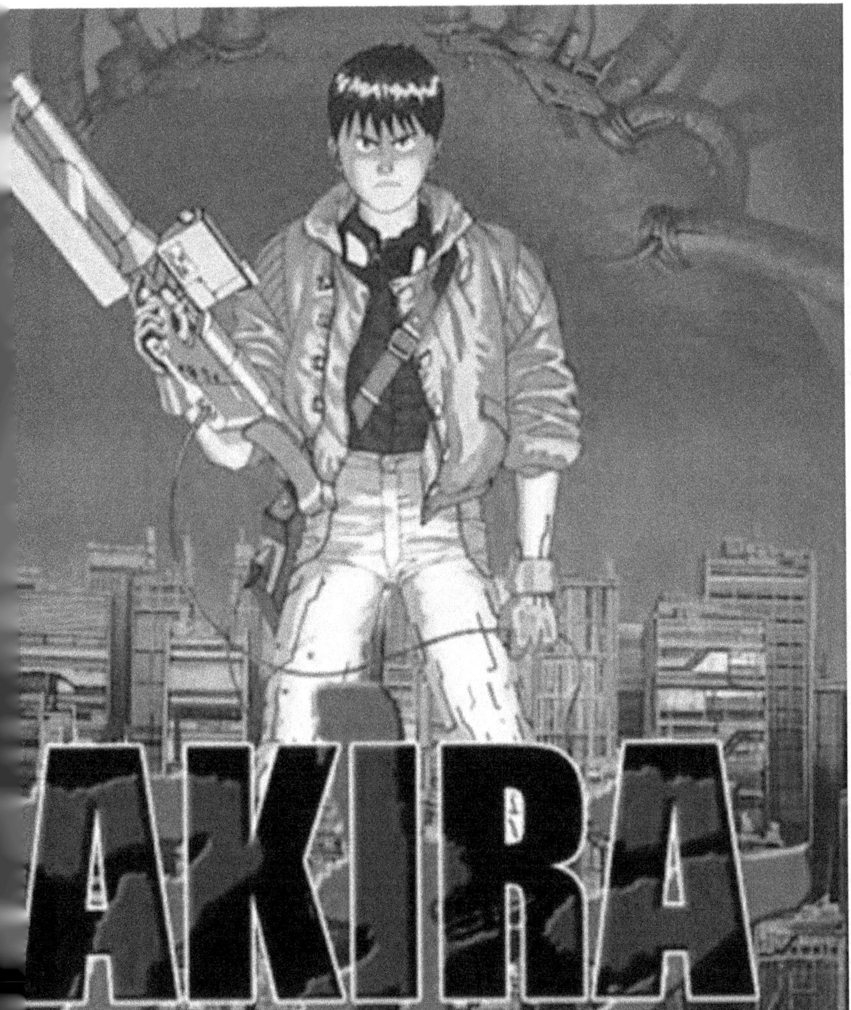
AKIRA

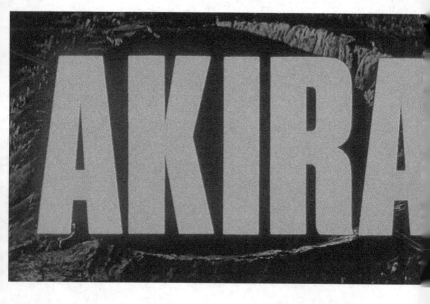

The title card for the Western release of Akira

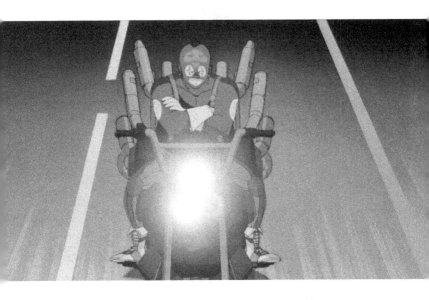

Images from Akira
(this page and over).

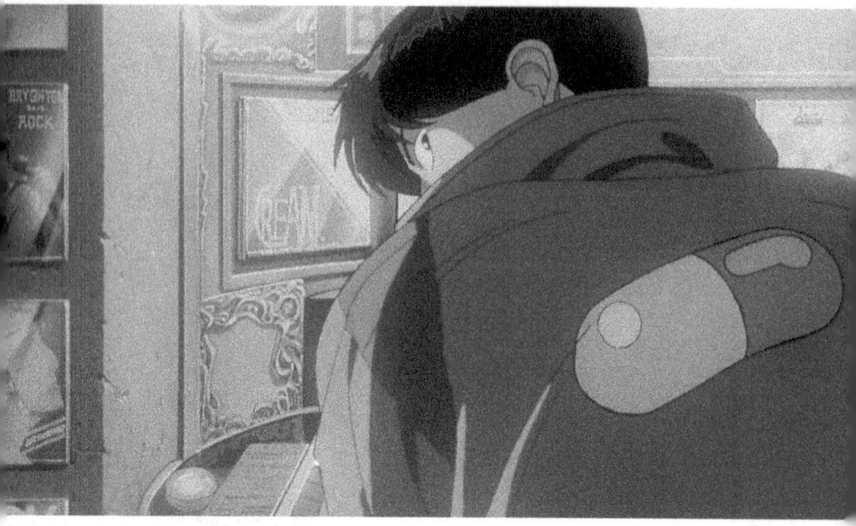
ROCK

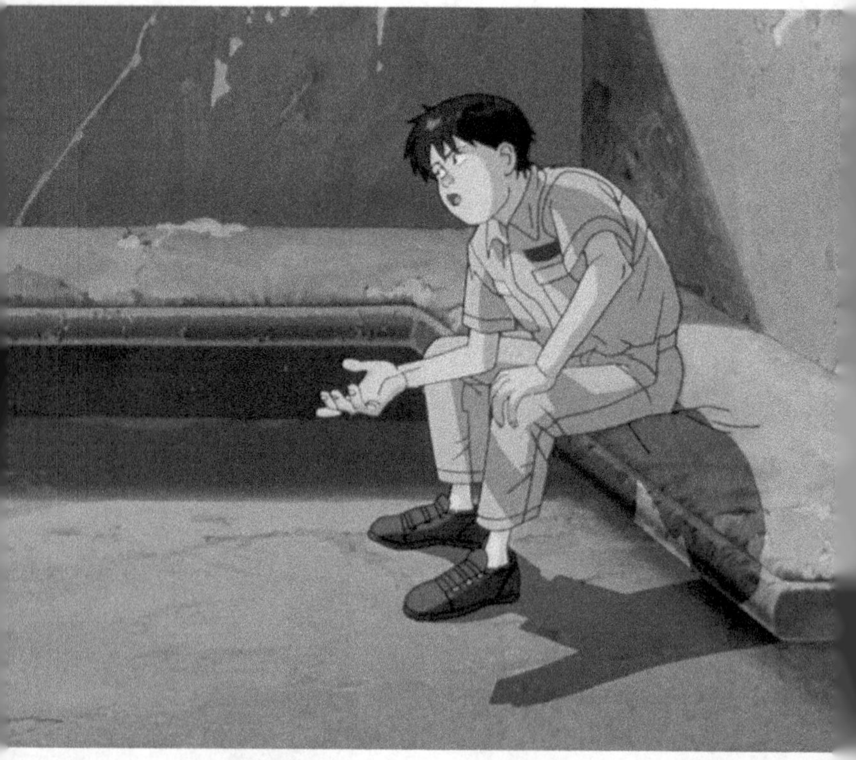

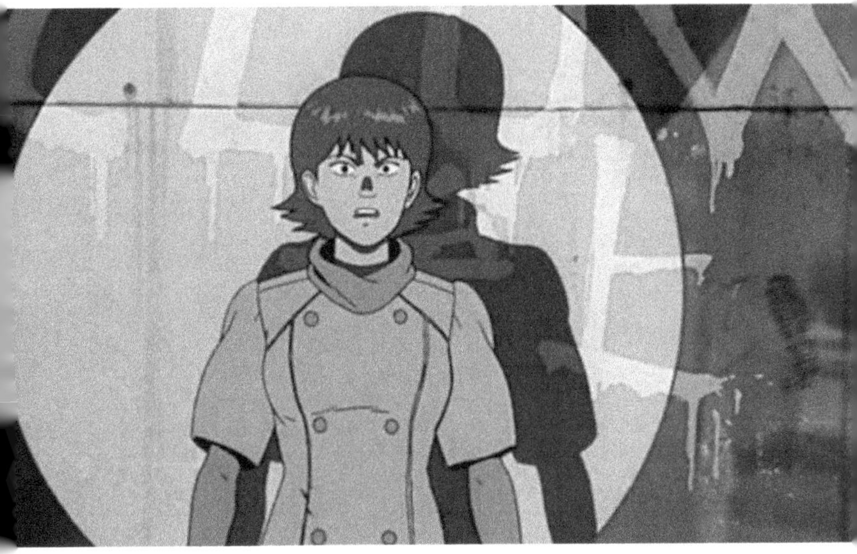

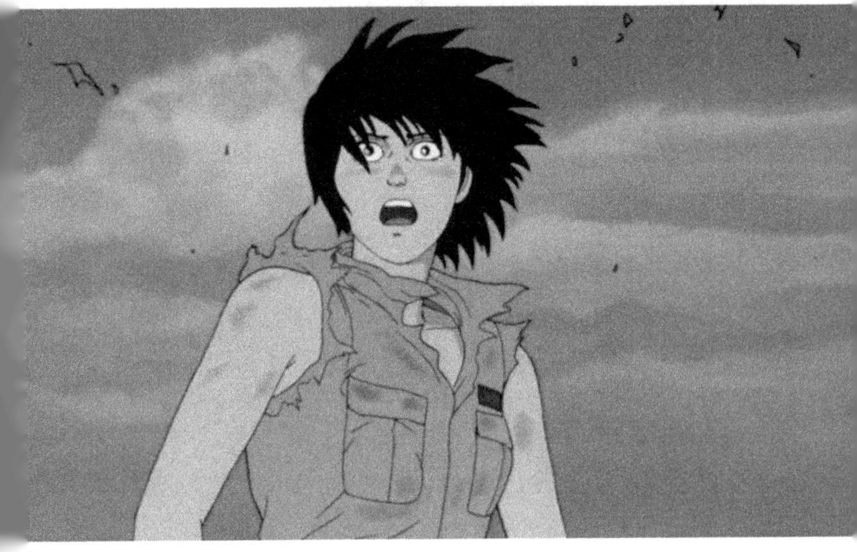

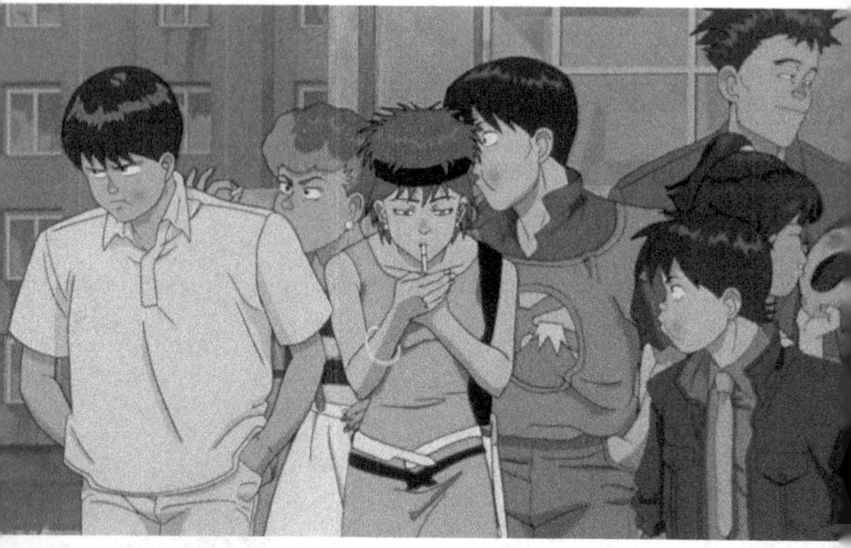

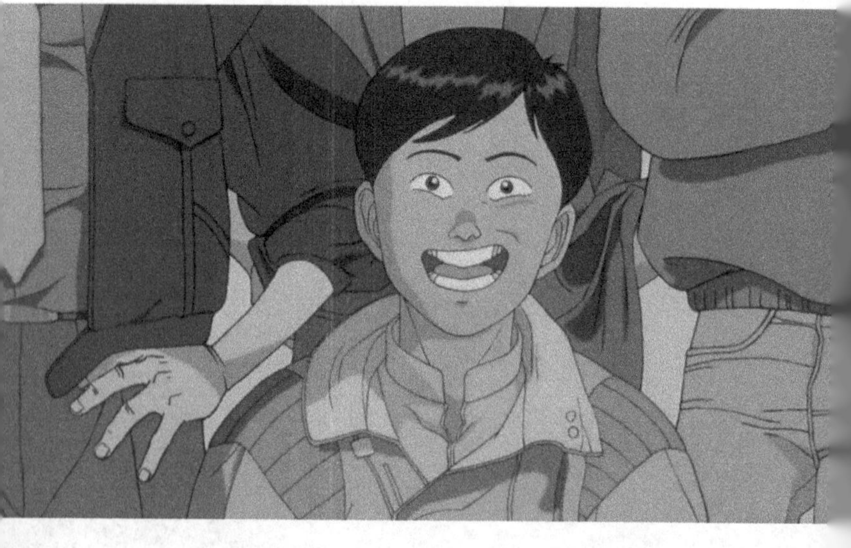

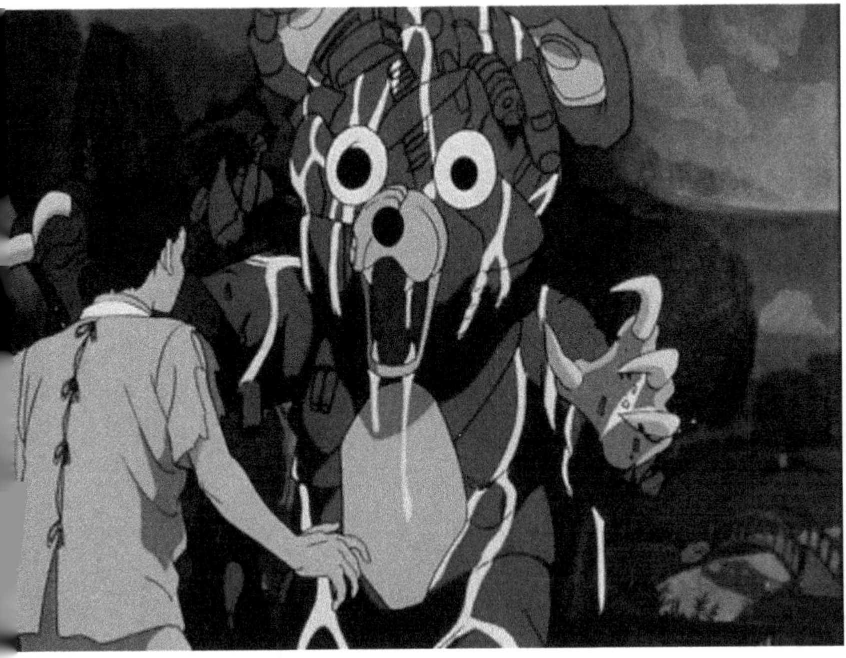

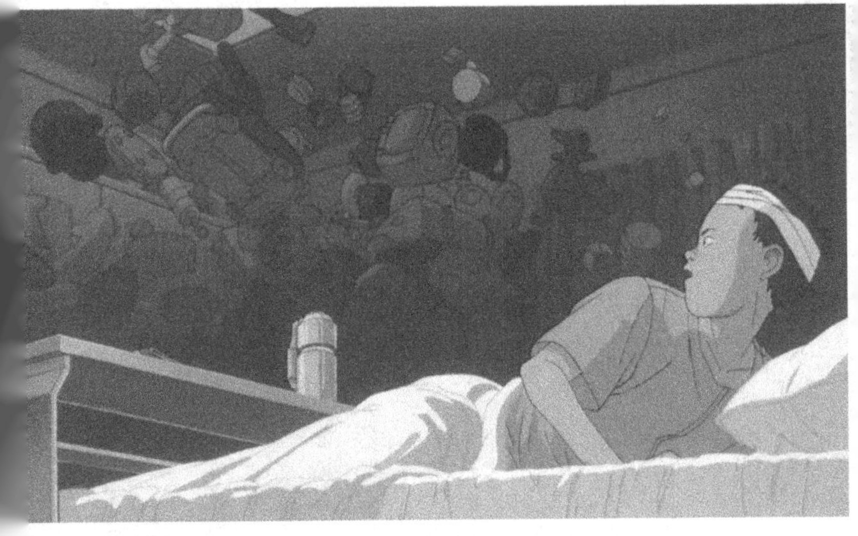

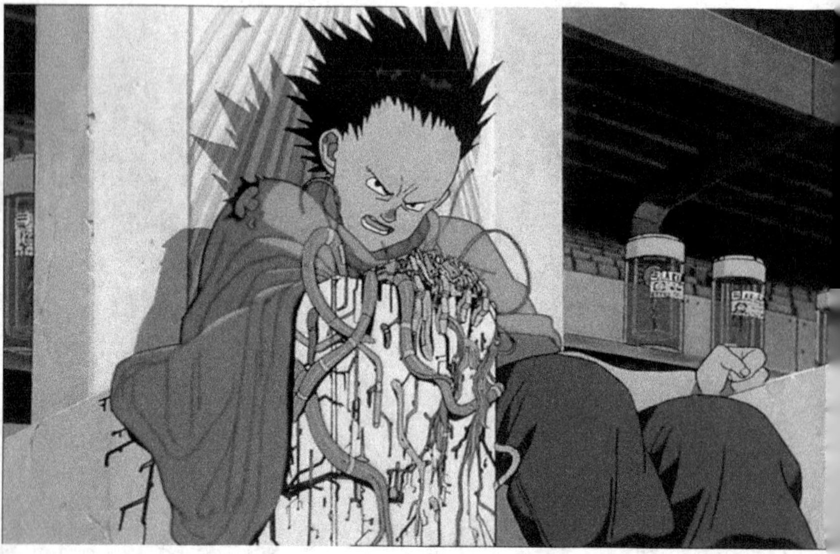

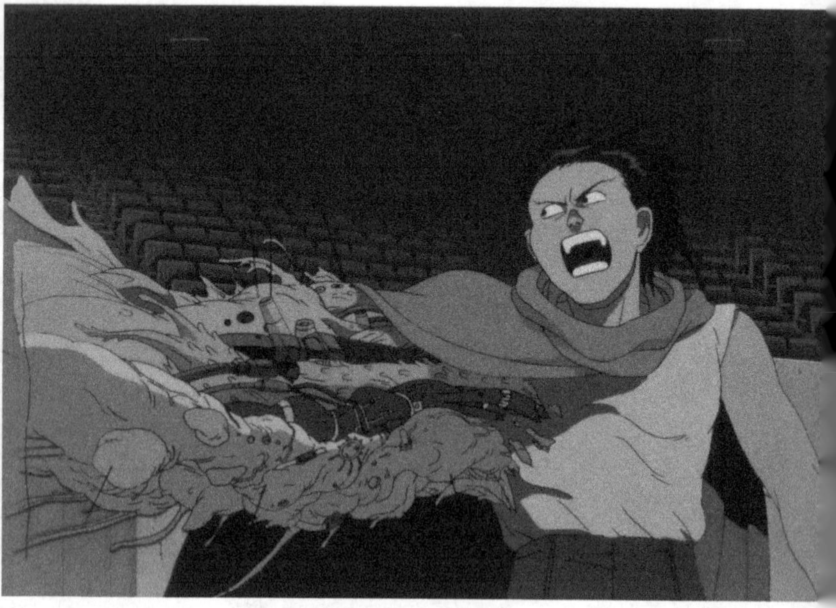

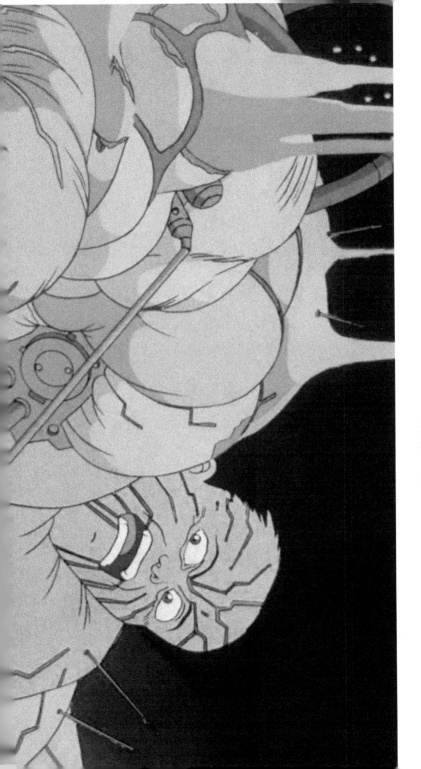

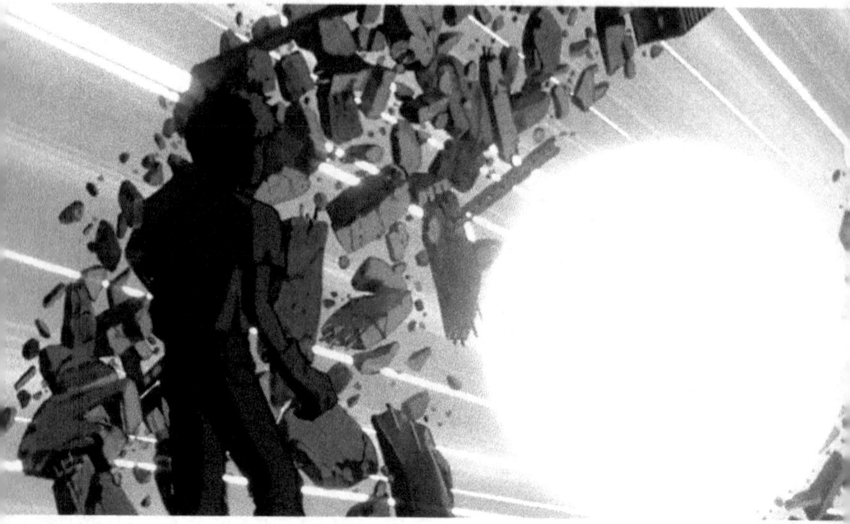

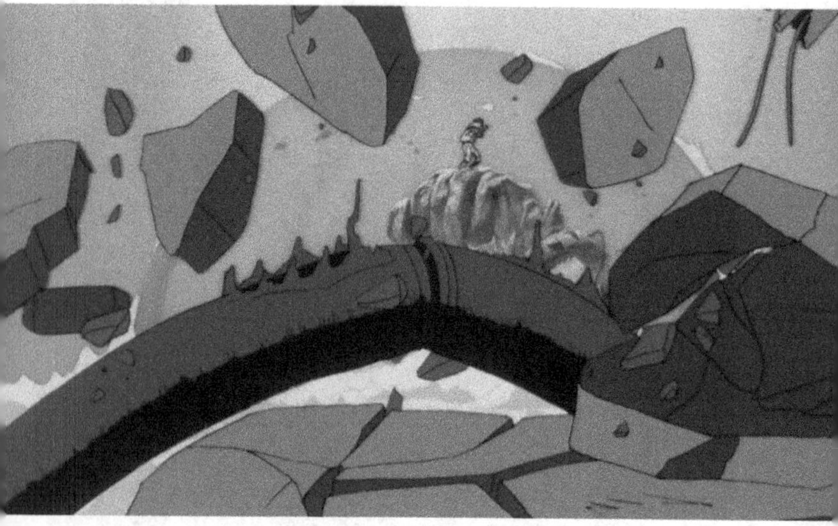

05

THE STORY OF *AKIRA*

The cinema, like the detective story, makes it
possible to experience without danger all the
excitement, passion and desirousness which
must be suppressed in a humanitarian ordering
of society.

Carl Jung

THE OPENING.
Akira is a GIANT of a movie that opens at full blast:
this movie *rocks* from shot one. I mean, it REALLY
ROCKS – at a *far* higher level of intensity than any
comparable movie, including all of the classics
regularly trotted out as hi-octane movie-making.

    Akira is totally overwhelming.

    The first half of the first act of *Akira* alone has
enough action, chases, explosions, fire, smoke, stunts,
hardware, vehicles, *mecha,* characters, and issues
(including political unrest, riots, police vs. rioter
confrontations, youth culture, gangs, etc), for a whole
movie – hell, for five whole movies. And by 15
minutes into the 1988 picture, it has already referenced (deliberately or unconsciously), *The Road
Warrior, A Clockwork Orange, The Warriors, The Wild*

One, Easy Rider, Rebel Without a Cause, Takeshi Kitano and Akira Kurosawa. Yes, and *Blade Runner,* naturally (is there a major Japanese science fiction *animé* that *doesn't* include nods to *Blade Runner*?! No!).

Akira is clearly one of those movies where the filmmakers have thrown *everything* they can think of into the mix, and it's a movie in which the filmmakers have given their *all.*

Akira opens B-I-G: the first shot is nothing less than an atomic bomb exploding in the middle of Tokyo (Akira created this explosion,[1] so it's not strictly a nuclear bomb dropped or exploded by humans – although humans have certainly created Akira and the psychic children – and to use them as weapons. So, yes, it is a human-made weapon… in the form of a 'human').

Captions tell us that the movie is set some 31 years after that apocalypse (the crater from the nuclear explosion looms ominously in subsequent scenes – it hasn't been flattened, and nothing's been built on it, as if it's been left as a warning, and a memorial). Like *Blade Runner, Akira*'s set in 2019, with World War 3 occurring in 1988 (it's slightly different in the *Akira manga*: WWIII starts in 1992 in the *manga* (thus, ten years ahead of its publication in 1982): it's December 6th, an echo of Hiroshima, of course (August 6th, 1945). The *manga* also states that the explosion was a 'new type of bomb'. The *manga* then tells us that the setting is Neo-Tokyo, 38 years later: 2030 A.D.).

---

1 To work on *Akira*, you had to be good at drawing explosions. Hayao Miyazaki once remarked that although you might have to draw explosions as an animator, the most important thing was to be interested in people, 'in how they live, and in how they interact with things' (2009, 125). Animators aren't just actors, Miyazaki also stated (in 1988), they have to know how to analyze, fuse and put into sequence movements 'involving gravity and momentum, elasticity, perspective, timing, and the fundamental properties of fluids' (2009, 74). Of course: *Akira* isn't a catalogue of exploding things, one scene of cataclysm followed by another: its foundation is in interaction, psychology, drama and characterization – all of the ingredients of classical literature and drama. Or put it like this, for all its spectacle, *Akira* is still storytelling.

Akira opens, unusually, with an ærial view of Tokyo looking straight down, onto a freeway (as if from a plane, perhaps); the camera tilts upwards slowly, to reveal Tokyo. The sound, a dull, muffled atmospheric effect, drops out *before* the explosion, which occurs over silence. (*Akira* was not the first or the last movie to depict a cataclysmic event like an atomic bomb in silence).

There's always a knock-on effect of opening Big and Loud – a movie has to slow down after that for some exposition and introduction of characters. *Akira* is no different: after that giant of an opening sequence, the movie shifts into more regular narration, and begins to clarify the characters, explore their relationships to each other, and offer some background on the strange events.[2]

INGREDIENTS IN *AKIRA*.

➤ Tokyo
➤ war
➤ catastrophes and post-apocalyptic scenarios
➤ WW2/ the Pacific War
➤ Japan and the U.S.A.
➤ technology, and the uneasy relation with it
➤ motorcycles and motorcycle gangs
➤ *mecha* and gadgets
➤ death and violence
➤ sex; rape
➤ drugs; pills
➤ anger
➤ suicide
➤ politics
➤ anti-governmental, anti-establishment movements
➤ references to cinema
➤ characters that lose it, shouting and yelling
➤ the colour red, above all, and green and blue, and orange and yellow

2 Flmmakers know that if you open with extended action, it has a delaying effect, and pushes back exposition until later.

- circles and spheres
- speed lines, exaggerated perspective
- pale tones for heightened scenes
- light
- giant numbers as decoration
- graffiti
- robots
- pebbles and rocks
- youth vs. age, sons vs. fathers, children vs. parents
- names beginning with a 'k': Kaneda, Kai, Kei, Kaori (echoing Katsuhiro)
- flashbacks
- superhero poses and cloaks
- guns and weaponry
- the military machine
- skyscrapers
- action, fights, duels, chases, explosions
- spiritual or mystical philosophizing
- psychic phenomena, flying, disappearance
- the 1964 Olympic Games
- messiahs

THE TIMELINE.

The time-scale of *Akira* is not made clear, as in many action-adventure movies, but it all seems to be occurring in a short space of time (maybe a few days). The movie, though, goes back several times to Tetsuo's childhood (maybe ten or eleven years), and briefly into the Colonel's past. *Akira* also starts 31 years in the past, in 1988 (that the Akira-explosion occurs in the year of the release of *Akira* is as expected in this kind of story. The date in the caption is July 16, 1988, when the movie opened in Japan). The time-scale of the *manga* is more thoroughly worked-out (tho' it still doesn't wholly match up).

---

3 Invisibility: in the *manga*, the psychic kids can disappear: it's used in the movie, but only Kei seems to see it; in the *manga*, Kaneda's amazed by it.

RIOTS.

The political dimension of *Akira* is further enhanced by the depiction of rioting citizens pitted against the police. The imagery comes right out of newsreels of the 1960s, with the filmmakers referencing Paris, London, Kent State, etc (as well as Tokyo in the early 1960s, of course). Civil rights, anti-government protests, manning the barricades – images of armed police in body armour firing on unarmed citizens or beating them with truncheons still carry an immense charge.[4] Large, red flags are waved, and the riots evoke Marxist, Maoist and left-wing movements, aligning the activists in *Akira* with the left-wing, battling against the oppressive, ruling, right-wing regime. It's the 1960s movies of Jean-Luc Godard, it's *The Battle of Algiers* (Katsuhiro Otomo has cited riots in Japan at the time of the 1964 Olympics as an influence, which were concerned with the uneasy relation between Japan and North America (such as the anti-A.M.P.O. movement, which protested against the American-Japanese Treaty On Mutual Cooperation and Security).[5] That is a recurring theme in many *animé* and *manga*, and also in Otomo's subsequent work: *Spriggan*, for instance, or *Roujin Z*).

Tokyo (now 'Neo-Tokyo') is rebuilding itself in a big way by hosting the next Olympic Games – it's next year, the city fathers say. The Olympic Games motif brings with it issues of international co-operation, and Japan's political relationship with the rest of the world. After the devastation of WW3 Japan really *needs* the Olympic Games.

✳

Dogs – how animators ♥ to put dogs[6] in movies! In *Akira*, one of the ten zillion details occurs in the

---

4 And cinema has occasionally gone back to that period, though often with self-indulgent romanticism (as in *The Dreamers* and *The Unbearable Lightness of Being*).
5 *Animé* director Mamoru Oshii (*Ghost In the Shell*, *Patlabor*) had participated in anti-state student movements in the 1960s.
6 In recent years, the king of doggy lovers in *animé* is definitely Mamoru Oshii. And Hayao Miyazaki.

opening scenes, when the kidnapper of Takashi shoots two dogs,[7] point blank, with a gun, in the midst of a traffic jam: you know this is no ordinary movie when someone kills two dogs while kids're watching from the nearby cars[8] (you couldn't do it in live-action – can't kill pets! And today you couldn't do it in animation). Of course, the guy is shot to pieces in an incredibly OTT manner moments later, by the police trying to control the crowd (an over-the-top death that recalls *RoboCop*, *The Godfather*, *The Wild Bunch* and *Bonnie & Clyde*. It's a crucifixion with bullets, far in excess of the dramatic requirements of the scene – however, you could argue that it has to be not simply a death in front of Takashi, but an ultra-violent death, to make Takashi's reaction even more extreme). One astounding beat follows another – because right after that, psi-child Takashi, in shock over the man's ultra-violent demise, explodes the glass in the buildings (and a water tower) so it rains down.[9]

This part of *Akira* is overtly political – far more than the opening of the *manga*. The riots, the State oppression, the atomic bomb – *Akira* very rapidly and intensely evokes numerous vivid moments from Japan's history. It can seem like a call to arms aimed at the youth of Nippon, to rouse them from their complacency in the economic boom of the 1980s.

IN THE SEWER TUNNELS.

There are two big action scenes inside sewer tunnels in *Akira*: in the first, Kei, on her own, is set upon by guards, and Kaneda skids down the steep sides of the sewer to her rescue (pretty brave for a high school kid of fifteen – but Kaneda is one reckless kid!). In the fracas, Kei kills one of the guards (the

---

7 The dogs're introduced with a match cut from a bank of televisions screening commercials featuring Disneyesque mutts in a store window (a time-consuming shot involving multiple images). *Akira* is full of such visual rhymes.
8 The reaction of the kids is the film warning its audience: *this is not for children!*
9 That would be a million dollar scene in live-action – fake glass raining on 100s of extras.

motive is solid, though, she is trying to save Kaneda from being shot by another guard). Her shock and remorse are brilliantly handled – and that the guy is dead there is no mistake: Kei shoots him in the face (in the eye, in fact), not the shoulder, not the leg, not the arm, not the hand, not the side, not the stomach. She doesn't wound him, so they can escape (as other movies might portray it), but shoots him in the head, and she fires first (it's a girl and a gun, in Jean-Luc Godard's famous remark). When Kaneda kills a guy (or seems to) later it's handled differently.

In the *Akira manga,* the setting's different, and Kei's response is very different: she yells, 'Don't make a move. Throw down your gun!' The guard turns, and she lets him have it. *SBLAM!* One dead guy: Kaneda is shocked – 'Shit...' – but Kei is already turning, yelling, 'Come on! follow me!' So there's no remorse; maybe *Akira*'s film producers reckoned that with a scene of a girl shooting a guy (and a soldier) and killing him, it oughta be played with more social conscience (many film producers would argue to delete that whole scene, or have her injure him). A girl killing a cop, a man dying in a hail of bullets, dogs being shot, unarmed rioters being beaten up – *Akira* doesn't hold back! And it's still act one!

Eye violence is extreme (and rare) in cinema, but there's no mistaking that the guy is shot in the eye by Kei, and there's no mistaking that the guy's dead: a direct hit in the eye is a way of showing that someone has definitely been killed. The movie also dwells on the guard sliding down the sewer wall into the watery filth: this is not a glamorous death.[10]

In the second sewer action scene in *Akira*, the activists, as they enter the scientific facility below the Olympic Stadium in disguise, are discovered by guards on flying sleds. The staging, timing and spectacle of the action is stupendous: water, for instance, is used to great effect, sending up high

[10] Eyes and eye violence offer postmodern theorists, college students and psychoanalysts plenty to discuss in terms of voyeurism, the gaze, scopophilia, and violence.

waves which (like the smoke) further complicates the scene. This is one of Kaneda's big moments – when he first of all controls one of the sleds (we know he's very skilled at riding a motorcycle, and jumping on and off 'em), and saves Kei from death in the crossfire (putting Kei and Kaneda on the flying sled also handily separates them from the rest of the activists, so they can encounter Tetsuo, who's going nuts in the baby room at this time, on their own). In this scene, Kaneda seems to severely injure or kill the second guy approaching on a flying sled (he falls off, then the sled explodes), but there is no time for grief.

DREAMS AND FLASHBACKS.

Especially impressive in *Akira* are the levels of flashback, fantasy and heightened reality. When Shima Tetsuo is being haunted to the point of nausea and agony by the E.S.P. experience, the animated movie shifts into an exaggerated, fantasy-laden mode: Tetsuo imagines his guts toppling onto the ground, or the earth cracking and falling away. The filmmakers employ every device available to deliver the fantasy and nightmare sequences, from slow motion, super-impositions, step-motion and black backgrounds to selective sound (and silence). The flashes of alternate realities, of childhood traumas, of, in short, an Akira-world, put the viewer right into Tetsuo's anguish.

Some of the first flashbacks in *Akira* occur when Tetsuo is in hospital, recovering. He dreams of his childhood, and being with Kaneda (when he wakes from his nightmare, he calls out Kaneda's name. Notice he doesn't call for mom or dad, or any family member – the parents of Tetsuo and Kaneda don't feature much in *Akira*, except, as he sees it, to abandon him). These flashbacks are picked up in small doses throughout *Akira*. They are stylized in selective colour (pale, dirty blues predominate), with an imaginative use of elongated shadows from a low light source (as well as flashcuts). There are also premonitions in voiceover – the word 'Ak-i-ra' is heard when Tetsuo flies over the Olympic Stadium in the helicopter (only later is it revealed that Akira is buried underneath the stadium).

There are flashcuts in the middle of Tetsuo's nightmares, some of which contain images which look forward to later events in the story (such as Tetsuo becoming a giant half-machine). The flash-forward images have greater resonance when the movie is viewed a second time.

Katsuhiro Otomo and the filmmakers have structured some poignant flashbacks in the midst of the chaos and spectacle of the final act of *Akira*: and, rightly, Kaneda figures large in the flashbacks to Tetsuo's time at school (getting beaten up, weeping, feeling lonely). Tetsuo might complain to Kaneda when he turns up with the laser rifle in the Stadium that he always comes to rescue him, and Tetsuo resents it (a development of their snippy dialogue in the baby room). But at least Kaneda was there in Tetsuo's childhood.

When, for instance, Tetsuo is crumpling up in pain after he's gone for a ride on Kaneda's red bike, and experiencing those horrific flashes of other realities, Kaneda tells him they came to find him because 'we were worried'. But Tetsuo still rejects any help, and tries to get away from both Kaneda and Kaori.

For many the stand-out fantasy sequence in *Akira* would be where Tetsuo is having another terrible night in hospital, and the three psychic children visit him in the form of giant teddy bears, toys, cars and fluffy rabbits. The animation is a *tour-de-force*, truly wild, and an animators' showpiece, like *Alice's Adventures In Wonderland* crossed with Ralph Bakshi in the early 1970s (*Fritz the Cat* and *Wizards*,[11] two out-there animated projects directed by Bakshi). At one point, milk seeps from the creatures' eyes and

11 The cult counter-culture hit *Fritz the Cat* (1972) was an X-rated cartoon of Robert Crumb's equally cultish comic book. *Wizards* (1977) was based on Vaughn Bode's comics.

mouths, and Tetsuo finds himself in a sea of milk (like Alice in her own tears in Lewis Carroll's book),[12] which gives him the clue that the monstrous creatures are in fact kids. The teddy bear forming from a coalescing collection of animated objects recalls the Czech animator Jan Svankmajer, and also Giuseppe Arcimboldo (1527-93), a painter from Milan taken up by Salvador Dali and the Surrealists. Arcimboldo, famous for his portraits of heads constructed out of fruit and food, is a favourite with Svankmajer and also animator and filmmaker Walerian Borowczyk.

The big action sequence in the nursery not long after that takes Surrealism crossed with late Sixties psychedelia even further. It follows the *Akira manga* quite closely at points, and also adds elements that aren't in Katsuhiro Otomo's comic. The scene is one of Tetsuo's *big* scenes of sulks and angry outbursts. He is fuming, and demanding, and bouncing about, unhinged (and ordering then coercing someone to tell him about Akira). Now his powers are beyond the capability of the authorities and their guards to contain. Towards the end of the scene, rubble is floating upwards as Tetsuo destabilizes everything around him, reflecting his own instability. Tetsuo is so out of control, he literally flies out of the building, like a bouncing ball, lurching towards the viewer, amazed at himself again (*I can fly too!* he cries).

Akira suggests that having such powers ain't gonna be easy, might hurt like hell, and one might end up destroying what one cherishes, plus innocent bystanders. Even the hard-headed Colonel Shiki-shima admits to Doctor Ônishi that they might be playing with forces that'd be better left alone (with god-size forces).

IN THE BABY ROOM.

The confrontation between Tetsuo and Kaneda in the baby room is a critical moment: witness Tetsuo's

12 Katsuhiro Otomo had produced a spoof of *Alice* in *Hansel and Gretel*.

amazement that Kaneda is there at all. Tetsuo's been having tantrums akin to a four year-old kid who can't get his own way (raising his arms to create cracks of destruction across the floors and walls). Tetsuo acts as the spoilt, angry child, the id gone wild – but he has a pretty good reason for going nuts!

So Shotaro Kaneda appearing at this particular moment is, for Tetsuo, completely unexpected (and it's brilliantly played). That his friend would come for him to help him escape hasn't entered Tetsuo's head (because he probably wouldn't do the same for Kaneda!). But when Kaneda *does* say that, the resentment builds up in Tetsuo (though it isn't voiced yet). This scenario will be repeated a number of times: Kaneda will arrive to help Tetsuo, and Tetsuo will reject/ resent that help, seeing in it only Kaneda exerting his superiority as the cooler, wiser, more heroic kid in the gang. Tetsuo is proud enough to think that *he* doesn't need 'rescuing'.

Prior to this, a particularly gruesome murder occurs in the hospital corridor in the government's scientific building, when a doctor and two orderlies who come to check on Tetsuo being out of bed are murdered – the first people that Tetsuo kills (blood and body parts are strewn around the corridor, a hand hanging from the ceiling – echoes of very similar scenes in *Legend of the Overfiend* – except in *Overfiend* the people were naked, after having group sex, as they usually are in *Urotsukidoji*!). The death scene is replayed in another corridor, when the guards can't stop Tetsuo, and he storms thru them on his way to the nursery.

TECHNIQUE VS. STORYTELLING.

It's irritating that even renowned commentators on *animé* point out that the animation techniques in a movie like *Akira* have been surpassed by newer technological developments (in digital and computer animation, for instance).

Junk. Wrrrong!

The animation in *Akira* is astounding, and hasn't aged a bit – because it's a masterpiece of *filmmaking*, of art. Yes, technology and techniques may have improved over time: yes, cameras may have better lenses (actually, do they? – there are counter-arguments), and photographic and reproduction processes may be better than those available in 1941 or 1937 or 1927 or 1916 (actually, are they? – there are more counter-arguments on this issue), but how many movies made today are as good, as technically inventive, as imaginative dramatically, and as historically important as *Citizen Kane* (1941), *Snow White and the Seven Dwarfs* (1937), *Sunrise* (1927) or *Intolerance* (1916)?

Emphasizing the technical or technological angle in animation is such bosh when comparing then and now (marketing teams and PR depts must take some blame – because they have to emphasize the 'now', that the latest product they're pushing has to be trumpeted as the best ever). It's like saying that *Pinocchio* was a lesser movie because it used 35mm celluloid, 35mm movie cameras and the multi-plane camera, compared to, say, *The Sky Crawlers* (2008), because it used state-of-the-art computers and amazing digital software. But *The Sky Crawlers* stinks (dreadful movie!), and *Pinocchio* is *still* magnificent. (Actually, many would argue that in some ways technology is *worse* now than before. For a start, *Akira* was filmed in 70 millimetre, rarely used today. Also, *Akira* was a very high budget production, for animation, and it's clearly technically superior to most animation, and certainly all television animation of recent times).

Akira is, first and foremost, *storytelling*. That's all a movie is, ultimately: *storytelling*. That's all *manga* is, in the end. Just a story. That's all the audience cares about: a good story, a good night out at the theatre, an entertaining experience. That's all. Audiences don't give a hoot whether something was produced using 170,000 cells (*Ponyo On the Cliff By the Sea*) and 100s of workers and companies, or if it was produced using 56,078 cells by a much smaller team (*Nausicaä of the Valley of the Wind*).[13] Because both are masterpieces, and both movies have entertained millions of people.

And, you know, just one person on stage can entertain thousands of people for two hours (a stand-up comedian, for instance, or a guitarist). On their own! Just a guy or a girl and a microphone. Wow.

ASPECTS OF THE STORYTELLING.

The narrative structure of *Akira* is unusual: not only does the movie split up to follow different characters – it will follow Tetsuo, then Kaneda, then Kaori, then the scientist and the Colonel, for instance – it also includes short flashbacks inserted into the middle of scenes. For instance, as the Colonel, the scientists and cohorts descend to the bowels of the facility below the Olympic Stadium, to take a look at the place where Akira is stored at near zero Kelvin temperature (brilliantly evoked with ice and cold imagery, and animated puffs of cold air), there's a flashback to another descending elevator scene (not in the *Akira manga*), with a dialogue exchange between the Colonel and the scientist (they are overlooking the Japanese capital). *Akira* is unusual in giving flashbacks to characters other than the principal characters, Tetsuo and Kaneda (notice, for instance, that the flashbacks to childhood that Tetsuo experiences come from him, not from Kaneda; we see Kaneda thru Tetsuo's eyes pretty much. If you go to the final volume of *Akira*, you will see Katsuhiro Otomo orchestrating the ending differently, but actually more emotionally).

At the start of the second act, around 30 minutes into *Akira* (the usual place for the start of act 2), the story shifts direction, and follows Kaneda and Kei: there are scenes where Kaneda is tailing Kei, not sure

13 Certainly *Nausicaä*'s not seen as 'inferior' to *Ponyo* because it used fewer animation cells!

what her mission is (and realizing he's being a jerk in following her), and gets involved in a fight between Kei and some guards. One of the most significant on-screen deaths in *Akira* occurs here, when Kei fires at one of the watchmen (who's grappling with Kaneda), and kills him. Kei saves Kaneda, but Kaneda also saves Kei twice in the movie (and, in a way, Kei helps to rescue Kaneda at the end, when he calls for her and he hears her calling to him,[14] and finds his way back to reality from the Akira-world and Tetsuo-world). The *manga* explains more of these calls from beyond the 'boundaries of the world', as Kei and Kaneda appear as spectres to each other (at different times). And in the *manga*, of course, the Kei-Kaneda romance is played out in full, tho' in the movie it remains a sub-plot.

One of the amusing dramatic turns in *Akira* is how Kaneda shifts from being the leader of the gang to being a lowly member of the activists' group: when he's hanging out with his buddies, he's the cocky captain of a motorcycle gang, confident in his leader-ship; but when he joins the activists, he becomes rather goofy and hopeless, more like a hapless, clumsy sidekick (when they're in the drain, for instance, and the guard on the flying sled approaches, Kaneda simply stands gormlessly in the middle of the flow while the others dive for cover. Whereas, if he'd been with his chums in the *bosozoku* gang, *he'd* be the one yelling at *Kai* to hide!).

It's striking just how much *Akira* is a buddy movie, or a brotherhood movie. The central emot-ional relationship is between Tetsuo and Kaneda. Although *Akira* is an ensemble piece in some respects, it's really about two kids, Kaneda and Tetsuo. They could've been combined in one character: certainly they are two aspects of one person, which's a classic narrative device.

Kaori (who doesn't appear in the first volumes of

14 When Kaneda floats down to a piece of road (hanging in the midst of the nowhere place), he lies down on it, and seems to be succumbing to sleep. We hear Kei's voice calling 'Kaneda-kun!'

the *manga* of *Akira* – she appears in *Book Four*), is featured in her own short sequence: she's depicted early in the 1988 movie's second act collecting her washing from the laundromat in her dormitory (it's one of the more modest and domestic scenes in *Akira*, but even that scene is pumped out with visual details; and there's a girl on the phone chattering non-stop).

It's here (departing from the *manga*) that Tetsuo, having fled the government hospital, comes to find Kaori (he appears in the corridor of her dorm, entering from the emergency stairs). After this the two have their brief talk outside, two vulnerable, teen kids in the hard-hearted city. So it seems even harsher when Tetsuo rejects Kaori after she's been beaten up.

TETSUO AS MESSIAH.

There's yet another wonderful superhero moment in *Akira* – in a movie stuffed to the gills with them (the filmmakers waste no opportunity to have Tetsuo emerging from flames or smoke, silhouetted, head tilted down, hair spiked up, brow furrowed, eyes glaring at the audience).[15] It's when Tetsuo faces the troops in downtown Neo-Tokyo, on his way to the Olympic Stadium (true, it does take him a long time to reach the Stadium! For someone who can fly!): his arrival is brilliantly announced by a helicopter crashing at an evacuated intersection in the distance (seen from the p.o.v. of the soldiers in a tank and a crowd of onlookers on the street behind barriers).

As he walks towards the mob, Tetsuo grabs some drapes from a store (bright red, of course – Kaneda's colours), rips them to size on the broken window, and swirls them around his shoulders, to produce an instant Superhero Cloak (now he's really getting into his stride!).[16] It's fab: who needs to mess around for days and weeks, as in N. American superhero movies, carefully fashioning Spider-man or

15 Tetsuo appearing in the flames just b4 the cloak moment, for instance, occurs first as a flashforward a few minutes earlier.
16 Of course, the cloak flaps in the breeze – cloaks simply must flap in the breeze – no use having one if it doesn't.

Batman outfits or a stupid Iron Man mobile suit?[17]
One majestic flourish with the cloak, and Tetsuo is all
set (it does help that he also has the wild, spiky hair
too, mandatory for an *animé* star. And he's got the
lowered head and the 'I mean business' glower
perfected).

This scene also includes a significant moment in
Tetsuo's new career as a Boy With Powers: a guy in
the crowd leaps onto a car and yells that Lord Akira
has come (and when another guy climbs up to contra-
dict him, to counter that he's a false messiah, he's
pushed off). The we-want-a-messiah motif had been
introduced earlier, and here, for the first time, (some
of) the crowd acknowledges Tetsuo as Akira, the One
They've Been Waiting For.

But it's left uncertain as to whether Tetsuo really
understands all of this. Does he realize that some
people in the crowd around the tank're calling him
Akira? No matter: because in a subsequent big action
scene, at the downtown bridge outside the tunnel
(presumably some time later the same day), Tetsuo
seems more comfortable with his new status as a
Worshipped One: he stands out in front of the crowd,
facing the military. Once again, he is attacked, and
deflects the assault. Once again, he reciprocates: in the
Tetsuo vs. tank scene, he blew up the tank, in this
scene, he blows up the bridge (Tetsuo retaliates when
he sees the soldiers firing at the crowd, and then at
him. It seems for a moment that Tetsuo is concerned
that people're being killed. In the *manga*, of course,
this worship of Tetsuo is in a very different context,
with the 'Great Tokyo Empire' convening in the
rubble of Neo-Tokyo to witness bizarre rituals run by
Tetsuo and Akira).

17 *Spider-man* (2002) had an amusing (but unnecessary) scene where
Peter Parker fixes up (badly) a Spider-man outfit. Meanwhile, most of
Iron Man (2008) was taken up with the hero building and testing and
trying out his iron man suit. Throughout, *Iron Man* was a movie as
an engineering course: no action, no drama, just the whole second
act comprising a super-rich playboy jerking around with robots in a
super-rich, Malibu mansion. How the hell did that get past the script
stage?

KANEDA VERSUS TETSUO.

When Tetsuo stands amongst the ruins of the spherical vessel that held Akira (and discovers nowt but a clutch of very disappointing glass containers holding parts of what may once have been Akira), there is a wonderful scene involving Tetsuo and Kaneda (handily, when Tetsuo opens the Akira container underground, the whole, metal globe rises up from its storage far below the Stadium, so the subsequent scenes can be staged in the open air. But even that scene, of raising the Akira-sphere, is another giant action scene, involving plumes of smoke, laser beams, lightning flashes, pipes and cables flailing about, tons of vfx, and a grating, industrial noise cue from Shoji Yamashiro. And a superhero duel between Tetsuo and psychic children working thru Kei – there is far, far more of the Kei-vs.-Tetsuo duels in the *Akira manga*. There's a shot of Kei speeding thru the air screaming in agony – the movie doesn't hold back from showing that it's painful for Kei to be the avatar of the psychic children).

The two (former) friends are not evenly matched, but at least Kaneda is armed with a laser rifle (there is an amusing beat earlier where Kaneda rides thru a wrecked, corpse-ridden toll-booth[18] and looks about craftily before taking the rifle). The conversation between Tetsuo and Kaneda is soon over (Tetsuo leaps from Sulk to Crazy in a flash, and he brings up the fact that Kaneda has always been telling him what to do since he was a kid). The pre-fight talk evokes many a movie, including Westerns.

Kaneda-plus-a-laser-rifle is no match for Tetsuo, of course, but Kaneda is a ballsy kid, and attacks Tetsuo a moment after Tetsuo has begun his energy-working (it's different to the ending of the first *manga* volume, where Kaneda can't bring himself to kill Tetsuo). In the movie, Kaneda has to shift to wanting to kill Tetsuo much quicker.

---

18 Which the biker gang has probably crashed thru a few times. It evokes the toll-booth at the start of the *manga*.

There's a classic exchange here – with Tetsuo tilting his head down and roaring:

Tetsuo: Kaneda!
Kaneda: That's Mr. Kaneda to you, punk![19]

The Tetsuo-Kaneda duel goes thru many beats and gags, with both kids being thrown about a lot, and careening off the shattered remains of the Akira storage capsule (the setting is a mound of smashed technology (rendered in painstaking detail), a recurring motif in Katsuhiro Otomo's fiction, as if our 'civilized', capitalist world is one step away from being just another trash heap. All those machines that we fetishize – *such a cool cel phone! wow, what a neat little gadget!* – is going to be tomorrow's junk).

Kaneda fires at Tetsuo repeatedly, but the laser beam goes right thru him – and he doesn't die. When the battery fails on the laser rifle, Kaneda still doesn't give up; he demands that Tetsuo fight with his fists (that's the way that Kaneda knows how to scrap, from the school playground, not with superhero powers! And Kaneda also knows (and Tetsuo does too) that if they fought with bare fists alone, he would win[20]).

However, the filmmakers add a complication to the duel here – the introduction of the S.O.L. weapons system on the orbiting satellite. This is unexpected (though it was foreshadowed in the Colonel's dialogue earlier, in the control room truck): a wide beam of white-blue light shoots down from the heavens, frying Tetsuo (and only just missing Kaneda nearby). It rips off Tetsuo's arm, but he survives. In the interval when the military prepare another strike (we cut back to the Colonel in the mobile control room a few times, as they react to what's happening), Kaneda is hefting a boulder above his head to attack Tetsuo with (he is not giving up until Tetsuo is dead).

19 This exchange is about getting the names correct in Japanese society. So it's Kaneda-san.
20 Because they've been involved in many scraps before.

This beat is pure Katsuhiro Otomo – when fancy technology like laser rifles and satellites fail, a good, old rock[21] smashed into the skull will probably do the trick! (And there are more rocks and stones flying around in this part of *Akira*, and all the way to the ending, than in 99.99% of other movies! Oh how Otomo-sensei loves rocks and pebbles![22]).

The second blast from the satellite system creates mayhem at the Olympic Stadium, but again both Tetsuo and Kaneda survive (Tetsuo protects himself with one of the domes of energy employed throughout the *manga* of *Akira* – the hemisphere also includes Kaneda. Otherwise, Kaneda would be fried). This is the moment where Tetsuo, in fury, speeds up into space (with a comic double take from Kaneda, where he looks at the audience), to destroy the satellite, which burns up as it falls to Earth (the space scenes are played without sound effects or dialogue, just a low, ominous rumble. No need for music or anything else when the visuals are this incredible. The evocation of *scale* is especially impressive – that satellite really is big! And how do you show that summat is big? Simple: you put your characters drawn very small next to it).

Meanwhile, Kei, Kai and Kaneda are making a rapid getaway from the site on a motorcycle (an echo of the scene where Kaneda jumps onto to Joker's flying platform with Akira in the *Akira manga*; the movie puts Kei and Kai together for a brief moment – echoing the touching, lighthearted scene in the *manga* where they're reunited at Lady Miyako's temple, in the aftermath scene). The imagery and action is vast and apocalyptic – and consciously religious (the image of Tetsuo hurtling upwards into a circular hole in the clouds is like something out of Gustave Doré's illustrations for the *Divine Comedy*).

Earlier, Kei and Kai ride into the chaos following the face-off between Tetsuo and Kaneda, though

21 A gag used in *A Farewell To Weapons*.
22 Some of the action around here is staged slightly comically – such as how Kaneda escapes one falling boulder after boulder.

the world is falling apart so rapidly, they soon tumble off the bike. They brace themselves for the impact of the satellite's beam, which they're trying to out-run, but they survive. (Even here, there are marvellous details, like the pebbles hanging in the air which drop to the ground).

The lighter moment (at night, round a campfire), when Kaneda is trying to recharge the laser rifle battery, using Kai's motorcycle (which catches on fire), is necessary – because much of the rest of the 1988 movie is pretty darn serious and is also wall-to-wall action (that scene also echoes a scene outside Miyako's temple in the *manga*, when Kaneda returns from his period in the spirit world). It also depicts the three kids together in a modest scene. Had the running time been even longer, several of these humble scenes around this point would be welcome.

SUPERMAN AND THE SATELLITES.

Superman (in movies as well as comicbooks) is consciously referenced in the scene where a very angry Tetsuo (he's had his arm ripped off)[23] hurtles into outer space to take out the military satellite system (in the mid-1980s, satellites for espionage and defence were big news – three quarters of satellites at the time were military). They've formed part of action cinema in *James Bond* movies (*Moonraker*), in *Star Wars*, *War Games* and of course the U.S.A.'s S.D.I. system was dubbed 'Star Wars' by President Reagan's administration (much to the irritation of George Lucas *et al*, even tho' *Star Wars* can be interpreted as an extremely right-wing movie – the perfect hi-tech reflection of Reaganite-Thatcherite ideology).

The sequence in *Akira* closes with an incredible

---

23 Arms were oddly a focus for violence in the *Star Wars* films: Ben Kenobi cut off the man's arm in the space bar, C3PO's arm was torn off, and Han Solo says that Wookies pull people's arms out their sockets when they lose at chess. The losing-an-arm motif continued in *The Empire Strikes Back* when Darth Vader cut off Luke Skywalker's hand. In *Akira* as in *Star Wars*, losing an arm has a clear castration element to it: a little comedy occurs when Tetsuo tries to hide his bulging, unruly metal arm from Kaori under his cloak.

image of satellites falling to Earth like meteorites in a distant view over the city, under a purple and crimson sky, accompanied by a hushed choral cue (with Tetsuo fashioning himself a new arm, from metal. Again, there's more to this sequence in the *Akira manga*. Indeed, in the *manga*, even Kei gets to play Superwoman, flying up to the SOL satellite to aim it at the Tetsuo-monster. The *manga* probably over-uses the satellites, however).

THE FINALE.

In the last act of the 1988 film of *Akira*, the destruction and action on screen is simply stupendous. Shots costing hundreds of thousands of ¥¥¥¥ are erupting across the screen, super-freighted with as many visual effects as the filmmakers can beg, steal or borrow from every animation house in Tokyo (the real Tokyo – not Neo-Tokyo!). I wish I'd seen *Akira* in Tokyo in a packed house on a Friday night on its first run in 1988 – the effect would be total overload and obliteration! (*Akira* is definitely one of those very rare movies where you walk out of the theatre in a state of bliss).

Why hold back now?! The filmmakers don't: *Akira* is cinematic war, a climactic, catastrophic conflict which beggars belief (only the last act of *Legend of the Overfiend* and the climaxes of Hayao Miyazaki's movies match it in Japanese – or global – animation for sheer intensity and fire). The energy is shooting out of the screen, to consume the audience.

The level of *imagination* on display in *Akira's* finale is mind-boggling. If the animators weren't burnt out after producing that last act of *Akira* (and I bet some of them were!), the viewers will be. There are many times in *Akira* when you think there's no way the filmmakers can top what they've just produced on screen.

But they do.

Tetsuo versus Kaneda...

...the Tetsuo-baby...

...the Akira explosion...

...the cosmic journey and flashbacks...

...the destruction of Neo-Tokyo...

So many magnificently realized sequences, each one containing many mini-scenes within the scenes.

Often money is running out as animation production goes into overdrive during the final months of the schedule, and sometimes the endings of TV shows, O.A.V.s and movies suffer for it (if they haven't been tackled earlier in the schedule – as they often are in live-action). Luckily, *Akira* saved a substantial part of the budget for the stops-all-out finale.

The ending of the movie of *Akira* influenced the *manga* – because Katsuhiro Otomo, who doesn't like to repeat himself, didn't wanna simply emulate the movie. The *manga,* Otomo thought,

> would end with Tetsuo and Kaneda somehow sharing their memories of the orphanage. Using that ending in the film meant I had to come up with something else for the *manga*; the ending there is a bit different.[24]

It begins with Tetsuo walking into the Olympic Stadium. When he finds out that Akira, the supposed messiah and answer to all his problems, is reduced to a bunch of golden liquids and body parts in glass tubes, he goes nuts. Well, *even more nuts*, because Tetsuo, as soon as he attains his powers, is one mean son-of-a-gun with a chip on his shoulder the size of Shinjuku.

The filmmakers have saved up astonishing mass transformations for this section of *Akira*, when the powers raging inside Tetsuo become too much for him to handle. Out come the organic and artificial body parts, the tubes, cables, blood vessels, pulsating organs and goopy stuff, with the animators delivering classic squash-and-stretch movements – it's like a

24 Katsuhiro Otomo, quoted in T. Ryans, *Monthly Film Bulletin,* Mch, 1991.

gory, steam-punk *Fantasia* (1940) where Walt Disney's cute cherubs have been eviscerated, and the dancing hippos are turned inside-out. Eruptive, erectile, super-phallic, with laserbeams slicing out to incinerate anything that gets in their way (there is plenty more of this kinda imagery in the *manga*).

A body without limits, a body you can't control, a body with impulses and energies raging thru it so your identity is no longer yours (and perhaps it was never 'yours' – do you *own* life? Do you *own* your body? How much of your identity is bound up in your body?).

Who cares what it 'means'?! Who cares what the story is or what the characters're doing?! Who cares if it doesn't proceed in a conventional cause-and-effect progress or a logical A-to-B pattern?! This is spellbinding, kill-'em-in-the-stalls cinema. This is animation whipped up to a frenzy of movement, colour and destruction.

And yet the drama among the humans – Kaori and the Colonel on the platform, and Kaneda down below – is all worked out precisely. Some of the time their reactions are, understandably, disbelief and shock: after all, seeing the giant baby Tetsuo (which nobody has seen before, and not in cinema, either), is gonna stop you in your tracks for a moment!

So incredible is the final act of *Akira*, the messiah plot (the appearance of Akira himself/ itself/ herself), almost gets lost in the mælstrom. It's notable that Akira is visualized as a young boy looking a little like Kaneda in the childhood flashbacks (which fits, because that's partly how Tetsuo might regard Akira – how Tetsuo looked up to Kaneda as a kid). There's plenty more of Akira the Kid in the *manga*, yet he doesn't emerge with any more personality than he does in the movie: Katsuhiro Otomo is clearly not really interested in Akira at all, in the *manga* or the movie – not when they're strong characters like Kaneda, Kei, Tetsuo, the Colonel and Lady Miyako in the mix. (Akira is partly a function of the plot, a pretext, a goal, an emblem).

The atomic bomb motif from the opening scene of *Akira,* which's linked to the re-appearance of Akira, is reprised when he/ she/ it re-assembles again. The molten, white hemisphere expanding outwards has featured in a number of *animés*, but never as skilfully as here. Somehow, the filmmakers manage to make white (a tricky colour to use in visual effects[25]) seem to be solid, dangerous, and deathly, as it eats up all in its path, when it's visualized as a giant, white half-globe (the movie also uses the familiar method of making something scary: have other characters react to it in awe and fear. Thus, the three psychic kids hurry away from it, but they also want to help Tetsuo, Kaneda and the others).[26]

But what 'happens', exactly, in the finale? The psi kids pray, and seem to evoke/ conjure Akira.[27] Who, when he appears, blows up! They seem to be calling on Akira to help with Tetsuo (which's sort of ex-plained to Kaneda by Kiyoko). But Akira doesn't absorb Tetsuo, in an 'Akira event' localized in the Stadium; he/ she/ it explodes, engulfing Neo-Tokyo! (Couldn't Akira 'absorb' Tetsuo without killing millions of people in the process?! No, not in a Katsuhiro Otomo story!).

I mean, what kind of help is Akira?! We see the white sphere eating up Tetsuo – good, yes, very good! – Tetsuo certainly needs to be taken care of! – but the white energy keeps expanding, devouring everything in its path! What kind of medicine or healing is that?!

There are so many beats to the action in *Akira*'s climax, it would take some time to consider them all. The invention of the filmmakers is just astounding. How they exploit that treasured red motorcycle, for example, bringing it back from the dead several times – Kaneda rides it to escape Tetsuo's wrath, but also

25 Colours in *anime* such as purple/ lilac or green're often used for nasty events or charas.
26 The moment earlier in the riot with the tear gas is recalled – where Kei steps into the smoke to hide from a cop.
27 The liquid in the glass jars bubbles seemingly in response to the psychic kids' efforts.

to charge at Tetsuo while wielding the laser gun (which he fires at his friend like a samurai shooting an arrow on horseback in an Akira Kurosawa *jidai geki*). The filmmakers are clearly big motorbike nuts (as well as weapon nuts, and tank nuts, and *mecha* nuts – like 100s of people in Japanese animation, including Masamune Shirow, Hideaki Anno and Hayao Miyazaki): they simply don't want to get rid of that bike until they've milked it to the max (indeed, they even revive it – battered to bits – for the final scenes, where Kaneda, Kei and Kai ride back to Neo-Tokyo. That scene is an altered version of the incredible finale of the *Akira manga* – where Kaneda and Kei have rustled up a gleaming, new bike).

✳

With the reformation of the entity called Akira in the final act of the 1988 Japanese movie, all hell breaks loose again: it has to: a movie such as this, which opens with a nuclear detonation destroying much of Tokyo, leading to WWIII, and swiftly following that with mass demonstrations, riots, and truly astonishing bike battles, can only end with a Big Bang. The images of the vast, white sphere eating up the Japanese capital as it expands outwards, the hurricane winds, the enormous clouds of smoke, and the buildings and debris being sucked upwards, and collapsing and crumbling downwards, the ocean flooding thru, are simply sensational. And the images are poetically counterpointed with a soft, haunting choral music cue, not the expected boisterous action-adventure music (or the usual low, bassy rumble). Because it's a very solemn scene: we are witnessing the devastation that humans have visited on themselves, by meddling with forces they don't fully understand (and also the deaths of a *lot* of souls, tho' individual deaths aren't shown).

The ending of *Akira* is ten disaster movies of the 1970s packed into one: *Earthquake, The Towering Inferno, The Poseidon Adventure, Airport et al.* Katsuhiro Otomo as a film director is the King of Catastrophe, the Master of Mayhem (he gives even filmmakers celebrated for on-screen carnage – like Cecil B. DeMille, Irving Allen, and D.W. Griffith – a run for their money – and that's not easy!). It's as if Otomo is putting on screen *his* version of the movies he grew up with – Irving Allen disaster flix, Ray Harryhausen stopmotion epics, *Thunderbirds, James Bond,* and of course Japanese *Godzilla* movies (and the cheapo rip-offs of them).

Yet *Akira* is not just about the joy of blowing stuff up produced by a bunch of boys (most key animators, and most of the key personnel in *animé,* are even today still mainly guys. Can you name ten female directors or producers of *animé*? No. Animators, yes (a few), colour designers, yes, in-betweeners, yes. But directors or producers? Not so many).

For the last ingredient of calamity, Katsuhiro Otomo and the huge team of filmmakers opt for a flood – so Neo-Tokyo is flooded (as it was in the movie *Neo-Tokyo*), with the Olympic Stadium handily surviving (though in bits. In *Steam-boy*, the film-makers used water again, and devastated another metropolis (Londinium), but it was so cold it turns everything to ice).

KANEDA'S TRIP.

There are multiple flashbacks in the final act of *Akira*, as Kaneda soars thru alternate realities, including Tetsuo's memories. Many of the flashbacks concern Tetsuo, and are vignettes of Tetsuo's child-hood (being taken to school by his mom,[28] on his own at school (weeping), in a tenement (out of *Domu*), and meeting Kaneda at school by a water fountain, where Kaneda hands a toy figure of a robot to Tetsuo, which, judging by his bloody nose, he's presumably just wrested from the school bullies. Kaneda's learnt the hard way that you have to stand up to bullies, or they'll walk all over you. School kids can exploit weaknesses as efficiently as murderous, fascistic

28 Or is that Tetsuo looking up at Kaneda as his dad?

governments[29]).

Now this is brave – to choose to go back to 5 or 6 year-old ages for Kaneda and Tetsuo – not, as many writers would've done, to teen years, to confront- ations at school, say, or disputes with teachers, or with parents, or fights over girlfriends (many writers would automatically put Kei in between the boys).

Some of the exposition about the psychic experi- ments on the children in *Akira* is played out here, too – so these memories are presumably also those of the three magical children Kiyoko, Masaru and Takashi (and Akira).[30] One of the kids manages to distort a video image on a TV monitor, which then blows up (to the delight of the other kids, who find some of the tasks dull). There are numerous images here – of doctors performing operations, of the children being led through educational tasks, and of kids resisting some of the treatments. (Kiyoko handles some of the exposition, in voiceover – in the *manga*, it's Lady Miyako who does that).

And some of the flashbacks are from not so long ago: for instance, we see Tetsuo and Kaneda on their motorcycles, with Kaneda and Tetsuo at their happiest (and boysiest), with Kaneda teaching Tetsuo how to ride, how to corner: lean into corners like you want to kill yourself – a classic Kaneda line, and a classic philosophy of (macho) teen rebellion. These ghostly images were part of the moving coda to the *Akira manga*, when Tetsuo (and Yamagata) appeared to Kei and Kaneda on their motorcycles, swooping around them, then zooming off into the future (the scene where the trio of 'K's' (Kei, Kai and Kaneda) race back to downtown Neo-Tokyo also alludes to the *manga*'s close).

✦

The last minutes of *Akira* enter *2001: A Space Odyssey* Stargate territory, with an assault of mad, abstract, trippy visuals. Every shot is a visual effects

29 Maybe that's where they learn it – in the playground.
30 One of the children in the scientific experiment looks like the young Tetsuo.

shot, every shot has out-of-control movement in it, as Shotaro Kaneda is taken on a flying journey thru space and time, seeing visions of Tetsuo and Akira in between images of the Japanese capital exploding and falling apart. (In fact, as impressive as *2001: A Space Odyssey* was and still is, *Akira* goes way, way beyond it in its masterful orchestration of psychology, childhood and visual effects).

What does it 'mean'? It goes further than 'meaning' or 'understanding' into cinema as pure experience, cinema as a series of abstract images and movements. The flying figure of Kaneda, wailing and screaming and reacting, is inserted in the frame in some of the abstract sequences to lend a sense of perspective and humanity to the proceedings (as in the *manga* of *Akira*).

The abstract visuals at the end of *Akira* employ: (1) shapes disappearing into the centre of the screen; (2) beams of light erupting from that infinite point; (3) waves of light sliding across the screen diagonally; (4) a variety of rotating effects; (5) over-exposed imagery; (6) a constant fragmentation of objects and patterns; (7) zigzag shapes echoing the serrated speed lines of the *manga*; (8) recurring circular forms and shapes; and (9) fades to black and white.[31]

Some of the abstract imagery in *Akira* recalls experimental movie-making and *avant garde* experimentation from the 1940s thru 1960s, such as: James Whitney (*Yantra, Five Film Exercises, Catalogue*),[32] Bruce Conner (*A Movie*), Robert Breer (*Fuji*), Stan Vanderbeek (*Science Friction*), Len Lye (*A Colour Box, Kaleidoscope*), Norman McLaren (*Begone Dull Care, Neighbours*), Oskar Fischinger, Harry Smith and Stan Brakhage (*Mothlight, Dog Star Man, Flesh of Morning*). And Jordan Belson, whose formal experiments

31 The imagery is reminiscent of 1960s abstract art – Dan Flavin with his white fluorescent tubes, for instance, the Colorfield and Post-Painterly Abstract painters, such as Frank Stella, Sol LeWitt, Kenneth Noland or Ellsworth Kelly, artists who worked with blocks of pure colour and nothing else. In 1960s art, paintings were objects in themselves, without any reference to anything outside of themselves.
32 Whitney worked on the titles for *Vertigo*.

in film included *Mandala* (1955), *Allures* (1961), *Re-Entry*, *Phenomena* (1965) and *Samadhi* (1967). Later, Belson's colourful blobs and liquids appeared in the movies *Demon Seed* (Donald Cammell, 1977)[33] and the wonderful *The Right Stuff* (Phil Kaufman, 1983), to evoke the visions the astronauts and pilots see).[34]

✦

Chotto – wait a second – just what is going on here? Thinking in conventional movie terms, what causes the Akira explosion? Presumably, the mixing of Tetsuo-energy and Akira-energy, two out-of-control powers. The three psychic kids heroically sacrifice themselves to help 'that boy', who hasn't asked for this (they mean Tetsuo, but also perhaps Kaneda). Unfortunately, their aid doesn't prevent the resurrected Akira going into meltdown. Instead of helping things along, millions die.

Yet Akira smiles when the children meet him (in part like a child meeting his old friends), suggesting that, now, Good Things Will Happen. Yes, Akira might be the messiah everyone's been waiting for, the one who's gonna Put Things Right, the literal *deus ex machina* who's gonna Save The World. The way that Akira materializes at the end of the 1988 movie (tho' not the *manga*), with the smile and the white light and the religious awe and all, hints at a magical or divine power who can reverse the rapid plunge into entropy.

But the opposite happens! Immense explosions and colossal devastation! This is typical of Japanese pop culture, and of Katsuhiro Otomo's art: Creating A New World in Japanese *animé* and *manga* means first of all *completely destroying the present world*! Every time! Japanese stories don't build on the existing society, they attempt to erase it. All of it. *Everything*. Nothing and no one will be saved (except the super-villain orchestrating it, of course).

---

33 Donald Cammell had been impressed by Belson's film *Chakra*, and used Belson's work in the 1977 movie *Demon Seed*.
34 G. Mast, 1992, 468.

AKIRA'S DÉNOUEMENT.

The startling scenes keep coming: *Akira* is relentlessly inventive to the final seconds: a tiny, white ball floats gently to the ground, right into Kaneda's hands (as he kneels on an outcrop of debris in the Olympic Stadium,[35] after his ordeal of travelling thru the wormhole of Tetsuo's psyche). The suggestion is that it's all that's left of Tetsuo, or the part of Tetsuo that he's left behind. His spirit, his soul, whatever. Peace at last, perhaps, for a very troubled boy (both Kei and Kaneda look up to the heavens as they discuss that all-important question: what happened to Tetsuo?).

That image of the white light falling into Kaneda's hands is ambiguous, like some of the key moments in *Akira*. But over the last of the abstract images which close *Akira*, it is Tetsuo's voice that's heard – *Bokura Tetsuo* ('We are Tetsuo'). Viewers will make of it what they will – certainly there are religious, mystical aspects to the ending of *Akira*, but it's worth remembering, when considering *Akira* from a Western perspective, that Shinto is the main religion of Japan, not Christianity, Judaism or Islam. For instance, Japanese animation likes the exoticism and otherness of many Western symbols (and Christian/ Catholic symbols, such as angels, churches and crosses), but less than one per cent of Japanese are Christian.[36] The moment can be related to the animism of Shintoism, the belief in millions of spirits or gods (that, in death, Tetsuo (and us, when we die) is literally everywhere, where death is a transformation into another form).

Little Kaisuke isn't wholly necessary in the *dénouement* of the 1988 movie (well, neither is Kei, really, though she has appeared in the climax, and was used by the 3 children to take on Tetsuo, and

---

35 This is a favourite motif of Katsuhiro Otomo's – rubble that forms a cone. The *Akira manga* is stuffed with people standing atop pillars, concrete blocks, roofs, rubble and skyscrapers. Again, a staple of *manga* and *animé*.
36 G. Poitras, 1999, 70.

watching from a distance and murmuring, 'Kaneda-kun'). But it's great that Kaisuke, the surviving motorcycle gang member, returns (the gang, after all, has been very important for Kaneda).

Kei, of course, plays a huge role in the *manga*, but in the effort to squeeze the story into a two-hour running time, and with Kaneda and Tetsuo taking up much of the screen time, there wasn't so much room for Kei.

As expected, *Akira*'s writers Izo Hashimoto and Katsuhiro Otomo keep the reunion scenes separate – so it's Kei who encounters Kaneda first. No hugs, no kisses[37] – this is Japanese animation, not Hollywood schmaltz, folks![38] – but Kei and Kaneda do exchange their warmest, tenderest look yet. Kaneda, kneeling, his back to Kei, thanks Kei – for calling to him.

Actually, this *is* a very significant act that Kei performs, because it brings Kaneda back to himself, as she calls to him – 'Kaneda-kun', and repeats his name (as she does in the *manga*, but there it's probably better achieved). In the movie, as soon as Kaneda wakes and responds to Kei's call, the sound rushes in and the movie cuts to Neo-Tokyo in turmoil. Kei calling is thus vital in bringing Kaneda back to the world of the living, rather than remaining adrift in the spirit realm, entangled with Tetsuo's memories. (In a lovely touch, notice that Kei is wearing Kaneda's red biker jacket).

(In the *Akira manga*, there is a superb ♥ scene, when Kaneda and Kei embrace passionately in Lady Miyako's temple; however, in Katsuhiro Otomo's quirky storytelling style, it's not a straightforward kissing scene, but one driven by Kaneda's anger, ambition and confusion, and Kei's patient acceptance).[39]

---

37 No kisses in *Akira* for the leads, but horny teenagers do grope each other and fool around.
38 Even in *animé* where you'd expect a kiss of reunion joy between lovers, such as at the end of the 26 episodes of *Escaflowne*, it doesn't come. Or *Princess Mononoke*. Or *Fullmetal Alchemist*.
39 If you wait long enough, even Kaneda's fury will die down! And you can get to say your piece!

Part of Kai's function is therefore to lighten the proceedings a little at the end of *Akira*, after all that carnage and filmic abstraction and colour, which he does by hurrying into the scene and gushing over Kaneda's survival (the animation, once again, is marvellous: Kai hastens up to Kaneda, and looks for a moment like he's gonna hug him; he remembers that he's part of a cool biker gang – boys don't hug boys – and stops himself at the last moment). Both Kei and Kai bring our hero Kaneda back to Earth, back to reality, back to something resembling 'regular life' (well, as 'regular' as you can have in a twice-post-apocalyptic city!).

THE ENDING OF *AKIRA*.

The ambiguity that is fundamental to *Akira* is played out in the final moments with the *dénouement* scene: who should survive, and who should die? (In 99% of movies, you can tell from the start). For killing so many people, including many innocent bystanders, Tetsuo should certainly die, using the rules of conventional action and fantasy cinema (or be punished – but, in action-adventure flicks, there's no time for that, so death it has to be). Well, Tetsuo kinda does die, and kinda doesn't: the ambiguous ending of *Akira* features multiple abstract images with Tetsuo's disembodied voice saying, 'I am Tetsuo' at the very end (a multi-purpose, open ending, it could mean anything. Perhaps that Tetsuo has become the new Akira, or a new messiah. Or he could be 'one' with everything. Or he might've fused with Akira. Whatever: the ending is a gift from the filmmakers to the audience, as if they're saying, oh, hell, we're *exhausted*, so *you* decide what happens!).[40]

Kaneda survives, as does Kei. The three psychic children don't. And poor Kaori doesn't, either: beaten to a pulp in the first act of *Akira*, then rejected by Tetsuo, she is swamped by the giant, bloated Tetsuo-

[40] The ending, according to Antonia Levi, is 'unresolved, unfair, and never fully explained,' adding: 'that happens a lot in anime' (92).

baby in the last act of *Akira* (is it another case of 'killing the ones you love?' – well, Tetsuo embodies that platitude: he repulses everybody who comes near him, including the two most significant people in his life, Kaori and Kaneda). If Tetsuo and Kaori play out yet another version of the Beauty and the Beast motif, a staple of sci-fi and fantasy fiction, that Kaori dies is another instance where the filmmakers have con- sciously altered the traditional fairy tale forms.[41]

So the ending of *Akira* is ambiguous, open-ended, and for many viewers I would guess it's also unsatisfying – really, it doesn't resolve some of the key issues, and certainly not some of the key plots. In fact, the more you think about it, the more the ending of *Akira* not only breaks many narrative rules (but who cares about them?!), it delivers abstraction and awe in the place of dramatic closure. (In fact, *Akira* announces early on that it will *not* be following the rules. Viewers familiar with Japanese storytelling will already know that. But *Akira* makes many narrative moves in the opening 30 minutes that not only go against expectations, they invent new ones).

Akira's ending is explosive spectacle, certainly, and stuffed with visceral action – oh yeah! – yet it also employs many unusual narrative devices: for instance, extensive flashbacks to the two protag- onists' childhoods (it also provides flashbacks for other charas, such as the Colonel). But much is left unclear – what or who is Akira? What happens to Tetsuo? Do they fuse? Is the military's telekinetic children project abandoned? Why does Tetsuo suddenly acquire those powers? Does the mass destruction of Neo-Tokyo lead to another World War, as it did decades ago? Even minor sub-plots, like the Kei-Kaneda romance, are left up in the air.[42]

But then, how *could Akira* have ended, anyway?

41 We know, from *Hansel and Gretel*, that Katsuhiro Otomo has enjoyed reversing the narrative expectations in classic fairy tales!
42 However, we do hear Kei calling Kaneda back from the nether- world, we do see the tender look they exchange, and they do ride on the motorcycle together at the end.

The primary plot – the Tetsuo and Kaneda rivalry and the psychic children project – oughta be resolved, right? But it isn't!

Has anybody learnt the error of their ways? No! Has Colonel Shikishima realized that exploiting humans to be used as weapons is immoral and downright nasty, and has led to the destruction of large parts of the Japanese capital? No! (You could say, tho', that at least the military-industrial complex probably won't be using children as weapons again. Controlling a teenage tantrum is simply not possible!).

But you can forgive the narrative non-sequiturs and the open-endedness in the ending of *Akira* for one simple reason: the filmmaking is simply *astounding*. This has nothing to do with whether it was achieved with traditional cel animation, or with 3-D animation, or digital animation, or toilet tissue finger puppets, or – what the hell – 568-D, multi-dimensional animation produced by an alien race who travelled back in time from the End of the Universe to 1980s Tokyo – it has to do with imagination and creativity. (And have you seen an animated movie since *Akira* that can even equal it?).

And there *is* an emotional impact to the ending of *Akira* – for example: that Tetsuo, standing in for all troubled, anxious, shy, belittled souls, has found peace at last. For me, *Akira* increases in emotion every time I see it – maybe because, knowing the*manga* so well, I can fill the bits the movie hasn't got time to show. But also, who can ignore the raw, elemental power of the filmmaking in the final 30 minutes? Which's at a level that hardly any other movies reach.

Rapture – that's a better word.[43] Or bliss. Or ecstasy – the ecstasy of filmmaking as pure experience.

---

43 Tho' not 'the rapture' in *The Simpsons*! (But there are similarities – the apocalyptic end of the world).

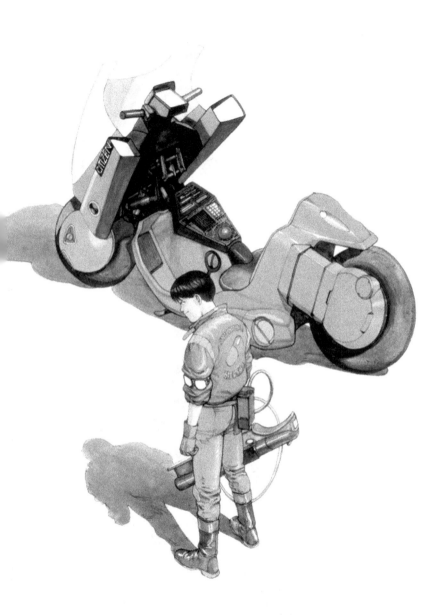

From Akira Club (this page and over).

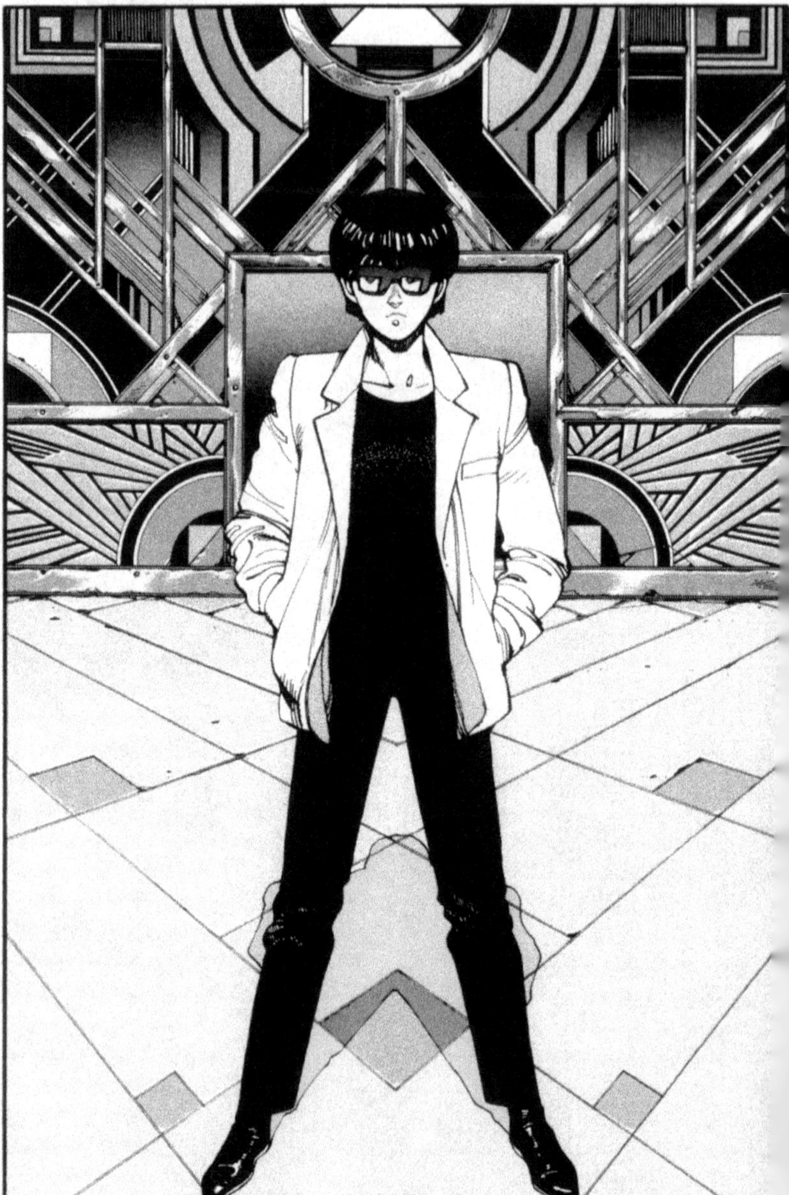

06

THEMES AND ISSUES

SOME INFLUENCES AND ALLUSIONS.
Katsuhiro Otomo has acknowledged *Astro Boy* and
Tetsujin 28 as influences on *Akira*. *Tetsujin 28*
(*Gigantor* in the West) ran from 1956 to 1966,
published by Kobunsha (the TV *animé* (from T.C.J.
Animation Center, dir. Yonehiko Watanabe & Tadao
Wakabayashi, 1963), ran from 1963 onwards for 4
seasons (96 episodes). Written by Mitsuteru Yokoyama, it featured the boy Shotaro Kaneda who
controlled the giant robot, number 28. *Tetsujin 28*
was a big inspiration on subsequent robot shows.)

References to *Gigantor* crop up in *Akira* – Kaneda,
for instance, is named after Shotaro Kaneda in
Tetsujin 28, and also Tetsuo, Ryusaku and Shikishima, Akira's codename is '28' (28 appears in many
places in *Akira*), and the Colonel is the son of one of
the scientists of the original project of Akira.

What can you compare *Akira* to? Really, it stands
on its own. It exists in its own cinematic space, like
The Color of Pomegranates (Sergei Paradjanov, 1969),
or *Vampyr* (Carl-Theodore Dreyer, 1932), or *Sunrise*
(F.W. Murnau, 1927). The depiction of young punks at
large has links to *A Clockwork Orange*, *The Outsiders*,
Rumble Fish, *West Side Story*, *The Wild One*, *Easy*

Rider, and *The Warriors;* the apocalyptic and post-apocalyptic *milieu* is reminiscent of *The Road Warrior* and *The Omega Man;* the bikers riding around evokes samurai movies and Akira Kurosawa's cinema; and the hi-tech, cyberpunk ingredients recall *Star Wars, Alien, 2001: A Space Odyssey,* and *Blade Runner.*

But, it's the *mix* of all those elements, plus many of its own devising, that makes *Akira* unique, un-repeatable, and very special. Talking about influences (such as from some of the above movies) only explains part of the movie. *Akira* is a genuine work of art, despite having 100s of people working on it (look at the long list of contributors in the closing credits!), and it carves its own niche in the cultural landscape.

If there's an X-factor, *Akira* has it in spades.

❖

Films of the Vietnam War era, such as *Five Easy Pieces, Bonnie & Clyde,* and *Easy Rider,* were touch-stones for Otomo-sensei. There's a reference to *Snow White* in the baby room (it's one of the *tableaux* on the walls; this may also be an allusion to the 1937 Walt Disney movie; it makes sense to reference the first North American animated feature in this ground-breaking, Japanese animated picture).

Dr Strangelove (1963) is a movie allusion in *Akira*: the design of one politico in the political debate scene definitely evokes George C. Scott's unforgett-ably out-size performance as the hawk Buck Turgid-son[1] – and the table in that scene is of course circular, as in *Strangelove*. When you're dealing with crazy politics in movies, particularly with a nuclear edge, *Dr Strangelove* is often referenced (other movies that nod to the 1963 Columbia movie include *The War Games, 1941, James Bond, Star Wars,* and of course the finest Western television show ever, *The Simpsons*).

There are a number of references to *A Clockwork Orange* (1971) in *Akira* – such as the Clowns crew (Alex and his droogs dressed up in masks), the rival motorcycle gang, the rivalry between the gangs, the

1 President Muffley is in there, too.

deserted theatre (actually called Star Bowling – it's in the *manga*), glimpsed behind one of the Clowns bikers as Tetsuo and Kaori hurtle past on Kaneda's bike (Alex and the droogs enjoy some ultraviolence with Billy-boy's gang in an abandoned theatre or casino in *Clockwork*).

Akira, tho', is a far more sophisticated piece of cinema (stylistically as well as ideologically) than the 1971 movie *A Clockwork Orange* (you could regard Katsuhiro Otomo as a Japanese Stanley Kubrick – tho' his movies are much warmer emotionally, and funnier, too).

Another influence on *Akira* is *The Demolished Man* by Alfred Bester, a sci-fi classic from 1953. Katsuhiro Otomo produced a *manga* entitled *Fireball* which was influenced by *The Demolished Man*, which he didn't finish; but he did re-use elements from *Fireball* in *Akira* (every *manga* artist re-cycles earlier works, especially ones that weren't published or completed). Among the elements in *Fireball* that turned up in *Akira* were the freedom fighters, the violent street demos, the government experiments, the psychics as superheroes, the infiltration of the psychic facility (in disguise), etc.

The film *Japan's Longest Day* (1963) may also have been an influence on *Akira*. The postwar vision of Poland after WWII in the *Ashes and Diamonds* trilogy of the 1950s (a film school favourite), may also be an inspiration.

The influence of *Akira* can be discerned in many places, in both Western and Asian art.[2] *Akira* has influenced numerous *animé*, including *Genocyber* (1993),[3] *Appleseed, Boah, Darkside Blues, Doomed Megalopolis, Toshinden, Serial Experiments Lain* (dir. Ryutaro Nakamura, 1998), *Lucy* (starring Scarlett

---

2 *Fist of the North Star* (1984) was a show that benefitted from *Akira*'s success overseas (and the *Fist* revamp of 2003 (by Takashi Watanabe) drew on *Akira*'s biker gangs).

3 A scene involving an aircraft carrier being taken over in *Genocyber* comes from *Akira*. And there's an *hommage* in *Hellsing*.

Johansson), and *Ghost In the Shell*.[4] *Sky Blue* (a.k.a. *Wonderful Days*, Kim Moon-saeng, 2003) is a Korean, C.G. movie pastiche of *Akira* (see appendix).

Otomo-sensei's influence can also be discerned in *manga* such as *Genocyber* (Tony Takezaki, 1991-93, in *Comic Nova*), *Godzilla* (Kazuhisa Iwata, 1985), *Hellhounds: Panzer Corps* (1988-90, in *Amazing Comics*), *Shion: Blade of the Minstrel* by Yu Kinutani (Sansheisha, 1988), *Hellsing* by Kohta Hirano (1997-2008), *Who Fighter With Heart of Darkness* by Seiho Takizawa (*Model Graphix*, 2004), *Project Arms* (Kyoichi Nanatsuki and Ryoji Minagawa, 1997-2002), *Raika* (Yu Terashima and Kamui Fujiwara/ Studio 28, 1992-97), *Naruto* (Masashi Kishimoto, 1999-2014), *Bleach* (Tite Kubo, 2001-16) and *A.D. Police* (1989-90). As Jason Thompson put it, *Akira* was 'the manga equivalent of a big-budget science-fiction movie' (284).

NARUTO AND AKIRA.

Masashi Kishimoto (b. 1974), creator of the astonishing *Naruto* franchise (200 million-plus copies sold!), is a huge fan of *Akira* and Katsuhiro Otomo (*Akira* is his favourite film). Kishimoto recalls obtaining storyboards from *Akira* and copying them endlessly as a teen. In his notes in *Naruto*, Kishimoto recalls being gobsmacked by a poster for *Akira*.

The influence of *Akira* can be discerned throughout the *Naruto manga*, from the designs of the villains (and their sometimes hysterical outbursts), to the depiction of the landscapes and even the explosions and the catastrophes. Several times in *Naruto*, for instance, Masashi Kishimoto draws huge, spherical objects (formed by ninja magic) which reference the Akira sphere (numerous other visual elements in *Naruto* draw on *Akira* – such as the clouds spinning, the waves of energy, and of course the emphasis on drawing every tiny detail).

---

4 Even down to the red leathers worn by Motoko Kusanagi in *Ghost In the Shell: Arise*.

The body of Gaara, the sand ninja, becomes deformed, like Tetsuo in *Akira* (Gaara, a fierce rival for Naruto until Naruto teaches him the value of the family and love, also evokes Tetsuo in his murderous rages).

In *Naruto*, brothers and rivals are a *big* deal. Yes, this is a staple of Japanese *animé* and *manga* (especially in *shonen manga*, where rivals are mandatory), but the rivalry between Naruto and Sasuke (the obvious example, but there are many others), clearly evokes that between Tetsuo and Kaneda (Naruto is a similar characterization, too: like Kaneda, he's non-intellectual (not great at school work), out-spoken, has boundless energy, is brave, a bit too loud and crude, but he has a heart of gold. And Naruto is the soul and centre of the piece).

Also, both Naruto and Kaneda are natural leaders, with an effortless charisma. And both do their bit in redeeming and humanizing their rivals (Kaneda with Tetsuo, and Naruto with many characters, such as Obito and Jiraiya, as well as, of course, with Sasuke). Even details like Naruto's famous, bright orange costume might be an *hommage* by Masashi Kishimoto to Kaneda's red, motorcycle leathers.[5]

CITIES IN *AKIRA* AND *METROPOLIS*.

Akira takes up the visual evocation of the futuristic city[6] as a multi-level environment that the great, German movie *Metropolis* developed so vividly (Katsuhiro Otomo wrote the screenplay for the 2001 updated *animé Metropolis* – in a way, Otomo's version of *Metropolis* is more his follow-up to *Akira* than *Steam-boy*). Thus, much of the life in

---

5 Let's not forget, tho', that Kishimoto-sensei has also cited influences on *Naruto* such as *Dragon Ball* and *Dr Slump* (both by Akira Toriyama), *Blade of the Immortal* (by Hiroaki Samura), *Ruroni Kenshin* (a.k.a., *Samurai X*, by Nobuhiro Watsuki), and *One Piece* (by Eiichiro Oda).

6 The metropolis was perhaps *the* site of cyberpunk fiction, urban conglomerates that swallowed up other cities (as in *Akira*, *Neuromancer* and *Blade Runner*), cities in crisis, urban dystopias.

Japan's capital in *Akira* occurs up in the skyscrapers, and in walkways, bridges, tunnels and upper levels built high above the streets. The scene where the gang is hanging about, bored and listless, while the girls gather nearby and mope, takes place high up in a recreation area, which includes a fountain, stairways, trees and gardens.

And *Akira* is also a version of *Metropolis* in other respects: the city of the future that's falling apart, that is corrupt within, that is riven with class conflict. *Metropolis* stylized social and political conflicts in a rather simplistic, dualistic fashion in the 1920s, reminiscent of the Eloi and the Morlocks in *The Time Machine*, the H.G. Wells novel

Yet, for all its political corruption, its martial law, its oppressive regime, and its run-down and poverty-stricken zones, the city of Neo-Tokyo in *Akira* is also celebrated. The scenes of the city at night from a distance are meant to be ecstatic and visionary (in both the *manga* and the *animé*) – the modern city as a sea of lights[7] (especially in the scenes of the biker gang in full flight, or of Tetsuo flying over the city). The glamour and magic of the contemporary city, even a city falling into the abyss, is palpable throughout *Akira*. The crater looms darkly in the background, true, but the city is still regarded as home (even by the disaffected youths). It might be falling apart, as Kaneda might put it, but it's *our city*.

It was the integration of the city and its life with the story and characters that impressed Helen McCarthy about *Akira*, how it included the whole hierarchy of society from the leaders and scientists to the hobos and homeless. 'There have been films as good, but few as dazzling, and few that have attempted so much and succeeded so far', McCarthy noted in *The Anime Movie Guide* (75).

---

7 It's the view from the Empire State Building, from Griffith Observatory in L.A., or Hong Kong harbour, or from the CN Tower in Toronto.

YOUTH VS. AGE.

Like many youth pictures, *Akira* is also a rite-of-passage movie, a rebel without a cause movie, a youth vs. age movie, a movie where young people find out just how complex, ambiguous, corrupt and dangerous the adult world, the real world, is. The story of *Akira* focusses on both Tetsuo and Kaneda to explore the issues of kids growing up and moving into a larger world. That's one reason why *Akira* is so successful: it's not only a giant action movie and fantasy movie and a triumph of animation, it's also a movie with a powerful basis in the psychology and relationships of young people. It's about teenagers who rebel against their parents and the older generation, about how they resent them, make fun of them, and kick against them when they can (notice how there are no parents depicted for Kaneda, Kai, Kei or the rest of the teen charas; instead, the movie focusses on the youngsters and their gangs. The parental generation comprises authority figures such as the Colonel and the scientist, Doctor Ônishi. The two older men embody the military-industrial complex. We don't need to see the parents of these wild, disaffected kids – we can imagine what they're like. Except, that is, for Tetsuo's folks – and when they leave Tetsuo at school, he interprets it as abandonment).

Akira is about the sins of the Fathers, how the older generation visits its mistakes, its fears and desires, on the younger generation. It's about how the older generation exploits the younger generation (cynically, thoughtlessly, and sometimes cruelly – they have forgotten what it was like to be a child). It's about how the older generation lies and cheats and hides its sinister sides (burying them far underground, for instance – a terrific image of literally hiding your head in the sand, of submerging your mistakes and failures deep in the Earth).[8]

The conflict between youth and old age crops up in the dialogue often in *Akira* – Kaneda calls the cop

8 Otomo returned to this burial motif in *The Legend of Mother Sarah*.

in the interrogation scene an old man, and he retorts, furious, that he's only 25! (though he looks older). But 25 to Kaneda is *ancient* (remember when being 25 seemed fossilized?). That the child psychics look old beyond their years is a visual embodiment of the theme. Their youth is stolen by the older generation (we see this in the flashback sequence in the movie, where the children don't enjoy a regular childhood, but are living in a special facility. There is more of this in the *manga*, but the essence is the same).

Akira also employs the familiar science fiction trope of scientists meddling with powers they don't quite understand, powers which release immense energy and side effects. It's *Frankenstein* again, it's World War Two and the urge towards atomic energy, it's advanced capitalism doing stuff just because it can, regardless of the consequences. That the scientific experiments in *Akira*'re being conducted on children and young people is a method of enhancing the drama, but it also helps to focus the moral and ethical issues. When you make the victims of scientific experiments children, you go for maximum emotion and sentiment. If you turn the victims into, say, professional soldiers, you don't have the same dramatic juice.

JAPAN SELF-DEFENCE FORCES.

It's worth noting that *Akira* takes place entirely in Japan, and almost entirely in Tokyo (or Neo-Tokyo as it's dubbed). There are a coupla moments where Tetsuo flies up to satellites or the moon, and the odd time where (what appears to be) an overseas location is visited (like the astronomical observatory, in the 'ravage the moon' sequence). But this is a Japanese story, about the Japanese people, set in Japan (and, as with many *animé* and *manga*, other parts of the world come to Japan: Americans, Russians and Chinese).

Akira leaves out references to Japan's Self Defence Force (Jietai). There are 247,000 members of the Japan Self Defence Forces, which includes 5 armies, 3 air defence forces, and 5 maritime districts. The military budget (in 2011) was $56 billion (1% of GDP; Russia, China, Germany, Britain, France and the U.S.A. all spend more on the military). The Prime Minister is the Commander-in-Chief.

The role of the Japan Self Defence Forces – created in 1954 by the Diet (the name for the Japanese government) – was defined (by the U.S.A. and the Allies), following Japan's defeat in World War Two as a military force that would provide defence for Japan; that could not be deployed overseas; that had to stay within Japan's islands; that could not develop nuclear weapons; that could not become a major military power or initiate hostilities; and that would have its arms exports limited.

There has been much debate over exactly what the Japan Self Defence Forces can or should do, and even how they are defined. The agreement, for instance, states that 'land, sea, and air forces, as well as other war potential, will never be maintained' (the 1947 Constitution forbade Japan having an army).

In *Akira*, Katsuhiro Otomo has opted to leave aside some of the aspects of the Japan Self-Defence Force, but at the same time he has consciously fore-grounded the debates over the controversial treaty with the U.S.A. and the West (which was part of the political unrest of the early 1960s, coalescing around the 1964 Olympics).

The 'Great Tokyo Empire' in *Akira* is thus a satire on what some of the Japanese population believe or endorse. That is, there are plenty of people in Japan who passionately resent the treaty which forbids Japan to exert its military power.

And in *Akira*, a Japanese teenager attacks a United States Navy aircraft carrier! And sets off a nuclear warhead! Talk about wish-fulfilment! – And he triumphs.

BODIES IN TRANSFORMATION.
As in *Legend of the Overfiend, Hellsing, Ninja*

Scroll, Basilisk, Nurarihyon's Grandson, Soul Eater
and other *animé*, the bodies in *Akira* are constantly
changing, twisting, contorting, oozing. Sweat, vomit,
tears, and plenty of blood are erupting all over the
place. In the 1980s, these were called 'body horror'
movies, in live-action, and included the movies
directed by David Cronenberg, Wes Craven, Dario
Argento and John Carpenter (like *The Thing* remake,
the *Alien* series, *Altered States, The Fly, Virus, Video-
drome, Eraserhead*, etc), movies where the human
body is feared, loathed, torn to pieces, and transformed grotesquely. Here, the body was in crisis,
under attack, undergoing unwanted and sometimes
horrific alterations. And it's significant that it's often
the *men's* bodies in 'body horror' movies (including
Akira) that are the site of terror, ambivalence, and
desire (they're also called 'masculinity in crisis'
movies).

An equivalent for the body horror and masochism and anxiety over the human-technology interface
in *Akira* is also reflected in the totally wild *Tetsuo*
movies (Shinya Tsukamoto, both 1991), which enact
bizarre horrors in live-action out of *Eraserhead* or
David Cronenberg, but *way* stranger (and the movie
Tetsuo is from the same era as *Akira*).

The bodies of Tetsuo in *Akira* and the youths in
the *Legend of the Overfiend* movies seldom stay fixed
in one state for long. They're bursting out in every
direction: the men strike superhero poses, or writhe in
agony as they're transformed, or they send out
octopus feelers into the air. The men're often half-
dressed, displaying manly torsos.

However, transformation is an absolutely fundamental concept in animation, and has been since its
beginnings in the early 1900s. Animation has *always*
portrayed transformations, and human bodies are
the favourite site of depicting change (for all of the
obvious reasons. I mean, everybody's got a body,
right? If you're alive, you're always *in* a body,
right?).

Also, Western/ North American movies and the 'body horror' movies are only part of the picture: Japanese culture, going back to *Kabuki* theatre and the woodblock prints of the 18th/ 19th centuries, has a tradition of depicting extreme or graphic scenes, including violence, death and sex. Masses of blood and severed limbs are part of a tradition which embraces Grand Guignol theatrical effects (as well as the high theatricality of horror), plus heightened, operatic emotions. So the movement towards extremes in feelings, violence and horror is part of a very long tradition in Japan (and all of Katsuhiro Otomo's work reflects that, not only *Akira*).

TEENAGE ANGST.

The crisis in the youths in *Akira* and the *Urotsukidoji* series and similar *animé* exaggerates emotions, fears, anxieties and desires up to the level of superhero battles and 300-foot tall demons. This crisis over masculinity is expressed in extraordinary scenes of masochism and sadomasochism (Tetsuo in *Akira* exhibits both masochistic and sadistic behaviour). While the right-wing lobby and the left-liberal lobby can correctly go nuts over the rape of women in the *Urotsukidoji* series (and the partial rape in *Akira*) – because the rape (of anyone) is a crime against life itself – there is also a disturbing amount of masochism and self-loathing in *Akira* and in the *Legend of the Overfiend* universe (and in other *animé*, such as *Ghost In the Shell: Stand Alone Complex, Death Note, Eden of the East, Evangelion, Vampire Knight, Ninja Scroll, Fullmetal Alchemist* and the works of Satoshi Kon).

The cries of loneliness, of the inability to express oneself, of the angst of being young and misunderstood, is passionately and brilliantly expressed in *Akira* and the *Urotsukidoji* series (you can also find those feelings in (in addition to the shows cited above): *Gunbuster, Paranoia Agent, Gantz, Blade of the Immortal, Naruto, xxxHolic, Lain, The Qwaser of*

Stigmata, Berserk, and *Escaflowne* – the lost, angsty teenager and outsider is a recurring figure in Japanese pop culture – the embodiment of the post-WW2 generation). While no one would mistake these *animés* for being sensitive explorations of male psychology in the manner of quiet, sombre films by Ingmar Bergman or Carl-Theodor Dreyer (!), they definitely address many of the same issues (indeed, in some of the finer *anime* outings there is a level of dramatic and psycho-logical sophistication that goes beyond even Bergman or Dreyer, or the other famous explorers of the damaged psyche in the history of cinema).

Akira and Katsuhiro Otomo certainly under-stand teenagers very well, and can express their concerns beautifully. But it's not only that the kids in Japanese fantasy animation rip themselves to pieces, or are torn to shreds by forces outside of themselves that they can't control, it's also that these young men are like black holes, and they suck in people around them, so that the damage can be enormous. Those near them are affected by their behaviour and nega-tive feelings. If these young guys went off to some distant, desert planet and fought it out, maybe it would be better (which's what we would like polit-icians and authorities around the world to do – just go someplace far away and fight it out and leave the rest of us to get on with living).

What *anime* of this masculinity-in-crisis kind also does is to reveal the creepy double standards that exist in contemporary society and culture. And how low self-esteem and self-loathing, particularly among young characters, is a significant ingredient in Japanese animation.

TECHNOLOGY VS. HUMANITY.

One could discuss at length the significance of technology, technofetishism, cyborgs, robots and hybrid lifeforms in *Akira*, in the light of the theories of Donna Haraway, Paul Virillio or Slavoj Zizek or numerous other theorists – you know the theories: the

'return of the repressed', the undead, zombies, ghosts
in the machine, animated machines, dolls, puppets,
computers with souls, the uncanny, etc etc etc... but as
I've already done that elsewhere, I'll leave it up to
other writers.[9]

Also, *Akira* is such an *intelligent* movie, it
contains *its own self-analysis*: that is, as the picture
plays, it is also examining itself, and providing a
commentary for the audience upon issues such as
humanity vs. technology (which's one of Otomo-
sensei's recurring themes), science vs. the military,
science vs. capitalism, and in particular the mis-use of
science and technology by people who should know
better.

What comes across very powerfully in *Akira* is
that the groups and institutions who have the money,
the resources and the power to develop technology, in
super-capitalist states such as Japan, Germany or the
U.S.A., seem unable to resist mis-using it (that is,
Germany, Japan, U.S.A., Britain, etc, are the very
people you *don't* want to see with vast power!). In
Katsuhiro Otomo's view, even when people begin
with good intentions, pursuing the heights of technological advancement too often results in anxiety at the
very least, and can also lead to catastrophe. Of
course, Otomo's stories are *exaggerating* existing
issues for the sake of drama and effect, but the issues
are already there in advanced, capitalist societies
(otherwise the story in *Akira* wouldn't have such an
impact).

WOMEN IN *AKIRA*.

No one can miss the fact that *Akira* in both movie
and *manga* form is very masculinist, very macho, and
very boysy. Yet, in amongst the motorcycle gangs, the
braggadocio, the ultraviolence, the tonnage of *mecha*,
the explosions, chases and full-on action, there *are*
some strong female characters: Kei, above all, the

9 See, for instance, D. Haraway's "A Manifesto For Cyborgs",
Primate Visions (Routledge, London, 1989), and *Simians, Cyborgs, and
Women* (Routledge, London, 1991).

feisty, independent, sensible, courageous and kind-hearted heroine, the necessary antidote to the eternal and restless teenage wrangling between Tetsuo and Kaneda. In the second half of the *Akira manga,* Kei becomes a fully-fledged action heroine, and it's very satisfying to see (Kei is also a more ruthless operator than Kaneda, and kills more victims). There is also Lady Miyako, the ageing psychic and venerated Mother Theresa to the sick and wounded in Neo-Tokyo, one of the authority figures in the region. And there's Kaori, the shy, awkward, nervous and plain girl who becomes a helpmeet for Tetsuo and nurse-maid to super-being Akira. Kiyoko, a psychic like Miyako, seems to be a satire on certain strains of femininity, but she is also brave and resourceful (and, from her invalid's bed, she is often the commander among the three psychics in Colonel Shikishima's protection). And not forgetting the giant bodyguard to Kei, Chiyoko, a female warrior, quiet, implacable, loyal, and tough as granite.

Some critics (such as Helen McCarthy) have seen in the way that women're depicted in *Akira* a more mature and non-sexist or non-stereotypical treatment of women. Maybe. Maybe the portrayal of Kaori, who's beaten in the first act, does depart from conventional cinema: her battered, bruised appearance following the near-rape is distinctly 'realistic', and very disturbing.[10] Feminists, however, could easily point out that not only is Kaori threatened, attacked and nearly raped, she dies in the final scenes, yet Kaneda survives (and maybe Tetsuo sort of does). That Kaori dies – and in trying to help Tetsuo – seems especially cruel on the part of the filmmakers (but her death in the *manga* of *Akira* is equally vicious – shot in the back, unprovoked and totally unnecessarily, by Tetsuo's aide. In the old, chivalrous days of Hollywood, shooting a woman in the back was pretty mean, and usually justified punishment).

---

10 A bunch of thugs kicking an innocent, unarmed woman on the ground is revolting. But it occurs elsewhere in *manga* and *animé*.

However, there is a realist (or pessimistic) streak in Katsuhiro Otomo's work: it acknowledges that humans are capable of acts many would interpret as cruel and pointless. You can analyze those senseless acts of cruelty from moral, psychological, social, ideological, etc viewpoints, but they continue, and have been a part of every period of human history.

AN APOCALYPTIC EPIC.

Akira doesn't disappoint as an action film: lots of motorbike chases, fights between rival biker gangs, gun battles (though not too many), a big fight inside a sewer with flying sleds, and extraordinary scenes of destruction as Tetsuo, lasers and then Akira chew up Japan's capital.

And there's a genuinely epic dimension in *Akira*, which's lacking in many action-adventure films ('big' doesn't mean 'epic'). *Akira* is certainly as big, loud, pacey (and silly) as the best action-adventure movies, but there's a genuine, mythic grandeur to the picture. It might seem to derive partly from *Akira* being animation: it can be much more extravagant, visually, than a live-action film, it can go places, use camera angles and compositions, that are impossible in live-action (even with CG embellishments).

But no, that's not it: live-action can include matte paintings and models as well as real vistas to suggest grandeur and scale. Rather, in visual terms, it's to do with the manipulation of scale, perspective, distance and atmospheric effects; it's the visual genius that artists such as J.M.W Turner and Gustave Doré wielded for making even an everyday scene seem so much larger and more grandiose. Look at the long shot of the end of the tunnels which lead out onto the bridge in *Akira*: there is an impressive feeling of immense *scale* in that image – it's akin to the images of the Swiss Alps that Turner sketched in the 1820s, or the pictures of Hell in the *Divine Comedy* drawn by Doré in the 1880s.

Like many sci-fi films of the 1980s, *Akira*

explored a post-apocalyptic society, a social break-down combined with draconian measures to keep the populace in place, with the military taking over from politicians in policing the city. *Akira* pitted young motorbike gangs against the military-industrial complex, against scientists, committees and generals.

Nuclear holocaust haunts *Akira*, reflecting the time of its creation – the mid-1980s, when anxiety over an escalation of arms resulting in an atomic conflict was intense. There's also a disturbing under-current in *Akira,* because it's made in and set in modern Japan, the only country (thus far) that has been bombed by nuclear weapons. This gives the images at the beginning and the end of *Akira*, of a colossal hemisphere of white light that expands outwards and eats up the city, an added *frisson* of despair and horror. For Freda Frieberg, *Akira* expresses 'the post nuclear sublime', a national experience of nuclear disaster which gripped Japan even more than the West (1996).

The anxieties and challenges of nuclear power and atomic warfare haunt so much of Japanese animation and fantasy filmmaking – from *Godzilla* in the 1950s onwards. *Akira* is very much a part of that sub-genre of Japanese cinema (in animation, some classics of nuclear warfare and WW2 in both a realistic and a fantastical context include *Barefoot Gen, Grave of the Fireflies, Nausicaä of the Valley of the Wind, Fullmetal Alchemist, Howl's Moving Castle* and *Legend of the Overfiend*. There is also a significant sub-genre of *animé* which replays the Pacific War in different, often science fiction settings:*Gunbuster, Darling In the Franxx, Patlabor, Escaflowne, Evangelion, Macross, Full Metal Panic, Nausicaä* again, etc. (And there's another sub-genre which has Japan (or Germany) winning WWII).[11]

The apocalyptic scenarios of Japanese animation clearly derive in part from the experience of having two atomic bombs dropped on Japan in aggression –

11 Such as *Jin-Roh: The Wolf Brigade* (2000).

the only time that nuclear weapons have been employed in war (so far).

Other reasons for the apocalyptic nature of Japanese animation would be the economic problems after the stock market collapse of 1989; a disenchantment with the traditional values and goals of post-war Japan; the alienation and loneliness of urban living; and growing tensions between men and women, and between the generations (S. Napier, 29). And Japan experiences 100s of earthquakes a year.

Although science fiction is one of the genres of *Akira*, and it is often placed in that genre (sometimes with fantasy included), with its story of telekinetic children and explosive powers, there is plenty of the horror genre in there, too (as well as the high school melodrama, the youth rebellion genre, the crime thriller, and the political conspiracy thriller). Horror – Tetsuo's predicament contains numerous horror genre ingredients, from his nightmares and hallucinations to the violent deaths he inflicts on those who oppose him (there're even more in the *Akira manga*). And Tetsuo's experience is a continuous cycle of horrific suffering, which combines elements of the 'body horror' genre, the drug addiction genre, and the rebel without a cause genre.

AKIRA AND THE SUBLIME.

Akira is one of a number of science fiction films which emphasized the sublime: *2001: A Space Odyssey*[12] is the obvious case, but also the films helmed by Steven Spielberg (*Close Encounters of the Third Kind, Jurassic Park, A.I., E.T.*), *Star Trek, Star Wars, Solaris, Nausicaä, Metropolis, Avatar, Blade Runner* and *The Abyss* (five of those movies are

---

12 The sublime had always been a part of cinema (from early films such as *Intolerance* onwards), but after *2001: A Space Odyssey*, it became an essential ingredient of sci-fi and fantasy films (think of *Star Wars, Close Encounters of the Third Kind, Blade Runner, Total Recall, Independence Day* and *The Fifth Element*). *2001: A Space Odyssey* set the precedent for the sublime in sci-fi films, for gigantic scale, infinite distances, mysteries, long, elaborate shots, and complex special effects.

consciously alluded to in *Akira).*

For a useful guide to the sublime in cinema, art critic Christopher Hussey defined seven aspects of the sublime (in art), derived from critic Edmund Burke: (1) obscurity (physical and intellectual); (2) power; (3) privations (such as darkness, solitude, silence); (4) vastness (vertical or horizontal); (5) infinity; (6) succession; and (7) uniformity (the last two suggest limitless progression).[13]

These tenets of the sublime in art can be applied to cinema – to films such as *Intolerance, Faust* (1926), *Blade Runner, Ghost In the Shell, Urotsukidoji, 2001: A Space Odyssey, Citizen Kane* and *Apocalypse Now*, movies which consciously encourage notions such as obscurity, darkness, vastness and infinity. Meanwhile, *Akira* is virtually a 'Guide To the Sublime In Cinema', running through the seven tenets of the sublime of Christopher Hussey, and adding some inventions of its own.

In the history of painting, the sublime can be found in landscape painters such as J.M.W. Turner, John Martin and Thomas Cole, with their grand visions of mountains and ancient civilizations, up to the 'Abstract Sublime' of the Abstract Expressionists, in particular Barnett Newman and Mark Rothko, who made huge canvases of single colours, or two or three hues combined. Theirs was a self-consciously religious art, deliberately mythic and heroic, with transcendent, timeless and tragic subject matter. Their art culminated in the enormous, austere and very dark paintings in the Rothko Chapel in Houston, and Newman's ascetic *Stations of the Cross* series. The more 'sublime' reaches of Abstract Expressionism have a melodramatic, operatic quality, which seems to be reaching for something it is not equipped either to grasp or to put to use. It is an art of striving or Nietzschean 'becoming', and this journey towards transcendence sometimes produces paintings that are so self-consciously 'sublime', 'epic' and 'heroic' that

13 C. Hussey: *The Picturesque*, Putnam's, New York, 1927.

they fall into bathos or fascism.

RELIGION AND SPIRITUALITY IN *AKIRA*.

The *Akira manga,* even more than the 1988 animated movie, contrasts different forms of religion, cults and beliefs.[14] For instance, the Buddhist temple run by Lady Miyako is very prominent in Katsuhiro Otomo's *manga*, and becomes a major location in the second half of the *manga* series, and is contrasted with the ramshackle, nationalistic, post-punk cult that develops around Tetsuo and Akira (the religion of Japan, Shinto, meanwhile, is relegated to the background. Yet it's always there. Even when it's derided or ignored, Shinto is still the religion of Japan. The ending of the *Akira* movie certainly expresses some Shinto tenets).

Steeped in Shintoism and Buddhism, the use of Christian and pagan/ occult imagery and motifs in *animé* reflects a flirtation with foreign, religious influences which typically occur in teenage (the Christian wedding ceremony, for instance, or *Harry Potter*-esque occultism and Greek mythology).

Animé will take motifs and symbols from all sorts of places, often just for the look or the feel, disregarding the theological, religious or cultural attributes (and often lifted from foreign movies). As long as it looks exotic and other-worldly, that's cool. Thus, the Star of David is employed without the filmmakers seeming to be aware of its enormous cultural and religious significance (characters that're as right-wing as Nazis will employ the Star of David in their rituals without realizing it!). It's the same with cruciform and angelic imagery.[15] (A whole subcategory of *animé* and *manga* is mad about Catholic iconography – angels, crosses, churches, priests, etc – usually deploying them in preposterous, sinister and OTT scenarios).

---

14 'When anime uses religion as a story element, it is usually because of its ability to generate conflict,' note J. Clements and H. McCarthy (2006, 533).
15 *Death Note* is a classic example of the flirtation with religion among teenage characters.

There is a strong messianic, religious strand to *Akira*: a project experimenting with telepathy and supernormal powers in children goes out of control. One of the Capsules biker gang members, Tetsuo, becomes super-powerful, in the traditional *animé* fashion (which means lots of superhero devastation); and, at the end of the 1988 film, in the apocalyptic climax, the real, long-awaited Akira arrives – glimpsed as a young boy enveloped in white light (we spend much more time with li'l Akira in the *Akira manga*, yet we know just as little about him).

YOU'RE NOT GOING TO BLOW UP TOKYO AGAIN?!

For Mamoru Oshii[16] (*Ghost In the Shell, Patlabor*), it shouldn't be so easy to destroy an entire city, as in *Akira*:

> The most frustrating thing I feel when I watch movies such as *Akira* is that they destroy Tokyo so easily. If you depict it as a city which you won't miss even if it were destroyed, as a fake thing made from only steel and concrete from the beginning, destroying it won't accomplish anything. It's far from being a real catharsis. Even in Tokyo, if you look carefully, if you dig up your memories, you can find some scenery which you are very much attracted to. It can be the evening at the train crossing, or it can be scenery of some vacant land with Seitaka-awadachisou in Tokyo Bay area.[17]

In *Akira*, though, the cataclysms have a strong ideological as well as psychological underpinning: this is not simply carnage for the sake of carnage. In your average sci-fi *animé* series, you do have stuff blowing up with little true resonance. But *Akira* earns

16 I wonder if Oshii, a major dog lover, disliked *Akira* because dogs are shot in it!
17 Yes, but Mamoru Oshii blows up plenty of Tokyo in *Patlabor 2* (1993), including many of its bridges! And some of the films directed by Oshii are influenced by *Akira* (even if Oshii himself *isn't* influenced by *Akira,* many in the production teams are).

its right to devastate Tokyo, so to speak, because it is making important points about humanity's Faustian bargain with science and technology (indeed, *Akira* is one of the most thematically rich of *animé* movies – the number of issues and themes it evokes is very impressive).

As well as the atom bombing of Japan, and WW2, and the Pacific War, another cataclysm has influenced Japanese animation – the Great Kanto Earthquake of 1923 (and the subsequent fires). The earthquake crops up in *animé* such as *The Wind Rises, Oshin, Doomed Megalopolis, Urotsukidoji* and *Smart-san* (Japan is one of the most earthquake-prone countries in the world, with about 1,000 earthquakes a year. And Tokyo is right in the middle of a volatile area. There are memorials to Kanto in Japan. So a Japanese audience seeing such gargantuan destruction in animation would be familiar with it in a realistic respect – having probably felt seismic tremors themselves).

Of all the carnage and destruction in Japanese *animé* – and there are *huge amounts* of it – you have to admit that the movies directed by Katsuhiro Otomo are among the wildest and densest.[18] Nobody puts more stuff blowing up, cracking, shattering, falling and crashing in their movies than Otomo-sensei (or more lovingly – this is lovingly destructive filmmaking). Ignore the story and the characters and the themes in *Akira* and you'll see a movie where something is exploding or being torn to bits every five minutes. Same with *Steam-boy*. And *Memories*. And *Roujin Z*. And *Spriggan*. The movies directed by (or supervised by) Otomo are simply obsessed with watching stuff splinter, shatter and smash. (And when he can't put devastation on film, he puts it in his comics – in *Domu* and *The Legend of Mother Sarah*, for

18 Others would include *One Piece, Hellsing Ultimate, Fairy Tail, Bleach, Appleseed* and Hayao Miyazaki's movies.

ex).

AKIRA AND HOMOSEXUALITY.

How is Tetsuo Shima first introduced in *Akira*? It says it all, if we use the crude simplifications of pop psychology: he is sitting on Kaneda's bike, and marvelling at the features and extras it has.[19] No need for your *Sigmund Freud Psychology 101* text-book here, we know what's going on! Tetsuo is sitting astride a big, shiny, red machine, drooling over it! That only Kaneda can handle! A machine that is heavily fetishized in the movie (and the *manga*)!

The elements of homoeroticism are there in *Akira*, if you want to acknowledge them at the level of caricature and popular cliché (between Tetsuo and Kaneda, but also some of the other characters). Male, heterosexual audiences of *animé* and *manga* may resist homoerotic interpretations of their favourite fictions,[20] but there is of course a category of Japanese *animé* devoted to it, called *shonen ai* and *yaoi* (however, the audience for *shonen ai*, dubbed 'pretty boys in pain' by Helen McCarthy,[21] is mainly female. 'Pretty boys in pain' actually describes a good proportion of *manga* and *animé*).

Tetsuo and Kaneda aren't gay lovers (they are both given girlfriends, for instance), but the homoerotic subtext in *Akira* is of the order of cowboy cinema, or gangster cinema, or military/ war cinema, where buddies become so close they're like blood brothers, action men who're loyal, who fight alongside each other.

The two girlfriends in *Akira* are contrasted with each other (Kaneda has two girls, actually). But

---

19 But, jeez, Tetsuo has a pretty cool motorcycle himself, and he's an amazing rider. So what's he complaining about? Simple: he's not the leader, he's not looked up to by the others in the gang, his self-esteem is *low*. Tetsuo, in short, has flaws, vulnerabilities and weak spots which won't be solved by getting a brand new bike just like Kaneda's (capitalist consumerism won't help), or getting that fantastic girlfriend, or being the captain of the gang. Tetsuo's problems are way deeper and more complex than that.
20 But lesbians getting it on is just fine – especially naked.
21 H McCarthy, 1998, 32.

notice too that Kei and Kaori are not sexualized along conventional dramatic lines: Kei is tomboyish, practical, and independent, with high ideals; Kaori is small, shy, and introvert (but both women are portrayed nude in the *Akira manga* in 'fan service' imagery).

However, Shima Tetsuo does display some aspects of stereotypical gay culture as it appears in the popular media – he is portrayed as a masochistic mother's boy (he has her picture in a locket), and his relationship with Kaneda veers into a deep attachment. Not obsession or compulsion, but something more intense than friendship (he dreams of Kaneda, for instance, a number of times – and even more in the *Akira manga*). There is little affection displayed between Tetsuo and Kaori, for example: in their scenes alone together, Tetsuo is not especially concerned with Kaori or how she feels. Well, he *never* asks how she feels. (Notice how at the end the two people that Tetsuo absorbs into his out-of-control body are Kaneda and Kaori – and the Colonel). In the *manga*, Tetsuo is tenderer towards Kaori, and is genuinely distressed at her death (ironically, it's his aide who kills her).[22] In the comic, Tetsuo over-compensates, acting the playboy in a sex scene with several girls (and they expire – if you get too close to Tetsuo, he's toxic).

Kaneda, meanwhile, is depicted as a horny, heterosexual guy – a 'skirt chaser', as the subtitles of the movie put it (that's how Kei sees Kaneda at first, for instance).[23] These are sometimes lecherous kids, too: in the bar a couple are making out, and Nezu and Ryusaku pass a kid groping a girl on a bench at night. In Otomo's *manga*, this is simply what some boys think about or do. (Otomo knows, as comedy writers know, that a quick and easy way to get laugh is

22 The relationship of Kei and Chiyoko has a lesbian undercurrent, though it's subtle (as lesbian undercurrents tend to be in mainstream entertainment).
23 Kaneda would fit in to the world of *Legend of the Overfiend* just fine.

crudity).

THE MORALITY AND ETHICS OF *AKIRA*.

What are the messages, the morality, the ethics of *Akira*? Very mixed, very ambiguous, to say the least. Take Tetsuo, one of the movie's two main protagonists (the *manga* of *Akira* has three – Tetsuo, Kaneda and Kei), and the issues and themes that coalesce around him: he rejects everybody who tries to help him: when Kaori comes to see him at the Olympic Stadium, Tetsuo, after a brief conversation, rejects her. He won't listen to the three paranormal children. Even the Colonel, in his blunt, no-nonsense fashion, tries to appeal to Tetsuo to come back to the laboratory where they can help him (true, when that fails, the Colonel does fire at Tetsuo repeatedly!). But no, Tetsuo is having none of it.

Only one person can truly get thru to Shima Tetsuo, and that of course is his double, his brother, his childhood friend: Shotaro Kaneda. It's Kaneda who races to the Olympic Stadium with one mission: to stop Tetsuo. If that means killing him (with the laser rifle he's snaffled), so be it. Kaneda does the right thing, or at least does something that will halt the total mayhem that Tetsuo is unleashing (is it right to kill one person in order to stop them killing 100s or maybe 1,000s? It's a moral question often raised by the action-adventure genre[24]).

So one of the lessons or moralities put forward by *Akira* seems to be that when a loser gains power and agency, he remains a loser. Tetsuo doesn't *want* to learn, to grow, to develop (or even to listen to reason or commonsense, or even the people that love him). But like all young rebels, he doesn't *know* what he wants. He just knows that whatever is being offered to him, he doesn't want it. As Marlon Brando said in *The Wild One*, he's rebelling against everything. And he's *very* angry.

---

24 Certainly, asking the Tetster to sit down for a calm chat wouldn't work! And neither would trying to capture him.

Yes, Tetsuo Shima didn't ask for any of this; yes, as the three E.S.P. children note, he must be helped; yes, Tetsuo is in agony and needs medical attention desperately; but he also, in moments of lucidity and clarity, acts in a resentful and violent manner (he certainly kills his gang buddy Yamagata in cold blood). He is the element of modern, Japanese youth that refuses to be integrated into society. He represents the impulses, the fears, the weaknesses, and the seething resentments of young people in Japan (the aching to belong coupled with the simultaneous repulsions and avoidance, the need to be recognized and accepted coupled with the simultaneous rejection and alienation).

Little Kaori comes to Tetsuo at the Olympic Stadium, which can't have been easy for her (she's not the most confident of people), and in great danger (and she probably walked all the way), but Tetsuo rejects her. At times, Tetsuo's self-loathing seems to manifest itself like a death wish.[25] Again, it's a replay of the moment following the near-rape and beating, when Tetsuo was too self-absorbed to recognize that Kaori was suffering mightily too. (Tetsuo is self-absorbed to a striking degree, and seldom seems interested in Kaori's life).

Another Kaori-alone scene (in the movie) puts the girl on the streets in a crowd that sees a newscast on television in a store (note the guys who turn to look at her, somewhat disdainfully). When the news show says Tetsuo's going to the bridge, Kaori follows the crowd who head in that direction (yes, that scene is partly a plot function scene, to explain how Kaori turns up at the stadium; similarly, there's a scene with Kai in a back alley, when he glimpses Kaneda and Kei hurrying by[26]).

Meanwhile, note how Kaneda, in the psychedelic

25 Suicide does occur in *Akira* – one of the politicians slits his wrists in a bathroom (in a Gothic horror moment, during the Nezu-Ryu sequence, when the door creaks open on its own to reveal the sorry sight).
26 This is a more artificial scene, narratively.

last minutes of the *Akira* movie, when he's flying all over the place in and out of different levels of reality, memory and dream, calls to Kei (at one point, he screams her name), and she helps him to come back to Earth, to reality, to consciousness (as she does in the *manga*, tho' it's a pity the movie didn't use her impressive spirit form from the *manga*). He's no romantic, he's not going to get all smoochy and cute (the gang members are characterized in the early scenes as skirt-chasers, though not romantics in the girlie, feminine sense), but he does acknowledge that it was Kei calling to him, or him calling to Kei, that helped to bring him back, at Kiyoko's prompting in voiceover (and the sweetest moment between the couple in *Akira* occurs here, when Kaneda, kneeling on the debris, acknowledges Kei, and she wears a mysterious half-smile. By the end of the movie, Kei has definitely warmed to crazy Kaneda – she calls for him in concern, and also brushes away tears (these are welcome tears – like, jeez, *someone's* gotta weep at the end of this incredible movie!). The *manga* of course makes so much more of the Kaneda-Kei romance, and their relationship is *far* more satisfying in the *manga* than in the movie, where it is never more'n a subplot).

Akira is similar to many sci-fi *animé* which feature a father scientist who gives their offspring a giant robot or some other ultimate toy (or weapon). *Akira* splits the father into two – the Colonel and Doctor Ônishi (meanwhile, the biological fathers or step-fathers of the street kids, as well as the magical children, are nowhere to be seen. Nor their mothers. And they're not mentioned, either. *Akira* is a movie in which parents are simply not part of the plan – except in some minor roles, like Tetsuo's folks in the flash-backs. But we can guess about the parents of Kaneda-kun and Kei-chan are). But the movie is also all about children's relations with parental figures, and the younger generation with the older generation.

Some critics have related Tetsuo's agony and

rage to the problems of puberty and growing up. Of course – that goes without saying; it's part and parcel of numerous *animés* of this type. But *Akira* is a *much* bigger movie than that, and goes way beyond the psychological or the psychosexual levels.

Shima Tetsuo you can also say embodies something in Japanese youth which doesn't want to integrate with society, or can't, or if it does it will be killing part of itself. *Akira* is a very *political* and *social* movie: it is much more than a story about a group of young kids who get involved with a government scientific/ military experiment which goes wrong. It is so obviously about conflicts between youth and age, between Japan's younger generations and the sins of the Fathers.

The youth vs. age, sons vs. fathers, children vs. parents motif is picked up throughout *Akira*. It's everywhere. Just look at the *mise-en-scène* of the Eighth District Youth Vocational Training School,[27] with its trashed corridors and graffited walls.[28] And what does coach Mr Takaba do? He beats the kids around the face! And the principal and the teacher in the office just ignore it! (The *manga* explains that the street punks are on probation, which enhances their uneasy relation with the school, which is, of course, boys only).

Thus, although *Akira* contains elements of conservative, rightwing ideology, in common with most of fantasy literature and cinema, you could also argue that the 1988 animation puts forward a leftwing and socialist politics which targets and criticizes the authorities – in the government, the military-industrial complex, science and education – and finds corruption, aggression, repression,

27 'Great if you're into bikes, drugs and serious rumbles as a way of life. Not so hot if you're female (you'll end up pregnant or on the game or both) or hoping to become a chartered accountant,' as Helen McCarthy put it in *The Anime Movie Guide* (196).
28 There's a bust outside the school with a bra and other trash plastered over it, and the graffito 'HOTEL' (a more detailed improvement on the drawing in the *manga*). That trashed statue is contrasted with the idealized, golden figure in the government room where the politicos debate the fate of Neo-Tokyo.

exploitation and dogma. (One of the key political messages of *Akira* is this: there is nobody who is pure, innocent or uncorrupted: every group or organization has its elements of distrust, violence and corruption. There is no John Wayne figure, no Sheriff, no cop, no hero, no one at all who is a beacon of light and goodness.[29] Even a character such as Kei, the heroine, who has more commonsense than most in *Akira*, has, by act one of the movie, killed a soldier (and, in the *manga,* blown up some other soldiers during an escape from a hide-out, and also sabotaged the Olympic Stadium with more fireworks). Kaori is one of the few figures in *Akira* (the *animé*) who is gen- uinely good-hearted and caring – and what happens to her! Beaten… and rejected – then killed!)

If the kids in *Akira*'re messed up, in the socialist and left-wing view, it's due to society, to the social conditions they live in, to social deprivation, to complicated structures like societies, laws, rules, and morality. Socialism points the finger at society, at systems, at laws, at environments. In pitting a bunch of young kids against the giant military-industrial complex, the screenwriters (Izo Hashimoto and Katsuhiro Otomo) turn *Akira* into a very intriguing and subtle movie. A North American/ Western movie would probably add characters such as soldiers or cops (or maybe neutral characters like journalists or observers), who would intervene and be caught in the middle, between the kids and the government, Army and scientists, or who would start out working for the military-industrial machine then end up fighting against it after uncovering what it was really up to (and a North American/ Western movie would almost certainly include some idealistic or righteous figure, someone to embody the morality and politics of Middle America).

But *Akira* is simply not black-and-white like that,

29 The Colonel is the closest personality to that kinda guiding light figure, but he is a more complex character (he embodies the right- wing military, for a start, the authorities who're keeping the Japanese capital under martial law).

not good guys vs. the bad guys: it is also sympathetic to both sides. The moral and ethical complexity of *Akira* is easy to see from the way it portrays the social hierarchy of the Neo-Tokyo world (which certainly draws on the 1927 movie *Metropolis*; Katsuhiro Otomo scripted the 2001 remake).

THE POLITICS OF *AKIRA*.

That Neo-Tokyo is under martial law, with Colonel Shikishima and the military taking control of the city, adds yet another layer of political resonance to *Akira* (the Colonel, however, is also not portrayed as a one-dimensional, nasty military man – the 1988 movie seems to take up his viewpoint often, giving him flashbacks and also voiceovers, cinematic devices usually only allocated to primary characters). Another layer still is the group of activists (or terrorists – for the government, they're terrorists), that Kaneda hooks up with (that it's a girl, Kei, who connects him with the freedom fighters, is wholly convincing – despite what Ryusaku and the other activists think, about him spying, it's simply a boy and a girl, a boy wanting a girl). The activists are also linked to corrupt politicians.[30] Yep, *Akira* sure is dense and multi-layered, and there sure are a lot of charas to follow. Yet it never feels confusing to me.

Although critics point out Katsuhiro Otomo's interest in the radical politics of the 1960s, and the anti-government movements in Japan of the early 1960s (as well as the political activism surrounding the 1964 Olympic Games), it's also worth recalling that Otomo was very young at the time: 10 years-old in 1964. By the time he was the age of Tetsuo and Kaneda in *Akira*, 15, it was 1969. So Otomo's interest (or involvement) in politics would probably have occurred in the 1970s.

However, *Akira* is certainly the work of a man who can remember what it was like to be fifteen, and to be fired up with idealism and rebellion as well as

30 A plot point that was included in the 2001 *Metropolis*.

cynicism (and the crushing disappointment when you realize that the world isn't quite what seemed to be promised). Otomo-sensei was 28 when the first installments of the *Akira manga* were published in 1982, and he was 34 when the *Akira* movie was in production.

❖

Would the whole world abandon Japan, one of the most important economies, if it suffered a cataclysm like the one depicted in *Akira*? According to Katsuhiro Otomo, yes! Well, it does seem as if Neo-Tokyo is left alone for a long time in the *Akira manga*, with rescue units from the United Nations only coming in to the Japanese capital after some time. Of course, the Yanks turn up, armed to the teeth, determined to solve the Akira crisis in the way they know best: blow everything up! *Send Japan to the bottom of the sea!* – That's what the commander of the aircraft carrier yells. (The North Americans detach secret military units to nobble Akira, and when that fails, they use the satellite laser cannon plus carpet bombing – it's WW2 all over again[31]).

VIOLENCE AND SELF-LOATHING.

Akira is phenomenally violent – characters are hurled about all the time, the violence is intimate and very physical, blood is flowing on the ground and gushing out of wounds, heads're slammed by weapons in motorbike fights, characters tumble off speeding bikes with loud crunches, and there're plenty of on-screen deaths and beatings. Kaneda is thrown about often, landing hard on the ground with a bloody nose; the guy with the dud grenade's leapt on by cops and hauled away leaving a trail of blood; and the activist who kidnaps Takashi is dripping blood copiously over the street.

It's not just the quantity of violence and conflict that's depicted in *Akira*, however, but the intensity and vehemence of it. There is, it has to be said, a real

31 Sometimes you wonder how *Akira* can be so popular in the U.S.A., due to its portrayal of Americans and American ideology.

nastiness and self-loathing about some of the aggression on display in *Akira* (Tetsuo embodies, perhaps
above all, an extraordinary self-hatred, and a lack of
empathy with other characters. A number of characters try to call Tetsuo off from harming others,
including Kaneda, Kiyoko, Masaru and the Colonel.
Does he listen? Not really).

Nastiest of all (in the *Akira* movie) is the beating
and near-rape scene: while Tetsuo is pinned to the
tarmac by the Clowns gang getting revenge, his girlfriend, Kaori, is threatened, hit, and stripped. It's
meant to be a repulsive scene, of course, like similar
scenes in *A Clockwork Orange* (which it clearly references), but there's also a glorying in the act.[32] The
scene is the only flaw in the *Akira* movie.

This will sound odd, but to me *Akira* seems more
grotesquely violent and twisted than the *Legend of the
Overfiend* series and similar fare, even though
Overfiend depicts numerous rapes and acts of sexual
violence. The most disturbing thing about *Akira*, at
the level of the characters, rather than the big,
political picture, is the self-hatred of the characters, in
particular Tetsuo, which erupts in phenomenal bursts
of anger (aided by Nozomu Sasaki's absolutely
incredible vocal performance as Tetsuo). That self-
loathing is also very striking and disturbing in the
Urotsukidoji series.[33] Both movies are clearly about
male youth in Japan in crisis in the 1980s. Forget the
giant fantasy and horror ingredients for a minute,
and just consider how these young kids are suffering.

Yes, it's true that Shima Tetsuo is undergoing a
horrible experience, in immense pain: but look at how
he deals with it, with acts of astonishing destruction
and violence. There's a million ways of dealing with

32 Notice that the guy Tetsuo beats up in revenge is dressed in red,
and even looks like Kaneda.
33 In the *Urotsukidoji* series *everybody* suffers, not only the female
characters. The men undergo incredibly painful tortures, with their
bodies ripped to shreds. What's arresting is the amount of *self-hatred*
in the *Legend of the Overfiend* cosmos: it's not only violence against
women, it's violence against men, and against everything. (Self-
loathing is a disturbing ingredient to discover in such quantities in
cinema and TV).

illness and injury, but lashing out at everything in the vicinity says loads about Tetsuo's weaknesses and fears.

Tetsuo is the kid that everyone picked on in school, the kid who was bullied (even more so in the *Akira manga*). Tetsuo is also the kid who was always second to Kaneda, the handsome boy, the sporty type, the jock, who gets to have the best motorbike, the best girlfriend,[34] and to be the leader of the motorcycle gang the Capsules.

With his new-found powers, Tetsuo is paying back everybody who looked down on him, who scorned him, who didn't respect him. The resentment Tetsuo feels has been building up all of his life. Notice that when his body undergoes horrific transformations at the end, it takes the form of a giant baby, the baby that part of Tetsuo has been all along (talk about an inner child!).

But it is also highly entertaining watching someone who's very unpredictable and explosive (and also very powerful), and seeing someone completely lose it. When it comes to depicting people really losing it, Japanese animation has no peers: Raito Yagami at the end of the truly extraordinary *Death Note* series; the prima donna vampire Hellsing in *Hellsing Ultimate*; Kenpachi Zaraki when someone foolishly stands in his way during a duel in *Bleach*; and Monkey D. Luffy when he's white-hot with rage during one of the many bust-ups of *One Piece*.

---

34 Tetsuo's girlfriend, Kaori, is a skinny, quiet type, not like the babes that hang around Kaneda, or like Kei, who pairs up with Kaneda.

07

THE STYLE OF *AKIRA*

MOTIFS, DEVICES, SYMBOLS.

One of the many motifs in *Akira* is the circle. Akira itself is housed in a spherical vessel (actually, it's a sphere within a sphere); the explosion at the story's beginning is spherical, as is the re-appearance of the Akira-like cataclysm at the end; the scientist's psychic-measuring device is circular (and spins); the testing machine that Tetsuo's strapped to is also circular; Tetsuo stands on a hemispherical play area in his nightmare; there're circular lamps, tunnels, sewers, manhole covers, entrances and signs, and even the faces (and hairstyles) designed by Katsuhiro Otomo & co. are spherical.[35]

Light – *Akira* is one of the great animated movies dealing with light (others in animation might include *Ghost In the Shell*, *Final Fantasy*, *Bambi*, *Memories* and *Princess Mononoke*). *Akira* makes light a key vehicle of the drama; for instance: in the flashbacks of Tetsuo's childhood, there's low level sunlight with lengthy shadows; the lamp trails from the bikes (like a slow shutter speed image in photography, or a retinal ghost); the blinding walls of fire and explosions; the

---

35 Kei and Kaneda are often drawn very alike at times: they have the same rounded faces, the same haircut – about the only difference is some panels is that Kei's given eyelashes, and Kaneda has a slightly squarer jaw. (In their orange overalls, they look almost identical).

very low light in the Harukiya Bar; and of course, during the apocalyptic climax, light becomes a physical force, an enveloping hemisphere of light (*Akira* employs light in the same manner as a religious movie – light as revelation, as signifying summat divine or holy or awe-inspiring, and light as the transmitter of energy or a force in itself).[36]

DESIGN AND STYLE.

The design work on the movie of *Akira* (courtesy of production designers Kazuo Ebisawa, Yuji Ikehata and Koji Ono, and art director by Toshiharu Mizutani), was staggering: the acreage of detail in every shot,[37] the inventiveness of the locations, the combinations of modern and postmodern architecture, the staging of the action, the choice of camera angles, and the framing. This was filmmaking of a very high quality and power of imagination.

The world that *Akira* depicts is not only hi-tech and futuristic, it's also incredibly scuzzy and messy, with trash, graffiti, and debris strewn over every set (and way scuzzier than even desperate-to-be-cool movies set in scuzzed-up worlds; graffiti is employed throughout the *Akira manga* and the movie not only as atmosphere and context, but also to wryly comment upon the narrative).[38] The high school that the punk kids attend is trashed (and the regime at the school is both inadequate and violent – there's a scene where the gym teacher Mr Takaba whacks each kid in the face, while the principal sits at a desk and does nothing).

The school in *Akira*, in both print and celluloid form, is a send-up of the familiar high school setting of a million Japanese comics and TV shows, where smug, middle-class students spend their days angsting over romances with unattainable beauties,

---

36 And in *Neo-Tokyo*, extreme lighting effects are employed – in particular characters moving between light and shadow.
37 'Every shot in the film is a spectacle of meticulous detail' (B. Camp, 363).
38 A piece of graffito in the first sewer scene reads: 'CLOWNS FUCK YOU'.

or wondering when they're gonna get the next glimpse of the school idol's panties. *Akira* subverts all of that superficial tripe, presenting a shabby, no-hope limbo, one step away from prison, where students are smashed in the face by teachers.

One of the most curious aspects of *Akira* is the character design – which, like the direction and the co-written script, was done by Katsuhiro Otomo. Big round eyes and oval eyes, round faces, and huge, domed foreheads – the Otomoan style is found throughout *Akira*, to the point where many characters look the same, whether they're girl, boy, old or young (the biker gang is differentiated, but everyone in the activist cell looks like Ryu – grim, frowning, with a moustache).[39] It might be not be everyone's favourite character design in Japanese *animé*, but it does the job at first; however, it grows on you, becoming a key ingredient – and it does make *Akira* (and Otomo's other artworks) distinctive. Otomo was noted for being one of the first *manga* artists to depict Japanese people as definitely Japanese (which was a controversial decision).

There is also a wonderful use of verticality all the way thru *Akira* – so many images include figures or objects floating gently upwards or downwards, or, like Tetsuo in his Superman mode, zooming up rapidly from the Earth into space.

Akira imaginatively employs the vertical axis to a striking degree: when Tetsuo goes nuts, debris is floating *upwards*, across the frame; when Tetsuo has his nightmares, the ground falls away from him, with the camera looking up at him; below the Olympic Stadium are enormous canyons that stretch down into darkness.

Akira piles on the visual effects, and is certainly one of the great visual effects movies in history, in animation or live-action, alongside *Jason and the Argonauts*, *Star Wars* or *Fantasia* (Takashi Maekawa

---

39 Moustache Man is a character design that crops up in Otomo's 1970s *manga,* including the lead character in *Sayonara Japan.*

and Noriko Takaya oversaw the visual effects). The futuristic visual effects in *Akira* are easy to spot – the laser beams, the psychic phenomena, the shattering debris. But many of the effects are practical effects, which in a live-action production are handled by the practical effects crew: smoke, fire, steam, ice, water, wind. Smoke, for instance, is employed as billowing clouds with a volume and dynamism (and pinkish colour) of their own, as in the movies of Hayao Miyazaki (Kei steps into tear gas to evade the cops in the riot, for instance, and Kaneda and the gang storm thru smoke in the tunnel).

The sound design (by Susumu Akitagawa, Shizuo Kusahashi, Tokuya Shimada *et al*) and editing (by Takeshi Seyama) in *Akira* gets more impressive every time you watch the 1988 movie. By the time you know the story, after seeing the picture a few times, you can ignore or switch off the subtitles (highly recommended), and appreciate the orchestration of sound effects, music and dialogue. And silence – there is a lot of silence in *Akira*. The atomic bomb/ Akira explosion, at the start, for instance, occurs over silence. Often the sound will dip out to silence. When Masaru appears with the helicopters behind him, for example, in order to bring back Takashi, the dialogue is echoey, and takes place in the mindscreens of Masaru and Takashi; then the sound roars back to something more objective, as the aircraft lands behind Masaru in his floating chair.

The producers of the *James Bond* flicks in the 1960s (Harry Saltzman and Cubby Broccoli) talked about the *Bond* movies as 'total cinema'. *Akira* is definitely like that, so OTT and rapid, you just have to go along for the ride. The *story* is only *part* of the appeal of *Akira*, as with the *007* movies, the *Star Wars* movies, the *Harry Potter* movies, and dumb-but-fun superhero movies – which are not about the story and the characters so much as the explosions, the chases, the gadgets, the stunts, the babes, the hunks, the thrills, the chills, the music, the visual effects, the costumes,

the designs, the cool quips and funny gags, the spectacle, and the high entertainment and attitude of the
whole thing. (Watch those movies with a large
audience – *that* is what they're about).

COLOUR.

Sometimes I wonder if Katsuhiro Otomo, working mainly in black-and-white as a *manga* artist, said
at some point: *you want <u>colour</u>? I'll give you <u>colour</u>!* As
if Otomo-sensei is revelling in the possibilities of
working in full colour, and in the 70 millimetre
photographic gauge, and on a giant scale, with a
large production crew.

The colours employed by the filmmakers in *Akira*
are wonderfully fresh and vivid (Setsuko Tanaka,
Michiko Ikeuchi and Kimie Yamana were the colour
stylists, production design was by Kazuo Ebisawa,
Yuji Ikehata and Koji Ono, with art direction by
Toshiharu Mizutani), although *Akira* is probably
thought of as a dark-hued piece, with blues and grays
predominating. In fact, the dominant colour is *red* (as
in the movies of Jean-Luc Godard and Ken Russell) –
the red of blood, of course, of the red flag, of a red
cloak, of red paint,[40] red lights, red floors, red walls,
red roads, red machinery. Even the pavement is red
in parts of Neo-Tokyo: in the explosion at the subway
station scene, the sidewalk is bright red. And the red
of Shotaro Kaneda, of course (red for Kaneda represents his passion, blood, his irrepressible liveliness
and recklessness, but also his anger and danger). And
the filmmakers explored using combinations of red
and green, rather than the more usual red and blue
(although there is blue everywhere, too).

Indeed, there's so much red in *Akira*, it looks as if
the city's going to explode anyway, without the aid of
an entity called Akira or a North American atomic
bomb. It's a volcano, an inferno.

Another of Katsuhiro Otomo's signature colours,

40 The religious fanatics, protesting on the elevated walkway in
Akira, paint huge *kanji* on the sidewalk with an enormous brush (b4
being set upon by the cops).

which he has made his own – absolutely *no one else* in the history of cinema has used it so much – is orange. Molten oranges like the centre of the sun (for Neo-Tokyo's buildings, in particular the scientific facility, overalls and the police cell), oranges coupled with sunflower yellows, oranges for interiors – orange is everywhere (orange is particularly aligned with Kei).

In the jail scene, the colour designers paint the cell with intense oranges – a very unusual choice of colour for a jail! (Is there another prison cell this orange in cinema?!). Even more when you consider that the utility uniforms worn by our heroes are also orange (and a very close orange to their surroundings, too).

And then there's yellow – as if he's bringing his beloved desert into downtown Neo-Tokyo, Katsuhiro Otomo has asked the colour stylists Michiko Ikeuchi, Setsuko Tanaka and Kimie Yamana to find as many places they could put yellow as possible.

But not only red and orange and yellow and green and blue in *Akira* – there are bright pinks (Kaneda's Tee shirt, Kiyoko's crib), pinkish smoke, and very pale greens (for the skin of the psychic kids). To contrast with Kaneda's all-red mode, the film-makers use for Tetsuo (at the beginning) a turquoise and pale blue (as if Tetsuo is still unformed, lacking the blood and vigour of Kaneda). The city at night includes pale pinks and lilacs, often for the far distance. Here using the pricier 70mm film gauge, and a very large number of cels (160,000), helps to enhance the details and the colours. (Achieving all of this intricacy ain't cheap – you can see why *Akira* cost $11 million).

Akira has its own colour design as few animated movies have: there's a deep, rich and glowing *saturation* to the colours in *Akira*, so it recalls the abstract paintings of the 1960s, the Colorfield and Minimal painters like Frank Stella, Morris Louis, Ken Noland and Ellsworth Kelly. And of course the great Pop artists, like Andy Warhol, R.B. Kitaj and Roy Lichenstein (with its *manga* origins, *Akira* really does look

like a comicbook that's come to life in movies, with
only the speech bubbles, sound fx and panels missing.
Yet, of course, the *manga* in *Young Magazine* was
b/w).

Akira is a genuinely inventive colour movie; most
movies are ultimately indifferent to colour, beyond
evoking prettiness. Why? 'Cos it takes time (and
plenty of experience) to design a colour plan for a
movie which's tied in to the material. *Akira* resembles
the great colour pictures of cinema in its attention to
detail in the coloration (the MGM musicals directed
by Vincente Minnelli come to mind, or *Shadows Our
Forgotten Ancestors*[41] and *The Color of Pomegranates*,
directed by Sergei Paradjanov).

Indeed – *Akira* is a truly astonishing work in
terms of colour design, and so refreshing to see after
so many contemporary movies which beat down
colours to dirty greys, blues and blacks, every colour
subdued, restrained. As if the thrillers, actioners,
dramas and all the rest have simply given up on
colour, on exploring colour, apart from the occasional
vague colour plan.

EDITING.

One of the key reasons that*Akira* is such a compelling movie is its pacing and its editing, those invisible elements which, if they're not working, can make
even 10 minutes of a movie seem like *forever*. *Akira*
locks the audience into its kinetic kaleidoscope of
cataclysm not simply by cut-cut-cutting from one shot
to another rapidly: it's not that straightforward.
Akira knows when to speed up and when to slow
down, when to hare off into full-on action and when
to halt for a moment (there's a simple shot of a piece
of white bandage blowing across the ground towards Kaneda's red bike, for instance, following the

41 *Shadows of Our Forgotten Ancestors* (1964) was the film that
brought Sergio Parajanov to the attention of film critics. It is a
completely extraordinary film. It is explosive filmmaking, as
incendiary as anything in the history of cinema, including all of the
usual movies – *Citizen Kane, Breathless, The Battle of Algiers,
Intolerance*, etc.

high drama of the authorities taking Tetsuo away. It's one of those interval or interlude shots (called 'pillow moments') which crop up everywhere in Japanese cinema – live-action as well as animation).

Akira was edited by Takeshi Seyama, the key editor for Hayao Miyazaki.[42] One of the reasons that the films of Miyazaki are so successful is that same invisible device: their editing, pacing and structure. Watching a Miyazaki movie, you know you are in the hands of a master editor, and a master storyteller.

EDITING AND INTRODUCING CHARACTERS.
Akira isn't wall-to-wall action: it knows when to slow down, when to insert backstory or motivations, and when to reveal elements of the plot. It's all intuitive: it's not something you can learn from a book or a training course, this feeling for pace and timing and structure; and each picture is different, with different demands and possibilities. And there are no formulas (there are screenwriting manuals that claim to have the mechanics of scriptwriting down, but it's not that easy).

But without this magical feeling for how time flows within a 90 or 120 minute movie, films soon become wearying and boring. A bad or disappointing movie is often one which hasn't been edited smoothly or successfully (of course, studios and producers meddle with filmmakers' work all too often).

Again and again, every time I watch *Akira*, it strikes me that one of the chief reasons for the impact of *Akira* is that opening act: *it really rocks*, it really ignites the movie with a scorching blast of energy that propels the show onwards to the end. And a chief ingredient in that rocking sequence of scenes is the editing and the pacing. It doesn't matter how spectacular your imagery is or how good your gags and stunts are, if you can't put them together in a clear, coherent, dramatic and imaginative way, the whole

42 Katsu Hisamura also edited Miyazaki's movies.

enterprise sinks.

Just look at how editor Takeshi Seyama and his assistants give each character in *Akira* a striking introduction, how they set up sequences of shots which not only tell the story but also introduce charas (and, also importantly, their *relationships* with each other), establish locales, introduce themes and issues, and also maintain a rock solid pace. In short, *Akira* is a masterpiece of editing, like *Citizen Kane*, or *Breathless*, or *Time and Tide*, or *The Man With a Movie Camera*.

AKIRA AND OVERFIEND.

Akira has numerous links to the *Legend of the Overfiend* (*Urotsukidoji*) series, the animated series (1987-1997),[43] based on the *manga* by the 'tentacle master', Toshio Maeda. If you saw *Akira* first (and for many folks in the West it was their first *animé* experience – and after *Akira*, everything probably disappoints!), then you might suspect that *Legend of the Overfiend* borrowed (or stole) from it. In fact, in *animé* at least, the first *Legend of the Overfiend* episode was released in 1987, while *Akira* was still in production (although the *manga* of *Akira* had been published earlier – but so had Toshio Maeda's *manga* of *Urotsukidoji*).

Far better to say that the content of *Akira* and *Legend of the Overfiend* is so similar because of the cultural and social climate: the excess and high consumption of the 1980s, with Japan's Bubble Economy at its height, and nuclear war and apoca-

---

43 The *Legend of the Overfiend* movies were produced by Japanese Audio Visual Network, Angel and West Cape (Jupiter Films produced the third movie, and MW Films produced the fourth movie). They were directed by Hideki Takayama, written by Noburu Aikawa and Goro Sanyo (the first two movies), Noburu Aikawa (III.1), Hideki Takayama and Yashito Yamaki (III.2 and III.3), Gonzo Satsuka (III.4), and Nobuaki Kishima (the fourth movie). Masamichi Amano composed the music. Eitaro Tono, Hidetoshi Ômori and Akihiko Yamashita designed the charas (first movie); Hidetoshi Ômori did the monsters (first movie); Shigemi Ikeda was art director (first movie); Rikizo Sekime and Shiro Kasami designed the characters (third movie). Sumilto Io designed the demons and critters (third movie). Art director was Kenichi Harada (third movie).

lyptic scenarios seeming closer to becoming a reality than ever. (And some other *animé* movies and O.A.V.s of the time have similar imagery and scenarios). We are also talking about a bunch of artists and filmmakers in one city, Tokyo, at the same time: there are bound to be crossovers everywhere in *manga* and *animé*.

Akira and *Urotsukidoji* share numerous other elements, such as fantasy, high schools, teenage angst, social rebellion, punky kids, excessive style, flamboy- ant colour, a post-apocalyptic *milieu*, and Tokyo settings (tho' some of *Urotsukidoji* is set in Toshio Maeda's hometown of Osaka). There is also an impossible-to-miss aspect of self-loathing and masculinity-in-crisis in the young, male characters of both *Akira* and *Overfiend* (Tetsuo might wander into the high school of *Overfiend* and be quite at home, while the hapless Nagumo would be quite at home as part of the motorcycle gangs in *Akira*).

Preliminary material by Otomo for the Akira manga
(this page and over).

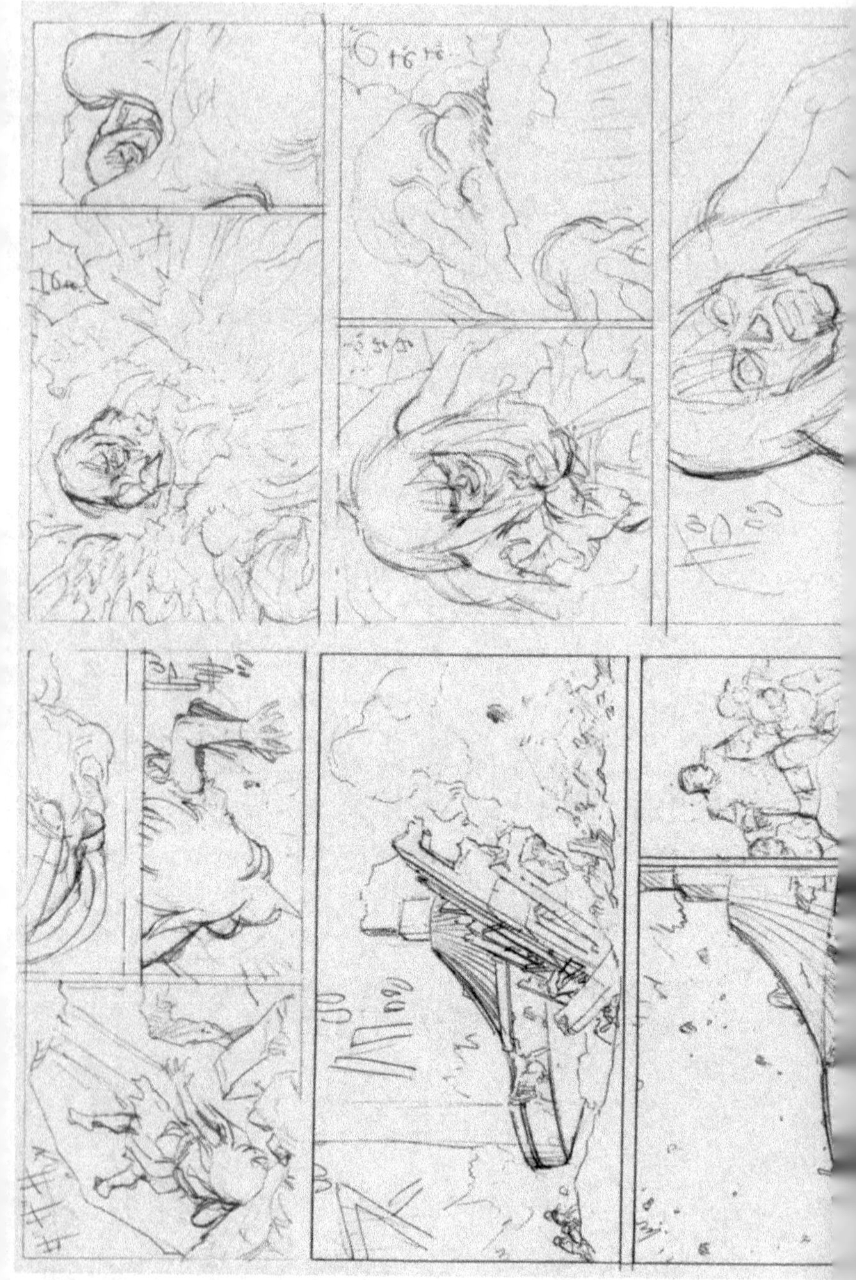

Akira covers for tankobon editions of the manga (this page and over)

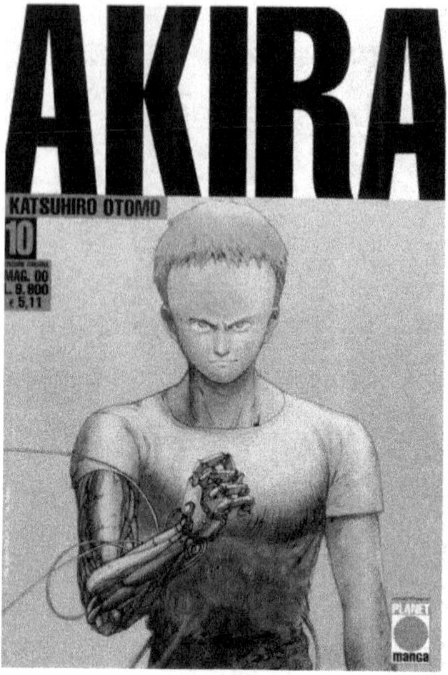
AKIRA
KATSUHIRO OTOMO
10
MAG. 00
L. 9.800
€ 5,11
PLANET
manga

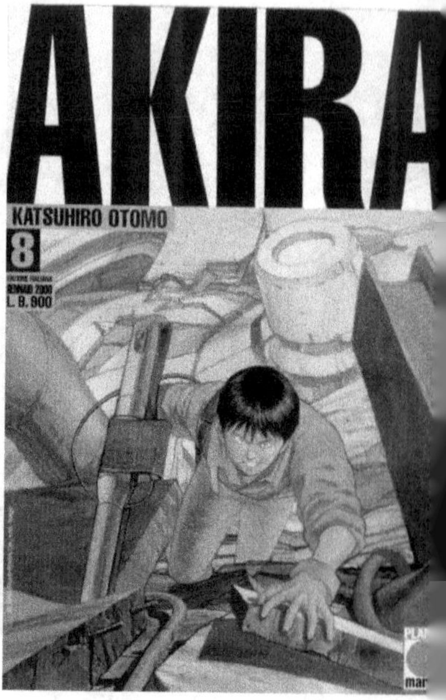
AKIRA
KATSUHIRO OTOMO
8
L. 9.900

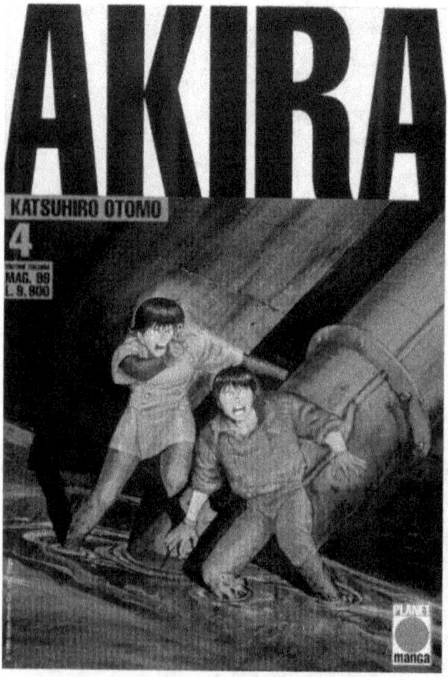
AKIRA
KATSUHIRO OTOMO
4
MAG. 99
L. 9.900
PLANET
manga

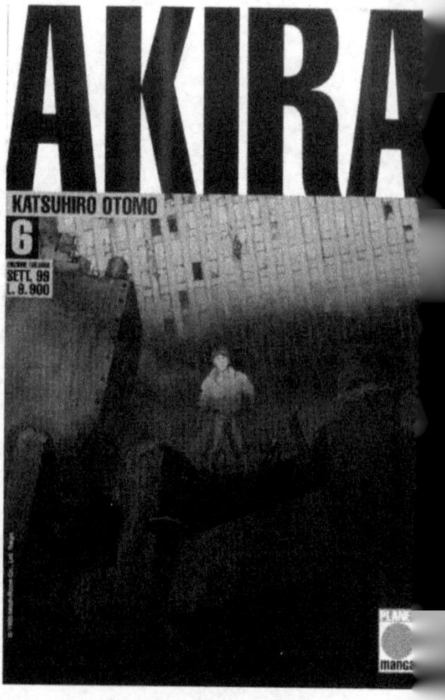
AKIRA
KATSUHIRO OTOMO
6
SETT. 99
L. 9.900
PLANET
manga

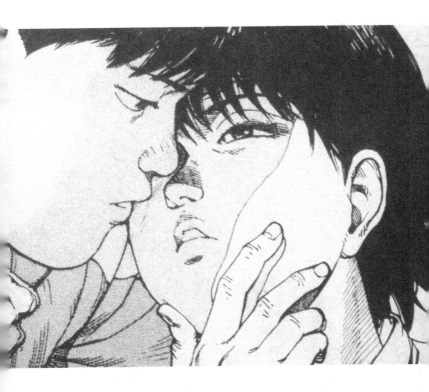

The romantic highpoint of the Akira manga,
for Kei and Kaneda (this page and over)

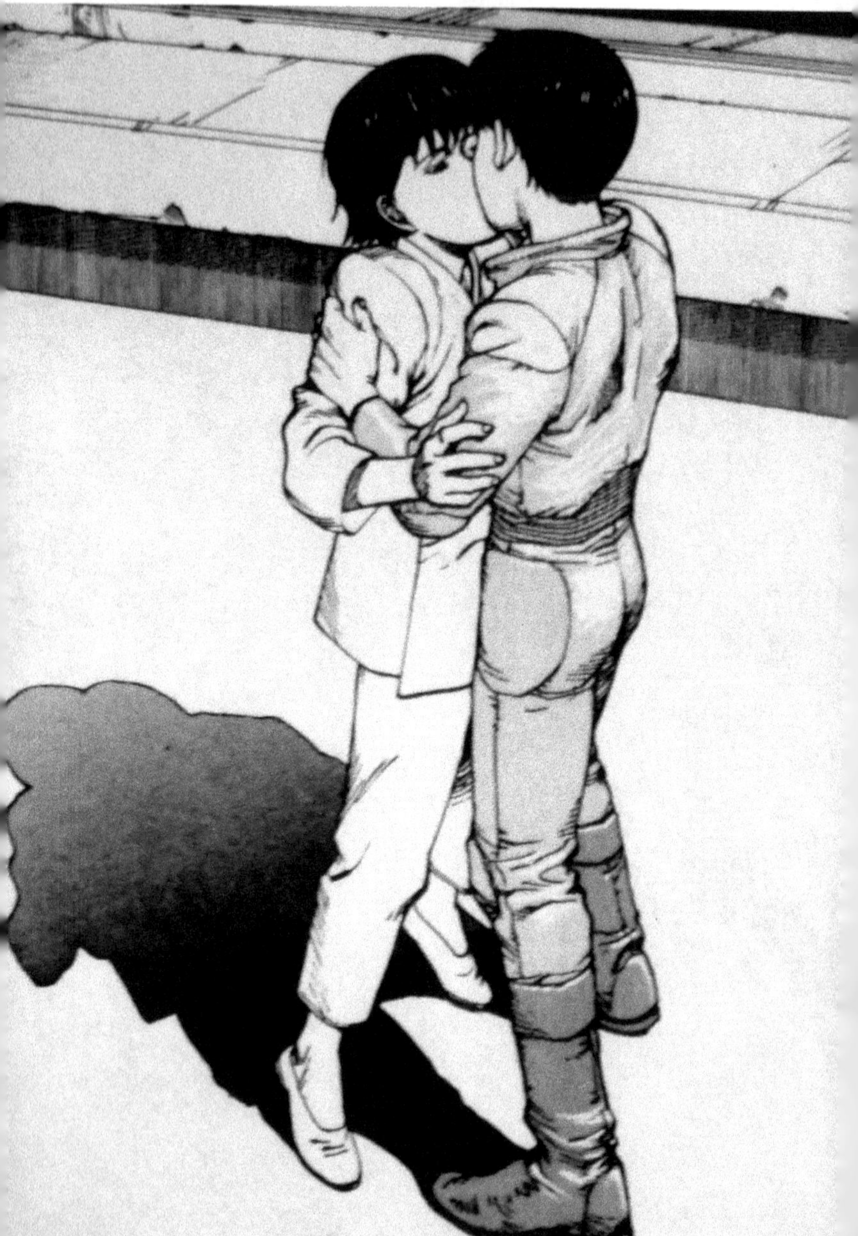

Kei, the heroine of Akira, takes a bath
in an unashamed 'fan service' moment.
She looks at us and vows to fight Tetsuo
'to the end!' Go Kei!

Tetsuo in one of his familiar rebel angel guises in Akira:
head tilted down, eyes staring, mean but playful frown,
spiky hair blowing, and he's topless.

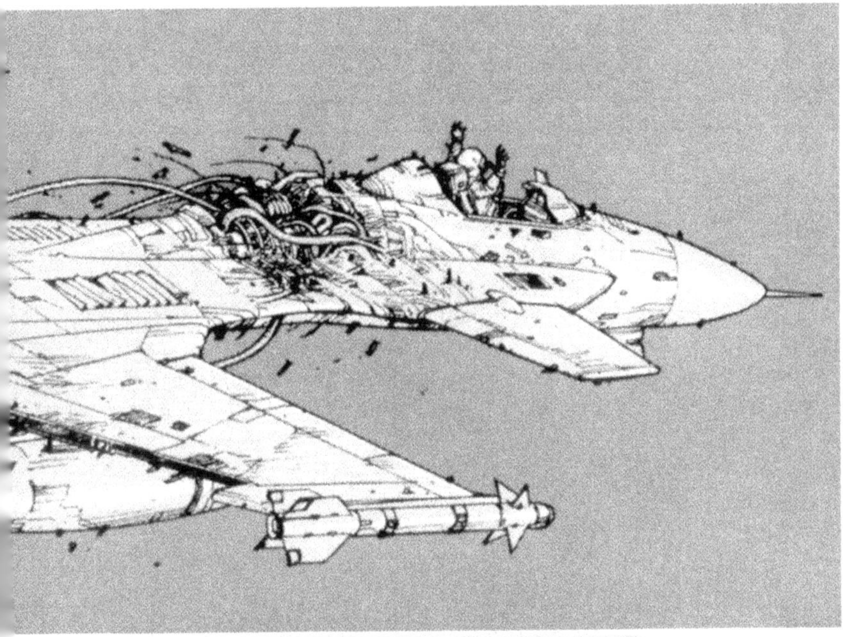

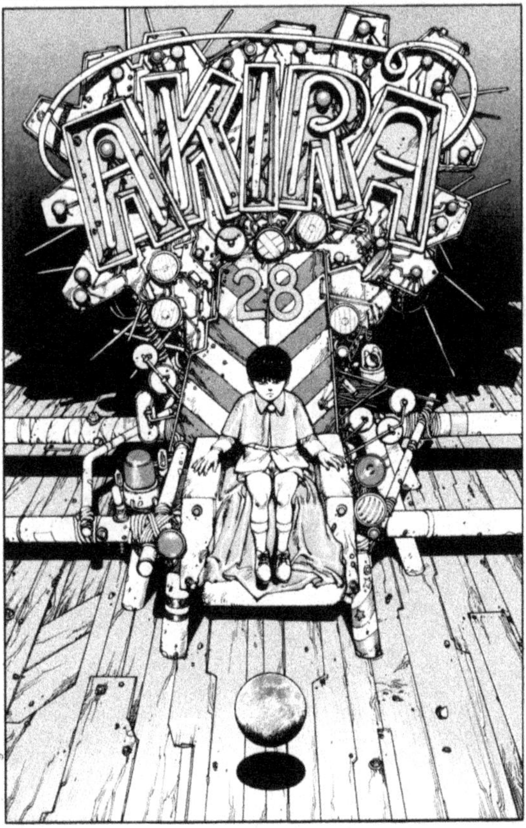
AKIRA
28

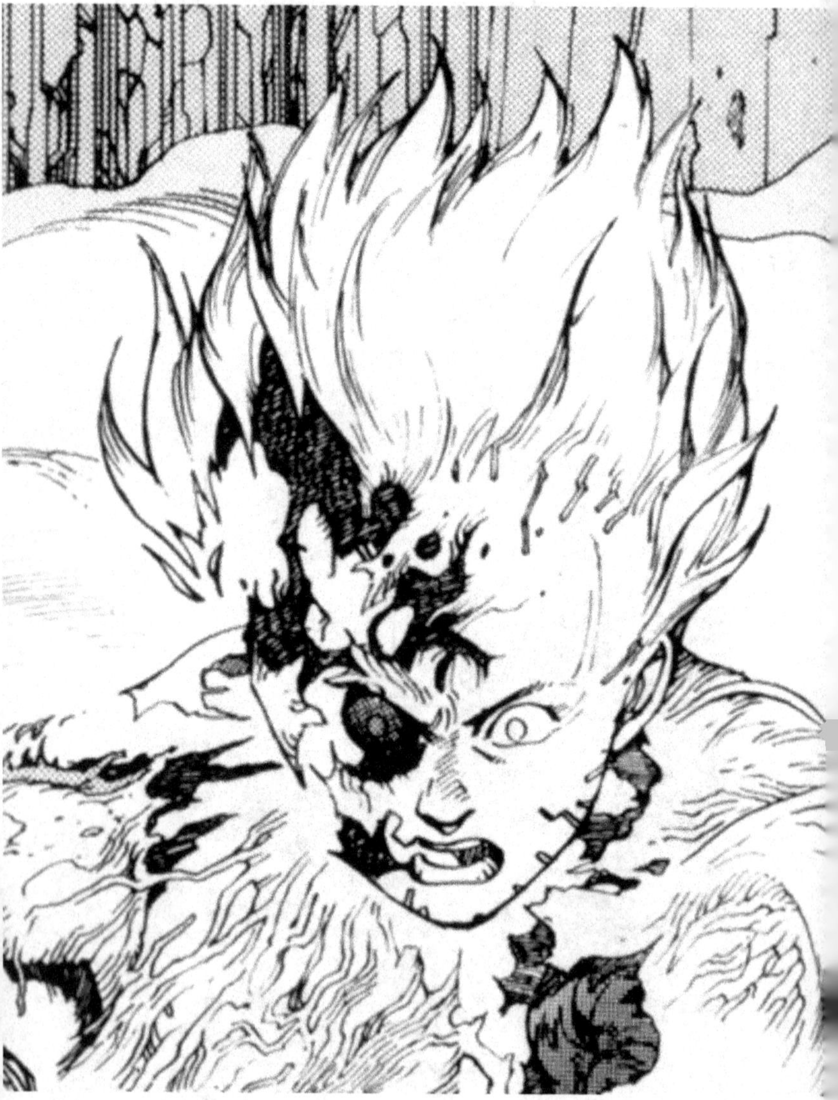

This page and over: images from the Akira Club
artbooks, including splash pages, title and
chapter pages, sketches and other additional
material created for the Akira manga.

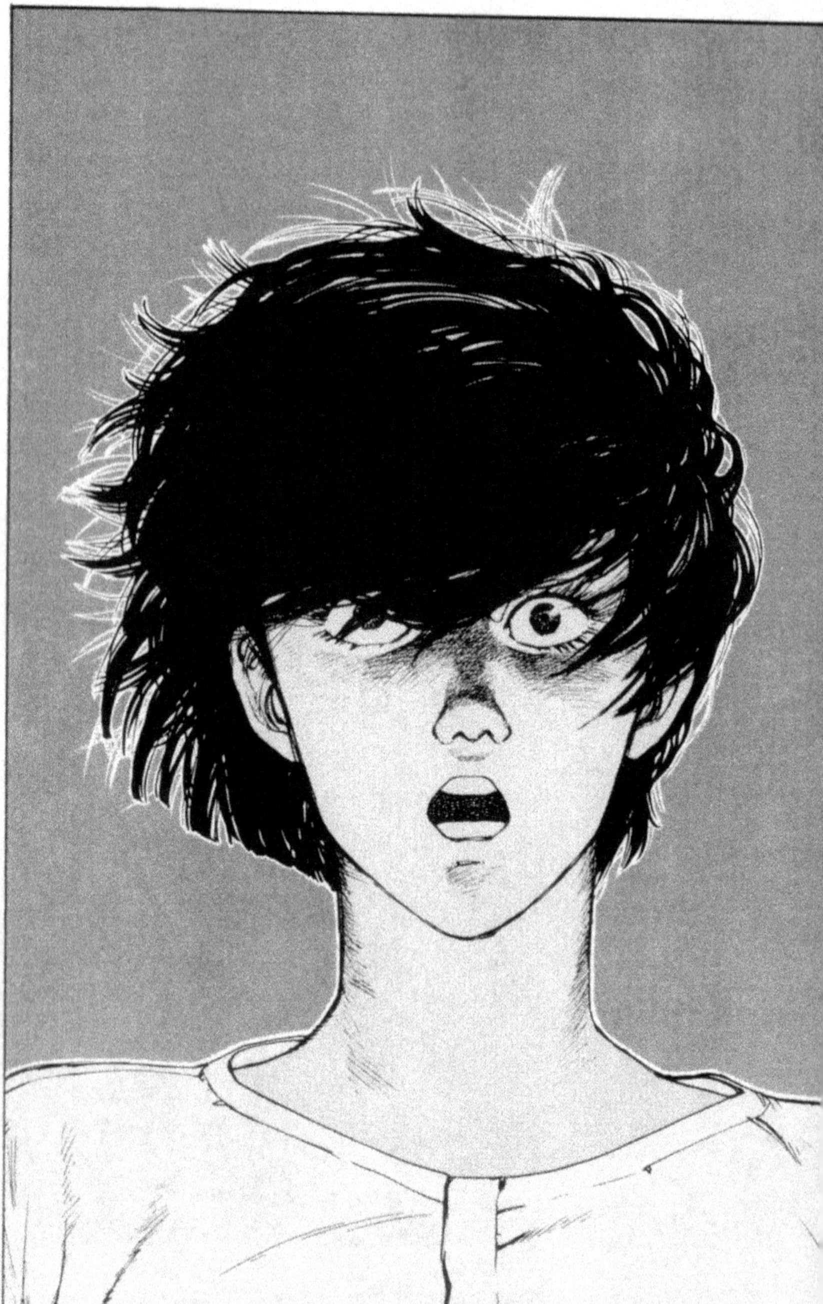

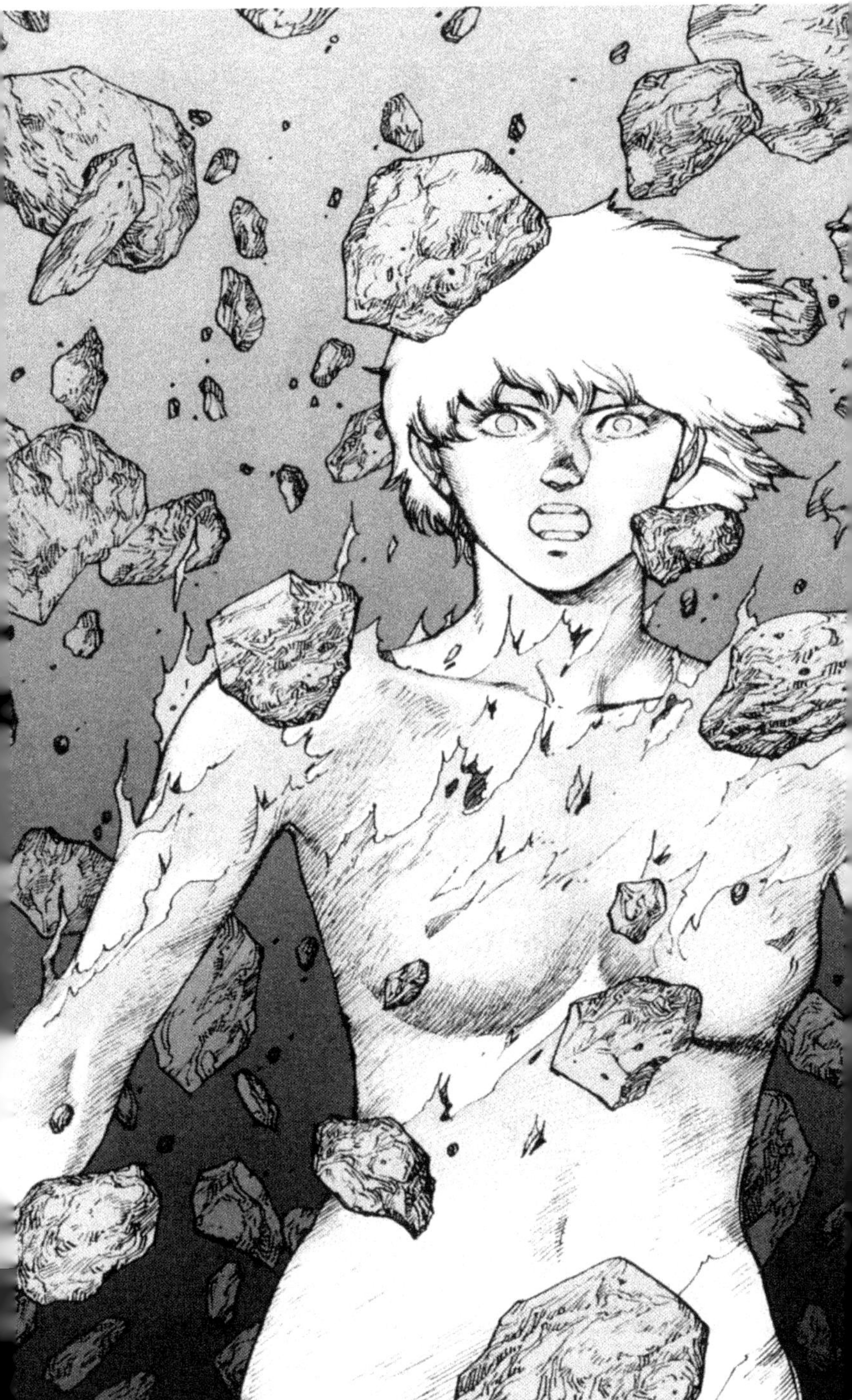

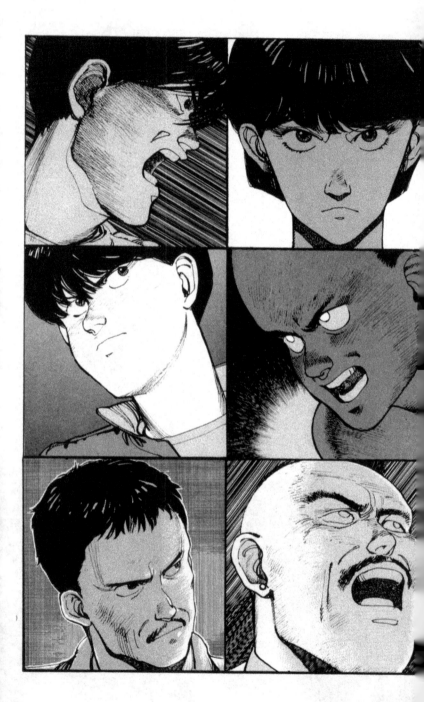

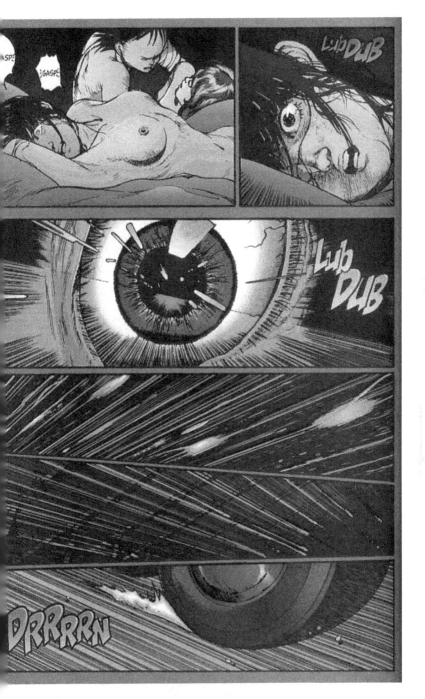

Akira, the Marvel colour edition
(this page and over)

WHAT THE HELL--?!

AAAHHH--

OouuUUUH!

HOLY SHIT!!

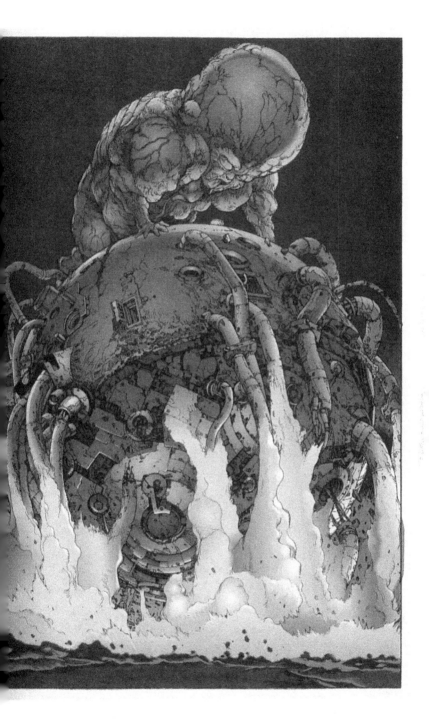

In the finale of Akira, a work of genius on every level,
the heroine Kei saves the hero Kaneda from beyond this world.

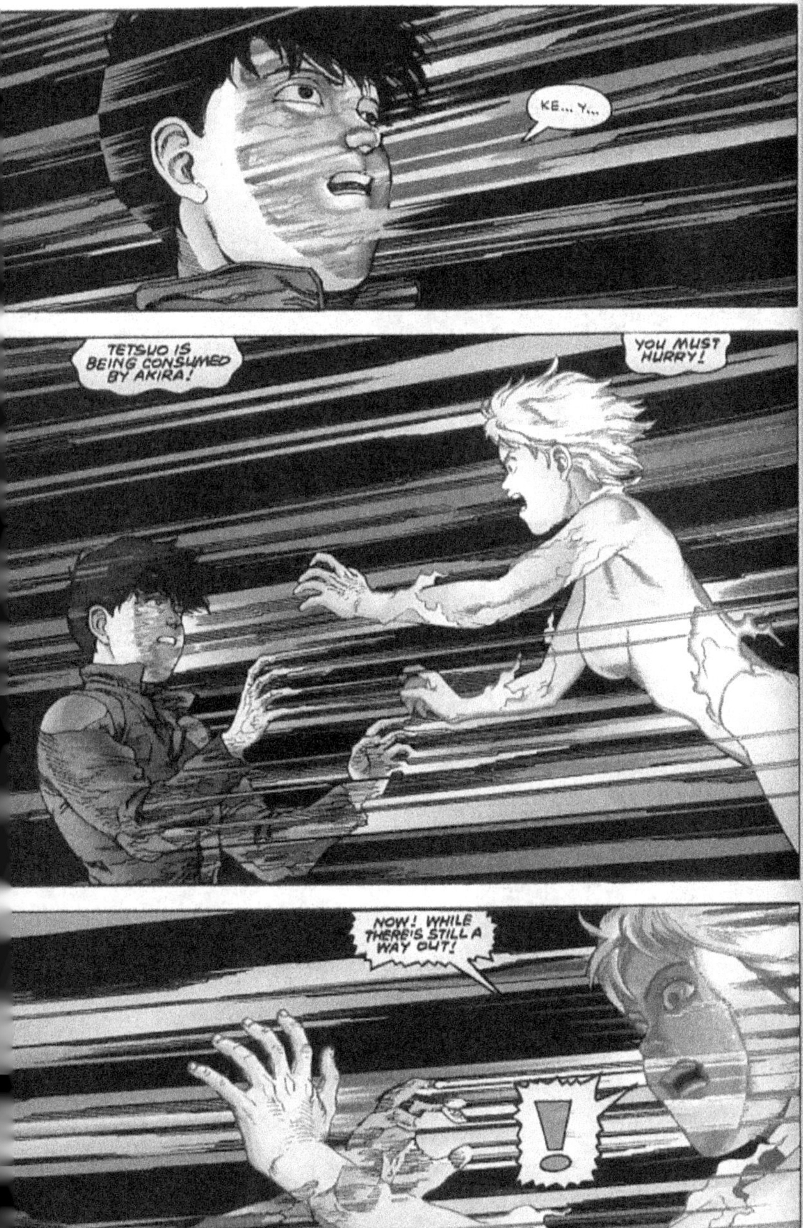
KE... Y...
TETSUO IS BEING CONSUMED BY AKIRA!
YOU MUST HURRY!
NOW! WHILE THERE'S STILL A WAY OUT!
!

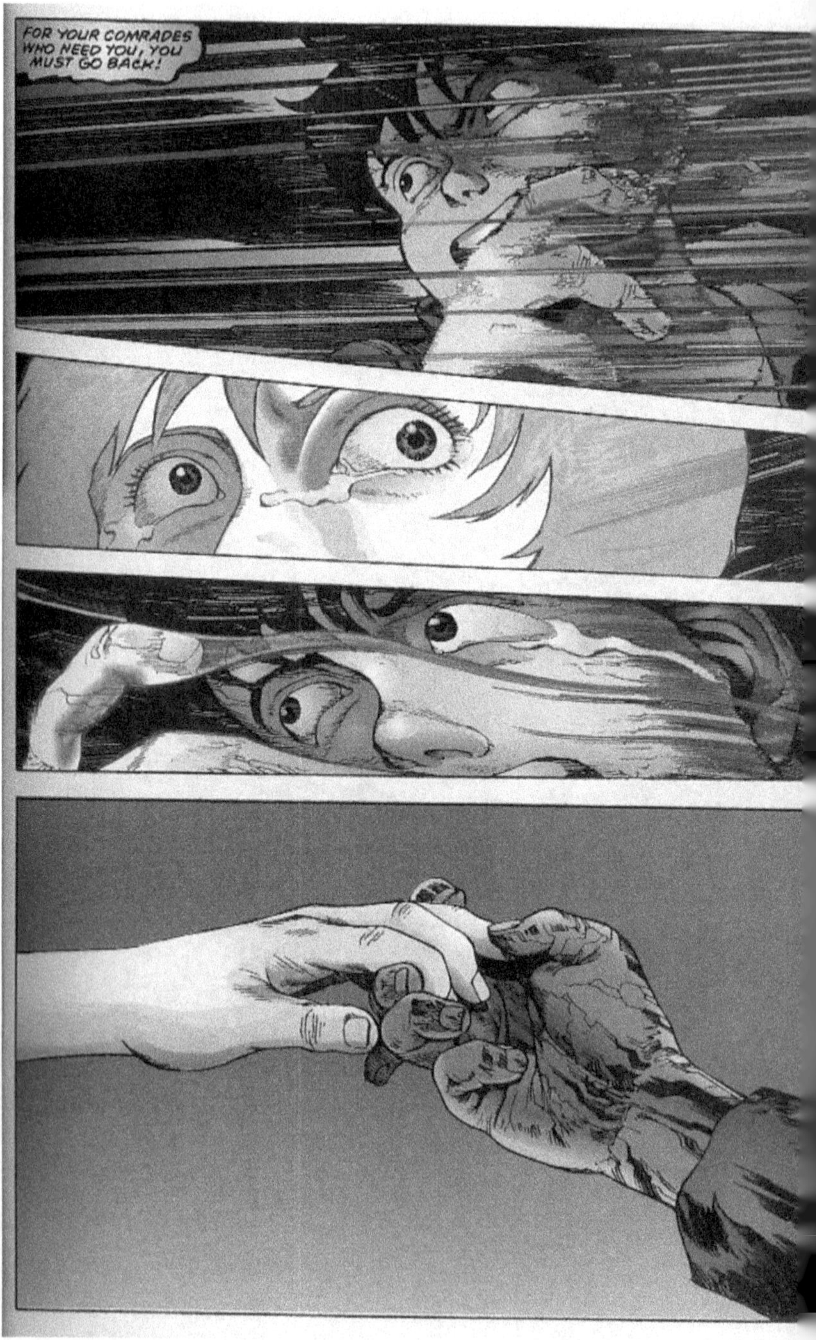
FOR YOUR COMRADES WHO NEED YOU, YOU MUST GO BACK!

Pages from the truly incredible finale of the Akira manga,
taken from the Marvel colour edition (this page and over).

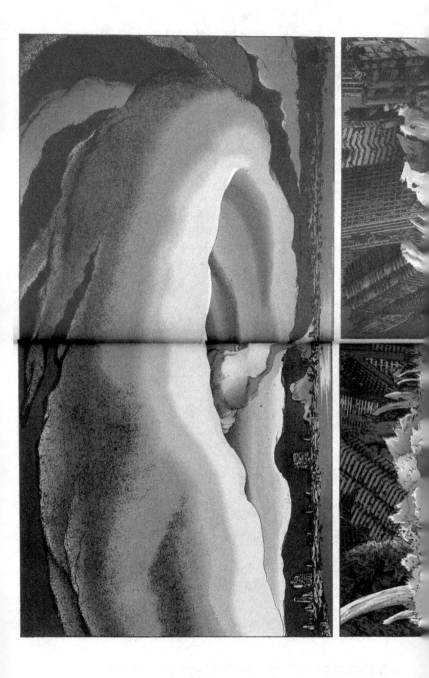

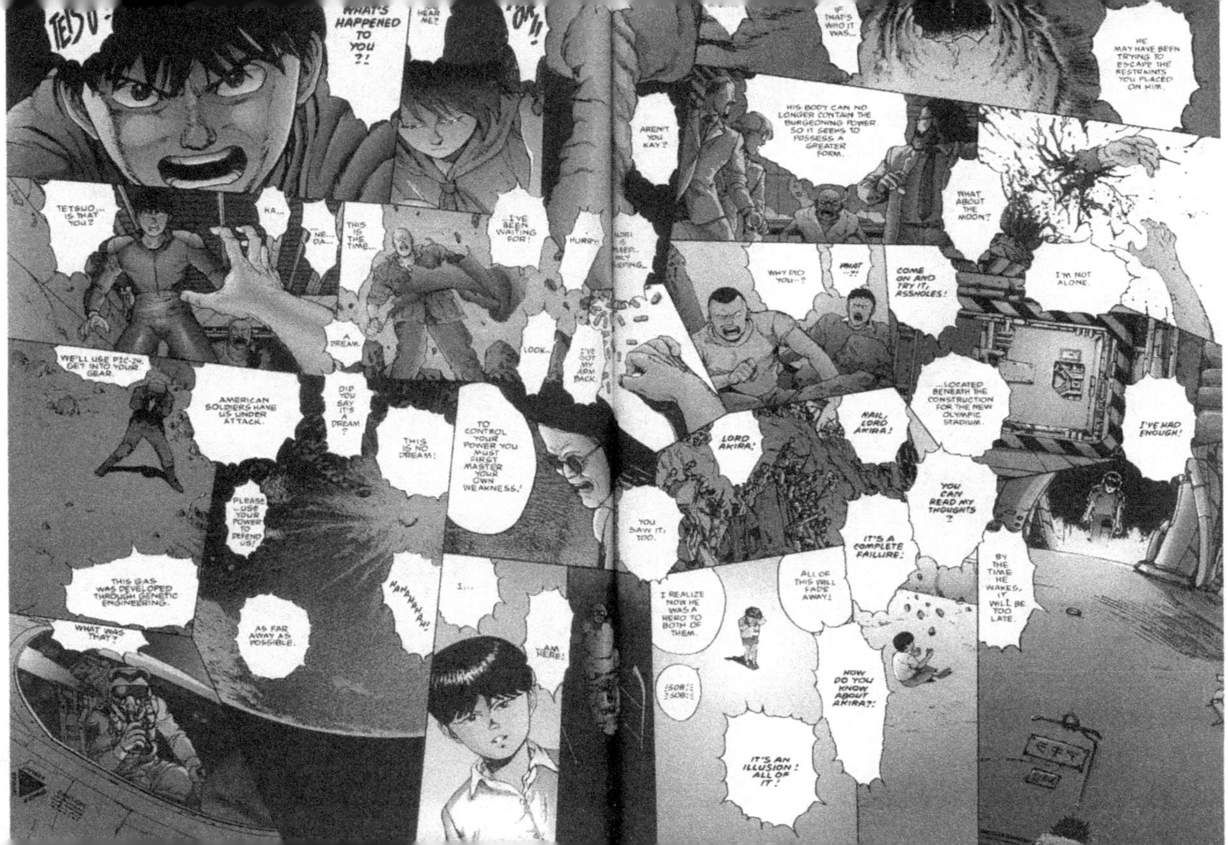
TETSU-
WHAT'S HAPPENED TO YOU ?!
HEAR ME?
"OH!!
TETSUO... IS THAT YOU?
KA...
...HE... DA...
THIS IS THE TIME...
...I'VE BEEN WAITING FOR!
HURRY!
A DREAM.
LOOK...
I'VE GOT MY ARM BACK.
WE'LL USE PIC-24. GET INTO YOUR GEAR.
AMERICAN SOLDIERS HAVE US UNDER ATTACK.
DID YOU SAY IT'S A DREAM ?
THIS IS NO DREAM!
TO CONTROL YOUR POWER YOU MUST FIRST MASTER YOUR OWN WEAKNESS!
PLEASE ...USE YOUR POWER TO DEFEND US!
THIS GAS WAS DEVELOPED THROUGH GENETIC ENGINEERING.
WHAT WAS THAT?
AS FAR AWAY AS POSSIBLE.
HAHAHAHAHA!
I...
AM HERE!
IF THAT'S WHO IT WAS...
HE MAY HAVE BEEN TRYING TO ESCAPE THE RESTRAINTS YOU PLACED ON HIM.
AREN'T YOU, KAY?
HIS BODY CAN NO LONGER CONTAIN THE BURGEONING POWER. SO IT SEEMS TO POSSESS A GREATER FORM.
WHAT ABOUT THE MOON?
WHY DID YOU--?
WHAT --?!
COME ON AND TRY IT, ASSHOLES!
I'M NOT ALONE.
LORD AKIRA!
HAIL, LORD AKIRA!
...LOCATED BENEATH THE CONSTRUCTION FOR THE NEW OLYMPIC STADIUM.
I'VE HAD ENOUGH!
YOU SAW IT, TOO.
YOU CAN READ MY THOUGHTS ?
IT'S A COMPLETE FAILURE!
BY THE TIME HE WAKES, IT WILL BE TOO LATE.
I REALIZE NOW HE WAS A HERO TO BOTH OF THEM.
ALL OF THIS WILL FADE AWAY!
SOB!! SOB!!
NOW DO YOU KNOW ABOUT AKIRA?!
IT'S AN ILLUSION! ALL OF IT!

Akira's golden couple, Kei and Kaneda, in the final scenes

PART FIVE

THE *AKIRA MANGA*

THE *AKIRA MANGA*

AKIRA AS A MASTERPIECE.
The *manga* of *Akira* exceeds all expectations – about storytelling, about what a comicbook or *manga* is, about how an action-adventure-fantasy story can work in a contemporary setting, and how a story can be genuinely thrilling, genuinely political, genuinely wild and epic.

In short, *Akira* ticks all of the boxes: (a) it has action and spectacle in spades, (b) it has fascinating characters and situations, (c) it is incredibly exciting, (d) it is very unusual, sometimes downright eccentric and out-there, (e) it is highly politicized, (f) it has plenty to say about living in the modern world, about contemporary, advanced capitalist societies, and (g) it establishes its own world, its own *raison d'être*, its own philosophy with supreme self-confidence.

Akira is the *manga* to top all *manga,* to end all *manga*. It is a *manga* designed to go further, louder and wilder than any other *manga*. And it does! *Akira* delivers on its promise: it really is every bit as great as everybody says it is.

For many fans, the *Akira manga* is the pinnacle for the form (along with classics such as *Nausicaä of the Valley of the Wind*, *Naruto* and *Blade of the Immortal*). *Akira* is certainly one of the important longer *manga* (some 2,000 pages), and embodies a certain obsession and compulsion on the part of its creator. The movie of *Akira* was the baby of Katsuhiro Otomo too: he was 34 when *Akira* was released: he directed the film, co-wrote the script, designed it, and it was based on his *manga* (which had begun in 1982 in *Young Magazine*).[1]

PRODUCTION OF THE *MANGA* OF *AKIRA*.
Kodansha was the publisher of *Akira* in Japan. Other publishers included: in Britain, Titan and Mandarin; in the U.S.A., Marvel, Random House and Dark Horse; in France, Glénat; in Spain, Norma and Ediciones B; in Italy, Panini; in Brazil, Globo; and in Taiwan, Tong Li.

The comics market in Japan is led by three big publishing houses: Kodansha, Shogakkan, and Shueisha. Other notable *manga* publishers include Futabasha, Shonen Gahosha, Hakusensha, Kobunsha, Akita Shoten and Nihon Bungeisha. The Japanese companies have links to Western companies: Shueisha and Shogakukan, for instance, own Viz, Kodansha has worked with Del Rey, and Square Enix with Yen Press.

The *manga* of *Akira* appeared first in the Western world in 1988 in a Marvel Epic Comics edition,[2] which flopped the artwork, and added colour (one of the early success stories of *manga* publication in the West. The colour was added by Steve Oliff; colour was necessary to give *Akira* the look of a North American comicbook). It ran until 1995 (with a two-year gap). Later editions returned the *manga* to its origins in a b/w, right-to-left format (however, the Dark Horse editions are flopped).

In *Dreamland Japan*, Fred Schodt noted that Marvel, one of the two biggest comicbook publishers

1 *Young Magazine* is one of the 'young' magazines – aimed at late teens and college-age men (others include *Young Jump* and *Young Sunday*). *Young* is a *seinen* magazine, publishing plenty of erotic material along with the usual sports, video games, crime, humour and drama stories.
2 The label has since folded.

in North America (the other is Detective Comics),
tried to make *Akira* look as 'American' as possible.
They colourized it (American readers much prefer
colour, while the *manga* culture in Japan is still, as
then, chiefly black-and-white). But *Akira* was already
a *manga* with a strong French and American influence
(in its look, but also in its story, themes and
characters).

In the West, the *manga* of *Akira* has been
published in six hefty *tankobon* volumes by Studio
Proteus and Dark Horse (in the U.S.A.). The artwork
was flopped, so it reads left to right (Japanese read
the other way).[3] Each book was pricey, too ($24.95 or
more), although the editions were standard trade
paperbacks, and only the first coupla pages were in
colour.

The *manga* was translated by Yoko Umezawa,
Linda York and Jo Duffy (three women, note);[4] the
graphics and lettering were re-drawn by David
Schmit, Digibox, Éditions Glénat, Digital Chameleon
and Dark Horse Comics.

The flopped artwork is irritating at times: it
means that characters shake hands with their left
hands, that Tetsuo has his left arm ripped off, not his
right, that characters shoot guns left-handed (and all
sorts of other business), and cars're on the other side
of the road. Flopping artwork also wrecks some of
the careful compositions: *manga* artists are very conscious not only of each panel, but how each panel
relates to other panels, and to a single page as a
whole, and to each double page spread. There're also
many visual rhymes and patterns, across the whole
2,000 page *manga*, which are spoilt by reversing all of
the drawings.

Tokyopop published a comicbook version of
Akira using stills from the movie with word balloons

3 On some pages, you can see both flopped and original format
artwork (to preserve elements such as numbers or letters).
4 Altho' *Akira* is a macho, boysy and ultra-violent *manga*, it was
translated in the West by three women: Yoko Umezawa, Linda M.
York and Jo Duffy. So it's Umezawa, York and Duffy who're
responsible for versions in English of the ballsy, often crude dialogue.

(called *animekomikkusu*, 'animation comics').

A video game of *Akira* was produced in 1988; a video game was made in 1994; and a pinball simulation created by Bandai for PlayStation in 2002.

Katsuhiro Otomo was aided by assistants during the production of the *manga* of *Akira* (only a few *manga* artists, such as Masaume Shirow, do without assistants[5]). Satoshi Takabatake was Otomo's chief assistant. Satoshi Kon was among the more well-known of Otomo's assistants on the *manga*. Kon, who died in 2010 aged only 46 (a huge loss to the *anime* industry), was himself a significant *anime* director – *Perfect Blue, Tokyo Godfathers, Millennium Actress, Paranoia Agent* and *Paprika.* Kon worked with Otomo a number of times – set designer for *Roujin Z* and co-writer of *Memories*, and the *manga* and story of *World Apartment Horror*, for instance. He also drew the *manga* by Mamoru Oshii, *Seraphim 266,613,336 Wings,* plus *manga* such as *Toriko, Kaikisen, Opus* and *Paprika*).

Hiroshi Hirata produced the calligraphy for *Akira*, and designed the *tankobon* (along with Akira Saito). The editors were Koichi Yuri, Hisataka Nishitani, Yuka Ando and Noriyuki Okazaki.

THE MARVEL COLOUR EDITION OF *AKIRA*.
The colour edition of *Akira* by Marvel (1988-95) was produced in conjunction with Katsuhiro Otomo and his Mash Room Studio. Proofs and translations were sent to Japan, to Otomo and his team, as well as to his publisher. The colour was by Steve Oliff and the Olyoptics Computer Crew; as with the text, ideas for colours were approved by Otomo and Mash Room. As with the b/w editions, panels and bubbles were re-arranged and re-drawn.

Colour adds an entertaining layer to the *Akira manga* which of course it doesn't really need: this is fantastically rich storytelling which's already immensely colourful. The colour scheme for the

---

[5] Shirow, tho', has used several assistants, including 'Pure'.

Marvel edition follows the 1988 movie (thus, if you wanted to know what colour Tetsuo's cloak was (red), the movie had already shown you).

However, the Marvel edition did create fascinating extra layers to *Akira* in the abstract and supernatural sections, where exaggerations and extreme stylizations are encouraged. Thus, when Akira is just about to explode (in chapter 13/ end of *Book 3*), sepia/ orange panels are employed, along with the lilac/ purple which in *animé* signifies præternatural occurrences. For Tetsuo's terrifying nightmare, when his mind's connected to Akira, the colour palette shifts into abstractions.

However, the Marvel edition is *not* Otomoan in its use of colour: Otomo, as we know, slaps reds, oranges and yellows all over his colour work. His colour style is like no other in comics. It is super-rich (and very Asian). The Marvel edition of *Akira* is instead produced in the North American style: more 'naturalistic' colours, with blues and greens and greys.

THE STYLE OF THE *AKIRA MANGA*.

The *Akira manga* is in a large format, with the usual 4, 5, 6 or 7 panels per page, in black-and-white, with big action set-pieces taking up more page space. Sound effects are added to the action ('BLAOM', 'VVVROOOOOO'). In *manga*, the sound effects are part of the graphic style (which's inevitably impaired during the English translation). The typical *manga* panel in *Akira* comprises circles and square shapes, often presented in exaggerated perspectives, with the characters inserted in the foreground.

The *manga* of *Akira* employs all the usual conventions of *manga*. The characters, for instance, drip sweat to an alarming degree – but it's there to indicate extreme feelings (like the blushes on the cheeks or the crosses indicating anger).

Giant numbers and letters are a recurring motif. Also: circles, stones and rocks, very low angles, symmetry, city-wide vistas, steep perspectives, high contrast in lighting, etc.

There are boulders and pebbles everywhere in the *Akira manga*: Katsuhiro Otomo clearly loves the look of stones in bright light, so they cast shadows. There's even bits of rubble on the characters' beds in the second half, as if the world is continually shedding debris everywhere (and the characters are so wasted or tired, they can't brush them off their bed clothes).

As in most *manga*, most of the panels comprise black line drawings over white, but there also are many panels where mid-tones are employed, and also darker tones, when the artist wants to emphasize something, or to offer something unusual in amongst the regular black-lines-on-white pages. And of course, there are speed lines and exaggerated perspectives during the action or high drama scenes.

Katsuhiro Otomo also maintains the level of interest by employing a variety of viewpoints on almost every page of the *Akira manga,* so there are high angles mixed with low angles, very much in the cinematic mold of comicbooks. However, Otomo will employ direct-to-camera views at eye-level, when characters are confronting each other, and talking face-on to each other.

Katsuhiro Otomo keeps the scales and size of the drawings varied, shifting continuously from medium close-ups (his favoured kind of close-up), to full body shots and long shots. To further maintain interest, the number of panels per page changes with almost every page, and of course there are many climactic and interval scenes which dispense with speech bubbles.

As an artist of *spaces* and *places*, and especially the urban jungle, Katsuhiro Otomo is very impressive; the *Akira manga* delivers a very intense feeling for cities and city life (loving and also critical). By the end of the six-volume *manga*, Otomo has explored every possible region of a contemporary city, from the very depths (way below tunnels and sewers), to the very tops (a large number of scenes take place on rooftops – particularly in the second half of the *manga*, where Neo-Tokyo is an immense bomb site, and often the only way across the metropolis is via the roofs and girders).

In a useful close reading of a confrontation in *Akira* between Kei and Tetsuo, David Brothers notes (in 2011):

> None of what I've discussed could be described as flashy. There are no Photoshop tricks, after-images, or anything like that. There's not even a particularly obsessive attention to detail. This is just straight up comics, the kind of story that uses an incredibly nuanced understanding of what makes comics go to give a fight scene some serious punch. Otomo takes the basics of comics art and executes them so well that he elevates a scene that could've been seen in any comic into something divine. *Akira* in particular is full of this sort of thing, and if you haven't read it, you should seek it out.

Of course there are numerous differences at the story level, and characterization, and other dramatic elements, between the 1982-90 *manga* of *Akira* and the 1988 *animé* movie. But on the whole, the movie is refreshingly close to the spirit of the *manga*. The main thing, above all, is that the movie works on its *own* terms, without relation to the *manga* or to anything else. And it succeeds: *Akira* is regularly cited as the number one *animé* for thousands of fans, and it would have to be in anyone's top five list of animation of any kind from anywhere.

So although some fans gripe about what was left *out* of the *manga* in its journey to the screen, you can also celebrate what was kept *in*. And also what was added: because the 1988 animated flick added 100s of elements to the *manga*: at the level of detail and visual information, for example, the *animé* enhanced the *manga* enormously in many areas (colour, obviously, scale, movement, and the sheer size of the movie screen). When you add music, sound effects, voices, editing, and all the rest, the benefits are huge.

But as the *story* goes, and characters, and the large number of incidents, the *manga* includes far, far more than the movie.

The *detail* in the *Akira manga* is one of the first – and last – things that strikes you about it. Skyscrapers and city streets aren't sketched in vaguely, with just a few lines. Instead, every single, goddamn window is delineated.[6]

The density of detail in the *Akira manga* is phenomenal – way, way beyond what is required to tell the story. Like many *manga*, *Akira* has moments (not always action scenes) where a whole page's taken up with an image (and occasionally two pages).

Though critical of technology, *Akira*, in both *animé* and *manga* form, also fetishizes technology to an extraordinary degree: look at the lovingly depicted helicopters, weaponry,[7] motorcycles, etc (down to every rivet!). Parts of *Akira* look like the design department of a car manufacturer. In the *manga*, Katsuhiro Otomo has taken his ruler to everything, so that buildings and vistas are drawn with an emphasis on straight edges (multiple black speed lines on the roads or in the air signify high velocity). The crisp, straight edges and jagged linearity are typical of *manga* aimed at boys (*shonen*), compared to the cutie, pretty, rounded approach of girls' *manga* (*shojo*).[8]

Some *manga* comics have very busy pages, with panels not only in different sizes but bleeding into each other. Even celebrated *manga* like *Ghost In the Shell* by Masamune Shirow can be a little confusing to read (even more so when the action comprises

6 No lazy photocopying of a photo of Tokyo and and slapping it onto the page for Otomo!

7 Hayao Miyazaki admitted: 'I am a bundle of contradictions. The love of weaponry is often a manifestation of infantile traits in an adult' (2013).

8 *Manga* aimed at older readers is called *gekiga*.

characters floating thru the abstractions and space-
lessness of cyberspace).

The *Akira manga,* thankfully, employs panels
with a black line around them, and a quarter of an
inch or so between each panel. So every panel is
separate and enclosed. Of course, Katsuhiro Otomo
does change that format from time to time, going to
double-page spreads at highpoints, or smaller frag-
ments of panels.

By the end of drawing the *Akira manga*, Katsuhiro Otomo must've sketched every single skyscraper,
real or designed or made up, on Earth: the *Akira
manga* is a *Collection of Skyscrapers*, a pocket guide to
the 20th century skyscraper. Although modern-day
Tokyo is at the heart of *Akira*, New York City, as the
King of Skyscraper Cities (and certainly the most
influential), is all over *Akira* (Otomo draws the line at
including the two most celebrated sky-rises in
Gotham, the Art Deco giants – the Empire State
Building and the Chrysler Building – but he did
include icons such as the Pan-Am Building (now the
Met Life Building), which looms over Grand Central
Station.

And, by the end of the long slog of creating *Akira*
on the *manga* page, Katsuhiro Otomo must've drawn
more debris, chaos and mayhem than almost any
other contemporary artist. Yeah, and he also drew a
wrecked city in more detail than anybody else: I can't
think of any other print work I've seen which so
enjoys evoking a rubble-strewn environment. Not
only is *Akira* a *Guide To Modern Skyscrapers*, it is also
a *Catalogue of Smashed, Teetering, Fallen and Demolished Skyscrapers*. Girders, windows, brick-work,
walls, foundations, ceilings, heating and air condit-
ioning systems, ducts, lamps – Otomo could have had
a second (or third or fourth) career designing cities of
the future or advising architecture companies.

THE STORY OF THE *AKIRA MANGA*.
By the end of the *Akira manga*, Katsuhiro Otomo

THE ART OF KATSUHIRO OTOMO ○ 594

and his assistants have shown us so many things, so many aspects of life. But not all – this is a young person's story, and altho' there're older characters, such as Lady Miyako (Miyako-sama) and the Colonel and the Scientist, this is about young kids, their glories, their desires, their fears and their vulnerabilities (but Otomo would make up for that with *Roujin Z*, his hilarious pæan to all things old, cranky, miserable and rickety).

In the *manga* Tetsuo Shima, Kaneda Shotaro and the rest of the kids are fifteen when the story starts (Tetsuo was born on July 29, 2004). That's quite young – these are not 18 or 19 year-olds.

Katsuhiro Otomo explained what he wanted to do with *Akira*:

> I wanted to revive a Japan like the one I grew up in, after the Second World War, with a government in difficulty, a world being rebuilt, external political pressures, an uncertain future and a gang of kids left to fend for themselves, who cheat boredom by racing on motorbikes.

The pace in the *Akira manga* is extremely rapid – it's a genuine page-turner: you really do want to know what happens next. Then, once you've got the story, you can go back at marvel at some of the artwork. And yet it never feels rushed: there are enough interludes and also places where the reader needs to know some background information. It's not just wall-to-wall action – that quickly becomes movement, weaponry and violence for the sake of it, and you tire of that easily. Even in the action scenes, there's a lot more going on in the *Akira manga*.

The *Akira manga* consciously takes up every post-war scenario from recent history, in its second half: it is war-torn Europe from 1945-1960, it is the Vietnam War, it is Korea, it is the Soviet Union in the Stalinist era, it is Spain in the Civil War, and so on.

Notice that the *Akira manga* stays within Japan

for the duration of the series. It might've been tempting to go to other countries, such as Russia, China or North America (the three obvious ones), but no, *Akira* remains in the homeland. When the cataclysms hit Neo-Tokyo, including the ravaging of the moon, presumably many other cities around the world would've been affected (especially by raging storms or rising tides). But Katsuhiro Otomo sticks to the principal charas and settings in Japan.

One of the subplots in the *Akira manga* has Tetsuo being taken to the Clowns gang's hide-out (in an abandoned bowling alley). There's a terrific scene where Tetsuo faces off against the portly Clowns' leader, Joker. Later on in the *manga*, it's reported (but not shown, except in a two-page flashback), that Tetsuo has become leader of the Clowns (which seems a little unlikely, though Tetsuo has also probably long resented Kaneda being the boss of everything, so being able to be the captain of a rival gang would appeal to Tetsuo. Kaneda can't believe it).[9]

THE INFLUENCE OF *AKIRA*.

Katsuhiro Otomo has of course influenced subsequent artists, such as Akemi Yoshida (*Banana Fish*), Masamune Shirow (*Ghost In the Shell*, *Appleseed*) and Yukito Kishiro (*Gunnm* a.k.a. *Battle Angel Alita*) – not least for his pioneering shift towards more realistically 'Japanese' faces. Kei Kusunoki (*Ogre Slayer*, *Jin-roh*, *Curse of the Undead: Yoma*) has admired *Akira*. *Hommages* appear in *Ghost In the Shell* and *Macross Plus*. There's a biker gang in the O.A.V. *Shonan Bakusozoku* (*Bomber Bikers of Shonan*, 1986), and in *Sky-Blue* (Kim Moon-saeng, 2003 – see appendix).

Among the other people who've cited *Akira* as an influence are Masashi Mishimoto (*Naruto*), who raves about it; Josh Trank; Sean Lennon; the Wachowski brothers; Kanye West; and James Cameron.

9 Joker, meanwhile, makes a surprise appearance in the later *tankobons* of *Akira*, forming an uneasy but ultimately brotherly alliance with our Kaneda.

*

In *The Rough Guide To Graphic Novels*, Danny Fingeroth remarked:

> *Akira* can legitimately be said to have changed everything in Western readers' expectations of what comics could and should be. But it's certainly no museum piece. It's a story that asks timeless questions in a distinctly modern manner. (65)

1001 Comics You Must Read Before You Die calls *Akira*

> a masterwork of action-fueled drama, and it contains some of the finest action sequences ever committed to page... *Akira* is a unique hybrid of Western and Japanese sensibilities, both in illustrations style and substance, and has become a cultural phenomenon. (436)

ADAPTING THE *MANGA*.

A film director will prefer to direct the movie version of their own *manga*, Katsuhiro Otomo admitted, but one challenge is to maintain the level of interest – because the artist has already lived thru the story once. A *mangaka* who is also the writer of the *manga* has already brought the story to life by telling it, and also telling it visually. As Otomo put it:

> I don't like repeating myself, and I feel that adapting my own *manga* is essentially repeating something I've already done once before.
> [...]
> I generally don't like revisiting or even reading my own *manga*. Maybe I just don't like my own work.

Manga weren't ideal to turn into movies for reasons such as the multiple plot-lines, Hayao Miyazaki said (2009, 62). Another reason was length:

Nausicaä of the Valley of the Wind was 1,000 pages long, and *Akira* is 2,000 pages.

Like many other *animé* adapted from *manga*, there is some confusion and incoherence about *Akira*'s story. Adapting *manga* usually means only part of a series can be put into a movie, and with long-running *manga*, that means only a small proportion (and adapting your own *manga*, as Hayao Miyazaki, knew, could be extra difficult, because it is your own work). However, as with many of the finest movies, the *story* in *Akira* is merely *one ingredient* in a vast display of spectacular elements. Yes, decent stories and characters are essential to the success of most movies, but with movies such as *Akira*, story and character isn't everything. It's the same with pictures such as *Kagemusha, Gertrud, Aguirre: Wrath of God, Pierrot le Fou,* Hong Kong martial arts movies, and, in *animé, Cowboy Bebop, Drifters, Escaflowne* and *Ghost In the Shell.*

As with a Hollywood musical, you don't need to know the story, or to be able to follow the story, or to know which character is which, to get so much out of the 1988 Japanese movie. You go along for the ride, you submerge yourself in the experience. With movies like *Akira* – or *An American In Paris, Seven Swords,* a Jan Svankmajer animation (*Alice*), a Walerian Borowczyk flick (*Immoral Tales*) – you submit to the experience, to the feeling, to the adrenalin rush.

Akira is telling a story, yes, but it is also doing so much more. It is clearly created to operate on a number of levels simultaneously. (One of the ways you can test this, and consider other levels to *Akira*, is to switch off the subtitles, and watch the movie in Japanese. *Akira* is a movie so overloaded with stuff, it works a treat like that. It's a good thing to do with other Japanese *animé*: watch the movie or TV show once to get the story that's carried by the dialogue, then enjoy it again without the subtitles).

Overload – a good term to describe *Akira*. *Overload* certainly describes the culture of the late

1980s: I can remember that period as having intense levels of political craziness and cultural saturation. It recalls David Selznick's advice about doing an epic movie like *Gone With the Wind*: if you're going to do a big movie like that, then you'd best *really* do it.

COMPARING THE MOVIE AND THE *MANGA*.

Yes: the *manga* of *Akira* is much more intimate and domestic than the movie (most of the panels present medium close-ups or medium shots of people, which's typical of the comicbook medium of course). Sometimes they're sitting around eating. And altho' the *manga* is a riot of action and movement, amazed looks and Moebius-level visual density, the movie explodes with colour and light, music and sound effects. Both the *manga* and the *animé*, though, share numerous elements: a breakneck pace, for starters.

It's true that the 1988 *animé* movie of the *Akira manga* changes so much, and only covers part of the epic story. But if you know the *manga* well, or read it just b4 seeing the movie again, you will find hundreds of smaller moments, right down to looks or gestures from the characters, which come from the *manga*, but which the movie employs in a different context (the movie was clearly storyboarded right out of the *manga*).

The production team – not only the writers, Katsuhiro Otomo and Izo Hashimoto, but layout artists, background artists, *mecha* designers, and of course the key animators – will have gone thru the *manga* again and again and again. They will have looked at the *manga* so many times it will have made them sick! (As artists who've worked on *manga* adaptations have admitted). But they also included 100s of elements from the *manga* in the movie.

Although the Neo-Tokyo in the *Akira manga* and movie draws on cinematic forebears such as *Metropolis*, *Blade Runner*, and many *animé* forerunners (such as *Macross* and *Gundam*), Katsuhiro Otomo makes it his own: his futuristic city, for instance,

THE ART OF KATSUHIRO OTOMO ○ 599

contains 100s of non-descript back streets, places which're run down and distinctly *un*spectacular, with dingy stalls and stores, the kind of downtown Tokyo and suburban Tokyo where people really live. The extraordinary images of downtown Neo-Tokyo at the beginning of the 1988 animated movie, with forests of skyscrapers rising above even more skyscrapers, only appear in the *manga* from time to time.

In the *manga*, Tetsuo Shima is introduced in a cursory manner b4 the accident; writers Izo Hashimoto and Katsuhiro Otomo recognized that he needs a fuller introduction for the movie, in particular his relationship with Kaneda, and the rest of the gang. And in *manga*, after the accident on the bridge near the toll-booths, Tetsuo disappears for a long section of the narrative: the movie elevates Tetsuo to a dual protagonist role with Kaneda much quicker (and it also cuts back to Tetsuo and what's happening to him many times).

In the *Akira manga*, the lovely Kei has a different introduction: she walks into the Harukiya Bar (to meet Ryu), and the kids hanging out there are wide-eyed and awe-struck – 'WAAA... OOOH' – no one that delicious has graced their home-from-home since forever.

Among the scenes added to the *manga* for the movie were Kaori introduced on her own (in a laundromat), and further scenes featuring Kaori alone. Kaori's beating and near-rape were additions. The wonderful scenes in the police interrogation room were additions, as was the scene where Kaneda tries to pick up Kei afterwards.

In the *manga*, Kaneda has a romance with a cute, young school nurse in the infirmary: when she tells him, 'I think I might be pregnant', his response is total dumb-ass: 'Hey great! Can I watch you have it?' (The school nurse tests the pills that Kaneda swiped from his encounter with the psychic children).

Some other differences:

▾ An enjoyable addition to the *manga* was the

terrific and humorous scene in the stadium where the cops question the motorcycle gang. It's not strictly necessary, in terms of the chief plot, but it does add characterizations for the gang, and for Kaneda in particular. It also leads into a brief scene where Kaneda gets to talk to Kei, b4 she hurries off.

There're six kids who are brought in the principal's office to be reprimanded in the *manga*: the movie tended to focus on four of the gang members: Tetsuo, Kaneda, Kai and Yamagata (for the purposes of the movie, four members is enough to represent the facets of the young generation, and also for dramatic purposes).

▾ Neo-Tokyo comprises a new city and an old city: it's to the Old City that the biker gang ride in the *manga*, across the very long bridge; the movie includes the bridge, as well as the toll-booths (in the *manga*, the bridge ends abruptly and symbolically at the bomb crater).

▾ Drugs play a bigger role in the *Akira manga*: the Capsules gang take their name from drugs, for instance, and the psychic children need a constant diet of mega-dosage pills. The movie was right to play down the drugs angle, allowing more time for more compelling material.

▾ The Colonel has two rather inept agents working with him, driving his car and running errands in the *manga*; thankfully, the 1988 movie dispensed with them (tho' they don't last long).

(The companion book to this volume, *The Akira Book*, includes a detailed, 350-page summary of the whole of Katsuhiro Otomo's *manga*).

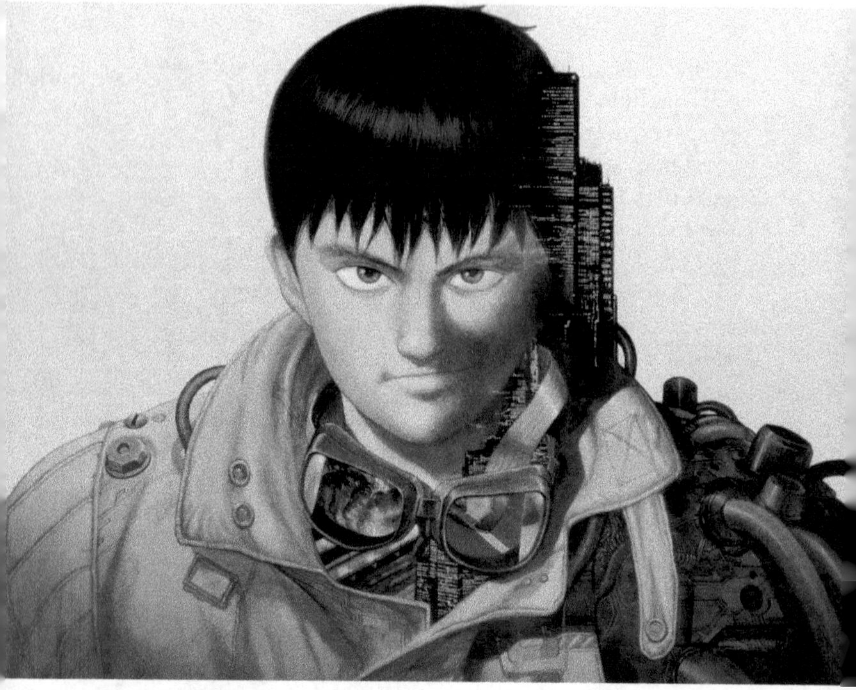

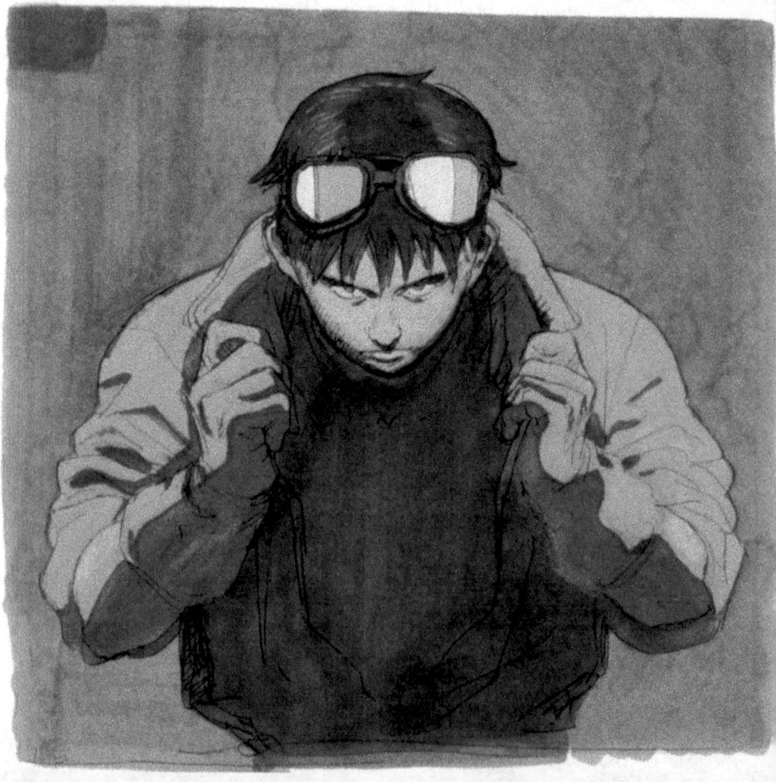

RESOURCES

WEBSITES

AKIRA AND KATSUHIRO OTOMO

   akira2019.com
   steamboy.net
   bbakira.co.uk
   cdn.halcyonrealms.com
   Otomblr.tumblr.com
   chronotomo.aandnn.com

   I would recommend: Anime News Network (animenews
network.com), which is excellent, and the first stop for any
online research on *animé*. Anime News Network has the
fullest credits on the web for animation, and each entry is
linked, so you can follow your favourite actors, directors,
producers and artists, across numerous shows.
   Also: Japanese Cinema Database.
   Japanese Movie Data Base.
   Gilles Poitras's site: koyagi.com.
   Fred L. Schodt's site: jai2.com.
   Otaku News: otakunews.com.
   Midnight Eye (for Japanese cinema): midnighteyec.com.
   Also: anipike.com and manga.com.
   There are fan sites, of course.

BOOKS ON *ANIMÉ*

Compared to, say, Walt Disney and Alfred Hitchcock, who
have stacks of books written about them, there is very, very
little on Katsuhiro Otomo in English. Most studies of *animé*,
however, have references to *Akira*, it being such an important work commercially and culturally as well as critically
(the books on *animé* which have a 'best of' section usually

include *Akira*).

Books by Frederik Schodt, Helen McCarthy, Trish Ledoux, Patrick Drazen, Fred Patten, Jonathan Clements, Simon Richmond, Antonia Levi, Susan Napier, Jason Thompson and Gilles Poitras are standard works. But apart from those key authors, there is surprisingly little available on *animé* in English.

And most film critics tend to focus on characters, stories, and the biographies of the filmmakers. So many books on *animé* simply tell us the stories. Very few critics grapple with the industrial, social and cultural aspects of *animé* (and even less with theory and philosophy). Which's why critics such as Fred Schodt and Helen McCarthy are so important, because they address issues such as the modes of production, the audience and the market, and social-cultural contexts.

The single most useful book on *animé* is *The Animé Encyclopedia* (2001/ 2006/ 2015) by Jonathan Clements and Helen McCarthy. If you buy one book on Japanese animation, get this one. *The Animé Encyclopedia* provides entries on pretty much every important *animé* show, O.A.V. and movie to come out of the Japanese animation industry, as well as numerous minor shows and oddities. This is the equivalent of a Leonard Maltin/ *Time Out/ Virgin/ Oxford/ Variety* guide to cinema. Clements and McCarthy are *animé* experts as well as fans (I would also recommend any of Clements' other books, including his history of *animé*, and his entertaining account of working in the *animé* business in translation and dubbing, *Schoolgirl Milky Crisis*).

All of Helen McCarthy's books have become standard works: *Anime! A Beginner's Guide To Japanese Animation, The Animé Movie Guide, The Erotic Animé Movie Guide, 500 Manga Heroes & Villains* and *500 Essential Anime Movies* (some of these were co-authored with Jonathan Clements). They contain facts, credits and background info to *animé* and *manga* which will greatly enhance your studies (and enjoyment) of Japanese comics and cartoons.

Other standard works on *animé* include: *The Art of Japanese Animation* (from Animage, 1988-89), and the *Dictionary of Animation Works* (2010).

Fred Schodt is one of the most valuable commentators on Japanese *animé* and *manga* in the West. His pioneering study of *manga, Manga! Manga! The World of Japanese Magazines*, is a marvellous book. Before it, there was virtually nothing. Because of the huge crossover between *manga* and *animé*, many of the chapters on *manga* in Schodt's studies also apply to *animé*. Schodt also offers one of the fullest and most detailed accounts of the history of *manga* and visual art in

Japan. (*Manga! Manga!* also includes samples from some famous *manga*, including *Barefoot Gen* and *The Rose of Versailles*, and the illustrations – from the history of Japanese art as well as from *manga* – are stunning).

Fred Schodt's follow-up, *Dreamland Japan: Writings On Modern Manga*, is equally riveting. It includes a huge number of illuminating studies of individual artists and their works (with illustrations), as well as another history of *manga*. *Dreamland Japan* is also probably the finest, most intelligent and best-informed analysis of the *manga* market in both Japan and overseas. As well as Osamu Tezuka, Frederik Schodt also discusses Hayao Miyazaki, the relation of *manga* to *animé*, artistic styles, Japanese publishers, and the big *manga* magazines. It enhances Schodt's books that he has also interviewed many of the chief artists of *manga*, including the 'god of manga' himself, Osamu Tezuka.

Trish Ledoux and Doug Ranney edited an early guide to *animé*, *The Complete Anime Guide*, that is now a standard work. It is packed with fascinating snippets, as well as hard information, credits, etc. The companion volume, *Anime Interviews*, culled from *Animerica* magazine, is wonderful, featuring many of the key practitioners in animation (such as Masamune Shirow, Shoji Kawamori, Mamoru Oshii, Leiji Matsumoto, Rumiko Takahashi and Hayao Miyazaki).

Gilles Poitras has produced a number of works on *animé*, including *The Animé Companion* and *Animé Essentials*. Poitras offers vital links between Japanese animation and Japanese culture and society. There are objects, gestures, words and customs in *animé* that often surprise or bemuse Western viewers: Poitras' books help to explain them. You will find yourself recognizing all sorts of elements in *animé* that Poitras includes in his books (which contain many illustrations).

Antonia Levi's *Samurai From Outer Space* is stuffed with information on Japanese society as well as Japanese animation. Clearly written and with an appealing sense of humour, Levi's book is a lesser-known but invaluable work. *Samurai From Outer Space* discusses all of the celebrated *animé* shows that've made the leap across the Pacific to the Western world. Published in 1996, you wish that Levi (like many other authors whose books came out in the 1990s), was able to update them. Many great shows have been released since 1996!

Simon Richmond's *The Rough Guide To Anime* is a superb, general introduction to the wild world of *animé*. Like other *Rough Guides*, it selects fifty must-see TV shows and movies, plus providing discussions of related topics like *manga*, adaptations of *animé*, and a history of animation.

Jason Yadao's *The Rough Guide To Manga* is a companion guide to the *Rough Guide To Animé*. It has the same format and is a terrific general introduction to the world of Japanese comics. Yadao's enthusiasm is infectious: you will want to hunt out many of his recommendations. Both *Rough Guides* were published in the 2000s, so they're able to include recent classics like *Fullmetal Alchemist, Cowboy Bebop, Love Hina* and the masterpieces of Satoshi Kon.

Manga: The Complete Guide (Jason Thompson and others) is another illuminating book, packed with short reviews and longer pieces on topics like games, sci-fi, martial arts, sport, religion, crime, *mecha, shojo*, and *yaoi*.

Zettai! Anime Classics is another of those books that looks at 100 classic movies: Brian Camp and Julie Davis spend more time, however, on each of the familiar masterpieces of Japanese animation, exploring the films, O.A.V.s and TV shows in much more detail than the usual single paragraph review.

Manga Impact! from Phaidon is an entertaining survey of Japanese animation, with a format focussing on characters and personnel. *Manga Impact!* has short text entries, but features numerous wonderful illustrations in colour.

Susan Napier's *Anime: From Akira To Princess Mononoke* is much more theoretical, and somewhat dry. (If you are familiar with the theoretical approaches to Western animation (see the studies noted below), you will find nothing new in Western authors exploring Japanese animation from a theoretical or philosophical point-of-view).

The guides to the art of comics by Scott McCloud (including *Understanding Comics*), are highly recommended general introductions to how comics work (delivered in the form of a comic, with plenty of humour).

BOOKS ON ANIMATION

On animation in general, I would recommend the following studies: P. Wells' *Understanding Animation*; E. Smoodin's *Animating Culture: Hollywood Cartoons From the Sound Era*; Leonard Maltin's *Of Mice and Magic: A History of American Animated Cartoons*; James Clarke's *Animated Films*; *From Mouse To Mermaid: The Politics of Film, Gender and Culture* (edited by E. Bell *et al*); *Animation Art* (edited by J. Beck); and *Reading the Rabbit: Explorations in Warner Bros. Animation* (edited by K. Sandler).

For information on Walt Disney, the standard works include: Leonard Maltin's *The Disney Films*; Richard

Schickel's *The Disney Version: The Life, Times, Art, and Commerce of Walt Disney*; R. Grover's *The Disney Touch;* Project on Disney's *Inside the Mouse: Work and Play at Disney World*; *Disney Discourse: Producing the Magic Kingdom* (edited by E. Smoodin); and *Walt Disney: A Guide to References and Resources* (edited by E. Leebron *et al*).

BOOKS ON CINEMA

For a study of cinema, there is one book that towers above *every other book* on film (even tho' the competition is fierce!): David A. Cook's *A History of Narrative Film*. If you want one book that covers everything, this is it.

David Bordwell and Kristin Thompson have written many meticulously researched and beautifully crafted books on cinema: *Film Art: An Introduction, Narration In the Fiction Film, Film History: An Introduction, The Classical Hollywood Cinema: Film Style and Mode of Production to 1960* and *Storytelling In the New Hollywood*. Anything by Bordwell and/ or Thompson is excellent.

I would also recommend Bruce Kawin's *How Movies Work,* Gerald Mast's *Film Theory and Criticism: Introductory Readings,* and Mast & Kawin's *A Short History of the Movies*.

David Cook, David Bordwell, Kristin Thompson, Gerald Mast and Bruce Kawin will give you all you could need for an in-depth study of cinema. Read their books: it's the equivalent of a degree or PhD in cinema!

AVAILABILITY

Akiira has had two English language dubs – in 1988 (by Streamline), and in 2001 (by Animaze/ Pioneer). You can buy editions of *Akira* which have both versions.

However, the original language versions are always the ones to go for. Why? Because Katsuhiro Otomo himself has overseen or approved of the voice casts and mixes (as well as the dialogue). Many elements are altered in a foreign language dub, including music, sound fx and even scenes.

Think of it in the opposite direction: a film by Orson Welles or Alfred Hitchcock that was dubbed into Japanese, even by the best technical staff and the best actors in the Japanese film business, could not be regarded as conforming completely to the filmmakers' vision (unless Welles or Hitch could speak or understand Japanese and were present at

THE ART OF KATSUHIRO OTOMO ✧ 607

the ADR and sound mixing and editing sessions). I also object to dubbing on social, cultural, personal, æsthetic, political and ideological grounds.

FANS ON *AKIRA*

FROM THE INTERNET MOVIE DATABASE

Akira is one of the most visually potent animated films of all time.

Akira is raw and uncompromising, the action is over-the-top and spectacular, the setting (Neo-Tokyo) is fantastic, and the characters intriguing. At the end of the movie, we also get a good dose of theology/ science ideas thrown at us for good measure. Combine all of these and you're in for quite a ride.

Akira is far underrated, and should be easily in the top 250 movies. The story is innovative, and draws you into the plot in a matter of minutes. The surreal and futuristic society portrayed, is one that few if any other movies can match. The music and cinematography intermix perfectly, as Kaneda and Tetsuo lead the cast in a whirlwind of explosions, mystery, and mesmerizing visuals.

The animation equals or exceeds Disney's best, the music is awesome, and the characters are complex, but *Akira* has its flaws.

This was the first Japanese animation movie I ever saw – I was totally unprepared what I was in for, and left the cinema stunned and amazed. For me, without any doubt, *Akira* is a seminal film.

Akira is without doubt the best animated film ever!

FROM AMAZON

THE FIRST TEN MINUTES OF THIS VIDEO SETS THE STAGE FOR ONE OF THE MOST INNOVATIVE, CREATIVE, AND STYLISH ANIMATED FILMS EVER.

⊖

Akira is one of those movies that you never forget. The images are extremely powerful and graphic, so that they stick with you long after the movie is over.

⊖

My favorite anime/ manga movie of all time. It got me into the genre, and this edition has all the dub versions and is super spectacular. I am a fan for life.

⊖

Saw this movie when I was thirteen and it changed my opinion on anime completely. I went from hating it, to loving it. This is a masterpiece.

⊖

One of the more interesting, confusing, convoluted, awesome, well made animes. If you've never seen an anime, this is the first one you should see!

⊖

This movie is good. This movie is beyond good.

⊖

This was the BEST anime ever! Two hours I bliss. I was amazed the entire movie. See this you will love it! END

CRITICS ON *AKIRA*

Put it up there with the most astonishing animated features ever made.

Derek Malcolm, *This is London*

▶▶

The most expensive animated feature ever made in Japan (over 1 billion yen) and it's easily the most impressive, as well.

Richard Harrington, *Washington Post*

▶▶

Style and substance run neck and neck in this thrilling, bold landmark film that just refuses to become dated.

Phelim O'Neill, *The Guardian*

▶▶

The movie, even at 124 minutes, has the densely packed sweep and go-for-it pep of a pop epic.

Jay Cocks, *Time Magazine*

▶▶

[*Akira*] is a blast and a half, a twisted dystopian parable of violence and rock and roll, Japanese-style. It's Disney on PCP, mean, rotten, psychotic, but incredibly vivid.

Stephen Hunter, *Baltimore Sun*

▶▶

The cityscapes are awesome, the camerawork is dizzying. If you're new to manga, prepare to be converted.

David Parkinson, *Radio Times*

▶▶

Akira is pure concentrated cinematic excellence – accept no substitutes.

Rob Daniel, *Sky Movies*

▶▶

Rightfully considered one of the greatest accomplishments in sci-fi storytelling.

Film 4

▶▶

Still one of the best techno science fiction thrillers of all time

Felix Vasquez Jr., *Film Threat*

▶▶

Plenty of superb recent blockbusters, including *The Matrix*, *The Dark Knight*, *Minority Report*, *Dark City* and *Inception*, are all in its debt – not to mention a fair number of shockers, like *Star Wars Episode II* and the most recent *Resident Evil* atrocity.

Robbie Collin, *News of the World*

▶▶

Moments that can only be captured as animation make *Akira* still worth watching: gusts of wind from chopper blades, ka-tooming bursts of fiery explosions, Tetsuo's visions.

Brian Gibson, *Vue Weekly*

▶▶

Some kind of fever-dream masterpiece, easily the most breathtaking and kinetic anime ever made and one of the most eloquent films about atomic afterclap.

Michael Atkinson, *Village Voice*

FILMOGRAPHIES

KATSUHIRO OTOMO

MOVIES AS DIRECTOR

Give Me a Gun Give Me Freedom (1982)
Neo-Tokyo (1987)
Robot Carnival (*Coming Soon* and *See You Again*) (1987)
Akira (1988)
World Apartment Horror (1991)
Memories (*Cannon Fodder*) (1995)
Steamboy (2004)
Bugmaster (2006)
Short Peace (*Combustible*) (2013)

MOVIES AS WRITER

Kôkô Erotopia: Akai seifuku (1979)
Give Me a Gun Give Me Freedom (1982)
Neo-Tokyo (1987)
Fushigi monogatari: Hachi neko wa yoku asagata kaette kuru
(*The Cat Often Comes Back In the Morning*, short, 1988)
So What (short, 1988)
Akira (1988)
Roujin Z (1991)
World Apartment Horror (1991)
Memories (1995)
Metropolis (2001)
Steamboy (2004)
Bugmaster (2006)
Hipira (2009)
Short Peace (*Combustible*) (2013)

FILMS DIRECTED AND WRITTEN
BY KATSUHIRO OTOMO

Credits: release dates are Japanese release. Cast are the main Japanese actors.

KOKO EROTOPIA: AKAISEIFUKU / HIGH SCHOOL EROTOPIA: RED UNIFORMS

1979. 63 mins.
Production – Nikkatsu
Director – Shin'ichi Shiratori
Script – Shôko Shikamizu and Katsuhiro Ôtomo

CAST
Etsuko Hara – Yoshiko Sawada
Tayori Hinatsu – Kikuko Kikuchi
Yûko Asuka – Yukiko Ôno
Moeko Ezawa – Sasae
Hiroshi Fujino – Yutaka Miyajima

GIVE ME A GUN, GIVE ME FREEDOM/ JIVU O WARERA NI

1982. 60 mins.
Director and script – Katsuhiro Ôtomo

NEO-TOKYO/ LABYRINTH TALES/ MANIE MANIE MEIKYU MONOGATARI

September 25, 1987. 50 mins.
Production – Project Team Argus, Madhouse and Kadokawa
Executive Producer – Haruki Kadokawa
Producers – Masao Maruyama and Rintaro
Directors – Rintaro, Yoshitaki Kawajiri and Katsuhiro Ôtomo
Animation Directors – Takashi Nakamura, Atsuko Fukushima, Koji Morimoto and Kunihiko Sakurai
Music – Micky Yoshino
Art Dir. – Takamura Mukuo
DP – Kinichi Ishikawa

Editing – Harutoshi Ogata

CAST
(for *Order To Stop Construction*/ *Koji Chushi Meirei*)
Tsutomo Sugioka – Yuu Mizushima
Iemasa Kayumi – Buchô
Jôji Yanami
Hiroshi Ôtake – Robot 444

ROBOT CARNIVAL

1987. 90 minutes.
Production – A.P.P.P., Studio A.P.P.P.
Executive Producer – Kazufumi Nomura
Directors – Katsuhiro Ôtomo, Atsuko Fukushima, Lamdo
Mao, Hiroyuki Kitakubo, Takashi Nakamura, Hiroyuki
Kitazume, Yasuomi Umetsu, Manabu Ôhashi, Hidetoshi
Ômori and Koji Morimoto
Script – Hiroyuki Kitazume, Koji Morimoto, Hiroyuki
Kitazume, Katsuhiro Ôtomo, Mao Lamdo, Takashi
Nakamura, Yasuomi Umetsu, Manabu Ôhashi and Hidetoshi
Ômori
Music – Joe Hisaishi, Isaku Fujita and Masahisa Takeshi
DP – Toshiaki Morita
Editors – Yukiko Ito, Harutoshi Ogata and Osamu Toyosaki
Sound Director – Yasunori Honda

CAST
Kôji Moritsugu – Toymaker
Yayoi Maki – Android
Keiko Hanagata – Wife
Kei Tomiyama – Sankichi
Chisa Yokoyama – Yayoi
Katsue Miwa – Fukusuke
Kaneto Shiozawa – Denjiro
Toku Nishio – Daimaru

AKIRA

July 16, 1988, Japan. 124 minutes.

Produced – Haruyo Kanesaku, Shunzo Kato, James Yosuke Kobayashi, Yutaka Maseba, Yoshimasa Mizuo, Sawako Noma, Ryohei Suzuki and Hiroe Tsukamoto

Production companies: – Akira Committee Company Ltd., Bandai, Kôdansha, Mainichi Broadcasting System (MBS), Sumitomo Corporation, Toho Company and Tokyo Movie Shinsha (TMS)

Director – Katsuhiro Ôtomo

Script – Katsuhiro Ôtomo and Izô Hashimoto

Manga – Katsuhiro Ôtomo

Original Music – Shoji Yamashiro

Takashi Nakamura – chief animator

Cinematography – Katsuji Misawa

Film Editing – Takeshi Seyama

Production Design – Kazuo Ebisawa, Yuji Ikehata, Koji Ono

Art Dir. – Toshiharu Mizutani

CAST

Mitsuo Iwata – Shôtarô Kaneda

Nozomu Sasaki – Tetsuo Shima

Mami Koyama – Kei

Yuriko Fuchizaki – Kaori

Tarô Ishida – Colonel Shikishima

Tesshô Genda – Ryûsaku

Hiroshi Ohtake – Nezu

Takeshi Kusao – Kai

Kôichi Kitamura – Priestess Miyako

Mizuho Suzuki – Doctor Ônishi

Michihiro Ikemizu – Inspector

Tarô Arakawa – Eiichi Watanabe

Masaaki Ôkura – Yamagata

Kazuhiro Kamifuji – Masaru

Tatsuhiko Nakamura – Takashi

Fukue Itô – Kiyoko

Yôsuke Akimoto – Harukiya Bartender

SO WHAT

1988.

Director – Naoto Yamakawa

Script – Yasushi Hirano, Toshiyuki Mizutani, Naoto Yamakawa and Katsuhiro Ôtomo

DP – Noboru Shinoda

CAST
Kazuki Minabuchi
Mikihisa Azuma
Kanako Fukaura
Risa Honda
Renji Ishibashi

WORLD APARTMENT HORROR

1991. 97 mins.
Producers – Yoshihiro Kato and Yasuhisa Kazama
Director – Katsuhiro Ôtomo
Story – Satoshi Kon
Script – Keiko Nobumoto and Katsuhiro Ôtomo
DP – Noboru Shinoda
Art Dir. – Terumi Hosoishi

CAST
Sabu – Ita (as Hiroki Tanaka)
Jazz Cutz
Mohammed Abdul Sahib
Hiroshi Shimizu
Hua Rong Weng

ROUJIN Z/ OLD MAN Z

1991. 80 mins.
Produced – A.P.P.P., the Television, Tokyo Theater,
M.O.V.I.C., TV Asahi and Sony
Executive Producers - Masayoshi Yoshida, Shugo Matsuo,
Tsuguhiko Kadokawa and Yutaka Takahashi
Director – Hiroyuki Kitakubo
Script and *Mecha* Designs – Katsuhiro Ôtomo
Music – Bun Itakura
Character Designer – Hisashi Eguchi
Animation Director – Fumi Iida

CAST
Shinji Ogawa – Suguru Ogawa
Chie Satou – Nobuko Ohe
Chisa Yokoyama – Haruko
Hikojiro Matsumura – Kijuro Takazawa

Kouji Tsujitani – Mitsuru Maeda
Masa Saito – Haru Takazawa
Rica Matsumoto – Satoh Tomoe
Shinsuke Chikaishi – Yoshihiko Hasegawa
Takeshi Aono – Old Man
Tamio Ohki – Professor Tachibana

MEMORIES/ *KANOJO NO OMOIDE*

1995. 115 mins.
Production companies – Bandai Visual, Kodansha and Shochiku
Production – Madhouse and Studio 4°C
Executive Producers – Shigeru Watanabe, Makoto Yamashina, Shoji Yakigaya, Teruo Miyahara and Katsuhiro Ôtomo
Producers – Atsushi Sugita, Eiko Tanaka, Fumio Samejima, Hiroaki Inoue and Yoshimasa Mizu
Directors – Koji Morimoto, Tensai Okamura and Katsuhiro Ôtomo
Script – Satoshi Kon and Katsuhiro Ôtomo
Music – Takuya Ishino, Jun Miyake, Hiroyuki Nagashima and Yoko Kanno
Animator Director – Yoshitaki Kawajiri
Sound Producer – Masakatsu Aida
Sound Director – Sadayoshi Fujino
Editor – Takeshi Seyama

CAST
Shigeru Chiba – Aoshima
Tsutomu Isobe – Heinz
Kôichi Yamadera – Miguel
Shôzô Îzuka – Ivanov
Ami Hasegawa – Emily
Kayoko Fujii – Sakiko
Michio Hazama – Nirasaki
Hideyuki Hori – Nobuo
Michitaka Kobayashi – Reporter
Keaton Yamada – Father
Keiko Yamamoto – Mother
Yu Hayashi – Boy (in *Cannon Fodder*)
Nobuaki Fukuda – Chief Shell Handler

SPRIGGAN/ STRIKER

1998. 90 mins.
Production – Tokyo Broadcasting System, Toho,
Shogakukan-Shueisha Productions, Bandai and Studio 4°C
Producers – Ayao Ueda, Eiko Tanaka, Haruo Sai,
Katsuhiro Ôtomo, Kazuhiko Ikeguchi, Kazuya Hamana
Director – Hirotsuge Kawasaki
Script – Hirotsuge Kawasaki, Yasuaka Ito and Katsuhiro
Ôtomo
Manga – Hiroshi Takashige and artist Ryoji Minagawa
Music – Kuniaki Haishima
Designer and Animation Director – Hisashi Eguchi
Editor – Takeshi Seyama

CAST
Showtaro Morikubo – Yuu Ominae
Ryuji Aigase – Colonel MacDougall
Takehito Koyasu – Jean Jacques Mondo
Ken Shiroyama – Dr. Meisel
Kenji Takano – Fat Man

METROPOLIS/ METOROPORISU

Released May 26, 2001. 107/ 113 mins.
Production companies – Madhouse, Bandai Visual,
Dentsu, Imagica, Kadokawa Shoten, Toho, Sony, Metropolis
Production Partners, Starchild Records and Tezuka Product-
ion
Executive Producers – Akihiko Terajima, Fumio Nagase,
Ken Munekata, Ryohei Tsunoda, Tadamichi Abe, Hisanori
Hiranuma, Takayuki Matsutan, and Toru Shiobara
Director – Rintaro
Script – Katsuhiro Ôtomo
Manga – Osamu Tezuka
Chief Animation and Character Design – Yasuhiro
Nakura
DP – Hitoshi Yamaguchi
Art Dir. – Shûichi Hirata
Sound Director – Masafumi Mima

CAST
Yuka Imoto – Tima
Kei Kobayashi – Kenichi
Kôki Okada – Rock
Tarô Ishida – Duke Red

Kousei Tomita – Shunsaku Ban
Norio Wakamoto – Pero
Junpei Takiguchi – Dr. Laughton
Takeshi Aono – Ponkotz
Masaru Ikeda – President Boon

STEAM-BOY / SUCHIMUBOI

July 17, 2004. 104/ 126 mins.
Production – Studio 4°C, Sunrise and Mash Room
Production companies – Bandai, Bandai Visual, Culture
Publishers, Dentsu, Imagica, Sony, Studio 4°C, Sunrise, Tokyo
Broadcasting System and Toho
Executive Producers – Shigeru Watanabe, Atsuhiko
Chino, Chikara Takano, Hiroo Murakami, Kazuya Enna,
Kenji Uchida, Kiyoshi Watanabe, Masao Seyama, and Ryohei
Tsunoda
Producers – Shinji Komori and Hideyuki Tomioka
Director – Katsuhiro Ôtomo
Script – Katsuhiro Ôtomo and Sadayuki Murai
Music – Steve Jablonsky
Editor – Takeshi Seyama
Art Dir. – Shinji Kimura
Character Designers – Atsushi Irie and Katsumi Matsuda
Mecha Designer – Makoto Kobayashi
Sound Director – Keiichi Momose
Chief Animation Supervisor – Tatsuya Tomaru

CAST
Anne Suzuki – Ray Steam
Katsuo Nakamura – Lloyd Steam
Masane Tsukayama – Eddie Steam
Manami Konishi – Scarlett O'Hara
Kiyoshi Kodama – Robert Stephenson
Sanae Kobayashi – Emma
Satoru Sato – Archibald Simon,
Osamu Saka – the Admiral
Ikki Sawamura – David
Keiko Aizawa – Ray's mother

BUGMASTER/ MUSHISHI

Mch 24, 2007. 131 mins.
Production companies – Ogura Jimusyo Inc.
Producers – Sunmin Park, Kiyoshi Inoue and Satoru Ogura
Director – Katsuhiro Ôtomo
Script – Sadayuki Murai and Katsuhiro Ôtomo
Manga – Yuki Urushibara
Music – Kuniaki Haishima
DP – Takahide Shibanushi
Prod. Des. – Noriyushi Ikeyawas
Sound – Yoshiya Obara
Editor – Soichi Ueno

CAST
Ginko – Joe Odagiri
Nui – Makiki Esumi
Koro – Nao Ômori
Tanyu – Yû Aoi
Tanyu's Nanny – Reisen Ri
Nui's Husband – Baku Numata
Maho – Reia Moriyama
Maho's Mother – Makiko Kuno
Nijirou – Nao Omori

HIPIRA/ HIPIRA-KUN

Dec 24, 2009. 18 mins.

Production – Bandai, Sunrise
Producers – Motoki Mukaichi, Yasumasa Tsuchiya
Story – Katsuhiro Ôtomo
Script – Shinji Kimura
Director – Shinji Kimura
Music – Conisch

CAST
Yumiko Kobayashi
Sayaka Ohara
Bin Shimada

COMBUSTIBLE/ HI NO YOJIN

July 20, 2013. 12 mins.
Producers – David Del Rio, John Ledford and Eiichi Takahashi
Production companies – Bandai Visual, Dentsu Inc., Lantis, Bandai Namco Games, Shochiku Co., Ltd., Short Peace Committee and Sunrise
Screenplay – Katsuhiro Ôtomo
Music – Makoto Kubota
Character Design – Hidekazu Ohara
Animation Director – Tatsuya Tomaru

CAST
Masakazu Morita – Matsuyoshi
Saori Hayami – Owaka

KATSUHIRO OTOMO

MANGA WORKS

MANGA

A Gun Report, Action magazine, 1973
Short Peace, 1979/ Futaba Shoten, 1986
Highway Star, Futabasha, 1979
Fireball, Manga Action Deluxe, Futabasha, 1979
Domu, Manga Action Deluxe, Futabasha, 1980
Sayonara Nippon, 1981
Hansel and Gretel (*It's a Crazy, Crazy World*), Sony
Magazines, 1981
Kibun wa Mou Sensou (*The Mood Is Already of War*),
Futabasha, 1982
Akira, Young Magazine, Kodansha, 1982-90
Akira, Marvel Comics, 1988-1995
Akira, tr. Y. Umezawa *et al,* 6 vols, Dark Horse, Milwaukie,
2000-02
Visitors, 1984
Kanojo no Omoide (*Memories*), Random House, 1990
The Legend of Mother Sarah, Young Magazine, Kodansha,
1990
ZeD, Glénat, 1991
SOS! Tokyo Metro Explorers, Kodansha, 1996
Batman: Black & White #4 (*The Third Mask*), Titan, 1996
Hipira: The Little Vampire, Dark Horse, 2001
Park (*Slice of Life*), Brutus, 2006
DJ Teck's Morning Attack, Shinchousha, 2012

ARTBOOKS

Kaba: Artwork 1971-1989, Kodansha, Tokyo, 1989
Akira Club, Carlsen Verlag, 1995 & 2007
Akira Animation Archives, Kodansha, 2003
Kaba 2, Kodansha, Tokyo, 2012
Genga: Original Pictures, Pie Books, 2013
Posters, Pie Books, 2014

OTHER

Interview, *A.V. Club,* 2005
Interview, in J. Clements, 2009

BIBLIOGRAPHY

OTHERS

Animage. *The Art of Japanese Animation*, Tokuma Shoten,
    1988-89
—. *Best of Animage*, Tokuma Shoten, 1998
A. Baricordi *et al. Anime: A Guide*, Protoculture, Montréal,
    2000
J. Beck, ed. *Animation Art*, Flame Tree Publishing, London,
    2004
E. Bell *et al*, eds. *From Mouse To Mermaid: The Politics of Film,
    Gender and Culture*, Indiana University Press, Bloomington,
    IN, 1995
J. Berndt, ed. *Global Manga Studies*, Seika University Inter-
    national Manga Research Center, Kyoto, 2010
D. Bordwell & K. Thompson. *Film Art: An Introduction,*
    McGraw-Hill Publishing Company, New York, NY, 1979/
    2010
—. *Narration In the Fiction Film*, Routledge, London, 1988
—. *The Way Hollywood Tells It*, University of California Press,
    Berkeley, CA, 2006
J. Bower, ed. *The Cinema of Japan and Korea*, Wallflower Press,
    London, 2004
P. Brophy, ed. *Kaboom! Explosive Animation From America and
    Japan*, Museum of Contemporary Art, Sydney, 1994
—. *100 Anime*, British Film Institute, London, 2005
—. ed. *Tezuka*, National Gallery of Victoria, 2006
J. Brosnan. *Future Tense: The Cinema of Science Fiction,* St
    Martin's Press, New York, NY, 1978
—. *Primal Screen: A History of Science Fiction Film,* Orbit,
    London, 1991
David Brothers. "Katsuhiro Otomo and the Perfect Panels of
    Akira", *Comics Alliance*, June 24, 2011
S. Bukatman. *Terminal Identity: The Virtual Subject In Post-
    modern Science Fiction*, Duke University Press, Durham, NC,

1993

E. Byrne & M. McQuillan, eds. *Deconstructing Disney*, Pluto Press, London, 1999

B. Camp & J. Davis. *Zettai: Anime Classics*, Stone Bridge Press, CA, 2007

D. Cavallaro. *The Animé Art of Hayao Miyazaki,* McFarland, Jefferson, NC, 2006

J. Chapman. *British Comics,* Reaktion Books, London, 2011

C. Chatrian & G. Paganelli, *Manga Impact!,* Phaidon, London, 2010

J. Clarke. *Animated Films,* Virgin, London, 2007

J. Clements & H. McCarthy. *The Animé Encyclopedia,* Stone Bridge Press, Berkeley, CA, 2001/ 2006/ 2015

—. *The Development of the U.K. Anime and Manga Market*, Muramasa Industries, London, 2003

—. *Schoolgirl Milky Crisis,* Titan Books, London, 2009

—. *Anime: A History,* British Film Institute, London, 2013

I. Condry. *The Soul of Anime*, Duke University Press, Durham, NC, 2013

D.A. Cook. *A History of Narrative Film*, W.W. Norton, New York, NY, 1981, 1990, 1996

J.C. Cooper: *Fairy Tales: Allegories of the Inner Life,* Aquarian Press, 1983

C. Desjardins. *Outlaw Masters of Japanese Film,* I.B. Tauris, London, 2005

J. Donald, ed. *Fantasy and the Cinema*, British Film Institute, London, 1989

P. Drazen. *Animé Explosion,* Stone Bridge Press, Berkeley, CA, 2003

Mircea Eliade. *Shamanism: Archaic Techniques of Ecstasy,* Princeton University Press, Princeton, NJ, 1972

—. *Ordeal by Labyrinth,* University of Chicago Press, Chicago, IL, 1984

—. *Symbolism, the Sacred and the Arts,* Crossroad, New York, NY, 1985

M. Eliot. *Walt Disney: Hollywood's Dark Prince: A Biography*, Andre Deutsch, London, 1994

D. Fingeroth. *The Rough Guide To Graphic Novels*, Rough Guides, 2008

F. Freiberg. "*Akira* and the Postnuclear Sublime", in M. Broderick, ed. *Hibakusha Cinema,* Kegan Paul, London, 1996

H. Garcia. *A Geek In Japan,* Tuttle, North Clarendon, VT, 2011

L. Goldberg *et al*, eds. *Science Fiction Filmmaking In the 1980s,* McFarland, Jefferson, 1995

J. Goodwin, ed. *Perspectives On Akira Kurosawa*, G.K. Hall, Boston, MA, 1994

P. Gravett. *Manga*, L. King, London, 2004

R. Grover. *The Disney Touch*, Business One Irwin, Home-
wood, Illinois, 1991

P. Hardy, ed. *The Aurum Encyclopedia of Science Fiction*,
Aurum, London, 1991

C. Heston. *In the Arena: The Autobiography*, HarperCollins,
London, 1995

Tze-yue Hu. *Frames of Anime*, Hong Kong University Press,
HK, 2010

J. Hunter. *Eros In Hell: Sex, Blood and Madness In Japanese
Cinema*, Creation Books, London, 1998

B.F. Kawin. *How Movies Work*, Macmillan, New York, NY,
1987

R. Keith. *Japanamerica*, Palgrave Macmillan, London, 2007

Sharon Kinsella. *Adult Manga*, University of Hawaii Press,
Honolulu, 2002

F. Ladd & H. Deneroff. *Astro Boy and Anime Come To the
Americas*, McFarland, Jefferson, NC, 2009

T. Lamare. *The Anime Machine*, University of Minnesota
Press, Minneapolis, MN, 2009

T. Ledoux & D. Ranney. *The Complete Animé Guide*, Tiger
Mountain Press, Washington, DC, 1997

—. ed. *Anime Interviews*, Cadence Books, San Francisco, CA,
1997

T. Lehmann. *Manga: Masters of the Art*, HarperCollins,
London, 2005

J. Lent, ed. *Animation in Asia and the Pacific*, John Libbey, 2001

A. Levi. *Samurai From Outer Space: Understanding Japanese
Animation*, Open Court, Chicago, IL, 1996

P. Macias. *The Japanese Cult Film Companion*, Cadence Books,
San Francisco, CA, 2001

—. & T. Machiyama. *Cruising the Anime City*, Stone Bridge
Press, CA, 2004

L. Maltin. *Of Mice and Magic: A History of American Animated
Cartoons*, New American Library, New York, NY, 1987

—. *The Disney Films*, 3rd ed., Hyperion, New York, NY, 1995

A. Masano & J. Wiedermann, eds. *Manga Design*, Taschen,
2004

G. Mast *et al*, eds. *Film Theory and Criticism: Introductory
Readings*, Oxford University Press, New York, NY, 1992a

—. & B. Kawin. *A Short History of the Movies*, Macmillan,
New York, NY, 1992b

H. McCarthy. *Anime! A Beginner's Guide To Japanese
Animation*, Titan, 1993

—. *The Animé Movie Guide*, Titan Books, London, 1996

—. & J. Clements. *The Erotic Animé Movie Guide*, Titan Books,
London, 1998

—. "The House That Hayao Built", *Manga Max*, Apl 5, 1999

—. *Hayao Miyazaki: Master of Japanese Animation*, Stone Bridge Press, Berkeley, CA, 2002

—. *500 Manga Heroes & Villains*, Barron's, Hauppauge, New York, 2006

—. *500 Essential Anime Movies*, Collins Design, New York, NY, 2008

S. McCloud. *Understanding Comics*, Harper, London, 1994

—. *Reinventing Comics*, Harper, London, 2000

—. *Making Comics*, Harper, London, 2006

H. Miyazaki. *Starting Point, 1979-1996*, tr. B. Cary & F. Schodt, Viz Media, San Francisco, CA, 2009

—. *Turning Point, 1997-2008*, tr. B. Cary & F. Schodt, Viz Media/ Shogakukan, San Francisco, CA, 2014

A. Morton. *The Complete Directory To Science Fiction, Fantasy and Horror Television Series*, Other Worlds, 1997

S. Napier. *Anime: From Akira To Princess Mononoke*, Palgrave, New York, 2001

—. "Interviewing Hayao Miyazaki", *Huffington Post,* Jan, 2014

S. Neale & M. Smith, eds. *Contemporary Hollywood Cinema*, Routledge, London, 1998

C. Odell & M. Le Blanc. *Studio Ghibli: The Films of Hayao Miyazaki and Isao Takahata*, Kamera Books, Herts., 2009

—. *Anime*, Kamera Books, Herts., 2013

A. Osmond. *"Nausicaä* and the Fantasy of Hayao Miyazaki", *SF Journal Foundation*, 73, Spring, 1998

—. "Hayao Miyazaki", *Cinescape*, 72, 1999

—. "Will the Real Joe Hisaishi Please Stand Up?", *Animation World Magazine*, 5.01, April, 2000

— *Spirited Away*, British Film Institute, London, 2003a

—. "Gods and Monsters", *Sight & Sound*, Sept, 2003b

—. *Satoshi Kon*, Stone Bridge Press, San Francisco, 2009

F. Patten. *Watching Anime, Reading Manga*, Stone Bridge Press, CA, 2004

L. Pearce, ed. *Romance Revisited*, Lawrence & Wishart, London, 1995

D. Peary & G. Peary, eds. *The American Animated Cartoon*, Dutton, New York, NY, 1980

J. Pilling, ed. *A Reader In Animation Studies,* John Libbey, 1997

G. Poitras. *The Animé Companion*, Stone Bridge Press, Berkeley, CA, 1999

—. *Animé Essentials*, Stone Bridge Press, Berkeley, CA, 2001

N. Power. *God of Comics: Osamu Tezuka and the Creation of Post-World War II*, University of Mississippi Press, 2009

K. Quigley. *Comics Underground Japan*, Blast Books, New York, NY, 1996

E. Rabkin & G. Slusser, eds. *Shadows of the Magic Lamp: Fantasy and Science Fiction In Film*, Southern Illinois

University Press, Carbondale, IL, 1985

D. Richie. *The Films of Akira Kurosawa*, University of California Press, Berkeley, CA, 1965

S. Richmond. *The Rough Guide To Anime*, Rough Guides, 2009

C. Rowthorn. *Japan*, Lonely Planet, 2007

B. Ruh. *Stray Dog of Anime*, Macmillan, 2004

K. Sandler. *Reading the Rabbit: Explorations In Warner Bros. Animation*, Rutgers University Press, Brunswick, NJ, 1998

R. Schickel. *The Disney Version: The Life, Times, Art, and Commerce of Walt Disney*, Pavilion, London, 1986

M. Schilling. *The Encyclopedia of Japanese Pop Culture*, Weatherhill, Boston, MA, 1997

—. *Contemporary Japanese Film*, Weatherhill, New York, NY, 1999

F. Schodt. *Inside the Robot Kingdom: Japan, Mechatronics and the Coming Robotopia*, Kodansha, Tokyo, 1988

—. *Manga! Manga! The World of Japanese Magazines*, Kodansha International, London, 1997

—. *Dreamland Japan: Writings On Modern Manga*, Stone Bridge Press, Berkeley, CA, 2002

—. *The Astro Boy Essays*, Stone Bridge Press, CA, 2007

J. Seward, ed. *Japanese Eroticism: A Language Guide To Current Comics*, Yugen Press, Houston, TX, 1993

C. Shiratori, ed. *Secret Comics Japan*, Cadence Books, San Francisco, CA, 2000

T. Smith. "Miso Horny: Sex In Japanese Comics", *Comics Journal*, Apl, 1991

E. Smoodin. *Animating Culture: Hollywood Cartoons From the Sound Era*, Roundhouse, 1993

—. ed. *Disney Discourse: Producing the Magic Kingdom*, Routledge, London, 1994

V. Sobchack. *Screening Space: The American Science Fiction Film*, Ungar, New York, NY, 1987/1993

J. Stieff & A. Barkman, eds. *Manga and Philosophy*, Open Court, Chicago, IL, 2010

J. Thompson. *Manga: The Complete Guide*, Del Rey, New York, NY, 2007

K. Thompson & D. Bordwell. *Film History: An Introduction*, McGraw-Hill, New York, NY, 1994

—. *Storytelling In the New Hollywood*, Harvard University Press, Cambridge, MA, 1999

P. Wells. *Understanding Animation*, Routledge, London, 1998

C. Winstanley, ed. *SFX Collection: Animé Special*, Future Publishing, London, 2006

J. Yadao. *The Rough Guide To Manga*, Rough Guides, 2008

J. Zipes. *Breaking the Spell: Radical Theories of Folk and Fairy Tales*, Heinemann, London, 1978/ 2002

—. *Fairy Tales and the Art of Subversion: The Classical Genre for*

    Children and the Process of Civilization, Heinemann, London, 1983

—. *Don't Bet On the Prince: Contemporary Feminist Fairy Tales In North America and England*, Methuen, New York, NY, 1986

—. *The Brothers Grimm: From Enchanted Forests To the Modern World*, Routledge, New York, NY, 1989

—. ed. *The Oxford Companion To Fairy Tales*, Oxford University Press, 2000

—. *Breaking the Spell: Radical Theories of Folk and Fairy Tales*, University of Kentucky Press, Lexington, 2002

—. *Sticks and Stones: The Troublesome Success of Children's Literature from Slovenly Peter To Harry Potter*, Routledge, London, 2002

—. *The Enchanted Screen: The Unknown History of Fairy-tale Films*, Routledge, New York, NY, 2011

—. *The Irresistible Fairy Tale*, Princeton University Press, Princeton, NJ, 2012

MEDIA, CINEMA, FEMINISM and CULTURAL STUDIES

J.R.R. Tolkien: The Books, The Films, The Whole Cultural Phenomenon
J.R.R. Tolkien: Pocket Guide
The *Lord of the Rings* Movies: Pocket Guide
The Ghost Dance: The Origins of Religion
The Cinema of Hayao Miyazaki

Hayao Miyazaki: *Princess Mononoke*: Pocket Movie Guide
Hayao Miyazaki: *Spirited Away*: Pocket Movie Guide
The Peyote Cult
HomeGround: The Kate Bush Anthology
Tim Burton : Hallowe'en For Hollywood
Ken Russell
Cixous, Irigaray, Kristeva: The *Jouissance* of French Feminism
Julia Kristeva: Art, Love, Melancholy, Philosophy, Semiotics and Psychoanalysis
Luce Irigaray: Lips, Kissing, and the Politics of Sexual Difference
Hélene Cixous I Love You: The *Jouissance* of Writing
Andrea Dworkin
'Cosmo Woman': The World of Women's Magazines
Women in Pop Music
Discovering the Goddess (Geoffrey Ashe)
The Poetry of Cinema
The Sacred Cinema of Andrei Tarkovsky
Andrei Tarkovsky: Pocket Guide
Andrei Tarkovsky: *Mirror*: Pocket Movie Guide
Walerian Borowczyk: Cinema of Erotic Dreams
Jean-Luc Godard: The Passion of Cinema
Jean-Luc Godard: Pocket Guide
John Hughes and Eighties Cinema
Ferris Buller's Day Off: Pocket Movie Guide
The Cinema of Richard Linklater
Liv Tyler: Star In Ascendance
Blade Runner and the Films of Philip K. Dick
Paul Bowles and Bernardo Bertolucci
Media Hell: Radio, TV and the Press
Detonation Britain: Nuclear War in the UK
Feminism and Shakespeare
Wild Zones: Pornography, Art and Feminism
Sex in Art: Pornography and Pleasure in Painting and Sculpture
Sexing Hardy: Thomas Hardy and Feminism

*The Light Eternal is a model monograph, an exemplary job. The subject matter of the book is
beautifully organised and dead on beam.* (Lawrence Durrell)
It is amazing for me to see my work treated with such passion and respect. (Andrea Dworkin)
Sex-Magic-Poetry-Cornwall *is a very rich essay... It is like a brightly-lighted box.* (Peter Redgrove)

CRESCENT MOON PUBLISHING P.O. Box 1312, Maidstone, Kent, ME14 5XU, Great Britain
0044-1622-729593 cresmopub@yahoo.co.uk www.crmoon.com

Printed in the USA
CPSIA information can be obtained
at www.ICGtesting.com
LVHW020233240124
769827LV00004B/35

9 781861 716873